Detroit Monographs in Musicology/Studies in Music, No. 47

Editor
Susan Parisi
University of Illinois

Music in Jewish History and Culture

by
Emanuel Rubin
and
John H. Baron

Harmonie Park Press   Sterling Heights, Michigan   2006

COVER:

**Reconstruction by Moshe Gorali of kinnor shown on a coin
of ca. 132-35 CE pictured in fig. 2.2 (p. 37)**

Courtesy of the Haifa Museum of Ethnology

FRONTISPIECE:

**Frieze from the Arch of Titus in Rome, showing two silver trumpets (right)
taken to Rome as booty from the conquest of Jerusalem**

Private collection

Printed and bound in the United States of America
Published by
Harmonie Park Press
Liberty Professional Center
35675 Mound Road
Sterling Heights, Michigan 48310-4727

Publications Director, Elaine Gorzelski
Editor, Susan Parisi
Cover design, Mitchell Groters
Book design and Typographer, Colleen McRorie

Library of Congress Cataloging-in-Publication Data

Rubin, Emanuel, 1935-
    Music in Jewish history and culture / by Emanuel Rubin and John H. Baron.
      p. cm. — (Detroit monographs in musicology/Studies in music ; no. 47)
    Includes bibliographical references and index.
    ISBN 0-89990-133-6
      1. Jews—Music—History and criticism. I. Baron, John H. II. Title. III. Series.

ML3776.R75 2006
780.89'924—dc22

2006043366

To my wife, Serene

*To my wife, Doris
and to my parents*

Contents

Contents ‖ ix

ILLUSTRATIONS

FIGURES

TABLES

ACKNOWLEDGMENTS

Like any large-scale undertaking, this book is the responsibility of its authors, but it is the product of an entire army of people and institutions that made it possible. Their number to be thanked for contributions would fill a small stadium. Here I would like to mention a few persons to whom I owe a special debt. It has been half a century since the late Cantor Mordecai Heiser awakened a love for Jewish music in me and encouraged my musical aspirations. Closer to the book's genesis, thanks must be given to a several others whose contributions played some part in making its realization possible. They are not responsible for my errors, but they provided a matrix for what understanding I was able to bring to this project. Scholars Israel Adler, of the Israeli Music Research Centre, and Yitzchak Kerem, who edits and broods over distribution of the Sephardic Music Newsletter, gave freely of their time and guidance, as did composers Zvi Avni, Yehuda Yannay, and Menachem Wiesenberg. Paul Landau, director of the Israel Music Institute, and Willi Elias its former director, helped in surveying the astonishing maze of musical activity in Israel today, and Yossi Tel-Gan, director of the Israel Music Festival, led me through the labyrinth of that undertaking's operations, of which I could only include a glimpse here. The indefatigable Moshe Jacobson regaled me with both funny and profoundly moving stories about teaching music in the early days of Israel's statehood, overwhelming me with his love of music and of the children and adults who make music. These Israelis, who were my informants, bore up bravely under time-consuming interviews and queries long past the point where lesser beings would have lost patience. The list also included friends like Rabbi Phillip Graubart, a scholar and himself a writer, and Dr. Chaim Cohen of Ben-Gurion University, who somehow found time in their overburdened schedules to read sections of this book in typescript and offer insights. "Acharon, acharon, haviv," they say in Hebrew (the dearest comes last), so the list of people to whom I am indebted for help concludes with my wife, Serene, whose editorial skills and critical eye remained sharp even while her support never wavered. To all these people go my thanks, with apologies for errors I might have let slip through in spite of their good offices.

Emanuel Rubin

University of Massachusetts at Amherst

My part in this book is the result of six decades of gestation. Many persons nurtured my interest in Jewish music and helped me understand it. At the beginning were my parents, Rabbi Joseph L. Baron from Vilna and Milwaukee, and Bernice Singer Baron, a violin graduate from the Juilliard School of Music. Also my great-uncle Rabbi Jacob Singer of Chicago provided an example of someone who was professionally a Jewish musician, while his father, my great grandfather Joshua Heschel *Chazan* (Singer) of Latvia and Buffalo, was always the icon of the perfect cantorial scholar. During the course of my education there were Cantors Sol Altschuler (Milwaukee) and Alex Zimmer (Boston) who helped me focus on what the composition of synagogue music was all about. Dr. Eric Werner was frequently a guest in my parents' home, and later he advised me as I wrote my honor's thesis on Jewish music. From him I learned much that has never been written nor should be about Jewish musicians and the reception of Jewish music among learned rabbis. I will always also be grateful to Herbert Fromm, who during my senior year at Harvard allowed me to visit him weekly in order to learn at a master's feet.

More recently I have benefited from the counsel of persons in all walks of life who have helped me understand the meaning of Jewish music, its variety, and its spiritual significance. A partial list includes Don David Lusterman, Emanuel Rubin, Israel (Joe) Katz, and Michael Shochet. Not least should also be mentioned the several hundred students at Tulane University who have taken my course "Jewish Music," which I first offered in 1981 and which has been transformed each year as I learn more from them. It is they who have asked for a book like this, so I hope this will show them how much they have taught me. To all the librarians, scholars, and professional Jewish religious and lay musicians who have given of their time and knowledge I say "todah rabbah" (thank you very much). I am forever indebted to my wife Doris who has patiently endured my daydreams so that the book could be written, and I hope that my three children—Beth the Jewish educator, Miriam the musician, and Jeffrey the solid businessman—will benefit from the finished book so that they can enjoy the kind of music which has given me so much satisfaction.

John H. Baron

Tulane University

At Harmonie Park Press we would especially like to thank series editor Susan Parisi for her thorough review of our manuscript and her invaluable suggestions; president and publications director, Elaine Gorzelski, who has been of immense help to us; and typographer, Colleen McRorie, whose careful work on our volume we greatly appreciated. We also fondly remember our late friend and colleague Bunker Clark, who encouraged the publication of this book, and we will always be indebted to him. Many institutions have made their libraries and archives available to us, particularly Jewish Theological Seminary, Hebrew Union College-Jewish Institute of Religion, Spertus College, Tulane University, University of Massachusetts, and Temple Sinai of New Orleans. We also thank the foundations, societies, and institutes that have allowed us to use illustrations and which are acknowledged within the book.

EMANUEL RUBIN
JOHN H. BARON

July 2005

INTRODUCTION

This survey is designed for those interested in the point at which music and Judaic Studies intersect. Since both the authors have been teaching college courses that cover this material, we were conscious of the need for a comprehensive survey, but we were also aware that interest in the subject was not restricted to students. Many people, after becoming acquainted with one or another form of music in Jewish life, have wanted to know more about it without becoming specialists. This book was conceived to fill such a need: it is addressed to those readers who are well versed in one of the two intersecting disciplines, as well as to those whose intellectual curiosity embraces both, but without expertise in either.

Containing this enormous, sprawling topic within the covers of a single volume necessitated some painful choices about what to include or omit from music of the last four thousand years. In making such choices we almost certainly left out someone's special interest, but there was simply no room in a one-volume work to cover all the details. Jewish music in the Byzantine world, the music of India's Jewish community, the many varieties of cantillation traditions, music of the Jews of North Africa, of Medieval France, of Holland and Belgium, of South and Central America, all had to be minimized or put aside, or the result would have been an enormous, multi-volume work. Other constraints also limited the contents of the book, often to our frustration. Examples in musical notation, so useful to the musician but not nearly as helpful to the non-musician were kept to an absolute minimum, as was the kind of analytical discussion that forms the essential backbone of studies aimed primarily at scholars.

Those omissions grew out of our desire to provide non-specialists with a concise, self-contained survey of the music characterizing selected Jewish communities from biblical times to the present. The areas we have chosen to treat have arguably made the most visible contributions to what some would call "Jewish music." For each we have constructed a social-historical frame-work bringing together cultural, historical, and linguistic information to show their interaction in shaping the musical expression of a particular Jewish society. Periodic "Historical Interludes" consider watershed events in Jewish history and supply a chronological orientation, while cultural, as well as musical, background is woven through the chapters to provide a context for understanding the place of music in Jewish society.

Each chapter focuses on a different aspect of music in Jewish history. To enrich that perspective, a list of suggested further readings and recordings is furnished, to encourage readers to pursue topics of interest in greater depth. Given the wide variety of backgrounds readers bring to such a book, all foreign words are defined upon their first occurrence, and are listed in a glossary at the end of the book. Detailed knowledge of Jewish religious and cultural traditions is not assumed. Instead, this material is concisely surveyed so that musical ideas can be placed in an appropriate context.

The story told here is about music in Jewish life. Music played an important part in the life of the Jewish people from the time of our earliest knowledge about them. Their music is defined not by any special musical features, but by its "purpose"—its function in Jewish society. Over time, or in different historical circumstances, the nature of those aims has changed. The Jews' sense of participation in—or isolation from—different host societies shaped the perimeter of Jewish purposes they perceived. To the extent that a defining thread runs through this survey, then, it is that when music—any music—serves the purpose of a Jewish community, it might be called Jewish music.

PRELUDE || *What Is Jewish Music?*

This seemingly simple question has posed almost insurmountable problems for those trying to answer it, or even parse exactly what it means. The initial interrogative "what" implies that a single statement can serve as an answer, while "music" is even more ambiguous. Does it mean compositions that have a recognizable identity with an identifiable beginning, middle, and end? If so, cantillation, one of the important bodies of Jewish music, would not qualify. If it refers to music for religious practice it would exclude *klezmer* music, folk songs, the Yiddish theater, and dances, all of which are too strongly associated with Jewish culture to omit. In reality, we cannot answer the question as posed.

Perhaps the most meaningful answer is that there is no such thing as Jewish music; that is, there is no particular chord or scale, no melodic type or harmonic sequence that is specifically "Jewish." Yet people seem to readily identify certain song types, prayer modes, or instrumental conventions as "sounding Jewish." Such identification, though, depends on the individual's experience. To a Jew raised in the Eastern European tradition, the liturgical singing of the great cantor Yossele Rosenblatt "sounds Jewish," but that style is as foreign to the Jews of India or Adjerzaiban as is the sound of their music to Western ears. We might interpret "Jewish music" to mean music written to Hebrew texts, but then what is to be done with instrumental music or the great treasury of song in Yiddish, the common language of most *Ashkenazic* (European) Jews since the Middle Ages? For that matter one must also consider Ladino, the language of *Sephardic* Jews, Judeo-Arabic, and Luganda, the language of the Abayudaya Jewish community of Uganda. Then, too, we could not exclude Jewish songs in English, French, Spanish, Russian, or more than a dozen other languages, so that neither liturgy nor language can encompass all of Jewish music.

Perhaps the answer could be framed as "music written by Jews." But then *Hatikvah*, Israel's national anthem, would have to be excluded, since it is based on an old central European folk song—the same one Smetana used as a theme for his nationalistic Bohemian tone poem, *The Moldau*. That interpretation would also exclude an astonishing number of synagogue hymns and table songs for the Sabbath which, like *Hatikvah*, had origins in non-Jewish culture.

Jewish composers themselves have been perplexed by the question, and some have opted simply to claim as Jewish any music written by a Jew. More perceptively, though, Israeli composer Alexander Boskovitch wrote, "When examining the question of Jewish music, we should not consider Jewish descent as a decisive factor."[1] If family lineage were a factor in determining what constitutes Jewish music, how "Jewish" would a composer have to be to be included in the register of Jewish composers? The nineteenth-century composer Ferdinand Hiller was born into an assimilated Jewish family; Georges Bizet was the son of a mixed marriage with no particular Jewish affiliation, but he married a Jewish woman, as did Paul Hindemith, a non-Jew. All this skates dangerously close to racist ideology, and has little relationship to musical considerations, so that a composer's "pedigree" can clearly be discarded as a qualification. Some excellent music has even been written for the synagogue by Christian composers such as Franz Schubert, and a particularly beautiful instrumental setting of *Kol Nidrei* was by Max Bruch, who was not Jewish himself, but used the melody from one of the most solemn moments of the Jewish liturgy. Conversely, Leonard Bernstein's ecumenical *Mass* might be difficult to consider as Jewish music even though it was written by a Jew, as would songs celebrating Christian holidays, such as "I'm Dreaming of a White Christmas" and "The Easter Parade," both written by Irving Berlin, who was Jewish.

Consider music written for Israeli adventure films or television comedies: Israeli, certainly, but does that make it Jewish? Secular musicals like *The Sound of Music* (Rodgers and Hammerstein) or *My Fair Lady* (Lerner and Loewe) did not suddenly become Jewish when they were translated into Hebrew; but one might ask whether they were Jewish even before translation, because their composers and librettists were Jewish. If so, does that make the song "Stormy Weather" or *The Wizard of Oz* Jewish because the composer, Harold Arlen, was a Jew? What about *Elijah*, an oratorio with an Old Testament subject by Felix Mendelssohn, a Christian who met with anti-Semitism because his grandfather was a Jew?

We could pursue this exercise endlessly, but the point is clear. There seems to be no parameter of musical style, language, nationality, religion, or even relationship to the liturgy that would allow one to point to "Jewish" musical characteristics in the same way we can when talking about Scottish, Italian, or Balinese music. Technical characteristics of klezmer or synagogue music that have been claimed as distinctively "Jewish" turn out, on examination, not to be so. Scales with augmented seconds, for example, that give a characteristic sound to many Eastern European synagogue and klezmer melodies seem to have been introduced by conquering Moslems in the late Middle Ages, while the klezmer sound itself is closely bound up with the style of Eastern European and Gypsy folk musicians. Even that quintessentially Israeli dance, the *hora*, turns out to have its origins in Rumania.

---

[1] Alexander U. Boskovitch, "A Zsido Problema" (The Problem of Jewish Music), *Kelet éts Nyugat Közott* (Cluj: 1937), 31; quoted by Jehoash Hirshberg in "Alexander U. Boskovitch and the Quest for an Israeli National Style," *Modern Jews and their Musical Agendas*, ed. Ezra Mendelsohn (New York and Oxford: Oxford University Press, 1993), 96.

Music played an important part in the life of the Jewish people from the time of our earliest knowledge about them. Archeology and biblical studies confirm a thriving musical practice going back thousands of years, so it is not surprising that the frequently-asked question, "What is Jewish music?" is so difficult to answer. Most often the question is posed as a challenge to define characteristics that can be identified as Jewish. Such postulates, though, are untenable in the end.

Any definition of "Jewish music" grows out of a questionable concern with national or ethnic identity. The ancient Greeks were aware of different musical styles, which they termed "modes" and named for the ethnic group identified with each. Plato spoke about Dorian or Phrygian modes, meaning the styles associated with those Greek tribes. The Dorians, Lydians, or far-off Scythians of the ancient Greek world were self-identified ethnic groups whose musical tastes were formed by generations of living within a defined area, hearing music created by local musicians who trained disciples by rote, and who thus passed on a locally familiar style—and a taste for it—from one generation to another. When we talk today about French or Brazilian music, we are talking about musical styles molded in the crucible of continuous geographical proximity. For at least two thousand years, though, such proximity was denied the Jewish people, and as a result there is no single Jewish musical style, especially if one tries to define it in terms of rhythmic, melodic, or harmonic features. Instead, the Jews absorbed music from every society in which they lived, and in doing so, their musical practice became uniquely multicultural.

Yet there was also a cement that bound Jews from those different contexts together, bridging distinctions of time or place. That bond—the belief system of Jewish civilization—swept aside parochial concerns and minimized esthetic differences with an overriding sense of brotherhood. Here we might turn again to Boskovitch, who, in the same article mentioned before, defined Jewish music as "the expression of the Jewish spirit and mentality in sound."[2] Unlike the music of West Africa, which was totally isolated from that of, say, Tibet until quite recently, there was constant, if constrained, intercourse between most communities of the Jewish Diaspora. Even geographically isolated groups continued to participate in a common religious-cultural base, and Jewish travelers, as well as Jewish texts, enabled the sharing of musical ideas, melodies, dances, or practices among Jewish communities with only the most tenuous communication. As a result, the Cochin Jews of India, who returned to Israel after a millennium of separation, shared a similar enough value system to integrate comfortably into the polymorphous society of modern Israel.

It is those commonalities to which we must look for characteristics that might define music as "Jewish." This line of thought goes beyond traditional musical analysis. To fully understand what gives any music its identity, four characteristics must be examined. The first and most apparent is "sound"—that is, melodic types, harmonic practices, vocal and instrumental timbres, etc. The second aspect is "logic"—the organizational processes underlying the music's progress through time. Most technical writing about music concentrates on those two, neither of which can define Jewish music, as we have seen. There are, however, two other properties that have

---

[2] Ibid.

received less attention: "affect," which embraces our psychological response to music, or more specifically, the musical features evoking such a response, and the "purpose" of music—its societal function.

Affect has indeed received attention in the past from those writers who describe their own feelings while listening to music and claim that those are inherent in the music itself. Thus, they would say that the music is "sad" or "happy." Such terms, though, describe a person's psychological response to the music, not the music itself. It is valid to look for what is happening in the music that evokes such a response, but the response itself is personal, and could not provide ethnic-defining features.

A more promising route lies in the often-overlooked features that fall under the heading, "purpose." Mordecai Kaplan (1881-1983) called Judaism a civilization in his 1934 book of that title: a way of living that subsumed sacred and secular, religious and historical, within a single unified world-view. Jewish civilization's core beliefs, such as monotheism, the task of humanity in perfecting the world (*tikkun olam*), the aspiration of the intellect to understanding, the mutual obligations of individual and community, and the tolerance of other belief systems consonant with those values, are a heritage expressed in the art, as well as the life, of its practitioners. The societal function of music is a part of that belief system, so that the "purpose" of music may bring us closer to finding commonalities among the diverse musical styles of Jewish societies than any characteristic of its sound. To characterize some melodic or harmonic expression as the irreducible core of Jewish music would be to misunderstand the historical experience of the Jewish people. The question is not whether this or that music *sounds* Jewish, but whether it meets the needs of the Jews.

With that in mind, let us adopt the following as a working definition: Jewish music is music that serves Jewish purposes. This is not circular, as it might appear at first glance. "Jewish purposes" differed over time as Jews discovered new opportunities or constraints shaping their identity and destiny. Those purposes sometimes expanded to embrace the larger society when Jews found acceptance. More often throughout history the Jewish community was forced to turn inward, focusing its musical interests on solely parochial concerns. Despite differences in "sound" or "logic," despite a wide range of "affect" crossing the entire gamut of human feelings, we can only conclude that any music having a Jewish purpose can be said to be Jewish music.

Music in
Jewish History
and Culture

1 || *Background and Orientation*

Judaism is more than a religious belief. It is a multi-layered civilization, a culture with a richly textured heritage, of which religious belief is one important part. The different aspects of Judaism exist in a tightly woven fabric that defies easy untangling. To some that poses a problem. There are those who would prefer to tease the threads of faith free of those threads representing social, political, educational, historical, and even gastronomical aspects of the total Jewish picture. Others would spend an equal amount of energy denying that the various strands are in any way separable. For many the result is not a tapestry, but a bewildering snarl of yarn without apparent beginning or end.

To trace even so narrow a subject as music through that tangle is a daunting task, with no obvious place to begin and few guidelines as to what should be included or omitted. The simple fact is that one cannot study the music of the Jews without setting it in the context of Jewish culture. For this reason a certain amount of historical and cultural background has been woven into the account of musical developments. That same reasoning dictated the content of this opening chapter, whose function is to introduce the uninitiated reader to information without which such a reader might find later discussions incomprehensible.

Thus, this chapter will introduce—or for some, review—key ideas, seminal texts, and cultural practices that form the screen against which the progression of Jewish music will be projected, paying special attention to musical implications. It will establish terminology for the social and religious practices that gave birth to different musical styles for similar social uses found in Jewish communities as disparate as Yemen and Chicago, as well as core concepts for discussing the different musical types of a widely dispersed people. For those who come from a different tradition, or whose knowledge of the Jewish tradition is less than they might wish, it outlines the frame of reference shared by Jews living in many different societies. The key topics to be covered are the Bible, the liturgical year, the synagogue, the worship service, other liturgical or paraliturgical uses of music, and music in secular life.

The Bible

The English word "Bible" (from the Greek, *biblios*: book) designates the holy writings of both the Jewish and Christian religions. In spite of that apparently clear definition, the word does not mean the same thing to everyone. Items included in one version of the Bible are omitted in another, and different translations render the same text in different ways. Here, we will talk solely about the Hebrew Bible. Note that Jews do not call it the Old Testament, because for Jews there is no New Testament. The Bible is also sacred to Christians and Moslems, because they find in it the history of what they see as the precursor religion to Christianity or Islam and the moral-ethical foundations of religious practices detailed in the New Testament or the Koran. The language of the Bible is almost entirely Hebrew. The only exceptions are a handful of passages in Aramaic,[1] the everyday language of the Palestinian Jewish community for several hundred years before the destruction of the Temple in Jerusalem in 70 CE.[2] Both prose and poetry are used, and much of the Bible is written in an elegant Hebrew using an elevated poetic narrative style.

The Bible has been translated innumerable times into almost every language known to man; however, because of their influence on later writers, certain early translations have special significance and should be mentioned here. The first of those, known as the *Septuagint*, is the oldest Greek translation, dating from as early as the second or possibly even the third century, BCE. Its name, based on the number "seventy," derives from a legend that the translation was completed in seventy days by seventy-two wise elders. Another important early translation is the so-called *Targum Onkelos* (Translation of Onkelos). This was a translation into Aramaic attributed to Onkelos the proselyte, probably made in the second century CE. That attribution has been questioned, but as yet no definitive proofs are available either supporting or denying the identity of the translator. It is cited so often that it is usually simply called "the Targum" (Translation), in spite of the fact that other translations also exist. Both of these translations owed their origin to the fact that much of the Jewish population of their times could no longer understand the Hebrew of the original. In the case of the Septuagint, it was the Jewish community of Greek-speaking Egypt, primarily in Alexandria, whose needs prompted the translation. The Targum grew out of a similar need on the part of Aramaic-speaking Jews of Palestine and Babylonia. Since in Jewish thought it has always been important for individuals to study the precepts of the Bible for themselves, those translations played an important part in enabling the people to continue to practice their religion in a meaningful manner.

Three different compilations of writings are collected into what we call the Bible. The core is the Five Books of Moses, also known as the Five Books of the Law, called *Chumash* in Hebrew, or *Pentateuch* in Greek—both terms refer to the number "five." It is also called the Torah ("Law" or "Instruction"), a word which, depending on its use, might designate the five

---

[1] For example: Genesis 31:47; Jeremiah 10:11; Daniel 2:4-7:28; Ezra 4:8-6:18, and 7:12-26.

[2] A word about the protocol of dates: In the ancient world years were calculated from the beginning of the reign of the reigning king. Thus we read, "in the third year of Cyrus," or "in the second year of the reign of Caesar Augustus." In the Western world today our calendar is dated from the assumed date of the birth of Jesus, and years are counted in relation to that time, being "BC" (Before Christ) or "AD" (*Anno Domini*, that is, "in the year of our Lord"). Many historians today prefer to use a more neutral terminology, designating the same dates by CE (Common Era) or BCE (Before the Common Era). That is the system that will be adopted here.

books of the *Chumash*, the entire Bible, the physical scroll on which the text is written, or even, in some contexts, the sum total of Jewish religious knowledge. In informal use, the term usually refers to the Pentateuch—the five books of Moses. In that sense, the Torah recounts the prehistory of the human race, summarizes the history of the Jewish people from their earliest beginnings to the death of Moses, and includes all the practices and laws incumbent upon one who professes Judaism.

One section of the Torah is chanted (see chapter 4, "Cantillation") sequentially every week in the synagogue so that all might become acquainted with its contents. According to one scheme, called the annual plan, the cycle of readings (i.e., cantillations) progresses serially through all five books of the Torah in the course of a single year, reading a different section (Hebrew., *parashah*) each week. An alternative, known as the triennial cycle, divides each of those longer extracts into three shorter ones, reading the first third of each section one year, the second third the next year, and completes the cycle by reading the last third in the third year. Accompanying the weekly readings from the Torah is a companion cycle of readings from the prophets. Specific passages from the prophets (pl., *haftarot*; sing., *haftarah*) were chosen to accompany each section of the Torah because they had some relevance to the Torah reading for that week.

For the orthodox Jew the Torah is wholly, literally true because it was revealed by God directly to Moses at Mount Sinai. From this perspective it contains not just the overt story written in the five books, but all the wisdom necessary for mankind, in concealed meanings that can only be understood by careful study and analysis. According to the medieval Jewish-Arab philosopher Moses Maimonides, who attempted to harmonize Jewish and Greek thought, the Torah does not deny later developments in the arts and sciences, but rather indicates paths by which mankind can achieve them. The five books of the Hebrew Bible are shown in table 1.1.

TABLE 1.1
The Five Books of the Bible
(called the *Chumash* in Hebrew)

Hebrew Name*	English (i.e., Greek) Name
B'reshit	Genesis
Shemot	Exodus
Vayikra	Leviticus
Bamidbar	Numbers
Dvarim	Deuteronomy

*The Hebrew titles are actually the first word of each book.

The second component of the Bible is the writings of the prophets, inspired men who preached to the ancient Hebrews, interpreting and applying the wisdom they found in the Jewish tradition to morals and ethics. The earliest of them seem to have been musicians who delivered their visions to the people dramatically, through ecstatic song and dance. Most of the earliest prophetic material was not preserved in writing, so that group is sometimes referred to as the "pre-literate," or "early" prophets. The work of the so-called "literate," or "later" prophets was collected into the Book of Prophets (Hebrew: *Sefer Nevi'im*). These writings contain not only what we might characterize as prophecy, but moral and ethical principles, social criticism, and history, both cultural and political. Much of that material is in elegant poetry, intended to be sung. To this day it is declaimed musically in the synagogue in a style called cantillation. The Book of Prophets is divided into the *Nevi'im Rishonim* (Early Prophets) and *Nevi'im Achronim* (Later Prophets), as follows in tables 1.2A-C.

TABLE 1.2A	TABLE 1.2B
Nevi'im Rishonim	*Nevi'im Acharonim*
(The Early Prophets)	(The Later Prophets)
Joshua	Isaiah
Judges	Jeremiah
Samuel (Books I & II)	Ezekiel
Kings (Books I & II)	

TABLE 1.2C
The Twelve Minor Prophets
(collected into eight books)

Hosea	Jonah	Haggai
Joel	Micah	Zephaniah
Amos	Nahum	Zecheraiah
Obadiah	Habbakuk	Malachi

The third component of the Jewish Bible is itself an anthology, called *Ketubim* (Writings) in Hebrew, or *Hagiographa* (Holy Writings) in Greek. This is a collection—or rather several collections brought together—of religious writings that were included in the final form of the Bible by its editors, the Pharisaic scholars of the late Hellenistic period (see chapter 3). The books included under this heading are given in table 1.3.

TABLE 1.3
Ketubim (Hagiographa) (Writings)

Psalms	Ecclesiastes*
Proverbs	Esther*
Job	Daniel
Song of Songs*	Ezra
Ruth*	Nehemiah
Lamentations*	Chronicles

The books marked with an asterisk (*) are often grouped together under the general heading, "The Five Scrolls." Again, most of this material was poetic and intended to be sung, rather than read, in the worship service. More properly, it was meant to be cantillated—that is, sung in an elevated kind of musical declamation that is described in chapter 4.

Those three large components of the Bible are often referred to collectively by a Hebrew acronym representing the first letters of each part: Torah (Law), *Nevi'im* (Prophets), and *Ketubim* (Writings). For reasons having to do with the morphology of the Hebrew language, the letter that makes the sound "K" of *Ketubim* softens to a "ch" sound (as in Scottish "loch") when it occurs at the end of a word or syllable. Thus, with the addition of vowels to make the word pronounceable, the usual Hebrew designation for the whole Bible is the acronym, *Tanach*.

In addition, a number of other writings were once considered for inclusion in the Bible, but for one reason or another, were excluded. One group of these, called the Apocrypha (Greek for "Hidden"), was included in the Septuagint and was therefore later included in the Vulgate, the Latin translation that became the basis for the Catholic Bible of today. Still others were attributed to false or nonexistent writers and excluded from the Jewish Bible because they were judged historically questionable. This group is called the Pseudepigrapha (Greek: "Falsely Inscribed").

While Orthodox believers of all three major faiths regard the Torah as having been revealed to the ancient Hebrews in a single revelation, most scholars today view its compilation as a historical process. According to that view, the Bible as we know it was compiled in stages over more than half a millenium, with the Torah receiving its present form in the fifth century BCE, *Nevi'im* (Prophets) about the second century BCE, and *Ketubim* (Writings) late in the first century CE, although there was still controversy over some of them for a long time after that. It should be noted, though, that most Orthodox Jews reject this interpretation, as do most fundamentalist Christians.

To insure the greatest accuracy in recopying the Torah in the days before printing, there were many rules about who could be considered a suitable scribe, the circumstances under which an acceptable copy could be made, materials to be used, and a precise format from individual letter-strokes to page layouts. The rules included the mandate that each Torah, in order to be judged suitable for use, or *kasher* (literally, "bound" [by the law]), had to be hand-copied in the traditional manner by a person meeting the same requirements for integrity, orthodox religious belief, intelligence, and knowledge of biblical literature that were established over two millenia ago, and that nothing—not even the slightest mark (such as modern vowels or punctuation)—could be added, changed, or taken away from the text. The meticulous procedures and rules surrounding the copying of a Torah are in force even today, when Torah scrolls can be scanned for errors electronically and checked by computer to be declared fit for use. The text itself may be reproduced by any means, including printing, photocopying, or optical scanning; and vowels, punctuation, or commentary can be added to those copies, which may be bound in book (codex) form, as loose-leaf notebooks, or even put on computer disks. Such formats, which are widely used for study, may not be used in the synagogue ritual. Useful as they may be, they are not *kasher*. Only when in the form of a scroll, copied on vellum by a specialist with the unique ink whose formula has been prescribed for more than a thousand years, can a Torah be used in the synagogue service.

Since each hand-copied Torah was unique, the ancient texts were not always completely standard. In spite of meticulous care exercised to create only perfect replicas, slight variations crept in between one copy and another. As a result, a group of scholars undertook to produce a single, clear text with those ambiguities resolved. To do this, they worked for some twenty generations—half a millenium—from a vast collection of manuscripts, rabbinic notes, Talmudic quotations and other sources, including the traditional melodies for cantillating the holy books. These sources were said to constitute "the Tradition" (Hebrew: *Masorah*), and the scholars who undertook that work were known as Masoretes. They worked from the sixth century (CE) through the tenth century. Their work resulted in a clear, carefully annotated version of the Bible known today as the Masoretic text. In addition to their principal mission of collating and studying existing versions of the *Tanach* to produce a single authoritative edition, the Masoretes developed the vowel signs that were adopted into Hebrew and a system of musical notation about which we shall read more in chapter 4.

Liturgical Calendar

The calendar may seem unrelated to a discussion of music; but since so many aspects of Jewish life and celebration are related to the religious holidays, it is necessary to understand the major religious celebrations and when they occur. When leaving the land of their origins, the Jews carried its geography with them in their calendar. Knowing, for example, that the liturgical year begins at the end of the desert's long, dry summer and just before the wheat and barley are to be sown, it becomes clear why an important feature of the liturgy for the High Holidays is the prayer for dew—and why that prayer is musically highlighted. Bound to a calendar based on the agricultural year of the Middle East, Jews of the northern hemisphere continue to celebrate the tree-planting festival of *Tu b'Shevat* in the snows of February.

The Jewish year is calculated according to both lunar and solar cycles. Beginnings of the months and dates of festivals are calculated by phases of the moon, but the seasons are determined by the sun's position. The lunar year is about eleven days shorter than the solar year. This means that in nineteen years the accumulated difference is about 209 days, or approximately seven lunar months. To accommodate this, the Jewish calendar inserts seven additional months into each nineteen-year period, sometimes called the "small cycle." The system was established by the Temple priests (*kohanim*) on the basis of their direct observations of agricultural conditions. Today the leap year cycle is fixed, as it has been for centuries past, with the third, sixth, eighth, eleventh, fourteenth, seventeenth and nineteenth years of each "small cycle" lengthened by one lunar month. Those adjustments produce a more accurate calendar than either the Greeks or the Romans had. The following chart (table 1.4) shows one nineteen-year "small cycle," with leap years marked by an asterisk.

TABLE 1.4
Jewish Calendar "The Small Cycle"
(Leap Years marked by *)

1	2	3*	4	5
6*	7	8*	9	10
11*	12	13	14*	15
16	17*	18	19*	

In leap years the extra month is inserted following the month of Adar, and is simply called Adar II when it appears. A lunar month equals 29 days, 12 hours, 44 minutes, 3.33 seconds. If you multiply those figures out, you will find that they only add up to a little more that 354 days for the year. To make that come out even in practice, some lunar months are 28 days and some 29 or 30, depending on the year.[3] There are still more refinements in calculating the year and the seasons, but this will be more than sufficient for our purpose.

The calendar was not just a theoretical construct, but served a practical function. Its most important use was in predicting the seasons for sowing and harvesting, which were marked by religious festivals. One function of the priests of the ancient Temple was to keep track of

[3] For more discussion and detail on this complex topic, see Richard Siegel and Carl Rheins, *The Jewish Almanac* (New York: Pacific Press, 1987).

the calendar and set those dates. While that was first based on observation of the heavens, it has been done by mathematical calculation since the middle of the fourth century CE. Originally, the months were simply designated by number, as are the days of the week in Hebrew (except for *Shabbat*, the Sabbath); but when the Jews returned to Israel in the sixth century BCE, following the Babylonian exile, they brought Babylonian month names back with them, which have continued in use until today. The Jewish day, it should be noted, begins at sundown, because the Bible says "It was evening and morning. . . ." Thus all holidays, beginnings of months, and calculations of time start with sunset, not, as in the Roman calendar, with sunrise.

In the following listing of the Hebrew calendar year, the word "civil" designates the "chronological" or "civil" cycle of the year, while "religious" designates the annual liturgical cycle. Tishre, for example, is the first month of the civil cycle, but the seventh of the religious cycle. Some holidays were assigned a two-day celebration outside of Israel because of the possibility, in early times, of error in calculating their dates, while they were celebrated for only one day in Israel.

Jewish Year

The Hebrew months, with a listing of their principal days of religious observation, are:

Tishre (First civil month; seventh month of the religious year)

1-2	*Rosh Hashanah* (New Year)
3	*Tzum Gedalya* (Fast of Gedalia)
1-10	*Y'mei ha-Nora'im* (Days of Awe)
10	*Yom Kippur* (Day of Atonement)
15-21	*Sukkot* (Festival of Booths)
21	*Hoshana Rabah* (Great Hosannah)
22	*Shemini Atzeret* (Eighth Day Assembly)
23	*Simchat Torah* (Rejoicing in the Torah)

Cheshvan (or **Marcheshvan**) (Second civil month; eighth religious month)
(no major religious observations)

Kislev (Third civil month; ninth religious month)

25	*Chanukah* (Festival of the Rededication of the Temple) continues to the second or third day of Tevet, depending on whether Kislev has 29 or 30 days)

Tevet (Fourth civil month; tenth religious month)

10	*Tzum Tevet* (Fast of Tevet)

Shvat (or *Shevat*) (Fifth civil month; eleventh religious month)

15	*Tu b'Shevat* (New Year of the Trees)

Adar (Sixth civil month; twelfth religious month)

13	*Ta'anit Esther* (Fast of Esther)

14 *Purim* (Feast of Lots)
15 *Shushan Purim* (Extra day of Purim for walled cities)

Nissan (Seventh civil month; first religious month)
15-22 (15-21 in Israel) *Pesach* (Passover)
16 (to 5 *Sivan*): *Sefirat ha-Omer* (Counting of the *Omer*)
27 *Yom ha-Sho'ah* (Holocaust Commemoration Day)

Iyyar (Eighth civil month; second religious month)
4 *Yom ha-Zikaron* (Memorial Day)
5 *Yom ha-Atzma'ut* (Israel's Independence Day)
18 *Lag b'Omer* (33rd Day of the Omer)

Sivan (Ninth civil month; third religious month)
6-7 *Shavu'ot* (Feast of Weeks)

Tammuz (Tenth civil month; fourth religious month)
17 *Shva 'Asar b'Tammuz* (Fast of the Seventeenth Day of *Tammuz*)

Av (Eleventh civil month; fifth religious month)
9 *Tishah b'Av* (Fast of the Ninth of *Av*)
15 *Tu b'Av* (Fifteenth of *Av*). Not observed for centuries, this may once have been a midsummer solstice holiday. There is a movement afoot to revive this in certain quarters in Israel.

Elul (Twelfth civil month; sixth religious month)
The entire month is a month of solemn preparation for the Days of Awe, including special *Selichot* (penitential) prayers.

Rosh Hashanah means, literally, "The Head of the Year," but there are actually three different points in the year at which there is a celebration for the beginning of some annual cycle. *Rosh Hashanah*, the best known of those, falls on the first day of the month of Tishre. It marks the point at which the legal year begins, therefore the time at which the year number changes. Another "new year," called *Tu b'Shevat* (15th of Shevat), the "New Year of the Trees," occurs at the height of the rainy season and determines the breakpoint from which the age of trees, crops, and vegetation are calculated for agricultural purposes. The religious year, though, is measured from the first day of Nissan, which marks the date from which all religious festivals are calculated.

Some complicated cultural considerations affect the calculation of festival dates. The date for *Rosh Hashanah*, to give one example, establishes the calendar for other holiday observances during the year, therefore it must be set so that *Yom Kippur* will not fall on either a Friday or a Sunday, which would conflict with the observance of *Shabbat*. *Rosh Hashanah* must also be set so that the *Hoshanah Raba* festival will not fall on a *Shabbat*, for if that were to occur it would be forbidden to carry and beat the willow branches as is done on that day. Consequently, *Rosh Hashanah* cannot fall on a Sunday, Wednesday or Friday.

Holy Days Occurring in Shorter Cycles

- The Sabbath (*Shabbat*). Rabbinic authorities concur that it is not the annual festivals, but the weekly celebration of the Sabbath (*Shabbat*) that is the most important of the holidays. The Sabbath begins at sundown on Friday evening and continues until sundown on Saturday.

- New Moon (*Rosh Chodesh*). Celebrated as a minor festival each month, with special insertions in the prayer service and women abstaining from work. That last reason has been one of the factors leading to its recent revival in some quarters as a women's celebration.

- The Pilgrimage Festivals. Three of the holidays are "Pilgrimage" festivals—i.e., holidays on which every adult male was charged with making a pilgrimage to Jerusalem, bringing ritual sacrifices to the Temple. Because those pilgrimages were often made in groups singing both religious and secular songs, they have some musical significance as well. The three pilgrimage festivals are:

  - *Sukkot*: 15-22 Tishre, comes at the fall harvest of dates and olives, ripening of the vineyards.

  - *Pesach*: 15-22 Nissan, is placed at the end of the rainy season and before the barley or wheat harvest, when it was possible to close up the house and go to Jerusalem.

  - *Shavu'ot*: 6-7 Sivan, falls at the end of the barley harvest, but well before the wheat would need to be harvested.

The above constitute the principal holy days observed in Jewish communities around the world. Most of them, as we shall see, are connected to specific songs, prayers, and chants.

The religious calendar also impacts on "civil" aspects of Jewish life as well. No joyous celebrations such as weddings, for example, are permitted during the period known as "the ten days of awe" at the beginning of the Hebrew month of Tishre. The same is true during the seven-week period of *Sefirat ha-'Omer*[4] in the spring, the period that leads up to the barley harvest and the celebration of *Shavu'ot* (The Feast of Weeks). Because that is such a long period to suppress all festivity, one day, called *Lag b'Omer* (The fifteenth [day] of the *Omer*), is set aside for celebrations in the middle of that solemn count. That day, tradition says, was created for young people, so that impatient brides and grooms would not have to wait a full seven weeks to be married. Such information is more than simply a folkway. It is a clue to the values of a community and a hint to the music historian about what to look for in the culture. The calendar is a key to Jewish life and the music created for it. It shows, among other things, that sacred

---

[4] Literally, "counting the measures" [of barley]. This identifies a seven-week period between *Pesach* and the harvest feast, *Shavu'ot*. In the early Middle Ages it became a solemn period during which marriages, wearing new clothes, cutting one's hair, or other elements of rejoicing, were forbidden. The tradition seems to commemorate the deaths of perhaps as many as 24,000 students of the great rabbi, Akiva ben Joseph. Some say their deaths occurred during a plague, but the incident may instead refer to students killed in Bar Kochba's rebellion against the Roman Emperor Hadrian (132-135 CE), which had been strongly supported by Akiva.

and secular events were intertwined, suggesting that there is likely to be a similar merge of functions in the music.

Music for Jewish religious life is designed for the home and the synagogue, not the concert hall. For reasons discussed later, great orchestral and choral compositions of sacred music have not played a significant part in Jewish communal life. On the other hand, there was always a rich fabric of sound woven from the traditional chant for cantillation of the holy books, the melodic traditions of the synagogue, music for home and communal festivities, songs of love, joy, and sadness, dance music, lullabies, and music for plays, weddings, and life cycle celebrations. In today's Jewish music, melodies of the ancient world mingle with electronic sounds and oriental[5] melodies are colored with jazz harmony. "There is a time for everything," wrote Kohelet. Both ecstasy and mourning have a place in life, and if in life, then also in the music that encompasses every phase of Jewish life.

Synagogue

The word "synagogue" names the building used for social and religious purposes by Jewish communities, although in some of the Christian patristic writings the word was used allegorically to refer to the Jewish community as a whole. In later chapters the synagogue will be examined historically and it will become clear that the synagogue is not the same thing as the Temple in Jerusalem,[6] nor is it quite the same as its Christian counterpart, a church. Here, though, we will look at the institution one might find today. In Hebrew it is called a *bet knesset*, or "house of the congregation." In its earliest manifestation, discussed in chapter 7, it filled the need for a community study and social hall, gradually taking on a worship function because of the close relationship of study and worship in Judaism. After the fall of the Temple it became the center of religious activity for each community. In recent times a parallel institution, the Jewish community center, has arisen to house multi-congregational, social, and athletic activities, but originally the synagogue housed all important communal functions, liturgical and non-liturgical. Today's synagogues provide community social and meeting halls, religious education for children and adults, and in some places have even added a gym and pool, although athletic functions have generally been relegated to community centers.

A synagogue service may be officiated by two professionals—a rabbi and a cantor (Hebrew: *chazzan*), but neither is essential, as anyone may lead a service. A rabbi ("teacher," or "master") is hired by the congregation as a scholar-in-residence, a legal as well as an ethical guide chosen for the attributes of piety, scholarship, and humanity. The rabbi's function is to study and teach Jewish law, to read the texts, and to interpret them meaningfully to the congregation. Usually, though not necessarily, that assignment includes organizing and leading the prayer

---

[5] The term "oriental" is used throughout this book to mean what most Americans would think of as "Middle Eastern." That meaning is general in Israel today and, in fact, stems from eighteenth- and nineteenth-century European usage, in which "oriental" was used as a descriptor for everything east of Europe.

[6] Some Reformed Jewish congregations refer to their houses of worship as a "temple," possibly to commemorate the Temple destroyed in Jerusalem in 70 CE. Here, though, we will distinguish between the Temple in Jerusalem (with a capital "T") and the synagogue as a communal house of worship other than that.

services, a task shared with the *chazzan* (see the next paragraph). A synagogue is not required to have a rabbi, and many small congregations divide that role among knowledgeable members of the community; however, because of the importance of study of the texts and the vast literature to be mastered for their interpretation, a rabbi's presence is highly desirable, and for most Jewish communities, is prominent among their priorities.

A large urban congregation will usually engage a full-time *chazzan*, a singer employed as cantor, or leader of the service, whose role is probably better understood from the Hebrew name for the position: *shaliach tzibbur* (representative of the public)—that is, one who "represents" the congregation with his/her own voice in prayer. This personage is also hired by the congregation and is of more specific interest here because the position encompasses everything that might touch on religious music. The *chazzan* is usually a professionally-trained singer chosen for his/her piety, knowledge of the service, and musical ability. The job description calls for leading the singing of traditional melodies and/or composing new melodies for worship, teaching all aspects of music (e.g., hymns, prayer melodies, cantillation), chanting the special prayers for weddings, funerals, and appropriate public occasions, being responsible for the organization and performance of subsidiary worship music, such as that performed by the organist, choir, a soloist, etc., overseeing the music curriculum of the synagogue school, and being knowledgeable about all aspects of Jewish music—that is, sufficiently acquainted with music theory, history, and performance to function as the synagogue's respected liaison with the professional musical community. The ideal *chazzan* is supposed to be a devoutly religious person with a glorious voice, a skilled professional musician with the patience to teach young children, a diplomat, conductor, composer, and, to top it all off, a tireless performer who can sing the equivalent of full operatic performances on each of the High Holy Days in quick succession (on *Yom Kippur* that is the equivalent of several operas in twenty-four hours without food or water). This is not a job for the weak of body or spirit.

A large congregation may also employ others: a professional education director and a staff of teachers, a beadle (*shammash*), whose job it is to keep the library of religious books in order, clean the candlesticks, deal with the poor who need assistance, assist the rabbi by leading some of the services, and in some cases, keep track of the condition of the physical plant, although the actual janitorial duties usually no longer fall to this post, as they often did in earlier times. If the congregation is large enough, there may also be one or more assistant or associate rabbis and subordinate music directors, as well as a secretarial and janitorial staff, depending on its size. Administration is in the hands of a lay president, elected by the members, who works with those officials and committees of congregants on everything from hiring/firing staff to having the carpets cleaned.

Most synagogues usually welcome visitors, with one exception: it would be wise not to drop in without pre-arrangement during *Rosh Hashanah* or *Yom Kippur*, as there is likely to be a shortage of seating on those days. Sabbath (Saturday) morning services last about ninety minutes to three hours from beginning to end, depending on the style of the congregation. Other services vary widely in the time they take and the nature of the service itself.

A word may be in order about some of the things you may see in a modern synagogue. In Orthodox synagogues, men and women will be seated separately. Either there will be a physical separation between the sexes called a *mechitzah* (divider) in such congregations if all are seated on one floor, or women and children will be seated on another floor, such as a balcony, if that is available. There are several reasons for this. The two most important are a belief that women's voices would distract men from concentrating on prayer (discussed at length later) and a tradition that women, whose primary obligation was felt to lay with their families, should be free to come and go from the synagogue as the needs of children or home demanded without disturbing the men, who were obligated to remain until the prayers were finished. More liberal (Conservative or Reform) congregations do not follow this practice, and prefer families to be seated together.

Adult men wear a skull-cap or hat (Hebrew: *kippah* or Yiddish: *yarmulke*) in most synagogues. Caps are usually provided near the entrance for those who do not have their own. In more traditional congregations married women wear a hat or head covering, but girls usually do not. Today some women have also adopted the wearing of a *kippah* in the synagogue. The more liberal branches of Judaism continue to respect the tradition of head covering although they do not insist on it, and practice may vary from one synagogue to another. Most men wear a prayer shawl (Hebrew: *tallit*; Yiddish: *tallis*) over their clothing, and today some women choose to do so as well. This grows out of a tradition that congregants should cover themselves with a simple wrap while praying to eliminate, or at least minimize, distinctions in dress. The specific form that the prayer shawl takes is dictated by Deuteronomy 15, read in every prayer service, commanding the Jews to "make a fringe on the corners of their garments," and assigning symbolic meaning to the fringe and most specifically to the specially knotted strings (Hebrew: *tzitzit*) at the corners.

The tradition encourages reading aloud or in a semi-vocalized manner or sing-song when reading to oneself, which may be accompanied by weaving and bowing (called *shukeling*, in Yiddish) on the part of some people. This is an age-old practice which is more pervasive in traditional synagogues, less so in more modern-oriented synagogues. The presence (or absence) of this mode of prayer is a cultural tradition, not a religious one.

Regardless of how the building is situated, the main prayer hall, or sanctuary inside it, should be oriented so that the worshippers face Jerusalem. In the Western world, that would be facing East, but of course the Jews of China, India, or Iraq would face West. Against the eastern wall of the sanctuary, or built into it, will probably be a large closet with ornate doors and a covering curtain. This is called the "ark," in which the handwritten scrolls of the Torah are kept. Every synagogue will try to have at least one scroll, and many have a collection of them, some of which may be quite old. In Western synagogues each scroll is tied closed with a soft cloth and covered with a richly-embroidered mantle. Eastern Jews are likely to house their Torah scrolls in beautifully decorated hard cases that stand upright. In either instance the covering may also have a silver crown and other handsomely-wrought ornaments hung on it. The doors and/or curtains in front of the ark are usually beautifully decorated.

There are three basic layouts for the sanctuary. One traditional ground plan places the rabbi at the eastern, or Jerusalem-facing, wall and the cantor at the western end (i.e., facing east), with the congregation seated along the north and south walls facing the center. A second design has the congregation facing the ark on the eastern wall, with a special lectern in their midst for the cantor, also facing the ark, to symbolize the cantor's role as their "musical spokesperson." In this plan the rabbi, who interprets the law to the congregation, faces them *from* the East. Both the rabbi and cantor are provided with reading desks, but that of the cantor is usually larger and more elaborate, because it is there that the Torah must be unrolled and read. A third layout for a sanctuary, common since the nineteenth century, is much like that of an auditorium: both the rabbi and cantor are located at the front (East) of the room facing the congregation, each with their own lectern. This has gained favor among more liberal congregations, especially those that look to the cantor as a virtuoso singer whose performance is *to* the congregation, but other synagogues have adopted that plan as well, including many that maintain the traditional view of the cantor singing on behalf of the congregation.

Liturgy

The synagogue service was developed over a period of almost a thousand years, approaching a relatively well-developed state by the first or second century, and a more fully-developed liturgy by about the seventh century CE. The service was not fixed in its modern format until the sixteenth century, when printing of the prayer book (Hebrew: *siddur*) standardized Jewish worship to a great extent. Even today the Jewish service is relatively open to change and development, especially in more liberal congregations. There is no central authority that dictates details of the synagogue service, and local variations can be many; however, on the whole, there is tacit agreement that one does not stray too far, lest the sense of *klal Yisr'ael* (community of Israel) be lost. Many, but not all, synagogues are affiliated with one of several denominational organizations that have a modicum of standardization in the worship service as one of their goals, but such affiliation is not mandatory.

To endorse communal responsibility and participation two supplementary practices were developed in connection with the synagogue service. In the first of those, certain prayers can only be recited in a public service—"public" being defined as a service with at least ten members of the community present to constitute a *minyan* (quorum). Originally this meant ten men qualified by *bar-mitzvah* (a public declaration of religious majority normally, but not necessarily, undertaken at age thirteen). The Orthodox adhere to that tradition, but liberal congregations today usually include women in the count. None have proposed altering the basic count, though, for the concept of communal worship is an important part of Jewish practice. Of course, one may pray at any time and in any circumstance, but if there is not a *minyan* present, such occasions are considered private prayer. Calling for the presence of a *minyan* for public prayer was one way of emphasizing communal responsibility.

Another such practice was the development of various modes of participation for community members with different levels of learning and literacy. For the learned, the "study" portion of the service offered the opportunity to introduce original commentary or interpretation, although today this is normally left in the hands of the rabbi. For those willing to invest the time and effort, there are opportunities to lead prayers, declaim a section of the law or prophets in the special song-like reading called cantillation (see chapter 4), and/or to lead the congregation in blessings before each section of the law or prophets is read. There are also occasions for children to lead the congregation and ritual honors for members that can be carried out by congregants who may not have such expertise; for example, opening the curtains covering the ark or carrying the scroll of the law in procession. In this way, the rabbis created opportunities for all to participate actively in the service.

Variations in Liturgical and Social Practice

There are a number of different branches on the Jewish tree. Aside from the cultural differences between Ashkenazic and Sephardic Jews, the best-known ideological divisions in the United States are Orthodox, Conservative, Reform, and Reconstructionist. Those are divided into subgroups of bewildering complexity, even to many Jews, and there is little point in chasing down all the subtle differences here. To oversimplify for the sake of clarity, Orthodox congregations, the most traditional, adhere closely to the Torah as the literal word of God and the Talmud, developed at the beginning of the Middle Ages, as the basis of its interpretation. Reform Judaism grew out of a modernizing movement called the *Haskalah* (enlightenment) that first grew up among German Jews in the early nineteenth century, and has undergone several sweeping institutional revisions since then. The *Haskalah* is discussed at length in a "Historical Interlude" later in this book. In response to the growth and leftward swing of Reform Judaism, the late nineteenth century saw the rise of Conservative Judaism as an attempt to find a more traditional path between Orthodoxy and Reform. Reconstructionism was primarily the devising of the American rabbi, Mordecai Kaplan (1881-1983), who, in his 1934 book *Judaism as a Civilization*, sought to harmonize the spiritual essence of Jewish practice with the realities of life in the twentieth century. In addition, there are many congregations that do not affiliate with any of those movements, but develop their own liturgies, rituals, and practices. All this makes it hard to predict in detail what you may find when you attend a synagogue service, for the liturgy in one place might differ noticeably from another. These nominally different groups share a common core of religious and cultural beliefs; but to one unacquainted with the Jewish community, their superficial differences can appear quite confusing.

Sabbath (Saturday) Morning Synagogue Liturgy

Prayer services vary for different holidays and different seasons of the year, and it would be impossible to detail that diversity in this brief introduction. Instead, because of the importance of the Sabbath, we will look at a basic Sabbath morning service. There are four large divisions of the Sabbath morning service, demarcated by a recitation of the Sanctification prayer (*Kaddish*). They are:

A. *P'sukei d'Zimrah* (Passages of Song)
B. The Prayer Service
C. The Torah Service
D. The *Musaf* (Additional) Service

The following provides basic descriptive detail of each of those.

A. Passages of Song. The morning service opens with the singing of preliminary benedictions, psalms, and hymns known collectively as "Passages of Song" (*p'sukei d'zimrah*). These conclude with a reading of a "Short" or "Half" Kaddish (Sanctification, see below), marking the conclusion of this section of the service.

B. The Prayer Service

- Invocation to Prayer. This begins with the sung "call to prayer," beginning with the words, "Bless the Lord, Who is to be blessed" (*Bar'chu et adonai ha-m'vorach*). It continues with psalms, hymns, and scriptural readings in preparation for the next part of the service:

- The Declaration of Faith: "Reading the *Sh'ma*" (*Kri'at Sh'ma*). This is a key part of the service, a statement of belief in the unity of God that was later echoed in the *Credo* of the Catholic Mass. The central verse, taken from Deuteronomy 6:4 (*Sh'ma yisra'el adonai elohenu adonai echad* [Hear O Israel, the Lord our God, the Lord is one]), is the principal declaration of faith. The congregation's response is "Praised be the sovereignty of God through all time" (*Baruch shem kavod malchuto l'olam va'ed*). That is followed by several paragraphs expanding on the significance of the creed and culminating in the hymn, "Who is like You, O Lord" (*Mi chamocha*).

- The "Eighteen Benedictions" (*Amidah*). This takes its name (*amidah* = standing) from the tradition of standing to recite the entire section. It is the original core of the service—so important that it is often simply referred to as "the prayer" (*ha-tefillah*). Each member of the congregation reads these benedictions silently (there are actually nineteen, as is explained in chapter 3). Congregants sit down individually as they finish. The entire section is then repeated aloud by the prayer leader, a practice instituted to help worshippers who had no books (which, long ago, were rare and expensive) or who were illiterate, to learn the benedictions. Since neither of those conditions poses the problem today that it did in the Middle Ages, some modern congregations have eliminated or truncated the repetition. A number of powerful and moving compositions have been written for cantor, or cantor and choir, to perform during the repetition of the *Amidah*.

C. The Torah Service

- Reading of the Law (Torah) and Prophets (Haftarah). The ceremony for the reading of the law and prophets is a ritualized mini-drama. It consists of five major parts:

  1. Taking out the Torah.

     - Invocation. Singing of various psalm verses, beginning "There is none like God," (*Eyn kamocha*) declaimed by the prayer leader announcing the opening of the ark and removal of one or more Torah scrolls, depending on the circumstances.

     - Opening the ark. This is accompanied by the sung verses "And it came to pass when the ark went forward" (*Vay'hi binso'a*, Numbers 10:35-36), and "For out of Zion shall go forth the law" (*Ki mi-Tzion tetzei Torah*, Isaiah 2:3), followed by the blessing for receipt of the Torah.

- Removal of the scroll(s). Various blessings and prayers are sung as one or more Torahs are removed from the ark, culminating in the singing of the core verses of the declaration of faith, *Sh'ma yisra'el*.

- Procession with the scroll(s). In response to the cantor's singing "Magnify the Lord with me" (*Gadlu ladonai iti*, Psalm 34:4), the Torah scrolls are carried around the synagogue in procession to congregational singing of the hymns, "Thine, O Lord, is the greatness" (*L'cha adonai hag'dulah*, I Chronicles 29:11) and "Exalt the Lord" (*Romemu*, Psalm 99:8-9). As the procession approaches them, many will venerate the Torah by touching their prayer shawl or book to its cover, then kissing that object. Other prayers and verses are recited by the cantor during the preparation of the scrolls for reading.

2. Reading (Cantillation) of the Torah.

- The scroll is unbound and prepared for reading.

- Members of the congregation are called up to the lectern one at a time to read a section of the Torah, which, on the Sabbaths, is done in seven "portions." A reading, called an *aliyah* (ascension), is first given to a descendant of the priestly class (*kohen*), if one is in the congregation. If not, another member of the congregation can be called as a substitute. The second aliyah goes to a descendant of the tribe of Levi, if one is present. The other readings are open to all. Readings are to be done in a special, musically-heightened declamation, called cantillation. If congregants given the honor of an aliyah are not prepared to cantillate the portion, they may just sing the preliminary blessing before it is read by someone more knowledgeable (such as the cantor) and then the concluding blessing after. When children reach religious majority—called *bar mitzvah* for boys, *bat mitzvah* for girls—they are given the honor of reading the blessings and verses for the first time. It takes months of preparation, and is an accomplishment in which the entire community takes great pride.

- After the sixth reading there may be a Short Kaddish or Half-Kaddish, then the concluding (*maftir*) portion is read, either from a second scroll or from the same one. If two scrolls are used the first will be closed before the second is read, using the procedure given immediately below. The first scroll will then be set aside until the second is closed so that both can be put away together. If a youngster is becoming a *bar* or *bat mitzvah* that day, they will usually be called up to cantillate the *maftir*.

- Each portion is prefaced by a preliminary benediction and followed by a closing benediction. As each reader takes his/her place, special optional prayers or petitions may also be read.

- Two members of the congregation are called to the front to ritually close the scroll, one (the *hagba*) to carry the heavy scroll, the other (*galilah*) to re-wrap it. The scroll is held aloft by the *hagba* with the text facing the congregation for all to see, accompanied by singing of the hymn "This is the Torah" (*V'zot ha-Torah*, Deuteronomy 4:14) and "It is a tree of life" (*Eytz chayim hi*, Proverbs 3:18, 17, 16). The *galila* then replaces the scroll's decorative covering. The Torah is then set to one side until later, when it is formally returned to the ark.

3. Cantillation of the Prophetical Reading (*Haftarah*).

   - A member of the congregation (or the youngster becoming a *bar/bat-mitzvah*) sings a series of blessings preceding the cantillation of the prophets, then proceeds with the prophetic verses. This is traditionally (but not necessarily) the same person who read the *maftir*.

   - A series of prayers and blessings then follows. These may include:

     - Prayers and blessings for scholars, leaders of the community and the nation, or international leaders. These petitions ask for wisdom on the part of those who make decisions affecting the population.

     - Specific seasonal blessings, such as those for a new moon.

     - The singing of Psalm 145 (*Ashrei*, "Blessed are they that dwell in Thy house"), preceded by verses from Psalms 84 and 144.[7]

   - A recitation of the Half-Kaddish occurs here in some congregations.

4. Returning of the Torah scroll(s) to the Ark. A second procession carries the scroll(s) once more around the synagogue, and Psalm 29 is sung. The scroll(s) are then returned to the ark, which is then closed, and a closing prayer is sung.

5. Sermon (Study of the Law). The sermon is normally given by the rabbi, who presents an interpretation of the Torah and/or *Haftarah* just read, exploring its ethical/moral dimensions. Using the sermon as a platform for a communal discussion or debate is another way in which a rabbi might deal with this part of the service, whose chief purpose is study of the Torah portion of the week.

D. The *Musaf* (Additional) Service. A short additional service follows without pause, consisting of:

---

[7] Psalm 145 is an alphabetical acrostic that, curiously, skips the letter "nun," the 14th letter of the Hebrew alphabet. One tradition alleges that the letter was omitted because, as the beginning of the word meaning "to fall," it had negative associations with the fall of the Temple. Prefacing the singing of Psalm 145 with two additional verses (from Psalms 84:6 and 144:15) appears to be a tradition dating from early rabbinic times.

- Another reading of the *Amidah*

- Singing of the Full Doxology (*Kedushah*)

- Singing of the Full Kaddish

- Hymn: "There is none like our God" (*Eyn keloheinu*)

- The Adoration (*Aleynu l'shabe'ach*, "We bend the knee"). This is a very old prayer, predating the destruction of the Temple. It was originally part of the New Year service, but from the twelfth century CE it began to be used as the concluding hymn for all services, a practice that seems to have become universal among Jews by the fourteenth century.

- Another recitation of the Kaddish, the so-called "Mourner's Kaddish," spoken by those memorializing either the death of a loved one within the last month or the anniversary of their death.

- Announcements of interest to the congregation

- Concluding Hymn (*Adon olam*, "Lord of the world"). The poem is by Solomon Ibn Gabirol (1021-58).

Liturgical Occasions Outside the Synagogue

In Jewish practice liturgy is not restricted to the communal setting of the synagogue. Many liturgical traditions center around the home as well. Two of the most important are the Sabbath eve meal and the Passover Seder. Both of those traditions are deeply invested with music, some of which will be discussed later in the book. Here, though, the idea is only to introduce the setting in which that music is sung.

The family dining table is an important setting for religious song. Blessings over food are recited at every meal, and any meal eaten by three or more people (three or more men in Orthodox practice) should conclude with a formal grace, sung communally or read silently, depending on the occasion and the family's tradition. This is especially true of the most festive meal of the week, the Sabbath dinner. Guests and the best tableware, clean tablecloths, and special dishes are customary. Even the poorest families try to make the Sabbath dinner special to the best of their ability. The tradition is so strong that even the most militantly secular of the socialist-oriented Israeli *kibbutzim* (collective farms) will go out of their way to make Sabbath meals special occasions. In a traditional household, Sabbath meals, even more than other festive occasions, are followed by the singing of joyous songs (*z'mirot*).

The Seder is a festive celebration of freedom from slavery that takes place on the eve of Passover. It is built on a family retelling of the Passover story from the book of Exodus and rejoicing over having been freed from slavery, interspersed with moral tales, historical observations, and the singing of hymns, songs of praise, and allegories. It is the most elaborate home holiday, and one in which song plays a major role. It is hardly alone in that, though. Both joyous and solemn festivals have given rise to a rich repertory of song.

Perhaps the Jewish wedding is the most notable of the community celebrations in which music plays an important part. Tradition demands that weddings command the resources of an entire community, if necessary, "to gladden the heart of the bride." That precept has given rise to a rich overlay of traditions. The obligation to make the wedding a time of honor and joy for the bride overrode the rabbinic proscription on music in solemn observance of the destruction of the Temple. The wedding tradition, more than any other single aspect of Jewish life, gave rise to the employment of musicians (*klezmorim*) and the wedding jester (*badchan*), whose function was to keep everyone laughing, often at the good-natured expense of family members. Both of those figures will be discussed in chapter 6. A Jewish wedding is, on the one hand, a solemn exchange of vows and obligations: personal, communal, and religious. The other side of that coin is a joyous celebration for family and the entire community, honoring the bride and groom in an atmosphere of festive music and dance.

In addition, Jewish practice prescribes a blessing (Hebrew: *bracha*) for almost every daily activity. Drinking, eating, washing the hands, leaving on a trip or returning from one, meeting a scholar or encountering a thunderstorm, are only a few of the many occasions for praising God in daily life. Each act of daily life is made sacred by a brief blessing praising God: for creating food, commanding cleanliness, etc. All these blessings begin with the formula, "Blessed are You, O Lord our God . . ." and conclude with the specifics of the particular benediction. An example would be the blessing to be said over bread before eating: "Blessed are You, O Lord our God, who brings forth bread from the earth." Each, too, is a potential occasion for song, depending on the individual and the circumstances.

Secular Music

Strictly speaking, one might almost say there is no such thing; or perhaps it would be better to say there is no clear-cut division between what most westerners in the twenty-first century might consider sacred and secular. A continuing flow of recited and sung blessings in daily life, extension of liturgical and paraliturgical song into the home, communal celebrations in which music and dance play important roles, are all visible signs of the fusion of sacred and secular in Jewish life, and hence in the music. This fusion can be further seen in the adoption of secular melodies for prayers and hymns, and in the absorption of distinctive musical styles of the surrounding non-Jewish culture into the synagogue. Examples of the wholesale embracing of musical styles will be seen throughout this book. The florid virtuosity of Italian opera, the contrapuntal texture of Renaissance madrigals, the melodic intricacy of Islamic song, and the forthright squareness of Christian hymns all found a place in the home or synagogue repertory. Sensuous love poetry, such as the Song of Songs, was visualized as an allegory of the holy, ballads of Spanish nobility became lullabies, and marching tunes were transmuted into Sabbath songs. Things flowed in the other direction, too, as when the melody for the hymn *Yigdal elohim chai* (Praise the living God) became first an Anglican hymn and then a drinking song in eighteenth-century England. The melody long used in many Ashkenazic synagogues for the hymn *Eyn keloheynu* (Lord of the World) is almost identical with the sixteenth-century German Christmas song, *Schönster Herr Jesu* (Beautiful Lord Jesus). More recently, at the Chassidic Song

Festival in Israel, updated "pop" style melodies were introduced for centuries-old prayers, and many of those melodies have since become commercial hits. One Israeli artist, Ofra Haza, became an international recording star performing modernized arrangements of sixteenth-century Yemenite hymns that appealed to Europeans and Americans who had only the vaguest knowledge of what the words meant—they just liked the music.

That fusion of sacred and secular, of tradition and renewal, has made it possible for Jewish communities across the world to adopt local modes of artistic expression without compromising the core of their common belief system. Jewish music from India, Uzbekistan, France, Iran, or the United States may be stylistically indistinguishable from the music of non-Jewish countrymen; but its content and cultural function remain distinctively Jewish. It is that musical heritage, built on a tradition with roots in prophecy and the Temple, in millenia of persecution and celebration, that made and makes Jewish music not just an expression of the beauty of song, but a vehicle for public declamation. In the twentieth century, when American Jews turned centuries of background as *chazzan* (cantor), *badchan* (jester, entertainer), and *klezmer* (popular musician) to Broadway and Hollywood, they brought that didactic legacy with them. It was the Jewish composers who first took up social issues in their musicals, thus departing from the bland "moon-spoon-June" stories that had dominated the form earlier. Jerome Kern, together with librettist Oscar Hammerstein II, was one of the first, tackling racial prejudice in the 1927 musical, *Show Boat*. Hammerstein then teamed with Richard Rodgers to deal with wife-beating in *Carousel*. Harold Arlen took an anti-war stance in *Bloomer Girl*, while Kurt Weill attacked apartheid in *Lost in the Stars* and the tensions of tenement life in *Street Scene*. Marc Blitzstein upheld unionism in *The Cradle Will Rock*. George Gershwin, who had earlier lampooned politics in *Of Thee I Sing*, wrote the greatest musical play to have yet come from the American stage, dealing with poverty, drug addiction, and racial prejudice in *Porgy and Bess*.

Ethnomusicologist Bruno Nettl writes that every society shapes music to its own needs. That has certainly been the case with Jewish music. It pervades the home, the synagogue, and daily Jewish life in such a way that separating the religious from the worldly is not always possible. One of the important features in defining a musical style is the cultural use to which it is put. It is that purpose, its vital function in the community's life, that imparts distinctive intensity to Jewish music. Perhaps that is the reason why so many people are discovering—or rediscovering—it today.

Suggestions for Further Reading

Abrahams, Israel. *A Companion to the Authorized Daily Prayerbook; Historical and Explanatory Notes*. New rev. ed. New York: Bloch, 1966.

Donin, Hayim. *To Be a Jew: A Guide to Jewish Observance in Contemporary Life*. New York: Basic Books, 1972.

Elbogen, Ismar. *Jewish Liturgy: A Comprehensive History*. Trans. Raymond P. Scheindlin. Philadelphia and Jerusalem: Jewish Publication Society, 1993.

Hallo, William W., David B. Ruderman, and Michael Stanislawski. *Heritage: Civilization and the Jews, A Source Reader*. New York: Praeger, 1984.

Idelsohn, A. Z. *Jewish Music in its Historical Development*. New York: Schocken Books, 1967.

_____, and National Federation of Temple Brotherhoods. *The Ceremonies of Judaism*. Cincinnati: The National Federation of Temple Brotherhoods, 1929.

Kaplan, Mordecai Menahem. *Judaism as a Civilization; Toward a Reconstruction of American-Jewish Life*. New York: Macmillan, 1934.

Neusner, Jacob, and Alan J. Avery-Peck. *The Blackwell Reader in Judaism*. Oxford: Blackwell, 2001.

Nulman, Macy. *Concise Encyclopedia of Jewish Music*. New York: McGraw-Hill, 1975.

Siegel, Richard, Michael Strassfeld, and Sharon Strassfeld. *The Jewish Catalog: A Do-It-Yourself Kit*. Philadelphia: Jewish Publication Society of America, 1973.

2 Music in the Bible

Music played an important role in the life of the Jewish people from their earliest recorded history. The book of Exodus tells us that following the Hebrews' escape from the Egyptian army at the Red Sea a spontaneous outburst of song and dance was led by Miriam, Moses' sister. Even though King Saul was known primarily as a warrior king, he can be credited with establishing a professional school for training Temple musicians. His successor, King David, gave us the first known example of music therapy while still a boy, by playing the lyre to soothe Saul in his fits of depression. As a vigorous young national hero, David again illustrated the importance of joyful music and dance to the ancient Hebrews when he danced in triumph before the ark. As might be expected from a king famous as a musician himself, David expanded professional music training in his own royal capital (Chronicles 15:22), where he created a music school whose outline was replicated more than a millennium later in the Roman *schola cantorum* created by Gregory the Great, pope from 590 to 604 CE.

Levitical Musicians

When the twelve tribes of Israel conquered the Land of Canaan, the country was divided into geo-political units. Tribes were each assigned one of those areas as their own territory except for the tribe of Levi, which was accorded special treatment. Within that tribe the families of Moses and Aaron were designated as priests (*kohanim*), who were to serve in the Temple. The rest of the tribe of Levi was assigned to the administration of all those tasks necessary to maintain the practice of a priestly religion. Instead of tilling the land, fishing, or herding, the Levites were accorded the honor of serving in perpetuity as keepers of the holy ark and providers for all its attendant needs. The Levites, then, according to their individual abilities, became the Temple architects and masons, accountants and gardeners, educators, scribes, and street sweepers. Among those duties was the performance of music for the Temple service, including psalms and hymns of praise to the Lord. According to I Chronicles 23:30, they were required "to stand every morning to thank and praise the Lord, and likewise at evening."

The post of Levitical musician was considered so important that those professionals were exempted from all other duties, "for they were employed in their work day and night" (I Chronicles 6:16). Public ceremonial music called forth special mention in the Bible. At the dedication of Solomon's Temple the chronicler made special note of the quality of the music: "It came about that the multitude of trumpeters and singers were as one—to make one sound together praising and thanking the Lord" (II Chronicles 5:12-13). On another important occasion of civil ceremony, the crowning of the boy-king, Joash, it was recorded that "All the people of the land rejoiced and blew with trumpets. The singers also played on instruments of music and led the singing of praise" (II Chronicles 23:13).

Apparently, at some later date, the singing of psalms was delegated to particular Levitical families, or so it seems from the statement of II Chronicles 20:19: "The Levites of the sons of Kohath, and of the sons of Korach . . . praised the God of Israel with a loud voice on high." One hundred seventeen of the psalms have superscriptions of one sort or another, many of which contain some type of musical terminology. Many superscriptions to the psalms mention the sons of Korach as performers. In Chronicles and elsewhere, we read of other musicians as well. Herman and Jeduthun were named to sound the silver trumpets (*chatzotzerot*), for example, and Chananiah seems to have been the principal conductor and teacher of the music school. A recent discovery in the rubble surrounding the destruction of the Temple in Jerusalem was a stone that had fallen from the parapet of the building 2,000 years ago, with an inscription that identified it as the location from which the silver trumpets were sounded (see fig. 2.7). Under David, for special occasions, the Levitical orchestra and chorus numbered "four thousand who pleased the Lord with instruments" (Chronicles 23:5), and, under the later kings music played an increasingly important role in both sacred and secular life. Songs of triumph, despair, faith, and love are woven through the biblical narrative. Many psalms were to be sung to existing melodies, and were rooted in the folk melos of the land of Israel. Centuries later, when the Jews were driven from their own land into a foreign culture, their poets in the Babylonian exile lamented, in Psalm 137, the impossibility of singing Israel's songs "by the rivers of Babylon."

Imagining the Music

If we could only hear those songs many puzzles about worship, melody types, and musical style would be resolved. What music soothed mad King Saul when, as it says in I Samuel (16:23), "David took a lyre, and played with his hand; so Saul was refreshed, and was well, and the evil spirit departed from him?" What martial blasts brought down the walls of Jericho? What music accompanied King David's dance before the ark, and what wild melodies inspired the ecstatic trances of the early prophets? The sad truth is that apparently nothing has been preserved from the music of the biblical world but the raucous sound of the shofar.[1] The best

---

[1] See pp. 40-41 for a description and illustration of this musical instrument and its function.

we can do is try to build a picture from the numerous accounts in the Bible and the Book of Psalms, and to look at what we have discovered about the music of the neighbors of the ancient Hebrews. Assyriologists have found writings about music from the ancient city-states of Assur, Nippur, Ugarit, and Ur, and have even transcribed what appears to be a Hurrian hymn to the moon goddess. Egyptologists have uncovered drawings and paintings of ancient musicians and their instruments; but when all is said and done, we still do not really know what biblical music sounded like.[2]

The prominence given to the art of music in the Bible shows that it played an important role in the life of the ancient Hebrews. We are provided with a description of the music for King Solomon's dedication of the first great Temple (the *bet hamikdash*, "consecrated house"), and in I Chronicles, chapter 15, we are given a critique of the dedication performance: "It came about that the multitude of trumpeters and singers were as one—to make one sound together praising and thanking the Lord." In the same place we are also told that Herman, Asaph, and Eitan were precentors (song leaders) and solo singers who conducted and gave cues to other musicians. Asaph is also said to have composed some of the psalms, but it is not clear whether that was the music, the poetry, or what is most likely, both. Eight others are named there as sub-precentors, or leaders of divisions, who led songs and accompanied themselves *al alamot*, an obscure term to be discussed later that may possibly mean "with psalteries," or as many modern scholars think, "with young women." Six more are named as prefects who either doubled the melody at the octave *al sheminit* (or "on 8-stringed harps," in another reading) or possibly even played some kind of accompaniment. Unfortunately, as with so many other clues about biblical music, the exact meaning is still uncertain.

An enormous variety of song types besides the well-known psalms are mentioned at one place or another in the Bible. Second Chronicles (32:13) describes royal ceremonial music as employing trumpets and other "instruments of music" as well as choral song. Shlomo Hofman, who combed the Bible for references to music, lists over 900 places in which mention is made of song or a type of musical instrument in his *Miqra'ey Musica*.[3] There are still other references to music in the Bible that he omitted because he felt the language was ambiguous. This attests to a culture in which music played more than an incidental role. Some of the other song types mentioned in the Bible are listed in table 2.1. Beyond these song types, there is no reason to doubt that mothers sang lullabies to their children, men boasted of their prowess in song, and children sang game-songs in their play.

Looking over such evidence allows us to draw a cultural picture in which a rich variety of music infused every aspect of life. While we cannot re-create that music, we can examine aspects of the biblical heritage that still exist in order to draw conclusions and make inferences

---

[2] As an example of that uncertainty we should note that the Hurrian hymn mentioned earlier has incorrectly been transcribed as the first example of polyphony in history. More recent work has corrected that misperception, but the error still stands in a number of quite recent books. For further information, see *Sounds from Silence: Recent Discoveries in Ancient Near Eastern Music* by Anne Draffkorn Kilmer, Richard L. Crocker, and Robert Brown (Berkeley, CA: Bit Enki Publications, 1976), corrected by Marcelle Duchesne-Guilleman in *A Hurrian Musical Score from Ugarit: The Discovery of Mesopotamian Music*; vol. 2, fascicle 2, *Sources from the Ancient near East* (Malibu, CA: Undena Publications, 1984).

[3] Shlomo Hofman, *Miqra'ey musica* (*Occurrences of Music* [in the Bible]) (Tel-Aviv: Israel Music Institute, 1974).

TABLE 2.1
Song Types found in the Bible

1. psalms and hymns of praise	8. love songs
2. war songs (Numbers 21:14-15, 21:27-30)	9. wedding songs
3. songs of triumph (Exodus 15:20, Judges 5:1 ff, Samuel 21:12)	10. drinking songs
4. marching songs	11. dance songs
5. work songs of the Temple builders	12. songs of the palace
a. laying the cornerstone (Job, 38:7)	13. songs of the courtesan
b. laying the top-stone (Zechariah 4:7)	14. songs of derision
6. field workers' songs	15. songs of mourning/lamentation
7. songs of the watchmen (Isaiah 21:12)	16. pilgrimage songs

about the nature of the music. Those fall into three categories: literature, artifacts, and traditions. The literature of the Jewish people has been preserved with great care. An important collection of music expressly designed for singing has come down to us in the Book of Psalms; also, other parts of the *Tanach*, such as the prophetical writings and the public declamation of the Torah, are known to have been rendered musically. Archeological investigations have provided us with both artistic representations of musical instruments and remnants of the instruments themselves, from which measurements could be made and conclusions drawn about the type of sound, and even, to some extent, the playing style employed. Tradition, while often cited as important, is actually the least reliable indicator of the distant past, because traditions can be altered, either consciously or unconsciously, by creative modification or distortion. By examining evidence from all three categories and cross-checking among them, though, some approximation of biblical music can be perceived, however imperfectly.

Psalms

Without question the best-known musical compositions of the Bible are the psalms, which have inspired both Jewish and Christian composers for thousands of years. Psalms were lyric poems created to be sung, either to a pre-existing melody or a new melody composed for that specific poem. Psalms were sung as part of the daily Temple ritual. To the best of our knowledge, they were performed by chorus and accompanied with instruments, but they also employed some solo songs and possibly choreographed choral movement, though the latter is not certain.

Psalm 68:24-25 gives a picture of one way in which music was used in certain ceremonies:

> They see thy processions, O God,
> The processions of my God, my King, in the sanctuary.
> The singers go before,
> The players on instruments (*nogenim*) follow after,
> Among them are maidens beating tambourines (*tofefot*).

Another example, taken from Psalm 43:4, reads:

> Then will I go to the altar of God,
> To God my exceeding joy,
> And I will praise thee with the lyre (*kinnor*)[4]

And again, from Psalm 71:22:

> I too will praise thee with the harp (*nevel*)
> Speaking of thy truth, O my God,
> To thee will I sing with the lyre (*kinnor*).

In performance, psalms were sung in the Temple service by various combinations of voices or voices and instruments. Certain performance practices influenced musical forms not only in the synagogue, but in the later development of music for the Christian church as well, and through that, the whole of Western music. Those seminal practices codified in the psalms were:

Direct performance. Performance straight through, either with or without instrumental accompaniment.

Responsorial performance. Alternation between a soloist and a choral response, or between the soloist and a simple communal response from the observers, such as *Amen* (so be it) or *Hallelujah* (praised be God).

Antiphonal performance. Division of the choir into two parts with the lines (or half-lines) of the psalm text sung first by one half of the choir, then by the other.

Direct performance, of course, was hardly an innovation, and can be passed by without comment. The influence of responsorial performance, though, was considerable. It can be seen not only in the important place of that practice in both synagogue and church liturgy, but because church forms shaped the thinking of so many Western composers, it formed a basis for purely secular musical expressions such as the concerto, and set the stage for musical expressions as diverse as the "call and response" work song and the jazz solo, both of which employ the formula of a musical leader to which a larger group "responds." To see the influence of the antiphonal mode of performance, we need only think of the polychoral motets of the late Renaissance or, in a very different context, the popular "battle of the bands" that are often a feature of night clubs, popular music events, or football games.

As we have seen, psalms were also used for processionals and were often used for special paraliturgical occasions as well, as they still are today. When the Jews returned from the first Babylonian exile (ca. 516 BCE), the governor Nehemiah wrote about the reassembly of the Levitical musicians. From his description, we see they were a double choir with instrumental accompaniment and that they performed antiphonally for the celebrations at the dedication of the rebuilt Temple:

---

[4] The Hebrew *kinnor* (lyre) is sometimes translated with the Greek word *kithara*, from which our modern word "guitar" is derived. The translation of these psalms is from *The Jerusalem Bible* (Jerusalem: Koren, 1988).

> And at the dedication of the wall of Jerusalem they sought the Levites out of all their places, to bring them to Jerusalem, to keep the dedication with gladness, both with thanksgiving, and with song, cymbals (*metziltayim*), harps (*nevelim*), and lyres (*kinnorot*). And the singers gathered together . . . and [I] appointed two great companies of them that gave thanks, whereof one went on the right hand upon the wall . . . [and the other to the left]. (Nehemiah 12:27-28 and 31)

The Book of Psalms seems to have been compiled over several centuries. In its present form it contains 150 poems.[5] Many people are under the impression that the psalms were all written by King David, but that is not only unlikely, it would have been impossible.[6] Certain psalms refer to events that happened after David was dead, while others contain words he would not have known, or use a poetic style that had not developed when he was alive. Additionally, there are psalms within the collection whose headings clearly attribute them to Korah and Asaph as well as David.

Many psalms are headed with superscriptions that tell us something about the composition of the psalm or its intended use. Psalms 51, 52, 54, 56, 57, 59 and 63, for example, are headed with a brief biographical note saying where and when, or under what circumstances, David composed them. Other superscriptions give different information, sometimes quite mundane, sometimes puzzling. None of this down-to-earth information makes the Psalms any less marvelous as one of the world's great bodies of lyric poetry. Their place is assured by the beauty of their language and imagery, which has colored the speech of every people to have come into contact with them, and by the profound spiritualism that infuses them.

The impulse to create religious poetry remained part of the Jewish heritage long after the destruction of the Temple. All through the Middle Ages, poet-musicians in Jewish exile communities continued to write religious songs and poems. After the compilation of the Bible, though, in which the psalms inherited from the ancient world were included, the collection of psalms was considered closed and no new ones were added. Later compositions in that vein, and there were many throughout the Middle Ages, were called *piyyutim*, and the authors who wrote them were known as *paytanim*.[7] Many *piyyutim* were used in compiling the prayer book (*siddur*)[8] while others remained alive in the tradition but were not utilized for formal prayer services.

---

[5] The Septuagint includes a 151st psalm, telling of the duel between David and Goliath; but this is regarded as apocryphal by Jewish authorities.

[6] Again, when dealing with biblical matters, one must note that the conclusions of scholarship are not always accepted by certain communities of faith.

[7] Note the resemblance between the Hebrew word *piyyut* and the English word "poet." Both the English and Hebrew words ultimately derive from the Greek *poenin*, meaning "to make or create" something.

[8] A linguistic aside: The Jewish prayer book is called a *siddur*, derived from the root letters *SDR*, meaning "to arrange, put things in order." The same root gives us the Hebrew name for the Passover ceremony, the *Seder*: an orderly arrangement for re-telling the story of the Exodus. Hebrew roots are discussed further in the following section.

Musical Information in the Book of Psalms

To understand the following discussion about biblical music most fully, it is first necessary to understand how Hebrew words are formed. As in other Semitic languages, most Hebrew words are based on a root form usually made up of three consonants that always remain the same, even as the word changes to reflect gender, number, tense, or even different (but related) meanings. Word-building proceeds by adding prefixes, suffixes, and infixes of other consonants or vowels to that root. For example, *LMD* is the root of both the word *LoMeD* (to learn) and *meLaMeD* (to teach). One can easily see, then, the relationship between that root and the words *LaMiD* (teachable), *LeMiDah* (learning), and *meLuMaD* (a learned person; i.e., a scholar). Just understanding those relationships will help greatly in untangling the following discussion.

The collection of religious poetry we know as the Book of Psalms is called *Sefer Tehillim* (Book of Songs of Praise) in Hebrew. The (plural) word *teHiLLim* (sing.: *teHiLLah*) comes from the root *HLL*, meaning "to praise," which is more familiar to English speakers as it occurs in the Hebrew exclamation *HaLleLujah* (Praise the Lord).[9] The Latin word *Psalmus* derives from the Greek *psallein*, meaning "to pluck a stringed instrument," which gives a strong suggestion about the intended mode of performance.

Fifty-seven psalms have headings with the word *mizmor* in them. This derives from the root *ZMR*, which seems to indicate a song independent of dance, most probably accompanied by the *nevel* (psaltery) or harp. *ZMR* is a root of Assyrian origin, where it meant "to play an instrument" or sometimes, "to sing." A second meaning for that word is "to pinch or pluck a string," which is how those instruments were played. Another designation found for some of the psalms is the word *ShIR*,[10] meaning "song" or "lyric poem for singing," particularly on joyous occasions. Eventually that term came to be especially applied to songs sung by the Levitical choir. One interpretation is that *shir* meant a psalm accompanied by instruments, and *shir mizmor* (note the root *ZMR* inside the word *miZMoR*) was a song for chorus alone. It is possible that the original Assyrian meaning had been lost and the word came to be applied in that new way. As a matter of fact, in Assyrian itself, the phrase *zamar sh'eri* meant "an elegiac song." Some psalms bore the barely different designation, *mizmor shir*. There appears to be no discernible difference between those headed *shir mizmor* and those headed *mizmor shir*; but again, the fact is that we really don't know. There may have been some unexplained difference in the way they were performed, but at the present we have no evidence one way or the other.

---

[9] The double-L in "hallelujah" occurs because Hebrew consonants are sometimes "strengthened." This is no problem in Hebrew, where it simply means placing a dot in the middle of the letter, but in English it requires writing the consonant twice, as in Hallelujah or Sabbath.

[10] This root contains a sound that must be represented in English by a consonant cluster (Sh). That sound is represented by a single Hebrew letter. We will encounter two more of those: "Ch" and "Tz."

Shir ha-ma'alot Psalms

A rather puzzling heading, *Shir ha-ma'alot*, appears before fifteen consecutive psalms, numbers 120-134. Scholars believe that this is the oldest group of Psalms sung by the Levitical choir in the ancient Temple service. There is some evidence that this may have been an independent collection, later integrated into the larger collection of psalms. The heading *Shir ha-ma'alot* has been translated variously as "Song of Degrees," "Song of Ascents," and "Pilgrim's Song." The root *'ALH*[11] always has the meaning of ascending, but it is used in several different ways. In the form *ma'ALeH* (pl., *ma'alot*)[12] it can be used to designate either "degrees" (as on a thermometer) or "steps." The relationship between those two is clear. In a third meaning whose relationship is also relatively easy to see, the word can signify "arise" or "ascend." When the word takes the form *'OLeH*, though, it has the meaning "pilgrim" or "immigrant," two terms that seem, at first, to be unrelated. There is a connection, though—one that has musical implications.

Since Jerusalem is in the mountains, one is said "to ascend" to Jerusalem, even today. That accounts for the translation, "Song of Ascents." Ascending to Jerusalem for the three pilgrimage holidays was an obligation for every Israelite, and those who made the journey were designated by this same root, which we would then translate as "pilgrim" (literally, "one who goes up"), which is where the third possible meaning comes from. It is on that basis that Alfred Sendrey asserts this group of fifteen psalms was a collection of popular songs that people sang while walking on the prescribed pilgrimages to Jerusalem.[13] The same word (*oleh*) is used not just for a pilgrim, but for anyone who "goes up" to Jerusalem, and by extension, to the country of Israel: an immigrant. In a fourth, liturgical, usage, the word is applied to the Torah reading in the synagogue. A person is said to be called from the congregation to an *'ALiyaH* (arising, or going up) to read the Torah.

To add still a fifth possibility, Martin Luther, in his translation of the term *Shir ha-ma'alot*, used the phrase, *ein Lied in höhern Chor* (a song in the upper choir), assuming that the term referred to the placement of the Levitical choirs on the steps of the Temple. That is not as far-fetched as it may sound at first, since the Levites actually did stand on riser-like steps in front of the Temple to perform. Modern scholars feel that was the reason one of the more elaborate musical sections of the medieval Christian Mass was called the "gradual," a word derived from the Latin word *gradus*, meaning "step"—the Latin translation of *ma'aleh*. It is quite possible that in the middle ages soloists in church performed the gradual from the steps in front of the altar, since tradition claimed the steps as the place from which the Levites made their music in the days of the Temple.

---

[11] The root of the word *ma'alot* is 'ALH, which poses some problems for English readers. First of all, the letter represented by 'A (note the apostrophe before it) is not a vowel, but a consonant—a silent one that we don't have in English, which can carry the sound of any appended vowel. It is probably easiest to think of it as the "glottal stop" that you use to begin each syllable of "Uh-oh." There are two such letters in Hebrew, both represented here by the sign ('). The consonant has various vowel sounds added so that you can pronounce it.

[12] The final "h," which is nowhere to be found in the plural form, *ma'alot*, is the last letter in the root, but it is replaced by the "-ot" ending of feminine plurals. You can find similar confusing changes in English, where "was," for example, is the past tense of "am."

[13] Alfred Sendrey, *Music in Ancient Israel* (New York: Philosophical Library, 1969), 138.

Other Musical Terms in the Psalms

Another six psalms bear the heading *miktam*. The meaning of that word has generated enormous controversy among biblical scholars, with interpretations ranging from "an unidentified wind instrument" to "an epigram with a hidden meaning." Sendrey suggests[14] that this may be the key word or title identifying a song whose melody was to be used for this psalm, as was not uncommon in Middle Eastern cultures and was true of some of the other psalms. However, that, like so many other things, is still an unresolved argument, and there is no single, agreed-upon meaning for *miktam*. Shlomo Hofman, in his survey of musical terms in the Bible, *Miqra'ey Musica*, does not even include that term. Still another problematic term that appears is *shiggayon* (e.g., Psalm 7), which also appears in the Book of Habbakuk (3:1) in slightly different form as '*al shiggyonot* (on [several] *shiggayons*). This may have derived from the Assyrian liturgical term *Shigu*, meaning a lamenting dirge in several stanzas.

The term, *la-m'natze'ach*, which heads fifty-five psalms, derives from the root *NTzCh*,[15] meaning "shine" or "triumph," and is now commonly believed to refer to the leader or precentor of the Levitical choir. In a similar analogy, the word is used in modern Hebrew to indicate "conductor" as well as "victor." It may mean that this psalm was to be sung by the leader as soloist, or, in another interpretation, that it was sung responsorially by soloist and choir. Sendrey suggests that the heading may have been put there at the insistence of the precentors, in recognition of their role as virtuoso in the performance.[16] There is more than a little evidence to support that theory, which, if true, suggests something about the nature of the soloist's part in responsorial performance of the psalms. If it was important to the singer to denote a particular psalm as a solo, we may venture a guess that the singer expressed enough individualism in the performance (by way of ornamentation and improvisation, for example) to mark it with his own style, much as many performers do today.

Another important word found in the Book of Psalms is *neginah*, or its plural, *neginot*, deriving from the root, *NGN*, meaning "to play by touching the strings." This is the term that was translated into Greek in the Septuagint as *psallein*, from which the English word "psalm" is derived. Thus, we can find the heading, *lam'natze'ach baneginot*, which might mean, in this interpretation, "for the precentor [to sing as a virtuoso solo] with [the accompaniment of plucked] string instruments." The term *nigun* will appear in other contexts, too. It appears later as the designation for a wordless melody, hummed, or sung to nonsense syllables such as "ya-ba-bam" or "la-la," that became popular among the *Chasidim* of more modern times.

Another term, '*al 'alamot*, appears only twice in the Bible: once in the heading of Psalm 46 and again in Chronicles (15:20). This is another controversial term. The majority of scholars today agree, with some hesitation, on the meaning: "in the range of women's voices," or "in the treble range." '*Al sheminit* has been translated as "on the 8-[string harp]," but another suggestion has been that it may refer to a specific ritual by name, to "the eighth act of purification," or even to

---

[14] *Music in Ancient Israel*, 104-08.

[15] The "la-" prefix means "to . . ." or "on behalf of. . . ."

[16] Sendrey, *Music in Ancient Israel*, 116-17.

"the eighth day," indicating that these psalms were to be performed on the eighth day of a festival. Recent scholarship suggests another intriguing possibility: that this term may indicate the same thing as "8ᵛᵃ basso" in modern musical notation—that is, it should be read as, "in the range of men's voices," or, "an octave lower." If so, the following puzzling passage (I Chronicles 15:21):

> *benaiah b'nevalim 'al-'alamot . . . v'azaziah, b'kinnorot al hasheminit l'natze'ach*

which has sometimes been given the obscure half-translation

> Benaiah, with harps *'al-'alamot* . . . and Azaziah, with lyres *'al sheminit*, to (lead? shine out? triumph?)

should really be read as rather straightforward performance directions:

> Benaiah, with harps in the treble . . . and Azaziah, with lyres in the bass, to lead.

The headings of Psalms 53 and 88 contain the rubric, *'al machalat*. Again, even the earliest translators did not seem to know exactly what this meant, so it appears in the Vulgate and Septuagint more-or-less unchanged as *pro maheleth* and *pro ma'eleth*, respectively. Others have related this word to three different roots, all with possible musical implications:

1. Deriving it from the root *ChLH*, as in *machalah* (sickness), some commentators feel that these are psalms written in thanks for recovery from illness. Others think this extremely unlikely, in the light of the contents, especially those of Psalm 53.

2. Deriving it from the root *MChL*, as in *machol* (dance), some have translated it as *pro chore* (for the dance) or (for the roundelay). While this is not out of the question, because choral movement *may* have played a role in the Temple service, the content of Psalms 53 and 88 makes that unlikely—though not impossible.

3. Deriving it from the root *ChLL*, as in *chalal*, provides a whole different set of interpretations. This root has two principal meanings: "to profane" and "to pierce."

   a. "To profane" has sometimes been used to translate these headings with an implication of the reflexive (*hitpa'el*) form of the verb, as "to profane, lower, or afflict oneself."

   b. The meaning, "to pierce" gave rise to the interpretation of the medieval scholar Rashi: "on a 'pierced' instrument" (meaning the flute or pipe). This is given credence by the fact that the Hebrew word for such an instrument is *Chalil*.

The majority of commentators accept Rashi's interpretation (3b), with that of "dance" (2, above) as the second most popular reading. There is more discussion of the *chalil* below (see p. 40).

Psalm 30 has the heading, *Shir chanukkat ha-bayit* (Song for the Dedication of the House). The title suggests that this might be the psalm described in Chronicles as having been performed at the dedication of Solomon's Temple (tenth century BCE), or if not then, at the dedication of the second Temple more than 400 years later. If so, that suggests an extraordinary performance, with large chorus and orchestra as described in Chronicles, including trumpets and percussion instruments (fig. 2.1).

FIG. 2.1   **Cult stand with musicians.**
Ashdod, late eleventh-early tenth century BCE
Courtesy of the Israel Museum

'*Al shoshannim* (On Lilies) is one of a number of superscriptions found in the Psalms that may indicate names of existing melodies to be used in the performance of the psalm. Some other such indications are: '*al yonat 'elem rechokim* (On a distant, silent dove), and '*al tashchet* (Do not destroy). Most scholars today interpret those as the names or opening words of well-known melodies of that time intended to be used for performance of those psalms, much in the same way that "The Battle Hymn of the Republic" ("Mine eyes have seen the glory of the coming of the Lord") makes use of a melody originally sung to the words "John Brown's Body." Musicologists refer to a new song set to an existing melody as a *contrafactum* (pl., *contrafacta*). Another well-known *contrafactum* would be the Christmas carol, "What child is this," sung to the melody of the decidedly secular song, "Greensleeves."

The word *selah*, along with *amen* and *hallelujah*, is one of the best-known, though least-understood, Hebrew words in the non-Jewish world. The reason is that people have not been able to agree on a translation for it, but its frequent appearance in the Book of Psalms and the Book of Habbakuk insures that it is sung or read countless times daily all over the world. The heated arguments swirling around this single word would fill—indeed, have filled—any number of volumes. Our current state of understanding is that *selah* indicates an interruption in the choral performance of a psalm for an instrumental interlude, possibly played on the silver trumpets (*chatzotzerot*) discussed below. To borrow an anachronistic, but parallel, term from the Baroque cantata, whose practice this closely resembles, it seems to indicate a *ritornello* (periodically returning instrumental interlude). After the instrumental interlude the choir apparently began again at the point where it left off, continuing the psalm to its finish, or to the next *selah* cue.

Musical Instruments of the Bible

Many different musical instruments were used to accompany the psalms in biblical times. It might occur to you to ask, "If there was such an active tradition of instrumental accompaniment to the psalms in the Temple, why is there so little instrumental music for synagogue use today?" It is true that the synagogue does not possess the great body of magnificent instrumental music that we find in the Christian tradition. The reason is that after the destruction of the Temple in the year 70 CE, the rabbis decided that music, being so enjoyable, should be one of the things that the Jews should foreswear as a sign of mourning for the national catastrophe of the destruction of the Temple and of Jerusalem itself. The people's love for music gradually won out over that drastic ban, though, and a modification of it grew up in which only instrumental music was forbidden, because it was associated with dancing and secular celebration on the one hand, and the grandeur of the Temple on the other. As a result, traditional congregations do not use instrumental music in the synagogue, although there have been a few notable exceptions in the history of synagogue music. Some liberal congregations have started introducing instrumental music into their services, but this has only been in the last 150 years or so, and even then only in a limited way. There is not much instrumental music for the synagogue, a striking lack when compared to the many towering masterpieces of Christian church music that utilize instruments with or without voices. Whether there will be, or should be, is a matter of some debate. A few composers in the past century have written Jewish liturgical music for the concert hall. Especially noteworthy in that regard have been "Sacred Services" by the twentieth-century composers Ernst Bloch and Darius Milhaud. It is a development to be watched.

The Bible confirms the grandeur of instrumental music in the ancient Temple. Strings, winds, and percussion instruments were numerous in both sacred and secular music. King David, as is well known, played the small harp (the lyre, or *kithara,* as the Greeks called it). In Hebrew, the name of that instrument is *kinnor* (fig. 2.2), although in modern Hebrew its meaning has changed from a plucked string instrument to "violin." A larger version of the lyre was the great C-shaped harp without a front pillar known as the *nevel* (fig. 2.3). There were no bowed instruments in biblical times. The Persians may have been the first to use bowed strings in that part of the world, instruments which they may have borrowed from the Indian subcontinent, but that was not until later. Bowed instruments did not come to the West until after 1000 CE, when crusaders returned with them from their first encounter with the more sophisticated Arab civilization.

FIG. 2.2 Image of a lyre (*kinnor*) shown on a bronze coin issued at the time of the Bar Kochba Rebellion, 132-135 CE

Courtesy of the Israel Museum

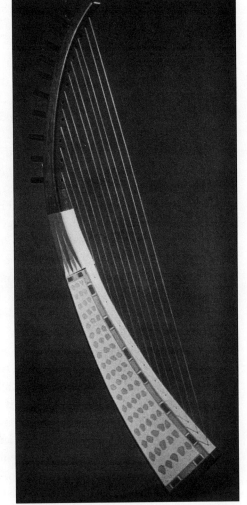

FIG. 2.3 Harp (*nevel*) reconstructed from Egyptian tomb paintings

Haifa Museum of Ethnology

Percussion instruments were popular in Biblical times, and a wide variety of them, in various sizes, were employed as an accompaniment for both singing and dancing. We find frequent mention in the Bible of an instrument called the *tof* (pl., *tuppim*). This was a small hand drum consisting of skin stretched over a wooden frame much like a tambourine, without metal jangles. The *tof* (fig. 2.4) is never mentioned in connection with Temple music. Instead it always appears in connection with secular song and dance or paraliturgical processions, apparently played almost exclusively by women, for:

> The drum in the Old Testament [is] a sexual symbol. In Judges 11:34 Jeptha's daughter bewails her virginity with a drum. The nude and decorated terra-cottas of the Israelite period clearly document this element of fertility and eroticism.... Later Old Testament books sublimate this sexual and erotic element by employing the metaphor "virgin Israel," as in Jeremiah 31:4: 'O virgin Israel! Again you shall adorn yourself with the [tof], and go forth in the dance of the merrymakers.[17]

The hand drum is still widely used in Eastern Mediterranean folk music. A similar, though larger, instrument is known in Arabic today by the related name *duff*. In Genesis 31:27 Laban reproaches Jacob for stealing away secretly, saying that instead of sneaking off, "I might have sent you away with mirth and with songs, with *tof* and *kinnor*." This suggests the celebratory circumstances under which the instrument was used, as does the passage in Exodus 15:20, in which Moses' sister Miriam leads the people in rejoicing "with a timbrel (*tof*) in her hand, and all the women went after her with timbrels and with *mecholot*." As discussed earlier, the word *mecholot* (sing., *machol*) also gives us some problems. Scholars differ as to whether the women in the preceding passage went out "with timbrels and dances," or "with timbrels and flutes." Translators as varied as Martin Luther and Martin Buber have opted for "flutes," while others have chosen "dances," or "round dances." Aaron Marko Rothmüller, in his book, *The Music of the Jews*, suggests that both translations may be correct, and cites evidence in support of both. Again, as in so many instances, we are not in a position to know for certain. Another popular percussion instrument was the *sistrum* (pl., *sistra*), a rattle constructed of a wooden handle with a wire or metal band running through it, on which were threaded several metal disks that jangled when shaken (fig. 2.5).

Among the instruments of the Temple itself we find mention of *metziltayim* made of brass. These were cymbals played by clashing two of them together, as we know from the suffix "-ayim," which is used in Hebrew to indicate things that normally come paired, such as eyes, arms, or scissors. Other percussion instruments included bells (*pa'amonim*; sing., *pa'amon*), of which a small, golden, set was sewn to the hem of the high priest's robe: "And Aaron shall wear it when he ministers, and his sound shall be heard when he goeth in unto the holy place before the Lord, and when he cometh out, that he die not" (see Exodus 28:33-34 and 39:25). Bells and rattles of all sizes and types were, and still are, widely used throughout the Middle East, and probably played a role in the music of the Temple just as they did in the music of the oldest Christian sects.

---

[17] Joachim Braun, *Music in Ancient Israel/Palestine: Archeological Written, and Comparative Sources* (Grand Rapids: William B. Eerdmans, 2002), 30-31; see also 29.

FIG. 2.4 Girl playing the timbrel (*tof*).
Terra cotta statuette of the
Second Iron Age from Tel Shikmona.
(Note the braids and uncovered hair,
signs that this is a young unmarried girl)

Haifa Museum of Ethnology

FIG. 2.5 Israeli rattles and *sistra* of the Roman period

Haifa Museum of Ethnology

Woodwind instruments were used as well. Most prominent among the woodwinds was the *chalil*, a recorder-like flute popular all through the Mediterranean basin, whose name probably derives from the root *ChLL*, meaning "pierced," since the body of the pipe was pierced with finger-holes as well as a fipple-hole to make the sound. Another wind instrument was the *ugav*. Genesis 4:20-22 tells us that Yuval was the father of all those who handle the *kinnor* (lyre) and *ugav*. The *ugav* seems to have been a wind instrument, a pipe with a reed, probably a double-reed, either enclosed like the ancient Greek *aulos*, or free, like the modern oboe. In modern Hebrew, *ugav* has been adopted for "organ," which is, after all, a collection of pipes.

Of the brass wind instruments played by vibrating the lips at the end of a tube, two are mentioned prominently in the Bible: the silver trumpet (*chatzotzerah*) and the ram's horn (*shofar*) (fig. 2.6). The latter was used only as a signal instrument, and had little musical value. It was used to give military signals or to alert the community that specific religious observations were being held in the Temple, so the sound was raucous by intent. It was meant to proclaim boldly: to terrify enemy troops, sound valiantly above the tumult of battle, or broadcast its message over a wide area. Its symbolic association with the function of community "announcer," coupled with the fact that it was not really a musical instrument to be listened to for pleasure, gained it exemption from the general proscription, and it became the only musical instrument retained in the synagogue. It has the distinction of being the only instrument from the ancient world that is still heard today, although it represents the music of the ancient world no more than the bugle would describe music in the twentieth century to people four thousand years from now.

Jewish tradition has preserved the names and musical renditions of three of the principal signals sounded by the shofar. The first of them is *t'kiah*, a word indicating a long, sustained blast. The second, *tru'ah*, calls for three sustained, but shorter blasts. The third, *sh'varim*, signifies nine short, staccato notes. Since these are merely signals, not melodies, the pitch does not really matter. They are not melodies of ancient song, but raucous blasts of large-scale public utterances. The shofar has been used for this purpose from ancient times to the present, especially on *Rosh Hashanah* and *Yom Kippur*, the most solemn days of the liturgical year. The "voice of the shofar" as featured in Jewish ritual, is a musical symbol representing the voice of God.

Another brass wind instrument was the *keren* (horn), which may—or may not—have been the same instrument as the shofar. The trumpet (*chatzotzerah*), on the other hand, was an entirely different instrument. In Numbers 10:1-10, Moses is commanded, "Make thee two trumpets (pl., *chatzotzerot*) of silver . . . that thou may use them for calling the assembly." These instruments were without question the instruments depicted, along with other booty stolen from the Temple, on the Arch of Titus (built around 80 CE), which is still standing near Rome. Raised to commemorate Titus's triumphal return to Rome from the military campaign in which Jerusalem was destroyed, a bas-relief on one face of the arch shows ceremonial objects borne by the victorious army, among them two straight, trumpet-like objects that appear to be about five feet or so in length. Recently an engraved stone that had fallen from high up on the wall of the ancient Temple was discovered in the rubble at the foot of that wall. On it was inscribed, in Hebrew, "The place of sounding the *chatzotzerah*." This not only confirms the use of these instruments for signaling in the days when the Temple was standing, it even shows from where on the Temple wall above the city they were sounded (fig. 2.7).

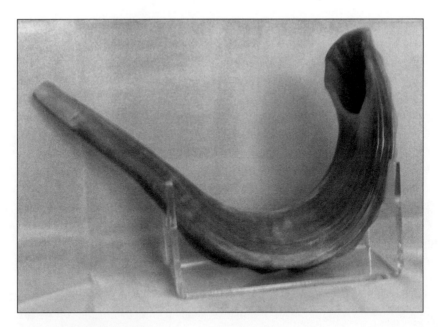

FIG. 2.6   Ram's-horn shofar

Courtesy of Emanuel Rubin

FIG. 2.7   Inscription: "To the Place of Trumpeting," Jerusalem, first century BCE.
Incised on a stone in the wall of the Temple

Courtesy of the Israel Museum

Biblical Music in the Context of the Ancient World

While uncertainty clouds an accurate perception of the musical culture of the ancient Hebrews, it is clear that music played an important role in both sacred and secular life, and that a wide variety of musical instruments lent color to the Hebrews' musical enjoyment. Voluntary abdication of the pleasures of music was adopted as a sign of national mourning after the loss of the Temple in Jerusalem. There is another aspect to consider as well. The ancient Middle Eastern world was divided between those peoples who adhered to religions of one God (Jews, and later, Christians) and those who remained faithful to the multiple gods of the Syrian, Greek, and Roman cultures. As the pagan religions gave themselves over increasingly to unbridled sensualism, the more sober monotheists distanced themselves from such debauchery. In the late Hellenistic period and after the destruction of the Temple, both Jewish and Christian leaders went to great lengths to spiritualize religious practice and reinterpret pagan concepts in light of their own belief system.

One of the ideas revitalized, for example, was music of the spheres, a mystical concept developed by Greek thinkers that envisioned music as an expression of the mathematics underlying the geometry of the universe. The music that we can hear, went the argument, was only the lowest kind of music, known as *musica instrumentalis*, meaning not just instrumental music, but all audible music. A higher level of music was called *musica humana*, referring to what we might today call our psychological well-being. Influenced by that concept, we continue to speak, even today, of people being "in harmony" with themselves, or their place in the world. Grandest of all, though, was what the Greeks called *musica mundana*, the music of the spheres—that is, of the worlds or planets. Just as the sounds of audible music reflected a mathematical relationship between a physical cause such as a vibrating string and the resulting sound, the motion of the planets in their orbits was imagined to occur in the same mathematical ratios as those that produce the overtone series.[18] It was then conceived that the motion of the planets therefore created sound, just as the motion of a vibrating string did, but sound on such a cosmic scale that only the gods could hear it. On that basis, music was viewed as a mathematical discipline that held the key to understanding the universe's structure, thus it was considered an essential part of education.

How did such an idea get translated into the monotheistic world view of the Jewish editors and compilers of the Bible? Perhaps even more importantly, why? To start with the second question, we need to remember the pervasive influence of Greek thought in all corners of the world of the Middle East. The closely woven network of music, mathematics, psychology, and cosmogony was an attractive idea, for it unified considerable philosophical speculation and practical wisdom into a single, interrelated system. Reinterpreting that system into Jewish thought accorded perfectly with the biblical command to "magnify and sanctify the name of the Lord." So it is not surprising to find the author/editor of the book of Job including the observation that "the morning stars sang together, and all the sons of God shouted for joy" (Job, 38:7), revealing how contemporary pagan concepts could be re-framed for adoption in a Jewish context.

---

[18] The overtone series is a natural phenomenon in which every sounding body vibrates not only along its whole length, but also in partial lengths, always in successive ratios of 2:1, 3:2, 4:3, 5:4, etc. Each of those partial vibrations also generates a sound (though softer than the fundamental tone), the whole complex of which is what we experience with each sound we hear.

Much music of the pagan world had long been associated with drinking, dancing, and licentiousness of all kinds. By the time of the Hasmonean (i.e., Maccabean) kings, as we will learn in chapter 3, music had earned a bad name among serious thinkers. Aristotle, for example, warned against free men associating themselves too strongly with music and musicians, for professional musicians, he stated firmly, were "low and vulgar people." No wonder that musicians gained such a bad reputation and that the rabbis, the church fathers, and later the judges and scholars of Islam, all shunned music as a potential danger.

In the following chapters you will read more about the rabbinic ban on joyful music. At first thought the ban seems harsh, perhaps even unreasonable, from a modern perspective, and there is no question that it played a large part in impeding the development of art music for the synagogue. Yet, in the light of the licentious reputation music had gained in the ancient world, the proscription on instrumental music in the synagogue may, on reconsideration, appear more like a solemn meditation on the loss of the Temple, and less like a misguided excision of pleasure. In another sense, that prohibition underlines the importance of music to Jewish culture, for had it not loomed so large in the eyes of the rabbis as a source of pleasure, they would not have limited it so severely as a sign of their pain.

Suggestions for Further Reading

Bradshaw, Paul F. *The Making of Jewish and Christian Worship*. In *Two Liturgical Traditions*, ed. Lawrence A. Hoffman. Vol. 5, part 1. Notre Dame: Notre Dame University Press, 1991.

Braun, Joachim. *Music in Ancient Israel/Palestine: Archeological, Written, and Comparative Sources*. Trans. Douglas W. Stott. Grand Rapids, MI, and Cambridge, England: William B. Erdmans, 2002.

Edelman, Marsha Bryan. *A Bibliography of Jewish Music: Resource Materials for Educators*. New York: Hebrew Arts School, 1986.

Gradenwitz, Peter. *The Music of Israel: From the Biblical Era to Modern Times*. Portland: Amadeus Press, 1996.

Idelsohn, Abraham Zvi. *Jewish Music in Its Historical Development*. 1st ed. 1929; 2nd ed. New York: Schocken Books, 1967.

Isaacs, Ronald H. *Jewish Music: Its History, People, and Song*. Northvale, NJ: Jason Aronson, 1997.

Sarna, Nahum M. *On the Book of Psalms: Exploring the Prayers of Ancient Israel*. New York: Schocken Books, 1993.

Sendrey, Alfred. *Music in Ancient Israel*. New York: Philosophical Library, 1969.

Stainer, John, and Francis W. Galpin. *The Music of the Bible, with Some Account of the Development of Modern Musical Instruments from Ancient Types*. Da Capo Press Music Reprint Series. New York: Da Capo Press, 1970.

Werblowsky, R. J. Zwi, and Geoffrey Wigoder, eds. *The Encyclopedia of the Jewish Religion*. New York, Chicago, San Francisco: Holt, Rinehart, and Winston, 1965.

3 | *The Greco-Roman World*

A Turbulent Period

One of the most turbulent yet productive periods for the religious and cultural development of Judaism was the late Hellenistic and Roman period. The adjective "Hellenistic" refers to the period when Greek culture became the norm for the Middle East, even though Greece itself had faded as an international power. In the last centuries of that era Greek culture and language shaped the ideals of upper-class life, even though political rule was in the hands of first the Hellenistic Syrians, then the Romans. Greek literature and athletics were imitated throughout the Middle East and much of Europe. The idealized life style of the Greek freeman was the model that much of the Roman world-tried to emulate. Rome itself reflected the ideals of the Greek life style, and throughout its Eastern empire Greek was used even more than Latin, except for administrative purposes, as the language of the upper-classes.

"In the past decade," wrote Tzvee Zahavy in 1988, "there has been renewed scholarly interest in the development of Jewish prayer in its most formative period, from 200 BCE to 200 CE."[1] This was a period in Jewish history that saw great triumph followed by great tragedy. At the era's finish the most basic tenets of Jewish thought were forced into reconsideration. From the Jewish perspective, this era may be said to have begun with the noble revolt of the Maccabees against the Seleucid king Antiochus IV about 167 BCE. It continued with the triumph (and later decadence) of the Jewish Hasmonean dynasty, and it came to an inglorious end with the fall of Jerusalem and Rome's crushing subjugation of the entire country fewer than 250 tumultuous years later. The era encompassed such far-reaching developments as the renewal of an independent Jewish commonwealth, the growth of Pharisaism that would change the balance

---

[1] Tzvee Zahavy, "The Politics of Piety: Social Conflict and the Emergence of Rabbinic Liturgy," in *The Making of Jewish and Christian Worship*, ed. Paul F. Bradshaw and Lawrence A. Hoffman (Notre Dame and London: University of Notre Dame Press, 1991), 42.

of power inside that commonwealth, the rise of Christianity, the destruction of the Temple, and a series of unsuccessful revolutions against Roman power. It was followed by the period of Constantine and the early medieval world of Yochanan ben Zakkai, who led the rabbis of the Sanhedrin, called the *Tannaim* (Great Teachers), in the movement that redefined Jewish practice from its focus on priest and Temple to Judaism as we know it today.

Fragmented Judaism

During those centuries Jerusalem, which had lost much of its centrality and influence in the face of the formation of large and successful Jewish communities outside the land of Israel, first reestablished itself as the spiritual center of Judaism, then squandered that position as its upper-classes became self-indulgent, self-satisfied, and sycophantic to the Roman overlords. At the same time, a new groundswell of spiritualism swept across the Middle East in reaction to the dissolute hedonism of Greco-Roman culture. The impact of that wave was seen in the appearance of charismatic prophets, isolationist monastic sects, and the outbreak of fundamentalist rebellions against religious establishments, not the least of which was the Jewish priesthood. Sectarianism was rife among the Jews. Such historical figures as John the Baptist have been identified with one or another of the many Jewish sects that divided the community in Palestine at the time. Some of the chief factions that we read about include the Sadduccees, an assimilationist party made up primarily of the wealthy and the priestly classes; the Pharisees, the party of teachers (such as the famous pair, Hillel and Shammai) who advocated scholarly reinterpretation of the Torah and the accessibility of religious study for every man; and the Essenes, one of many zealot groups that retired into monastic communities in the desert. The scholarly class known as the Pharisees, would later, after the Temple's destruction, become known as rabbis (teachers) when, in the resulting vacuum, they effectively took over the religious direction of Judaism.

That outline barely scratches the surface in mentioning the many divisions and subdivisions that ran through the contentious Jewish community. The Sadduccees, led by corrupt priests, were drawn by the attractions of Hellenistic culture. The Pharisees, for their part, were attempting to institute a religious revival, while at the same time fanatic religious zealots went so far as to murder "transgressors" of the religious laws. It was during this turbulent period that one Jewish monastic sect hid the Dead Sea scrolls in a cave at Qumran. Some of those recently-discovered scrolls reveal details of the sect's daily regimen, showing it to have had an almost military organization, along with the sect's belief in "The Teacher of Righteousness," a messiah-like figure supposed to have been killed by the machinations of a priest.

Birth of Christianity

This was the atmosphere in which, about fifty years after the "Teacher of Righteousness" died, a young man by the name of Yeshua ben Yosef, or to give him his Greek name, Jesus, preached a reform of Jewish practice. He asserted that he was the Messiah (*Christos*, in Greek), who had been sent to make a new covenant between God and the Jewish people. The Jewish sect that formed around this teacher developed into what later became a new religion called Christianity: followers of the Christ (or Messiah). The chief architect of that development was a former rabbinic student, Saul of Tarsus, who, after becoming a follower of Yeshuah, took the new name Paul. In Jerusalem it was not unusual for arguments among partisans of the various groups to become heated and even violent—indeed, the Jewish metropolis was a political powder keg whose citizens were angrily divided among themselves.

The Fall of the Temple

When the revolution against the Roman rulers occurred, the population of Jerusalem was not united under a single will and could not withstand the terrible siege that followed. In spite of petty victories in the early skirmishes, when the full power of the Roman war machine was brought to bear against Jerusalem, the city, reduced to starvation and internal squabbling, was crushed in the year 70 CE.

As punishment for defying Rome, and as a lesson to other subject populations in the empire, the city of Jerusalem was razed, the Temple burned and destroyed, and the inhabitants slaughtered or sold into slavery. As final humiliation a law was promulgated that forbade Jews to even approach the Temple mount on a pilgrimage. The treasures of the Temple were sacked and carried in triumph to Rome in a forced march memorialized by friezes that can still be seen today on the triumphal arch built by Titus to brag of his conquest (see frontispiece). Thousands of prisoners were dispersed to all corners of the empire through Roman slave markets. Surviving guerrilla bands of Jews, hiding in mountain fortresses such as Masada in the south and Gamla in the north, were destroyed one by one. The remaining rural population, cowed, and stripped of political, spiritual, and intellectual leadership, was abandoned by the Romans to their own devices in the ravaged country. Jerusalem would later be rebuilt by the Romans as a puppet city-state, Aeolia Capitolina, but the conquerors tried to make sure the city would never again serve as the capital of a Jewish commonwealth.

To non-believers as well as followers of Yeshua, and even to many Jews, this crushing blow seemed to signify that the Jewish time in history was past, that God had deserted the Jews. Their survival as a people depended on recovering from that disaster. The recovery was achieved, as we shall see, by redefining the practice, but not the core beliefs, of their religion. At the same time the Christian movement, trumpeting a revitalized covenant with God, a "New Testament," succeeded in rebuilding a spiritual life based on Jewish precepts, but for political reasons carefully separated from Judaism. What is significant about this to our interest in music is that both Judaism as we know it today and Christianity were forced to define themselves at the same time, in the same culture, and in some cases, at the hands of the same people. Christianity interacted with Jewish practice directly, in the adoption of modes of thought, melodies, and prayer forms, and indirectly, as spiritual leaders of both communities reacted to the larger culture of their time in somewhat similar ways. Ideas and practices of Judaism, the "mother religion," were absorbed into the new worship forms of Christianity, though with great care, so as not to appear to prospective converts as simply another sect of the defeated Jews.

Music as Vehicle of Liturgy

When concerned with sacred music, the history of Western music has always been primarily a history of Christian religious music. The reasons are not hard to fathom. The first was that, since its very beginning the church was the largest institution unstintingly devoted to the development and application of music. The church's appreciation of the importance of music in liturgy was partly aesthetic and partly utilitarian. Music had played a key role in the Temple, and the Jewish roots of Christianity made it inevitable that many of those values and practices would be adopted by the daughter religion, where music was used to create an ambience of soul-soothing beauty that separated the worship experience from a world that was often coarse, crass, and ugly. The new church developed a keen appreciation for music's ability to attract recalcitrant minds to religious thought. Then too, singing hymns and psalms unified individual voices in communal praise and fixed sacred teachings in the mind through repetition. Such assumptions can be seen in the writings of the early church fathers.

Saint Paul, speaking from his early background as a rabbi, advised the Ephesans to "[speak] to yourselves in psalms and hymns and spiritual songs, singing and making melody in your heart to the Lord" (Ephesans 5:19). In the fourth century Saint Augustine wrote, "I perceive our minds to be far more religiously and zealously blown up into a flame of devotion, whenas these ditties [i.e., psalms] are thus sung, than they would have been, had they not been so sung."[2] St. John Chrysostomos (the "Golden-tongued") also praised music as a valuable complement to worship. "What if drunkenness or gluttony does make our minds dull and foolish? Where psalmody [i.e., psalm-singing] has entered, all these evil and depraved counsels retreat."[3]

Christianity at first absorbed Jewish liturgical practices and even Jewish melodies, because it sought to present a familiar face to the population most likely to adopt what was viewed, in its earliest days, as a Jewish reform movement. The inheritance from the Jewish tradition," writes musicologist Karl Gustav Fellerer, "received a form and shape that for many centuries determined the final 'Gestalt' of Christian worship."[4] As the new religion spread to a wider, non-Jewish audience, changes were made to appeal to prospective new converts. In the fourth century, when Christianity emerged as a state religion, it constructed a wholly new edifice over the existing framework. Like the wooden infrastructure that supports a marble dome, it requires a discerning eye to envision the framework underlying the finished edifice.

Relating Jewish and Christian Liturgy

"Since music history began to be written, it was considered an ecclesiastical matter, and was viewed from a theological base,"[5] wrote twentieth-century scholar Eric Werner. This was never more true than for the Hellenistic period now under consideration. Accepting that truism

---

[2] "Confessions," trans. Oliver Strunk, *Source Readings in Music History* (New York: W. W. Norton, 1950), 74.

[3] St. John Chrysostom, "Exposition of Psalm XLI," in ibid., 69.

[4] Karl Gustav Fellerer, "Jewish Elements in Pre-Gregorian Chants," in *Proceedings of the World Congress on Jewish Music, Jerusalem, 1978*, ed. Judith Cohen (Tel Aviv: The Institute for the Translation of Hebrew Literature Ltd, 1982), 115-18.

[5] Eric Werner, "Hellenism and Judaism in Christian Music," *Three Ages of Musical Thought* (New York: Da Capo Press, 1981), 49-112.

is necessary to gain genuine understanding of the musical developments of that time, for the Roman period laid down the musical-liturgical roots of both Judaism and Christianity.

Werner recommends several principles to keep in mind when discussing the music of that confusing time. The first and most important of them is that Hellenism must be seen as a fusion of Greek culture with that of the Near East. Most of the scholars who wrote the seminal histories of music in the eighteenth, nineteenth, and early twentieth centuries visualized Hellenism as a specifically "Greek," (i.e., European) phenomenon. As Martin Bernal charges in *Black Athena*,[6] such scholars believed that the achievements of the Greeks sprang from an Aryan culture, from which it flowed to the superior minds of Caucasian Europeans, who alone were capable of appreciating it. However, that was not quite the case. Culturally, politically, and economically, Greeks looked eastward to Asia Minor and southward to Egypt to derive much of what was once believed to be their own innovations. Greek values, art, and thought were nurtured in the crucible of Eastern Mediterranean culture, a relationship that could be symbolized by the derivation of the Greek alphabet from Semitic letter-forms. Hellenistic culture must be seen as a descendant of Near Eastern, not European, development. When Rome conquered and absorbed Hellenism, it was not simply a matter of employing "Greek" slaves as teachers (many of whom were Jews, Syrians, or Egyptians who spoke Greek), but of integrating the whole combination of cultural assumptions that constituted the Greek-imbued thought of the Near East into Roman civilization.

A second point that seems self-evident today, but that apparently escaped many earlier European scholars, is that the historic development of Asia Minor during those crucial centuries must be understood to be continuous with the previous millennia, not a radically new era. This now seems so obvious as to hardly need stating. But it is possible to read again and again, especially in older books, that statuary, music, painting, drama, or a whole host of cultural features "came into being" among the Greeks, as if the Minoans, Sumerians, Chaldeans, Egyptians, Babylonians, Assyrians, Persians, Nabateans, Jews, or for that matter, the races of the Indian subcontinent, Far East, and Africa, had existed without such amenities.

Archeological research has irrevocably destroyed that myth with evidence of high art practiced in what we are now embarrassed to remember were formerly called "primitive" areas of the world. How could earlier scholars have been so restricted in their vision as to think that the Hellenic world created their culture out of whole cloth? The answer to that question brings us to Werner's third consideration, that the ancient traditions of the Near East were often transformed into, and disguised as what he calls Hellenistic "pseudomorphoses," by which he means that existing forms from preceding cultures were adapted by the Greeks for their own needs. The Greek genius was to creatively transform those practices into vibrant new expressions that retained their roots in antiquity, but took on new life. Here we must recognize the Greeks for what they *did* achieve. Their transformations of earlier intellectual and artistic traditions were often brilliant, and unquestionably played an important role in all the cultures that inherited them, among which we must certainly number the barbarians of Western Europe. To recognize the Greeks' role as inheritors as well as creators of tradition is not to denigrate the importance of Hellenic culture; it simply puts Greek achievements into the broader perspective of human culture as a whole.

---

[6] Martin Bernal, *Black Athena: The Afroasiatic Roots of Classical Civilization* (London: Free Association Press, 1987).

Werner cautions that in examining the Hellenistic period we should not fall into the trap of evaluating phenomena exclusively in ecclesiastical or systematic terms. This, of course, is part and parcel of late twentieth- and early twenty-first-century historiography: scholarship must view all cultures, including our own, with the greatest possible objectivity. That we subscribe to a certain set of religious, political, or cultural beliefs should not restrict our vision, or at least we should recognize the limitations it might impose. On the one hand, ancient customs persist in new guises, while on the other, human institutions, for whatever estimable purpose they were conceived, are subject to the comedy of human failings as well as the nobility of human aspiration. History must be studied in the harsh light of reality, which sometimes reveals uncomfortable truths and wide gaps between intent and realization.

Buttressed by those principles, we are better prepared to step into the potential quagmire of musical and liturgical developments in the period of the Hellenistic religious turmoil. Again, it is Werner who admonishes us that we must strive to see as a whole what has so often been treated only as separate parts:

> It must be clearly understood . . . that the development of Jewish and Christian worship is so closely interrelated and mutually involved that the knowledge and study of *both* liturgies is indispensable to every serious student of either.[7]

In other words, we have become so accustomed to thinking of the separateness of Judaism and Christianity over the centuries, that we have not given sufficient attention to their commonality.

A final caveat must be kept in mind when dealing with Hellenistic sources: they are often contradictory, self-serving, and sometimes border on being xenophobic, making clear inter-pretation problematical. The reasons are not hard to fathom. Source material is drawn primarily from three different origins: Greek, Jewish, and Christian. These references tend to be mutually distrustful, condescending, and even hostile to one another, so we must read them with some caution. Greek intellectuals of the time lamented that music was no longer a serious art as it had been in the heyday of Greek hegemony. The music of their own day, they believed, was corrupted by "Asiatic" influences, grossly sensual, and lacked intellectual virtue. Those opinions are frequently accepted without question by modern Grecophiles, for whom such writers are the principal sources of information. On the other side, Jewish intellectuals feared the incursions of Hellenism on Jewish cultural and religious life. In the light of their desire to "build a fence to protect the Torah,"[8] their defensive stance hardly qualified them as an objective source for the evaluation of musical life of the day.

The third group, the Christian church fathers, displayed a slowly changing attitude during the centuries that Christianity developed. At the outset, their view of Hellenistic philosophy

---

[7] Eric Werner, *The Sacred Bridge: Liturgical Parallels in Synagogue and Early Church* (New York: Schocken Books, 1970), 54.

[8] *Pirkei avot* (Ethics of the Fathers), 1:1.

and art concurred with the Jewish view; that is, they held a low opinion of it. They gradually came to terms with Greek philosophy, though, as they came to grips with the entire Roman Empire, and began to appreciate its nobler implications. The victory of the Roman church over the Judeo-Christian sects at the Council of Nicea in 325 enshrined that new syncretism, and played an important role in the church fathers' unwillingness to acknowledge Jewish roots of their worship and musical practice. The view of any one of those three camps of thinkers, then, must be tempered by balancing it with that of its opponents, and the rationale for its artistic and cultural standards seen in the light of its response to the others.

It was just such a blend of Middle Eastern and Hellenistic-Roman thinking that led both Judaism and Christianity at this time to conceive the need for a fixed liturgy. Christian thought arrived at that point via Roman legalism, and the need to forge a bond to the mother religion while at the same time maintaining a political distance from it. The Jews reached the same point by requiring a spiritual substitute for the Temple and the capital. The earliest Christians seem originally to have viewed themselves as what we might today call "reformed Jews," rather than as originators of an entirely new religion. Feelings of rivalry between Jews and Christians certainly gained impetus through the first two hundred years of Christianity; but the separation was not complete until the conversion of Constantine and the adoption of Christianity as an obligatory state religion after 313 CE. It becomes more realistic to think in terms of two separate religions at that point; before then, the idea of Christianity as just another of a number of Jewish sects might be a more useful construct.

If it were necessary to pinpoint a watershed in the parting of the two groups, it would not be the time of the crucifixion or even the ministry of Paul, but the year 325, when the Emperor Constantine called the Nicene Council. It was then that the development of the Nicene Creed, a carefully-formulated legalistic statement of Christian belief for interpolation in the Mass, marked the point of no return. Such statements of belief had long played a role in the developing Christian liturgy, dividing the early "Mass of instruction" from the "Mass of sacrifice." With the elevation of Christianity to a state religion the new formulation took on the status of law. Even after that, unquestionably there were many who continued to view the "other side" as sectarians who needed only to be convinced of the wrongness of their cause, not as subscribers to a different belief system.

It is helpful, then, to envision the development of what became two independent liturgies as liturgies that only gradually separated. They were, at first, two Jewish sects groping for an appropriate mode of expression as they progressed along slowly diverging paths. Both looked to Jewish practice as a model; but each saw something quite different to be learned from the ancient rituals. The great break codified by the Nicene Council imposed different obligations and opened different possibilities to each, at which point each set about reinterpreting the tradition to suit its needs. The resulting differences, extending out like spokes in a wheel from a common center two thousand years ago, give the appearance today of being quite distinctive. But examination of the roots of the two liturgies will show that there is more commonality than is generally thought.

Jewish Liturgy at the Time of Early Christianity

"Liturgy," according to Plato's *Laws*, originally meant a kind of public service or obligation.[9] Wealthy Athenians were obligated to provide such "liturgies" for their city, such as serving in an unsalaried public office, financing plays or participating in choruses for the plays, subsidizing part of the army or navy budget, or undertaking public works (e.g., paving streets and building statues or temples for the gods). By extension, the word came to indicate a regular prayer obligation and the structure organizing prayers into fixed schedules for public worship. The Hebrew word *avodah* (literally, "work") reflects that origin in its secondary meaning of "prayer service," as, for that matter, does the English word, "service." The Jewish liturgy as it stands today primarily represents developments that took place during and immediately after the Hellenistic era. In the period itself, though, the Jewish liturgy was not as highly organized as it came to be later.

In Jewish religious thought there were five categories of prayer: 1) praise and exaltation of the deity, 2) expressions of thanksgiving, 3) petitions and supplications, either individual or communal, 4) professions of faith (doxology), and 5) blessings sanctifying acts and experiences of daily life (*brachot*). Saint Paul, who before his conversion had been Saul, a student of the great Rabbi Gamliel, was well aware of those categories, and played a role in their absorption into Christian practice. When the Temple was still in existence, the priestly celebration of ritual moved in a carefully-defined path, from which it could not deviate in the slightest. Several incidents recounted in the Bible warn that departure in any detail from the prescribed sequence was a crime that was punishable by nothing less than death.[10] What was true for the Temple, the province of professionally trained priests, was not necessarily true for the synagogue, developed as a demotic religious institution of and for the general population, not the priesthood.

The synagogue, or in Hebrew *bet knesset* (congregational house), developed as an independent institution even before the Second Temple was built. There were 394 synagogues in Jerusalem itself in the time of the Temple. The institution seems to have first developed during the Babylonian exile (597-538 BCE), then continued as a special location for religious activities, both among those who returned to Jerusalem after the exile and those who remained in Babylonia. While the sacrifices and activities of the priests had their place in the Temple, the synagogue was, at first, a house for study and debate about interpretations of the Torah, or for the celebration of community-wide events. In modern terms, it might be visualized as a combination of library, classroom, and meeting hall. Both before and immediately after the destruction of the Temple, rabbis expressed discomfort with the idea of fully prescribed prayer such as one finds in a formal liturgy. The synagogue service of the period preceding the fall of the Temple was thus not firmly fixed, for the still-standing Temple was the primary venue for the public practice of religious ritual; but with the destruction of the Temple the synagogue became the logical institution around which to rebuild the spiritual life of the Jewish community.

After destruction of the Temple in 70 CE the rabbis took the practices of the synagogue, not the Temple, as their primary liturgical model. There were two major reasons for this: 1) The rituals of the Temple required a *kohen*, or hereditary priest, to carry them out under

---

[9] See Plato, *The Laws*, Book 12, esp. the section "Refusal to Contribute to Public Expenses."

[10] See, for example, the account of the death of Aaron's sons in Exodus, or of the death of Eli's sons in Samuel I, in which departure from liturgical detail resulted in death or severe punishment.

special circumstances available only in the Temple, while there were no such limitations on the synagogue, and 2) the aristocratic priestly class, with its wealth, power, and all-too-human abuses exercised by the last occupants of those posts, was de-emphasized in the redefined Judaism developed by the Pharisees after the destruction of the Temple, except for a handful of vestigial practices that served as historical—or perhaps nostalgic—reminiscences. It would have then been unthinkable to reestablish the centrality of the priestly Sadducean party in the new, pharisaic (that is to say, rabbinic) Judaism. When the rabbis of the Sanhedrin saw the need for a prescribed liturgy (and such recognition was not unanimous), they did not visualize it in terms of Temple practices, but in terms of that more democratic institution, the synagogue.

Jewish-Christian Liturgical Links

The young Christian church, on the other hand, saw the situation differently. Claiming precedence as rightful heir to the spiritual tradition which they saw as deserted by the Jews, Christians had no hesitation in adopting Temple practices into their liturgy, as well as practices of the synagogue and other rituals they found appropriate, such as the Passover Seder. On the other hand, many Christians, like Jews of the post-destruction period, viewed the Temple with some antagonism. As Werner aptly puts it, "The monopoly of the Temple, its festivals of pilgrimage, its minutely regulated sacrificial rituals, were the jealously guarded prerogatives of the aristocratic hierarchy of priests and the nationalistic zealots."[11] The synagogue had always been the people's place, and with the orientation of Christianity towards increased proselytization among the common people, it, too, provided an attractive model for design of the Christian liturgy.

Along with much of the rest of the world at that time, Christians saw the destruction of the Temple as a sign of God's abandonment of the Jewish people. Jewish views ranged over a wide variety of interpretations, but the one that seems to have gained most currency was that the destruction was permitted by God as a punishment for not maintaining a sufficiently spiritual commonwealth. While the Jews went into mourning for the destruction of their religious center, Christians celebrated the same event as authentication of the reforms advocated by Jesus. Christian liturgists, therefore, borrowed freely from both modes of Jewish worship as they saw fit, while Jewish liturgical development studiously avoided too close an identification with Temple practice.

Ban on Women Singing

Both Jewish and Christian spirituality, though, were in agreement about the rejection of the rampant sensuality of the pagan world. Many of the more puritanical attitudes of the later Middle Ages, shared by Jews and Christians alike, had a common inception during this time. Among those reactions seems to have been a change in the attitudes of both Jews and Christians towards women. This is not the place to discuss the social and spiritual havoc wreaked by that

---

[11] Werner, *Sacred Bridge*, 2.

change, except insofar as it touches on our musical focus. For in spite of the fact that sources from early Jewish antiquity speak without prejudice of women's voices, Jewish sources under the influence of this response began to view women's singing with suspicion.

It is noteworthy that neither the church nor the synagogue countenanced women singing in their respective liturgies. In all likelihood, this was because of the association of such singing with female slaves who were required to perform love songs and lascivious entertainment for their masters' and guests' amusement. Slave women, as a matter of fact, constituted the majority of musical performers in the pagan world. That unwholesome alliance of music, slavery, and prurience formed the background for much of the early medieval attitude toward music, musicians, and women. It was in reaction to such associations that the rabbis of this period also forbade a woman to sing in the presence of any man outside her immediate family, promulgating that doctrine under the general proscriptions against women's participation in the liturgy.

The ban on women singing together with men, referenced in Jewish legal code under the heading *Kol isha* (a woman's voice), is a topic that has generated a great deal of writing among Jewish authorities over the centuries, and in recent decades has become the focus of harsh polemic on all sides. One of the best introductions to this heated topic is an article written by Emily Taitz in 1986 that identifies and evaluates the important medieval sources.[12]

The root of the issue was the Talmudic contention, *Kol isha ervah* (A woman's voice is forbidden). To understand this charge, we must begin by recalling the circumstances out of which it grew. Those included the recent prohibition against music as a sign of mourning for the profound devastations of the first century: the loss of nationhood, the Temple, and tens of thousands of slain compatriots, and the loss of a generation of the survivors sold into slavery. Threatened by the extinction of their two-thousand-year-old religion, the rabbis were assailed on every side. A vigorous Christianity appeared to be displacing Judaism, and recruitment to the pagan sects was growing, while immorality, cynicism, and anti-intellectualism infused the entire culture that surrounded them. Inheritors of a tradition that distinguished sharply between the social roles of each sex, they perceived all the "modern" incursions on that tradition as destructive of a civilization they were trying to uphold. Woman's song was attacked with the same zealotry that was aimed at the enjoyment of music itself. One of the greatest of the rabbis of the Talmud is supposed to have said, "If you hear a [secular] song, uproot it."

Questions about the propriety of women singing in the presence of men are first raised in Jewish law in the Talmud. The most influential of them occurs in the context of a discussion about distractions to prayer. There, Rav Shmuel lists the sound of a woman's voice among other circumstances to be avoided, for "A woman's voice is sexually stimulating, as it says, 'For your voice is sweet . . .'" (Talmud: *Brachot*, 24a). In another passage Rav Yehudah, in the course of an argument with Rav Nahman, cites Shmuel's opinion as the basis for his own. In still another place (Talmud: *Sotah*, 48a), Rav Yosef, obviously referring to secular entertainment, avers, "When men sing and women join in, it is licentiousness; when women sing and men join in, it is like fire in flax." Some later medievals, such as Rabbi Isaac Alfasi (known by the acronym *Rif*) and Maimonides (whose acronymic designation was *Rambam*), cite no such prohibition, although

---

[12] Emily Taitz, "Kol Ishah—The Voice of Woman: Where was it Heard in Medieval Europe?," *Conservative Judaism* 38 (Spring 1986): 44-61.

Maimonides suggests that "even to listen to the voice of a forbidden woman . . . is forbidden." Here, though, the scholar specifies "a forbidden woman"—that is, one with whom close relationships would not be permitted, such as another's wife. Nevertheless, once established, this prohibition became part of the elaborate code of modesty (*tzni'ut*) imposed on both sexes, and entered the social practice of a society that looked on such legalisms as a way to insure appropriate conduct.

What was it about the art of music that elicited such strong reactions? The most important reason probably was not the music itself, but the circumstances in which it was made. In the world of professional musicians most performers were women, slaves, or both. Many, though not all, entertainers at wealthy courts were little more than prostitutes. Conversely, the more exclusive brothels were often renowned for the quality of their singing and dancing girls. Because of the questionable moral character of its practitioners, music and musicians were viewed askance by more conservative elements of society. This was certainly the reputation that Aristotle had in mind when he had earlier warned against free men associating with musicians or attempting to gain too much musical proficiency: "for indeed, performers do become vulgar, as the object at which they aim is a low one."[13] To drive the point home, he avers that "professional musicians . . . are vulgar people."[14]

That reputation led to a negative view of music held by the more sober-minded. In that view, which Islamic scholars would later share with their Jewish and Christian counterparts, music was seen as a kind of "attractive nuisance" against which serious thinkers railed. Because music was pleasing to the spirit, went this reasoning, many became attracted to it and invested their time in frivolous entertainment, decadent activities, and bad company at the expense of attention that might better be given to religious and philosophical pursuits. Athenian-born Christian patriarch Clement of Alexandria (ca. 150-ca. 215), wrote, "We must be on guard against whatever pleasures titillate eye and ear. . . . [Those things] corrupt men's morals, drawing to perturbation of the mind, by the licentious and mischievous art of music."[15]

Taitz shows that while there were always rabbis who adhered strictly to those tenets, the restrictions gradually eroded. Mixed singing at weddings was reinstated almost immediately after it was banned, and the prohibition on women singing with the men at synagogue services was soon felt to be excessive (although not the separation in seating). On the one hand, the eleventh-century commentator Rashi agreed with the warning against men listening to women sing. "He nevertheless points out, in commenting on the Talmudic passage (*Ber.* 57b) about the three things that soothe the spirit, that one of them is the voice of a woman singing an evening song."[16] In a heartbreaking poem praising the virtue of his wife and daughters, who had been killed by rampaging crusaders, the great Rabbi Eleazar of Worms wrote that his wife "sang songs and prayers," and that she taught songs to other women. His older daughter, Bellet,

---

[13] H. Rackham's translation, as cited in Strunk, 21.

[14] Ibid., 17.

[15] Clement of Alexandria (Titus Flavius Clemens), *The Instructor*, trans. G. M. Butterworth, book 2, chapter 4; cited in A. Z. Idelsohn, *Jewish Music in its Historical Development* (New York, 1929; 2nd ed., Schocken Books, 1967), 94.

[16] Taitz, 47.

only thirteen, "learned all the prayers and songs from her mother," and the younger, only six, "knew how to chant the *Sh'ma* and sang songs for his entertainment."[17]

The stringency with which this ruling was applied seemed to depend largely on the liberality of those doing the interpreting. The Sarajevo *Haggadah*, from ca. 1350, shows pictures of Jewish girls singing and dancing, including one playing the tambourine. The tradition of women mourners, too, seemed exempt from the prohibition on women singing before men, as the Mishnah urged parents to "teach your daughters a lament." Two of the most notable medieval women singers were the female cantors Urania of Worms and Richenza of Nurenberg, who officiated at women's synagogue services. Urania's tombstone has inscribed on it:

> This headstone commemorates the eminent and excellent lady Urania, daughter of R[eb] Abraham, chief of all synagogue singers.... She, too, with sweet tunefulness, officiated before the female worshippers, to whom she sang the hymnal portions. In devout service her memory shall be preserved.[18]

The contribution of Jewish women to music was only partly limited by the doctrine *kol isha ervah*. Northern Europe was generally more repressive on all matters pertaining to women than was the case in the South. Depending on the time, place, and rabbinic temperament, women's musical participation ranged from the imposition of their near-silence to their exuberant participation in the bands of professional *juglares* and *jongleurs* that roamed the continent. Bearing in mind that the women of the Bible did not seem to suffer from any musical constraints, many women did, in fact, take part in the singing of prayers, blessings, and hymns, of table songs and lullabies, and even in the public performance and teaching of music.

Liturgical Intertwining

To summarize, both church and synagogue discovered the need to develop a fixed liturgy at the same historical moment and in the same part of the world. They both looked to the same sources for this purpose, but because of their different needs, their motivations and attitudes toward the Jewish prayer tradition were dissimilar. Both synagogue and church shared the attitude that the sound of women singing was a likely cause of sinful thoughts (for the men), and took steps to limit that danger. In many parts of Europe, Jewish suppression of women's singing was less widely observed than in the church; but vestiges of that attitude continue to exist today in Orthodox Judaism, as well as in the more conservative branches of Christianity and Islam. In this parallel development, ideas and images crossed from one to the other religious group. Practices of one evolved in reaction to practices of the other, and concepts that had at first served both gradually diverged as the history of the two institutions separated over the next two millennia. Without going into undue detail, it is worthwhile to examine the liturgies of both church and synagogue for such intertwining.

---

[17] Ibid., 48.

[18] Cited and trans. by Israel Abrahams, *Jewish Life in the Middle Ages* (Philadelphia: Jewish Publication Society, 1896; reprint, New York: Athenaeum Press, 1981), 26.

Even before the destruction of the Temple a morning prayer seems to have been said in local synagogues before the dawn sacrifice in the Temple. Afternoon prayer would correspond accordingly to the time of the afternoon sacrifice. There was no evening sacrifice in the Temple, but there was a public service. As the liturgy took on definition, rabbis cited both Temple practice and biblical authority for the establishment of fixed liturgical hours of three times a day, pointing to such passages as Daniel 6:11 ("And he kneeled upon his knees three times a day and prayed and gave thanks to God . . .") and Psalms 55:18 ("At evening and morning and noon will I make my complaint and moan, and He heareth my voice"). Following the destruction of the Temple, the hours for synagogue worship were fixed at times more or less standard to this day: *Shacharit* (morning, between 7 and 10 AM), *Minchah* (variable with the season, in the late afternoon) and *Ma'ariv* (twilight). Later, in the Talmud, dawn and dusk were reinforced as the most appropriate time for morning and evening prayers. In more recent times, those fixed times have not always been interpreted so rigidly in synagogue practice.

By the end of the first century CE the synagogue liturgy was regularized. Three days a week—Monday, Thursday, and *Shabbat*—the Torah and Prophets were also chanted, using prescribed cantillation formulas that were virtually inseparable from the text and served to assist in understanding it. A service in a synagogue of Roman times might consist of the recitation of one or more psalms, biblical verses (chief among which was the *Sh'ma*), and, as the central prayer, the *Amidah*. On Mondays, Thursdays, and the Sabbath, the weekly Torah passage was cantillated, and was followed by prophetical writings originally chosen by the reader, and later codified into prescribed passages that went with particular Torah readings. The service ended with congregational recitation of the sanctification of God's name, known as the *kaddish*. As we know from stories of the life of Jesus, synagogue services often included oral interpretation of the readings by a rabbi or another learned member of the congregation, after which discussion might follow. Conclusion of each section of study was marked by recitation of the sanctification (*kaddish*) in the vernacular of the day, Aramaic.

In a similar manner, the church developed a schedule of Christian worship hours, which became part of the cycle known as "The Proper of the Time." The New Testament (Acts 2:15, 3:1, 10:3) gives times for prayer similar to those mentioned above. Special late evening prayers for Christians were recommended, but normal prayers were to be held at about 9:00 AM, noon, and late afternoon, with the optional evening prayers not closely regulated. By the fourth century, with the growth of monasteries under the Benedictine rule, an elaborate plan for religious communities was developed, with seven prayer services during every twenty-four-hour period, based on Psalm 119:164, "Seven times a day do I pray to You because of Thy righteous ordinance."

The five categories of Jewish prayer enumerated above (see p. 52) were assigned a hierarchy of value by the rabbis. Most esteemed were prayers of praise and exaltation, least esteemed were individual petitions or supplications. In between came expressions of individual thanks or general- ized thanksgiving. There were other prayer types as well: doxologies (professions of faith) and the *brachot*, or blessings.[19] All of the preceding were absorbed into Christianity; for example, the opening formula of blessings, "Baruch atah adonai," became, in Greek, "Eulogetos sy, kyrie."

---

[19] This word (sing., *bracha*; pl., *brachot*) is derived from the root, *berech*, "knee," implying that at some point there was a connection between blessing and genuflection, as is still seen in certain prayers. If that was once true, it no longer applies, and daily blessings are not associated today with kneeling.

To look at the contents of that liturgy, two of the earliest prayers to become regularized into the synagogue service were the *Sh'ma Yisrael* and the *Tefillah* or *Amidah*, also known as the "Eighteen benedictions." The *Sh'ma* was an unequivocal statement of the unity of God, the core of Jewish belief: "Hear, O Israel, the Lord our God, the Lord is one." These were originally two unrelated items, but rabbinic leadership molded them into a unified liturgical framework some time after the defeat of Bar Kochba in 135 CE. The additional paragraphs following the *Sh'ma*[20] were probably also added during the second century. In the Passover Haggada, a story appears in which students interrupt an all-night discussion of the second-century rabbis Eleazar, Yoshua, Elazar ben Azariah, Akiba, and Tarphon, saying "Masters, the time has come for the morning recitation of the *Sh'ma*." It can be inferred from this that the *Sh'ma* alone may have constituted the morning prayer at that time, perhaps even without the *Tefillah*, or it may be that recitation of the *Sh'ma* constituted the obligatory part of morning worship.

The *Tefillah* (prayer) or *Amidah* (= "standing," because it is recited in a standing position), originated sometime after 200 BCE, and had become part of the daily sacrificial service in the Temple after about 145 BCE, when it was recited privately prior to the sacrificial offering by the officiating priest. The question of when it was first introduced and when it reached its current form, though, "is very intricate and very difficult to answer because of the lack of sources," writes Idelsohn.[21] Zahavy points out that "priestly and aristocratic themes were central to the Tefillah,"[22] confirming its origins in the Temple. Such themes, especially the metaphor of God as King, provided support for the hierarchy and the autocratic position of the priests. By the first century the *Tefillah* was a central pillar of the synagogue liturgy and its daily recitation obligatory. In addition to the alternative name, *Amidah*, the *Tefillah* is also known by the problematic name *Sh'moneh esrei*, meaning "eighteen," supposedly reflecting the number of blessings it contained. However, as it has been recited for centuries, there are not eighteen, but nineteen blessings. For generations scholars hypothesized that the nineteenth blessing was one that had been added by the great Rabbi Gamliel, "against heretics," and that the heretics under fire were the Jewish Nazarenes, or Christians. However, Ismar Elbogen, after studying newly discovered documents from the Cairo *genizah*, was able to demonstrate that the original eighteen blessings had been expanded to nineteen by Babylonian Jews, who chose to divide the fourteenth of the original blessings into two. That Babylonian practice eventually predominated, but the name, "Eighteen," reflecting the original form, stayed with the *tefillah* through the centuries.[23] Its prominence in synagogue prayer may have been a concession to priestly authority, with the hope that the Temple would be reestablished in the future; or it may have been the unifying features of the *tefillah*, focusing the wishes of a dispersed people on the centrality of the Temple, that contributed to its retention.

Two other important prayers in the developing Jewish liturgy were the Kaddish and *Kedushah*. Both words are based on the triliteral root *KDSh*, meaning "holy." These were the principal

---

[20] ¶1 "Love the Lord your God with all your might . . ." (Deuteronomy 6:4-9); ¶2 "If you will earnestly heed . . ." (Deuteronomy 11:12-13); and ¶3 "The Lord said unto Moses . . ." (Numbers 15:37-41).

[21] Idelsohn, *Jewish Liturgy*, 109.

[22] Zahavy, 50.

[23] Paul F. Bradshaw, *The Making of Jewish and Christian Worship* (Notre Dame: University of Notre Dame Press, 1991), 23 ff.

doxologies, speaking of God in the third person (rather than being addressed *to* God) and stressing the eternity of the supreme being. Both *kaddish* and *Kedushah* became important musical items in Jewish liturgy, with the latter often incorporating more lyrical qualities, the former a simpler, more syllabic style for congregational singing. The Kaddish, which pre-dated the destruction of the Temple, was not in Hebrew, but Aramaic, the language of everyday speech in Palestine of that time. It originated in the sentence, "May His great name be blessed for ever and for all eternity," traditionally spoken by teachers (rabbis) at the close of a study session, discussion, or lecture. It was adopted into the liturgy to mark the division between large structural sections of the service, much as it had originally been recited to mark the close of a section of study.

Specific recitation of the Kaddish by mourners is relatively recent in Jewish history, probably not pre-dating the Middle Ages, although there are signs that it may have been employed like that for centuries in some places before general acceptance. A medieval folk tradition, never sanctioned by the rabbis, claimed such powerful properties for the Kaddish that, by its regular recitation, a son could gain his parents' admission to heaven. In the twelfth century CE Rabbi Elyakum ben Joseph of Mayence (d. ca. 1150) felt it necessary to caution, "It is not generally accepted that through the recitation of Kaddish the son brings his father and mother to paradise." Instead, most rabbinic authorities agree that the use of Kaddish as a memorial prayer stems from its praise of God in the face of painful, as well as joyous, occurrences, since the death of a parent or spouse is the most traumatic experience that befalls most people.

The *Kedushah* originally consisted of three biblical verses: Isaiah 6:3 ("Holy, holy, holy is the Lord of hosts . . ."), Ezekiel 3:12 ("Blessed is the glory of the Lord . . ."), and Ps. 146:10 ("The Lord will reign for ever . . ."). It seems to have originated as part of the Temple service, but over the centuries there have been additions and changes reflecting the practices of different communities and different outlooks. This was especially true during the first millenium following the destruction of the Temple, after which the variations to the *Kedushah* stabilized in various locales. Changes were not adopted uniformly into all Jewish rites, so that there are variations not only in the text itself, but also concerning when it is to be recited. All the versions, though, share the three verses cited above.

There are Christian parallels to the core of the Jewish liturgy. These verses sometimes consisted of direct translations, including even the careful preservation of the original rhythm. As an example, here, taken from the Roman Catholic Mass, is the Latin translation of the Hebrew *Kedushah*, faithfully preserving the threefold rhythmic repercussion the opening word ("Holy, Holy, Holy"), as can be seen in the following comparison:

Hebrew:	*Kadosh, kadosh, kadosh, adonai tzeva'ot* . . .
Latin:	*Sanctus, sanctus,* sanctus, *domine deus sabaoth* . . .

Note that the ambiguous Hebrew word *tzeva'ot* is preserved untranslated in the Latin, where it is simply transliterated as "Sabaoth" because of uncertainties about its meaning.[24] One more such example will suffice to demonstrate the point. Here is a phrase from the Kaddish, in Aramaic, compared with its counterpart in the Latin *Te Deum*:

---

[24] While most scholars agree that it means "hosts," or "armies," a significant number of others argue that it may here mean "high places."

Aramaic: *V'yitpa'ar, v'yitroman,v'yitnaseh . . .*
Latin: *Adoramus te, glorificamus te, magnificamus te . . .*

Here we can see that the Latin translation preserves both the meaning of the original and the structural idea of a strong, reiterated "upbeat-downbeat" rhythm.

The fact that, beyond simply borrowing concepts, such Latin translations went on to incorporate the poetic structures of the originals, strongly suggests that those prayers were intended to serve as allusions—reminiscences, perhaps—to their sources, and as such would be comfortably received by former Jews among the Christian congregants. It also implies the possibility, even the likelihood, that the rhythm may have been imported expressly to allow those prayers to be sung to melodies imported from the synagogue or the Temple. While it may not yet be possible to substantiate such a hypothesis on the basis of available evidence, new research in the music of Jerusalem's earliest Christian communities may provide support for that line of thinking.[25]

There were other ways, too, in which Jewish practice left its mark on the church liturgy. The singing of psalms, for example, which dates back to the Temple, became a central practice in the Christian liturgy. The Mishnah (*Tamid* 7:4) tells us that psalms appropriate to each day of the week were performed by the Temple Levites. On the first day of week they performed Psalm 24; the second day, Psalm 48; the third day, Psalm 82; the fourth, Psalm 94; the fifth, Psalm 81; the sixth, Psalm 93; and on the Sabbath, Psalm 92. In other places in the Mishnah we learn that the psalms were sung in three sections (*Sukkah* 4:5), and that the "sons of Levi" (i.e., the Levitical musicians) blew trumpets after each section (*Tamid* 7:3).

In Christian monasteries psalms were sung as a continuation of the practice of psalm singing in the Temple, and because of that tradition, it was incumbent on every Christian monastic order to sing the entire Book of Psalms each week. In like manner, the Jewish practice of cantillation was applied to the earliest Christian psalm singing, where it gradually underwent modifications to bring it into line with Western musical practice. While Christian psalm singing soon developed a musical style of its own that was quite different from Jewish cantillation, the idea of the Christian psalm tones, or lection (reading) tones, grew directly out of Jewish cantillation practice.

Other Jewish influences on Christian practice can be seen in the adoption of Hebrew words left untranslated in the Christian prayer vocabulary, as we saw with the pair *tzeva'oth/sabaoth*. The best-known of those is unquestionably *amen* (Hebrew, "so be it"), but there is also the congregational response, *hallelujah* (praise God), and *selah*, the musical cue for an instrumental interlude—perhaps the sounding of the trumpets between sections of the psalms. Hymn singing was itself an import from Jewish practice, noted by the Roman-Jewish historian Philo of Alexandria as a feature of worship among the Jewish monastic sect of *Theraputae*.[26] On still another level that influence can be seen in the singing school (*schola cantorum*) begun by Gregory the Great, pope from 590 to 604, modeled on the music school begun by King David and described in

---

[25] See, for example, Peter Jeffery, "The Earliest Christian Chant Repertory Recovered: The Gregorian Witnesses to Jerusalem Chant," *Journal of the American Musicological Society* 47/1 (1994): 1-38.

[26] See Egon Wellesz, *Eastern Elements in Western Chant* (Copenhagen: Munksgaard, 1974), esp. chapter 4, "The Liturgical Significance of Bilingual Singing."

the biblical books, Kings and Chronicles. The very structure of the Christian liturgical year is patterned after that of the Jewish liturgical year, and the justification for the use of musical instruments in church, originally shunned as being too worldly and reminiscent of instruments used for secular entertainment, lay in the use of instruments in the ancient Temple.

Transmission of Musical and Liturgical Practice

How were those practices transmitted between two groups that seem so distinctively different today? The two most obvious modes of transmission were physical proximity and shared membership. Early Christians adopted practices that they found among the Jews simply because they lived together and shared a culture, especially in the earliest days of the church. We must remember that the first Christians saw themselves as sectarian Jews—not bearers of a new religion, but bearers of a new revelation to the Jewish people and anyone else who cared to listen. Many of the Jewish followers of this new sect saw no reason to disassociate themselves from their friends, relatives, and communities. Nor, in all likelihood, did they feel any great need to abandon comfortable melodies that they viewed as a continuing part of their heritage. Musical practices were freely exchanged among members of the overlapping Jewish and Christian populations. Even as the two groups drew apart, the back-and-forth flow of people did not entirely stop until the establishment of Christianity as a state church, after which the practice of Judaism was viewed as tantamount to treason.

We are not always provided with a clear picture of how such cultural transmission took place, but there are enough concrete facts to allow us to draw certain inferences. Some of those facts require interpretation to understand their full import, such as can be seen in the story given by Werner of an otherwise unremarkable grave in the first/second century Roman Christian catacomb of St. Calixtus. The name of the man buried there is given as Deusdedit, and on his crypt are carved both a fish, the emblem of early Christianity, and a shield of David, an identifying symbol of Judaism. Below that are inscribed the Latin words:

> *Hic levitarum primus in ordine vivens, Davitici cantor carminis ipse fuit.*
> (Here lies a Levite of the first order in life. He was a singer of David's songs.)

The name Deusdedit is a direct Latin translation of the Hebrew name Jonathan ("Given by God"). Judging from the presence of both Jewish and Christian symbols on his grave, his presence in a Christian burial ground, and the reference to him as a Levite, it is not unreasonable to infer that this was originally a Jew named Jonathan, one of the Temple musicians who became a follower of Jesus and remained a singer of the liturgy, practicing the same skills in his new community that he had used in the now destroyed Jewish Temple. Sendrey makes note of still another such tomb, that of the convert Redemptus (whose name had originally been Reuben), praised on his gravestone for producing a "nectar-like melody."[27] Such people would have played a key role in the vital religious and musical interchange that took place in the tangled Greco-Roman world.

---

[27] Alfred Sendrey, *Music of the Jews in the Diaspora* (Cranbury, NJ: Yoseloff, 1971), 226.

Suggestions for Further Reading

Bernal, Martin. *Black Athena: The Afroasiatic Roots of Classical Civilization*. London: Free Association Press, 1987.

Bradshaw, Paul F. *The Making of Jewish and Christian Worship*. In *Two Liturgical Traditions*, ed. Lawrence A. Hoffman. Vol. 5, part 1. Notre Dame: Notre Dame University Press, 1991.

Fellerer, Karl Gustav. "Jewish Elements in Pre-Gregorian Chant." In *World Congress on Jewish Music*, ed. Judith Cohen, 115-18. Tel Aviv: The Institute for the Translation of Hebrew Literature Ltd, 1982.

Galambush, Julie. *The Reluctant Parting: How the New Testament's Jewish Writers Created a Christian Book*. New York: Harper, 2005.

Jeffery, Peter. "The Earliest Christian Chant Repertory Recovered: The Gregorian Witnesses to Jerusalem Chant." *Journal of the American Musicological Society* 47, no. 1 (1994): 1-38.

Sendrey, Alfred. *The Music of the Jews in the Diaspora (Up to 1800): A Contribution to the Social and Cultural History of the Jews*. New York: T. Yoseloff, 1971.

Steinberg, Milton. *As a Driven Leaf*. Indianapolis and New York: Bobbs-Merrill, 1939.

Taitz, Emily. "Kol Ishah—The Voice of Woman: Where was it Heard in Medieval Europe?" *Conservative Judaism* 38 (spring 1986): 44-61.

Werner, Eric. *The Sacred Bridge: Liturgical Parallels in Synagogue and Early Church*. New York: Schocken Books, 1970.

HISTORICAL INTERLUDE | The Great Diaspora

Consider, for a moment, the cataclysmic destruction of Jerusalem and the Temple in the year 70 CE. What happened to the abject few who survived that catastrophe? What happened to their religion, rooted in animal sacrifice by a priestly class at a single holy site to which all Jews were expected to make pilgrimages? The answer to those questions lies in the Jewish experience of the coming centuries. The Jews were the first people to preserve their ethnic and cultural unity without either a political center or the military might to defend themselves. That national experience lasted until the reestablishment of the State of Israel—actually the Third Jewish Commonwealth—in 1948, a two-thousand year period known in Jewish history as "The Diaspora" (dispersion).

The Diaspora has a complex history—it is, after all, almost ten times as long as the entire chronicle of the United States. During those centuries Jewish communities were dispersed and could be found from the farthest reaches of East Asia to the New World, from Russia or Canada in the North to South Africa or Tierra del Fuego at the earth's other pole. Jews became part of the local culture in China and India, in Africa, Russia, England, and the Americas, as well as the Middle East. In each of those far-flung lands the local Jewish populations maintained their religion, adopted and absorbed the customs, languages, and musical traditions of their hosts to the extent that they found in them modes for the expression of their religious life. The infiltration of local musical styles into such a seamless system was superficial in circumstances where political or religious prejudice enforced separation from the indigenous population, but was also very deep in societies that raised no social barriers against cultural interpenetration.

The idea that the Diaspora resulted solely from the Roman destruction of Jerusalem is not entirely correct. It grew out of a Eurocentric perception of Jewish history, as did the myth that Jews were totally absent from the area during the intervening millennia. When tens of thousands who had survived the fall of Jerusalem were sold into slavery in all quarters of the Roman empire, well-established Jewish communities that already existed in Europe, North Africa, and the Middle East sacrificed their own treasures to buy many of their brothers from servitude. Pre-exilic Jewish communities had also sprung up in Spain, North Africa, and other trading centers of the Roman Europe, as well as in the Arab world. In addition, the Jewish community remaining in Israel, though no longer permitted to be in Jerusalem after the fall of the Temple, was strong enough to support a continuing series of rebellions: in the South at Masada, in the Galilee at Gamla, and, the largest of them, the revolt of Shimon Bar Kochba (or Bar Koziba) from 132 to 135 CE, sixty-five years after the fall of the Temple. Bar Kochba issued coins celebrating "the redemption of Israel" in each of the three years of the revolution's success. In the first year one of those coins was stamped with the picture of a lyre (*kinnor*), which provides some idea of the strong association between the Jewish people and music in their own minds (see fig. 2.2, p. 37). Some 580,000 Jewish soldiers and an untold number of civilians were slain in that bloody uprising, according to Roman sources, which reported 985 villages destroyed.

In spite of that wholesale slaughter more than forty Jewish communities still existed in the Land of Israel in the fifth and sixth centuries, when they mounted still another failed attempt to regain independence. European crusaders who arrived in the eleventh century found Jewish communities thriving under Moslem rule throughout the country, in Jerusalem, Tiberias, Ramleh, Ashkelon, Caesarea, and Gaza. The late Middle Ages saw the growth of Jewish mysticism, centered in the city of Safed, which by 1577 became a center of Hebrew publishing, where the first printing press using moveable type was created outside Europe. So on the one hand, large Jewish expatriate communities had existed in foreign countries long before the destruction of the Temple, while on the other, there was a continuing Jewish presence in the homeland all throughout the Diaspora.

What was lost in the year 70, then, was not the Jewish connection with the land of their forefathers, whose restoration became a part of daily prayer for every Jew. What had been lost was the Temple and the priesthood: the locus and means for the maintenance of biblical Judaism. However severe that loss, it was offset by a group of scholars—the Pharisees—who gathered in the little town of Yavneh to work out the changes necessary to maintain their religion and culture even while the razing of Jerusalem was still under way. Led by the visionary rabbi Yochanan ben Zakkai, they set about to redefine normative Jewish practice in the absence of two of the principal features on which it had been focused for two thousand years: the Temple and the priesthood. They achieved this by formalizing the training of religious teachers (the rabbinate), and, over the next three centuries or so, by deducing religious practice for those new circumstances from biblical Judaism, by a process of rigorous Greek logic.

> Pharasaism . . . fought resolutely against Hellenism while absorbing its
> most distinguishing features—in a subtle and creative way. . . . The Pharasaic
> revolution was thus a novel form of Judaism fashioned by men of genius
> out of raw materials from both the [Greek] *polis* and the Pentateuch.[1]

The resulting system was codified in the Mishnah: six volumes of ethical and moral law extracted, or logically extrapolated, from the Torah. Its further expansion by thousands of pages of legalistic debate, historical pondering, and systematic, if non-linear, ethical and judicial thought, created the complex compilation called the Talmud. The contents of the Talmud were spread

---

[1] Ellis Rivkin, *The Shaping of Jewish History: A Radical New Interpretation* (New York: Charles Scribner's Sons, 1971), 81.

across centuries of scholarship that virtually obliterated time, or at least ignored it. In the Talmud, rabbis of the fourth century take issue with authorities from the first century, and long-dead scholars are quoted to refute points made by contemporaries. One version of the Talmud grew up within Palestine itself, while a different one developed in what had become a center of perhaps even greater intellectual brilliance, the Jewish academies of Babylon (Iraq). It was the Babylonian version that was to prevail for most, though not all, Jews.

The Talmud became the key to law and practice for the rekindled Jewish religion. Its universal study among Jews served, in many ways, as the link binding most Diaspora Jews to their brethren. The Talmud, as a gloss on the *Mishnah*, which was in turn a gloss on the Torah, was the glue that held Judaism together during the long centuries of dispersion. Having a sense of their history and mission from the Torah, along with an understanding from the Talmud of how those ideals from the days of an independent commonwealth could be applied to the very different life of the Diaspora, Jewish communities felt free to adopt the manners (and from the vantage point of our interest, the music) of their host cultures without needing to sacrifice the essence of their religion. Thus armed, the main body of Jewry entered into the history of other peoples as a minority culture: sometimes tolerated, occasionally welcomed, and frequently oppressed.

The complexity of Diaspora history and the wide differences between the experiences of communities in different parts of the world, or at different historical moments, make it impossible to treat the music of the Diaspora as a whole. Instead, this book will concentrate on two of the largest population groups, and perforce give no more than passing attention to a mere sampling of others. The two largest groups were the Jews living in the spheres of Islam and of Christianity. Even within those, there were dozens of cultural subdivisions, while the social and political fortunes of each group varied widely at different times in their history. We must necessarily oversimplify, generalize, and omit large sections of the picture if we are to get even an inkling of the overall story. It must be remembered that the Jews of Ethiopia, of India, of the North African Mughrab, Khazakstan, China, Buenos Aires, or Milwaukee, all have their own rich and complex histories, as do numerous other Jewish communities of the Great Diaspora. Our survey here must necessarily be cursory in what it does treat, and parochial, in that disproportionate attention will be given to the Western world.

Even so, we should not lose sight of the breadth of the Jewish Diaspora and the impact it has had on Jewish consciousness generally, and specifically, on its music. Jewish communities of many cultures, with roots that go deep into the history of their host communities, have brought widely varying music to their common social and religious practices. In the past century or so, communication among those far-flung communities has made them conscious of the plurality of Jewish musics. With the reestablishment of the Jewish homeland in the twentieth century those communities have been brought together again. The result has been a gradual fusion of musical styles in Jewish life, in spite of attendant cultural and social problems. The State of Israel has begun to formulate a unique musical language, one that may eventually blend Kurdish, Indian, and Iraqi influences with Yemenite, European, American, and Russian to produce a new, syncretistic lyrical expression. If that occurs—and it already appears to have begun— the Diaspora experience will have shaped an entirely new vernacular for music in the Israeli community, one that is multicultural, yet at the same time, local.

4 ‖ Cantillation

If there is any part of the musical tradition that can be claimed as distinctively Jewish, it is the practice of cantillation. The term refers to the use of pre-existing musical motives in a song-like declamation of the Bible passages (Torah and Prophets) read weekly in the synagogue. Its purpose, though, is more than musical, as we shall see. Cantillation has a uniquely Jewish identification not just because it is used in the synagogue, and not even because it is restricted to the holy books. Its claim grows out of the fact that this musical system was conceived and designed for the express purpose of conveying the meaning of the central Jewish texts clearly and accurately, and of preserving the Hebrew language in which they were written.

Cantillation Tradition

Tradition requires that the Torah be declaimed aloud in public on the Sabbath and public market days (Monday and Thursday of each week) in the special musical-dramatic way known as cantillation. In the Jewish worship service, the Torah is read—that is, cantillated—serially throughout the liturgical year in a cycle of weekly readings (sing., *parashah*; pl., *parashot*), completed annually on a holiday called *Simchat Torah* (Rejoicing in the Torah).[1] On that day the final verses of Deuteronomy are read, followed immediately by the first verses of Genesis to symbolize the endless continuum of reading and study. The day is one of celebration, featuring apples and candy for the children, with marching, singing, and even joyous dancing with the

---

[1] The joyous holiday *Simchat Torah* is an addition to the liturgical calendar made in the diaspora. It seems to have been instituted when an older Babylonian tradition of reading the complete Torah in a three-year cycle was replaced by an annual cycle of reading. In the fourteenth century Rabbi Jacob ben Asher instituted the custom of immediately following the reading of the final verses with the opening verses of the next year's cycle, "so that Satan might have no opportunity of accusing the Jews of having finished with the Torah."

Torah scrolls to commemorate receipt of the law at Mount Sinai. In addition to the Five Books of Moses, other parts of the *Tanach* are cantillated at services as well. Every week a passage from the Prophets (*Nevi'im*) is also read, and on certain holidays special readings from the other writings (*Ketubim*) are read. On the festival of Purim, for example, the entire Book of Esther is cantillated, while Jeremiah's Book of Lamentations is cantillated on *Tishah b'av* (the ninth of the month of *Av*), when the destruction of the Temple is mourned.

For westerners accustomed to thinking of musical compositions in terms of individually composed works that exist as unique artistic constructs, cantillation is a new concept. To understand the practice fully means discarding preconceived notions of what constitutes "music." Western music assumes that each vocal or instrumental composition is an independent work that can be uniquely identified as something separate from all other compositions. That is why we can speak of "knowing" a particular composition: "The Star-Spangled Banner," for instance, or Beethoven's Fifth Symphony. Cantillation is built on a different premise and has style features not familiar in Western music.

The first unexpected characteristic that one encounters is that the melodies are non-metrical: there is no regular "beat." They flow, instead, according to the length and sequence of melodic motives assigned to particular textual situations. Those motives are chosen from a pool of melodies appropriate to each book being read and are combined into a kaleidoscopic chain that utilizes motives only from that specific group in constantly changing combinations. This kind of a system is called centonization, a method of structuring music common to several cultures of the Middle East. The practice of centonization also nourished the earliest roots of Gregorian chant and the Islamic *tajwid* (cantillation of the Koran). Some scholars feel that Hebrew cantillation played a major role in shaping the chant of the Christian church of antiquity, since its earliest musical forms were developed in the Middle Eastern Church, and as we saw in chapter 3, there was a great deal of interplay between Christian and Jewish liturgies in their formative period.

In order to "sing" a passage from the Torah correctly, one must first memorize all the musical motives belonging to the appropriate group, then choose the correct melody for each word from an existing pool of motives according to a complex set of rules expressed in written signs. Musical considerations play only a minor role in determining the sequence in which motives are strung together. According to the logic governing the chant, only when the other rules allow a choice of several possibilities does one make a selection based on musical taste, and even then, the choices are restricted to a small group of the total that qualify for that textual situation. Appropriate motives are chosen on the basis of rules bound to the text, such as the number of syllables in a word, the word's position in the sentence, or the number of unstressed syllables between stressed ones. It is the text that determines what the resulting cantillation sounds like. We call music built on such a plan "logogenic," meaning that its structure is determined by the words to which it is attached rather than by musical considerations.

There is good reason to believe that the practice of logogenic cantillation goes back to the very introduction of public recitation of the Torah in the time of Ezra the Scribe more than 2,500 years ago. As a result, most people are under the impression that the cantillation melodies are also very ancient. In fact, the music used today is from much later. Surprising as it may seem, we cannot with certainty date any of the western melodies in use today much earlier than the end of the fifteenth or beginning of the sixteenth century CE, although there is reason to believe that melodic patterns of some of the oriental Jews may be older than that. As studies by Abraham Z. Idelsohn and Hanoch Avenary have shown, within the last four-and-a-half centuries or so for which we have written records, those melodies have undergone quite a bit of change.[2]

It is likely that the basic logical rules for cantillation served as a vehicle for different melodies over time, as the orally transmitted musical motives were continually adjusted to conform to musical styles of host cultures. As a result, there is not just one family of cantillation melodies. Jewish communities all over the world developed their own, possibly all branching off from the original melodies of biblical times, now lost. Early in the twentieth century Idelsohn demonstrated certain structural resemblances in the melodies of far-flung communities isolated from one another for millennia, which strongly suggested that the melodies may all have derived from a common model. The structural resemblance of cantillation from different diaspora communities is rarely apparent to a casual listener, though, and research since then has cast some doubt on Idelsohn's hypothesis. Although there are now scholars trying to reconstruct what the cantillation of biblical times might have sounded like, we must fall back again on the disappointing phrase, "We don't know for sure." It is probable, though, that the original melodies had only the slightest, if any, resemblance to those heard in the modern synagogue.

Melodic Motives (Te'amim) of the Tradition

Where did today's cantillation motives originate, then, and how does the reader know what to sing? Since the Middle Ages the melodic motives of the Jews have been written in what is known as ekphonetic notation, in which each musical motive is represented by a sign inserted into the text. Ekphonetic signs do not represent pitches, as in modern musical notation. Rather, each sign is associated with a brief melodic motive in the same sense that a button worn by a political conventioneer displaying the picture of an elephant informs you that the wearer is a Republican. Each of those symbols is called a *ta'am* in Hebrew (pl., *te'amim*), and each represents a brief melodic motive to be sung on a single unit of text. Those textual units are normally single words; however, words can be combined into hyphenated complexes that are treated as single units either because of their grammatical relationship or by some other close connection. It is probably better, then, to talk about "word-units" rather than simply "words," remembering that most, but not all, such word-units are individual words.

The *te'amim* cannot be "read" like modern musical notes—nothing about them identifies pitch or rhythm. The reader must begin the study of a passage to be chanted by first memorizing the motives associated with each written sign. It is as if the letter "X" stood for the first measure of "Frère Jacques" and "O" represented the opening notes of "The Star-Spangled Banner." Knowing those two songs, you could then perform the series "XOX"; but if you did not know the songs, you would have no way to deduce the correct melody from that ekphonetic notation.

The *te'amim* are sometimes referred to as "accents" in Western languages; but because that term is also used for word stress, we will use the Hebrew here to avoid any confusion.

---

[2] See Hanoch Avenary, *Ashkenazi Tradition of Biblical Chant Between 1500 and 1900* (Jerusalem: World Congress on Jewish Music, 1978), and Abraham Zvi Idelsohn, *Hebräisch-Orientalischer Melodienschatz, zum ersten Male gesammelt* (Leipzig: Breitkopf and Härtel, 1914).

Some writers refer to the collective body of *te'amim* as "the trope," while others reserve that word for the melody of a specific *ta'am*, so that, too, is an ambiguous term that will be avoided here. Melodic families specific to a particular region or culture are often called a *nusach*, a word that is probably best translated in this context as "melodic type" or "melodic tradition."

While someone who is cantillating has a certain amount of freedom for musical interpretation, it is not an improvised performance in any sense. The centonization of motives proceeds according to carefully worked-out formulas developed by a succession of early medieval scholars known as Masoretes (a Greek formation built on the Hebrew word, *masorah*, meaning "tradition"). To understand their system, we must begin by understanding the world of those Masoretes who created and codified the system. We will make a brief excursion, then, to learn who those people were, what they did, and why they did it, then return to examine the results of their work.

Masoretes

In the centuries immediately after the fall of Jerusalem and destruction of the Temple, the Mishnah (the code of Jewish law) was written down for the first time and the Talmud (the interpretation of that code) was compiled, providing the basis for today's normative Judaism. It was after this that the generations of medieval scholars known as the Masoretes took on the task of preparing a meticulously correct edition of the *Tanach* and finding ways to insure its transmission with complete accuracy. There were several centers of Masoretic scholarship. The principal ones were the Babylonian academies of Jewish learning (primarily at Sura and Pumbedita), and parallel Palestinian academies in Jerusalem and Tiberias. At some point by about the sixth century CE, those groups of scholars recognized the need for written signs to help readers correctly cantillate the books they were so painstakingly editing. Each school developed its own scheme for solving that problem. Knowledge of musical notation, which had existed in a rudimentary form in the ancient world, had been lost; therefore it was necessary for them to invent a system for that purpose. Their efforts may have been based on musical signs found in Syrian and Greek manuscripts of the fifth century, at least judging from the similarity of appearance, but they also show some resemblance to the still earlier thinking of the Alexandrian grammarians. Gradually, the signs of the Tiberian school gained the widest adoption because of their clarity and precision. By the eleventh century the *te'amim* of the Tiberians had supplanted the others in all but a few locations.

Within Tiberian notation two different logical systems for applying the *te'amim* were developed. One was for the twenty-one so-called "prose" books of the Bible and the other for the three poetical books: Job, Proverbs, and Psalms (sometimes grouped together into the abbreviation "*Sifrei* [books of] EMeT." EMeT is an acronym made from the initial Hebrew letters of those three books, which assemble into an acronym resembling the word "truth." The logical rules for that second system have been lost, and all we know about them today is that the rules—and the melodies—were different, even though the signs were the same. Perhaps the rules had to be different because the verses of the three poetic books were shorter than those of the prose books. Two interesting exceptions to that rule exist. The first is that Job 3:1 and 42:7-17 are cantillated according to the system of the prose books. The second is that Psalm 18 occurs twice in the Bible: once in *Tehillim* (The Book of Psalms) and again in the prose book, II Samuel 22, where it is cited in full. Some specialists think that this might provide enough clues to someday rebuild the lost system of the poetic books if only a few more pieces of information can be found.

To complicate the matter still further, the same signs represent different melodies for different publicly read books of the twenty-one for which we know the system. There is an entirely different pool of melodies used for those signs in, say, the Book of Esther, from that for the five books of the Torah, and those melodies are themselves subject to variation for special liturgical situations. In all, there are six separate sets of melodies referred to by the same signs. Additionally, widely separated communities of the diaspora have developed their own melodic traditions (*nusachim*) for the *te'amim* over centuries, each in accordance with the local musical culture, so that the Yemenite *nusach* has little in common with that of the Turkish, Russian, or Romanian community.

In short, there is not a simple one-to-one correspondence between the signs and their melodies. The signs are symbols in what we shall see is a complex logical system, but the melodies they represent vary according to a complex overlap of melodic systems, regional traditions, books of the Bible, and special variations. To avoid dealing with all of these complications, the discussion here will be restricted to the structure of cantillation used for the twenty-one prose books of the Pentateuch, in the system developed by the Tiberian Masoretes that is in almost universal use among Jews today.

Creation of the *te'amim* was only a minor part of the work of those scholars. The Tiberian Masoretes worked from about the sixth to the eleventh century CE on their edition of the Hebrew Bible, and the fruit of half a millenium of their labor exists today as one of the most exhaustive editing jobs ever undertaken. The problems faced by those scholars were many. The text inherited from the ancient world was flawed. It existed in a number of manuscripts that displayed variant readings, had no vowels, failed to distinguish the ends of verses or even the division between words, and had many points of internal inconsistency, variant spellings, and unknown terms. To complicate matters, it was written in Hebrew, a language that had not been in general use, even by the Jews themselves, for over a millennium by the time this project was brought to fruition. In addition to collating existing versions to produce an authoritative text, the Masoretes created the vowel and punctuation signs of modern Hebrew as well as developed this musical notation. They studied and assiduously collated texts over some twenty generations of scholarship, leaving as their legacy a perfected edition of the *Tanach* known today as the Masoretic Text.

Their concerns in developing the *te'amim* were not primarily musical. The cantillation was designed to serve grammatical and logical functions first and foremost, with musical considerations taking a back seat. The musical aspects incorporated a long-standing tradition of cheironomy (musical hand-signs), reflected in the names the Masoretes gave to some of the written signs; for example, *tip'cha* (hand-breadth).[3] The assignment of musical signs was based

---

[3] In cheironomy, a system still in use among some oriental Jewish communities today, positions of a teacher's hands or fingers indicated corresponding melodic motives to be sung by the student. The practice may have extended to the public reading itself, where an experienced cantillator would assist a neophyte in reading the Torah portion by using hand signs as a reminder of motives to be sung on specific words.

on their reading of the text, which had been preserved with surprising (though not total) fidelity through centuries of scribal copying, and which was painstakingly studied, debated, edited, and reedited over hundreds of years in the course of producing their final version.

Traditional centonization before their time had utilized music for centuries to provide design to an undifferentiated string of text. The addition of music provided inflection and intonation that clarified their content, and the cantillator imparted structure to what was often ambiguous on the page by inserting pauses, emphasizing key words or passages, and making musical connections between ideas. That is, no doubt, the reason the sages of the Babylonian Talmud took the unusual step of commanding that the Bible "should be read in public and made understood to the hearers in a sweet, musical tone."

Biblical texts had been cantillated from the beginning of the institution of their regular weekly readings after the return from the first Babylonian exile (ca. 538 BCE). At that time Ezra the Scribe decreed that the holy books should be read in public for the edification of the populace. While it was once thought that cantillation was common in the ancient world, Idelsohn had concluded by 1929 that "there is . . . no foundation for the current notion that the cantillation of the Bible is derived from the Oriental manner of reading in public."[4] Formal cantillation may have been an innovation of the returning exiles, the same generation that sang of their return from Babylon in Psalm 126: "We were like dreamers; our mouths were filled with laughter and our tongues with song."

The most important sources from the Hellenistic period—Philo of Alexandria (25 BCE-40 CE), Josephus Flavius (Joseph ben Mattityahu ha-Cohen, ca. 38-ca. 100 CE), and the Christian Gospels—all attest to a long-established practice of public Torah reading in this fashion by that time. By the second century CE the rabbis of the Talmud were already referring to the centonization melodies with the quaint phrase *halachah mi-Sinai* (law from Sinai), a colorful figure of speech used to designate practices they believed dated from the very distant past. To insure that this atypical practice, which had already acquired the status of hoary antiquity, was properly carried out, the Babylonian Talmud contained such caveats as, "Whoever reads the Pentateuch without its tune shows disregard for it and the vital value of its laws."[5] On the other hand, it also cautioned against vulgarizing the practice, saying, "Whoever intones the Scriptures in the manner of secular song abuses the Torah."[6]

The original melodies may have been lost after the destruction of the Temple, or they may have continued through the centuries during which the Talmud was compiled, although they are likely to have changed with use over time, as often happens to orally-preserved music. They would not have fallen under the rabbinic proscription against instruments or secular music, and it is possible that the melodies already known to the Masoretes might have reflected an ancient tradition, at least to some degree. The antiquity of the melodies, though, is of little consequence. The texts were cantillated long before the Masoretes came on the scene. They did not create the melodies. What they did was to systematize the use of existing motives to serve the purpose of unambiguous oral transmission and semantic clarification of the biblical texts.

---

[4] Idelsohn, *Jewish Music*, 35.

[5] *Megillah*, 32a.

[6] *Sanhedrin*, 101a.

That purpose gained increasing urgency with the rise of Islam and the triumph of Arabic as the Middle Eastern *lingua franca* in the seventh century. Jewish communities had given up Hebrew for daily speech some two hundred years before the Christian era, when Aramaic became their common language. Still later, as we have seen, Aramaic was replaced by Greek. By the seventh century it appeared that Greek would give way to Arabic throughout the Middle East (which is what happened), and the possibility that Hebrew might disappear entirely loomed as a credible danger. One goal of the Masoretes was to maintain the language, even artificially, for that distant day when they firmly believed that the diaspora would return to Zion.

With that in mind, the Masoretic scholars devised two systems of signs to be added to the text. One system designated the vowels, which served a grammatical function in Hebrew as in other Semitic languages, but which had no letter-forms in the alphabet. A second innovation was creation of the *te'amim*. The earliest reference to the names of the signs themselves seems to be in a fragment containing a "Kara'ite[7] List of Terms" dating from the eighth century. It was found in the nineteenth century in a depository of medieval manuscripts above an old Cairo synagogue. Their next mention as musical representations is found in a mid-ninth century manuscript of Semach ben Chayyim Ga'on (883-896), who discusses "Vowel points and conjunctive and disjunctive *te'amim*," pointing out differences between Babylonian and Tiberian usage. The culminating figure of the Masoretic line was Aaron Ben-Moshe Ben-Asher, the last of a family of Masoretic scholars, who lived in the late tenth and early eleventh centuries. Around the turn of the eleventh century Ben-Asher wrote the first major treatise on the subject of cantillation: *Dikdukei ha-te'amim* (Grammar of the *Te'amim*). Ben-Asher's treatise circulated widely in manuscript, but was not published until 1515 (after the invention of moveable type), still highly regarded five hundred years after its compositon.

The Masoretic *te'amim*, as Israel Yeivin explains, perform three functions:

> Their primary function . . . is to represent the musical motifs to which the Biblical text was chanted in the public reading. This chant enhanced the beauty and solemnity of the reading, but because the purpose of the reading was to present the text clearly and intelligibly to the hearers, the chant is dependent on the text and emphasizes the logical relationship of the words. Consequently, the second function is to indicate the interrelationship of the words in the text. . . . [A]ccentuation [i. e., the *te'amim*] marks semantic units, which are not always identical with syntactic units. . . . [T]he third function of the accents is to mark the position of word stress.[8]

The last point, identification of word stress, requires some explanation. A *ta'am* placed on a particular syllable may be the only way to distinguish between identically spelled words—for example, between *shávu* (they returned) and *shavú* (they captured). The melodies have no

---

[7] The Kara'ites were a sect of Jews who adhered to the written text of the Torah exclusively, denying the "oral [i.e., interpreted] Torah" of their opponents, the rabbinites (pharisees). It was the rabbinites, of course, who prevailed as the majority of normative Judaism. A handful of kara'ite congregations still exist in Israel to this day.

[8] Israel Yeivin, *Introduction to the Tiberian Masorah* (Missoula, MT: Scholars Press, 1980), 158.

"expressive" function. Mordechai Breuer points out that the same sequence of *te'amim* is used for Genesis 1:1, "And God created the heavens and the earth," as for Genesis 36:26, "And these are the sons of Ishan: Chemdan and Eshban and Itran and Charan." He makes this quite clear:

> The music of the [*te'amim*] . . . does not express sorrow or happiness that arises from the content of the verses. . . . This music is equal for all verses of the Bible and does not distinguish between the lofty and the mundane. . . . The verse, "And Timnah was a concubine" is no less the word of God than "And God created the heavens and the earth."[9]

Cantillation System

There are twenty-eight symbols for *te'amim* in common use, each with its own name and function. Each is associated with a specific musical motive and each conveys information about—and in turn is determined by—the grammatical organization of the text. The *te'amim* are divided into two classes. The first type is called "Disjunctive" *te'amim* (Hebrew: *mafsikim*), sometimes called "Masters," or "Lords," because the signs of the other group are subservient to their placement. The second group is called "Conjunctive" *te'amim* (Hebrew: *mechabrim*), or "Servants," because they are dependent on the "Lords" for their placement and musical function. Conjunctives function to connect syntactically related words into a continuous melodic flow, while disjunctives reveal the grammatical structure of a verse by introducing pauses that provide oral punctuation for the listener. Disjunctives are further subdivided into four levels of importance according to what is called in Hebrew their *ko'ach pisuk*, or "separating power." The four levels of disjunctives were given fanciful designations by Christian scholars of the sixteenth century to indicate their relative importance in the hierarchy: "Emperors, Kings, Dukes, and Ambassadors," in one such scheme. Their melodic core is always the same and, as the Masoretes made clear, each ends with a distinct separation from the next word, signified in musical notation by a rest. The melodies of conjunctive *te'amim*, on the other hand, flow directly into the following word without any pause.

The Anglican clergyman William Wickes, a principal figure in the revival of scholarly interest in the *te'amim*, explained in 1881:

> [T]he logical pauses were duly represented—and that according to their gradation—by musical pauses; and when no logical pause occurred in a sentence, then the syntactical relationship of the words . . . decided which among them were to be sung together and which were to be separated by a musical pause. In this way the music was made to mark not only the broad lines, but the finest shades of distinction in the sense.[10]

---

[9] Mordechai Breuer, *Te'amei ha-mikra be-21 sefarim uve-sifre eme"t (Te'amim of the Bible in the 21 Books and the Books of EMeT)* (Jerusalem: Michlalah, 1981), 4.

[10] William Wickes, *Two Treatises on the Accentuation of the Old Testament*; reprint of the original treatises of 1881 and 1884, with a prolegomenon by Aaron Dotan (New York: Ktav, 1970).

There are eighteen disjunctive *te'amim*, subdivided, as noted above, into four categories of decreasing importance. Each *ta'am* has its own unique melody. To understand how they are used, one must be aware that most biblical verses have a two-part poetic structure in which the second half amplifies or comments on the first. An example would be the opening of the twenty-third psalm: "The Lord is my Shepherd / I shall not want." The most important category of *te'amim*, the so-called "Emperors," contains two major pause markers: 1) *silluk* (also called *sof pasuk*), which marks the end of a verse and functions as an audible period, and 2) *etnachta*, which marks the middle of a verse and functions more or less like a semicolon. The *silluk* looks like a short vertical line drawn under the accented syllable of a word. Thus, in a word like *ha-shamayim*, where the accent falls on the penultimate syllable, it would occur as a vertical stroke underneath the "a" (or its Hebrew equivalent). The *etnachta* has the appearance of a half-circle with a short vertical sticking straight up from it. Both of those can be seen in context in fig. 4.4, below.

A clause of the verse that has enough syllables to warrant it may be subdivided again, using one of the five signs in the next lower category of disjunctives, called "Kings." If any of the resulting clauses are still long enough to warrant it, they, too, may be subdivided into halves by one of the next class down, the "Dukes," in which there are five different signs. Finally, if at that point there is still any clause of the verse requiring further subdivision to insure clarity in the reading, one of the six signs in the last class, the "Ambassadors," is used to effect that. That continuous halving of clauses prompted one scholar to coin the phrase, "the principle of continuous dichotomy" to describe the process by which the Masoretes structured the *te'amim*.[11] The purpose of introducing a disjunctive *ta'am* of any class is to put oral punctuation— a pause—into the reading. The category of disjunctive *ta'am* to be used at any given point in a verse, reflects the importance of the pause.

The other major class of *te'amim* is the conjunctives: signs indicating that the reader must *not* stop, but should connect smoothly to the next musical motive. Conjunctives are the glue that hold the musical narrative together. There are eight conjunctives, but here things get a little complicated. The musical motives of the conjunctives are not "fixed," as are those of the disjunctives. Rather, each sign may be realized in several different ways, depending on which *ta'am* precedes or follows it. This may be partly because the function of a conjunctive is to insure a smooth flow of text from one word to the next, and musical considerations would play a role in the seamless transition into the next motive. The choice of which conjunctive to use depends on the relation between specific conjunctive and disjunctive *te'amim* and the syllable count in a particular clause.

Finally, two remaining signs should be mentioned for the sake of completeness. Even though strictly speaking they are not *te'amim* (that is, they have no musical motives of their own), they are part of the musical system. The first of those is the *meteg* (also called *gaya* by some writers), the second is called *pasek*. Their function is to modify the other musical signs, and they will be discussed at greater length in the section on textual exegesis (see pp. 81-82).

---

[11] Miles Blicker Cohen, *The System of Accentuation in the Hebrew Bible* (Minneapolis: Milco Press, 1969).

Structure of Individual *Te'amim*

Each individual *ta'am* consists of three segments: a nucleus that carries the distinctive musical motive applied to the accented syllable, and two optional segments enclosing it fore and aft, the presence and length of which vary according to the number of syllables in the word. The melodic identity of each *ta'am* resides in the nucleus, which may be as brief as a single note; but for many of the *te'amim* the nucleus is neumatic (two, possibly three, notes on the accented syllable) or melismatic (four or more notes on the accented syllable). The melody of the nucleus may differ from one tradition to another, but within each cultural tradition it is invariable. The nucleus is the key musical motive identified with each *ta'am*. For a one-syllable word, only the nucleus would be sung. In words with more than one syllable additional notes would be added for syllables before the accent, and/or added to syllables coming after it as needed.

Notes on unaccented syllables that precede the nucleus are called the prefix; notes on unaccented syllables following the accent constitute the suffix. Prefixes and suffixes are often sung on a single pitch, repeated as necessary to obtain the appropriate number of syllables. In certain cases they can extend over several pitches, and, for a few *te'amim*, constitute florid melismas. The schematic diagram for all *te'amim*, then, would be Prefix-Nucleus-Suffix, with the understanding that the prefix and/or suffix only occur if there are unaccented syllables in the word to be sung. In addition to memorizing the nucleus of each sign, then, it is also necessary to understand how to form prefixes and suffixes for *te'amim* when needed.

Words or word-units in the Pentateuch range from a single syllable to as many as six, or even seven, syllables. Approximately seventy percent of all words in classical Hebrew bear final-syllable accents, while a little less than thirty percent are accented on the penultimate syllable. Most of the exceptions are words borrowed from Arabic or Greek, or in modern Hebrew, foreign coinages like *televíziah*, *biológiah*, or *svéder*. The Hebrew grammatical term for words with final-syllable accents is *mileil*. Words with unaccented final syllables are said to be *milra*. *Te'amim* are primarily structured for *mileil* words—that is, words with a final-syllable accent. When a *ta'am* falls on a *milra* word, a musical suffix must be created either by repeating the last note of the nucleus or by adding one more note to account for the final, unaccented syllable. In the same way, a prefix must be created for any syllables that precede the accent.

The Masoretic procedure in placing the signs seems to have been that once all the verses were bisected and re-bisected by disjunctive *te'amim*, the words between disjunctions were connected by conjunctive *te'amim*. The resulting melody can vary greatly, depending on the structure of the verse and the choice of *te'amim*, especially since certain conjunctives show considerable melodic variation, depending on what precedes or follows. The musical effect is not so much logical or developmental as we are accustomed to in Western music; it is kaleidoscopic, with ever-changing patterns of the same basic elements.

The length of the pauses following disjunctives vary according to the level of disjunctive being used; that is, an "Emperor" should be followed by a longer stop (i.e., a musical rest) than a "King," which in turn should be longer than a "Duke" or "Ambassador." The cantillation would then flow in short, continuous phrases interrupted by brief pauses marking greater or lesser logical divisions in the text.

It must be remembered that the primary goal of the Masoretes was preservation and accurate transmission of the texts, not interpretation, and that most of the congregants for whom these scholars prepared their painstaking editions no longer understood Hebrew. For that reason an oral interlinear translation accompanied the public reading of the Hebrew text, so that following each *silluk* the verse would be repeated in the vernacular. Such performance insured that the words would be heard clearly, and even those who might not understand the language could learn the sound of the text and associate it with its meaning. It was that need for vernacular translations that had spawned the Septuagint in Greek for the Alexandrian community and the *Targum* in Aramaic for the Palestinian and Babylonian communities. The Masoretes did not doubt that the time would come when people would once again use the Hebrew language, and those future people would need to know what it had sounded like. Their approach assured that the sounds of the language would not be lost in the interim.

Like the Masoretic vowel signs, the symbols used for cantillation were small dots, curved lines, and angles affixed above or below the letters of the text. Here are the opening verses of the Bible (Genesis 1:1-5) shown in three different states to demonstrate their appearance. Figure 4.1, below, shows the words with no Masoretic signs, the way they appear in the Torah scroll itself.

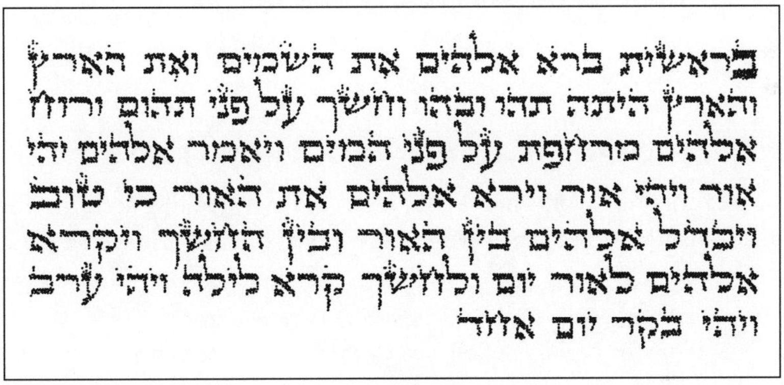

FIG. 4.1 Text of Genesis 1:1-5 as it is in a Torah scroll, without Masoretic signs

Figure 4.2, following, shows those same verses as they appear in a modern transcription of the Torah printed in a book for study (Hebrew: *tikkun*). A comparison of the two will quickly show that while fig. 4.2 has exactly the same letters, a number of little marks have been added above or below the letters. Those are the vowel signs added by the Tiberian Masoretes.

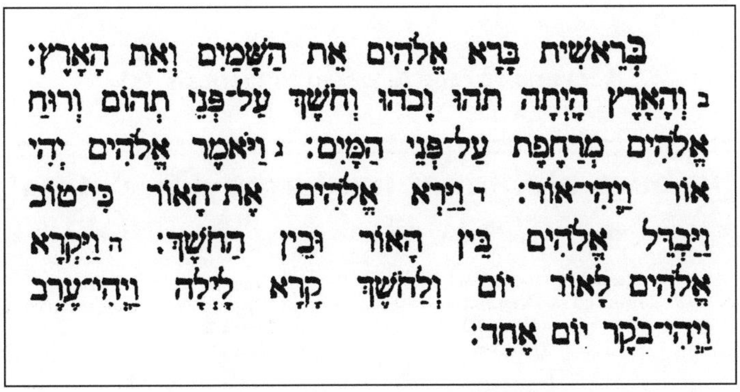

FIG. 4.2 Same verse in modern transcription with vowel signs added

Now compare fig. 4.2, above, to fig. 4.3, below. Notice that still more signs have been added above and below the letters of the same text. Those additional signs are the *te'amim* that indicate to a knowledgeable reader the melody to be used for each word.

בְּרֵאשִׁית בָּרָא אֱלֹהִים אֵת הַשָּׁמַיִם וְאֵת הָאָרֶץ׃
ב וְהָאָרֶץ הָיְתָה תֹהוּ וָבֹהוּ וְחֹשֶׁךְ עַל־פְּנֵי תְהוֹם וְרוּחַ
אֱלֹהִים מְרַחֶפֶת עַל־פְּנֵי הַמָּיִם׃ ג וַיֹּאמֶר אֱלֹהִים יְהִי
אוֹר וַיְהִי־אוֹר׃ ד וַיַּרְא אֱלֹהִים אֶת־הָאוֹר כִּי־טוֹב
וַיַּבְדֵּל אֱלֹהִים בֵּין הָאוֹר וּבֵין הַחֹשֶׁךְ׃ ה וַיִּקְרָא
אֱלֹהִים לָאוֹר יוֹם וְלַחֹשֶׁךְ קָרָא לָיְלָה וַיְהִי־עֶרֶב
וַיְהִי־בֹקֶר יוֹם אֶחָד׃

FIG. 4.3   Same verse with *te-amim* signs added

Constructing the Cantillation of a Biblical Verse

To see how cantillation works in practice let us begin by looking at fig. 4.4, an analysis of the *te'amim* in a transliteration of the opening verse of the Bible. The verse reads:

> B'reishit bara elohim et ha-shamayim v'et ha'aretz.
> (In the beginning God created the heavens and earth.)

In fig. 4.4 the signs for the *te'amim* are circled and enlarged below the transliterated words of the verse. Beneath each sign its name is given, and below that each *ta'am* is categorized as conjunctive or disjunctive, with the disjunctives classified according to their level in the hierarchy. Heavy horizontal bars show the primary division of the verse into two halves, with an *etnachta* at the end of the first distich and a *silluk* marking the end of the verse. Both halves of the verse are again subdivided, as shown by the lighter black bars above the text, and a second-level

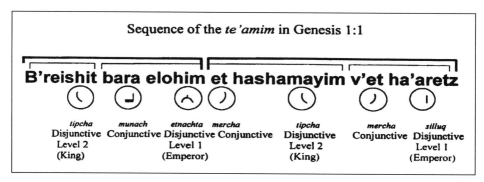

FIG. 4.4   Analysis of *te-amim* in Genesis 1:1-5

disjunctive (*tipcha*, one of the "kings") is used to mark the subdivision for both halves. Each of the disjunctives must be followed by a pause, with the intervening conjunctives smoothly linking the rest of the words together.

An accomplished reader, called a *Ba'al Kri'ah* (master reader), goes through that analytical process in glancing at each verse to be read, and, to apply one melodic tradition (*nusach*), sings the following (fig. 4.5):

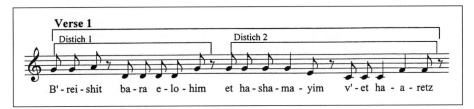

FIG. 4.5   One tradition's cantillation of Genesis 1:1

Most people who know cantillation do not have a sufficient level of skill to go through that process at first sight. They can only perform the public reading after long study and memorization of the specific verses they plan on reading, so that cantillating a portion of the Torah requires intensive preparation. The prophetical readings follow the same procedure, except that those same *te'amim* represent an entirely different set of melodies for those books. Many Jews have some understanding of cantillation, but few gain the appellation *ba'al kri'ah*. Such people are not necessarily cantors by profession. The training is accessible to all, and to have mastered enough of the art of cantillation to be able to take a turn reading a portion of the holy books is an honor open to all, depending solely on skill. In most congregations this honor is given to lay members rather than to the professional cantor. For the cantor to have to read those portions could be construed as a sign that the community is not carrying out its commitment to fully educate young people, who would be denied the opportunity for the honor of reading the Torah correctly in public, or put in the position of reading it in some less time-honored manner.

Traditionally, many adult men in most congregations were capable of some level of cantillation. In the past such training was only given to boys, who were taught the basics of cantillation by the age of thirteen so that they could read the appropriate weekly Torah portion publicly for the first time at their religious coming-of-age ceremony when they become a *bar mitzvah*, which loosely translates as "son of the covenant," meaning a religiously responsible member of the community. Not all, though, had the ability or inclination for additional training that would enable them to become a skilled *ba'al kri'ah*. Today, among Ashkenazic Jews, all but orthodox congregations extend this privilege to women as well, and a girl becomes a *bat mitzvah*, to use the feminine form.

Since the biblical reading had to be done from an acceptable (i.e., *kasher*) scroll, into which no extraneous marks of any kind could be entered, the punctuation, vowels, and *te'amim* were not in front of the reader at the time of public reading. Instead they were provided in ancillary books used for study and preparation of the reading. Those books were normally in codex format (i. e., folded and bound) rather than scrolls. It was into such a codex that the Masoretes entered not only the helpful vowels and cantillation signs but also extensive analytical notes on the text. Those notes were neither interpretative nor prescriptive; they were descriptive. The concern of the Masoretes was with structural or statistical data, such as spelling anomalies, the number of occurrences of this or that word, the fact that this was the second of three appearances of an unusual form or meaning, and such details as noting the middle word of a book or the middle verse of the Torah. Interpretation, it was felt, must be undertaken anew by each generation as the circumstances of Jewish life changed.

The most important of those books was compiled at the opening of the eleventh century by, or under the editorship of, Aaron ben Asher, who has already been mentioned. Maimonides seems to have described that codex as being in Fustat (Cairo) in the twelfth century. It then dropped out of sight until modern times, when what appears to be the same manuscript once again surfaced in Aleppo, Syria. Its English name is taken from that city: the Aleppo Codex. It was revered by the Jewish community of Aleppo as an ancient manuscript with almost mystical powers, and it was carefully guarded in the synagogue—strangers were not allowed to see it. At the founding of the State of Israel in 1948 anti-Jewish riots broke out in the city and the synagogue was set afire. Through the heroic efforts of the rabbi and some of the congregants, the invaluable codex was saved, but much of it was burned beyond recognition. As a result, the Syrian community sent what remained of the codex to Israel, where it can be seen in "The Shrine of the Book," a museum in Jerusalem given over to the study and display of ancient texts.

Over the years, didactic texts without musical notation were compiled for learning the cantillation by rote, but there was no systematic study of the music until the sixteenth century. Text-critical and linguistic studies did exist, though. Not too long after Ben-Asher's seminal work at the turn of the eleventh century came the Arabic-language treatise *Hidayat al-kari* (Advice to a Reader), parts of which are preserved only in later quotations.

It was the Christian Humanists of the sixteenth century, such as Johannes Reuchlin (*De accentibus et ortographia linguae hebraica* [Hagenau, 1518]), Sebastian Muenster (*Institutiones grammaticae in hebraeum linguam* [Basel, 1524]), and Johannes Vallensis (*Opus de prosodia hebraeorum* [Paris, 1545]), who were the first to move beyond rote memorization to notation. Reuchlin went even further, treating the cantillation melodies as a tenor part and commissioning pedestrian (and totally out-of-place) four-part harmonizations for them by his student, Christoph Schilling. In their dissatisfaction with the defective translations of the Vulgate, the humanists turned to Hebrew sources and took to heart Rabbi Abraham Ibn Ezra's pronouncement: "Any interpretation inconsistent with the *te'amim* you must reject." Their use of Western notation to display *te'amim* motives in so-called *Zarka* Tables is invaluable to the modern study of cantillation.

Te'amim as a Resource for Textual Exegesis

An additional aspect of the *te'amim* is the role that the strict logic of their placement plays in textual exegesis. David Freeman and Miles Cohen have demonstrated this in two articles. One uses the *te'amim* to show that the two different enumerations of the Ten Commandments in the Bible resulted from the different demands of "private" versus "public" reading.[12] The second traces the degradation of several texts through various editions of the Bible as a result of editors' inadequate

---

[12] David Freeman and Miles Blicker Cohen, "The Dual Accentuation of the Ten Commandments," *1972 and 1973 Proceedings of the International Organization of Masoretic Studies*, 1 (1974): 7-20.

understanding of the *te'amim*.[13] Cohen's article, "Masoretic Accents as Biblical Commentary"[14] is virtually a textbook for understanding the exegetical possibilities inherent in the *te'amim*.

Still another area in which *te'amim* contribute to understanding the Bible is in their clarification of ambiguous word chains. Anticipating this problem, the Masoretes added two special modifying signs to deal with situations in which the succession of words might possibly suggest a second meaning. A modern analogy might be a sign reading "Hospital Complex Parking," for which the addition of a comma, and its position, would make a difference in meaning. The first of those added signs is the *pasek*, a vertical stroke placed between words, which serves that purpose by inserting a disjunction following a conjunctive *ta'am* where no such break would ordinarily occur. This was a later "corrective" added by one of the last generations of Masoretes, to places where the meaning might have gotten distorted by the normal, unbroken flow of music. An example occurs in Genesis 1:5 preceding the word *la'or* (light), where a *pasek* can be found in the next-to-last line. The Hebrew reads:

> *Vayikra   elohim* | *la'or yom.*
> And God called | the light day.

In that verse a *pasek*, represented by a vertical bar, stands between the words *elohim* (God) and *la'or* (the light),[15] where the pause it inserts precludes any possibility that God might be, or be called, "light." It rules out as well any attempt to read this text to mean that God might have conversed with the light, since the verb *vayikra* is ambiguous in that it can have several different meanings (call, cry out, shout, read).

The other such sign that has sometimes erroneously been dismissed as inconsequential is the *meteg* or *gaya*, a short vertical stroke placed beneath an unaccented syllable. In appearance it is indistinguishable from the *silluk*, discussed above, but it never occurs on the last word of a verse, which is the only place a *silluk* can occur. Placement of the *meteg* was important enough to have become the principal preoccupation of Ben-Asher's last years, and the primary sticking point in an unresolved dispute between Ben-Asher and his colleague, Ben-Naphtali. The *meteg* indicates a momentary slowing of the pace in order to emphasize what would otherwise be an unaccented and perhaps inadvertently slurred or swallowed syllable, as occurs, for example, in a word such as *Ya'akov* (Jacob). The eleventh-century reader's guide, *Hidayat al-kari*, says, "[*Meteg*] is neither a disjunctive nor a conjunctive accent, but indicates that the syllable must be lengthened a bit."[16]

---

[13] Freeman and Cohen, "The Masoretes as Exegetes: Selected Examples," in ibid., 35-46.

[14] See *The Journal of the Ancient Near Eastern Society of Columbia University* (January 1972), 2-11.

[15] Here is another example of a possible ambiguity in translation. The word *la'or* might be carelessly interpreted as "to the light," which would be unidiomatic and mindlessly literal. Such a misreading could produce the nonsense sentence: "God shouted to the light, [saying] 'day.'" However, the prefix *la* does not here signify "to" or "toward," but indicates that the noun "light" is an indirect object. Biblical translation is full of such traps for the unwary.

[16] Yeivin, *Introduction*, 243, 315. An earlier scholar, Yehoash Hacohen, writing in 1890, called attention to the biblical use of the word *meteg* to mean "bit," referencing Psalm 32:9, "Be not like a senseless horse or mule, whose movement must be curbed by bit and bridle" (*meteg v'resen*). The "bit," which forces a running horse to slow down, is indeed a good metaphor for this sign.

The *meteg* has the effect of restoring full syllabic value to a vowel that might otherwise be "swallowed." In doing so, it restores the rhythm of the prosody, maintaining the poetic rhythm in verses that might otherwise be disturbingly "three-legged." The sign might be best considered to be a musical *tenuto* (lengthening) mark over the appropriate note.

Cantillation of the Pentateuch constitutes a living centonization tradition, the vibrant remnant of a practice carried forward from the ancient world for two-and-a-half millennia. It forms a vital aural bridge back to the Middle Ages and beyond, to the sixth century BCE, when the practice was initiated. As such, it is one of the most historically meaningful aspects of Jewish music—totally different in concept from what we think of today when we speak of religious music, but nevertheless a characteristic Jewish musical style that carries with it the weight of history. Perhaps that is why a composer such as Leonard Bernstein turned to the motives of cantillation as a basis for his own music, most notably in the *Jeremiah Symphony*, which is based on motives taken from the cantillation of Jeremiah's Book of Lamentations.

Suggestions for Further Reading

Avenary, Hanoch. *Ashkenazi Tradition of Biblical Chant between 1500 and 1900.* Jerusalem: World Congress on Jewish Music, 1978.

Binder, Abraham Wolf. *Biblical Chant.* New York: Philosophical Library, 1959.

Heskes, Irene. *Passport to Jewish Music: Its History, Traditions, and Culture.* Westport, CT: Greenwood Press, 1994.

Idelsohn, Avraham Zvi. *Jewish Music in its Historical Development.* New York: Schocken Books, 1929; 2nd ed., 1967.

Jacobson, Joshua R. *Chanting the Hebrew Bible: The Art of Cantillation.* Philadelphia: Jewish Publication Society, 2002.

Neusner, Jacob. *Judaism's Theological Voice: The Melody of the Talmud.* Chicago Studies in the History of Judaism. Chicago: University of Chicago Press, 1995.

Werner, Eric. *The Sacred Bridge: Liturgical Parallels in Synagogue and Early Church.* New York: Schocken Books, 1970.

5 | *Jewish Music in the World of Medieval Islam*

The Arabs sing of Love and Lust,
The Christians sing of War and Revenge,
The Greeks of Wisdom and Cunning,
The Hindus of Proverbs and Riddles;
But Israel's song is to the Lord of Hosts.
—Abraham ibn Ezra (1092-1167)

A Powerful and Sophisticated Arab Culture

Across the Mediterranean from medieval Europe a vigorous new culture was flowering. By the seventh century the heterogeneous peoples of the Arab world were swept into the embrace of monotheistic Islam, whose meteoric expansion soon engulfed all of North Africa, Asia Minor, and large parts of southern Europe. Within a generation of Mohammed's death in 632 CE the tightly-knit social structure and honor code of his militant followers, coupled with their effectiveness as warriors and the unifying zeal of their new religion, allowed Arab conquerors to impose a semblance of peace across a vast empire. In less than a century Islam held dominion from the Iberian Peninsula and the straits of Gibraltar to the edges of the Indian subcontinent, threatening Christian Europe with total conquest.

In most of those places medieval Arab civilization was at a higher level than that to which Europe had sunk after the fall of Rome. The desert tribesmen were quick to absorb and adapt the achievements of the more sedentary peoples who came under their sway. In the larger settlements of the Islamic conquest civic administration was practiced, trade flourished, and a rich multiplicity of cultures was subsumed into the Arab empire. Life in Persia was not the same as it was in Turkey, and the Kurds were quite different from residents of Baghdad. Yet for all those distinctions, there was a commonality imposed by the conquerors' thought.

Islamic society incorporated advanced economic tools such as letters of credit and private foundations to dispense grants for artistic or scientific work. Poetry and mathematics, music and medicine, business, law, international trade, and above all else, the religious doctrines of Islam flourished, supporting a sophisticated culture of learning and elegance. Under Islamic law the status of Jews and Christians was one degree higher than that of the pagans who had been conquered, though they still occupied a lower niche of citizenship than their Moslem conquerors. They were protected minorities (*dhimmi*) whom Mohammed himself had once recognized as "People of the Book" (meaning, of course, the Bible). As long as they observed the conditions laid down by the so-called "Pact of Omar"[1] they could live in relative peace. To many, this was a tolerable price to pay for living in the most powerful, sophisticated, and artistic culture of the time.

Practice of Music in the Arab Empire

Since before the lifetime of the prophet Mohammed, Jewish life had been thriving in the Arabian Peninsula. In the early seventh century, just before the rise of Islam, the city of Yathrib, or Medina, as Mohammed would later rename it, was largely populated by Jewish tribes who were famous for producing the finest musicians. Singing-girls and instrumentalists of the *Banu Amalik*, one of those Jewish tribes, were particularly highly regarded, and were sought by other courts as well. According to Bar-Hebraeus the Syrian (d. 1289), Jubal, the son of Cain in the Bible, was credited with the first song, an elegy on the death of Abel. The very word for singing-girl, *qaina*, was attributed to the fact that it was Cain's daughters who invented musical instruments.

When Mohammed's army conquered the city of Yathrib/Medina in 624 CE, the Jewish tribe of Qainuqa was offered the alternatives of conversion or expulsion. Most chose the latter course, refused to change their religion and accepted exile. A contemporary account of their eviction offers a flickering glimpse into the place of music in Jewish culture of the Arabian peninsula during the sixth century. At the expulsion of the Jews from Medina, al-Waqidi wrote:

> Their women were decked out in litters wearing brocades, velvet and
> fine red and green silk. They passed by in a train one after the other,
> borne by 600 camels. . . . They went off beating on tambourines and
> playing on pipes.[2]

---

[1] Caliph Omar ibn Abd al-Aziz (717-20) codified decades of loose practice when he established a code for the treatment of conquered Jews and Christians as "protected minorities" (in Arabic: *dhimmi*). In exchange for protection of their lives and properties, the state exacted special taxes and applied the *sharia*, or Moslem law, in a long series of humiliating conduct codes that enforced permanent underclass status. The *sharia* required *dhimmi* to refrain from dressing as elegantly as their Moslem neighbors, build no religious buildings higher than the local mosque, and dismount to walk in the gutter when their betters passed. *Dhimmi* were also put in charge of such unpleasant necessities as removal of garbage and feces from the towns, and individuals of that class were barred from holding civil office.

[2] Al-Waqidi, *Kitab al-Maghazi*, ed. Marsden Jones (London, 1966), 1:363-75; quoted in Norman A. Stillman, *The Jews of Arab Lands* (Philadelphia: Jewish Publication Society, 1979), 136.

Such a show of bravado must have been calculated to raise the spirits of the exiles as much as to demonstrate devotion to their faith. Interestingly, al-Waqidi's account does not speak of the expelled Jews singing psalms or hymns, but notes the use of secular music on tambourines and pipes to raise their morale. Another observer wrote that they had decided "to go into exile with their heads held high. They departed for the Jewish oasis of Khaybar in an impressive caravan . . . through the heart of Medina to the music of pipes and timbrels."[3] Their bravado was to be short-lived. After his stronghold at Medina had been solidified and the Jewish tribe of Nadhir expelled some two years later, Mohammed then turned on the Jews in fury for not accepting Islam:

> Most tragic was the fate of the [tribe of] Quraiza, who were betrayed by their Arab companions. After a mock trial by the latter's chief, all males of the tribe were condemned to death unless they changed their faith. Remarkably, only three or four weak-kneed men chose apostasy, while all the remaining Jews, estimated at between 600 and 750, after a night spent in study, suffered martyrdom.[4]

Despite the discomfort of religious leaders of all three faiths, poetry and music flourished in the Arab world among the Jews as well as their rulers. Music, especially secular music, had always had an unfavorable association among the pious. According to historian Henry George Farmer, the rise of male professional musicians was a generally undesirable social innovation that first appeared in Arab culture during the reign of the Caliph Uthman (644-56 CE). "These people," he writes, "were an effeminate class who dyed their hands and affected the habits of women."[5]

Nevertheless, the people's love for music prevailed over the opposition of religious leaders. A twelfth-century Jewish traveler, Benjamin of Tudela, admiringly recorded the wonders of the Islamic lands, especially of Baghdad, the seat of the Caliphate, or central government. Baghdad, noted Benjamin, had a Jewish community of 40,000. "The Jews of the city are learned men, and very rich," he wrote. Baghdad's Jews were headed by a powerful community leader called the exilarch, who answered only to the Caliph. Benjamin describes the ceremonies accompanying the appointment of a new exilarch as a festive occasion for the entire population:

> At his installation, the Head of Captivity [i.e., the exilarch] gives much money to the Caliph, to the princes and ministers. On the day that the Caliph performs the ceremony investing him with authority . . . [he] is escorted from the palace of the Caliph to his own house with timbrels and fifes.[6]

---

[3] Stillman, 14.

[4] Salo Baron, *A Social and Religious History of the Jews*, 14 vols., 2nd ed. (Philadelphia: Jewish Publication Society of America, 1957), 3:79.

[5] Henry George Farmer, *A History of Arabian Music to the Thirteenth Century* (London: Luzac and Co., 1967), 44-45.

[6] M. N. Adler, trans., *The Itinerary of Benjamin of Tudela* (London,1907; reprint, Malibu, CA: Pangloss Press, 1983), 101.

Again, one sees timbrels (tambourines, small hand drums) and fifes (flutes?) being associated with secular celebration.

Intellectual life in the Jewish community of Baghdad was maintained by an impressive array of educational institutions, with curricula organized along the lines of the Greek trivium and quadrivium.[7] Here is the course description for a music class taken from a late twelfth century curriculum of advanced studies in a Jewish school for both religious and secular subjects:

> After studying the science of astronomy the teacher will lecture on music to his students. Music embraces instruction in the elements of the melodies and that which is connected with them, how melodies are linked together, and what condition is required to make the influence of music most pervasive and effective.[8]

The Arabic language, with its beautiful script and effusive sentiment, became the vehicle of a rich poetic tradition that was invariably tied to music. Arab tradition tells of many great musicians, both slave and free, who earned lasting names as performers in the earliest days of Islam. Many of the best-known musicians and teachers of the Arab world were women. Azza al-Mayla (d. ca. 705) and Djamila (d. 720) were two who gained renown for their musical skill and beauty. They were treated with all the adulation given to popular music stars today. On the occasion of Djamila's pilgrimage to Mecca she was accompanied by some of the most famous musicians of the time, many of whom were her students, as well as by a retinue of fifty singing-girls. One of her famous students, a male singer by the name of Ma'bad, held her in great reverence as a teacher, writing, "In the art of music Djamila is the tree and we are the branches."[9]

The love of music and the sensual life that flourished in Arab capitals did so in spite of reproaches from religious authorities. One can readily imagine pious mullahs (religious scholars) shuddering, just as their Jewish and Christian cousins did, at the songs of pleasure-loving poets like the Caliph al-Walid II (743-44 CE), who wrote, "There is no true joy but lending ear to music / Or wine that leaves one sunk in stupor dense."[10] In spite of a steady downpour of scorn from intellectuals and religious conservatives, music was enjoyed in many forms by the upper classes, who cultivated their own skills as amateurs, enjoyed the performances of a large class of professional musicians, and often went beyond providing patronage to take musicians as close personal friends. One writer described the social circumstances during the Umayyad Caliphate (661-750) thus:

---

[7] Those terms outlined the educational curriculum of the ancient world (the "Seven Liberal Arts") as handed down to the medievals through the writings of such scholars as Martianus Capella (b. ca. 400) and Flavius Magnus Aurelius Cassiodorus (b. ca. 485). The course of study was divided into the trivium, or language arts: grammar, logic, and rhetoric; and the quadrivium, or mathematical arts: arithmetic, geometry (including what we would today call science), astronomy, and music.

[8] Stillman, 227.

[9] Amnon Shiloah, *Music in the World of Islam, A Socio-Cultural Study* (Detroit: Wayne State University Press, 1995), 12.

[10] Ibid., 18.

> Some of the best known musicians turned their residences into schools
> of music where rich dilettanti came to develop their aptitude and where,
> in particular, talented slave girls who belonged to notables and wealthy
> men were trained in music and other cultural matters. Indeed the houses
> of the rich bourgeoisie competed with one another in attracting the best
> musicians to enhance their gatherings in which the singing-girls who lived
> in the house participated.[11]

Jews who lived in that milieu were not immune to those tastes and seem to have shared most of them. Like their Moslem neighbors they viewed music with mixed feelings, fearing its attractions, yet drawn to song, both sacred and secular, by their own natures. That explains why, during the long period under Arab rule, one finds poet-composers writing for the synagogue side by side with rabbis voicing anxiety over the erotic danger for men in hearing female singers, or disregarding the mandate to mourn the temple's destruction by abjuring instrumental music. As had happened before, the people's natural love of music prevailed.

Musical Instruments in the Arab World

Arab music-lovers enjoyed a wide range of both string and wind instruments as well as percussion of various kinds and sizes. A small number of preferred instruments formed a core of favorites, and those will be singled out here. The most important were the *ud* (lute), *nay* (flute), and *duff* (drum). The *ud* was the chief instrument for both vocal accompaniment and instrumental virtuosity. Its Arabic name produced the western designation for that instrument brought back from the crusades. The preceding Arabic article ('*al*) was conflated with the noun ('*al 'ud*), producing what sounded to European ears like "a lute." The *nay*, or flute, was associated with love songs and dancing, a connection that had also existed in the ancient world. An Arab legend avers that the first flutes were made from reeds growing around the well into which Adam had discarded secrets he learned while still in the Garden of Eden. Melodies of the flute, then, whisper of undefined, secret pleasures. The *duff*, or hand drum, was one of the most popular of many percussion instruments. This was probably the instrument we know as the timbrel from the King James translation of the Bible. It could be played subtly with different strokes of the fingers, the thumb, or parts of the palm to produce complex rhythms in different tone qualities. A skillful drummer was capable of producing a stunning variety of timbres. The term *duff* could be applied to any type of frame drum, and these came in a wide variety of sizes, both with and without jangles. Drums could also be made of a membrane stretched over a clay vase-shaped frame, such as the popular *darbukkah*. Some, held under the arm, had cords holding the drumhead against the frame in such a way that the pressure of the player's arm could tighten or loosen the cords, changing the tension on the head and making it possible to play different pitches. Other percussion instruments included larger drums of various sizes and the *kasat* (cymbals), both large and small. Some cymbals, called *sunuj* or *sajat*, were small enough to be worn on the fingers, and were often played by dancers.

---

[11] Ibid., 19.

Beside the end-blown flutes, wind instruments included double-reed types in various sizes called, variously, *zurna*, *zamr*, or *ghayta*; there was also a single-reed instrument known as the *mujwiz*. A stored-wind bagpipe instrument has a long history in the Arab world too, predating by far the rather late seventeenth or eighteenth-century entry of the bagpipes into Scotland. Single and double-reed instruments were also made with a second pipe, a drone, paralleling the first.

The two most influential string instruments were the *ud*, the sophisticated lute of courtly life often played with admirable virtuosity, and the *rebab* or *rabab*, a one-stringed violin having a square sound box and played with a convex bow. The *rebab* tended to be used in folk music and in less refined settings. Both types were brought back to Europe in the Middle Ages by crusaders who encountered them, and they were the ancestors of the European family of bowed viols and lutes. The harp (*simsimyya*), with a heritage in both shape and function from the harp of the ancient world, was also found, especially in informal environments such as in Bedouin encampments and villages. This hardly exhausts the long list of instruments in use in that music-loving culture, but gives some idea of their variety.

When the sweeping conquests of the seventh and eighth centuries carried their culture across a far-flung Islamic empire, the Arabs, as conquerors often do, adopted attractive local traditions, so that the music of each part of the empire developed its own distinctive sound while sharing the same root tradition. That tradition was monophonic (i.e., without harmony), poetic, and built on melodic modes, each of which was associated with a particular emotional state, season, or even condition of the body. Each mode consisted of a number of different melodic formulas built on a common scale tuning, and was felt to have a powerful and unique emotional impact on the listener.

The medieval Fatimid Caliphs "spent fabulous sums on musicians, singing-girls, dancers, and banquets."[12] Favorite musicians were highly rewarded, and many became close drinking companions of high members of the court—even of the Caliph himself. Ibrahim al-Mawsili (d. 804), who is believed to have written some nine hundred compositions and was credited with introducing a new rhythmic mode into the court's music, was elevated by the Caliph Harun al-Rashid to the role of "boon companion." Music received such support not only for the pleasure it brought to individuals, but even more, as a public display of court splendor. The great medieval Arab historian ibn Khaldun (Abu Zayd Abd-Ar-Rahman ibn Khaldun, 1332-1406) remarks that five hundred trumpeters played in one parade band, and that for a celebration of the New Year in 975 the court employed fifty kettledrums and fifty cylindrical drums. At the climax of that celebration:

> As the Caliph approached the city gate, a golden horn with a curved head emitted marvelous sounds, and other horns replied. Following the Caliph through the gate was a vast ensemble of drums, cymbals, and whistles, "making the world hum."[13]

---

[12] Ibid., 71.

[13] Ibid., 71.

While none of the music of those large Arab bands has been preserved, it was heard with awe by Western travelers of the time, who brought stories of their experiences back home, in some measure stimulating the growth of such music's public function in Europe as well. By the fifteenth and sixteenth centuries European rulers were making use of wind and percussion bands for ceremonial purposes. Such ensembles were called "Turkish music" or Janissary bands, after the marching bands of the Janissary brigades that played so important a role in Turkish military strength. Such bands were marked by large percussion sections featuring drums of two or three different sizes, cymbals, tambourines, and triangles in addition to such wind instruments as shawms and fifes. Early in the eighteenth century Augustus II of Poland boasted a full Turkish military band received as a gift from the Turkish sultan. His rival, Empress Anne of Russia, topped that by importing a still larger band from Constantinople.

Jewish Poet-Composers of Arab Lands

In the atmosphere of their relative acceptance that characterized the earlier period, Jews, like their Arab neighbors, flourished in the art of music. It is not unexpected, then, to find that Jewish poets, singers, and instrumentalists continued to play a visible role in Arab culture. Both Jews and Arabs placed a high value on poetry, so that we find, during the period of Islamic ascendancy, a number of Jewish poet-musicians who composed secular poetry in Arabic while continuing to express their religious thought in Hebrew. The Hebrew word *piyyut* (pl., *piyyutim*) designates a poem with religious content. Those who wrote such poems were called *paytanim* (sing., *paytan*), and their *piyyutim* were a continuation of the long tradition of Hebrew psalm writing. Like the psalms, *piyyutim* were written to be sung rather than simply read. Some of the *paytanim* lived in Christian Europe, but the majority by far flourished under Arab rule. Many *piyyutim* of the Middle Ages were based on Arabic melodies. Some were expressly headed with instructions to be sung to an existing Arab tune, as in certain Judeo-Spanish prayers, while others were sung to newly composed melodies in a similar style.

Though the *paytanim* concentrated much of their efforts on religious songs and poems, we also have examples of love and heroic poetry from those same hands. Most wrote with equal fluency in Hebrew and Arabic; others included Aramaic in their repertoire, too. The poetic meters and styles of their contemporaries infused both secular and religious compositions, which combined the rich imagery of the Arabic language with the wit and clever turns of phrase of their intellectual environment. Passionate love poems might turn out, on reflection, to be religious allegories, while the most mundane matters—the price of a goat, for example—could reveal the hierarchy of the universe, as in the song "Chad gadya." Most *piyyutim* had an overtly religious cast, but some of the most popular of them seem, at first glance, to have only a tenuous connection to the religious occasion with which they are associated. One must keep in mind the kind of society in which such poems were created to experience the full dimension of their meaning.

The most important works created by the *paytanim* were intended for liturgical or para-liturgical settings. Those included two important forms of *piyyut* called *s'lichot* (penitential prayers) and *z'mirot* (songs), both of which are based in Jewish tradition and found in Ashkenazic, as well as Sephardic, practice. *S'lichot* go back to unknown *paytanim* of the sixth century. Some of these poems are used as part of the liturgy today, although they are now sung to much later melodies.

Z'mirot are sung at the table following the Sabbath meals, or for that matter, any time a festive meal is spread in connection with some religious occasion, such as at *Pesach* (Passover) or a wedding dinner. The Jewish family or community get-together provides the setting for the singing of these paraliturgical songs. This is especially true when more than three men are present at a meal, which requires an expansion of the required blessing after eating, the "Benediction After Meals," into an extended form, usually chanted and sung. On such occasions, in many Jewish communities, the event is extended still longer by singing joyous *z'mirot* afterwards.

New texts for Passover *z'mirot* were created in the Middle Ages and more are constantly being added even today, for Passover centers on home celebration, and its commemoration can be quite open-ended. The Haggadah[14] contains many *piyyutim*, making it a veritable treasury of their widely varied forms. "Ki lo na'eh" (For it is due to God) for example, is constructed so that every verse consists of three declarative statements, each of which begins with the next consecutive alphabet letter, followed by a responsive refrain between verses. A similar, but slightly more complex, scheme marks the *piyyut*, "Adir hu" (Mighty is God). The Seder closes with two marvelous examples of "additive" *z'mirot* that seem, at first, to be extraneous to the holiday: "Echad mi yode'a" (Who knows one), and "Chad gadya" (One kid). Their inclusion is partly in the spirit of fun and partly didactic, for they come at the end of a long evening, with children at the table who are inevitably tired and restless; but these rousing songs can be counted on to reawaken the slumbering attention of the little ones. "Echad mi yode'a" outlines some of the important images of Jewish tradition in a merry numbers game. "Chad gadya," a tongue-twisting allegory, teaches the subservience of all beings to God, the final judge.

Other lyrics for Chanukah, Purim, circumcision and wedding feasts, etc., were created by *paytanim* over the centuries. Many of them are still in use today. But in no time or place since the ancient world were there the number of fine poets writing outstanding religious songs as were found in the medieval Arab world. The Jewish liturgy has always been open to infusions of new musical styles, and there are many parallels between the situation today and that of medieval Spain and the Levant; but we have yet to see a modern poetic flowering of the excellence that those times provided.

Important *Paytanim*

Important musician-poets of the period included leading religious figures such as Rabbi Yehuda Ga'on, the eighth-century head of the Talmudic academy at Sura in Babylonia. He may have introduced the "Kol Nidre" text into the synagogue, although only a few archaic elements of the original music still remain in the Ashkenazic version. Many of the Sephardim, however, still sing an old, possibly medieval, tune for that prayer. Other important *paytanim* of the period include Shmuel ibn Nagrela, also known as "The *Nagid* of Grenada" (fl. 1020-1055), Joseph the Scribe (fl. ca. 1042), and Shlomo ibn Gabirol (ca. 1020-1058), who wrote one of the best-known hymns, "Adon Olam" (Lord of the World). Ibn Gabirol wrote both secular and religious poetry. His secular poems deal imaginatively with nature and love, while his religious poems convey a burning

---

[14] Hagaddah, which means "retelling," is the name of the book used in the home service (Seder) for the holiday of Pesach, which commemorates the exodus from slavery in Egypt.

intensity. The confession of sin that concludes his "Keter malchut" (The Kingly Crown) was integrated into the liturgy of Yom Kippur. He also wrote widely used books on philosophy and ethics.

Moses ibn Ezra (ca. 1070-1138 or 39) and his brother Abraham (ca. 1092-1167) were Spanish writers (in Arabic) of speculative philosophy as well as religious poetry. Moses wrote about one hundred twenty *piyyutim*, many of which have been absorbed into the Sephardic ritual. Abraham traveled widely for most of his life, living in North Africa, England, France, and Italy. He was best known for his biblical commentaries, but also wrote on mathematics, astronomy, medicine, philosophy, and astrology. His poetry, written in Hebrew, is primarily secular. He seems to have been the inspiration, some seven hundred years later, for Robert Browning's poem "Rabbi ben Ezra." Yehuda ben Shmuel ha-Levi (ca. 1075-ca. 1141), was a physician and philosopher who is acclaimed today as the greatest Jewish poet of the Middle Ages. Born in Tudela, he settled in Toledo, where he worked as a physician. There he wrote his *Divan* (Poetic Anthology), Hebrew poems on friendship, love, and nature, as well as religious poems that were adopted in the Jewish liturgy. He eventually left Spain and undertook the long and arduous journey that would enable him to live in Jerusalem. He is known to have reached Alexandria and Cairo; but legend says that he was trampled to death by an Arab horseman just outside the gates of Jerusalem. Another *paytan* of that same time was Meshullam ben Kalonymos (ca. 1100), who wrote the hymns "Ata hu eloheinu" and "Ein kamocha," still sung in the synagogue today.

Daniel ben Yuda (thirteenth century) was the composer of the hymn "Yigdal elohim chai" (Praise the Living God). Abraham bar Yitzchak Abalufia (fourteenth century), who also wrote a treatise on music theory, was the patriarch of an entire family of musicians. Still another outstanding *paytan* was Shlomo ha-Levi Alkabetz (ca. 1505-before 1584), who wrote the beautiful hymn "L'cha dodi" (To You, My Beloved) that incorporates the letters spelling his own name as an acrostic in the poem. Born in Turkey, he immigrated to Palestine, where he settled in Safed (Zfat). To this day, in synagogues all over the world, "L'cha dodi" is sung near the beginning of the Sabbath evening service on Friday evenings. In its text the poet visualizes the Sabbath approaching with the radiant beauty of a bride approaching her bridegroom.

Sixteenth-century Safed was a hotbed of Jewish mysticism (kabbala) and home to many religious poets besides Alkabetz. The kabbalist Isaac Luria (1534-72), known as the "Ari" (The Holy Lion), was one of them. He wrote mystical songs in Aramaic that are still popular among the Chassidim. Israel Najara (ca. 1555-1628), another *paytan* of Safed, published *Z'mirot Yisrael* (Songs of Israel) in 1587, which was the first songbook ever published in the Orient. The songs in his collection were grouped according to their melodies, a practice taken over from the Arabic *Divan*, or poetic anthology. Some of the melodies were his own, others were borrowed from Turkish, Spanish, Arabic, and Greek sources. His religious poetry was condemned by more conservative rabbis because of its impassioned, almost erotic, imagery. "Israel Najara," wrote Idelsohn, "was the last poet, *hazan*, and composer in the direct succession of *paytanim* who created their religious-lyrical songs in Hebrew for use in the houses of worship and introduced beauty, poetry, and lively rhythm into a service that had become stilted and was lacking in creative force."[15]

That rich tradition of religious songwriting was revived in modern times, attracting great interest and a number of talented composers in the United States and Israel. A variety of

---

[15] Idelsohn, *Hebräisch-Orientalischer* Melodienschatz, vol. 4.

institutions have grown up encouraging its practice, ranging from the Society for Jewish Music in the United States to the more pop-oriented Chassidic Song Festival in Israel, and a significant number of today's young composer-poets have been attracted to the composition of this music, often using the style of folk or popular music. It remains to be seen, though, whether these new *paytanim* can produce works of either the quality or quantity of their medieval forebears.

Jewish Contributions to Arab Musical Thought

The world of medieval Islam was fascinated by the life of the mind, and like many other topics of philosophical interest, music was the subject of much theoretical thought. As one might expect from their generally rationalist position, Jewish musicians were active in the development of speculative music theory in the medieval Arab world. Yitzchak ibn Sulaimann (Isaac Israeli, ca. 842-932), the first prominent Jewish philosopher of the Middle Ages, regarded music as the most rewarding of the major disciplines to be studied. Saadia ibn Yosef (ca. 892-942) is better-known as Saadia Ga'on; that is, he was the *ga'on*, or principal, of the Academy in Sura (Iraq). Between 930 and 938 he composed (in Arabic) his influential *Kitab al-amanat wa'l-itiqadat* (Book of Beliefs and Doctrines), later translated into Hebrew by Judah ibn Tibbon (d. 1190) as the *Sefer emunot v'de'ot*. In the introduction to that book he divided music into "natural" and "artificial" types, after the manner of the Islamic philosopher Al-Kindi. He believed that just as single colors or aromas cannot produce a beneficial effect on the soul, in music only a "mixture of colors," that is, a succession of rhythms and tones—a melody, could exert a beneficial influence on the soul and character. Henry George Farmer, who wrote extensively on Arab music in the first half of the twentieth century, concluded that Saadya might have been referring to different rhythmic modes, a concept that did not become current in Europe until almost four centuries later. It may be that only after Europeans were exposed to Arab art music during the crusades did they develop a rhythmic theory. This hypothesis is given weight by the fact that the earliest rhythmic notation is not found in Europe until after the middle of the twelfth century, by which time writing on rhythmic theory was well advanced in the Arab world. On the other hand, it should be noted that no conclusive evidence has yet been found to support that line of thought.

Another Jewish writer, Shemtov ben Joseph (ibn Falaquera, ca. 1225-ca. 1295) speculated at great length on music and its relationship to society, intellectual life, and individual health in his influential book, *Reshit Chochma* (The Beginning of Wisdom). His observations often strike the modern reader as quite up-to-date, dealing with such topics as the sociology of music and its relationship to intellectual life and mental health. His work shows a close acquaintance with music and musicians, rather than purely theoretical conjecture. He wrote:

> The science of music falls into two divisions, that of theory and that of practice. Musical practice consists of producing audible tones by means of instruments, both natural [the throat, mouth] and artificial [harps, psalteries and the like]. The experts at musical practice devise such melodies and harmonies as are customarily extracted from musical instruments *because they are latent in those instruments.* [emphasis added]

Here Falaquera raised the idea of musical styles appropriate to particular instruments, which indicated a sensitivity to the nature of instrumental sonority that would not be formally recognized in European music until the late sixteenth and seventeenth centuries. Even his more speculative passages rang with common sense and practicality. "Musical theory," he wrote, "admits, in turn, of five large subdivisions":

1. principles of investigation, which we might equate to some extent with the modern term "musicology";

2. arithmetical elements, or "music theory" in today's language;

3. rules of instrumental composition, or compositional methods for abstract music un-structured by a pre-existing text;

4. rhythm, dealing with the practice and notation of the time element in music; and

5. composition of metrical melodies, or the practical application of all the preceding.

His writing not only showed an intimate knowledge of classical authors on music such as Boethius and St. Augustine, but also drew on the most important music theorists of the Arab world. All this gave his writing a richer texture and more practical musical approach than could be found in most of his Western contemporaries.

Another Spanish-Jewish thinker, Moses ben Isaac, known as Bottarel, defined music in his *Commentary* of about 1409[16] on the *Sefer Yetzirah* (Book of Tendencies), as "the science of melody, the motion of ascending and descending tones as well as the study of intervals." Contrast the clarity of this with the narrow definition of even so practical a European writer as Odo, Abbot of Cluny, who defined music in his tenth-century *Enchiridion musices* as "the science of singing truly and the easy road to perfection in singing." As a further illustration of the common-sense approach taken by Jewish theorists, Isaiah ben Isaac wrote a commentary on the music treatise, *Al-Kanun*, by the Arab philosopher ibn Sina (known in Europe by the Latinized name Avicenna), in which he noted that:

> The task of music is the composition of *lahanim* (melodies). The elements of which melodies consist are divisible into two groups: 1. The individual tones (*ne'imot*), and 2. structure or shape (*chibur*). The first one is [the] matter (*chomer*) [out of which melodies are constructed] and the second is the form of the completed melodies.

Such pragmatism in the Arab-Jewish writers on music bespeaks a close and practical acquaintance with the real world of music-making, as opposed to theoretical speculation alone.

---

[16] Bottarel's *Commentary* was composed about 1409, but not published until 1562. He was that strange combination of brilliance and fraud that is found more than once in Jewish history: both a prolific scholar and a charismatic messianic pretender.

When Jewish theorists of the Arab world did deal with more abstruse aspects of music, such as its ultimate purpose, they expressed psychological insights that may have predated European thinking by several hundred years. The great composer-poet Yehuda Halevy, in his book, *Khuzari*, expressed the opinion that "[Already by David's time] music was a perfect art. It wielded that influence upon the soul which we attribute to it, namely, that of moving the soul from one mood to another." Such a statement might easily have been made by any late seventeenth- or eighteenth-century European musician trained in the Baroque concept of the passions of the soul. But to find it in a twelfth-century writer is exceptional, suggesting that in that period there was an Arab tradition of speculation about music far richer than that available to Christian contemporaries.

In another place Halevy affirms the importance of mathematics as the structural basis of music, writing, "Measures, weights, the proportions of various movements, the harmony of music, everything is in number." Numbers truly played a large part in the medieval understanding of music, both in understanding the harmonic proportions that produced the tones themselves, and, even more influentially, in the elegant metrics of Arab poetry. In the eleventh century Iberian Jewish lyric poetry was often based on Arabic metric schemes, and probably because Arabic melodies were used to such an extent, Hai (Chiya) ben Sherira ha-Gaon, Isaac Al-Fasi, and Yehuda of Barcelona all felt it necessary to express opposition to the excessive use of Arabic poems and melodies in the synagogue.

Maimonides (Moses ben Maimon), writing at the end of the twelfth century, permitted the use of Arabic poetry in the service provided it did not interrupt prayers and benedictions; but he did not approve of popular and instrumental music. He quoted the twelfth-century Arab writer, Al-Ghazali, that there can only be opposition to music if one listens to it "for its own sake and not for recreation."[17] Yehudah Hadassi (d. 1271), on the other hand, felt that worshippers paid better attention when a chazzan with a fine voice intoned a beautiful melody, and that his song could "purify and ennoble" their minds. In *The Book of the Pious* he wrote:

> If you cannot concentrate in prayer, search for melodies, and if you pray,
> choose a tune you like. Then your heart will feel what your tongue speaks;
> for it is the song that makes your heart respond.

He obviously felt strongly about the cultural identification lodged in music, because he specifically forbade Jews to teach Hebrew prayer melodies to Christians, or to learn melodies from Christians, and specifically prohibited using religious songs for secular purposes—even for lulling a baby to sleep. Other Jewish figures of the Jewish Middle Ages who wrote on music included Abraham bar-Chiyah (d. ca. 1136), Yehuda ben Shmuel ibn 'Abbas (thirteenth century), Shem Tov ben Palakera (thirteenth century), the fourteenth-century Italian-Jewish poet, Immanuel ben Shlomo, and his contemporary, the cabalist Abraham ben Yitzchak of Granada.

---

[17] Quoted in Peter Gradenwitz, *The Music of Israel from the Biblical Era to Modern Times* (Portland, OR: Amadeus Press, 1996), 106.

This active state of musical speculation in the Islamic world provided a receptive critical context for Jewish writers on music. The great scholar Al-Farabi (ca. 873-950) was the most famous and influential of the Arab music theorists, and many later writers—Jewish, Moslem, and Christian—referred to his authority with great respect. His *Al-Kanun* was translated into Latin, and many of the concepts embedded there found their way into western music. Most of the Jewish writers on music theory mentioned here were familiar with his work to some extent, and they frequently cited his authority for one or another point. His influence on European music, rediscovered by Henry George Farmer, has not yet been fully evaluated, but it is much greater than many western historians realize. Other Arab philosophers of that time who wrote on music include some of the most distinguished thinkers of the culture, such as Honein Al-Harizi, who, in his *Maxims of the Philosophers*, made the observation that "music . . . stirs up that which is at rest and brings to rest that which is in motion." He posited three kinds of arts: those in which speech preponderates over action [such as telling stories], those in which there is more action than speech [such as the art of the physician], and those in which speech and action are balanced [such as music]. Music, he therefore concluded, was the best art.

One aspect of music that underwent development during the Middle Ages was the theory of rhythm, especially the notation of rhythm. Although we have reason to believe that complex and interesting rhythms may have been used in European music before the thirteenth century, we have no way of knowing for sure, because Western music lacked any notation for rhythm until the end of the twelfth century. A type of music notation was known to the ancient Greeks and Persians, but that knowledge seems to have been lost in the period of destruction and trauma that accompanied the end of the ancient world and the beginning of the Middle Ages. Medieval Jewish and Arab theorists spoke of eight basic rhythmic modes, any of which could be further developed by skilled improvisation. The basic rhythmic modes of Arab music theory are given in fig. 5.1.

Each of those eight rhythmic modes goes back to four principal patterns, which appear in two versions, a slow one (*taqil*) and a fast (*kamil*). Thus there seems to have been recognition of variable tempo as well, an idea that only worked its way into European music during the Renaissance. In Europe, pitch notation seems to have further developed around the late ninth and tenth centuries, but at that time western composers could not represent rhythm. That development did not occur until almost three hundred years later, when the Parisian master Leoninus started using six rhythmic modes patterned after poetic meters. While the music of the Arab empire was primarily monophonic, there was also some evidence for the occasional use of more than one simultaneously sounding pitch. However, those "chords" are likely to have consisted of sporadic drones, an occasional emphatic strum across the strings of the *ud*, or possibly passages of free-flowing melismas over sustained tones in a lower voice.

Music as Therapy

Given the focus of both Hebrew and Arabic medieval sources on the ability of music to elevate the spirits of the depressed and calm the agitated, it is not surprising that musicians were called upon to relieve the physical pain of the sick in the hospital, as well as illnesses of the spirit. Fanciful as this may sound at first, one must realize that music therapy is in wide

FIG. 5.1   The eight rhythmic modes of Medieval Arab music

use today for all kinds of medically-related purposes, from use in dentists' offices to the treatment of autistic children, aid with speech training for aphasic patients, and assistance with the
relaxation of hypertension. H.G. Farmer describes an ancient Hebrew manuscript that has a
drawing of a lutenist sitting in a physician's anteroom, waiting to be called on to "cleanse the
mind of the possessed"—or, to restate that in more modern terms, to calm an overly stimulated
patient. Is that so different from piping recorded music into waiting rooms today? A long
tradition of music therapy can be traced back to the young David in the Bible, who, according
to I Samuel (16:23), played his harp to soothe Saul much as a modern therapist might:

> And it came to pass, when the evil spirit from God [madness? depression?]
> was upon Saul, that David took a lyre, and played with his hand; so Saul
> was refreshed, and was well, and the evil spirit departed from him.

Here it is only possible to give a brief, though fascinating, summary of the philosophical
medical-musical therapy system accepted by both medieval Jews and Arabs. It was widely
believed, for example, that the 'ud (lute) possessed curative powers, an idea that finds an echo
in modern therapy's reliance on the sound of the acoustic guitar to induce relaxation. In the
Aristotelian environment of Arab science that idea led to speculation about the causes of those

well-observed effects. One theory attributed the psychological power of the instrument to differences in the range, pitch, or tone color, and surmised that there might be a relationship between those things and the workings of the body. Today many mental hospitals and nursing homes employ specially trained music therapists for precisely the same reasons that Arab physicians found were effective a thousand years ago.

One version of that theory is summarized in fig. 5.2, below. The first column indicates which string of the ʻ*ud* should be played for treatment of a specific condition; the second column indicates which of the four universal elements comprising our bodies each string represents; the third column shows which of the four body "humors," or fluids, it can treat; and the last column equates each string with one of the four seasons of the year. Presumably, one played on the appropriate string at certain times of the year for injuries caused by one of the four elements to one of the four humors of the body. Perhaps medieval Arab physicians prescribed melodies, then, the way we might prescribe drugs.

Ud String	Element	Humor	Quality	Season
Zir (1ˢᵗ or treble)	Fire	Yellow Bile	Hot	Summer
Mathna (2ⁿᵈ)	Air	Blood	Humid	Spring
Mathlath (3ʳᵈ)	Water	Phlegm	Cold	Winter
Bam (4ᵗʰ or bass)	Earth	Black Bile	Dry	Autumn

FIG. 5.2   Influence of strings of the *ud* on aspects of bodily health

The most learned of the medieval Jewish physicians in the Arab world was the great Maimonides (Moses ben Maimon), who made careful distinctions among the different social functions of music. While subscribing to the ban on vocal and instrumental music in the synagogue, this careful scholar admitted music to festive occasions of a religious nature or spiritual song, since its ultimate goal was not simply entertainment, but a desire "to approach the creator and to strive . . . to know God." In his role as a physician, Maimonides also endorsed the therapeutic value of music "for the preservation of body health and for the cure of psychiatric illness such as melancholy."

> He recognizes the relationship of the soma to the psyche and asserts that mental and physical health are dependent on each other. Both are necessary to attain wisdom and to strive for the acquisition of the knowledge of God. . . . He thus foresaw . . . that music therapy is useful for the treatment, rehabilitation, and education or training for people suffering from physical, mental or emotional disorders.[18]

---

[18] This and the preceding two brief quotes are all taken from Harry Rosner, "Moses Maimonides on Music Therapy in His *Responsum* on Music," *Journal of Jewish Music & Liturgy* 16 (1993-94): 12-13.

Sound of the Music

Despite the mass of evidence showing Jewish musical activity in medieval Arab lands, none of it was preserved in a form that we can make use of today, and although theorists wrote voluminously about it, we are not certain what it actually sounded like. This was partly because there was not yet a good system of music notation available. But that was only a small part of the problem, for a form of notation had existed in the Arab world since the early Middle Ages, although it did not come to Europe until much later. A bigger problem was that music was considered by its practitioners to be a secret science, and little was entrusted to notation. Students studied and practiced for their masters "by ear." If a student did not have the skill to grasp melodies quickly, reproduce them accurately, and improvise his own musical elaborations, then he just was not cut out to be a musician. While this method seems to have produced exciting performances, from what we read in sources of that time, it left little in the way of notation for later generations to reconstruct. While we often know the names of tunes that the *paytanim* used for their songs, we have no record of the music. Songs handed down over the centuries probably changed melodies any number of times, and existing melodies and rhythms were gradually altered over time to suit the tastes of new generations. As *piyyutim* moved from one congregation to another, or to another location altogether, local tunes were substituted, or more modern ones supplanted the originals. At this point, we are no longer certain whether or not we have any traces of the original melodies left. What we can say is that a wide range of Jewish composer-poets were active in the medieval Islamic world, and that their work was widely adopted, attesting to its popularity.

While scholarship has as yet unearthed little that represents the actual sound of the medieval Arab tradition, medieval practices have survived among a number of relatively isolated Jewish communities that may at least support speculation about the nature of that music. If nothing else, it fires the imagination to try to visualize the sound of the Middle Ages on the basis of what we can hear today. It is true that to speculate about the sound of medieval Jewish song in the Islamic world we cannot rely on recordings of the Bukharan Jews, the Kurds, or isolated communities from the Moroccan highlands. And it would be a mistake to think that what we hear today represents the sound of the Middle Ages, for musical styles have changed over the centuries in the Arab world, just as styles have changed in the West.

We can hypothesize, though, that in such remote societies the rate of change was probably less precipitous than in recent Western history. There is a possibility that music in these communities may have traveled less far from its roots than would have occurred over the same period in western Europe or in the metropolitan centers of the East. Our best hope for imagining the sound of this music would be to study the music of a conservative Jewish community isolated in some out-of-the way place and segregated from the international electronic culture of the twentieth century so that there would be minimal disruption of its traditions. In a sense, and with some limitations, such a community does exist. Its members have moved to Israel, where their music has attracted the attention of scholars and the fascination of the rest of the world.

Music of the Jews of Yemen

Yemenite Jews brought a rich culture of music and dance with them to modern Israel. It was not only attractive in its own right, but played an influential part in shaping the music of their new country. Isolated for centuries by fiat of their Arab rulers, the Jews of Yemen were subject to the discriminatory rules of the Pact of Omar before their migration to Israel. Partly due to their long-standing persecution and partly because of their faithful maintenance of the ban on instrumental music, they were forbidden to own or play musical instruments. Instead, they developed a tradition of song and dance accompanied by intricate rhythms improvised on percussion instruments consisting of trays, silverware, tin cans, and gasoline containers, as well as hand-claps. "Of all the Jewish communities of the Orient," wrote Idelsohn, "that of Yemen accomplished most in the creation of folk-poetry."[19] In the sixteenth and seventeenth centuries, almost without antecedent, this oppressed community burst forth with a number of remarkable poetic talents.

The greatest of them was unquestionably Rabbi Shalom ben Joseph Shabazi (1618-70), compiler of the collection of religious lyric poetry known as the *Yemenite Divan*. Influenced by kabbalist poet Israel Najara of Safed, Shalom Shabazi wrote *piyyutim* suffused with sentiments of love of God, Zion, and of his fellow man. His poems, some of which were adopted into the Yemenite liturgy, were sung continuously by Yemenite Jews in melodies handed down by a rigorous oral tradition. That method may have preserved even more of the music than might have been the case had the poems been written down and lost, to be rediscovered in torn, deteriorated manuscripts. His vibrant songs stayed alive for generations, and found renewed popularity not long ago at the hands of such pop stars as Ofra Haza. "Even if there is no mercy left in the world," he wrote, "the doors of heaven will never be closed." That song ("Im ninalu"), among others, was recorded in the mid-1980s with electronically engineered sound and a throbbing percussion accompaniment. The recording sold in the millions, not just to Jews, but to European and American Christians whose only knowledge of it was that they were captivated by the music. It was such a hit that the singer was presented with two gold and two platinum awards by the recording industry.

Many Yemenite songs are cast in the form of love poems in which a young man sings of passionate yearning for his bride-to-be. Their secular character, though, masks a deeper allegorical meaning in which the groom represents the People of Israel and the bride, the Land of Israel. Other songs are allegorical wedding narratives, meant to be understood on two levels. On the personal level they often tell a tale of love in which there is an argument, parting, and reconciliation, which was to be understood on a more profound plane as an account of the people of Israel's love for the Land of Israel, her exile, and the hoped-for return.

Perhaps the most characteristic circumstances under which those songs were performed was at a *muwwasha*, which is not so much a compositional form as a community event that blends sacred and secular. The *muwwasha* has three parts. It opens with the *nashid*, a *piyyut* usually sung by one of the elders of the community in a free rhythm. The *nashid* often represents

---

[19] Idelssohn, *Jewish Music*, 364.

a bride's musing on how she wishes her suitor to present himself, and is set forth in two-line stanzas. It serves as a kind of prelude to the next section: the *shira*.[20] The *shira* is the groom's statement of love, and is a lyric poem of great beauty and intensity. During the *shira* many of those present, especially the younger men, dance to the singing, which becomes faster as it goes along. It is accompanied by increasingly complex rhythms beat out by the assembled company on spoons, dishes, trays, and whatever containers might be at hand. As dancers begin to tire, the celebration enters its third phase: *hallel*, which are songs of praise, beginning with the declaration, "Praise the Lord." Here the music grows slower and more lyrical, becoming less frenetically rhythmic as the event moves to its end. Other song types interpolated into those playlets include the *tzafat* (wedding procession) and *chidduyot*, which are joyous songs following the nuptials.

The greatest attention was lavished on the groom's love song, the *shirah*, whose poetry was more often than not cast in one of the most important poetic forms, the so-called girdle form. In its most common appearance, girdle-form poetry took the configuration of four long lines followed by three shorter lines in a different rhythm, ending with a couplet of longer lines that matched the rhythm of the opening, as you can see diagrammed in fig. 5.3.

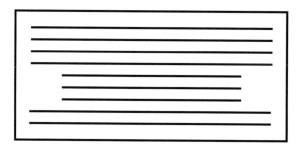

FIG. 5.3   Girdle form: schematic representation

That structure maintained a long popularity in Middle Eastern poetry. Its name comes from its appearance on the written page, where it appears to have a cinch, or "girdle," around the middle, as you can see in the schematic diagram.

The *muwwasha* was essentially an all-male occasion. Women's songs, on the other hand, centered on the celebration of life cycle events: love, marriage, birth, child care, death. A rich repertory of these songs filled the days of Yemenite women, but the most elaborate of them centered on the wedding ceremony. Both the *henna* ceremony and the formal dressing of the bride were accompanied by a whole litany of women's songs bearing marriage advice and singing of love. The wedding itself was—and remains today—a high point of communal celebration, including joyous singing and dancing. Yemenite Jews still sing those songs today, providing a glimpse into the vigorous rhythms and lyrical melodies of the world from which they came, a world in which, in a sense, the Middle Ages has lasted until the present.

---

[20] It should be noted that the term *shirah* was also used for an entirely different class of songs: those for the Sabbath.

Music of a Medieval Egyptian Jewish Community

It became possible to get closer to the actual sound of medieval Arab music at the end of the nineteenth century, when an exciting discovery was made by the scholar Solomon Schechter in a Cairo *genizah*.[21] There, manuscripts were found containing documents of Jewish life in medieval Egypt. Included among the treasure trove discovered there were hymns transcribed in the twelfth century by a Sicilian monk of Norman descent named John or Giovanni, who converted to Judaism in 1102, taking the Jewish name Obadiah. While still a Christian monk in Italy he had been trained to read and write the rudimentary musical pitch notation of his day, a skill that he would exercise later in his life in a very different community. After his conversion he traveled widely in the Middle East, at one point obtaining support from the Jewish community of Baghdad while learning to read and write Hebrew "studying the Pentateuch and the Prophets 'with the orphan boys.'"[22] He eventually settled in Egypt, sometime after the year 1121. There he notated the music of his new Jewish community, most notably that of the hymn "Who stood on Mt. Horeb" ("Mi al har horeb") (fig. 5.4) by Amr ibn Sahal, a *paytan* of Fustat (near Cairo). This was the community that would be headed by the great Maimonides only a generation or so later. The hymn was transcribed into modern notation in 1969 by Israeli musicologist Israel Adler, and arranged for performance by the composer André Hajdu.[23] It is the oldest Jewish music for which we have notation. Several different recordings of the music are available. Because the notation of Obadiah's time was not detailed, modern transcriptions are ambiguous and should be viewed as an outline rather than as precise directions for performance. Recordings, therefore, vary widely, depending on the performer's interpretation. Still, it is thrilling to be able to hear those melodies, now over eight hundred years old, which constitute the earliest synagogue music whose sound we can know with any certainty.

Iberian Song: The Western Sephardim

Under Arab rule for almost eight centuries (711-1492 CE), the Iberian Peninsula was a meeting place for the best of the Jewish, Christian, and Islamic worlds, a culture in which Jews felt relatively free to participate in the arts and sciences. For at least three of those centuries (ca. 900-1200 CE) the Iberian Peninsula was the most sophisticated kingdom of the Western world, vying with Attic Greece as one of the most attractive societies of all history. This was, indeed, a "Golden Age." Spain housed some of Europe's first universities and was receptive to poets of all three faiths. Elbogen wrote with admiration, "In Spain sacred poetry attained its fullest flowering and its most perfect expression; never again did there appear so many religious poems that

---

[21] A *genizah* is a repository for old books and manuscripts, especially those that contain the name of God, which Jews considered too sacred to be simply thrown out once they had reached an unusable state.

[22] Israel Adler, "The Notated Synagogue Chants of the 12th Century of Obadiah, the Norman Proselyte," in *Contributions to a Historical Study of Jewish Music*, ed. Eric Werner (New York: Ktav Publishing House, 1976), 170.

[23] Israel Adler, *Trois chants synagogaux du XIIe siécle (Three Synagogue Chants of the Twelfth Century)*, notation and arrangements by Andre Hajdu (Tel Aviv: Israeli Music Publications, 1969).

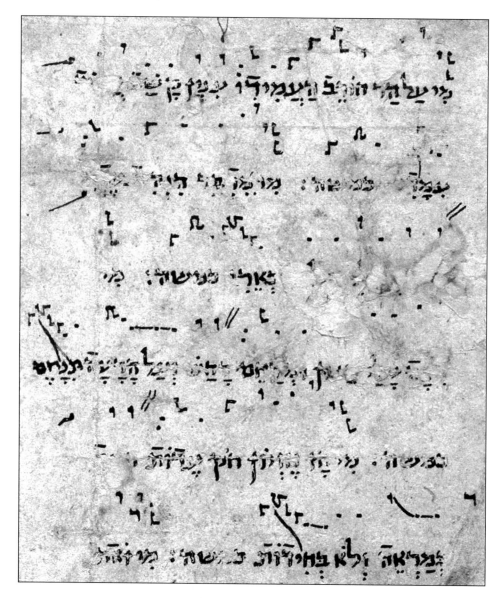

FIG. 5.4   Hymn "Mi al har horeb" from 12th century Egypt.
Hebrew text with music notation, probably in the hand of Obadiah the Proselyte

Courtesy of the Library of The Jewish Theological Seminary

were so perfect in form and content."[24] The situation began to deteriorate with the rise of the Almohade dynasty in the twelfth century, and declined still further as the Christian reconquest of the land progressed at the end of the fourteenth century. In the fifteenth century, persecution of the Jewish minority became a policy of the government and the church. The establishment of the Inquisition in Spain, then Portugal, marked one of the darker periods in Jewish history.

The importance of Spain to Jewish music reached beyond the country's borders. As an Arab state, Spain was a dynamic conduit of Jewish and Islamic musical, literary, and scientific thought to Christian Europe. After the expulsion of the Jews in 1492 it remained a focal point for reminiscences of the Sephardim, the musically productive Ladino-speaking culture that spread to the Netherlands, southeastern Europe, North Africa, new settlements in the Western Hemisphere, and the Levant. The list of Jewish poet-musicians in the golden age of Islamic rule in Spain was long and distinguished. Around 800, for example, a Jew with the Arabic name Al-Mansur was court musician at the Spanish court of Sultan Al-Chakam I (796-822), where Jewish performers had long been a part of court life. Even in Christian enclaves there was more openness to religious plurality than could be found in northern Europe. An example of that can be seen in two beautifully illustrated manuscripts: *Las Cantigas de Santa Maria* (Songs for St. Mary), attributed to Alfonso X ("The Wise"),[25] and the *Cancionero de Ajuda* (Ajuda Songbook) from the court of Alfonso III, King of Portugal from 1248-79. Colorful marginal decorations in both of those show Moslems and Jews making music and working alongside their Christian counterparts. Alfonso, though a Christian king, was highly regarded by his Jewish subjects until he later turned against them. One poet-musician, Todros ben Yehuda Abulafia, dedicated a canzone (a metric, rhymed song) to him, declaring:

> Good faith is avenged over lies
> Since, as King, Alfonso did arise.
> I hail thee, with chalice inscribed
> With this song, to Alfonso the Wise:
> As God said, "Go not empty-handed,"
> Accept then, my Lord, this humble prize.[26]

One is deluged with the names of Jewish musicians and poets in the Iberian Peninsula. Many were *juglares*, wandering musicians hired for short engagements, like their French counterparts, the *jongleurs*, about whom we will read in chapter 6. Others, especially those skilled in writing poetry, were employed at noble courts in long-term positions, some even earning the sobriquet "troubadour," a word usually reserved for musicians of noble birth who practiced their art as skilled amateurs (see chapter 6). One of those was Meshullam ben Solomon de

---

[24] Ismar Elbogen, *Jewish Liturgy: A Comprehensive History*, trans. Raymond P. Scheindlin, ed. Joseph Heinemann et al. (Philadelphia and Jerusalem: The Jewish Publication Society, 1993), 261.

[25] Alfonso X, King of Castile and Leon from 1252-84, was a poet as well as a distinguished general. But this manuscript was probably compiled by artists and musicians at his court.

[26] Translated by Judith Kaplan Eisenstein in her article "Medieval Elements in the Liturgical Music of the Jews of Southern France and Northern Spain," *Musica Judaica* 14 (1999): 12.

Piera, who flourished early in the thirteenth century in the vicinity of Gerona. Another well-known musician referred to as a troubadour was Rabbi Santob (i.e., Shem Tov) de Carrion, who wrote, among other things, a long poem of moral counsel for the new King Pedro (later called "Pedro the Cruel") at his accession to the throne (1334). A man by the name of Charliot, designated as "le Juif" (the Jew) is also mentioned in manuscripts of the time as a troubadour. Alfred Sendrey lists many other well-known fourteenth-century *juglares*,[27] including the entire family Bonafos and Jacob Evanyon of Pamplona, who played with their ensemble on at least one occasion. Samuel Alfqui, a famous physician from Pamplona, also appeared as a *juglar*, and we read of another father, Solomon de Besers, and his two sons, Vitalis Ferrari and Vitalonus Bertelay, who played at a Purim festival "ut moris est juedorum" (according to the custom of the Jews). One Saçon (Sasson) Salomon was lauded as a fine lutenist at the royal court, and another, Johann Baruch, *judeu*, appears listed as the leader of Queen Sibile's string instruments. In addition to these and many others, various accounts of royal entertainments mention entire bands of Jewish instrumentalists. Just as we shall see in other countries of Christian Europe, Jewish musicians in Spain earned especially high marks for musical talent.

When the Spanish finally succeeded in wresting their country back from the Muslims in its entirety after some eight hundred years, many Jews were unprepared to live under the conditions of serfdom and uncertainty once again imposed on Spain as a Christian country. In 1492, with a final victory over the Moors and the political marriage of Ferdinand and Isabella uniting the country, the Jewish community of Spain was given the alternative of conversion or exile. A similar law was promulgated in Portugal just five years later. Thus a thousand years of brilliant, cultured Jewish life on the Iberian peninsula came to an end.

Spanish and Portuguese Jews fled in abject misery. Their exodus was carried out in chaos and suffering. Shiploads of fleeing Jews were abandoned at sea after having paid their fare. Others were dumped unceremoniously onto coasts where they had no intention of going and where they found themselves unwelcome. Processions of weary exiles attempted to cross the Pyrenees on foot, with the result that there were as many deaths as successful crossings. Unscrupulous shipowners, and even royalty, greedily accepted money with the promise of transport to safety, then abandoned their charges. It is hardly surprising that many Jews chose outward conversion so that they could remain in their ancestral homes rather than face exile. Many of those *conversos* (converts) continued to practice Judaism in secret. Such people were known by the pejorative name, *Marranos* (pigs). With the installation of the Inquisition they were hunted down by zealous Christian inquisitors and forced to recant by torture, sometimes meeting their end by being burned alive.

Those who escaped took with them the Iberian culture with its tradition of song and poetry, the Judeo-Spanish language called *Ladino*, and a deep yearning for the civilization they had left behind. Those things, and precious little else, they carried to settlements throughout the Mediterranean basin and to the New World. There they sang the songs of fifteenth-century Iberia and maintained, to the extent that it was possible, a life style based on the golden days

---

[27] Much of the information in this paragraph is taken from Sendrey, *Music of the Jews*, chapter 5, "Jewish *Juglares* in the Iberian Peninsula."

of peace and prosperity in Toledo or Lisbon. High on the scale of their memories were the popular story-songs known as *romanceros*. Those ballads wove long, often quite involved, stories of love and fantasy, dreamy narrations about sins of the noble, or warnings of a worried mother. They sang of handsome princes who loved milkmaids, of kings and queens, of sleeping babies, sibling rivalry, and murdered lovers. They formed the core of women's strophic songs in a culture that segregated the sexes by interest as much as function. Just two brief examples will give some sense of the romantic content of these beloved songs:

¡Ay! Mancebo

¡Ay! Mancebo, ¡Ay! Mancebo	Ay! Young man, Ay! Young man
El amor me haze llorar.	Love has brought me tears.
Si por la Francia vos irex	If you will go to France,
Al mi amor saludez.	Take greetings to my love.
¿Que señal vos me dariax	What signs can you give me,
Que lo podré conocer?	That I can know him?
El es alto como un pino	He is tall as the pine,
Derecho como un fenar.	Straight as a beam of light.
La su garón es alta	His neck is [held] high,
Que parece Imán, él.	He resembles a chief.
En su mano la derecha	In his right hand,
Una lança lleva el.	He carries a sword.
En la punta de la lança	At the point of the sword
Hay un rico cimer.	There is a sharp edge.
Un caballo blanco tiene	He has a white horse,
De los que vienen al rey.	That comes from the king.
Que se lo mandó la reina	That is what the queen ordered,
Que su enamorada es.	Because she was his lover.

La Rosa Enflorece

La rosa enflorece	The rose blooms
En el mes de May.	In the month of May.
Mi alme se escurece	My soul darkens,
Sufriendor del amor.	Suffering from love.
Los bilbilicos cantan	The nightingales sing
Sospiran del amor.	And they sigh of love.
Y la pasión me mata	And the passion kills me
Muchigua mi dolor.	Intensifying my pain.
Más presto ven paloma	Go quickly, dove
Mas presto ven a mi.	Go quickly, and return.
Más presto tú mi alma	Go quickly, you my soul,
Que yo me vo morir.	For I am going to die.

The Ladino *romancero* took root wherever emigres from the Iberian Peninsula found themselves: in the Balkans, the Middle East, North Africa, Holland, and England. *Romanceros* were folk creations, passed through the hands of many who re-worked them, some of whom were bound to have been non-Jews. Yet their melodic beauty and poetic fantasy spoke to the heart of Sephardim nostalgically remembering the golden age of medieval Spain and Portugal, and many of them have been preserved intact for over five hundred years.

Unlike the great body of secular *romanceros* that have been collected, there is barely any evidence of the underground religious music of the Marranos, or crypto-Jews. That is quite understandable, since they risked their lives to practice Judaism in secret while trying to appear Christian in public. Bathing, having guests for dinner, or changing linens on a Friday could lead to denunciation to the inquisition, resulting in torture and death for all members of the family. Committing a Jewish hymn to writing would have been a foolhardy piece of incriminating evidence to agents of the inquisition. About a dozen manuscripts exist which may possibly point to a formal Marrano liturgy before the expulsion from Spain in 1492.[28] In one, dubbed a *Kedushah*-motet by Eric Werner, the cantus (top voice) sings the ancient Ashkenazic tune of the preamble to the high holy day *Kedushah*; the tenor (middle voice) seems to imitate the *shofar*, and the contratenor (lowest voice) sings the Latin hymn, "Alma redemptoris mater," possibly in an attempt to disguise the Jewish function of this composition behind a well-known Christian melody. The piece displays a high degree of contrapuntal skill, the kind that only comes with good training and much practice. It is unlikely that it existed in total isolation; that is, the survival of this isolated piece suggests that there may have been more such music. On the other hand, the furtive circumstances of Marrano life were such that the preservation of music on paper was unlikely, and we must assume that a great deal of unwritten liturgical music was lost when songs of the grandparents disappeared from the memory of later generations through disuse. Because of that, other scholars doubt the authenticity of this piece, some feeling instead that it might have been a satirical composition, written to ridicule Jewish religious practice for the entertainment of the wealthy.[29] If that were the case, it would not be an isolated example, for the practice of mocking the Jews and their music found great favor in Christian courts.

While we are once again left in the frustrating position of having to admit that we "don't know for sure" what Jewish music in Moslem Spain sounded like, the lack in this case is not as absolute as that of earlier historical periods. The *romanceros* have been carefully preserved by oral tradition, and while changes certainly must have crept in over the centuries, those folk melodies bear a stamp of overall authenticity that has not been completely eradicated. Many of the *cantigas* from the beautiful manuscript of King Alfonso *El Sabio* (The Wise) have now been recreated and recorded, and from those we can get a good idea of the way thirteenth-century music sounded. Even when we do not have notated melodies for the specific pieces we would like to hear, we can listen to performances of contemporaneous music that re-create the sound and style. In that, we are far ahead of the students of Jewish music of just a few years ago, who had to be content with what they could imagine. Where notation of any kind existed, scholars

---

[28] See Eric Werner, "The Oldest Sources of Synagogue Chant," *Proceedings of the American Academy for Jewish Research* 16 (1947): 228, ff. There is a picture of this manuscript in Gradenwitz, facing p. 64.

[29] The controversy is summarized by Sendrey in *Music of the Jews*, 165-68.

have generally been able to re-create good approximations of the original. Alas, in many cases the notation either has been lost or may never have existed, so our knowledge is still far from perfect.

This, then, was the world in which the Jewish poet-musicians of the Arab world found themselves. From Persia to Portugal, from Khartoum to Khazakstan, stretched the empire of Islam, one of the greatest the world has ever known. It was an empire that prided itself on great poetic, scientific, artistic and literary achievements. It was, on the whole, wealthy, sophisticated, and hedonistic. For much of its history and over much of its geography the empire was, if not hospitable, at least not excessively hostile to Jewish thought and practice. Here, for most of a millennium, the practice of Jewish music flourished. Using musical styles of their own time, the Jews of the medieval Arab world were able to "sing the songs of Israel in a strange land," as, according to Psalm 137, they could not do in ancient Babylon.

Suggestions for Further Reading

Adler, Israel. "The Notated Synagogue Chants of the 12th Century of Obadiah, the Norman Proselyte." In *Contributions to a Historical Study of Jewish Music*, ed. Eric Werner, 168-99. New York: Ktav Publishing House, 1976.

Armistead, Samuel G., Joseph H. Silverman, and Israel J. Katz. *Judeo-Spanish Ballads from Oral Tradition, Folk Literature of the Sephardic Jews*, 2-3. Berkeley: University of California Press, 1986.

Avenary, Hanoch. "A Genizah Find of Saadya's Psalm-Preface and Its Musical Aspects." In *Contributions to a Historical Study of Jewish Music*, ed. Eric Werner, 37-54. New York: Ktav Publishing House, 1976.

Farmer, Henry George. *A History of Arabian Music to the XIIIth Century*. London: Luzac, 1967.

Golb, Norman. "Aspects of the Historical Background of Jewish Life in Medieval Egypt." In *Jewish Medieval and Renaissance Studies*, ed. Alexander Altman. Cambridge, MA: Harvard University Press, 1967.

Marks, Paul F. *Bibliography of Literature Concerning Yemenite-Jewish Music*. Detroit Studies in Music Bibliography, 27. Detroit: Information Coordinators, 1973.

Menasseh, Sarah. "A Song to Heal Your Wounds: Traditional Melodies of the Jews of Iraq." *Musica Judaica: Journal of the American Society for Jewish Music* 12, no. 5754/1991-92 (1992): 1-29.

Rosner, Fred. "Moses Maimonides on Music Therapy in His *Responsum* on Music." *Journal of Jewish Music and Liturgy* 16 (1993-94): 1-16.

Shelemay, Kay Kaufman. *Let Jasmine Rain Down: Song and Remembrance among Syrian Jews*. Chicago/London: University of Chicago Press, 1998.

_____. *Song of Longing: An Ethiopian Journey*. Urbana and Chicago: University of Illinois Press, 1991.

Shiloah, Amnon. *The Dimension of Music in Islamic and Jewish Culture*. Collected Studies Series. Brookfield, VT: Variorum, 1993.

_____. *Music in the World of Islam: A Socio-Cultural Study*. Detroit: Wayne State University Press, 1995.

_____. *The Musical Tradition of Iraqi Jews: Selection of Piyyutim and Songs*. Studies on History and Culture of Iraqi Jews, 3. Or Yehuda: Institute for Research on Iraqi Jewry, 1983.

Touma, Habib. *The Music of the Arabs*. Trans. Laurie Schwartz. Portland: Amadeus Press, 1996.

6 | Secular Music of the Jews in Christian Europe in the Middle Ages

Jewish Life in the World of Christianity

There were a number of thriving Jewish settlements in late Roman and early Christian Europe. Jewish communities had spread beyond the Land of Israel from as far back as the days of the Babylonian exile, and in all likelihood even before that. A voluntary diaspora of merchants, soldiers, and technicians existed long before the destruction of the Temple, planting Jewish communities throughout the Middle East and the Roman empire. Significant numbers also moved west into North Africa and Europe, particularly in such places as the Rhine valley, the Iberian Peninsula, and Southern Britain. The existing communities were enlarged with Jewish slaves ransomed from captivity by their co-religionists after the carnage in Jerusalem. That was compounded by the annihilation of the Jews of Alexandria, the largest and most prosperous community outside Israel, less than fifty years later, in 116 CE. Housing the greatest library in the ancient world, with about a half million volumes, Alexandria had been home to a large, comfortably assimilated Jewish community whose immersion in Greek philosophy produced such influential writers as Philo and Josephus.

As the new order took shape in Western Europe, Jews found their religion to be a distinct social and economic disadvantage there. The culture and military power of Rome had stabilized Western Europe through the second century CE; but as Rome slipped into its long, slow decline and eventual fall in 476 CE, a power vacuum was left behind. In Europe it was occupied by raiding barbarians, by brutal struggles between petty warlords and local bandits, as well as by pirates on the high seas and corrupt officials. Much of the population was ignorant and super-stitious, sinking into what might best be described as a brutish existence. It would take centuries for Europe to recover from the demise of the ancient world. During that time, a vigorous Christianity spread outward from Rome, sweeping much of the continent into its fold. It was to the pacifist and intellectual tendencies of that new belief, more than anything else, that Europe owed its recovery. Had it not been for the growth of monasteries and monastic schools, the continuance of Roman political structure in the hierarchy of the church, and the civilizing influence of Christian benevolence, the West might have sunk into barbarism.

As Europe came under the aegis of the Church, though, a new and more threatening element was added to Jewish life. As the state religion, Christianity was inextricably bound up with civil law. Nonconformity became a crime whose punishment lay largely in the hands and at the whim of local authorities. With the fall of Rome and the rise of Christianity, the situation of the Jews deteriorated from relative acceptance by local barons of the Roman Empire to active hostility from the Church and the recently-converted population, who reacted predictably to such Gospel passages as Mark 14:65:

> Then all [the Jews] condemned Him [Jesus] saying He must die. Some of them started to spit at Him. They covered His face, hit Him with their fists, and told Him, "Prophesy!"

or Matthew 26:25:

> Then the [Jewish] people as a whole answered, "His blood be on us and our children."

Religious persecution often resulted in an entire community being uprooted. Jews fled to escape oppressive circumstances in one place, establishing a new center in another. Scattered ever more thinly through what had become a hostile environment, Jewish communities of the Middle Ages tried to stay in touch with one another to share the hope that some day there would be a return to Zion, a longing that they wove into their prayers and songs.

Jews in the Middle Ages

"Middle Ages" is something of a problematic term in the European context, for in Europe the era known as the Middle Ages is generally felt to have ended by the middle of the fifteenth century when the rebirth of classical learning and science ushered in the era known as the Renaissance. For Jews, though, especially the Jews of Eastern Europe, conditions prevalent in medieval times hardly changed even as Europe entered the seventeenth century. Indeed, in many parts of Russia and Poland such difficult circumstances extended into the nineteenth century. Thus, any terminus for the *Jewish* Middle Ages in Europe would have to be flexible, arriving first at the western edge of the continent and slowly advancing eastward.

Most Jewish music still preserved today is from the end of that period, and the line between folk music and composed art music grows quite permeable in the late nineteenth and early twentieth century. Often the only difference was that songs written after the introduction of a popular Yiddish press and the literature it generated were published with composers' names, while unpublished songs by their contemporaries entered the realm of folk music.

More than anything else, it is the commonality of the Yiddish language that defines this chapter's discussion. Yiddish, a conglomeration of German, Polish, Russian, and Hebrew, with an older layer rooted in Old French and Italian, became the *lingua franca* of most European Jews. This was not by intent, at least not at first. During Roman rule Jewish immigrants had learned the local tongue as well as Latin, just as immigrants all over the world have had to do from time immemorial. In central Europe, where the Jewish population was centered in the Rhine Valley, the German language predominated. To the extent that persecution and legal obstacles later increased their isolation from the local population, Jews were left speaking archaic dialects while their Christian neighbors adopted the changes that occur normally in spoken language. As successive expulsions drove Jews from one part of Europe to another, they took their insular speech patterns along, until the resulting polyglot became a separate Germanic dialect called Yiddish. For generations it was denied the status of a language and learned Jews long scorned it as low jargon. That view has gone out of fashion in recent years as its status as a language in its own right has begun to be reevaluated, for, as Yiddish scholar Max Weinrich put it, "A language is only a dialect that has an army and a navy." The degree to which Yiddish was the primary language of the European Jews was directly related to their insulation from the rest of European society, so that even into modern times East European Jews spoke nothing but Yiddish in their daily lives, while in France or England it grew to be more of a second language.

From the fourth to the eighth centuries Europe gradually integrated the administrative structure of the Church of Rome into its political infrastructure. At the beginning of the ninth century Charles Martel, known as Charlemagne (Charles the Great), was appointed Holy Roman Emperor by the pope in an attempt to unify all Europe under the wing of a "catholic" (i.e., universal) Christianity. The period of Charlemagne is sometimes called the "Little Renaissance," for it marked the reemergence of Europe from the depths to which it had sunk. Charlemagne, even while upholding the laws discriminating against the Jews, nevertheless encouraged Jewish participation in commerce and the sciences, and even employed a Jewish physician himself. All this changed over the next several centuries as the Church strove to impose a single administrative model that would unify Europe. In doing so, the Church, perhaps unwittingly, encouraged the spread of vicious xenophobia.

The Jew and the Feudal System

The political structure of medieval Europe was loosely based on the model of the Church hierarchy, which in turn was taken from the administrative plan of Imperial Rome. It transformed that model into what is known as the feudal system. Every person held a place in society that owed allegiance, ultimately, to the pope. Kings accepted the pope's authority in exchange for the support of the Church in affirming their divine right to rule and collect taxes over whatever land they could hold by force of arms. The king, in turn, demanded those taxes from noblemen to whom he granted subsidiary rights—that is, they could collect as much as they wanted from the people in their districts, so long as they passed the required amount along to the king and supported him by raising armies to fight in the numerous bloody skirmishes over land or inheritance that plagued Europe. The nobles, in turn, farmed out smaller fiefdoms on the same terms to petty nobility, who employed local officials to enforce the collection of taxes. At the bottom of the heap was the individual peasant or serf, who worked on land allotted to him by virtue of his ability to pay taxes and provide himself and his sons as foot soldiers for armies of the nobility. The cement that held the entire system together was the oath of fealty to one's immediate overlord, taken "in Jesus's name." To break that oath was a religious as well as a civil crime, punishable not only by death, but even worse, by eternal damnation.

Obviously, Jews could not take such an oath, and in most places would not have been allowed to even if they wished to take it. Locked out of a secure haven within the feudal system, they were forced into finding other ways to stay alive. Squeezed out of trades and professions in which they had engaged for generations, they were forbidden to participate in civic life or own land, and were barred from employing Christians in their businesses and homes. They were reduced to living hand-to-mouth, easy prey for bandits, religious fanatics, and rapacious nobility who sold "protection" to beleaguered Jewish communities. By the tenth century, when Jewish life in Arab Spain entered its "golden age," Jewish life in the rest of Europe was precarious, at best. Then, just as things looked bleakest, the situation became catastrophically worse.

On 27 November 1095, Pope Urban II urged an assembly attending a church council at Clermont in France, to take up arms against the Seljuk Turks and capture the holy city of Jerusalem from the Moslems. He promised eternal forgiveness of sin for those who participated in the enterprise. In a wholly unexpected response, Europeans rose by the hundreds of thousands to join that great crusade against the Moslem "pagans." By the following August (1096) an unguided, disorganized band, including ignorant, opportunistic, zealous, and rapacious combatants, swept across Europe, creating havoc in their wake. It was not long into their arduous journey before many of them sought to earn heavenly bliss closer to home, without the difficulties of marching all the way to Jerusalem. "Why go to all the trouble of traveling so far to kill the enemies of Christendom," they must have thought, "when satisfactory substitutes were right at hand?" Soon the rioting marchers began to shout, "Kill a Jew and save your soul." Entire Jewish communities along the Rhine were decimated: Worms, Speyer, Mayence (Mainz), Cologne— communities that had lived in peace for centuries. Jews were burned alive in their synagogues, their goods pillaged, and those who tried to flee slaughtered by joyfully rioting mobs who believed—or pretended to believe—that the murder of Jews was commanded by the Church. Regardless of efforts by local rulers to preserve the rights of the local Jews, the lesson of that first crusade, which would be repeated in later crusades, was to establish in the eyes of the ignorant that killing Jews was pleasing to God.

The response of the Church was ambiguous, at best. On the one hand, papal pronounce- ments were issued abhorring the pogroms that arose from time to time and warning local communities that it was un-Christian to persecute the Jews. On the other hand such high- minded pronouncements were difficult to police from a distance, and local nobles often found it convenient to borrow money from Jewish sources, then provoke anti-Jewish riots and expel the Jews in order to avoid repayment. In the upper echelons of the Church those who were knowledgeable about history and philosophy were well aware of the debt Christianity owed to Judaism; but the lower clergy, often woefully ignorant and closer to the uneducated masses, found it personally rewarding to unite their impoverished flocks in hatred of the Jews.

As a result of increasingly oppressive laws, few legal ways remained for Jews to earn a living: tanning leather, the lowliest of all skilled trades because of the constant smell of rotting flesh that permeated one's person and clothing, was permitted, as were the trades of dyer and felt-maker, both of which led to insanity and/or early death by absorption of toxic chemicals used in the manufacturing process. Wood-cutting (with permission of the estate owner or manager to whom one paid a kickback), butchering, and unskilled contract labor such as that performed by a porter, were also permitted. By special permission (which generally meant bribes) of local officials, some small groups of highly skilled craftsmen such as jewelers, goldsmiths, and silversmiths, were allowed to practice their trade. But more often than not any economic success resulted in the bribes being raised beyond the Jews' ability to meet them, or in pogroms led by rival Christian artisans. For an even smaller handful of Jews, international commerce became a viable way of life. Their learning, linguistic ability, contacts abroad, and understanding of finances made them invaluable in the courts of many European princes. But a single miscalculation could quickly bring personal retribution, financial ruin, or even death to such highly visible "court Jews." Another possibility for a few who could amass the capital was moneylending at interest, ostensibly forbidden to Christians, but nonetheless necessary for the growth of the fledgling European economy. Again, this occupation was fraught with peril, as Jews could not testify in Christian courts, and the only frail means of collecting an unpaid debt was the threat of not lending money the next time it was needed.

Music as a Jewish Profession

Thus the Jews eked out an existence and, to maintain their families, sought fissures in the feudal system into which they could creep. One of those "cracks" in the system to which some Jews gravitated was the performing arts—especially music and theater. This was true to such an extent that in the Middle Ages in some parts of Southern France the word *juif* (Jew) had a secondary slang meaning of wandering musician. Such low-class performers, whom we have already encountered as *juglares* in Spain, were known as *jongleurs* in France and *gleemen* in England. They juggled, sang, played instruments, acted in plays, did acrobatics and bear-wrestling, or played the role of jester. Some of them became famous enough to acquire some degree of renown, like Joseph ben Benjamin or Schloime, "the joyous Jew" of Prague. To this day the names of many Jews indicate their ancestors were professional performers somewhere back along the line—e.g., such common Jewish names as:

Musicant (musician)	Geiger (also fiddler)
Cantor (singer)	Pfeiffer or Feiffer (flutist)
Singer (singer)	Feikler, Feckler, or Pauker (all mean "drummer")
Trebes, Trevis or Travis (treble singer)	Becker (cymbal player)
Discount (discantus, or melody singer)	Zimbalist (cembalo player)
Altmann (alto singer)	Tanzer or Tansmann (dancer)
Bass (bass singer)	Dichter (poet, songwriter)
Fiedler (fiddler)	Schreier (shouter, barker)

The absence of brass players from the list was because medieval trumpeters, an adjunct of nobility, had their own separate guild, from which Jews were excluded. Professional guilds for Jewish musicians were founded during the sixteenth and seventeenth centuries in many European cities as a way of protecting Jews in the entertainment trades. There is conclusive evidence of this in Frankfurt and Prague, but anecdotal evidence points to such trade unions of artists as a Jewish phenomenon throughout Europe.

From time to time particularly talented and charismatic personalities arose from those anonymous ranks to a modicum of fame as performers. In the thirteenth century, the German Jew Süsskind von Trimberg became well known as a *Minnesinger* (love-singer). Such figures were the popular musicians of that elegant, romantic age. Like their northern and southern French counterparts, the *trouvères* and *troubadours*, or the Italian *trovatori*, *Minnesingers* were usually adventurous young noblemen who roamed from castle to castle, bringing news to those in relative isolation, singing refined or suggestive songs of courtly love, and often wooing ladies of the castle. A picture of "Süsskind, the Jew of Trimberg" can be found in the Manasseh Codex, an illuminated manuscript prepared about 1300, now in the Heidelberg Library. It shows him dressed in the required Jewish regalia next to a nobleman and a clergyman.

In spite of his Jewish background, Süsskind seems to have filled these roles with success; but at some point he tired of that life, for he retired suddenly from his wanderings and returned to his home. Süsskind and his music are mentioned admiringly on a par with Walter von der Vogelweide and Hartmann von Aue, two of the best-known and most talented *Minnesingers* in the history of German music.

Twelve poems are attributed to Süsskind, six of which have been proven genuine. While his poems and melodies (none notated) were generally similar to those of his contemporaries, a few interesting differences are observable. Some of his verses derived from biblical phrases, from the Talmud, or even from Jewish prayers. Then, too, Süsskind sang in praise of the perfect wife, whereas most *Minnesingers* sang abstractly of a noble lady to be won or the Virgin to be served. As a matter of fact, not one of his poems dealt with the most common subject of other *Minnesingers*: secular love. At his retirement, whether forced or not we do not know, he wrote a poem which spoke eloquently, if sadly, of his life as a wandering entertainer, and which declared that, because his "race" was discovered, all he wanted to do was to return home to a quiet life, scorning his wealthy, unappreciative audiences.

Süsskind's Last Poem[1]

Why should I wander sadly,
    My harp within my hand,
O'er mountain, hill and valley?
    What praise do I command?

Full well they know the singer,
    Belongs to race accursed;
Sweet love does now no longer,
    Reward me as at first.

Be silent then, my lyre,
    We sing 'fore Lords in vain.
I'll leave the minstrel's choir,
    And roam a Jew again.

My staff and hat I'll grasp then,
    And on my breast full low,
By Jewish custom olden,
    My grizzled beard shall grow

My days I'll pass in quiet,
Those left to me on earth,
Nor sing, for those who not yet,
Have learned a poet's worth

---

[1] Manasseh Codex, Heidelberg University Library.

In another poem that goes well beyond the usual trite idealization of the beloved that makes up most *Minnesinger* fare, Süsskind offers a prayerful meditation on mortality that deserves a place alongside the *piyyutim* of the great Jewish-Arab poets:

> When I consider what I was and what I am,
> And what I yet will be—all my joy is fled.
> For the days of my life fly quickly by,
> And it is the burden of my tearful fate,
> That I must live in fear of death from day to day.
> Will loathsome worms be my end?
> How can I ever be joyful,
> When fear and loathing sicken me?
> Nowhere can my heart find peace,
> For I must always consider:
> Will my soul find bitter pain?
> Why do I abandon myself to sin?
> You, Lord, who alone are almighty and merciful,
> Help me, so my soul will find favor before you.[2]

Another piece of evidence toward solving the puzzle of Jewish participation in European musical life is an elaborately notated, beautifully copied manuscript known as the *Lochamer Liederbuch* (Locheim Songbook). Compiled around 1450, it is one of the most historically important manuscripts of German music extant. Its story not only informs us about a Jewish musician of the fifteenth century, but it also throws light on the efforts of anti-Semitic German scholarship of the nineteenth and twentieth centuries.

The modern half of the story begins in 1867, when a German-Jewish musicologist by the name of Friedrich Wilhelm Arnold examined this manuscript and published an article about it. Arnold pointed out its importance as the earliest known manuscript of German polyphonic songs. What created a disturbance was his assertion that the manuscript's owner was not a German nobleman, as had been thought, but a Jew. His chief evidence for this was an inscription at the bottom of page 17 that reads, "Der allerliebsten Barbara, meinem treuen liebsten Gemaken" (To the most beloved Barbara, my faithful and dearest spouse.) The most astonishing thing about that sentence is that the words are spelled out in Hebrew letters. Other Hebrew letters spell out the phrase, "ihr zu lieben" (to please her).

Arnold argued that no Christian in the middle of the fifteenth century would know how, or have any reason, to write German in Hebrew characters. Jews, though, regularly wrote German-based Yiddish that way. It was unlikely, too, for those words to have been added later by, say, a Jewish servant or wandering minstrel, as it would have been a serious crime to have stolen this beautiful manuscript or scribbled those lines into a nobleman's handsomely prepared book. Finally, Arnold argued that the name Wolf and its diminutives, Wölflin, Wölflein or Wölfl (or Velvel, in Yiddish) had long been a common name among Jews as a Yiddish translation of the Hebrew name Z'ev. On the basis of this and other internal evidence, Arnold concluded that

---

[2] Translation by E. Rubin, from *Die Lieder des Süsskind von Trimberg*, ed. B. Badt (Berlin: Fritz Gurlitt, 1920), 5.

the owner of the manuscript and the copyist of the music were the same Jewish musician, and that the designation, "von Lochamen," was simply the name of his town, not a term of nobility, as the prefix *von* ("of" or "from") seemed to imply.

In an immediate riposte to that article, German musicologist Johann Friederich Bellerman leaped in to save German honor from any admission that its earliest manuscript of polyphonic song might have been written by a Jew. Just a few key sentences from Bellerman's article give the tenor of his argument:

> The assertion voiced with such certainty . . . that Wölflein von Lochamen had been a Jew, appears to us thoroughly unfounded, inasmuch as it is based solely on a few Hebraic letters which spell out a German name and a German thought. . . . Arnold's theory is best disproved by the inner characteristic of the manuscript. *The songs express German mind and Christian ideas throughout, such as hardly could have been the utterance of a Jew living at the time.*[3] [emphasis added]

And so, on the strength of that flimsy refutation, Wölflein von Lochamen became enshrined in German music history as a South German nobleman, an assertion taught as fact until after the Second World War.

Just what were the contents of that manuscript? What "German" and "Christian" sentiments did it contain that "hardly could have been the utterance of a Jew living at that time?" The *Lochamer Liederbuch* contains forty-eight rather inoffensive love songs in metrical, rhymed poetry. They are all set in three voices, with the middle part texted, which suggests a performance style standard for the day: one voice (the tenor, or middle part) and two accompanying instruments. That hypothesis is borne out by the lyrical nature of the middle voice, with faster-moving, decorative counterpoint in the outer voices. Bellerman's weak argument would seem difficult to sustain in the light of the linguistic and internal evidence cited by Arnold. In recent years this controversy has all but died away and Arnold's original conclusions are accepted today as fact.

So far, so good; but what was a German Jew residing in a small Bavarian town doing with this handsomely written, expensive manuscript in the middle of the fifteenth century, when no other collections of German polyphonic songs are to be found? One attractive hypothesis is that Wölflein was a professional musician, not just a simple player, but the leader of a performing group, and the "Barbara" of the dedication, his *Der allerliebsten Gemaken* (beloved spouse), was another performer in the troupe.

In Italy, earlier in the Renaissance, a number of Jewish musicians had been active at Christian courts, not only in a musical capacity, but in the related profession of dancing master, a profession heavily populated by Jews. Dancing at that time was not only one of the most popular mixed-gender court entertainments, it was considered a key social grace, a required accomplishment for anyone with social aspirations. Families of wealth employed full-time musician-dancing masters, partly to see to it that everyone, especially the children, was well-schooled in the demanding steps of all the latest dances. These dancer-musicians were hired

---

[3] Translated by Sendrey, in *Music of the Jews*, 146-47.

partly to choreograph and lead the dancing for performances and social occasions, and partly to direct the musicians and provide new music for those events. Less wealthy families employed itinerant dancing masters, so many of whom were Jews that the profession became identified with them. In 1313 Rabbi Hacén ben Salomo was even called upon to teach dance in a Spanish church. Dancing masters had to be musicians themselves, and often carried small violins or flutes in the pockets of the long tails of their waistcoats to provide music for their lessons.

Occasionally one of these men would rise to prominence and find his way into a court situation. That was the case for one called Musetto ("Little Moses," or "Moishele," in Yiddish), dancing master to the children of Sigismondo Pandolfo Malatesta (1417-68), Duke of Pesaro. Another Jewish dancing master and composer of Italian madrigals was Giuseppe Ebreo. Two other Jewish dancing masters from Ancona were given special permission to teach dancing and singing in Rome by Pope Gregory XIII. Perhaps the most famous of those Jewish dancing masters was Guglielmo Ebreo, author of the important dance treatise, *Trattato del'arte del ballo* (ca. 1463), who was well-known as a choreographer for several different Italian courts, including the splendid house of the Medici in Florence. For one sumptuous event, the marriage of Costanzo Sforza and Camilla d'Aragon in 1475, he was said to have employed a troupe of one hundred twenty dancers with musicians, and arranged a solemn procession of the entire Jewish community of Pesaro.

In the sixteenth century, after King Henry VIII turned to English rabbis for advice on the legality of his first marriage (to Catherine of Aragon), the pivotal issue on which Henry based England's break with the Church of Rome, many Italian Jewish musicians gravitated to Protestant England. As a Protestant country free of the Inquisition, England became an attractive destination for some of the finest musicians from Italy, Portugal, and Spain. Apparently foreign Jews, especially Italians, outnumbered native English musicians in the court musical establishment. One writer catalogues nineteen Jews as members of The King's Musick in the 1540s.[4] Not only musicians, but instrument builders as well came to Tudor England, and contributed to the building of lutes, viols, and other instruments for which Renaissance England was famous.

The Jewish community in Amsterdam included many Marrano families who had fled the inquisition in Spain and Portugal. Finding themselves free to practice their religion openly in the Netherlands, they established synagogues and began to participate in the rich cultural life there and in The Hague. Synagogue schools sprang into operation, and the children were taught not only the fundamentals of their religion, but were also tutored in cantillation and sacred music. Perhaps because of its association with King David, the harp seemed to have been a favored instrument played by Dutch rabbis. Issac Uziel (d. 1622), Isaac Aboab da Fonseca (1605-93), and Abraham Pereira were rabbis who were also well-known harpists. Other members of the community gained renown as performers, too. In the early eighteenth century one of the most active composers of the community was Abraham Cacares (fl. ca. 1728), who composed the music for a prayer for the dedication of the synagogue in The Hague, setting a new text by the synagogue's *chazzan*, Daniel Cohen Rodriguez. In 1736 the Jewish community sponsored a "spiritual concert," as was done in many churches, featuring Cacares conducting from the harpsichord. Such concerts were not necessarily made up of religious music, but consisted of serious, as opposed to "light" compositions.

---

[4] Roger Prior, "Jewish Musicians at the Tudor Court," *Musical Quarterly* 69 (1983): 253-65.

Wealthy members of the Jewish community played an important role as music patrons, too, supporting professional concerts and operas that made Amsterdam a brilliant musical center in the eighteenth and nineteenth centuries. One music-loving amateur, Francesco Lopez de Liz, sponsored operatic performances and concerts at his grand home in The Hague from 1734 to 1742, for which he engaged one of Europe's most famous violinists, Jean-Marie LeClair, as concert-master and conductor. The roster of musical activities, from the composition of new music for voices and instruments to the hosting of visits by artists such as Leopold Mozart, who toured Europe to display the musical genius of his eight-year-old son, Wolfgang, is extensive, and is examined in Israel Adler's invaluable *Musical Life and Traditions of the Portuguese Jewish Community of Amsterdam in the XVIIIth Century* (Jerusalem: Magnes Press of The Hebrew University, 1974).

Holland, though, was one of the few exceptions to the unending succession of massacres, expulsions, kidnappings, and pogroms instituted elsewhere that formed a litany of horror and sorrow for European Jews. Their songs reflected this in a growing chorus of suffering, sometimes aimed at the oppressing culture, sometimes cast back on themselves in the form of barbed jokes. By the eighteenth and nineteenth centuries that body of song, catalogued by Ruth Rubin in her *Voices of a People* (Philadelphia: Jewish Publication Society, 1979), had grown into a rich repertoire of folk music.

Folk Music of the Yiddish-Speaking Jews

The term folk music is used here to include any music not prescribed by the liturgy, fixed in notation as a discrete art object, or composed for a formal public venue. Folk songs were obviously composed by individuals at particular points in time, but their original forms became irrelevant to the ever-changing sounds in actual performance. Whether instrumental or vocal, the primary characteristic was plasticity. A song was shaped and re-shaped by many voices, changing constantly to meet the needs of its users. In Western culture, only in the last two centuries or so has any concerted attempt been made to collect and notate folk music. Given such an ephemeral tradition, one can see that it can be difficult to locate folk music, or even to identify it as such when found; yet it is the largest repertory of music, easily surpassing all the instrumental compositions, operas, and art songs of any given time.

What we have today as certifiable Jewish folk music from the early Middle Ages in Europe is miniscule, and much of the repertory is open to argument. Lovers sang of their passion, mothers crooned lullabies, workers sang to make the hours pass, and lusty tunes could be found everywhere, from tunes for noble weddings to those for village dances. Only ragged remnants are left of that rich musical fabric today: bits and pieces that survived in oral trans-mission, which may or may not bear any resemblance to what was heard a thousand years ago. A little more is known about the period of Middle Yiddish (1250-1750), but most of the music we have represents the period after about 1750.

In 1791 Catherine the Great of Russia decreed that Jews would be restricted to the western periphery of her kingdom, the so-called Pale of Settlement.[5] At the same time Jews in Western

---

[5] Most of Poland was at that time a part of the Russian empire and Catherine's policy essentially dumped the Jewish population into the Russian-Polish border area and what had been Poland proper.

Europe were entering the period that would be called, in Hebrew, the *Haskalah* (enlightenment),[6] those in Eastern Europe were cut off from contact with the rest of the world and forced into isolated poverty. Living among uneducated, and for the most part unsympathetic and suspicious peasants, Eastern European Jews increasingly used Yiddish as their primary language just as it was losing its centrality for their cousins in the West.

Yiddish was scorned by learned Jews as a language fit only for the marketplace or for ignorant people. The language for prayer and intellectual discourse was Hebrew, and writers who wanted their work to be taken seriously would not publish in Yiddish. It earned the reputation of being a "women's language," because few women had the opportunity to learn Hebrew. One result of this was the growth of a literature in Yiddish aimed at enlightening the unlearned in a culture that prized learning: systematic "adult education." Retellings of biblical material in simple language, psalms, homilies, and prayers translated into Yiddish were published for women. They were widely read by poor men, too, who often began working by the age of seven or eight and had no opportunity to progress in their education beyond the recitation of basic prayers in Hebrew. The most popular of those translations were poetic verses designed to be sung to well-known melodies, so that children often had their first exposure to the Bible through their mother's Yiddish songs. One special category was called *tchines*, blessings and devotional prayers in Yiddish for women, often written by women. These circulated in cheap little booklets, and contained not only Yiddish translations of standard prayers and blessings, but special petitions for the childless, or for a wife whose husband was away on a long journey. Many of those prayers were ascribed to the half-real, half-mythical figure, Sarah bas Tovim. According to the legend, the rebellious young Sarah was condemned to wander eternally. She composed these prayers years later, it was said, in recompense for the sins of her youth, encouraging women to become godly and pious.

Among the very oldest manuscripts of Yiddish music that we know about is the *Shmuel Buch* (Book of Samuel). It is an epic retelling of bible tales, featuring the adventures of the kings and heroes of ancient Israel as recounted in the biblical book of Samuel. The poem consists of about 1,800 rhymed stanzas composed to be sung in the manner of such romantic epics of the Middle Ages as the "Song of Roland" or "Romance of the Rose." It is believed to have been written in the fourteenth century, "current [with] or possibly prior to the Black Death," according to Yiddish folk song authority Ruth Rubin, and remained popular up to the beginning of the eighteenth century. It circulated in manuscript and by word of mouth for some two hundred years until it was first published in Augsburg in 1544.

A different kind of book was written by Elias (Elijah) Levita, also known as Eliahu Bachur (1469-1549). In addition to being an outstanding scholar and author of the important biblical study *Masoret ha-Masoret*, he was the best-known Yiddish poet of his day. In 1545 he published a Yiddish translation of the Book of Psalms; but his most popular work by far was the *Bovo-buch*, published in Padua about 1507, based on an older story. This Yiddish fiction recounted the adventures of righteous Sir Bovo d'Antona in the eleven-syllable ottava rima that was popular for Italian poetry of the time. Its complicated provenance has been summarized as "A Yiddish adaptation of the Italian version (*Buovo d'Antona*) of the Anglo-French romance *Sir Bevis of Hampton*

---

[6] See the Historical Interlude *Haskalah*.

of the early fourteenth century."[7] The *Bovo-buch* was reprinted endlessly through the nineteenth century, and was so widely known that it gave rise to the Yiddish expression *bovo-maiseh* (deed of Bovo), used to stamp any unlikely adventure tale. As the *Bovo-buch* lost its currency, the hero's name was conflated with the word for grandmother (*bobbe*) and the widely used Yiddish expression metamorphosed into *bobbe-maiseh*, or "grandmother's tale."

The first collection of secular songs in Yiddish was compiled by Eisik Wallisch of Worms from about 1595 to 1605. It contains texts only for fifty-four poems: love songs, humorous songs, etc. Many of them are identical to German songs of the period with Christian references changed to appropriate Jewish ones. Twelve of them seem to have been written by Jews, for they are "peppered with Hebrew words and phrases," as Idelssohn puts it. It is of some interest to note that Wallisch's collection contains no songs of mourning, woe, or self-pity, even though they are taken from the area of Worms, which suffered greatly from pogroms in the time of the crusades and again in the time of repeated waves of bubonic plague in the latter part of the fourteenth century, when Jews were charged with having poisoned the wells. These songs concentrated instead on celebrating the joyous aspects of life.

In all those cases only the text was printed, not the music. Readers of the *Shmuel Buch* were instructed to sing it "in the tune which is known and popular among all Israel," but however popular that melody may have been at one time, it has now been lost.

One reason for its loss may have been a dramatic break in cultural continuity that occurred about the middle of the seventeenth century, when Eastern Europe was struck by an appalling series of events that shattered Jewish life there. In 1648 a former officer of the Polish army, Bogdan Chmelnitzki, led a cobbled-together army of Cossacks and Tatars in a revolution against the oppressive Polish regime. A three-year reign of terror ensued, with especially horrifying results for the Jews, who were singled out by the marauding hordes for murder, rape, and torture, although the Polish population did not escape unscathed. Weakened by the cost of putting down the Chmelnitzki rebellion, Poland was an inviting target for invasions, which followed immediately. Russia attacked from the East and Sweden from the North. While the Russian troops laid waste to everything indiscriminately, the Swedish armies progressed in a slightly more civilized manner, even protecting Jews against lawless elements in the Polish population that took advantage of the chaos to pillage local Jews. The result, though, was that after the war the Polish population believed that the Jews had been in league with the invading Swedes, and "the pogroms from which they had been spared by the Swedes were loosed upon them by the Poles, their own neighbors."[8] In ten years of unremitting wars, pogroms, and massacres, at least 100,000 Eastern European Jews were killed, and the tattered remnant of what had been a thriving Jewish culture survived in the direst poverty and unremitting fear.

If that were not enough, hopes of return to Zion that had been raised in the same fateful year (1648) by the self-proclaimed messiah Sabbetai (or Shabtai) Zevi, were dashed in 1666 when that widely admired hero cravenly chose conversion to Islam over death after being presented with those alternatives by the Sultan of Turkey. The spirit of the entire Jewish community, aroused

---

[7] "Bovo-Buch," *Encyclopedia Judaica* (Jerusalem: Keter, 1971), 4:1276.

[8] Solomon Grayzel, *A History of the Jews from the Babylonian Exile to the Establishment of Israel* (Philadelphia: Jewish Publications Society of America, 1963), 511.

to fever pitch by the charlatan's dramatic posturing, was cast into deepest despair. The sense of hopelessness that followed the Chmelnitzki massacres, wars, pogroms, and the great let-down of Sabbetai Zevi, virtually crushed any creative spark left in the Jews of Eastern Europe.

It was not until the eighteenth-century rise of mystical Chasidism under the leadership of Israel ben Eliezer (ca. 1700-60), called the "Baal Shem Tov" (Master of the Good Name), and his unwilling opponent, Elijah ben Solomon (1720-97), the *Ga'on* (sage) of Vilna, that the situation in Eastern Europe changed. The basis of Chassidism was anti-intellectual, while the *Ga'on's* reforms called for a return to the roots of Judaism by stripping away the hyper-sophisticated overlay of obtuse *piyyutim* and talmudic hair-splitting. The "Besht," as the followers of the Baal Shem Tov abbreviated his title, emphasized self-knowledge achieved through ecstatic prayer, song, and dance, and stressed the role of the charismatic, wonder-working *rebbe*; the *Ga'on's* road was one of objective study and wisdom. A bitter rivalry arose between the two schools of thought, creating a rift that, in some circles, exists to this day.

That rivalry had at least one constructive aspect in that it blew aside the torpor of the preceding generations and energized renewed Jewish creativity. A specialty of the chassidim was the *nigun*, a wordless melody hummed or sung on nonsense syllables such as "ya-ba-bam," or "bim-bom." These infectious tunes were sung as table songs or at celebrations, where they might be repeated endlessly in an almost hypnotic manner, inducing a fervent sense of community and rising religious ecstasy that played a part in attracting many young people into the Chasidic fold. They were sometimes composed by the *rebbe* himself, but might just as often be written by one of his followers and attributed to the group's spiritual leader. Hundreds of those *nigunim* became current in the late eighteenth and nineteenth century. Most were specific to a particular Chasidic sect or its *rebbe*, and were often prescribed for a specific circumstance, such as following the *Shabbat* meal, accompanying certain religious observances and life-cycle events, or particular days of the week. Many of those melodies have been published in recent years in collections such as the *Sefer ha-nigunim* (Book of Melodies), a compilation of melodies from the *Chabad movement* edited and annotated (in Hebrew) by Rabbi Samuel Zalmanoff, with melodies notated by S. Silbermintz (Kfar Chabad, Israel: "Nichach", n.d.).

Parallel to those *nigunim* the nineteenth century saw the growth of an entire body of new settings—or borrowed music—for medieval *piyyutim* that had long served as table songs or celebration songs. Others were transformed into hymns for the synagogue service, while a third class of newly composed songs took the place long held by secular folk songs. A resurgence of Jewish folk song grew in the last years of the nineteenth century that was to find its echo in the explosion of the popular music industry in the twentieth century.

Jewish Entertainment Professionals

Jewish entertainers were known by different names in local languages, as we have already seen, but among early Yiddish-speaking Jews all such designations were secondary to the Yiddish term *shpilman* (player). By the Middle Ages there was already a long tradition of the *shpilman* as a community entertainer whose principal employment was to provide entertainment for weddings, because the responsibility to "gladden the heart of the bride" was virtually an article of faith. At those occasions the *shpilman* might himself act as jester (Hebrew: *badchan*, or *leitzan*, "clown"), or might call on the talents of another who was quick of tongue and wit to serve as a *badchan*.[9] It was the role of the *badchan* to poke good-natured fun at the young couple, their families, and assorted guests, in cleverly improvised rhymed couplets.

The merriment of the Purim holiday afforded a professional opportunity for the entertainer, who might perform songs in praise of Queen Esther's beauty or Mordechai's staunch faithfulness, not to mention songs and dances poking fun at the sensual, but basically good-willed King Ahashueros, or the scheming villain, Haman. Such performances often expanded into *Purimshpils* (Purim plays), complete with music and dancing. On other joyous holidays the *shpilman's* talents were also called upon to provide Torah songs and dances at *Simchat Torah*, or songs about the exodus for *Pesach*. Most of this music was improvised, so most of the earliest examples have been lost, or at best, preserved in later transcriptions altered to conform to the style of subsequent generations. But the influence of the *shpilman* and Purim plays extended far beyond their original audiences. Their heritage laid the groundwork for strong musical institutions and a tradition of performing excellence in the Jewish community.

Klezmer

The musicians who shaped this tradition came to be known as *klezmorim* (sing., *klezmer*), a Yiddish term conflating the two Hebrew words *kle zemer* (musical instruments). Some villages had their own village musician and a few even boasted their own band, though it might be only two or three players; but the musical needs of the people were met, more often than not, by traveling musicians. Leo Rosten writes:

> As characters, the shabby *klezmorim* were familiar to all Ashkenazic Jews: they were regarded as drifters, odd types, itinerant minstrels. . . . In many places Jewish musicians played at Christian religious ceremonies. They were, indeed, preferred . . . because of their reputation for "modesty and sobriety."[10]

Some of the larger towns, especially toward the end of the period, had real orchestras with a dozen or more musicians, but the wandering ensembles of klezmorim usually consisted of a handful of players who performed for dances, weddings, funerals, or other occasions calling for the expenditure of a few *kopeks* or *pfennigs* to provide entertainment. Between engagements they might perform in the streets of some town, hoping grateful listeners would throw out a coin or two for them. Occasionally they would even play for a church festival or town fair. The

---

[9] The term is built on the Hebrew root *BDCh*, signifying "joke." The *badchan* was what we would today call an "emcee," or "stand-up comic."

[10] Leo Calvin Rosten, *The Joys of Yiddish: A Relaxed Lexicon of Yiddish, Hebrew and Yinglish Words Often Encountered in English . . . from the Days of the Bible to Those of the Beatnik* (New York: McGraw-Hill, 1968), 183-84.

most common instrumentation consisted of a melody instrument and bass, sometimes with a singer, who might be a third member of the troupe or might be one of the instrumentalists. The addition of a drummer was highly desirable, if available, or alternatively a *tsimbalum* player might do double duty in providing both harmonic and rhythmic support on that zither-like instrument. Medieval and Renaissance pictures show such musicians playing recorders, krummhorns, shawms, bagpipes, viols, lutes, and percussion of various kinds. By the nineteenth century the melody instrument was most often a violin, and the musical style tended toward a mixture of Eastern European folk song and oriental modal formulas from the synagogue tied together by the performers' improvisatory skill.

The influence of such musicians and their place in the history of European music is hard to gauge, because they left little in the way of written records. Most of their music was memorized and/or improvised, and they played under informal circumstances, so no newspaper reviews or learned articles were written about them. Occasionally, though, some small piece of evidence, such as the *Lochamer Liederbuch*, seeps through the historical net to afford a glimpse of the thriving world of the *klezmer*. One such item comes up in a brief account of the Czech composer and violin virtuoso Franz Benda, published by the English musician Charles Burney in 1775. Burney had undertaken a tour of Europe to meet and hear musicians and assess the musical achievements of different countries on the continent in preparation for writing his great *History of Music* (London, 1776). He carried letters of introduction to Europe's most important musicians from colleagues working in England at that time. It was through such a letter given to him by the Italian violinist Felice Giardini, that he obtained an interview with the famous virtuoso, Franz Benda, already past sixty and no longer playing in public.

According to Burney, "The gout has long enfeebled his [Benda's] fingers; however, there are fine remains of a great hand."[11] Burney goes on to sing the praises of his subject, once renowned throughout Europe as a most extraordinary violinist with a "fine tone, so remarkably full, clear, and sweet . . . a very affecting player . . . several able professors have assured me that he has frequently drawn tears from them."[12] Burney then recounts Benda's life story from his beginnings as a choirboy to the height of his fame. He tells us that when Benda's adolescent voice broke and he could no longer sing in the choir of the Kreuzhorn convent at Prague, he turned to playing dance music to earn his living. Here is Burney's account of that period in his life, as told to him by the aging musician:

> After losing his voice, he [Benda] had no other means of turning his musical talents to account, than by playing dances about the country with a company of Jews, in which, however, there was a blind Hebrew, of the name of Löbel, who in his way, was an extraordinary player. He drew a good tone from his instrument, and composed his own pieces, which were wild, but pretty: some of his dances went up to A in *altissimo*; however, he played

---

[11] Charles Burney, *The Present State of Music in Germany, Netherlands, and the United Provinces or, A Tour Through Those Countries, Undertaken to Collect Materials for a General History of Music*, 2 vols. (London: J. Robson and G Robinson, 1775), 1:173.

[12] Ibid.

them with the utmost purity and neatness. The performance of this man excited in Benda so much jealousy, that he redoubled his diligence in trying to equal him; and not to be inferior in any part of his trade, he composed dances for his own hand, which were far from easy. He often speaks of his obligations to the old Jew for stimulating him to excel on the violin.[13]

Here one of the great virtuosi of the eighteenth century speaks not just of the presence of *klezmorim* but of the high quality of musicianship found among them. It also shows that Jewish and Christian musicians could work together professionally in the world of popular music at a time when that was not true for society as a whole.

Late Developments in Western Europe

The extent to which Jews and Christians worked together professionally was colored by the nature of the society in which they lived. Italy, as we have seen, honored Jewish musicians for their talent for a number of generations, overlooking their religion to the extent that Christian law and zealous authorities permitted that to happen. Protestant England was another such country. An act removing civil disabilities from citizens of the Jewish religion was first submitted to the House of Commons in 1753, and such bills actually passed the House of Commons but were struck down by the House of Lords several times (1833, 1834, 1836). Civil rights of Jews in England remained circumscribed by law until 1858, 105 years after the first Jewish Naturalization Bill had been submitted, but active persecution of the Jews was not government policy after the Restoration (1660) and re-admission of Jews into the country. So it is not unexpected to find notable Jewish musicians in eighteenth-century London.

Perhaps the first of those to be mentioned should be James Cervetto, whose birth name was Giaccobe Basevi Cervetto (1682-1783), an Italian cellist who may have come to London as early as 1728. He seems to have been invited to England by George Frederick Handel, who had known Cervetto when they were young musicians together in Italy. Cervetto's presence in London is documented as fact by 1738, and soon after that he gained prominence as England's most famous cellist. It is unlikely that he "introduced the playing of the cello into England," as the *Encyclopedia Judaica* would have it;[14] but there is little question that he was one of the first—or perhaps the very first—to bring that instrument to prominence with his virtuosity, and he, more than anyone else, was responsible for its rise in popularity and the eclipse of the gentler viola da gamba in his adopted country.

It is possible that information about Purim plays passed along to Handel by Cervetto influenced the composer's choice of subject for his first oratorio, *Haman and Mordechai*, later reworked as *Esther*, presented around Purim to great acclaim, especially from London's Jewish community. Cervetto became the principal cellist at Drury Lane Theatre, from which vantage point he may have conducted the orchestra, since many writers attribute that post to him,

---

[13] Burney, 1:175.

[14] *Encyclopedia Judaica*, 4:289-90.

although he does not seem to have held the title formally. He was a favorite with musicians, actors, and the audience, who often called for him by his nickname, "Nosy." He was also on good terms with the actors. According to one anecdote, he yawned noisily one evening while the great actor David Garrick was portraying a drunkard on stage. Garrick, offended, stopped the scene and censured his friend in the orchestra pit. "I beg your pardon," Cervetto is supposed to have answered loudly enough to be heard throughout the theater, "I always yawn when I am very pleased."[15] In spite of his Jewish origins, which he never denied, Cervetto left orders in his will to be buried in the Anglican Church. He left a sizable fortune of £20,000 to his son James (1747-1837), who was also a cello virtuoso. Both father and son left a handful of virtuoso chamber compositions for their own instrument alone or in combination with others that, while never rising to greatness, were characteristic and pleasing.

Other musicians of Jewish origin in eighteenth-century London ranged from a stage singer-comedian who performed under the name "Jew Davis" to the popular Abrams sisters, Theodosia, Elizabeth, and Harriet, who sang individually and as a trio. Of those three, Harriet also made her mark as a composer and concert promoter. Perhaps the most famous of them, though, was John Braham, who, at the end of the eighteenth century and into the nineteenth, was acclaimed one of the finest tenors England had ever produced. In recognition of that he was chosen by composer Karl Maria von Weber to create the leading role of Max in his popular opera, *Der Freischütz* (The Magic Bullet). Braham was born in 1774, the son of Abraham Prosnitz (d. 1779), a chorister in London's Great Synagogue. After his father's death he sold pencils on the streets of London while still a boy, but his musical talent was soon recognized, and he was taken up by Meyer Leoni, *chazzan* of the Great Synagogue, who introduced him into services there as his "assistant"— that is, as a *meshorer*.[16] At the age of thirteen he sang his first engagement at the famed Covent Garden (21 April 1787), where he sang a song by British composer Thomas Augustine Arne, "The soldier, tired of war's alarms," known for its "truly alarming roulades, in a style which challenged comparison with Madame Mara, a celebrated coloratura of those times, when, let us not forget, the art of coloratura singing was at a very high pitch of perfection."[17] He adopted the name Braham as a memorial to his father, Abraham. A skillful composer of popular songs as well as a singer, he wrote about a dozen operettas and many songs himself, including "The Death of Nelson," which was still in print at the beginning of the twentieth century. Braham converted to the Anglican faith early in his career, but was almost universally known as "the little Jew" (he was quite short). He led a scandalous life, touring with the well-known soprano Nancy Storace, who bore him an illegitimate son who would later become a clergyman in the Church of England. He died in 1856 at the end of a long career in opera, on the concert stage, and as an (unsuccessful) owner-manager of a London theatre. Before the end of his career his concert tours included almost every country in Europe, and in 1840-41, the United States as well.

One final Jewish-British musician who deserves mention is Isaac Nathan (1790-1864), who will be cited again in our discussion of synagogue music. Nathan was a fascinating, scholarly sort of musician, who attempted to earn his living as a singer and composer, and failed at both.

---

[15] V. Wasielewski, *The Cello* (London: n.p., 1888), 51-52.

[16] For further discussion of this term see chapter 7.

[17] John Mewburn Levien, *The Singing of John Braham* (London: Novello and Co., 1944), 10.

He seems to have served his country as a spy in France (with less than desirable results for himself) and, in 1841, fled England under an ignominious cloud of debt. "Not much of a success story," one might think, but it is a story more worth telling than the bare facts might suggest.

Isaac Nathan was the eldest son of Menachem Mona of Canterbury, one of the many Jewish-Polish refugee cantors found all over Western Europe. What was different about Isaac's family was his claim that his grandmother had been the mistress of Stanislaus Poniatowski, the last king of Poland, which might have made him an (unlikely) heir to the no-longer-existing Polish throne. To this day there is no evidence to either prove or disprove his doubtful, but entirely plausible, story. Trained in *chazzanut* by his father, he was apprenticed to the London musician Domenico Corri in 1809. While doing advanced studies with Corri, he assisted the master by teaching piano and voice to well-bred young ladies on occasions when that worthy was hiding from his creditors, which in Corri's case, was frequently. It was in that capacity that he met Rosetta Worthington, a non-Jewish young woman who would become his wife.

Nathan became acquainted with the poet, Lord Byron, and collaborated with him by making musical settings based on synagogue melodies for some of Byron's poems. The result was a collection of twenty-six songs first published in 1815 under the title, *Hebrew Melodies*. The unknown twenty-five-year-old musician enlisted the famous John Braham to promote sale of the collection not only by singing the songs, but by adding his name to the book as co-composer. The ploy worked, but Nathan's name was eclipsed by Braham's enormous popularity, and all notice of him was lost in the popular adulation of Braham and Byron. Nathan went on to attempt appearances as a singer in light operas, but his voice, though sweet and well modulated, was too small for theatre in those days before microphones. He was a little more successful as a composer, and wrote several light musicals as well as a number of songs. In 1823 he published an important tome, *Musurgia Vocalis*, about which more will be said in chapter 7.

The last act of Nathan's life opened with what is said to have been a secret assignment to France spying for King William IV. Unfortunately, though Nathan claims to have sent back much valuable information, the King died while he was abroad, and since the assignment was secret, he was denied any salary for his services by the new Chancellor of the Exchequer. Hard pressed for money, he fled with his wife and child to Australia, where he successfully concertized, composed light music, took up music publishing, and conducted the first studies of Australian aboriginal music. His grandson was also a composer, best known for the jaunty song, "Waltzing Matilda." Five generations later, the most recent musician stemming from his line is the well-known Australian conductor, Sir Charles Mackerras.

Writers on Music

There was far less theorizing about music among Jewish musicians in Medieval Europe than we saw among those of the Islamic world. European life became oppressively difficult for Jews, and simply surviving took enough of their resources that fringe subjects such as music theory received little attention. For a while, Jewish life was a bit freer in Southern France, the culturally and linguistically distinct region known as the *Langue d'Oc*. There, Jews fared some-what better, at least until a heady mixture of politics, economics, and religion resulted in the so-called "Albigensian Crusade," in which the Northern French Christians crushed Southern France, decimating its population and virtually destroying its brilliant, poetic culture.[18] During the flowering of Southern France's greatness, enormous energy was devoted to poetic and philosophical introspection by Jews as well as their Christian counterparts. Most noteworthy among the Jewish philosophers of was Rabbi Shelomo Itzchak (1040-1105), better known by the acronym Rashi, from the first letters of his title and name. Rashi was not a musician, but a tireless and brilliant religious commentator. His common-sense readings of the most abstruse passages of the Bible are still studied today, yet he had the humility and intellectual honesty to simply say, when he encountered material he could not clarify, "I cannot explain this." It would be too much of an excursion to try to cover all his accomplishments, but one in particular comes to mind in connection with our topic. Rashi transliterated many terms of the Bible into the *Langue d'Oc* using Hebrew letters and vowels to explain them to his readers. His transliterations preserved the pronunciation of that language, and are used by its students to this day. Among the many terms he transcribed and explained were names of musical instruments mentioned in the Bible. Much of what we know about those instruments we owe to Rashi and his thorough research.

In the fourteenth century the phenomenal Jewish polymath Levi ben Gershon (1288-1344), known to western scholars by the Greek name Gersonides, in Hebrew by the acronym "Ralbag," and in scholastic Latin as Magister Leo Hebraeus, played an unusual and influential role in European music. Known primarily for his books on philosophical and theoretical speculation, in 1343 he wrote a Latin treatise, *De Numeris harmonicis* (On Harmonic Numbers) further developing the mathematics by which he had earlier laid the theoretical basis for Bishop Phillipe de Vitry's book, *Ars Nova* on special commission from the Bishop. De Vitry's book is credited with revolutionizing music notation and paving the way for modern music, but its mathematical basis was provided by "the Ralbag."

The rich culture of the southern French Jewish community was related to that of Northern Spain by proximity, of course; but even more, Jewish melodies were exchanged through the close relations maintained by those communities and later, by the stream of Jewish refugees who fled the Inquisition. Judith Kaplan Eisenstein has demonstrated that significant melodic content of modern Jewish synagogue music of Southern France draws on medieval Sephardic sources.[19] She cites a computer study of musical motives from synagogue melodies of this area showing that Jewish melodies not notated before the late nineteenth century can be stylistically identified as different from those of their non-Jewish contemporaries. Her analysis of those melodies reveals ties to medieval song styles of the Sephardic tradition, showing Hispanic roots for what we might expect to be purely French melodic blossoms.

On the whole, Southern Europe was generally a little less inhospitable to the Jewish presence than the North. The relatively greater freedom of Jewish life in Italy encouraged more speculative writing about music, just as it had produced more professional opportunities for Jewish musicians. In the fifteenth century Jacob Haim Farissol and Yohanan ben Isaac Alemanno reflected the

---

[18] The *Langue d'oc* area and much of its population were brutally destroyed in the first half of the thirteenth century when Pope Innocent III, in league with the northern French, launched a crusade against the Albigensian heresy in the South. The area was so disastrously desolated that it did not completely recover until the twentieth century.

[19] Eisenstein, "Medieval Elements," 9-29.

new attitudes of the Renaissance in praising the importance of music in general education. Juda ben Isaac authored a treatise ca. 1567 translating the notational methods of the fourteenth-century Italian theorist Marchetto da Padua into Hebrew.[20] The late sixteenth-century rabbi Yehuda Moscato was noted for his sermons on music, which were collected and published only two years before his death as *Nefuzot Yehuda* (Dispersions of Judah, Venice, 1588-89). In 1612, the famous Mantuan physician, Rabbi Abraham ben David Portaleone (1542-1612), devoted several chapters of his last book, *Shiltei ha-Gibborim* (Shields of the Heroes, published posthumously in 1612), to the music of the Bible. His book was "the first and most all-inclusive attempt of a Jewish commentator steeped in Renaissance culture, to describe systematically the musical theory, songs, and instruments that were used for ritual purposes in the Temple."[21] As we will see in the next chapter, all this activity was reflected in music for the synagogue as well.

Suggestions for Further Reading

Abrahams, Israel, and Cecil Roth. *Jewish Life in the Middle Ages*. London: E. Goldston Ltd., 1932.

Binder, Abraham Wolf. *Studies in Jewish Music: Collected Writings of A. W. Binder*, ed. Irene Heskes. New York: Bloch Pub. Co., 1971.

Elon, Amos. *The Pity of it All: A History of the Jews in Germany, 1743-1933*. New York: Henry Holt & Co.; Metropolitan Books, 2002.

Glückl (of Hameln). *The Life of Glückl of Hameln 1646-1724 Written by Herself*. Ed. Beth-Zion Abrahams. New York: Thomas Yoseloff, 1963.

Greenbaum, Masha. *The Jews of Lithuania: A History of a Remarkable Community 1316-1945*. Jerusalem: Gofen, 1995.

Lowenthal, Marvin. *The Jews of Germany: A Story of Sixteen Centuries*. Philadelphia: The Jewish Publication Society, 1936.

Rothmüller, Aaron Marko. *The Music of the Jews*. Trans. H. S. Stevens. Cranbury, NJ: A. S. Barnes and Company, 1967.

Saminsky, Lazare. *Music of the Ghetto and the Bible*. New York: Bloch Publishing Company, 1934.

Shiloah, Amnon. *Jewish Musical Traditions*. Detroit: Wayne State University Press, 1992.

Slobin, Mark. *Old Jewish Folk Music: The Collections and Writings of Moshe Beregovski*. Philadelphia: University of Pennsylvania Press, 1982.

---

[20] See Israel Adler, "Le traité anonyme du manuscrit hébreu 1037 de la Bibliothéque Nationale de Paris," in *Yuval: Studies of the Jewish Music Research Centre* (Jerusalem: Magnes Press of the Hebrew University, 1968), 1-47.

[21] Amnon Shiloah, *Jewish Musical Traditions* (Detroit: Wayne State University Press, 1992), 64.

7 | Synagogue Music from the Destruction of the Temple to 1800

The Early Synagogue and the Growth of its Liturgy

The music of the synagogue from the destruction of the temple to about 1800 was characterized by two distinctive developments: the adoption of polyphony and growth of the unique soloistic style known as *chazzanut*. Following the destruction of the temple, the synagogue, which had been a peripheral institution, moved to the center of religious life. Creating a liturgy for synagogue worship was one of the first priorities for Jewish life in exile, but couching that liturgy in an appropriate musical setting followed not far behind. The requirements of the synagogue were quite different from those of the temple, and developing suitable music became an important part of that religious redefinition. An overview of the contemporary liturgical plan was given in chapter 1, and the informally structured worship service of Hellenistic and Roman times was outlined in chapter 3. Here we will trace the main elements of the Jewish worship service from the synagogue's post-destruction move into the center of Jewish worship to the more-or-less final shape it took after the sixteenth century.

Before the first Babylonian exile, prayers of supplication were only given communal voice in time of distress. Daily and seasonal sacrifices were conducted in the Temple by the *kohanim* (priests) with music provided by the Levites. Participation of all other attendees in those ceremonies was restricted to responsive affirmations such as *hallelujah* (praised be God) or *amen* (so be it). The idea of regular public worship outside the temple did not exist in pre-exilic Judaism. Only after returning from Babylon in the sixth century BCE did any such practice begin to take shape. Gradually, during the period of the second temple, those occasional prayers developed into a set ritual, "performed at certain times and with certain stipulated texts in a certain order."[1]

---

[1] Idelsohn, *Jewish Music*, 72.

Although the Jewish commonwealth boasted a royal house and a priestly hierarchy, Judaism harbored a democratic streak that saw everyone as equally near to God and equally subject to God's law. The prophet Nathan did not hesitate to attack King David for thinking he was above the law (II Samuel 12), and Micah raised a flag of popular religion, subversive to the priestly cult, in writing, "What doth the Lord require of thee: to act justly, love mercy, and walk humbly with thy God." No mention is found there of obeisance to royalty or of sacrifices and subservience to the priestly class. Even within the Temple service itself an institution developed to provide for representation of the populace. Selected inhabitants of Judean villages who were not of priestly descent were divided into twenty-four groups called *ma'amadot* (representatives), and invited to take part serially in the daily sacrifice at the temple. Since not everyone could go to Jerusalem, a few were chosen from each group, while those who remained at home gathered to read the required portions of the Pentateuch. That became one of the roots of the synagogue service. Only in the last years of the Hasmonean dynasty did the synagogue become primarily a place of worship, and only then did any need begin to be felt for a fixed liturgy.

The *Mishnah* tells us that the service during the reign of Herod, in the last years of the Temple, consisted of reading the Ten Commandments and selected psalms by the priest officiating at sacrifices. The Ten Commandments were later replaced by the *Sh'ma Yisrael*, the song of the Israelites at the crossing of the sea, and the priestly benedictions, all taken from the Pentateuch. The rabbis of the *Mishnah* did not originally favor a predetermined plan for prayer, as we have seen. Nevertheless, dispersion of the Jewish people led to the conclusion that a standardized liturgy was necessary to keep widely separated communities from developing local variations that could, over generations, lead to schisms. Even though a liturgical plan was developed, controversy still occasionally arose between liturgical practice in some Diaspora communities and those of the homeland. Some of those differences were settled, others led to variations between Palestinian and Babylonian or Alexandrian practice, or between Ashkenazim and Sephardim; but on the whole, the overriding sense of communal responsibility, expressed in the often-reiterated phrase *klal Yisrael* (community of Israel), led to more-or-less amicable resolutions of those disputes. As a result, Talmudic Judaism entered the Middle Ages with a unified, though not monolithic, ritual tradition. During that early period of liturgical fluidity new blessings based on verses from the Prophets (*Nevi'im*) and Writings (*Ketubim*) were composed to introduce biblical readings. Other blessings and time-linked pronouncements were added to announce new months, festivals, or seasons of the year. Their adoption, together with the desire to have a common prayer practice for all Jews no matter where they lived, favored the development of a formal liturgy.

That, then, was the situation in the late Roman period. It was not until the fourth century CE that either the founding fathers of Christianity or Jewish scholars of the Talmud developed any real theory about how one worshipped outside the Jerusalem Temple,[2] but the framework of a rabbinic liturgy was in place by then. That was about the same time that the Nicene Council (ca. 325 CE) fixed the content of the Christian liturgy, showing similar concerns on the part of the Church. By then Christianity had separated from Judaism and, as we have already seen, each group formulated its own ideas about the role of communal worship. Pharisaic/Rabbinic Judaism,

---

[2] Stefan C. Reif, "The Early History of Jewish Worship," in *The Making of Jewish and Christian Worship*, ed. Paul F. Bradshaw and Lawrence A. Hoffman (Notre Dame: Notre Dame University Press, 1991), 111.

striving to maintain continuity with the history and traditions of the ancestral faith while redefining its practice, resolved the question of liturgy with several far-reaching decisions of a practical nature that shaped synagogue worship from that time forward. Those included the abandonment of ritual sacrifice, downplaying the centrality of the priestly class without abolishing it, and structuring a participatory worship service. A few of the temple's specifically public ceremonies were absorbed into the synagogue to stress continuity. Among those were sounding the *shofar*, reciting the priestly benedictions, and celebrating the major festivals. Great stress was laid on the communal aspects of Judaism. A *minyan* of at least ten men was required to hold a full public service, and the reciprocal responsibilities of each individual to the community, and conversely, of the community to the individual, became a mainstay of Talmudic thought. As the liturgy coalesced, blessings, prayers, supplications, and even confessions of sin were couched in the first person plural to stress that communalism. In addition to biblical passages that had been recited in the days of the temple, new prayers were written expressly aimed at supporting a Diaspora existence. The ritual was continually enriched to about the end of the seventh century, by which point it had taken on much of its present form. Additional passages and *piyyutim* were added until as late as the sixteenth century, when the first printed *siddurim* (prayer books) made some degree of standardization of the two major forms of the liturgy—Ashkenazic and Sephardic—a reality. Exactly how it got to that form, though, is not always clear, because there are so few documents that discuss what must have seemed, to those taking part in it, natural growth and development. "By the time we find literary sources about the liturgy," wrote its most famous historian, "it is already a finished product, with no witness to the centuries of its emergence and the first steps of its development."[3]

What we do know about the early formation of the liturgy may be summarized as follows. The *Sh'ma* and Tefillah, as discussed in chapter 3, became the basis of the synagogue service. The *Kedushah*, a form of doxology, was an early adoption, as was the *Kaddish*, which originated in synagogue study and predated the emergence of a formal liturgy. Other prayer types found in the Jewish liturgy incuded *Hallel* (hymns of praise), *Techinah* or *Tachanun* (petition), *Selicha* (intercession for pardon), *Viddui* (confession), and *Kinah* (lamentation). In addition, the ancient practice of reading from the Torah became part of the synagogue service, as did the rabbinic *drash*, or interpretation of the reading. Originally, those called up to read the Torah could choose any reading from the prophets they thought would be a suitable accompaniment to the Torah portion, but that was changed during the Middle Ages by the assignment of fixed prophetical verses to accompany each weekly Torah reading. Additional prayers and *piyyutim* were added as late as the sixteenth century, when the first printed prayer books (*siddurim*) made it a more realistic possibility to standardize the worship service.

Position of Music in the Liturgy

Post-destruction rabbis, as we have seen, decreed a ban on music and musical instruments as a sign of communal grief over the temple's destruction. Rab Huna, of third-century Babylonia, went so far as to prohibit all music in that community, which effectively crushed—or at least dampened—all festivities. His colleague at the Sura academy, Rab Hisda, took a more humane

---

[3] Elbogen, 188.

tack, canceling that over-zealous ruling and permitting the use of instruments for joyous celebrations such as weddings. If nothing else, that debate demonstrated that the place of music in
society was a matter that could even cause the two famous "Pious Ones of Babylonia" to disagree.

It was universally agreed, though, that no instruments were to be used in the synagogue,
for instrumental music continued to have negative associations that made it inappropriate for
a people in bereavement. Two important exceptions were generally recognized: weddings, where
the tradition of "gladdening the heart of the bride" overrode the prohibition of instrumental
music, and funerals. In the matter of funerals, the ancient Middle East sustained a long tradition
of mourning music provided by the family of the deceased. For this, women professionally
skilled at *kinah*,[4] or mourning laments, were hired along with players of the flute, in proportion
to the mourner's wealth. In those two cases powerful social traditions overrode rabbinic proscription. But the full restoration of instrumental music for worship, it was felt, should await the
restoration of the temple, when it could be practiced once again by Levites within the prescribed
confines of those sacred premises.

While instrumental music suffered from its association with the tavern and brothel, vocal
music did not have such strong negative connotations, and was welcomed into the synagogue
as a means of encouraging congregational participation. Congregational hymn singing offered
at least two culturally attractive features. The first was the sense of spiritual community that
resulted from singing together. One sang as an individual, but participation in the congregation
blended single voices into a qualitatively different sonority, one that symbolically expressed
both the importance of music's indivisible source in each singer and its communal expression
as a chorus. The second function, while more prosaic, was no less important. In those days of
hand-copied books, few had the prayers written in front of them and even fewer would have
been capable of reading them had they been available. Experience showed that prayers set to
music could be remembered more easily and fixed in the memory more permanently than
those memorized as speech.[5] The rabbis therefore scorned what they called "Greek virtuosity,"
and advocated simple, unadorned melodies that could be easily sung by all.

They were not the only ones concerned with the role of music in worship. In the fourth
century, Saint Augustine, Bishop of Hippo in North Africa and himself quite knowledgeable
about music, pondered whether he was enjoying the musical performance of certain church
singers at the expense of the song's religious content. He reached the same conclusion as the
rabbis: religious music must be beautiful enough to please the ear, and thus draw the listener
into worship; but it should not be too beautiful, lest hearers focus on the beauty of the music
itself and not on the texts for which it was a vehicle. Where to draw that line would continue
to be a problem for the church, as well as the synagogue. Admittedly, Hellenistic music seems

---

[4] From *kinah* we get the English word "to keen," meaning "to wail with grief." As such songs were normally
sung by women, *kinah* may also be related to the Arabic word *qaina*, meaning a singing-dancing girl, which ultimately
refers back to Cain's daughters, reputed by the Arabs to have invented the first musical instruments.

[5] This has been borne out by modern research into mapping of the brain, which shows that music is commonly
stored in the right half of the brain, text in the left. Texted songs, however, appear to be stored in the right brain as
a single *Gestalt* (i.e., music and text together), and again in the left brain, where the meaning of the text is stored
separately, so that the two reinforce each other. This also strengthens the case for the old method of rabbinic study in
which everything from the letters of the alphabet to complex Talmudic argument was memorized in a musical chant.

to have been sensual and its texts licentious. In the second century CE Rabbi Elisha ben Abuyah, though recognized as a brilliant thinker, was ejected as an apostate for his admiration of Greek thought. One of the charges laid against him was that he sang Greek songs.[6] The compilers of the Talmud, while acknowledging his contributions, never mention him by name, but register his thought only as *ha-acher* (the other). Rabbinic opposition to such music was so strong that Abba Areka (beginning of third century CE) scowled, "an ear that listens to [secular] music shall be torn out." That was an especially strong condemnation from a man who was reputed to have been a fine singer himself, although he restricted his singing to the synagogue.

The importance of Jewish converts to Christianity in the formation of Christian worship modes has already been noted in chapter 3. In the following centuries there would be still more such activity, leading many to believe that there may be more evidence of the nature of ancient Jewish music in the earliest church than exists today in the synagogue. Peter Jeffery, reversing the opinion of earlier scholars who doubted the extent of Jewish influence on Christian chant, shows that the forms and melodic material of Jerusalem chant exercised great influence on the Latin, Greek, Armenian, and Syriac chant repertories.[7] A composer known as Romanos (d. sometime after 555 CE), a Jew from Homs (Syria) who converted to Christianity, was a prodigious writer of *kontakia*, metrical Greek Christian hymns based on oriental models. He was highly esteemed by his contemporaries, who called him *"Melodos"* (Song-Maker). An astonishing total of about one thousand Byzantine church hymns are attributed to him. To what extent those hymns adhered to Jewish models is not clear, but if he was like most composers it would be unlikely that he completely abandoned the style of his youth.

Initially, then, synagogue music was restricted to congregational song in simple, straight-forward melodies. It was only a matter of time, though, before the people's natural inclination for song triumphed over the prohibitions of the rabbis, and music began to grow in importance within the synagogue as much as in the general community.

"Modes" of Synagogue Music

The music of the early synagogue, like all music of the ancient world, was monophonic—that is, it consisted of a single melodic line without harmony. Structurally, it was based on melodic modes. The word "mode" describes a collection of musical characteristics that a society has recognized as belonging to a single family, based on learned psychological responses evoked by music in that culture. A particular mode usually has three musical qualities that identify it: interval structure, range, and melodic type. It may also be marked by being centered on a particular home pitch, as will be seen in the following discussion of the separate modes. If that sounds rather abstract, try thinking of the interval structure of a mode as the alphabet of musical intervals out of which melodies might be made. Such an alphabet can be most easily represented by using pitch names (*A*, *B*, *C*, etc.), but those should not be construed as actual pitches. It is not the notes themselves that are important, but the intervals between them, for it is the interval

---

[6] Milton Steinberg wrote a fascinating novel, *As a Driven Leaf* (New York: Bobbs-Merrill, 1939), which fictionalizes the life of that exiled sage.

[7] Jeffery, "The Earliest Christian Chant Repertory," 1-38.

structure, not the pitches, that form what is here called the "alphabet" of the mode. Pitch-names make a convenient short-hand, but they must not be construed as constituting the mode any more than mile-markers on a highway constitute miles.

As to the second feature, "range," the actual pitches used for a mode would depend on the range of the singer's voice—for we are only talking about vocal performance here. In practice, a mode might be sung a little higher or lower ("transposed up or down," in musical terminology) to another set of pitches that produced the same intervals, as long as it remained in more or less the same placement in the voice. Some are "high" modes, others, "low," but "high" in a tenor's voice would not be the same set of pitches as "high" for a baritone.

Finally, there is the aspect of "melodic type." The intervals of a modal scale and its vocal range are not the whole story in defining a mode, any more than the letters of the alphabet or their font size define a literary style. Melodies in each mode are designed around musical "gestures" common to each mode, so that one mode may have a concentration of certain rhythmic tricks or melodic twists that play a part in imparting a particular feeling, such as sadness, to a sophisticated listener, while a different mode might suggest joy. Just as one would not normally introduce a trumpet fanfare into a lullaby, each mode is host to certain melodic motives that typify it. Think of the difference, for example, between the kinds of melodies found in jazz as opposed to those of funeral marches. The overall effect can quite convincingly convey states of mind to a listener immersed in the culture.

The principal modes used in the temple were also used in the early synagogue. The first of those we will mention is the *tefillah* mode, or, as it was called in later synagogue music, the *Adonai malach shteiger* ("God reigned" mode).[8] This is a hybrid term in which the first two words are taken from a Hebrew prayer that uses this mode, while the last word is Yiddish for the musical term "mode." The pitch alphabet for the *tefillah* mode is approximately equivalent to the seventh of the Gregorian chant modes, also called mixolydian.[9] Idelsohn says that it derives from the ancient Pentateuch mode[10] used for cantillation of the Five Books of Moses in the temple. Its melodic features include focus on a bright major third and a (usually) flattened seventh tone of the scale (see fig. 7.1).

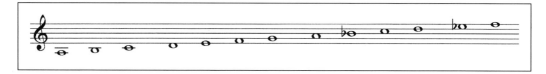

FIG. 7.1 **Interval alphabet of the *Tefillah* mode**

---

[8] *Shteiger*, the Yiddish word for mode, gives little problem here; but the opening words of this prayer, pronounced "Adonái malách" in Sephardic Hebrew, are pronounced "Adonóy móloch" in Ashkenazic Hebrew. The latter transliteration, while not representing modern pronunciation (except among the ultra-orthodox), will often be found in older writings about synagogue music by Ashkenazic Jews.

[9] Idelsohn (see *Jewish Music*, 73), calls it the equivalent of the Hypodorian, or second church mode, but his examples (see p. 75) appear to be Mixolydian.

[10] Ibid., 73.

Another of the modes was known as the *selicha* (pardon) mode. As the name suggests, it was used for prayers of *selicha* (pardon), *bakkasha* (request), *techinah* (petition), and *kinnah* (mourning). It seems to have shared some characteristics of the first, or Dorian, of the later church modes, but had a narrow melodic range, often restricted to just five or six notes. This mode took a different form in Eastern Europe, where it featured a lowered second step and an ambiguously large third scale step, which produced an augmented second between the second and third tones of scale. One can approximate its interval structure on the piano by playing the notes of fig. 7.2, remembering that the uppermost notes of that scale were almost never used.

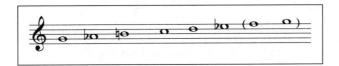

FIG. 7.2　Interval alphabet of the *Selicha* mode

The *viddui* (confession) mode is not unlike our major scale, except that phrases often cadence to the sixth tone of the scale (submediant, marked by an arrow in fig. 7.3), which to western ears, gives the effect of an unexpected change to the relative minor. It is also often marked by a lowered (minor) seventh step.

FIG. 7.3　Interval alphabet of the *Viddui* mode

The *Magen avot*[11] (shield of [our] fathers) mode takes its name from the prayer of that name, which is a summary of seven of the benedictions of the *amidah*, and was composed in third century Babylonia. The prayer was supposedly inserted for the benefit of late-comers, so that they could catch up on the essentials of the service. The mode follows the contours of the natural minor scale, but frequently raises the seventh tone at cadences. In addition, *magen-avot* melodies tend to dwell on and emphasize the fifth note of the scale. The scale, approximated on the piano, would look like the scale shown in fig. 7.4.

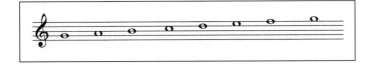

FIG. 7.4　Interval alphabet of the *Magen-avot* mode

---

[11] Also found as *Mogen-ovos*, in Ashkenazic Hebrew.

The last of these modes to be taken up here is the *Ahavah-rabbah* (great love) mode,[12] which again takes its name from a prayer in which it is employed. Here the scale is similar to that of the third (Phrygian) church mode, but with an augmented second between the second and third degrees (see fig. 7.5). *Ahavah-rabbah* was not derived from a biblical mode. Idelsohn suggests it was not a Jewish mode at all, but was "adopted as a result of the influx of Mongolian and Tartarian tribes into Asia minor . . . [and] the Balkans, beginning with the thirteenth century."[13]

FIG. 7.5   Interval alphabet of the *Ahavah-raba* mode

As we get into the late middle ages the advent of polyphony begins to force gradual change and homogenization of the monophonically-based modes until only three modes are distinguished by the time we approach the modern period: *Ahavah-rabbah*, *Magen-avot*, and *Adonai malach*, with the widest range, extending over the interval of a twelfth.[14] The *Adonai malach* mode has several fascinating musical characteristics, such as the two ascending five-note scale patterns, each repeated three times, as shown in fig. 7.6. The first of those (pattern A) corresponds to the first five notes of the western minor mode, the second (pattern B) to the first five notes of the western major mode. In neither case, though, is the major or minor scale completed in the manner we would expect in western music.

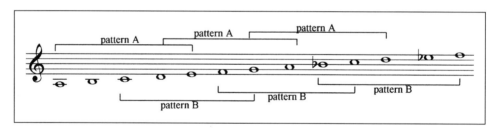

FIG. 7.6   Two repeated patterns in the *Adonai malach* mode

To the extent that composers of Jewish liturgical music adhered to those modes, they continued to play a role in giving the music of the synagogue a unique color. But you will see that most composers abandoned the old modes in favor of the western major-minor scale system, while others attempted to find some compromise between the two.

---

[12] Also found as *Ahavoh-rabboh*, in Ashkenazic Hebrew.

[13] Idelsohn, *Jewish Music*, 87.

[14] This synopsis is itself summarized from composer-theorist Isidore Freed's valuable book, *Harmonizing the Jewish Modes* (New York: Sacred Music Press of The Hebrew Union College, 1958).

The Cantor (Chazzan)

Among the ancient Egyptians, Assyrians, and Babylonians, an officiating priest led the service. The priest alone mediated between the people and their gods. In Jewish belief any person could pray directly to God, but many were unlettered, and did so only in a stumbling fashion. Thus arose the institution of *mitpallelim* (prayer leaders), knowledgeable members of the lay community who led the prayers. They might be rabbis or scribes, but could just as easily be anyone capable of directing the service, because rabbis had no automatic standing or authority as congregational heads.

In the second century CE we begin to read of another synagogue official, bearing the title *chazzan ha-knesset* (overseer of the congregation). Although that term was first defined in the second century by Rabbi Judah ben Ilai, it did not designate a service leader or singer as we use the word today, but denoted someone responsible for watching the building, calling people together for prayer, keeping order in the synagogue, and preparing the scrolls to be read during the service. Leo Landman suggests that it is a word borrowed from the Assyrian term *hazzanu* (overseer). The *chazzan* might lead the prayers as well, but that office more commonly fell to an educated member of the community who served as the precentor, or prayer leader. Another term that came to refer to prayer leaders was *shaliach tzibbur* (representative of the people), already found in the second century CE when the sages described such a position to Rabbi Gamliel as someone who could offer prayers on behalf of those who did not know how to pray themselves. The term *shaliach tzibbur* is often found abbreviated as *shatz*, combining the first letter of each word into a Hebrew acronym. This contraction was especially beloved by later *chazzanim* because, coincidentally, it is a homonym of the word that means "treasure" in Yiddish, and the bilingual pun seems to suggest that prayer leaders were a "treasure" of the community. None of those words originally carried the later meaning of professional cantor.

Over the first six centuries or so following the destruction of the Temple, *chazzanim* began to absorb functions of the lay precentors, and a pleasant voice became, if not exactly a requirement, a desirable characteristic for those holding the office. Those early *chazzanim* frequently composed hymns (*piyyutim*) at the urging of the community. Many rabbis were not entirely pleased with this. Some felt that music entered the service only to the degree that knowledge declined. One eleventh-century *chazzan* described the growth of his profession by writing, "When learning decreased and became marginal, they [*chazzanim*] composed hymns in lieu of exegesis."[15]

Cantor-poets also provided interlinear translations of the Torah reading, sometimes incurring the wrath of rabbis for their poor or overly imaginative translations, poor Hebrew pronunciation, or overly long-winded improvisations. Nevertheless, as the number of prayers increased and the liturgy grew in complexity, the leadership of someone more knowledgeable than the average layman became indispensable, and by the late sixth century a need was felt to professionalize the office. Besides the growing intricacy of the service and its enrichment with ever more devotional *piyyutim*, that need was prompted by an even more pedestrian problem: fewer and fewer of the congregants were themselves conversant in Hebrew, and the few capable volunteers could not keep abreast of changes, additions, and new tunes that were introduced for old prayers.

---

[15] Benjamin ben Samuel, of Byzantium, quoted in Leon J. Weinberger, *Jewish Hymnography: A Literary History* (London: The Littman Library of Jewish Civilization, 1998), 29.

Until the eighth century the practice of writing down prayers was frowned upon, so they were memorized or recited responsorially after the leader. Later, when hand-copied prayer books were deemed acceptable, they were so expensive as to be out of reach of all but the wealthiest members of a community. Before the invention of printing in the mid-fifteenth century, the *chazzan* was often the only person at a service who had a written text to read from if, indeed, even he did. In some European synagogues this problem was solved—at least for those who could read—by writing the principal prayers on various walls in large letters that were visible to the entire congregation.

By the seventh century the post of *chazzan* had pretty much taken the form it was to have for the next thirteen hundred years, and by the twelfth century Jewish leadership insisted that every congregation search out and hire a qualified *chazzan*. As the musical aspects of the position grew more important, a fine singing voice became an increasingly important requirement, along with some ability to compose new music and hymns. Not all of those people were skilled composers, so many of the tunes were borrowed from melodies popular in the surrounding culture, and have since become traditional through generations of use. Some of the earliest melodies, whose origins have now been lost, are so firmly melded into Jewish liturgy that many refer to them as *mi-sinai* or *missinai* (from Sinai) tunes—that is, melodies so ancient that they seemed to go all the way back to the covenant at Mt. Sinai.

In the ninth century the *Sefer Yuhasin* described a choir of boys accompanying the *chazzan* at the installation of a new Babylonian exilarch,[16] although only monophonic singing of responses was mentioned. The twelfth-century traveler Benjamin of Tudela, writing around 1170, says that in Baghdad he encountered "R[eb] Elazar, the son of Zemach . . . [whose] pedigree reaches [back] to Samuel the Prophet, the Korahite. He and his brethren know how to chant the melodies as did the singers at the time when the Temple was standing."[17] Just a few years later another Jewish traveler, Rabbi Petachya, who traveled between 1175 and 1190, praised Babylonian psalm-singing, saying:

> There is a youth . . . singing the songs with a fine voice. On the half-holydays they sing psalms to musical instruments. Since they have a tradition with regard to the melodies, they have [for the] *'asor* psalms ten melodies and for the *'al-hash'minit* [psalms] eight melodies. There are several melodies for every psalm, and they have a tradition how many melodies are [to be sung] in one psalm; one extends [a psalm] over several melodies in one extended time.[18]

With the medieval professionalization of the cantor's job, appointees were held to ever-increasing standards of musicianship and congregations took special pride in the vocal abilities of their *chazzan*. While *chazzanim* were ostensibly chosen for maturity, seriousness, and knowledge of the service rather than for their voices, vocal skill quickly took precedence in congregational choice. Many *chazzanim* looked on themselves primarily as performers, maintaining close

[16] Cited in Leo Landman, *The Cantor* (New York: Yeshiva University, 1972), 65.

[17] Benjamin of Tudela, *The Itinerary of Benjamin of Tudela*, ed. Michael A. Signer (New York: Pangloss Press, 1993), 99.

[18] Quoted in Hanoch Avenary, "A Genizah Find of Saadya's Psalm-Preface and Its Musical Aspects," in *Contributions to a Historical Study of Jewish Music*, ed. Eric Werner (New York: Ktav, 1976), 56.

relationships with other professional musicians, both Jewish and non-Jewish. As poets, they borrowed tunes from the culture in which they lived, sometimes transforming them by adapting them to one of the synagogue modes, and sometimes simply putting Hebrew words to the original melodies without change. As musicians, they composed new melodies or adapted old ones by changing them to suit the times and adding increasingly florid decorations to demonstrate their skill at improvisation. Rabbis inveighed against such "profanations," but they were popular with congregations. After a grueling week of hard work in grinding poverty, members of the congregation were only too happy to enjoy a beautiful voice and join in the satisfying ritual of singing hymns or psalms. With such encouragement, the *chazzan* would only redouble his efforts, while the rabbis cried out in vain against what they perceived as excessively elaborate music. "They care only for their songs without regard for the real sense of the words," complained Herz Treves (1470-1550), the rabbi-cantor of Frankfort-am-Main.[19]

In synagogues of the East there was more interest in straightforward melodies for communal singing and less emphasis on showmanship. Thus exhibition of piety and of correct Hebrew took precedence over flowery improvisation. The *piyyutim* of the Sephardim tended toward simple, dignified melodies with a limited range and a relatively declamatory style. Among the Ashkenazim, though, the *chazzan* became an important musical personage, and great stress was placed on his virtuosity and ability to move a congregation's emotions. Straightforward tunes for congregational song were interspersed with dramatic solos for the *chazzan*, featuring ecstatic cries, sobs, long melismas, and elaborate improvisations that were now and then extended to unnatural lengths. *Chazzanim* borrowed vocal tricks from opera such as trills, runs, swoops, and even the infamous "goat-bleat" ornament, or *trillo* of the seventeenth century, in which, as Hanoch ben Abraham ben Yechi'el charged about 1650, they used "the irritating habit of . . . [putting their] hands on the chin or throat while singing, evidently for the purpose of increasing the vocal vibrato or facilitating the trilling or producing high and shrill tones."

There is no question that the cantor's status as an artist—and sometimes the life style of one, too—was abused by men whose primary concern was their own fame. Having said that, though, it was also true that over the centuries *chazzanim* contributed enormously to Jewish liturgy and music by preserving traditional melodies and modes of prayer and creating new musical expressions that revitalized the worship service. The post of *chazzan* has been held by thousands of talented individuals over the ages. To many of them we owe a great debt for enriching the liturgy with the beauty of their song.

Rise of Polyphonic Art Music in the Synagogue

Western *chazzanim* adopted all the musical devices of the European culture in which they lived. So it was only a matter of time before polyphonic singing was introduced into the synagogue as it had been in the church beginning in the tenth and eleventh centuries, and in all probability earlier, when polyphony seems to have been improvised rather than written down. Polyphonic music, of course, required additional trained singers to carry the dependent voice parts; therefore it became necessary to have trained assistants available to the *chazzan*. This was accomplished

---

[19] Quoted in Landman, 13.

in a few wealthier congregations by the hiring of paid assistants; but in most places any cost had to be borne by the *chazzan* himself. The apprenticeship system suited that need nicely, providing apprentice singers as accompanists for mature *chazzanim* and at the same time making a path available for training young cantors. Such accompanist-trainees were called *meshorerim*[20] (accompanying singers) in Hebrew. They often bolstered their income and experience by serving as occasional *chazzanim* for small congregations that could not afford to pay a full-time professional, or by filling in for a sick colleague. Their principal job, though, was to provide a rest for the *chazzan's* voice now and then, or to sustain a background for his colorful melismas.

In Europe, during the eleventh, twelfth, and thirteenth centuries when their Christian counterparts were experimenting with the introduction of true polyphony in the Church, *chazzanim* would not have remained ignorant of those developments. The *meshorerim* became the nucleus of a choir. Where choirs did exist, and that was only in larger congregations, choristers were usually volunteers: men and boys whose good will sometimes outshone their voices. Judah Harizi could not resist scolding a cantor and choir who prolonged the service mercilessly while the congregation fled, leaving behind "four donkeys who bray and yell in harmony with the cantor and who think they are a choir."[21]

A professional choir, though, was an extravagant expense, more money than most congregations could afford. Then, too, for many it seemed to go too far, making synagogue music more elaborate than was necessary. While congregations in cultures with strong musical traditions often supported a choir of some sort, the majority opposed them on religious, social, or financial grounds. However, in Italy, where music was part of the cultural life-blood, it is possible to find not only choirs, but instruments, too, used in synagogues. In the sixteenth century the Jewish community of Padua had an organized choir that accompanied *chazzan* Benzion Zarfati, who later became a rabbi in Venice. Ferrara, too, boasted a choir of six young men who harmonized the liturgy in the style of contemporary Italian music. Such a development was not without opposition, though, and it would require the decision of an Italian rabbinical court to put the stamp of approval on those practices.

Salamone Rossi

Italian Jews were especially noted as professional musicians and choreographers, and were in demand as far away as England. In the fifteenth century there were Jewish schools of music and dance in Pesaro, Parma, and Venice, home of the first "ghetto."[22] Despite being at the very heart of Christian Europe, the pressures of the Inquisition did not weigh as heavily on the Italian Jewish communities as it did on their brethren in Spain and Portugal, and sufficient musical ability might allow one's religion to be temporarily overlooked. Raphael Mahler describes the situation in these terms:

---

[20] This word is sometimes given as *meshoyrerim*, a phonetic spelling of its Yiddish pronunciation, especially in the work of Ashkenazic writers.

[21] Landman, 66.

[22] The Venetian *ghetto* was the district where, in 1516, Jews were segregated into a separate neighborhood in which a cannon foundry (*ghetto*) had stood for over two hundred years.

> Assimilation [of the Jews] by choice did not extend to Italy. In contra-
> distinction to their brethren in Germany, the Jews of Italy had been firmly
> embedded in the Italian population for many generations. They were
> linked to it by language, culture and social relations . . . the Jews of Italy
> gave fine expression to their national allegiance in Hebrew poetry and in
> other literary media in Hebrew and Italian.[23]

This, then, was the setting from which Salamone Rossi *Ebreo* (ca. 1570-ca. 1630?), the first musician to gain equal stature as a composer of Jewish and mainstream European music, emerged. Rossi is an Italian translation of his Hebrew name, Shlomo ha-*Adumah* (Solomon the red[-haired]), with the added suffix "Ebreo" (Hebrew) marking him as a Jew. He worked as a musician and occasional director of string ensembles at the court in Mantua, the home of the Gonzaga family, who were known as great patrons of the arts. Jewish musicians besides Rossi in Mantua included Abraham dall' Arpa Ebreo (Abraham the Jewish Harpist) and his nephew (or grandson) Abramino (Little Abe); composers Davit da Civita, author of a set of seventeen three-part *canzoni* published ca. 1616 marked *Madrigali Ebrei*,[24] and Allegro (or Alegre) Porto[25] (whose first name was probably a translation of the Hebrew name, *Simcha*); and Isacchino Massarano. Massarano, one of the best-known dancers and choreographers of his day, was also a lutenist and singer. He was commissioned to do the choreography for Bernardo Pino's *Gli Ingiusti Sdegni*, performed by the Jewish Theater of Mantua for the wedding of the future duke, Vincenzo Gonzaga. In addition, Rossi's sister, known as "Madame Europa" was a well-regarded singer. Mantua was a truly extraordinary city. Ruled by the Gonzaga family since 1328, music at the Mantuan court reached its high point during the reign of Duke Vincenzo Gonzaga (1587-1612), when it could boast of employing some of Europe's finest composers. First Giaches de Wert, then Claudio Monteverdi came to Mantua, the latter beginning as a violist and eventually rising to become *maestro di capella*. It was during his time in Mantua that Monteverdi developed a new, more vigorous model of the Baroque style that would dominate European music for over two centuries. Monteverdi created history's first successful operas at Mantua. Then in 1612 he became *maestro di capella* at St. Mark's in Venice, one of Europe's grandest cathedrals.

Beside those colleagues, Rossi was blessed with patrons in the Jewish community who encouraged his efforts in both sacred and secular music, Rabbi Yehuda Arieh (known as Leone) da Modena and Moses Sullam. He was active as a violinist, singer, and composer. His works included at least thirteen books of madrigals, canzonas, sonatas, and other musical forms. He published the very first continuo madrigals in two books brought out in 1600 and 1602, and earned a reputation as one of the finest violinists and teachers in Europe. Gradenwitz feels that he may have given birth to the school of Italian violinists "who spread Italy's fame through-out the seventeenth and eighteenth-century world."[26] Combining his avant-garde approach to

---

[23] Raphael Mahler, *A History of Modern Jewry: 1780-1815* (New York: Schocken Books, 1971), xxii.

[24] *Premite armoniche a tre voci.* The only known copy of this book was housed in the Royal Library at Berlin, but has disappeared.

[25] Possibly a member of the well-known family of scholars that included Rabbi Isaac ben David (d. ca. 1577) and Zemach ben Isaac Porto (d. ca. 1666), both of whom were rabbis of the Jewish community in Mantua.

[26] Gradenwitz, 148.

composition with his love for the violin, he developed—may have even created—the quintessential Baroque instrumental form, the trio sonata, by applying the principles of Baroque monody to the instrumental canzona. His sonata *La moderna*, established the four-movement alternation of tempos that became standard for the Baroque *sonata da chiesa* (the "church," or "serious" sonata). He was so highly regarded as a musician that in 1606 the duke formally exempted him from having to wear the yellow badge required of all Jews at the time. The privilege was renewed in 1612 as the first official act of Duke Francesco Gonzaga after his father's death.

For all that, Salamone Rossi never held a formal appointment at the court, possibly because of his religion. He was *chazzan* of the Mantua congregation, and while his work at the court must have been both challenging and remunerative, it was as a *chazzan* that he would earn his greatest fame. Two leaders of the Italian Jewish community lent their support to Rossi: the wealthy Moses Sullam, a leading citizen of Mantua, and Rabbi Leone da Modena. It was primarily through Moses Sullam that Rossi was engaged to undertake his most renowned compositional project: religious songs to Hebrew texts in the "modern" (i.e., Baroque) style for synagogue use. These were published in 1622 under the title *Ha-shirim asher li'shlomo* (The Songs of Solomon), a pun on the biblical *Shir ha-shirim asher li'Shlomo* (The Song of Songs by Solomon). Rossi was fifty-eight years old at the time of their publication. These thirty-three compositions represent his mature work. They also represent the first and only surviving examples of polyphonic synagogue music in that style.

Anticipating some negative response to his innovative work, Rossi enlisted the aid of Rabbi Leone da Modena (1571-1648) of Venice. The music-loving rabbi was director of the Jewish academy of theater and music in the Venetian ghetto. A charismatic and well-known figure in Italian Jewish history, he has been praised as "brilliant and gifted," and at the same time damned as "unstable."[27] A rabbi who advocated novelties in religion as well as music, Leone had been the conductor of the above-mentioned polyphonic chorus at his synagogue in Ferrara as a young man. There, the rabbinic assembly had upheld the use of polyphonic singing in the synagogue against the opposition of certain rabbis and members of the congregation. Now, almost a generation later, he was in a position to further the cause of modernizing Jewish music.

In his capacity as a rabbi, Leone da Modena wrote a studied opinion (*responsum*) as a preface to Rossi's book, stating that polyphonic choral chant was acceptable in the synagogue. His essay provided the rabbinic approval necessary for acceptance of the greatest monument of Jewish polyphonic music written to that time. "There will certainly be found among us [Jews] some people who fight against all that is new," he wrote, "and so I have thought fit to refer to the answer I wrote with regard to this question eighteen years ago . . . and all great scholars of Venice agreed with me."[28] He appends to his argument the conclusion that the Talmud permits singing and the use of instruments provided it is in accordance with the custom of the times.

Rossi's collection contains thirty-three settings of liturgical texts using Baroque harmonizations in the latest style. His compositions make use of trio sonata-like textures and Italianate vocal devices, such as *messa da voce* and melisma. They are conservative, however, in their use

---

[27] Both epithets here are taken from the same article in *The Encyclopedia of the Jewish Religion*, ed. R. J. Z. Werblowsky and Geoffrey Wigoder (New York, Chicago, San Francisco: Holt, Rinehart, and Winston, 1965), 267.

[28] Translated and quoted by Gradenwitz, 154.

of canzona-like forms and a basically homophonic texture. Agogic accents with full-stop cadences mark most phrases, and frequent passages of homophonic writing are interspersed with occasional motet-like contrapuntal passages. They are, in fact, quite beautiful, but there is not even the slightest hint of the synagogue tradition in them. Even today, there are many who feel that Rossi's music, while it may have been Jewish in function, is not recognizably Jewish in form. And so the argument rages: is it the music's form or function that mark it as Jewish?

There is one last chapter to the story of Rossi's collection of *Shirim*. It concerns an idea far ahead of its time, one that would have enormous implications for the future. The idea was what we would today call intellectual property rights, a concept that had not yet been voiced in European law at that time, but that would, within the following century, begin to protect authors and composers from the theft of their works by unscrupulous printers. The last section of the preface states, in part:

> Having been granted permission from the distinguished court authorities.
> we, the signatories to this document, herewith issue a strict prohibition
> . . . that no Jew, wherever he may be, may print under any circumstances
> within fifteen years from this day the above-mentioned work, the music,
> or part thereof, without the consent of its author or his heirs, nor may any
> Jew, according to this decree, buy from any person, whether Jewish or not,
> copies of these compositions, without the composer's having authorized
> their sale by a special mark on them.[29]

The statement, dated Cheshvan 5383 (winter 1622), is signed by elders Izhak Gershon, Moses Cohen Port, Yehuda Arieh (i.e., Leone) of Modena, and Simcha Luzzato. In addition to being the first publication of Jewish music, Rossi's *Shir ha-shirim* can rightfully be claimed as the first copyright declaration. Even noting that such a statement would not be legally binding on Christians, it still acknowledges the composer's right to the proceeds of his talent and labor, a right that would only later be recognized around the world and would eventually enable composers to free themselves from patronage to enjoy financial and intellectual independence.

We do not know exactly where or when Salamone Rossi died. His last published work was dated January 1628. Shortly after that Mantua was invaded by Austrian troops, and in the ensuing seven-month siege much of the city was destroyed. Thousands fled, plague wracked the survivors, and in the ensuing confusion history loses sight of Salamone Rossi. There is some evidence that he may have fled Mantua before the siege and settled in Venice, where his friend and patron, Leone da Modena, lived; but that is uncertain. There is evidence that polyphonic music had been sung in synagogues before Rossi: in Ferrara, for example, where Leone da Modena had been the choir leader some eighteen years earlier. Nevertheless, Rossi's *Shirim asher li-shlomo* was the first publication of such music, and hearing those pieces is convincing evidence of their beauty.

That the synagogue songs of Salamone Rossi left no immediate impression on Jewish music is a result of the vagaries of history. The destruction of the Mantuan Jewish community and subsequent degradation of the city's formerly sophisticated court life, the death or exile of Jewish

---

[29] Cited in Gradenwitz, 157.

musicians who had once shone so brightly under the Gonzagas, the virulently anti-semitic turn taken by Protestantism in the later sixteenth and seventeenth centuries, matched by an equally aggressive anti-semitic stance on the part of the Catholic church in the mid-seventeenth-century counter-reformation, all had a role in ringing down the curtain on what had appeared, for a historical moment, to be a renaissance of Jewish religious music. Rossi had no surviving Jewish students to carry his approach into the next generation, and the disasters that befell the Italian Jewish community quashed any immediate chance for further debate about the nature of Italian synagogue music.

A new climate was abroad. New kings appeared who "knew not Joseph," and once again strict separation between Jews and Christians was enforced so that Jewish musicians were no longer welcome in Christian courts. Under this renewed oppression, Jewish communities hunkered down in a frightened, defensive stance, seeking comfort in their tradition and refuge in their "otherness." In such an atmosphere, even if any *chazzanim* had known Rossi's music, none would have dared to perform it. The *Shirim asher li-shlomo* would be rediscovered, but not until more than two centuries later, when the French *chazzan* Samuel Naumbourg would republish Rossi's work. For the moment it was as lost to the synagogue as if it had never been.

Secular Influences on Synagogue Music

Rossi's synagogue music was symptomatic of a new state of affairs that came to the fore in the European synagogue: a growing tension between the sacred and secular. In the ancient world of the Jewish commonwealth no such division existed, and as we have seen, many biblical psalms were headed with the names of quite worldly tunes to which their sacred words were sung. In the Diaspora, though, because Jews were interspersed among people of other faiths, preserving what was recognizably Jewish from the incursions of Moslem or Christian culture became a matter of concern. In Christian Europe, beginning quite early, there was a sharp line of demarcation between those two worlds in keeping with Jesus's saying, "Render unto Caesar what is Caesar's and unto God what is God's." It was an attitude foreign to biblical Judaism, but it had a growing influence on Jewish life in the Diaspora.

As the acceptance of Rossi's music indicated, Italian Jews of the sixteenth and seventeenth centuries seem to have been more receptive to incursions of such foreign practices into the synagogue than their brethren further north. Leone da Modena did not hesitate to advise that appropriate instrumental music could be used in the synagogue, and indeed, we read of orchestras and instrumental ensembles playing for the services in the synagogue of Venice, where Leone resided as head of a Jewish music school formed in 1629. Gradenwitz suggests that this school might have been established by refugees from Mantua following that city's occupation by imperial troops and an outbreak of the plague there, and it is even possible that Salamone Rossi may have been among the refugees.[30] Whether or not that was the case, concerts were given at the school twice weekly, which only enhanced the reputation of Jews for music-making. That reputation brought many Christians to synagogue services to enjoy the singing of the *chazzan*

---

[30] Gradenwitz, 169.

and choir, and encouraged synagogues to bolster their musical reputations still further by the addition of instruments. The Venetian synagogue, after all, was located in the city of St. Mark's Cathedral, one of the most glorious musical venues in Europe, and some spirit of competition must have been felt. The synagogue even went so far as to install an organ for the festival of *Simchat Torah*. The new organ brought out such a crowd that the police had to be called and the organ was removed—not for musical, or even religious reasons, but because its presence had generated a crush of traffic that destroyed any semblance of a worship service and created a public nuisance. In Mantua, too, Rossi seems to have introduced instruments into the synagogue.

The *bet din* (rabbinic court) of Prague permitted the organ to be played in the synagogue on week days and at the afternoon services introducing Sabbath and other holidays, but wrote, "those in our community who play an instrument on *Kabbalat Shabbat* (the preliminary "welcoming the Sabbath" service) must stop playing a half-hour before *Bar'chu* (the beginning of the Friday evening Sabbath service itself)."[31]

> All of us have prohibited the playing of the organ on *Shabbat* and *Yom tov* [holiday]. We permitted its use only on the *hol ha-mo'ayd*,[32] *erev shabbat* and *erev yom tov*, prior to the onset of these holy days. Even this was permitted to take place only for Jews who feared the Lord in their heart.

There is evidence that instrumental music was used in this fashion in some Dutch synagogues, too. A *siddur* published at Amsterdam in 1693 contained this inscription over a song placed just before "L'cha dodi," the traditional *piyyut* welcoming the Sabbath by Shlomo ha-Levi Alkabetz: "A beautiful song by Reb Shlomo Singer which is sung in the Meisel Synagogue with flute and lyre before *L'cha dodi*."[33]

As one might imagine, while such customs often found local acceptance, they were just as frequently the objects of scorn, derision, and attack from conservative elements of the Jewish community. The practice of adapting love songs, lullabies, or hymns of a different religion for the synagogue came under increasingly harsh criticism from rabbis who wanted to maintain cultural uniqueness. Such separatists saw in the division between sacred and secular the only means of preserving Jewish particularism while still participating in the cultural life of a non-Jewish majority.

This battle would culminate in the nineteenth century, when, in the spirit of the *Haskalah*, liberal synagogues began to install organs. The rationale for that breach of the rabbinic injunction against instrumental music was ostensibly to beautify their services; but underneath that may have lain the ulterior motive of making their worship service more closely resemble that of their Christian neighbors. Max Wohlberg asserts that this produced two important tendencies in Synagogue music:

---

[31] David Zevi Hoffman, "The Use of the Organ in Responsa Literature," trans. Winifred Wolfson, *Journal of Jewish Music & Liturgy* 18 (1995-96): 9.

[32] *Chol ha-mo'ayd* (or ha-mo'eid) = intermediate day of a multi-day holiday; *erev shabbat* = evening initiating the sabbath; *erev yom tov* = evening initiating a holiday. Because the Jewish day begins at sundown, the evening preceding a holiday is actually the beginning of the holiday.

[33] Hoffman, 12. Again, it should be noted that "before *l'cha dodi*" means that the instruments played before the Sabbath was formally initiated.

1. the free adoption of music characteristic of the Protestant Church, and

2. the "dejudaizing" of the retained traditional modes. The latter was accomplished by altogether eliminating or de-emphasizing their "Eastern" or "Polish" qualities.[34]

The *chazzanim*, whose main interest was sometimes musical ràther than religious, did not hesitate to borrow dance tunes or love songs, especially if they had good melodies or a rhythm that neatly fit one of the Hebrew prayers. It was a trend whose influence was to grow. It was not long before melodies from the secular world were applied to Jewish prayers by *chazzanim*. This only occurred in scattered locations at first, but the practice proved so attractive that Sendrey mentions fifteen or so such melodies over the following centuries, including such strange mixtures as the Kaddish sung to the tune of "La Marsellaise," or Psalm 115 sung to an aria from *La Traviata*.[35] German tunes, Turkish tunes, French tunes, and even the World War I song, "The Girl I left Behind Me," all found employment as prayer melodies at one time or another. This continuous stream of new melodies upset those who simply wanted to hear or sing the "good old" tunes with which they were already familiar and which held profound religious connotations; but it pleased many others, who were charmed by the novelty. Such divisions of musical opinion led to controversy within congregations, which reflected badly on the *chazzan*. So most congregations attempted to reign in their *chazzanim* and keep their liturgical music isolated from the world around them. But even the best of intentions did not serve to screen out all the worldly tunes.

Beside the influence of melodies from the outside world, there was the matter of the increasingly colorful singing style of the cantors, known as *chazzanut*.[36] The crowning glory of *chazzanut* was the recitative. In Western music that term referred to a non-metric style for declaiming the poetry introducing an aria, or song, in an opera or oratorio. It was generally considered to be only a means for "setting up" an emotional situation that prompted the more song-like aria. By contrast, cantorial recitative was considered the height of the *chazzan's* vocal artistry. Rather than being preliminary, it was used as the emotional climax of intense prayer, a free-rhythm exploitation of the extremes of a singer's range, declamation, vocal pyrotechnics, and emotional hyperbole. Many *chazzanim* were hired or fired principally on the strength of their ability to move the congregation to ecstasy, awe, or tears through recitative.

Reacting to the adulation of those in the congregation who were drawn to the service by the sweetness of song, some cantors prolonged prayers with elaborate improvisations, long melismas, and florid vocal displays. Words or phrases were repeated several times with increasingly extravagant vocal tricks such as sobs or trills, syllables were drawn out into elaborate coloraturas, or entire paragraphs were repeated with improvised embellishments. We read of cantors taking over an hour to sing the single prayer, *Baruch she'omar*, extending it so that an

---

[34] Max Wohlberg, "Significant Aspects of the Ashkenazic Hazzanic Recitative," *Proceedings of the World Congress of Jewish Music, Jerusalem, 1978* (Tel Aviv: The Institute for the Translation of Hebrew Literature Ltd., 1982), 161.

[35] Sendrey, *Music of the Jews in the Diaspora*, 239.

[36] This word is used in two different senses: either as the liturgical repertoire sung by cantors or, as here, the cantorial style of singing.

appreciative audience could immerse themselves in its kabbalistic connotations through the music. For ghettoized Jews denied the opportunity to attend the opera or symphony, *chazzanut* became their art music, and *chazzanim* reveled in their resulting renown.

All this would have been innocent enough—a tempest in a teapot—if it had not carried with it the Europeanization of synagogue music. Folk songs and dance-hall tunes in themselves might not have debased the music of the synagogue, any more than the adoption of the melody to "John Brown's body lies a-mold'ring in the grave" debased Christian music when it was sung as a hymn to the words, "Mine eyes have seen the glory of the coming of the Lord." A more lasting impact of such borrowing was the displacement of the old synagogue modes by the European major/minor scale system.

The development of harmony in Western music had necessitated a number of adjustments, made gradually over the centuries, to accommodate the system of chords that grew up. Most of those were microtonal tuning adjustments hardly noticed by most listeners. As the system of tuning settled into place, small differences in similar intervals that had once helped to distinguish one mode from another gave way to artificially standardized intervals, called "tempered" tuning. From the point of view of Western music that proved to be an advantage, for it allowed composers to change freely from one key to another (modulate), knowing that a keyboard instrument with fixed pitches would sound equally good in any key.[37] Gradually, as harmony entered the synagogue, the modes were modified to fit into the Western "tempered" tonal system so that Jewish music—that is to say, music written for the synagogue—sounded more and more like the music of the community's neighbors. The combination of western tunes, the introduction of harmony, and the desire of Jews to appear less different in the hope that this might soften the harsh attitudes they encountered, gradually eroded distinctions between Jewish and Christian music. Probably by the seventeenth century, certainly by the eighteenth, a kind of musical assimilation had taken place, almost unnoticed.

Idelsohn mentions the innovations of Christian religious poet Erdmann Neumeister (1671-1756) as symptomatic of a similar problem in the Lutheran church. About 1700, Neumeister wrote a series of poems interpreting stories from the Bible in simple allegorical terms that could be easily grasped. They were cast in the form of secular cantatas, which had been very popular, and featured arias, duets, and all the set pieces that made it appear like "a piece out of an opera," to use his own words. Bach's use of Neumeister's texts for his church cantatas converted those insipid poems into musical masterworks. But the more church music was expressed in operatic arias, love duets, and sonata-like instrumental interludes, the more it lost its separateness as church music, and soon any distinction between sacred and secular music was eradicated. Whether this was a good or bad thing depended on your point of view, and convincing arguments exist on both sides of that question. The invasion of secular music into the church and synagogue was a matter of some import to both. But for Jewish society it was crucial, for outside the core of Talmudic religion, music was one of the most important artistic expressions shaping the unity of Jewish practice and culture.

---

[37] It might almost be better to say "equally bad in any key," because the most effective system of tuning turned out to be one in which almost all notes were out of tune, but by such a small amount that most people could not detect it.

Jewish and Non-Jewish Music Interblend

As we move forward into the eighteenth century we begin to find that music for the synagogue has fewer and fewer identifiably Jewish characteristics. *Chazzanim* appropriated secular tunes or composed new melodies in the style of secular music; they carried to the congregations all the vocal tricks of the opera stage, and some of them moved back and forth between the secular world of opera and that of the synagogue, blurring the line still further. The cantor had become more than a precentor, or leader of the service. He had become a star, a personality who was recognized primarily for his vocal prowess. Recognition came not just as admiration, but in the form of salary, too. Such "stars" could command large fees, and often traveled from place to place, as one community outbid another for their services. One such star was Michael ben Nathan of Lublin, who officiated as *chazzan* in Amsterdam from 1700 to 1712, where he introduced the Eastern European tradition of *meshorerim*. Another was the Polish *chazzan* Jokele of Rzeszow, who appeared in Prague, then in 1715 moved to Metz. There, we read that he was just singing the morning prayer for *Shavuot* when people thought they heard the sound of the roof giving way. A panic ensued as worshippers tried to rush from the synagogue, and six women were crushed to death trying to force their way down the stairs from the women's gallery. As it happened, there was nothing wrong with the building—the panic was unwarranted. And where was the great *chazzan* in all this? "The cantor, Reb Jokel, went home in the middle of the prayer, and another cantor took his place, but sang little or nothing at all."[38] Reb Jokel was not the only Polish cantor in Western Europe. Partly as a result of the Chmielnitzki massacres of 1648, Eastern European Jews streamed into Western Europe and the British Isles. Among them were a number of outstanding singers who left their mark on Jewish music.

Notable among the great stars of Western Europe was the *chazzan* Meyer Lyon (ca. 1755-97), cantor of the Great Synagogue of London, who migrated to the opera stage around 1775 after a salary disagreement with synagogue leaders. Already widely admired among London's Jewish and Christian music-lovers, who flocked to the synagogue to hear his voice, he was welcomed with open arms at the opera, where he sang as Michael Leoni, or as he was styled in the newspapers of the day, "The Great Leoni." The Great Leoni was a brilliant singer, but a "stick of wood" as an actor. His greatest success was as Don Carlos in Sheridan's play, *The Duenna*, a part written specifically for him that featured much singing but little acting. After making several unsuccessful attempts to earn a name as a singer and then as a manager, he negotiated a better salary with the synagogue elders and returned to his post in the Jewish community. There he proceeded to exhaust the patience of congregants by, among other things, singing in a performance of Handel's *Messiah*. He later immigrated to Kingston, Jamaica, where he ended his days.

Leoni is best known as composer of the melody for Daniel ben Yuda's *piyyut*, "Yigdal elohim chai" (Praise the living God), which was not so much an original composition as a pastiche of existing melodic clichés assembled into a new tune. Leoni's melody was given a larger audience

---

[38] *The Life of Glückel of Hameln 1646-1724 Written by Herself*; ed. and trans. Beth-Zion Abrahams (New York: Thomas Yoseloff, 1963), 182.

by Wesleyan cleric Thomas Olivers (1725-99), who heard the *chazzan* sing it, and liked the song so much that he set English words to it as the hymn, "The God of Abraham Praise."[39] Here is how Olivers told the story to a friend:

> Look at this. I have rendered it from the Hebrew, giving it as far as I could a Christian character, and I have called on Leoni the Jew, who has given me a synagogue melody to suit it; here is the tune and it is to be called Leoni."[40]

To bring that story full circle, the melody became so well known in eighteenth-century London that it soon popped up as a soldiers' drinking song with an entirely different text: "Now pass the glass around."

Writings about Synagogue Music

Until the late eighteenth century most synagogue music was in the hands of those who, regardless of native talent, were musically illiterate. The earliest notated Jewish music for the synagogue may have been the *piyyut* "Mi al har Horev" (Who [stood] on Mount Horeb) notated by Obadiah the Proselyte in the twelfth century, but for centuries after that, little else appeared in notation, though we know that *chazzanim* were constantly creating new melodies. In chapter 4 a number of books were introduced that discuss how the *te'amim* were structured, but none of those included music until the end of the fifteenth century. The earliest musical notation we have for cantillation is a manuscript in the hand of the Christian cleric Caspar Amman (1460-1524), whose melodies seem to have been transcribed from the singing of his cantillation instructor, Johannes Boeschenstein (1472-1540).[41] Several Christian humanists of that time, in an effort to get at the Hebrew sources underlying the Latin Vulgate, undertook study of the Hebrew language, prosody, and music. In the sixteenth century those studies resulted in the publications of Christian humanists such as Sebastien Meunster, Johannes Reuchlin, and Johannes Vallensis, discussed in chapter 4, above.

After a long fallow period, the next item of interest written about Jewish music once again comes from the hand of an interested Christian. This was the Italian composer Benedetto Marcello (1686-1739), who published *Estro poetico-harmonico*, eight books containing settings of fifty psalms, in Venice between 1724 and 1726. The psalms are set for different vocal groupings accompanied by and interspersed with instrumental sonatas. For some of those psalms he used melodies that he had heard in the synagogue—some Sephardic, some Ashkenazic, from which we can infer that melodies from both rites were combined in the Venetian service. In a preface, Marcello explains that he "introduced recitatives . . . to approximate . . . characteristic[s]

---

[39] See *Hymns Ancient and Modern Revised* (#631), and *Songs of Praise* (#398).

[40] Quoted from the Jewish Chronicle of 1873 (642) by Idelsohn in *Jewish Music*, 220-21.

[41] See Avenary, *Ashkenazi Tradition of Biblical Chant*, 12.

of the Jewish people."[42] Marcello, a keen musician, recognized the stylistic differences between Ashkenazic and Sephardic tunes. He took the liberty of adjusting pitches, where necessary, and regularizing meters and phrases to conform to the expectations of his Christian audience. He also eliminated the swoops, glides, sobs, and other vocal devices that played so important a part in the original musical style. What was left, then, was only a pale reflection of synagogue song, reduced in much the same fashion as a translation from one language to another might be. For all that, his collection shows the rich and beautiful lyric tradition of the Venetian synagogue, still flourishing a century after Leone da Modena and Salamone Rossi.

After Marcello's publication the slate remains blank until 1823, when a British *chazzan* of Polish descent by the name of Isaac Nathan published the first volume his massive study, *Musurgia Vocalis, An Essay on the History and Theory of Music, and on the Qualities, Capabilities, and Management of the Human Voice* (London: G. and W. B. Whitaker, 1823). A second volume of that work followed three years later. What purported to be a treatise on singing was actually a monumental, if meandering, series of essays on various topics touching on the art of singing. Among those topics was cantillation, treated by Nathan at some length. "The Hebrews," he announces, "chant with particular pathos and effect . . . the whole of the Bible, after the manner in which it was delivered to them from the mouth of Moses."[43] That hyperbolic pronouncement is followed by a history of the development and purpose of Masoretic notation, culminating on page 106 in a so-called *zarka* table[44] listing musical notation for each of the *te'amim*, as they were sung in London at the turn of the nineteenth century. Nathan's was not the last exploration of the te'amin to appear, but later publications such as that of Abraham Dov Baer in 1883[45] or the two studies by William Wickes[46] discussed in chapter 4, properly belong to the nineteenth century.

Isaac Nathan's book came out just as Jewish life in Western Europe was on the verge of a major change. The sweeping social reforms of the French and American revolutions were paralleled by growth of the *Haskalah* movement among Jews themselves and were soon followed by the extension of basic civil rights to Jews in the Napoleonic era. All those changes converged to open new opportunities for European Jews over the next half-century, when we will see Jewish performers in the concert and opera halls, Jewish composers moving into the world of art music, and Jewish teachers appearing on the faculties of major European conservatories. The repercussions were both positive and negative. The invisibility that had marked long periods in the history of Jewish music was replaced in the nineteenth century by the vibrant presence of writers, teachers, composers, and performers of Jewish origin. The question "What is Jewish music?" in that age takes on a whole new coloring.

---

[42] Quoted in Gradenwitz, 166.

[43] Isaac Nathan, *Musurgia Vocalis* (London: G. and W. B. Whitaker, 1823), 98.

[44] *Zarka* tables show the *te'amim* with their equivalent musical notation in tabular form.

[45] Abraham Dov Baer of Ovruch, *Baal T'fillah oder "Der Practischer Vorbeter"* (The Prayer Leader, or "The Practical Cantor") (Frankfurt: J. Kaufmann, 1883).

[46] Wickes, *Two Treatises*.

Suggestions for Further Reading

Abrahams, Israel, and Cecil Roth. *Jewish Life in the Middle Ages*. London: E. Goldston Ltd., 1932.

Eisenstein, Judith Kaplan. "Medieval Elements in the Liturgical Music of the Jews of Southern France and Northern Spain." *Musica Judaica: The Journal of the American Society for Jewish Music* 14 (1999): 9-29.

Fellerer, Karl Gustav. "Jewish Elements in Pre-Gregorian Chant." In *World Congress on Jewish Music*, ed. Judith Cohen, 115-18. Tel Aviv: The Institute for the Translation of Hebrew Literature Ltd., 1982.

Glazerson, Matityahu. *Music and Kabbalah*. Jerusalem and Northvale, NJ: Jason Aaronson Inc., 1997.

Harrán, Don. *Salamone Rossi: Jewish Musician in Late Renaissance Mantua*. Oxford; New York: Oxford University Press, 1999.

Hoffman, David Zevi. "The Use of the Organ in Responsa Literature." *Journal of Jewish Music & Liturgy* 18 (1995-96): 8-15.

Jeffery, Peter. "The Earliest Christian Chant Repertory Recovered: The Gregorian Witnesses to Jerusalem Chant." *Journal of the American Musicological Society* 47, no. 1 (1994): 1-38.

Padwa, Mia Diamond. "'For Your Voice Is Sweet . . .': An Overview of *Kol Isha*." *Jewish Orthodox Feminist Alliance Journal* 2, no. 1 (winter 2000): 4-5.

Prior, Roger. "Jewish Musicians in the Tudor Court." *Musical Quarterly* (spring 1983): 253-65.

Reif, Stefan C. "The Early History of Jewish Worship." In *The Making of Jewish and Christian Worship*, ed. Paul F. Bradhaw and Lawrence A. Hoffman, 28. Notre Dame: Notre Dame University Press, 1991.

Rossi, Salamone. *Complete Works*, ed. Don Harrán. Neuhausen: American Institute of Musicology, 1995-2003.

Taitz, Emily. "Kol Ishah—The Voice of Woman: Where was it Heard in Medieval Europe?" *Conservative Judaism* 38 (spring 1986): 44-61.

Zahavy, Tzvee. "The Politics of Piety: Social Conflict and the Emergence of Rabbinic Liturgy." In *The Making of Jewish and Christian Worship*, ed. Paul F. Bradshaw and Lawrence A. Hoffman. Notre Dame and London: University of Notre Dame Press, 1991.

HISTORICAL INTERLUDE

The Haskalah

The *Haskalah* (Hebrew: "Enlightenment") movement was born when, after many centuries of isolation from the host cultures in which they found themselves, Jews began to interact with the surrounding culture and altered their practices to accommodate themselves to that culture. A central tenet of the *Haskalah* was for Jews to recognize non-Jewish authority on a par with Jewish authority in secular matters and, as a result, to alter their way of life so as to fit in with the non-Jewish way of life.[1] Before the nineteenth century, individual Jews like Baruch Spinoza (1632-1677) took part in the intellectual life of their times but remained aloof either from the Jewish population for doing so or from the Christian population for remaining steadfast in the traditional Jewish life style. By the second half of the eighteenth century, however, both Christian and Jewish intellectuals and artists began to interact in more significant ways, and with the arrival of Moses Mendelssohn in Germany came the real birth of the *Haskalah*.[2] When Mendelssohn (1729-1786) arrived in Berlin in 1743, he found that as a German-speaking intellectual he was accepted by some Christian intellectuals, most notably by Gotthold Ephraim Lessing, whom he met at a chess table. Lessing (1729-81) had written works defending Jews when, offended by King Frederick the Great of Prussia's refusal to grant Jews citizenship, he published his most important and last play, *Nathan der Weise* (*Nathan the Wise*, 1779), which is a defense of the Jew. While Jews in other parts of Germany had no chance to advance and be recognized, in Frederick's modern court the King became the patron of the Jewish philosopher, Moses Mendelssohn,

---

[1] Michael Stanislawski, *Tsar Nicholas I and the Jews: The Transformation of Jewish Society in Russia 1825-1855* (Philadelphia: The Jewish Publication Society, 1983), 49.

[2] On the German *Haskalah* movement see Marvin Lowenthal, *The Jews of Germany: A Story of Sixteen Centuries* (Philadelphia: The Jewish Publication Society, 1936), 198-216 and passim. Salo Baron, *The Russian Jew Under Tsars and Soviets*, 2nd ed. (New York: Macmillan Publishing Co., 1976), 375, believes that "there was an Italian and Dutch *Haskalah* before that of Berlin, Galician, and Russian periods."

who had translated the Torah into German, not just because it was vernacular speech, but also because it was considered the most precise language for scholarship.

In Germany, after Mendelssohn's death, the *Haskalah* had many repercussions. Rich Prussian Jews "achieved legal equality," even if only temporarily, in 1812.[3] The new philosophy of progress swept all German youth, not only Jewish youth, and throughout the nineteenth century most German Jews aspired to modern education, modern science, contemporary styles of living, and the arts. In 1862 Baden granted full citizenship to Jews and allowed Jews to enter German schools. A decade later some other German states followed. Deep-seated hatred of Jews by some Germans never disappeared, but enough Christians were tolerant and enough opportunities for Jews to participate in German affairs appeared that German Jews were led into the twentieth century with hopes for the ultimate victory of the *Haskalah* movement. With Hitler it all came to an end.

Emancipation of the Jews in Europe did not start in Germany, despite the leadership of German Jews in the development of the *Haskalah*. Rather it was in France that Jews first obtained citizenship and some measure of equality. In eighteenth-century France the *Haskalah* was already practiced by many Sephardic Jews who lived in the Southwestern parts of the country, primarily in Bordeaux and Bayonne, while until the Revolution and for a time thereafter the Ashkenazic Jews who lived in the Eastern part of the country, with centers in Alsace-Lorraine and Metz, were opposed to any integration of Jewish and French cultures. During the Revolution and for the next two decades, however, the Jews found themselves in a political situation which encouraged integration with the rest of France. Declarations of 1790 and 1791 suddenly made Jews citizens, and by the first decade of the nineteenth century the premise for Napoleon's organization of the Jews living in France was the assumption that Jews would cease many of their former practices and adopt many French ways. Only by being French nationals of the Jewish faith could Jews persuade the French parliament, and eventually Napoleon, to legislate their equality. In 1807 at the call of Napoleon, the Jews agreed formally to the terms of separation of synagogue and state. The following year, Napoleon consented to Jewish requests for the establishment of a centralized Jewish organization modeled on the minority Protestant consistories. There was one overall Jewish consistory, plus seven regional Jewish consistories.[4] Once citizenship and the hope of equality became realities for Jews, Jews began to come to France from all over Europe.

But legalized equality did not mean acceptance of their equality on the part of non-Jews. Christians called for the regeneration of the Jews—that is, educating Jews in the French language and French culture and converting the Jewish economy away from livelihoods of usury and begging to industrial, agricultural, and professional livelihoods. Behind the concept of regeneration was the opinion of many Catholics that most Jews were degenerate because of religious beliefs. Consequently, the Jewish consistories emphasized religious, educational, and economic changes to help remove the "stigma of degeneration" from Judaism. Individual Jewish intellectuals gained admittance to the universities and technical colleges to which they had previously been denied entrance, and many became close friends of Christian intellectuals with whom they shared liberal and republican ideals. Individual Jews were acceptable, but Judaism was not. As a result, those

---

[3] Eric Werner, *Mendelssohn: A New Image of the Composer and His Age* (London: The Free Press of Glencoe, Collier-Macmillan, 1963), 29.

[4] Eventually this was increased to nine.

individual Jews were accepted only to a point beyond which their religion became an impediment. The period from the 1820s to the 1860s, then, was one of turmoil for Jewish intellectuals. What started in the 1820s as the exciting expectation of a breakthrough and of Jewish acceptance in France, by 1860 had become for Jews the sad realization that Jew-hatred would not go away.

In Eastern Europe the political and social conditions did not allow the *Haskalah* to develop as rapidly as in the West, but many individual Jews—cognizant of the *Haskalah* in Germany and France—wanted for themselves a reform of Jewish customs and practices that would make them more modern. Such Jews were called *maskilim* (sing., *maskil*: enlightened one). Prior to the 1820s there were practically no *maskilim* in Russia. A Jew enamored of non-Jewish science, arts, and life style generally either converted to Russian Orthodoxy or went abroad. The overwhelming mass of Jews in Russia remained Orthodox or Chasidic throughout the nineteenth century, and until a handful of enlightened Jews gained governmental endorsement, the traditional Jewish leadership kept the *Haskalah* out.

There had always been some Jews aware of the surrounding culture, but they remained very small in numbers and on the periphery of Jewish life. When the great Gaon of Vilna studied non-Jewish science and letters, incorporated some of it in his work, and allowed some of his disciples to study it, he did so with the clear understanding that it never replaced the primacy of Jewish authority.[5] He was no *maskil*; "he considered the *Haskalah* an assimilationist movement that would estrange Jews from their values and traditions; he even approved the burning of their books."[6]

The most important pioneer of the *Haskalah* in Russia was Isaac Baer Levinsohn (1788-1860), whose book *Te'udah be-Yisrael* (*Testimony in Israel*, 1828) became the manual for the movement in Russia during the next few decades. In this work Levinsohn preached that pious Jews should study the Hebrew language and grammar as a science and should learn foreign languages and secular sciences.[7] Although Levinsohn was called a heretic by traditional Jews, his viewpoint was much approved by the government and inspired a whole new generation of Russian *maskilim*. The Tsar remained anti-Semitic, and nearly all Jews were highly suspicious of anything that the government did pertaining to Jews. The small group of *maskilim* who dissented from this view, however, had now gained recognition; at last they could come into the open with their beliefs. Their strongholds were in Vilna and Odessa, where they could challenge the great Jewish institutions of those Jewish capitals. The main result of Levinsohn's *Te'udah be-Yisrael* was to draw the lines between those who believed in a Jewish enlightenment (the *Haskalah*) and those who adamantly opposed it (traditional Judaism).

Equally important for the rise of the *Haskalah* in Russia during the 1820s was the establishment of modern schools. The most successful one was in Odessa, which opened in 1826 under the leadership of Bezalel Stern, supplementing Talmud study with Hebrew and modern languages, Mendelssohn's German translation of The Bible, and a full range of secular subjects.[8] A modern

---

[5] Stanislawski, 50.

[6] Masha Greenbaum, *The Jews of Lithuania: A History of a Remarkable Community 1316-1945* (Jerusalem: Gofen, 1995), 87-88.

[7] S. Baron, 125, and Stanislawski, 52-56.

[8] Stanislawski, 58.

school for girls opened in Odessa in 1835. Odessa was an ideal city for these schools since a large number of enlightened Jews from the western city of Brody had just arrived in Odessa, where, in 1840, they opened the Broder Synagogue, one of the most important synagogues for music in all of Russia.

While the emphasis was on the establishment of modern schools for pupils through their high school years, two modern rabbinical seminaries, too, were organized in 1847 in Vilna and Zhitomir. There were no communities who would accept their graduates for rabbinical positions, however, since the modern seminaries could not compete with the Orthodox schools in Jewish studies and there were no Reform congregations in Russia. Therefore the graduates went on to universities and received a secular education. Polemics for religious reform in Russia would come later, during the 1860s and 1870s with the efforts of Moshe Leib Lilienblum. Under the reign of Alexander II, Russian was "timidly" introduced into the synagogue;[9] German, the foreign language most used by Russian *maskilim* because of its similarity to Yiddish, was not used. But Reform Judaism, as practiced in Germany and later America, never gained a foothold in Russia.

When Tsar Nicolas II died in 1855, he was succeeded by his son, Alexander II, the most "liberal" of all the nineteenth-century tsars. During the ensuing two decades modern Jews were caught up in the various political and social movements that affected the Russian intelligentsia in general. The *maskilim* operated under the delusion that the Tsars were becoming friendly to the Jews and preparing the country for liberal reforms. The Jewish intelligentsia urged the use of Russian over Yiddish, and Joachim Tarnopol (1810-1900) suggested cleansing the Oral Law to bring it in line with modern (non-Jewish) customs. They wanted to break out of the narrow confines of the traditional Jewish life. Poet Yehudah Leib Gordon (1830-92) coined the expression, "Be a Jew at home and a man in the streets," which became their battle cry. While some of this had positive effects, the results were mostly negative. Thus, although Kalman Schulman (1819-99) popularized modern science and history in Hebrew among Jews, most *maskilim* used their new learning in a negative way: to attack the orthodox and hasidic communities. The Society for the Promotion of Enlightenment among the Jews was founded in St. Petersburg in 1863,[10] as support for the *maskilim*. The government's intent, however, was to end the separation of Jews from mainstream Russians by converting all Jews to Christianity, and by attacking their fellow Jews the *maskilim* fell unknowingly into the trap.[11]

Jewish hopes, however unreal, were dashed when Alexander II was assassinated in 1881. Terrified that Jews and other foreign, subversive intellectuals were threatening his kingdom and his life, Alexander III, son of the previous Tsar, initiated the infamous pogroms that totally changed Jewish life in Russia. Instead of encouraging Jews to become integrated in Russian society, the brutal butchering of Jews across the land made them aware that they were far from equal, and that they had no rights. One million Jews left the country during the next thirty-five years, most immigrating to America. Those who remained behind suffered incredible mistreatment by ordinary Russians and the Russian government. For the majority of *maskilim*

---

[9] S. Baron, *Russian Jew*, 132.

[10] Ibid., 374.

[11] Ibid., 129.

the *Haskalah* had become sterile and negative, and many of the younger intellectuals of the late nineteenth century turned to Zionism or converted.[12] For those intellectuals who remained, the *maskilim* regrouped and had added incentive to integrate into Russian life in order to try to bridge the gap between Jews and the larger community.

The development of the *Haskalah* in Germany, France, and Russia opened Jews to all facets of modern life which the ghetto mentality of Orthodoxy had forbidden. For the first time, Jews in large numbers took part in the musical life of Europe, interacting with non-Jewish musicians and with their own musical ancestors. On the one hand, Jews participated in all aspects of the general European musical scene, sometimes drawing on their Jewish heritage for musical inspiration; on the other hand, many Jews found aesthetic and spiritual satisfaction bringing their outside musical experiences into the synagogue.

---

[12] Ibid., 133. See also Louis Greenberg, *The Jews of Russia*; vol. 1, *The Struggle for Emancipation* (New Haven: Yale University Press, 1944), chapter 14.

8 The Cantor of the Nineteenth and Twentieth Centuries

As a result of the *Haskalah* and the subsequent emancipation of the Jews of Central and Western Europe during the Napoleonic period, the role of the cantor (*chazzan*) and the music of the cantor (*chazzanut*) among Ashkenazic Jews went through a number of changes. These changes, profoundly influenced in the twentieth century by the development of two new musical traditions (*minhag* America and *minhag* Israel[1]), made the lives of cantors and their music something far different from what it had been in 1800. Consequently, the situation of both *chazzan* and *chazzanut* among the Ashkenazic Jews today has little to do with that of two centuries earlier. As the nineteenth century opened, the cantor continued a thousand-year tradition. From the 1820s to the 1940s the cantor became the star performer in the synagogue, which led to the claim that this period was the *chazzanut's* golden age. Today, however, the cantor in most Western synagogues serves more as part-time *shaliach tzibbur* and part-time assistant rabbi, while in the East his role remains primarily as *shaliach tzibbur*, and has scarcely changed over time.

Itinerant Cantors

At the beginning of the nineteenth century most cantors in Europe, however talented, were musically illiterate—that is, they could neither read nor write musical notation.[2] They depended entirely on memory to learn and teach their repertory of synagogue music. Many were itinerant cantors who roamed the countryside performing their music in whatever village

---

[1] *Minhag* means "tradition"; in Jewish studies, each major Jewish cultural and religious group of the past millennium belongs to a particular tradition, such as *minhag Ashkenazi* and *minhag Sefardi*. Post-Holocaust alignments have resulted in two new major Jewish cultural and religious centers: in North America and in Israel.

[2] Pinchas Sherman, "Polishe Hazanut in Fargangenheit un Tzukunft," in *The History of Hazanuth Issued to the 30th Anniversary of the Jewish Ministers Cantors Association of America, Sunday, February 3rd, 1924*, ed. Aaron H. Rosen (New York: The Jewish Ministers Cantors Association of America, Pinski-Massel Press, 1924), 49-51.

would have them. They usually did not sing the entire service, which was in the hands of the local *shaliach tzibbur*; instead they sang only certain prayers which enabled them to move the congregation to heights of spirituality. They experienced great poverty, and they struggled to receive recompense for their musical enhancement of special events such as weddings, *brit milahs*, funerals, and Jewish holidays. For these occasions the *gabbai* (an officer of a synagogue or a Jewish community, usually responsible for the business affairs of the synagogue) doled out a small portion of the intake to the cantor, which often would barely pay for bread. No general regulations or customs protected the cantor from starvation or gave him any sense of security. Since the Jews of the small villages had little money to spend, the cantor moved from town to town, staying just long enough to earn whatever a single village could afford to pay him. For the High Holidays, however, a well-respected cantor was always welcome in the same city year after year. Such was the case with Salomon Weintraub (1781-1829), also known as Kashtan, a musically illiterate, itinerant cantor famous for his elaborate embellishments, who found rest from his wanderings each year during *Rosh Hashanah* and *Yom Kippur* in Dubno, Poland.

The itinerant cantor often traveled with two additional singers (*meshorerim*) who accompanied his solo singing. One of these was a bass, usually a young man who earned his meager subsistence by sharing the handouts which the cantor managed to eke out. The other, called the "singer," was a child, a boy whose voice had not yet changed. The *meshorerim* were entirely dependent on the *chazzan*, and they felt very fortunate indeed when their *chazzan* was of the caliber of Salomon Weintraub, an honest man who had much to teach them and whose reputation ensured a modicum of financial security.

Accompanying an itinerant cantor, however, meant that the *meshorer* forsook not only his own family but also the rigors of education in a *cheder*[3] or an apprenticeship to a skillful artisan. Since many singers grew up to become the next generation of cantors, the general educational level of the itinerant cantor was minimal—even in Hebrew. Thus was perpetuated a profession of men who were not highly esteemed and were often the butt of jokes. Their low educational background, musical illiteracy, and often unstable domestic lives, together with the poor pay they received, had an effect on the quality of what they performed. And in the hands of such cantors traditional Jewish *chazzanut* was in peril of being corrupted beyond recognition.

Salomon Sulzer and the Reform of the Cantorate

In the early nineteenth century in Central and Western Europe some cantors saw this sorry state in Jewish liturgical music and set out to stop it. Their aim was to approach *chazzanut* with extensive knowledge of Hebrew and of the Talmud, with solid, literate musical foundations, and with respect for traditional synagogue modes and melodies still encountered in the less ornate singing of the *shaliach tzibbur*. As Moritz Deutsch observed,[4] by the mid-nineteenth century three

---

[3] A traditional European Jewish school where Hebrew, Biblical interpretation, and other Jewish subjects were taught to children.

[4] *Vorbeterschule: Vollständige Sammlung der alten Synagogen-Intonationen* (Breslau: Julius Hainauer, 1871), as quoted in Aron Friedmann, *Lebensbilder berühmter Kantoren* (Berlin: C. Boas Nachfolger, 1918), 1-44.

traditions of *chazzanut* were cultivated: 1) that of the new "reform" cantors whose aim was to preserve tradition but modernize the music through the use of meters and up-to-date harmonies, to be sung by a trained four-voice choir, and even at times accompanied by an organ—a position at the time promulgated by a minority of Europe's cantors; 2) that of the traditional itinerant cantors who knew little of traditional *nusach* and who continually created new, faddish songs and intonations with no lasting value; and 3) that of the *shaliach tzibbur* who stubbornly clung to the oldest group of songs which had widespread use and were typical of the synagogue's oldest *chazzanut*. The reform cantors reacted negatively to the position of the second group but deeply respected that of the third group. They also feared that the old songs would be lost if not immediately preserved in notation and arranged in modern, nineteenth-century styles of performance.

The most important pioneer in this reform was Salomon Sulzer (1804-90; see fig. 8.1), arguably the most significant cantor of the nineteenth and twentieth centuries. It was he who changed the role of the cantor from scorned, illiterate, itinerant beggar to respected, educated, well-positioned purveyor of great Jewish music.

FIG. 8.1   Salomon Sulzer.
Synagogue Music no. 8 (New York, 1954)
Used with permission of
Hebrew Union School of Sacred Music

Sulzer was born in the south German town of Hohenems near the Alps.[5] His parents originally intended for him to go into business, but his intense interest in Judaism and beautiful voice convinced them to allow him to pursue the career of a singer. He started as a *meshorer* for a cantor in nearby Endingen and at thirteen returned to his birth town where, despite his age, he was engaged as cantor. He was granted a three-year sabbatical so that he could learn the art of *chazzanut* from Solomon Eichberg (1786-1880), the former cantor in Hohenems whom Sulzer greatly admired, and from the itinerant Swiss cantor Lippmann, who brought Sulzer along as he traveled through France and Alsace-Lorraine. Sulzer also studied music for a year in Karlsruhe before returning, at age sixteen, to assume his responsibilities as cantor in Hohenems. In 1826, at age twenty-two, he was appointed chief cantor at the newly organized Seitenstettengasse Synagogue in Vienna, where he remained for the rest of his life–sixty-four years in one place. He was greatly admired not only by the members of the Jewish community but also by the professional composers of the city and all who visited it, including Schubert, Liszt, and the important music critic Eduard Hanslick.[6] Jewish music and Cantor Sulzer achieved reputations and status unknown in Europe before then.

Sulzer was hired to work with Rabbi Isaac Noah Mannheimer to establish a synagogue in Vienna that would be acceptable to the Kaiser. It was commonplace in earlier synagogues for each congregant to recite prayers independently of anyone else standing in the same room, and the resulting polyphonic cacophony often mystified non-Jews who were used to the composed polyphony in churches.[7]

Since the Kaiser would not allow a synagogue with such noise (whether real or imagined) in his imperial capital Vienna, Mannheimer and Sulzer were compelled to bring "Christian" order, dignity, and solemnity to the service. Fearing that a rabbi would only perpetuate old customs, Mannheimer was allowed to stay in the city as a minister, preacher, or teacher but not as a rabbi. The cantor was himself to be a respected gentleman, able to speak perfect German and accepted by Viennese society, not a typical impoverished itinerant. The music had to be performed in a way that made it agreeable to a congregation accustomed to hearing the finest music (in 1826 Vienna was, after all, the city where Beethoven and Schubert were living). The cantor would lead the congregants in singing, educate them in the proper music, and teach them how to sing. He would bring synagogue music into the modern age, arranging it for four-voice choruses in specific keys, meters, and tempos that would be recognizable to an educated European musician of the time.

Sulzer fit the bill. He was educated in Hebrew, the Talmud, general studies, and music, had thorough knowledge of South German Jewish traditional *nusach*,[8] and was well aware of the distortions that itinerant cantors had imposed on Ashkenazic chant. He had conservatory training and was such an accomplished singer of German art song that during his first two years in Vienna he often performed with possibly the greatest composer of German song, Franz Schubert.

---

[5] Friedmann, 2:46-49.

[6] Eric Werner, *A Voice Still Heard* (University Park, PA: Pennsylvania State University Press, 1976), 215-17.

[7] A witness to Christian misunderstanding of the singing of synagogue prayer is captured in Orazio Vecchi's *L'Amfiparnaso* and referred to by the *Breslauer Zeitung* (15 April 1845, p. 803) in its praise of Cantor Moritz Deutsch who brought order to his synagogue prayers. See Werner, *A Voice*, 208.

[8] *Nusach* is a term used to refer to the collective musical repertory of a particular Jewish tradition.

Through nearly all of the nineteenth century he was in fact a congenial participant in the artistic life of Vienna.

Sulzer composed two large collections of synagogue music which reflect the aims of his reform of Ashkenazic music: *Schir Zion* 1 (1839) and *Schir Zion* 2 (1865). The most informative description of *Schir Zion* is by Eric Werner:[9]

> The difference in style between volume 1 and volume 2 of *Schir Zion* clearly indicates essential changes in Sulzer's approach to *minhag ashkenaz* and, notably, his painstaking revival of older traditions, both of Western and Eastern origin.... In the first volume he stated: "I see it as my duty ... to consider as far as possible the traditional tunes bequeathed to us, to cleanse their ancient and decorous character from the later accretions or tasteless embellishments, to restore their original purity, and to reconstruct them in accordance with the text and with the rules of harmony ...". The preface of the second volume stressed the tradition originating in the time of Maharil,[10] and also the inclusion of a good number of eastern Ashkenazic (Polish) elements. It mentioned a few pieces that he had provided with modest organ accompaniments. "The volume performs a mediatory mission between the past and the future."
>
> Most characteristic of the first volume are the numerous five- to eight-part *a cappella* settings. . . . His cantorial recitatives are quite impressive without many embellishments, and traditional in a noble— one is tempted to say classical—style, with impeccable taste.... In the second volume ... Sulzer abandoned his original intention of introducing *a cappella* art music to the synagogue. He now realized that this aspiration was not realistic. [*Ed.*: Instead of sophisticated polyphonic models he now turned to the example of simple folk-like tunes which were known in synagogues throughout Europe.] Some of the tunes in this collection came from far away places, yet they had already been chanted early in the century, and several are found in the manuscripts in the Birnbaum collection.[11] The modal flavor is more stressed in the second volume than in the first. . . . The great choral structures recede in the second volume, and the *hazan* comes more into his own than before. A few recitatives are accompanied by organ; the finest composition is the priestly benediction for the festivals [which] breathes a high and quiet solemnity.

---

[9] Werner, *A Voice*, 213-14. A third volume of *Schir Zion*, published posthumously by his son Joseph Sulzer (Frankfurt a/M: Kaufmann, 1922), is a distortion of the earlier volumes.

[10] Rabbi Jacob ben Moses Moellin (ca. 1360-1427), who ran a yeshivah in Mainz and was one of Germany's most important Talmudists, was also a cantor who preached the preservation of traditional synagogue tunes. See Ephraim Kupfer, "Moellin," in *Encyclopaedia Judaica*, 12:210-11.

[11] Cantor Eduard Birnbaum (1855-1920) was a pupil of Sulzer and later Hirsch Weintraub's successor as cantor in Königsberg (1879-1920). He took over a large collection of synagogue music amassed by Weintraub (son of Kashtan) and added greatly to it, including many Sulzer manuscripts. Since 1923 the collection has been housed in the Klau Library at Hebrew Union College in Cincinnati. Cf. Irene Heskes, *Passport to Jewish Music: Its History, Traditions and Culture* (Westport, CT: Greenwood Press, 1994), 7, 51.

Sulzer also compiled a collection of short responses and choruses for home and school entitled *Dudaim* (1850). All of his works became models for dozens of publications by cantors throughout the rest of the nineteenth and into the twentieth century.

Followers of Sulzer

At the beginning of the nineteenth century the Jewish community in Munich had the same aspirations as the Jewish community in Vienna. Here Maier Kohn (1802-1875) effected changes similar to those of Sulzer—that is, the enhancement of the service with artistic song and choruses, changes that were supported financially as well as philosophically by the congregation. Maier had arrived in Munich with his wife in 1825 to open a school for Jewish girls. In 1832, after much effort, he founded a four-voice choir to sing responses, intermittent polyphonic choral compositions, and the choral exchanges between the congregation and the cantor. Since there was as yet no repertory of such choral works, local non-Jewish composers such as Franz Lachner, Caspar Ett (Kohn's music teacher), and Karl Ludwig Drobisch contributed new compositions. Eventually Kohn wrote his own works, which he published in 1839 with the assistance of his congregation.[12] These choruses were added to the Orthodox service, whose liturgy was not changed and where most of the prayers and all the readings continued to follow the traditional *nusach*. It was very important for Kohn that these compositions not be confused with the new liturgical music of liberal German synagogues which copied Protestant models outright in the use of chorales and hymns. Rather, Kohn's songs were Jewish works which followed only some aspects of Protestant music (i.e., the norms of classical art music). Kohn did not come to the cantorate through the usual routes. It was only in 1843, after his contributions to Jewish choral music had been made, that he was appointed second cantor in Munich at the side of the first cantor, Max G. Löwenstamm (1814-81).

Cantorial Reform in France

Into this setting came Samuel Naumbourg (1817-80; fig. 8.2), who as assistant to Kohn learned the taste and style of the new synagogue music based on Bavarian *nusach*, which he then, in 1845, brought to Paris. The Jewish community in Paris had a status in that city which was the envy of all the Jewish communities in Europe. Under Napoleon the Jews had been granted equality with non-Jews and their synagogues had been organized into regional consistories. The first cantor hired by the Paris consistory was Israel Löwy, who served there from 1818 to 1832. He was a talented singer but had little impact on the daily prayers. After more than a decade in which inadequate cantors served following Löwy's death in 1832, the Paris consistory hired Naumbourg. He was not just a fine singer but was also an accomplished composer capable of introducing the new musical reforms to the French capital. On the selection committee to

---

[12] *Vollständiger Jahrgang von Terzett- und Chorgesängen der Synagoge in München nebst sämtlichen Chorresponsorien zu den alten Gesangsweisen der Vorsänger (Chasunus)* (Munich: Johann Palm, 1839).

FIG. 8.2   Samuel Naumbourg.
Synagogue Music no. 14 (New York, 1954)
Used with permission of Hebrew Union School of Sacred Music

choose the chief cantor in 1845 were Jacques-François-Fromental Halévy (1799-1862) and Charles-Valentin Alkan (Morhange, 1813-88), the former the outstanding Jewish composer of opera and the latter a leading piano virtuoso who was an ardent Jew.

Aided by such backers, Naumbourg flourished in the post until his death. He remains one of only a few true rivals to Sulzer in the composition of artistically great reform synagogue song. Naumbourg published three volumes of synagogue music containing traditional music, settings of various prayers and psalms by distinguished Jewish musicians such as Halévy, Meyerbeer, and Alkan, and his own choral compositions.[13] A work like "S'u She'orim" (Lift up your heads), which is sung while the Torah is taken from the ark on Sabbath mornings, reflects a triumphant grand opera march and is one of Naumbourg's most enduring reform compositions.

---

[13] *Semiroth Israel [Zemirot Yisra'el]*, vol. 1 (1847), vol. 2 (1852), and vol. 3 (1857). See John H. Baron, "A Golden Age for Jewish Musicians in Paris: 1820-1865," in *Musica Judaica* 12 (1991-92): 30, note 1, for a discussion of the correct dating of Naumbourg's collections.

Louis Lewandowski and the Berlin Community

Even before Vienna and Paris, Berlin could boast one of the outstanding cantors of the turn of the century in Aaron Beer (1738-1821), who served in Berlin from 1765 to 1821. An exception to the prevailing low level of the cantorate at the time, Beer was a musically literate cantor who compiled two large collections of synagogue music. He not only wrote down his own versions of the *nusach*, but he also copied out the tunes of many of his contemporaries. His collection is one of the most important resources we have for understanding what synagogue music was like during the eighteenth century before the reforms of Sulzer, Naumbourg, Lewandowski, and others.

Beer was succeeded by Ascher Lion (1776-1863), who came to Berlin's Heidereutergasse Synagogue in 1818. Lion was well schooled in traditional Prussian *chazzanut* and taught it to a number of choir boys who eventually became cantors: Jeretzki and Mirkin, among others, and Louis Lewandowski, who became the most important composer of synagogue music in nineteenth-century Germany.[14] Lion, however, was not as competent as his predecessor; he was not well trained in music and could not read it. In 1840, after Hirsch Weintraub performed concerts of Sulzer's music in Berlin, the Jews of Berlin, not wanting to lag behind Vienna in music for the synagogue, impelled Lion to form a four-voice choir, acquire Sulzer's music, and establish a Berlin repertory. Since he did not have the skills to teach music to such a choir, the Berlin community hired a well-trained musician who had served as a choirboy under Lion to coach him and train a choir. The choice—Louis Lewandowski (1821-94; fig. 8.3)—was most fortunate: soon Lewandowski would be known as Sulzer's principal disciple in musical reform.

Lion never learned to read music (nor did he recognize Sulzer's reforms), and an assistant cantor was hired to accomplish what he could not. This was Abraham Jakob Lichtenstein (1806-80), who arrived in Berlin in 1845 and soon forced Lion into retirement.[15] Lichtenstein was a modern cantor with a gorgeous voice, who could read music and was an outstanding musician. He started in the traditional way, leaving home at age nine to sing in Cantor Leib Conrad's choir in Königsberg. While there he also studied Hebrew and music and developed into a virtuoso violinist. After his voice changed, he became, at sixteen, a bass *meshorer* to Chazzan Lowe in Glogau, Germany. He later served as cantor and kosher butcher in Posen, Frankfurt am Oder, Schwedt, and Stettin. In this last city he worked closely with the well-known Christian composer Karl Loewe (1796-1869), whose songs he sang and in whose orchestral music he often played violin. When Lichtenstein went to Vienna years later to sing for Sulzer and learn from him, Sulzer is said to have remarked: "You, dear colleague, could only be taught by God."

In Berlin there ensued an artistically profitable collaboration between Lichtenstein and Lewandowski, who continually influenced each other. Lewandowski was by far the best trained and most talented composer of synagogue music in the nineteenth century. He had studied at the Akademie der Kunst in Berlin (not an insignificant feat for a Jew at that time) and was the composer of a symphony and a string quartet that saw public performances. Lewandowski had decided to devote his life to the synagogue following his recovery from a serious illness.

---

[14] Friedmann, 2:37-38.

[15] Ibid., 1:70-71, 77-86.

After the Berlin community hired him in 1840 he was sent to Vienna to learn about Sulzer's reforms. Upon his return, he persuaded the unsympathetic Lion to throw out the singer/bass choir and establish a four-voice one. In his first publication, *Kol Rinnah u-Tefillah* (1865), Lewandowski demonstrated his ability to write elegant responses to traditional chant, and in his second, *v'Zemirah* (1876-82), he revealed himself to be a great polyphonic choral composer. In 1866, when he moved from the old synagogue in Berlin to the new one on Oranienburgerstrasse, he had an organ at his disposal; consequently, he added organ accompaniment to his music and composed a series of organ preludes based on traditional chant.[16] Later, for the dedication of a new liberal synagogue in Nürnberg, he set over forty psalms in German, which are among his most elaborate pieces.

With such a composer and choir director at his side, Lichtenstein excelled in creating a new Berlin repertory, and with such a singer for whom to write, Lewandowski was inspired to new heights. The former sang his learned and artistic recitatives, which Lewandowski wrote down; then from the printed recitatives Lichtenstein elaborated on them. Lichtenstein was ardently orthodox, and the music that he and Lewandowski produced, including the four-part choruses, was meant for a liturgy that remained orthodox. Yet the music was so compelling that the German liberal synagogues also took it up and made it a standard part of their *nusach*.

---

[16] For descriptions of Lewandowski's organ, the controversy about building organs in Berlin synagogues, and a brief overview of organs in synagogues in Prague, Italy, and Germany, see Tina Frühauf, "Louis Lewandowski's *Five Festival Preludes Op. 37* for Organ," trans. Harvey Spitzer, *Journal of Jewish Music and Liturgy* 21 (1999): 20-40.

In the wake of the reforms four-voice choirs were organized throughout the country,[17] and numerous editions of the new music by lesser composers circulated throughout Western Europe. The reform music of Sulzer, Naumbourg, and Lewandowski was based on the assumption that synagogue music should be modernized following the rules of European music, which was tonal, metric, and conceived in four voices. Such rules were entirely contrary to traditional Jewish chant, which was modal, non-metric, and solistic, with the accompaniment, sometimes, of two vocal assistants. The three great composers of Western European synagogue music knew this and thus retained traditional chant for most of the service. The purpose of music in the synagogue was to spiritually uplift the congregation and enhance the liturgy, which should always remain more important than the music. Since the German, French, Swedish,[18] Dutch, and Swiss Jewish communities were liberated and were immersed in the secular concert and opera music of the time, their response to European classical music in the synagogue was full acceptance. In their desire to become part of the mainstream of Western European society, they were willing to sacrifice that part of their Jewish heritage that sounded exotic and would have emphasized their differences from the host societies.

Eastern European Reaction to the Western Reforms

This situation did not exist in most of Eastern Europe. Most Jews were not liberated, did not attend operas and concerts, and had no positive emotional responses to the music of the great classical composers of Western Europe.[19] Yet there were some cantors in Russia who desired to improve the status of the cantor in the East and observed with envy the reform music of Sulzer, Naumbourg and Lewandowski. They were aware of the Western-influenced classical music of the Russian and Polish aristocracy and sought to make some accommodation with the surrounding higher-class culture.

Probably the most important such cantor, initially, was Chayim Wasserzug (1822-82),[20] who was trained by his father, a cantor in Poland. In 1840 Wasserzug became himself a cantor in Konin, near the German border, while continuing as an itinerant cantor during the summer. Later he became a cantor in a village near Warsaw. Uncharacteristic of his Russian and Polish Jewish forebears, he traveled twice a week to study the science of music. He held several more small posts as cantor, continuing to travel through Poland, Russia, and Hungary as an itinerant

---

[17] Hermann Ehrlich (1815-79) published a treatise on how to organize and run such a choir: *Praktischer Stufengang zur Gründung und Bildung zweck- und zeitgemässer Synagogenchöre, zugleich als theoretisch-praktische Gesanglehre für höhere israelitische Lehranstalten und Volksschulen* (1859).

[18] The most important Swedish reform cantor was Abraham Baer (1834-94), who served in Göteborg for thirty-seven years.

[19] Concerts and operas performed in Russia prior to the 1860s were primarily for the aristocracy in the major cities of Moscow and Saint Petersburg, where few Jews were allowed to live. Thus even the average non-Jewish Russian would have had little or no contact with classical art music before late in the nineteenth century and a Jew in Russia would scarcely have had opportunity to hear any. Rather, when copying the music of their surroundings, the Jews of Russia drew from a wealth of Russian folk music.

[20] Friedmann, 1:106-10.

cantor. Since he traveled so much and made a sensation wherever he went, his reputation spread quickly and widely, and around 1858 he was called to the Great Synagogue in Vilna as cantor. His voice was so strong that he was often offered a chance to sing opera, but he refused on the grounds that it was against his faith. God gave him his voice, and he owed it to God to use it in His service. In 1878 he published *Sefer Shirei Mikdash, alte und moderne Synagogenmelodien*, which includes many traditional chants but also new four-part choral responses. Ten years earlier he had emigrated to London, where he served the North Synagogue, and where he remained for the rest of his days (see below).

More significant for the history of Russian synagogue music was Nissen Blumenthal (1805-1903). No illiterate, itinerant cantor, the Rumanian-born Blumenthal had studied the Bible and the Talmud as well as music and singing. Serving first in Berdichev and Yekaterinoslav, where he perfected his craft, in 1841 he was hired as the first cantor of the new Broder Synagogue in Odessa, founded the year before. He remained there for the next sixty-two years. He knew that his congregation would not accept reform music outright, so he gradually introduced elements of it while retaining most of the traditional *nusach*. He established the first Jewish liturgical choir in Russia—that is, an all male choir that could read music and was trained in both homophonic and contrapuntal singing. He brought the young David Nowakowski (1848-1921) to the Broder Synagogue in 1869 and placed him in charge of the choir.[21] Minkowsky describes Blumenthal's contributions as two-fold: he collected and introduced Western European song into the Russian synagogue, and he composed his own synagogue music imbued with the Jewish spirit. He did not publish music, but his manuscripts and manuscript copies of these circulated widely in Europe as his influence on the modernization of the cantorate spread eastward.

The institution of the itinerant cantor continued in Eastern Europe after the Western European cantors had changed course, though under the influence of both Western and Eastern reformers many itinerant cantors eventually studied music and settled down. For example, the twelve-year-old orphan Isak Lachmann (1838-1900) joined the *meshorerim* of the itinerant cantor Salmen Huminer as a singer, and when his voice changed he continued as a *meshorer* under Pitsche Abrass and then under Bazalel Odesser, as they traveled through Russia and Poland.[22] Lachmann differed from most itinerant *meshorerim*, however, in that he had begun Hebraic studies before his parents died and he then continued these studies, along with music and singing lessons. He was thus ready to assume more permanent positions influenced by the new status of cantor and cantorial music. He moved to Germany and eventually settled in the Bavarian town of Hürben, where he served as reform cantor to the substantial and highly regarded Jewish community.

Likewise, Hungarian cantor Moritz Friedmann (1827-91) started traveling as a poor Talmudic student when he was thirteen years old, and, because he possessed a beautiful soprano voice, he earned his keep in whatever village he found himself by leading the singing of prayers.[23] In Ödenburg

---

[21] Nowakowski remained as choirmaster until his death; after Blumenthal he also served Minkowsky. His compositions for cantor and choir—published in *Shirei David* (1895 and 1901)—became standard for Russian synagogues. There is a Nowakowsky Society now reediting his music, found after World War II buried in the yard of a house. See Emanuel Rubin, "David Nowakowsky (1848-1921): A New Voice from Old Odessa," *Musica Judaica* 16 (2001-02): 20-52.

[22] Friedmann, 2:108-23.

[23] Ibid., 1:131-40.

he met Cantor Rubin Goldmark, father of the famous composer Karl Goldmark,[24] and stayed for four years to sing in his choir and learn how to be a cantor. Then in the late 1840s Friedmann apprenticed himself to Sulzer in Vienna, so that when he began his formal career as an adult cantor he was thoroughly imbued with the ideals of the reform *nusach*. In 1850 he established a synagogue in the Viennese suburb of Fünfhaus and became both its cantor and substitute rabbi, which he could do because of his Talmudic training. Seven years later he became chief cantor in Pest.

Friedmann's stature in Pest was similar to that of Sulzer's in Vienna. He was much honored by the Jewish community, which he served in many capacities besides singing, and he was also the recipient of non-Jewish honors, particularly since he espoused Hungarian nationalism and used the Hungarian language in the liturgical service along with Hebrew. Franz Liszt described his music as very sensitive, musically powerful, and tasteful.[25] The twenty-three songs in Friedmann's *Israelitischen Tempelgesänge*, which demonstrate his ability to combine modern musical rhythm and form in compositions of a traditional Jewish character, came to be standard repertory in Hungary.

Schools for Reform Cantors

In an effort to replace the old-fashioned method for learning how to become a cantor, several reform cantors created schools to train young men for the profession. In the old days boys and young men traveled with itinerant cantors or joined the choirs of established cantors in cities. What was learned varied considerably; knowledge imparted depended upon how much the cantor knew and how good a teacher he was. In many cases this worked well, but there were no controls by the Jewish communities as to the quality. With the establishment of cantorial schools in Europe, there were clear-cut regulations and requirements, and a youthful aspirant for the profession knew that study in a particular school meant proper preparation for the career of a modern cantor. Among the best established schools were those directed by Moritz Deutsch in Breslau (founded in 1859) and Abraham Birnbaum in Lodz (founded 1906).

While cantors in Eastern Europe gradually upgraded their status as professionals, thanks to the efforts of Wasserzug and Blumenthal, the poverty they lived with from day to day continued. On the other hand, emancipation during the Napoleonic times had enabled Jewish communities in Western Europe to thrive; there Jews came to be better educated and many achieved comfortable living conditions. But as emancipation allowed more Jews to enter the mainstream of European art music, the number of practicing cantors in Western Europe diminished. Fewer applicants from the West, coupled with the West's improved capabilities of supporting cantors, meant that more cantors from Eastern Europe took over cantorial posts in the West.

---

[24] He was also great-grand-uncle of the Rubin Goldmark, head of the composition department of the Juilliard School of Music who had studied with Dvořák at the National Conservatory in New York. His students there included Henry Brant, Aaron Copland, Abram Chasins, Arthur Cohn, Lehman Engel, George Gershwin, Vittorio Giannini, Frederick Jacobi, and Bernard Wagenaar, among many others who played leading roles in twentieth-century music. See Emanuel Rubin, "Jeannette Meyer Thurber (1850-1946): Music for a Democracy," in *Cultivating Music in America: Women Patrons and Activists since 1860*, ed. Ralphe P. Locke and Cyrilla Barr (Berkeley: University of California Press, 1997), 159.

[25] Deutsch, *Vorbeterschule . . .*, as cited in Friedmann, 135.

Some, such as Wasserzug, who, as pointed out above, abandoned one of the most prestigious chief cantor's positions in Eastern Europe (in Vilna) for a cantor's position in London, preferred the enlightened life-style of a Western country over tyrannical rule in Poland and Russia. Others in this category were Marcus Hast (1841-1911), born in Praga near Warsaw,[26] who spent the last forty years of his life as cantor of the Great Synagogue of London and not only sang in oratorios but composed them, and Arnold Marksohn (1839-1900), also Polish,[27] who left his early post as cantorial assistant to Wasserzug in Vilna to become Lichtenstein's assistant and successor in Berlin and who thrilled non-Jewish audiences with his performances at the Berlin Tonkunstverein.

In moving West, Eastern cantors usually had to make compromises, such as performing with an organ and singing some prayers in German, but for the most part they continued to practice all the rites and *nusach* that they had brought with them. They thus bridged the gap between the ever-increasing German liturgical reforms and the ancient Western Ashkenazi tradition that was then surviving mainly in adaptations with westernized harmonizations and rhythms.

Caught in the middle, between the enlightened communities in Germany, France, and England and those in Russia and Poland, was Hungary. Living in close geographical proximity to Vienna, many Hungarian cantors were influenced by Sulzer's reforms, but they also retained a traditional Hungarian version of the *chazzanut*. Among these cantors was Leon Kartschmaroff (1842-1915), himself a son of a cantor in Cherson, Hungary, who remained his entire life in Hungary. At his synagogue in Nagykanizsa, where he served from 1865 to 1915, he organized a four-voice choir sometimes with, sometimes without organ, but he also always considered himself a *shaliach tzibbur* and never lost himself in virtuosity.[28]

Most significant of all the Hungarian cantors was Josef Singer (1841-1911), from the village of Illinik, who did leave his native country and spent the greater part of his career in Nürnberg (1874-81) and Vienna (1881-1911), the latter as Sulzer's successor.[29] Influenced by Weintraub's music and trained as a music scholar, Singer produced the first important theoretical study of synagogue music, *Die Tonarten des traditionellen Synagogengesanges (Steiger)*, which is an attempt to understand Jewish liturgical music in the framework of Christian European theoretical terminology.

By the end of the nineteenth century, with the increasing pogroms in Russia, a new exodus of Eastern European cantors took place. Some went to Western European synagogues, but there were not enough positions. Few British synagogues were interested in hiring cantors, and those that did were primarily Liberal (the English term for American "Reform"); the Orthodox synagogues relied on traditional readers or *Shlichei tzibbur*.

Thus originated an entirely new dimension to the migration of cantors: to North America, South America, and even to South Africa. America had imported minor cantors for at least a century when in the 1870s congregations in the United States began advertising for cantors in East-European Jewish journals.[30] A few of these earlier cantors achieved prominence among

---

[26] Friedmann, 1:160-69.

[27] Ibid., 1:154-59.

[28] Ibid., 1:180-84. He published *Shirei Bet Yosif* in 1911.

[29] Ibid., 1:170-79.

[30] Heskes, *Passport*, 63.

Jews in America, such as William Sparger (1860-1904), who served Temple Emanuel in New York, and Daniel Levy (1826-1910) and Edward Stark (1863-1918), who were scholars and cantors at Temple Emanuel in San Francisco. After the pogroms of the early 1880s following the assassination of Tsar Alexander II, more prominent cantors began to take the American invitations seriously. The situation in the United States presented new challenges.[31] There was relatively little shock for the immigrant cantor serving immigrant congregations. The shock came as the traditional cantor came into contact with the increasingly secularized American Jewish congregations, growing Reform and Conservative branches of Judaism, and daily assaults on Eastern European values which were simply not accepted by Americans. An example of that is portrayed in the Warner Brothers movie *The Jazz Singer* (1927), where the Americanized son of a traditional cantorial family no longer wishes to follow his father's religious ways, but instead becomes a secular singer of non-Jewish music and marries a Christian woman.[32] Most of the cantors of the nineteenth century were sons of cantors, and this chain was broken in America. Indeed, the tragedy portrayed in this movie is lost on modern American audiences, even Jewish ones, who are unaware of the strength of the family traditions of cantors.

The immigrant *chazzanim* in America, whose voices were recorded and who thus achieved a popularity unmatched by any other generation of cantors, were great singers, educated Hebraists, and pious purveyors of traditional synagogue music evolved over hundreds of years. They usually remained poor by American standards, but such poverty was wealth compared to what they had left in Eastern Europe. They thrilled American congregants with their singing in falsetto, their virtuosity, acrobatic vocalizes, sobbing outbursts, and melodic flourishes that sometimes suggested opera (for example, of Puccini); yet they also chanted the Torah and sang with reverence like any *shaliach tzibbur*.

Among the early arrivals of this sort of cantor was Pinchos Minkowsky (1859-1924; fig. 8.4), one of the most important cantors in Eastern Europe. A Talmudic scholar, he had studied *chazzanut* with Nissan Spivak and David Nowakowsky and was the leading cantor in Odessa from 1884 to (with interruption) 1920. Yet in 1884, during a brief period of conflict with his Russian synagogue's leaders, he emigrated to New York and remained for six years. Apparently America was not yet the bustling center of Jewish life which it was to become shortly thereafter, and not a match for the thriving Jewish city of Odessa.

The experience of Boruch Schorr (1823-1904) was similar. Raised in a Chassidic home in Lemberg (Lvov), Schorr sang in the choirs of distinguished cantors Bezalel Schulsinger (ca. 1790-1860) and Yeruchom Blindman (ca. 1798-1891), and later served as cantor in Khotin, Bessarabia (1846-48), Kamenets Podolski (1848-50), Iasi (1851-54), Budapest (1855-59), and Lemberg (1859-90). Then from 1891 to 1896 he was in New York, but his congregation fondly called him back to Lemberg where he remained for the rest of his life (1896-1904).

---

[31] Much of the description of the American cantorate over the past sixty years is based on personal observation by the authors and on Mark Slobin, *Chosen Voices: The Story of the American Cantorate* (Urbana: University of Illinois Press, 1989).

[32] John H. Baron, "Music as Entertainment and Symbol in the Yiddish Cinema from the 1920s and 1930s," in *Muzik und Szene: Festschrift für Werner Braun zum 75. Geburtstag*, ed. Bernhard R. Appel, Karl W. Geck, and Herbert Schneider, Saarbrücker Studien zur Musikwissenschaft, n.s., vol. 9 (Saarbrücker Druckerei und Verlag, 2001), 413-28.

FIG. 8.4   Pinchos Minkowsky.   From *History of*
Hazanuth (1924), ed. Rosen, 83
Reproduced by permission of the Jewish
Ministers Cantors Association of America

By the 1880s there were many excellent cantors in America whose professionalism helped perpetuate traditional Ashkenazic *nusach* in the New World.   Typical of these professionals was Cantor Joshua Heschel Singer (1848-1925), born in Ponivez (Province of Kovno) who, after twenty years as cantor in Kreutzberg (Latvia) emigrated in the mid-1880s and was hired by the Orthodox synagogue Beth Jacob in Buffalo, New York.[33]   He was not a cantor famous for his virtuosity or falsetto, but he was revered by his Pine Street Synagogue in Buffalo as a Talmudic scholar and *shaliach tzibbur*.   He developed a reform choir modeled after that of Blumenthal, and among his choirboys he trained future song-writer Jack Yellen.

---

[33] Selig Adler and Thomas E. Connolly, *From Ararat to Suburbia: The History of the Jewish Community of Buffalo* (Philadelphia: The Jewish Publication Society of America, 1960), 190-91.   He published two scholarly tracts that have nothing to do with music: *Zekhoron Basefer* (Vilna) and *Mishneh Zekhoron* (Jerusalem).

FIG. 8.5 Yosele Rosenblatt. From *History of Hazanuth* (1924), ed. Rosen, 188.

Reproduced by permission of the Jewish Ministers Cantors Association of America

Those who came over after the turn of the century, however, found America to be quite different. By 1900 New York had become one of the most important Jewish cities in the world, and there was plenty there for pious Jewish scholars and singers to do. In addition, there was the lure of Jewish communities west of the Atlantic seaboard, where Jews had established a comfortable lifestyle devoid of the virulent anti-Semitism of Europe. These communities, too, offered the distressed European cantor, like Joshua Singer, a haven and a chance for development of his art. A large number of cantors then immigrated to America and remained, and this time the European superstars were among them. The most famous immigrant cantor was Yossele (Josef) Rosenblatt (1882-1933; fig. 8.5),[34] whose many records retain their popularity more than half a century after his death. Born in Belaya Tserkov, Ukraine, Rosenblatt grew up in a Chassidic community where he learned both Chassidic tunes and traditional *nusach*. After serving as cantor in Czernowitz, Munkacs, and Bratislava, he spent several years with a synagogue in Hamburg, Germany, where he became well-acquainted with reform synagogue music. In 1912 he moved to America, and was affiliated with a Hungarian synagogue in Brooklyn for the next twenty years. During that time his reputation soared, largely through records but also through public performances in concert halls and even in the movies (his cameo appearance in *The Jazz Singer* helped make him famous among non-Jews). But despite his fame and an invitation to sing at the Metropolitan Opera in New York, he never agreed to sing opera or non-Jewish music.

The First World War hastened the emigration of cantors from Europe. Among those who came at this time were Jacob Samuel Maragowsky (*alias* Zeidel Rovner, 1856-1943) and Jacob Beimel (1880-1944). Maragowsky was also from a Chassidic background and sang in choirs as a child, but when he reached maturity, he made his living at first as a merchant. He also studied violin. Finally persuaded to become a cantor because of his beautiful voice, he served as cantor in Rovno (1882-84), Kishinev (1884-96), Berdichev (1896-1903), London (1903-04), Lemberg (1904-11), and Rovno again (1911-14) before immigrating permanently to New York in 1914.

Beimel, born in Russia and a pupil of Nisson Spivak, left a post in Berlin to immigrate to New York in 1916. All these cantors were trained in Europe and came as mature *chazzanim* to America. Their success in America—they were able to earn a living and they achieved considerable respect and some fame in the New World—encouraged many other cantors to emigrate from Europe and seek fame and fortune across the ocean.

---

[34] *History of Hazanuth*, ed. Rosen, 188-189; Samuel Rosenblatt, *Yossele Rosenblatt, the Story of his Life* (New York: Farrar, Straus, and Young, 1954).

The host of cantors who then made their way from Europe to America following the World War and the Russian Revolution is legendary. They quickly found congregations throughout America who relished their great voices, respected their piety and learning, and were inspired by their intense and sincere singing of the liturgy. To name just a few of the most important, there was Zavel Kwartin (1874-1953),[35] who came to Brooklyn in 1919, left for Palestine in 1926, and returned to Newark's Brisker Synagogue in 1937; David Roitman (1885-1944),[36] who came in 1924 and served Congregation Shaare Zedek in New York for most of the ensuing years until his death; Mordecai Hershman (1888-1940; fig. 8.6),[37] who arrived in 1920 and became cantor at the Borough Park synagogue Beth El in New York; and Berele Chagi (1892-1954),[38] whose first American position was in Detroit, then Boston, and finally in New York. All were tenors renowned for their coloratura, who became famous throughout the

FIG. 8.6   Mordecai Hershman. From *History of Hazanuth* (1924), ed. Rosen, 123
Reproduced by permission of the Jewish Ministers Cantors Association of America

American Jewish community through their numerous recordings and concerts. So many distinguished European cantors came to America that Gershon Sirota (1874-1943),[39] the great *chazzan* of Warsaw (at the Tlomacka Street Synagogue 1908-27 and at the Norzyk Synagogue 1935-43)

---

[35] Eliyahu Zaludkowski, *Kulturträger von der jüdischen Liturgie* (Detroit: n.p., 1930), 331. Kwartin was born in Nova-Archangelsk and worked with his father in a manufacturing business until he was twenty-one. Then he took up music studies in Charkov, Kiev and eventually in Vienna. In 1898 he became cantor in Yekaterinoslav where he also was a businessman, but in 1903 he sold the business and devoted his full time to the cantorate. He returned to Vienna to study *chazzanut* and then served congregations in Vienna, St. Petersburg, and Budapest before coming to America.

[36] Zaludkowski, 342. As a child Roitman served in the choirs of Jakov Soraker, Lieb Shapira, Moses Hoverman, and Zeidel Ravner, and by the time he was twenty he was a professional cantor in Yelisavetgrad. Subsequently he served in St. Petersburg (twice, the second time just before the Revolution in the Great Chor-Shul), Bakhmut, Vilna (Stadt-Shul), Odessa, and Besarabia before immigrating to America.

[37] Ibid., 275. A choirboy of Zeidel Ravner in Berdichev and later Shimai Margliot, when his voice changed he joined the choirs of Nissan Belzer and Meir Pisak. He was briefly cantor in Chitomirer, then in 1913 he was appointed *Stadt-Chazan* in Vilna where he officially remained until 1920. However, during the First World War he was drafted into the army, but a sympathetic officer ordered that he serve as cantor in Kremenstok rather than serve in the field. Before and after the War he gave many concerts throughout Poland and Russia and also sang in many synagogues as a guest. By the time he left for America he was one of the most famous of all European cantors.

[38] Ibid., 299. Son of a cantor, Chagi was a prodigy with the nickname "Pure Angel," and at eight was already *dovening* (praying)—i.e., knew the prayers and their melodies. He soon joined the choirs of Boruch Leib Rosowsky in Riga and Rachinovitch in Dvinsk. At eighteen he was cantor in Smolensk. Shortly afterwards he immigrated to America.

[39] David Olivestone, "Sirota," in *Encylopaedia Judaica* (Jerusalem: Keter, 1972), 14:1620-21. Sirota did concertize in America but never settled there.

stood out as the only one who did not emigrate; he paid for it dearly with martyrdom in the Warsaw ghetto uprising.

The Europeans continued to supply America with its most important cantors until shortly after the Holocaust. During the 1930s Germany still had a number of outstanding cantors, such as Hugo Adler[40] (1894-1955) in Mannheim and Manfred Lewandowski (1895-1970) in Berlin, both of whom escaped to America just before the War. But with the Nazis' destruction of Jewish life in many countries, and the communists' squelching of it in Russia, by the late 1940s Europe could no longer supply American synagogues with cantors. Such stars as David Putterman, Moishe and David Kousevitzky, and others continued through the 1960s and 1970s, but the number of European cantors serving in North America diminished significantly and was not replenished. Instead, American congregations had to depend on younger cantors either born in America or raised there.

Earlier in the twentieth century such cantors were brought up in environments not much different from those in Europe; the cantors were trained by previous cantors through singing in their choirs, and they spent a good part of their younger lives in synagogue. Cantor Isidore Frank, for example, was the son of Cantor "Summervogel" of Siedlitz, Poland, and was born there, but he immigrated to New York as a child.[41] He continued to study with his father, studied music with local teachers, and attended New York public schools and Cooper Union. He became a cantor in 1906, served as assistant cantor to Theodore Ginsberg of Central Synagogue, and then was cantor of Mount Neboh Temple from 1918. He was also interested in social work and was chaplain of the New York House of Refuge from 1915.

On the other hand by the 1920s and 1930s other would-be cantors found that in America their voices could be turned to more profitable areas than the synagogue, and so they entered the arenas of popular music or opera. Even earlier, Al Jolson (originally Asa Yoelson, 1886-1950), for example, the son of a cantor, found show business around 1910 more to his liking than singing in a synagogue. Jolson, of course, was the model for the character of Jack Robin in *The Jazz Singer*. Both Jan Peerce (1904-84) and Richard Tucker (1913-75) were born in New York to Russian Jewish immigrants and got their start as choir singers in synagogues;[42] both were trained as cantors and served frequently as cantors, yet they were first and foremost famous opera singers. Both loved to chant the cantillations and sing the festive songs and more elaborate prayers, and their recordings of these made them both famous as cantors, and known to a wide audience even today, but they earned their living singing opera. If Peerce and Tucker had been born in Europe, they would probably have been cantors and not opera singers. Their success encouraged many other young Jewish boys of their generation and the next to go into opera or popular music rather than into the synagogue. With the waning of traditional European-like *cheder* education in America, fewer Jewish boys had knowledge of Hebrew, the *siddur*, and Judaism or, most importantly, had the missionary spirit to want to be

---

[40] About his son Samuel Adler see below.

[41] *History of Hazanuth*, ed. Rosen, 18.

[42] Jan Peerce (originally Jacob Perelmuth), *The Bluebird of Happiness*, ed. Alan Levy (New York: Harper and Row, 1976), 38: "I never discovered my Jewish identity; I always had it. I can't think of a time when I wasn't going to synagogue. I must have started at the age of two. It was only when I began going to school and moving around the Lower East Side as a kid that I discovered there were people in this world who weren't Jewish—or rather, weren't like us."

cantors. While America relied for another generation on the older immigrant cantors, with their demise largely by the 1970s the cantorial world had been changed.

The Second World War had altered the position of the cantor in most of the Jewish world. The Jewish world was now basically divided between Israel and North America, with smaller communities in South America, South Africa, and a few other locales. After the war North America assumed the greatest responsibility for the future development of synagogue music, but most Jewish young people here were ill-equipped to do so. The desire was there; some Jewish youth felt the need to return to the synagogue, and this increased by the 1970s. In some cases young men wanted to become cantors and possessed good voices but did not have much knowledge of *nusach* or Jewish tradition and only a weak knowledge of Hebrew. The growth of Jewish day schools during this period produced many more knowledgeable Jewish youth, but most Jewish children in America did not attend such schools, could barely read Hebrew, and knew only Reform or Conservative liturgy.

To rectify the situation, the three main branches of American Judaism created cantorial schools, all in New York.[43] In 1947 the Reform Movement opened the School of Sacred Music associated with the Hebrew Union College-Jewish Institute of Religion. Four years later the Cantor's Institute of the Jewish Theological Seminary was established for Conservative cantors. In 1954 the Orthodox Cantorial Training Institute was started at Yeshiva University.

As a result of the post-World War II developments, most of the professional cantors in America today bear little resemblance to their counterparts a century ago. Although in New York there still are cantors like Moshe Schulhof and David Lefkowitz, or in Chicago one like Alberto Mizrahi, or even in New Orleans singers like Joel Colman and Seth Warner, whose outstanding voices, musicianship, knowledge of traditional *nusach*, and demeanor are Sulzer-like, the modern American cantor is prized primarily for his or her ability to work with the children, substitute on occasion for the rabbi, and direct various volunteer choirs.

Because of the shortage of young male cantors and especially ones with good voices, the Reform and Conservative schools have trained cantors of both sexes, with many of the young women possessing as excellent voices as their male counterparts. The admission of women to synagogue music had already occurred in America. Following the lead of liberal German choirs in the late nineteenth century and in American Reform ones, choirs in most American synagogues today have mixed voices and are accompanied by organ.

The Modern American Cantor

Present-day American cantors see themselves as the transmitter of Jewish values and as a leader, teacher, and counselor as well as a singer. "Cantors get involved in all aspects of Jewish life whether visiting a patient in the hospital, comforting the bereaved, or celebrating life's joyous moments."[44] The cantor is trained and prepared to serve as clergy. While the traditional

---

[43] Slobin, *Chosen Voices*, 94.

[44] Michael A. Shochet, "The Cantor: A Calling for Today," a video cassette produced by Thomas Kalamar for Hebrew Union College-Jewish Institute of Religion, 1994.

roles of rabbi and cantor were distinct until the mid-twentieth century (the rabbi interpreted Torah, the cantor interpreted sacred prayer), the distinction is no longer so clear. The issue of instrumental accompaniment has been so resolved that guitars and other so-called "secular" instruments are now as accepted in many non-orthodox synagogues as the organ. Some congregations that cannot afford to hire an invested cantor turn either to a knowledgeable member of the congregation or to the cantorial soloist, a part-time singer with limited training in Jewish music who performs the duties of the old-time cantor but in the musical style of the modern cantor. With the return of emphasis on cantillation and simple chant, away from extremely ornate *chazzanut*, this alternative has become possible. The *shaliach tzibbur* is now, once again, the main singer in the American synagogue as in most of the non-Ashkenazic synagogues of the rest of the world. Only in those few Ashkenazic synagogues that have been able to find a cantor of the old school, have some remnants of the golden age of *chazzanut* lingered on.

Meanwhile, under the influence of Ashkenazic cantors, some Sephardic cantors have expanded their singing roles. At the turn of the twentieth century in such cities as Istanbul and Vienna, and in other North Mediterranean centers where both Ashkenazic and Sephardic Jews had separate but neighboring synagogues, Sephardic cantors envied the star roles that Ashkenazic cantors had achieved and desired to emulate them. The elaborate melismas were added at the end of prayers since the Sephardic could not interrupt the prayers themselves, whereas Ashkenazic virtuosic cantors elaborated the prayers in process, interrupting the words and traditional melodies. Some Sephardic cantors achieved fame for such singing comparable to that of Ashkenazic cantors. Generally, however, the Sephardim remained *shlichei tzibbur*. With the disruptions of the traditional life of the Sephardic and oriental Jews since the formation of Israel, several traditions of Sephardic are now merging into what is referred to as the Syrian-Jerusalem Sephardic rite, and a school for training cantors for this rite has recently opened in Israel.

Suggestions for Further Reading

Baron, John H. "A Golden Age for Jewish Musicians in Paris: 1820-1865." In *Musica Judaica* 12 (1991-92): 30-51.

Heskes, Irene. *Passport to Jewish Music: Its History, Traditions and Culture.* Westport, CT: Greenwood Press, 1994.

Peerce, Jan (originally Jacob Perelmuth). *The Bluebird of Happiness*, ed. Alan Levy. New York: Harper and Row, 1976.

Rosenblatt, Samuel. *Yossele Rosenblatt: The Story of his Life as Told by his Son.* New York: Farrar, Straus, and Young, 1954.

Shochet, Michael A. "The Cantor: A Calling for Today," a video cassette produced by Thomas Kalamar for Hebrew Union College-Jewish Institute of Religion (New York), 1994.

Slobin, Mark. *Chosen Voices: The Story of the American Cantorate.* Urbana: University of Illinois Press, 1989.

Werner, Eric. *A Voice Still Heard.* University Park, PA: Pennsylvania State University Press, 1976.

9 | Music of the Yiddish-Speaking World in the Nineteenth and Twentieth Centuries

The last flowering of the Jewish medieval minstrel tradition in Germany was in the sixteenth century when the *badchanim* sang their epics at weddings. While the tunes were carried eastward with the migration of Jews to Poland, in Germany they soon disappeared in favor of new poems and music which Jews there copied from their Christian neighbors. The epic tradition lingered, perhaps, a little longer in Eastern Europe, but by the beginning of the nineteenth century, when epics had not been sung for several generations, the tunes were forgotten there, too. Since nearly all this music was passed on through oral tradition, it was permanently lost. Only the texts survive.[1]

During the nineteenth century Jews hotly debated whether Yiddish was a language or merely a jargon. If it was a jargon, some felt it was only a bastardized version of German, and Jews would be better off learning modern German and German literature. If Yiddish was a language, was it the universal Jewish language? And where was its literature? These latter points became crucial, especially as the Zionist movement gained momentum after the pogroms in 1881, when many Jews turned to Hebrew as the universal Jewish language. The revival of Hebrew became an important rallying point for Zionists because they realized that Hebrew was the language that belonged to all Jews—those in Arab countries and Spanish Jews as well Ashkenazi Jews—and that historically, Hebrew was connected to the homeland, Israel. These Jews therefore considered Yiddish an unfortunate accident of history and defamed it.

Most Jews belonging to the *Haskalah* (the *maskilim*) adopted the modern European languages of the countries where they lived: German, French, Italian, English, Russian, Polish, Hungarian, and so forth; to them, too, Yiddish represented the traditional Jewish life which they rejected. Most religious Jews, however, were against Hebrew as a modern language because they feared

---

[1] Leo Wiener, *The History of Yiddish Literature in the Nineteenth Century* (New York: Charles Scribner's Sons, 1899), 1-6.

it would defile the sacred Hebrew tongue. They simply had little opportunity to learn modern European languages. For them, Yiddish was the living language.

During the middle of the nineteenth century many *maskilim* in Eastern Europe decided to write in Yiddish. They felt that only in that language could they reach the vast majority of Jews and promote their ideas. By the end of the nineteenth century not only Yiddish writers, but also critics and general readers in Europe and America had come to realize that Yiddish as a language had intrinsic qualities not duplicated in any other language.

Revival of Yiddish Song in Nineteenth-Century Eastern Europe: Anonymous Yiddish Folk Song

The loss of the music for the old epic songs precluded any revival of them in a later period. Instead of these large poems, the Jews of Eastern Europe shifted their focus to popular, everyday folk songs. Learned Jews spoke Yiddish but concentrated their scholarly writing in Hebrew or, under the influence of the *Haskalah*, German, and to some extent, Russian. Less-educated men, and women, the latter excluded from the schools and rabbinic academies, were the primary market for Yiddish poetry. They began to sing about their own lives rather than the lives of legendary kings and queens. Their songs were often functional—that is, they sang work songs, children's play and learning songs, lullabies, songs for dancing, and so on. Most of the songs were simple and much shorter than the epic songs. A large number were sung by women about women's issues. There was no pretense to art song, and the authors of the texts and tunes almost always were anonymous. The songs bore recognizable similarities to Polish, Ukrainian, and other Slavic tunes.

The first attempts to write down modern Yiddish folk songs occurred in the 1860s in Russia. Composer Modest Mussorgsky copied several such songs in several of his compositions, though we do not know how true to the originals these adaptations are.[2] Stepan Karpenko copied some dances in 1864 and G. E. Golomb copied some songs and dances in 1887.

Although Yiddish songs were originally transmitted orally, the large repertory of songs that survive today do so because of two developments in Russia at the turn of the twentieth century.[3] The first of these occurred at the end of the nineteenth century when the Russian government assigned two Jewish ethnologists, Saul M. Ginsberg (1866-1940) and Pesach S. Marek (1862-1920), the responsibility of collecting and preserving Jewish folk songs. The publication of the texts of many of the songs in *Yevreiskia Narodnia Pesni v Rossii* (*Yiddish Folk Songs in Russia*, St. Petersburg, 1901) gave rise to study of Jewish folk song both on a systematic, scholarly level and on a practical, performance level.

---

[2] The most well-known is the picture of arguing Jews in his *Pictures at an Exhibition*. See Mark Slobin, *Old Jewish Folk Music: The Collections and Writings of Moshe Beregovski* (Philadelphia: University of Pennsylvania Press, 1982), 288.

[3] For a bibliography of published Yiddish song before 1960, see Eleanor Gordon Mlotek, *Mir Trogn a Gezang!*, 3rd ed. (New York: Workmen's Circle Education Department, 1982), 234.

Since Ginsberg and Marek were not musicians, they hired the young, distinguished Russian Jewish composer Joel Engel (1868-1927) as their musical advisor. Engel took up the cause with enthusiasm. Even before the book was published, he gave an important lecture in Moscow in 1900 on Jewish music, and followed it with a concert of Jewish folk music, to demonstrate to both the Jewish and non-Jewish intelligentsia that Jewish folk music existed and that it was worthy of performance and study. Most of Engel's original ethnographic material is housed today in the Institute of Jewish Proletarian Culture of the Ukrainian Academy of Sciences, Kiev.

The second event occurred in 1906, when the composer Ephraim Skliar (1871?-1943) founded the Society for Jewish Folk Music, which remained in existence until 1918 in St. Petersburg and Moscow. Skliar was a pupil of Rimski-Korsakov, whose suggestion it was to form the society. Skliar was assisted by some of the most talented Jewish music students in Russia at the time, including Lazar Saminsky, Solomon Rosowsky, Joseph Achron, and Joel Engel. Moral support from leading Russian composers Glazunov, Liadov, and Cui (who was half-Jewish) provided further impetus. The purpose of the group was to collect Jewish music, perform it publicly, and utilize Jewish folk music in the creation of new Russian art music.

Simultaneously with these two occurrences two other scholars, Yehudah Leib Cahan (1881-1937) and Moshe Beregovski (1892-1961), whose published works are the basis for any analysis in this field, began research into late nineteenth- and early twentieth-century Jewish folk song. Cahan was born in Vilna, lived in Warsaw from 1881 to 1901, then spent three years in London. From 1904 until his death he lived in New York, where he worked closely with YIVO (The Yiddish Institute for Jewish Research), the central archive for Yiddish culture, from its inception in 1925, both in New York and in Vilna.[4] Cahan's collections stem largely from his own recollection of songs his informants sang to him as part of their own folk song heritage, and which he then sang to a cantor, who notated the songs.[5] His *Yiddishe Folkslider mit Melodien, oys dem folks-moyl gezamlt*, 2 vols. (*Yiddish Folk Songs with Melodies Collected from the Mouths of the People*, New York and Warsaw: Die Internationale Bibliothek Farlag Co., 1912), was the most scholarly anthology of Yiddish songs in its day and remains the starting point for any modern scholarly work on Yiddish song. Two subsequent collections containing 560 items followed in 1927-28 and 1931; all four were edited and reprinted in New York in 1957.

Beregovski spent nearly his whole life in Kiev, where he did pioneering ethnomusicological work at various institutes entirely under the eye of the Soviet government. Much of his work was lost or is missing inside the Ukraine, but two of his large collections of folk songs (from 1934 and 1962) were republished with introductory essays by Mark Slobin in 1982. The songs were recorded between 1912 and 1938 and include some of Engel's; they are housed in his Institute in Kiev. Recently these recordings have been reissued on compact discs. In addition, in 1945 Beregovski transcribed a large number of songs ascribed to the popular cantor and Yiddish singer Yosef Volinets (= Yosl Tolner, 1838-1919), as sung by an old acquaintance of Volinets.

---

[4] Y. L. Cahan, *Yiddish Folksongs with Melodies*, ed. Max Weinreich (New York: YIVO, 1957), 559. YIVO was founded in Vilna in 1925, and moved to New York just at the outbreak of World War II. Cf. Lucy Dawidowicz, *From That Place and Time: A Memoir 1938-1947* (New York: Norton, 1989). YIVO originally translated its own acronym as the "Yiddish Scientific Institute," but in English it is now known as The Yiddish Institute for Jewish Research. It houses the most extensive Yiddish library in the world.

[5] Slobin, *Old Jewish Folk Music*, 2.

Cahan collected songs from all regions of Eastern Europe that were brought to America by immigrants, whereas Beregovski concentrated on songs of Ukrainian Jews, especially those in the city of Kiev (though he also had access to songs collected in St. Petersburg, 1912-14, now in Kiev). Yet, no matter where the songs come from, their nature is similar. Both Cahan and Beregovski recognized the utilitarian purpose of the songs, which were meant to be sung, unaccompanied, by persons performing specific duties, such as making shoes, tailoring, putting the baby to sleep, and sewing. These are not songs generally sung by rabbis and learned Jewish men, but rather songs sung by women, children, and less-educated men involved in the manual jobs described in the songs. The folk songs are basically simple, syllabic songs, often strophic, which fit easily into the range of amateur singers. Beregovski analyzes the music of his two collections and finds that in half of the songs the scale utilized is the natural minor, often with a flattened second step resulting in an augmented second from the second to third degree, while the major scale is "insignificant."

The 1957 edition of Cahan's folk songs is divided into various categories according to text: ballads, love songs, dance songs, wedding songs, family songs, lullabies, children's songs, songs about recruiting soldiers and other military songs, work songs, religious songs, riddle songs, humorous songs, Purim songs, and others. While in his 1912 volumes Cahan gives few notes besides identifying the European locale for the songs, he gives more precise information in the subsequent collections, often referring back to his earlier volumes. Max Weingrad, editor of the 1957 volume, has been able to reconstruct some of the bibliographical information for all four volumes. All the songs are in a minor scale, though a few also modulate briefly in the middle to a major scale (for example, "S'shteyt zikh a sheyn meydele," no. 37). Beregovski, too, finds the appearance of a brief major phrase in some of his songs. In any case, since many of the folk songs in Cahan's anthology express happy sentiments it is clear that use of the minor scale in no way suggests unremitting sorrow for Jews in Eastern Europe. Some songs, such as the workers' songs, do agonize over the sad plight of the Jewish laborer, but in Cahan's collection the songs, sometimes even coupled with laughter, help conquer the sorrow of the people. Songs like "Fun vanen heybt zich on a libe?" (Where does your love come from?) and "Papir iz dokh vays, un tint iz dokh shvarts" (Paper is truly white, ink is truly black), an adaptation of a song by Zunser, are pleasant love songs, while "Zolst azoy lebn un zayn gezunt" (So live and be healthy) is possibly a unique example of a lullaby by a baby sitter who wants to get out and have fun.

Beregovski analyzes the songs in his 1934 collection in a Marxist manner as befitting a survivor in Stalin's Soviet Union. He accuses Cahan, Engel, and the others of being bourgeois in that they seek to generalize a national Jewish type from the repertory that they studied and apply it to all social and economic classes of Jews. Instead, and with more astuteness, he recognizes that Yiddish song is continually developing, always influenced by the music of its surroundings, and never so rigid that it can be fixed as a musical type beyond the moment and place in which it is sung. This is true, he finds, of all folk music. What is more, Yiddish song of the later nineteenth century and during the first half of the twentieth reflects life and song in general in a society that in a short span of time underwent a wrenching revolution from feudalism to socialism.

Initially Beregovski categorizes the subject matter of the songs into two basic groups: "(1) songs created before the arising of an organized workers' movement and (2) songs created under the immediate impact of an organized revolutionary workers' movement and reflecting its various stages."[6] What Jews are experiencing has a corollary in Ukrainian society in general at the same time. In the first group are songs that Jews sing of their own personal suffering, such as: "Hard and bitter as death is the worker's life, Oh, he must spend his strength for a crust of bread" (no. 1); "I get up early and sit at my sewing, my heart is dried up and I want a glass of tea" (no. 2); "It's pouring outdoors, and the snow is falling, thus all my young years have passed always sitting at my sewing" (no. 3); and so forth. In the second group the Jews have joined the proletariat and sing together with all working people for their improved lot, such as the next group in the 1934 anthology: "Brothers and sisters, take each other's hands, come to the fire, which flickers, we're the proletariat, that means the working people. Let us break the iron chains, throw off the heavy yoke" (end of no. 60); "Brothers, if God won't help us, let us liberate ourselves, let us break the chains and walk together" (no. 65); "Oh you foolish Zionists . . . You want to take us to Jerusalem so we can starve there; we would rather stay in Russia and liberate ourselves" (no. 66); etc.

The songs fall into four genres: lyric, ballad-like, satiric, and hymn-like. The lyric, ballad-like and some of the satiric texts are usually set as solo songs, while the rest are choral songs. Solo songs belong to the first group of pre-revolutionary folk song, a time when Jews usually were engaged in solo forms of labor. Once Jews joined the Ukrainian proletariat in revolution, the songs became choral. Jews then were no longer confined to private labor but began to engage in collective labor, such as in construction, hauling, and communal farming. Choral singing often utilized nonsense syllables, while solo singing is rhythmically and tonally freer (in the latter the soloist does not have to adjust to others). Pre-revolutionary songs, furthermore, often borrowed tunes from the romances of the nineteenth-century bourgeoisie and from synagogue melodies, whereas Yiddish revolutionary songs copy non-Jewish Ukrainian heroic songs and marches, which were foreign to earlier Jews.

In Beregovski's 1934 collection nearly everything is seen in terms of the worker and the crushing capitalistic society. Thus, even in songs that deal with daily life and with families, he notes how women seek husbands who can earn them a living and try hard to avoid husbands who, because of their hard trades, harm their wives.[7] Widows and orphans face an even crueler world. Songs about the draft and about war before the revolution are a special case. Jewish boys were drafted into the Tsar's army for twenty years and all but disappeared from their families forever; thus, mothers cry out in folk songs about their grief at the loss of their sons, while the sons sing of the miserable army life they endure.

By 1962, however, Beregovski was enjoying somewhat greater freedom and published such non-worker, non-revolutionary types of songs as love songs, domestic songs, lullabies, and textless songs, along with dances. The love song is surprising, since until the twentieth century Orthodox Jewish marriages were arranged by the parents. Despite that practice Beregovski found and published a considerable number of love songs; Cahan, too, found them, though much earlier. The *maskilim*, apparently, were not so rigid about arranging marriages.

---

[6] Ibid., 31. All translations from the Beregovski collections are by Slobin.

[7] It should be noted that song no. 95 in the 1934 anthology claims that a girl who marries a musician is the best off of all girls because "A musician-boy is not bitter, he plays and beams, girls dance and give money."

Composers of Great Yiddish Songs

The folk songs described above are anonymous and were probably created by ordinary people expressing their personal situations with borrowed tunes from Jewish and non-Jewish sources. There also were Jewish poets and composers of considerable skill who began to write "folk music," that is, artistic or idealized folk music. The mere act of writing it down was a sign of a different origin from the folk songs that were orally conceived and transmitted. Written songs may have been composed as art songs, but many were so beloved by audiences that individual Jews began to sing them, hum them, and transmit them orally, often unaware who wrote the poems and the music. In this manner some songs were eventually established as folk songs. Likewise, in creating original songs, composers copied what they conceived to be Jewish folk style, and those pseudo folk songs, accepted by musically illiterate people, could over time also become established as folk songs.

The majority of the songwriters were poets, whose tunes may or may not have been written down. Those that were written down may have been so not by the poet but by some musically literate colleague or admirer. Although many such songs were eventually published, they gained their fame by being performed continually by roving *badchanim*, who performed them at weddings and other occasions throughout Eastern Europe.

Among the most significant writers of Yiddish song in the nineteenth century was Berl Margulies "Broder" (1817-80), who took the name of his native city, Brody in Galicia. He studied the Talmud, but to prepare for a living he was trained as a bristle-worker. He then took a job as a buyer for an export firm. Wherever he went on business travels he entertained other travelers, and he soon realized that he had another career in the making. In 1857 Broder formed a troupe of professional *badhanim* and toured Southern Russia, Galicia, Hungary, and Rumania, performing his Yiddish songs at weddings or in public gatherings in wine cellars and inns. There was no stage, only a table in the room around which the singers, sometimes in simple costumes, sang and gestured. Later he returned to Brody and sang there in a coffeehouse, accompanying his performance with mimicry. He died in Bucharest. A few of Broder's own songs survive, but most of his repertory was by his more famous poetic associates Wolf Ehrenkrantz, Eliakum Zunser, Isaac Joel Linetzky, and Abraham Goldfaden.[8] His principal theme was the sorrows of the work in which the Jew engaged.

Abraham Baer Gottlober (1810-99) was another early writer of popular Yiddish songs. Although Gottlober appears to have borrowed most if not all his subjects from foreign writers, mostly German, his development of a Yiddish repertory and the popularity of his songs earn him a place in the history of Yiddish folk song. His passion for Yiddish literature was passed on to his most famous pupil, Abraham Goldfaden. Gottlober was a fervent believer in the *Haskalah* until 1881 and thereafter became an ardent Jewish nationalist. He also produced important Hebrew works.

This earlier generation of nineteenth-century Yiddish songwriters also includes Michel Gordon (1823-90) and Sholem Berenstein (d. 1880), who both published their collections in Zhitomir, one of two Russian cities that maintained official (*Haskalah*) rabbinical seminaries approved by the Russian government. Both were modern Jews who saw Chassidic Jews in a very unfavorable

---

[8] Surviving songs by Broder, his son, and his grandson appear in B. Margolis, *Dray Doyres* (1957).

light, but also attacked the outmoded customs and superstitions of all traditional Jews. Berenstein, whose songs were published in *Magasin vun jüdische lider far dem jüdischen folk* (Store of Jewish Songs for the Jewish People) (Zhitomir, 1869), sings of the suffering Jews in a popular style. His "Sholem aleichem malochim fayne" was so popular that it became a folk tune often sung without attribution; the same fate befell his lullaby "Dos vigele." Meanwhile Gordon, whose collection *Bord . . . un andere . . . Yidishe Lider* (*The Beard and Other Yiddish Songs*: Zhitomir, 1868) contains most of his songs, calls vigorously for reform. The song "Di Bord" (The Beard) is a sharp attack on traditional Jews who cannot accept a Jew who cuts his beard.[9] Gordon's most ardent revolutionary song, "Shtey oyf mayn volk" (Arise My People) was written in 1869.

One of the most famous writers of Yiddish songs was Wolf Ehrenkrantz (= Wölwil or Velvel Zbaraschler, 1826-83). Born in Galicia, son of a *shochet*, he received a good Hebrew education and developed early a special interest in poetry. He joined the *Haskalah* movement to participate in secular Russian developments, and, when he was required to marry against his will, escaped to Rumania. There, to earn a living, from 1844 to 1869 he became a *badchan*. He was famous for biting satire and empathy with the sufferings of the Jewish people. Like Broder, in many songs he expressed antagonism toward Chassidism. Ehrenkrantz wrote equally in Hebrew and Yiddish, and published many of his poems. Many tunes he invented were based on synagogue modes and melodies, but since he did not write them down, most are forgotten. He returned to Galicia for a time, then moved to Constantinople, where he died.

Ehrenkrantz's poems cover almost every possible topic. He reflects on the vicissitudes of Jewish life in Eastern Europe, upon specific events ("The Cholera in the Year 1866"), on love, on labor, and on death. Frequently the song has a *Zuspiel*, an afterthought, which puts the main song into a new or contradictory light. In the satiric song "*Der* Filosof," which consists of four strophes with a refrain, the music is simple and is indistinguishable from so many folk songs collected by Cahan and Beregovski.[10] The voice's range is a sixth, and the scale is in the natural minor with the lowered leading tone. It is a spoof on the so-called miracles performed by Chassidic rabbis.

Yet another member of the Brody Singers, and one of its leading writers of Yiddish songs, was Eliakum Zunser (1836-1913), a *badchan*, born in Vilna.[11] As a youth he sang in a synagogue choir and was one of the Jewish boys tragically drafted into the Tsar's army.[12] He settled briefly in Kovno as an embroiderer, but from 1861 on he became a *badchan* in Vilna and achieved fame throughout Lithuania and Russia. At this point he was a rover in the fashion of other *badchanim* and cantors. Zunser was so good at composing and performing songs that he quickly became the most sought-after *badchan* in Russia. As the first *badchan* to have musical knowledge and one of the few Yiddish songwriters who could write music, he began to publish a series of collections

[9] Printed in Mlotek, 128-29.

[10] Ibid., 124-25.

[11] Sol Liptzin, *Eliakum Zunser, Poet of His People* (New York: Behrman House, 1950). His songs with melodies are published in *Verk*, ed. Mordkhe Schaechter (New York: YIVO, 1964), 2 vols.

[12] Jews drafted into the Tsar's army were normally in for much longer periods (sometimes 20-25 years as opposed to just a few years for "Russians") and were usually put in the front ranks for attacks so that they were the first to be shot. Added to that, they were terribly mistreated as the prejudice against them was strong.

of his songs, starting with *Shirim Hadashim* (= New Songs) (1872). Since he published his songs with music, we can trace his songs' popularity much better than the songs of most other Yiddish songwriters of the time. Zunser raised the profession of *badchanim* to a more dignified level. When he lost his wife and seven children in a cholera epidemic, his poems took a tragic turn. After the pogroms of 1881-82, he turned his attention primarily to Zionism and nationalism, detected in such songs as "Di Sokhe" (The Plow), written in 1888.[13] Zunser moved to the United States in 1889 and settled in New York as a printer. He wrote around 600 songs.

Also in Zunser's generation was the Yiddish writer Isaac Joel Linetzky (1839-1915), who helped establish modern Yiddish song. Born into a Chassidic family in Podolia, he later joined the *Haskalah*. His most famous work is the novel *Dos Poylishe Yingl* (*The Polish Jew*, 1869), a satiric attack on Chassidism, which remained in print until World War II. He also wrote satiric folk songs in *Der Beyzer Marshelik* (1879),[14] the best of which compare favorably with Ehrenkrantz's works. Although Linetzky is not regarded as one of the great Yiddish writers, he was a pioneer in raising Yiddish to a literary language.

Also at this time was the Galician Yiddish poet Bahrach Benedict Schafir (ca. 1858-1915), whose collection *Melodies from the Country near the River San* contains serious songs (longing for Israel or for his Galician home, laments on another blood accusation in 1883) and a great many comic songs (often taking jabs at *Chassidim*).

Mark Warshawsky (1845-1907) was another prolific and important composer of Yiddish songs. Born in Zhitomir, Russia, he was first a lawyer in Odessa who wrote Yiddish songs in imitation of Jewish folk songs on the side; he also adapted real folk songs. Many times it is hard to tell whether a song is an authentic folk song or whether Warshawsky invented it, but by the early twentieth century Warshawsky's songs had been accepted as folk songs—both his words and music. His most famous song, the beloved lullaby "Oyfn pripetshik brent a fayerl" (A flame burns in the fireplace) is such a case.[15] Few Eastern-European Jews did not know this piece from birth, and when during the mid-twentieth century it was converted into a resistance song against the Nazis and Soviets, probably few could name its composer. Certainly by the time it was quoted in the movie *Schindler's List* at the end of the twentieth century, it was accepted as the epitome of Yiddish folk song. No wonder that when Shalom Aleichem (see below) discovered Warshawsky, he promoted his songs.

At times these songs shout out against the injustices heaped on Jews, such as, for example, "Dem Milners Trern" (The Miller's Tears), which recounts the expulsion of Jews from their villages following tsarist pogroms. But in general Warshawsky was not a bitter poet or one who wrote to rouse people to resist intolerance; rather he wrote songs that made people chuckle or feel content. "Di Bobe un der Zeyde" (= "Akhtsik er un ziebtsik zi") celebrates all grandparents who live to a ripe old age (he at eighty, she at seventy), and in comical social satire pieces like "Di Mekhutonim geyen" (The In-laws are coming), Warshawsky pokes fun at the in-laws at a wedding. A few years after Warshawsky died in Kiev, Ernest Bloch took the melody of his

---

[13] Mlotek, 96-97.

[14] Wiener, 82, believes these were composed in 1863 and published in 1869.

[15] Published in Mlotek, 2-3; and in Jerry Silverman, *The Yiddish Song Book* (Briarcliff Manor, NY: Stein and Day Publishers, 1983), 46-47.

"Di Mizhinke Oysgegebn" (The Youngest Daughter's Wedding) and set it as the theme of "Simchas Torah," the second movement of his *Baal Shem Tov Suite*.

Abraham Goldfaden (1840-1908) was trained in Yiddish grammar schools and in the Zhitomir rabbinical school in Russia from 1857 to 1866. He published his first collection of Hebrew poems in 1865, his first collection of Yiddish songs in 1866, and *Di Yiddene*, the first popular collection of Yiddish poetry in 1869. From 1866 to 1875 he was a school teacher in Simferopol and Odessa, then, in 1875, a journalist in Lvov. Both professions resulted in financial failure. Goldfaden moved around Russia and then Rumania, where with the Broder Singers he founded the Yiddish Theater, which later spread to Russia, Poland, France, England, and America (see below). He visited the United States for a few years beginning in 1887, then immigrated there in 1903. When he died he was poor but famous. His funeral was attended by thousands. Goldfaden is buried in Brooklyn's Washington Cemetery. His song "Rozhinkes mit mandlen" (Raisins and Almonds), from the musical *Shulamis* (1880), remains possibly the most famous Yiddish song of all times;[16] during World War II it was adapted several times to the horrific experiences of the camps, in one case under the title "No Raisins and Almonds."

Among the other Yiddish songwriters of the latter part of the nineteenth century are Jehuda Loeb Gordon (1831-92) and Sholem Aleichem (= Shalom Rabinovitz, 1859-1916). Both were famous Jewish writers in genres other than song. Gordon, perhaps the finest Hebrew poet of the nineteenth century, was regarded as the chief spokesperson for the *Haskalah* in Russia during the second half of the century, while Shalom Aleichem was one of the ablest Yiddish storyteller of all time. Songs form only a minor part of their output, but the quality of these requires their inclusion. Gordon has only nine or ten folk songs, including "A Mother's Parting" and "A Story of Long-Ago," both which reflect on contemporary woes in the Jewish community, and "The Law Written on Parchment," which gives strength to Jews who are being persecuted. Shalom Aleichem's songs were written over many years and appeared mostly in journals. His most important song is the lullaby "Shlof, mayn kind" (Sleep, my child, 1892), for which he wrote the text and David Kovanovski the music.[17]

Yiddish songs continued to be written in great quantity in Eastern Europe during the first part of the twentieth century, but the nature of the songs changed radically. The increased emigration from Eastern Europe to America brought a new category of song which spoke to the difficulties of traveling away from the familiar *shtetl*, of leaving parents and friends behind, and of adjusting to a new world in America. This led to a whole new kind of Yiddish song: the American variety (see below). For those left behind the songs spoke of longing to see again the emigrants and of imagining their new world.

As Zionism became a vibrant force to young Jews of the early twentieth century, new pioneer songs in Yiddish were popular. World War I brought a new set of songs as Jews were dislocated within Europe and met tribulations. Opposed to these after 1917 were the new Communist songs, such as those promoted by Beregovski. Composers such as Mikhl Gelbart (1889-1962) wrote "Makhnes Geyen" (Forward Brothers) in 1934 as a workers' marching song and, in the same vein, "Ikh vil nit keyn ayzerne keytn" (I want no iron chains).

---

[16] Nearly every collection of Yiddish songs contains it; see Mlotek, 4-5.

[17] Printed in Silverman, 48-49.

Mordechai Gebirtig (1877-1942) was the most popular creator of Jewish songs in folk style in Poland between the two World Wars and the last great European Yiddish songwriter. Although he earned his livelihood in Cracow as a carpenter, he wrote hundreds of songs, some of which became folk songs, such as "Yankele," "Reyzele," and "Hey, Tsigelech."[18] These songs were eagerly sung by Jews throughout the Yiddish-speaking world. "Moyshele Mayn Fraynd" is fancier than the average true folk song with its wide range of a tenth and its smooth phraseology, but "Yankele" is a simple lullaby in a narrow range and only twelve measures long. Tragically, Gebirtig and his family were shot by the Germans during the liquidation of the Cracow ghetto, on 4 June 1942. But the many poems he wrote during the Holocaust survive (see chapter 13).

American Yiddish Song

The Jewish immigrants to America experienced a new life as well as a new world, and this changed the nature of their songs. As they came over on hundreds of boats from Europe, they faced the discomforts of riding on high seas, often with resulting seasickness and always in crammed quarters. The uncertainties of the ports of disembarkation—Castle Garden or, after 1892, Ellis Island—the unfamiliar speech of the immigration officials, and fear of being denied entry and returned to Europe, haunted their first moments on American soil. Once in New York they sought relatives and friends or simply philanthropic Jews who would help them settle into American society. The food was different, the streets were unfamiliar, the customs were incomprehensible.[19] Work, education, apartment-dwelling, life-cycle events, and the synagogue were of utmost concern. They worried, too, about their families and friends back in the Old Country, and they dreamed of how they would come to enjoy the great wealth and freedoms of America. All of this we know from the songs which they sang and which have been preserved in Yiddish. Some were composed by European Yiddish poets such as Zunser, who wrote "Kolombus un Vashington" (Colombus and Washington) as he sailed for America in 1889. Some were new texts to old, favorite melodies. Some were composed by new American composers such as Solomon Golub (1887-1952), who was born in Riga and came to America in 1906. Others sprang from anonymous Jews with something to sing about.

Before they left Europe, Eastern European Jews heard stories of how a few Jews went to America, made fortunes, and escaped the unremitting anti-Semitism that was a way of life in Europe. They sang "Lidl fun goldenem land" (Song of the Golden Land) by Mordechai Gebirtig, which put the dream of going to America in their heads, and they pleaded with their relatives and friends who had already gone to America to "Shikt a tiket" (Send a Ticket) so they could escape the poverty and troubles of the Old World.[20] "Eyn zach vel ich" (One thing I ask), they sang, was to leave the slavery of the tsar for the hard work of America, for nothing in America

---

[18] Many songs by Gebirtig are printed in Mlotek.

[19] See Moses Weinberger's scathing account of his immigration experience, in *Jews and Judaism in New York* (1887), translated from the Hebrew and republished as *People Walk on their Heads,* by Jonathan D. Sarna (New York: Holmes & Mercier, 1982).

[20] The following songs are reprinted in Silverman, 150-79; in Mlotek, 244; and in Neil Levin, ed., *Songs of the American Jewish Experience* (Chicago: Board of Jewish Education, 1976), 52-165.

could be as bad as life in Russia. When they finally got on a boat and neared New York, they saw the Statue of Liberty ("Frayhayt statue," a song by Abraham Liessin [1890-1931] and Lazar Weiner) and extended their hands to her in greeting. The poet Morris Rosenfeld (1862-1923) wrote a song with music by Warshawsky about the hopes that Castle Garden ("Kesl Gardn") invoked in the minds of the immigrants, while the fear of flunking the entrance examination on Ellis Island is remembered in the song "Elis Ayland."

Once in America the hard realities of immigrant life hit home, as reflected in "New Yorker Trern" (New York tears) by H. Altman, "Eyder ich leyg mich shlofn" (No sooner do I lie down), "Mayn yingele" (My little son) with text by Morris Rosenfeld, and "Dem pedlers brivl" (The peddler's letter) by Y. Brisker. The first sings of the moaning and sighing that is heard everywhere in New York; the second tells of the hard life of a laborer, always hungry and out of work if he complains; the third bemoans the grief of a father whose son never sees him because the father must work such long hours; the fourth is the sad letter of a son to his mother in the Old Country telling of his exhausting life as a peddler, "in heat and in cold and in wind and in rainstorm." Women, too, are always working, as A. Schwartz and J. Leiserowitz describe in "Di grine kuzine" (The Greenhorn Cousin), and as David Edelstadt (1866-92) says in "Arbeter froyen" (Women Workers), which is an early call for women to rise up and gain their freedom. Children were prepared to fight rich tyrants on both sides of the Atlantic in "Hert ir kinder" (Listen children) by Morris Winchevsky (1856-1933).

Was it worth it? Some agonized over this, particularly if they missed a parent who had stayed behind, as noted in Warshawsky's "A briv fun Amerike" (A Letter from America), or if they could not adjust, as lamented by A. Olshanetsky in "Ikh vil tsurik aheym" (I want to return home). With few exceptions, Jews who could not forget the oppression of life in Europe could not go back, so they had to make life in America better. They formed unions and worked hard to make their dreams of freedom and security come true. The Yiddish songs reflect the struggle, not the success, because by the time the struggle was won and Jews had achieved success, they had sufficiently assimilated into American society that their Yiddish was forgotten and they were singing praises of America in English.

Yiddish songs lingered on in America until after World War II because there were always immigrants from Europe who kept singing them. In New York, where the largest Yiddish speaking population in America lived between the two World Wars, there were many Yiddish newspapers and theaters, and even full-time Yiddish radio stations which broadcast many Yiddish songs (WEVD). In its heyday (1930s), Yiddish radio had as many as thirty stations in New York alone. In smaller cities in America, too, wherever Yiddish was still spoken, there were occasional Yiddish radio programs. In Milwaukee, for example, a weekly "Yiddishe Stunde" (Yiddish Hour) was broadcast to several thousand Yiddish-speaking Jews into the 1950s. The integration of Jews into American society is reflected in the most famous Yiddish song of the 1930s, "Bei mir bistu sheyn" (I find you pretty) from 1933, with music by Sholom Secunda to a text by Jacob Jacobs, 1890-1977.[21] By this time many Yiddish-speaking Jews spoke English as their main language. The song was in fact popularized throughout America by a non-Jewish group, the Andrews Sisters, with both Yiddish and English words, and it became one of the most well-known songs among non-Jews as well.

---

[21] Heskes, *Passport to Jew Music* (1994), 202.

Development of the Yiddish Theater in Europe and America

Since the destruction of the Temple in Jerusalem, rabbinic authorities had opposed Jewish theater. During the spring holiday of Purim, however, the rigid constraints of Jewish religious practices were relaxed to allow freer conduct, and eventually to permit the performance of plays or skits specific to the light-hearted celebration of the holiday. Purim commemorates a Jewish victory over intolerance and persecution, so it is a moment when Jews can be joyous publicly. In the early fifth century Jews near Antioch gathered in the synagogue courtyard in a happy, disorderly procession which sometimes took them outside the city gates, where an effigy they carried representing Haman, the villain of the holiday, was hanged and then burned in a bonfire. Around the fire they sang, told jokes, and traded jibes.[22]

In the Middle Ages Purim festivities in Europe resembled the annual carnival festivals of Christian Europe. By the sixteenth century it was the custom to present plays, usually about the Purim story, in the vernacular—that kind of Yiddish described above. The *Purimshpil* (Purim Play) of this early period corresponds to Christian mystery plays with the insertion of commedia dell'arte stock characters. While such plays became popular in most Jewish communities during the sixteenth century, the earliest published *Purimshpil* text was printed in Frankfurt am Main only in 1708.[23] From the sixteenth to eighteenth centuries the plays usually were performed without scenery (by the eighteenth century, however, a backdrop was used) in the living rooms of the wealthiest Jews in the ghetto. In the course of the eighteenth century a few public halls were built for these plays. Some were also performed outdoors, though most continued to be heard in parlors.

The Purim players were a band of boys from one of the local religious schools, or the sons of poor laborers, sometimes accompanied by extra musicians, absurdly dressed. Women were not only not allowed to perform but as viewers were segregated in their own seating areas just as in the synagogue. Along with the other performers were cantors and choirboys who "scandalized the pious by using the same melodies both for rowdy Purim songs and for prayers." Accompanying the play were songs and dances, and, by the eighteenth century, also interludes featuring music between the play's scenes, a practice that corresponds to the *intermedi* between acts of an Italian opera common in the seventeenth and early eighteenth centuries. In one guise or another, the *Purimshpil* has continued until the present, though since the Holocaust it is performed in Hebrew, or English, French, or Spanish, rather than in Yiddish.

Theater other than the *Purimshpil* was not accepted by the rabbis. The idea of actors representing others—producing images—was forbidden in Jewish law. Orthodox Jewish men could not tolerate a Jewish woman singing or dancing before them, and rabbis also strictly forbade men dressing like women. Purim plays were the exception because they reinforced the story of the Book of Esther, the reading of which in the synagogue itself was traditionally accompanied by children making lots of noise with the encouragement of the rabbis, but even

---

[22] Nahma Sandrow, *Vagabond Stars: A World History of Yiddish Theater* (New York: Limelight Editions, 1986), 2.

[23] Ibid., 4. Sandrow presents an excellent overview of the history of the *Purimshpil*; the quotations that follow are from *Vagabond Stars*.

they had severe restrictions. In addition to internal Jewish controls, the outside Christian authorities clamped down on any Jewish plays that depicted Christians in a bad light or were perceived to disturb the outside community. The *Purimshpil* had some legitimacy, but other plays in Yiddish had none.

The situation took a major turn around 1830, when the Polish physician Solomon Ettinger (1803-56) wrote *Serkele*. An early product of the *Haskalah* in Poland, Ettinger proved that in the theater Yiddish could be raised to a high literary level and could, at the same time, raise audiences to that level.[24] Since his play was outlawed by the Orthodox communities, it was not published until 1861. Performances were by amateurs, and the first audiences were other *maskilim*. Yet *Serkele* began a movement—legitimate Yiddish theater—which was to have a major impact on Ashkenazic Jews from 1876 to 1945, and on world musical theater and cinema until the present.

Ettinger's first impact was on the poet Abraham Baer Gottlober, who was so inspired by *Serkele* that he composed his own play, *The Bridal Canopy* (1838; published 1876). In addition, Israel Aksenfeld (d. ca.1868) began his career at this time with his *The First Jewish Recruit in Russia*, a tragedy about a boy who is drafted into the tsar's army for twenty-five years. This work, too, remained unpublished until 1862, though it circulated widely in manuscript. The plays represented the new, modern, middle-class Jew in secular situations that called on his or her sense of Jewish morality to survive, or that portrayed societal and political upheaval in the nineteenth century and its role in destroying ordinary Jewish families.

Yiddish musical theater took off a generation after Ettinger when the Broder singers began to sing little comedies, often basing their characters on those familiar to Jews in the Purim plays. While comedy was their mainstay, they occasionally performed more serious playlets. The Broder singers were *maskilim* and were quick to satirize the upholders of the old order, such as Chassids or rich Jews who exploited poor Jews. Their primary means of performance was singing; the acting was not yet professional.

Professional Yiddish theater began in 1876 when Abraham Goldfaden, a pupil of Gottlober who had moved to Jassy, Rumania, linked up with Israel Grodner, a Broder singer, to create a play with songs, all in Yiddish.[25] Until then Goldfaden's songs were popular with the *badchanim* crisscrossing Eastern Europe, and especially with the Broder singers. When he watched Grodner perform his songs in comic routines, he realized the potential of Yiddish musical theater—of setting the songs within a story. His early musicals were small affairs, but by 1880 he had produced two masterpieces, *Shmendrik* and *The Fanatic*, and shortly thereafter came *Koldunye*, an operetta. Other works poured from his pen, and he enlarged his acting company. Within a few years his performers included many of the stars of Yiddish theater for the next generation or two, such as Jacob P. Adler, Sigmund Mogulesko, David Kessler, and Keni Liptzin.[26] A major breakthrough was reached when Goldfaden decided that women had to play the parts of women.

---

[24] Precursors of Ettinger's play are Isaac Euchel's *Reb Hennoch* (1793) and Aaron Wolfsohn's *Frivolity and Religiosity* (1796), both in Yiddish but not in as high a tone as *Serkele*.

[25] Sandrow's account of Goldfaden's career is the best available; see *Vagabond Stars*, 40-69.

[26] One of the liveliest accounts of the early years of the Yiddish theater is recounted by Lulla Adler Rosenfeld, *The Yiddish Theatre and Jacob P. Adler* (New York: Thomas Y. Crowell, 1977; rev. ed. New York: Shapolsky Brothers, 1988).

In 1881, just as his Yiddish theater was experiencing tremendous success, Tsar Alexander II was assassinated and severe pogroms were started against the Jews. Suddenly many of the wealthier Jewish communities could no longer afford theater, and many communities were even obliterated. Goldfaden turned to biblical and Jewish themes, such as *Doctor Almasado*, *King Ahashuerus*, *The Sacrifice of Isaac*, *Shulamis*, and *Bar Kokhba* (1883), the last of which so infuriated the Russian censors that, according to one historian, they banned Yiddish theater altogether.

Disgusted with the situation in Europe, Goldfaden sailed for America in 1883. But America was not yet ready for him, and he returned to Europe after a short stay. In the 1890s Goldfaden took to Zionist stories, such as *The Messianic Age* (1891). Music played a major role in all these works, the latter which Goldfaden referred to as a "comedy with music," "musical melodrama," or "romantic opera." He often borrowed tunes from operas or folk music and transformed the melodies with his Yiddish texts. By the turn of the century New York had replaced much of Europe as the center for Yiddish theater, and even Goldfaden spent his last years (1903-08) there.

A large number of immigrants to America, especially to New York City, spoke Yiddish. Soon an active and artistically successful Yiddish theater had formed. The Lower East Side, eventually Second Avenue downtown from 14th Street, became the center for the Yiddish stage during the 1880s and 1890s. A series of playwrights, composers, directors, actors, and singers active there became famous not only among the Jewish immigrants but among the general population as well.[27] An area of New York that had once housed immigrant Irish and German theaters now turned to the newest group to arrive in its neighborhood: East European Jews.

In the early years, as Yiddish theater was getting started, a few prominent Europeans came to America and helped move it forward. Among these was Goldfaden, as already mentioned, and also the distinguished cantor Baruch Schorr, who so shocked his Orthodox congregation in Brooklyn with his opera *Samson* that he was forced to resign and return to his former synagogue in Lvov, Poland. Many lesser composers wrote the music to plays by professional dramatists; they included many popular Yiddish songwriters like Louis Friedsell (1850-1923), Joseph Brody (1877-1943), David Meyerowitz (1867-1943), Herman Wohl (1877-1936), Peretz Sandler (= Jacob Koppel, 1856-1931),[28] Louis Gilrod (1879-1956), Isidore Lillian (1880-1960), Rubin Doctor (1882-ca. 1960), Solomon Schmulewitz (= Solomon Small, 1868-1943) and later Joseph Rumshisky (= Rumshinsky, ca. 1879-1956), Abraham Ellstein (1907-63; fig. 9.1), and Sholom Secunda (1894-1974).[29]

The leading playwrights, most of whom started their careers in Europe, were Jacob Gordin (1853-1909), whose *Yiddishe King Lear* (1892), *Murder on Madison Avenue* (1893), *The Pogrom* (1893), and *Mirele Efros* were among his most popular; Leon Kobrin (1872-1946), famous for *East Side Ghetto* and *Two Sisters*, David Pinski (1872-1959), whose *The Treasure* was staged by Germany's most famous director, Max Reinhardt in Berlin, and whose *The Zwie Family* (1904), *Yankel the Smith*

---

[27] The best early account of music in the American Yiddish theater is Irene Heskes, "Music as Social History: American Yiddish Theater Music, 1882-1920," *American Music* 2 (1984): 73-87. Much of the following is based on her article.

[28] Sandler's "Eili, Eili" (My God, my God), composed for Thomashefsky in 1896, became one of the all-time leading hits of the American Yiddish theater.

[29] See Heskes, *Passport*, 194-208.

FIG. 9.1   Abraham Ellstein. From *History of Hazanuth*, ed. Rosen, 161.

Reproduced by permission of the Jewish Ministers Cantors Association of America

(1910), and *Sabbattai Svie* were among the most highly regarded, Sholem Asch (1880-1957), well known for *Three Cities*, *The God of Vengence* (1910), *Motke the Thief* (1917), *Uncle Moses* (1926), and *Kiddish Hashem* (1928), Perez Hirshbein (1880-1948), who started a more modern Yiddish theater with *Farvorfen Vinekl* (1913), *Blacksmith's Daughters*, *Green Fields*, and *Haunted Inn* (1919), S. An-ski (1863-1920), whose *Dybbuk* (1914) was the most popular production of the Vilner Troupe and earned the respect of non-Jewish playgoers,[30] and H. Leivick (= Leivick Halpern, 1888-1962), for *Rags* and *De Goylem*.

Among the distinguished actors and directors were Boris Thomashefsky (1868-1939), Jacob P. Adler (1855-1926), David Kessler (1860-1920), Sigmund Mogulesko (ca. 1856-1914), Bertha Kalisch (1872-1939), and Maurice Schwartz (1890-1960). All of them sang, and some even composed the music or the text to their arias. Thomashefsky flourished on Second Avenue for forty years; he was also a dashing actor who had a large fan club, though the quality of his acting was sometimes attacked for catering to popular taste. When he opened the first Yiddish Theater in New York in 1882 with a performance of Goldfaden's *Die Kishifmakherin* (*The Sorceress*), audiences were thrilled. They were eager to escape the hardships of daily living in New York for the fantasy of the stage. Thomashefsky enjoyed great success, and soon there were other Yiddish theaters rivaling his. He tried to bring Yiddish theater to Broadway but failed, though in 1924 he helped arrange the New York appearance of the famous Vilner Troupe, the best Yiddish ensemble in Europe. After their American run, several company members chose to remain in America and contribute to the American Yiddish stage.

After appearing in a Goldfaden European touring company, Jacob Adler wandered around Europe and America for a number of years before settling in New York in 1890. It was a time when the city finally had enough Yiddish-speaking persons to patronize Yiddish theater on a regular basis. He teamed up with Jacob Gordin to produce some of the most memorable Yiddish theater New York has ever witnessed. Adler's third wife, Sarah (ca. 1858-1953) and their very talented children Cecelia (1889-19?), Julia (1899-19?), Stella (1901-92), and Luther (1903-84) continued their father's Yiddish acting troupes well into the twentieth century, with Luther known especially for his portrayal of Tevye in *Fiddler on the Roof*.

Schwartz was the last of the great Yiddish actors, and when his theater—the Jewish Art Theater on Second Avenue—closed in 1950, it signaled the end of Yiddish theater. An attempt to reopen it five years later failed. Most surviving Yiddish actors found that they could no longer make a living just in Yiddish productions. Luba Kadison (b. 1907) and her husband Joseph Buloff

---

[30] See Sandrow, 217-21, for more on the original Yiddish production of *The Dybbuk* in 1920.

(d. 1985), for example, who had made their names in the Yiddish theater, turned to the American stage and movies in English.[31] A revived Yiddish theater since the 1990s plays mostly to non-Yiddish-speaking visitors, for whom translations are provided—a far cry from the early years of the century when Yiddish theater spoke the language of the man and woman in the street.

The subject of American Yiddish theater included the Jewish experience both in Europe and in America, with emphasis on the crises facing the Jewish immigrant in America. This differs from the European Yiddish theater with its themes of the separate problems of living in a hostile environment without hope for betterment. Music played a big role in many of the Yiddish plays, and some had so much music that they were referred to as operas. Women and men sang songs even when they portrayed heavy roles in serious dramas like *The Jewish King Lear*, the *Jewish Faust*, or the *Jewish Hamlet*. In Europe there was no need to bring synagogue music into the theater. But for many immigrants this was necessary; since their lives in Europe had been so bound up with the synagogue, retaining identity as Jews in the New World meant leaning on synagogue music more forcefully than before. The music was extracted from the shows and sold as sheet music to eager Jewish consumers not only in America but also back in Europe. Arrangements were made for violin solo or solo piano, as well as for voice with piano accompaniment.

While Yiddish theater flourished on Second Avenue, many of its performers also began to perform in American non-Jewish venues as well. Some appeared at the same time in vaudeville and burlesque, two types of theater that were virtually the same from 1900 to the 1930s. This is consistent with the practices of the early Yiddish theater representatives, Broder and Goldfaden, who were *badchanim* before they started the theater. Some entertainers remained *badchanim*, influenced by Yiddish theater but not actually taking part in formal theatrical events there. Irving Berlin, for example, did not get involved with Yiddish theater, though his early Jewish music reflects what was popular in contemporary Yiddish theater.

Jewish comedy was also a part of Yiddish theater. Many comedy acts in vaudeville and burlesque were in fact an extension of Yiddish theater. Among the most famous of the comic Jewish entertainers were Fanny Brice (1891-1951), Sophie Tucker (1884-1964), Eddy Cantor (1892-1964), Al Jolson (1886-1950), Red Skelton (1913-97), Danny Kay (1913-87), Jack Benny (1894-1974), George Burns (1896-1996), and Gracie Allen (1906-64).

Broadway had been home to Jewish composers and theater persons from the early twentieth century. By the 1920s chief among the leading writers of Broadway music were Irving Berlin (1888-1989), Richard Rodgers (1902-79), Jerome Kern (1885-1945), George Gershwin (1898-1937), and Harold Arlen (1905-86). Though the distinction between the two New York theater districts was maintained—Yiddish on Second Avenue and English on Broadway—their connection increased when Jewish performers such as Paul Muni (1895-1967) stepped from one stage to the other.

By the 1940s many Jewish performers eschewed the Yiddish stage and moved directly to Broadway. Movies had accepted Yiddish theater from the beginning (see below). But only with the arrival of the Broadway production of *Fiddler on the Roof*, however, did Yiddish theater finally conquer Broadway. Once Yiddish theater was dead on Second Avenue, it thrived on Broadway, albeit missing its principal characteristic: the Yiddish language. *The Rothschilds*,

---

[31] Luba Kadison and Joseph Buloff, *On Stage, Off Stage: Memories of a Lifetime in the Yiddish Theatre*, ed. Irving Genn (Cambridge: Harvard University Press, 1992).

Two-By-Two, *Rags*, *Ragtime*, *Cabaret*, *The Producers*, and *A Chorus Line* are among Jewish or partly Jewish musicals of the post-Yiddish theater and post-*Fiddler on the Roof* years. Each has elements that would have been accepted on Second Avenue in the 1920s: Jewish stories, with Jewish humor and Jewish characters reflecting Jewish modes of life and Jewish daily problems, and with some elements of Jewish folk and liturgical music. To a great extent, these Jewish elements were synonymous with what American musicals had come to be through the assimilation of Jewish artists and their audiences into American life in the first half of the twentieth century. Today the musicals on Broadway reflect their connection to Yiddish musicals of the past as well as to traditional English musical theater.

While Yiddish theater thrived in New York during the first forty years of the twentieth century, it continued to be important as well in Europe, despite revolutions, World War I, immense poverty, and unabated anti-Semitism. At the beginning of the new century professional and amateur Yiddish theater groups sprang up all over Poland, Russia, and elsewhere in Eastern Europe. At the same time that playwrights, actors, and directors were honing their skills, new songs and dances formed part of the productions. During World War I, the occupying German soldiers could understand the Yiddish plays and showed a tolerant attitude toward Jews, and so the theater in Vilna thrived, whereas in Poland and Russia the local authorities repressed Jewish activities even more than before the War. The Vilner Troupe began in 1916 in Vilna, moved to Warsaw in 1917 and quickly established a reputation as the best Jewish acting company in the world, with modern ideas of theater. Their most famous production was of *The Dybbuk* by S. An-ski (= Shloyme-Zanvl Rappoport, 1863-1920), in which traditional Chassidic music helps create the mysterious, mystic atmospheres so essential to this drama. After a 1924 tour to New York, the Vilner Troupe split into two groups, some company members remained in New York and others returned to Warsaw.

After World War I in Poland, though the country was finally freed from foreign control, a government based on vicious anti-Semitism came to power, and the anti-Semitic stance was reenforced in the 1930s by Poland's President, the pianist Ignaz Paderewski, and by its head Catholic cardinal. Rumania, despite its large Jewish population, including many refugees, preceded Hitler's Germany in condemning Jews to starvation and mass poverty. Yet Yiddish theater continued during the 1920s and until the outbreak of the War, in such cities as Paris, Brussels, Budapest, Vienna, and, yes, even in Cracow, Lodz, Bialystok, Grodno, and especially Vilna and Warsaw. In Vilna the Friends of Yiddish Theater, established in 1928, not only produced plays but also promoted theater through many ancillary activities. There was so much activity that in 1935 alone fifteen different Yiddish troupes performed there. In 1939-40 the Lithuanians made the performance of Yiddish plays difficult, but when the Poles and Russians established Communist state theaters there, they favored a Yiddish stage. In 1940 the German invaders, ousting the Poles and Russians, allowed the Vilna Yiddish theater to perform briefly, but it was only for sinister reasons; following the last performance the Germans killed all the performers and audience.

Warsaw, whose pre-War Jewish population was 300,000, was a much more cosmopolitan city than Vilna, and its Yiddish theaters were more sophisticated and westernized. Many older Yiddish plays and musicals were revived—even Ettinger's *Serkele*—and new dramas and farces were created in a city that now took for granted that Yiddish was indeed a living language with a vibrant literature. The Warsaw Yiddish Art Theater (acronym: VYKT) was formed out of two older Yiddish theaters in 1921, and although it struggled financially, it brought productions of all sorts to villages in Poland and Lithuania as well as to the major cities. Joseph Kaminsky (1903-72), the scion of a family of Yiddish actors who controlled VYKT, wrote new music for the theater; he later immigrated to Israel and was one of the Israel Philharmonic's famous four concert-masters. In 1926 the Nawósci Theater was built in Warsaw primarily for Yiddish theater, and it was a luxurious, state-of-the-art hall. Other theaters and other performing troupes sprouted up throughout Poland until the Holocaust, with songs as a central part of the productions. One such company was started in Lodz by the writer and comedian Moyshe Broderson (1890-1956), famous for his silly songs. Even opera in Yiddish occurred in Warsaw during these years.

Meanwhile, in Russia, after World War I things got worse. Starvation was everywhere in the wake of the Revolution and the Polish invasion of the Ukraine, and pogroms continued. Yet the new Soviet government considered theater to be important, and in 1919 established a Central Theater Committee to organize proletariat and peasant theaters. Yiddish theater fell under its jurisdiction, and suddenly, very surprisingly, Jews found their theater had governmental financial, as well as political, support. By the 1930s there were more than twenty such theaters in Russia. Not only Yiddish, but even a modern, Hebrew theater was established—the Habima Theater of Moscow, which in 1931 moved permanently to Tel-Aviv. The most important Yiddish theater was the Moscow Yiddish State Art Theater (acronym: GOSET). Initially the Soviet government used this theater to reach Jewish audiences with its communist propaganda; the only thing that was Jewish about the theater was its language. By 1921, however, the theater returned to the older Yiddish repertory, and it hired Jewish artist Marc Chagall to do the sets.

The music drew on what was remembered of the old *badchan*, or it introduced new music for portrayals of old *badchanim*. Works of Yitzchok Leib Peretz (1895-1915), Abraham Goldfaden, and Shalom Aleichem received such masterful productions that they were viewed by non-Jews as the equivalent of the best non-Jewish theater. In 1928, when the Moscow ensemble had reached its pinnacle, though, its director, Alexander Granovsky, defected to Hollywood, and shortly thereafter Stalin began a reign of terror; these occurrences led to a decline in the fortunes of Yiddish theater in the Soviet Union. As an attempt to appease the Soviets, and in particular Lazar Moisevitch Kaganovitch, one of Stalin's chief officials and a Jew, the theater revived Goldfaden's *Shulamis* and *Bar Kokhba* (1937). But in the end, all Russian theater—Yiddish and non-Yiddish—came under fire from Stalin and many theater persons were murdered by the government. When the new war came, Yiddish actors and singers entertained soldiers and moved away from the former centers of Jewish life in Western Russia to new Jewish communities toward Asia, where they also entertained Jewish refugees.

After World War II, though only half of the pre-War Yiddish theater personnel remained, GOSET made an attempt to revive Yiddish theater in Moscow and endeavored to use the stage to deflect a new barrage of Russian anti-Semitism. But Stalin was now determined to end Jewish culture in Russia and, in 1948, ordered the theater closed. He also had its director, its leading comic actor, and many Yiddish writers murdered.

Although after the Holocaust Yiddish life in Europe was moribund, there were still a few last gasps. Soon after they returned from the camps, Rumanian Jews established a new Yiddish theater in Jassy, where Goldfaden had started one in 1876, and in Bucharest a new Yiddish State Theater was founded in 1958. Survivors in Poland, too, resuscitated Yiddish theater, but by

1955 few people in that country were left who knew Yiddish. Political events and occasional post-War outbursts of anti-Semitism further decimated the Jewish population there. By the 1970s the Warsaw theater still existed but had no audience.

Stalin had closed Yiddish theater in Russia after 1948, and there, too, after two generations of Communism few Jews spoke Yiddish. Paris had two Yiddish theaters in 1945, made up of refugees from Eastern Europe, Amsterdam had cabaret in Yiddish, and London continued, unabated, to mount occasional resident Yiddish theater shows and intermittent tours by survivors from the East. In all these productions, music—songs in Yiddish—and dances were essential ingredients, just as they had been throughout the history of Yiddish theater.

Yiddish Cinema

The decade that preceded the invasion of Poland (1939) saw a unique flourishing of Yiddish films, both in America and in Europe. Many of these films included music not only in the form of songs, dance pieces, and background music, but also as subjects of the films. Films dealt with musicians, and the social struggles of many films were symbolized by the competition between various styles of secular and sacred Jewish music and between Jewish music and non-Jewish music.

The first milestone in this development was actually a non-Yiddish-language film, *The Jazz Singer* (1927), produced by Warner Brothers and starring Al Jolson. Although no one spoke Yiddish in the picture, and there were no Yiddish titles (this first "talkie" movie actually was mostly a silent movie with titles and occasional songs), most of the persons involved in making the film spoke Yiddish on the set. The story is a Jewish story. Also, at one point, the famous cantor Yosele Rosenblatt sings a Yiddish song.

The story of the movie is this: Jackie Rabinowitz, a cantor's son, portrayed by Jolson, is enamored of "jazz," which is condemned by his father. After being whipped by the cantor for singing in a saloon, Jackie runs away (on Yom Kippur evening) and joins a traveling theatrical group where he can sing what he wants. Interestingly, this is exactly what Jolson did in real life. Only near the end of the movie and many years later does Jackie return to his father, who is dying on another Yom Kippur evening, and as a gesture to the cantor Jackie sings *Kol Nidre* in the synagogue. But after his father dies, Jackie resumes his career as a tin-pan-alley or vaudeville singer. The struggle between traditional Jewish music and modern American music reflects the struggle that all immigrants faced between their traditional way of life and an assimilationist American way of life.

The Jazz Singer provoked numerous and vicious replies by Yiddish audiences and traditional Jewish theatrical people. Although the Warners were Jewish and spoke Yiddish, the film glorified the assimilationist viewpoint rather than the traditionalist one. Among the strongest reactions to the film came in another great Yiddish film, *Der Vilner shtot khazan* (The Chazzan of Vilna) (1940), which takes place not in America but in Warsaw and Vilna. While *The Jazz Singer* was produced for American audiences who spoke English, *Der Vilner shtot khazan* was directed at Yiddish-speaking audiences, both in America and Europe. Here a cantor, known as the Vilner Balebésel (a real cantor in the nineteenth century), deserts his family and his synagogue in Vilna for a career as an opera singer in Warsaw. The decision devastates his family and his community. Only when he learns that his thirteen-year-old son has died does the cantor realize his error and return, humbled, to Vilna. Once again it is Yom Kippur evening, and as the *Kol Nidre* prayer is being recited, he joins in with his powerful voice to ask God's forgiveness for his sins. Forgiven or not, he dies on the *bima* as he finishes the prayer. The message is the opposite of that of *The Jazz Singer*. But as we know from history, the traditionalists were almost completely annihilated in the next five years.

Among the extras in *The Jazz Singer* was Joseph Green (1900-96), a young actor who in the 1930s became America's leading producer of Yiddish films. Green recognized the strength of musical allegory, and continued it in some of his movies. He also felt that there was a vast Yiddish-speaking public worldwide who craved films in their own language and with their own cultural settings. In *A Brivele der Mamen* (1938) a simple Yiddish song unites a Jewish family. From immigration to America, death, and the vagaries of World War I, the family is asunder; in Europe only the mother, Dobrish, survives, and in America, only her youngest son. Through a series of adventures and misadventures she is finally reunited with her boy, whom she recognizes by his singing a song known only to the family. The title song itself became a standard Yiddish folk song, and the whole episode was further depiction of the Jewish experience through Yiddish music.

Probably Green's most successful film and one that is still popular today among Jewish audiences is the 1936 classic *Yidl mitn Fidl* (Yidl with a Fiddle), a comic story of four klezmer musicians in Poland. It was shot in Warsaw and in a Polish village just three years before the Nazi invasion. The music was written by Abe Ellstein and includes, besides the title song, various love and comic Yiddish songs. The title role was taken by one of the leading Jewish musical comedy stars of the twentieth century, Molly Picon (1899-1992). The film depicts the extreme poverty of the Jewish people of Poland and the joy that klezmer music brought to their drab lives, and in this latter point it goes beyond what Hollywood had to offer at the time.

Hollywood films after *The Jazz Singer* focused on idyllic, all-American stories, with music used only as background; whenever someone sang or danced, it was clearly forced on the movie and not the essential ingredient of the story. However, the four Yiddish films discussed above are different: in those films the music is the story and the story never loses focus when someone sings or dances. Movie historians refer to the Yiddish use of music as *diegetic*. The singing in the saloon and synagogue is integral to the story of *The Jazz Singer*, as the singing in the opera house and synagogue is in *Der Vilner shtot khazan*; a family song unites the plot in *A brivele der mamen*, and the klezmer music is the essence of *Yidl mitn Fidl*. What this shows quite clearly is that Green and the other directors realized that Jewish music is what holds the Jewish people together.

Klezmer Music of the Nineteenth to Twenty-First Centuries

As we have already seen, Jewish musicians frequently performed dance music at Jewish weddings and at weddings of Gentiles. They also performed for other joyous occasions within and outside the ghettos. Before the nineteenth century Jewish dance bands (Yiddish = *Klezmer Kapelyes*) in Central and Eastern Europe consisted of violinists and performers on both modern and folk instruments; this combination of instruments continued in the next two centuries.

Klezmer bands of the early nineteenth century followed the tradition, established many centuries before, of Jewish musicians entertaining both Christians and Jews at public and private dances. One such group, ca. 1800 in a small German town comprised five musicians: two violinists, one clarinetist, one violoncellist, and one *Hackbrett* (dulcimer) player. We know that Jules Offenbach, the son of a German cantor, went to Paris as a child with his older brother, and that they played violin and violoncello in a Jewish dance band there during the 1830s. By 1840, Offenbach had converted to Catholicism, gallicized his name to Jacques, and had begun composing light operas and operettas, and there is no further indication of an involvement with klezmer music. Like Offenbach, most Jews in Western Europe during the nineteenth century turned away from the folk dance tradition of their forebears and instead adopted the dances of their host countries. Jewish folk instrumentalists were looked down upon by assimilationists who were embarrassed by their lack of manners and lack of conservatory training.

In Central and Eastern Europe, however, the klezmer tradition continued in both villages and such Jewish-populated cities as Vilna and Dubnow, but with a whole new set of influences. The music was adapted from synagogue chant and song. With the Chassidim the tunes went in both directions: some synagogue *nigunim* made their way into klezmer music, while some klezmer music reappeared as Chassidic synagogue tunes. The klezmorim also heard and played the dance music of their non-Jewish neighbors and revised these dance tunes, rhythms, styles, and actual dance steps for Jewish parties. In Rumania dances of the Gypsies were particularly popular; the *longa*, for example, a "Turkish" tune similar to Rumanian Gypsy music, was heard among klezmorim. In some cases even the military music of the tsar's army influenced styles of klezmer music.

During the nineteenth century European klezmer musicians played mostly dance music. Until the 1930s there was a core repertory and there were regional repertories, often shared with non-Jews. Many of the dances were termed *freylach* in one locale, *skokne*, *khosidl*, or *sher* in another; there seems to have been no musical differences among them.[32] On the other hand, the *bulgars*, *horas*, and *zhoks* were special to certain regions of Bulgaria, Bessarabia, and Rumania.

In addition to dances, a common klezmer piece is a *doina*, which is a work with solo improvisations that is executed before a dance (often a *hora*) begins. Characterized by extreme *rubato* and by exploration of the modes utilized in Gypsy music, it is performed by a solo instrument—since the end of the nineteenth century usually by clarinet. The sound is also found among Rumanian Gypsies. An earlier term for doina-style music was *taksin*. "We know, for instance, that Jewish musicians in the nineteenth century played an improvisatory genre called *taksim*. Little is known about this genre, which seems to have been derived from the Rumanian *tacsim*, part of the *ballada* (*cintec batrinesc*) genre, and probably with some influence of the Turkish *taksim* genre. Around the turn of the century, in the Jewish repertoire, the *taksim* was replaced by the *doina*, an improvisational genre of Rumanian folk music that Jews played in a manner indistinguishable from that of the Rumanian Gypsy violinists."[33] Klezmer improvisation is called *dreydlekh* and *shleyfer*.

---

[32] Walter Zev Feldman, "Bulgaresasca/Bulgarish/ Bulgar," in Mark Slobin, *American Klezmer* (Berkeley: University of California Press, 2002), 93.

[33] Judit Frigyesi, "The Historical Value of the Record 'Máramaros—the Lost Jewish Music of Transylvania," in the record jacket of the CD *Muzsikás—the Lost Jewish Music of Transylvania* (Rykodisc USA, HNCD 1373, 1993).

These were string-dominated groups, with violins, violas, cellos, and string basses forming the core of the ensemble. The violin was the lead instrument. Many Jewish violinists in Europe were famous klezmer players first, and then, allowed to enter conservatories, they developed into virtuoso classical violinists. The typical string dance band could be as small as two players but often was slightly larger. While the violin had the melody, the instrument emphasizing the rhythm of the piece was the *tsimbl*, a large dulcimer whose strings were struck with a wooden or cloth-wrapped mallet. In the early twentieth century, the *tsimbl* was replaced by the accordion and, in America, also by the jazz trap set, but in recent klezmer bands the *tsimbl* has made a comeback. The clarinet gradually made its way into the klezmer band during the second half of the nineteenth century and by the turn of the century it had displaced the violin as the dominant melody instrument. Brass instruments such as the trumpet and trombone also were occasionally found in nineteenth- and early twentieth-century dance bands. Photographs of Russian klezmer bands in the early twentieth century show in one band three violins, a string bass, a flute, a clarinet, a trumpet, and one unidentified instrument (1912, see fig. 9.2), and in another band three violins, a clarinet, one tuba, two trumpets, and a bass drum (1905, see fig. 9.3).[34] An undated photograph from the same period shows a Polish klezmer band of four violins, a violoncello, and a *tsimbl* (see fig. 9.4).

FIG. 9.2   Russian klezmer band in 1912
(YIVO Institute for Jewish Research, New York)
Reprinted with permission

---

[34] See *Klezmer Pioneers: European and American Recordings 1905-1952* (Cambridge, MA: Rounder CD 1089, 1993), booklet.

FIG. 9.3   Russian klezmer band in 1905
(YIVO Institute for Jewish Research, New York)
Reprinted with permission

FIG. 9.4   Russian klezmer band, early 1900s
(YIVO Institute for Jewish Research, New York)
Reprinted with permission

With the massive emigration of Jews from Eastern Europe from the end of the nineteenth century and to about 1924, many performers of klezmer and their main Jewish audiences were transferred to America. These musicians dominated the American klezmer scene until the early 1950s when *Yiddishkeit* in general nearly disappeared in the United States. During their heyday, the klezmer bands in North America not only accompanied dances as in Europe, but also performed in the Yiddish theater, accompanied Yiddish singers, played concerts on the radio, and even performed radio advertisements.

Among the most distinguished of the new klezmer musicians to arrive in America was Naftule Brandwein (1889-1963), a dazzling clarinetist. He was born in Galicia and immigrated to the United States ca. 1913.

Clarinetist Dave Tarras (1897-1989), one of the most famous of the immigrant klezmer players, was born in a *shtetl* in the Ukraine. He learned music from his father, a musical *badchan*, and served in a Russian army band during World War I. In 1921 he left his ravaged and anti-Semitic homeland for America, where he resumed his musical activities with the help of the Progressive Musicians Benevolent Society, an organization designed to help newly-arrived musicians in New York. Soon he replaced Brandwein in Joseph Cherniavsky's Yiddish-American Jazz Band; he started making records with that band and also recorded with Abe Schwartz's Orchestra. By the late 1920s the so-called "Borsht Belt" in the Catskill Mountains near New York had become a center for Jewish entertainment, and Tarras was featured in many resorts there. Throughout the 1920s and 1930s he performed arrangements by the leading Jewish composers of the time— Sholom Secunda, Abe Ellstein, Alexander Olshanetsky—and accompanied some of the greatest Yiddish theater performers—Aaron Lebedeff, Michl Michalesko, Lucy Levin. But most of Tarras' activities then and into the 1950s continued to be playing at the traditional klezmer venues: weddings, bar and bat mitzvahs, *brisses* (circumcision ceremonies), and anniversaries. He outlived nearly all of the klezmer musicians who dominated the scene before World War II and lived long enough to become the godfather to those who were to revive klezmer in the 1970s.

Other early twentieth-century Klezmer musicians in America include Max Weissman, clarinet; Mishka Tsiganoff, accordionist; Abe Schwartz, violin and piano (ca. 1880-ca. 1960), whose bands ranged in number from five to nine players, among whom were Shloimeke Beckerman and Dave Tarras; Harry Kandel; Israel J. Hochman's Orchestra; Belf's Rumanian Orchestra; Viteazul, trumpet; Leon Ahl; Sid Beckerman, clarinetist; Howie Leess, tenor sax; Shloimke Beckerman, sax; Emil Bruh, violin; Epstein Brothers; Mickey Katz, clarinet; Raderman's Orchestra; Josef Solinski; Max Leibowitz; Joseph Moskowitz, *tsimbl*; Ray Musiker, clarinet.

Merging with jazz, in America klezmer music gradually dissipated between the 1930s and the 1950s. Benny Goodman and Ziggy Elman, two famous klezmer stars, moved to the American mainstream big bands. Even Dave Tarras played Jewish swing (his recording "Bridegroom Special" of 1940 is an example). Although the Holocaust ended klezmer in Western and Central Europe, some klezmer survived in the Soviet Union and in Rumania. The last klezmer musician in Poland was Leo Kozlowski.

In the middle 1970s a revival of klezmer music began which has continued to the present.[35] As interest was rekindled in old Jewish customs which assimilationist modern American Jews

---

[35] Much of the information on the klezmer musicians and bands of the revival klezmer period comes from *A bisl Yidishkayt* (Cambridge, MA: web page, www.yiddishmusic.com, 1999).

had shed, interest was also reawakened in the dance music which had surrounded the most joyous Jewish occasions of the past. From the 1980s on, in North America klezmer music has become not only accepted but also expected for these special occasions. Besides weddings, for which klezmer music was traditionally supplied, the occasions employing klezmer have expanded to include bar and bat mitzvah parties, *bris* parties, anniversaries, synagogue dances, and private dances. With the merging of traditional klezmer dance music with various modern popular genres, concerts of this music have become common in coffeehouses, nightclubs, schoolyards, college quads, Radio City Music Hall, and even football stadiums.

During the hiatus period from the late 1930s to the early 1970s, there were always some bands announcing that they were playing "klezmer" music, but in fact these bands were playing Jewish tunes in a foreign style—such as the Original Klezmer Jazz Band or the Jerusalem Jazz Band, which applied jazz to Jewish tunes. To a certain extent, this is what Benny Goodman was also doing whenever he used a Jewish tune with his swing orchestras. Even Dave Tarras, who had to make a living, reverted to swing and bop with Jewish tunes—sounds that hardly sound Jewish. In the late 1960s Balkan dancing was popular on college campuses, and the Israeli *hora* was included as a Jewish dance type, but the bands were not klezmer bands. Then in 1975 Lev Liberman and David Skuse founded the Klezmorim in Berkeley, which started the revival. As Liberman has stated, "I'd like to think that the current klezmer revival had its origins in our early experiments with tight ensemble playing, improvisation, klezmer workshops and neo-klezmer composition, street music, world beat, and New Vaudeville."[36] When the recording company Arhoolie issued the Klezmorim's *Streets of Gold* in 1978, it sparked a national, and eventually international, interest in the special sounds of klezmer music.[37] That interest was already out there is evinced by David Owens who notes that his Los Angeles-based band NAMA had issued a single klezmer piece in 1976 on a disc that was primarily devoted to Balkan folk dance. The klezmer revival sparked by Arhoolie's recording spread beyond California to the East Coast, where in 1980 the Klezmer Conservatory Band of Boston was organized under Hankus Netsky. From its first album *Yiddish Renaissance* (1981), it became clear that the high quality set by Klezmorim could be matched and that the country was eager for more such groups.

Among other early klezmer revival groups, some still in existence, were Kapelye (under Henry Sapoznik); Muszikas; The New Shtetl Band (New Mexico); Chicago Klezmer Ensemble (led by Kurt Bjorling, clarinet); Finjan Klezmer Ensemble (Winnipeg); Flying Bulgar Band (Toronto); Golden Gate Gypsy Orchestra (San Francisco Area); Machaya Klezmer Band (Maryland); West End Klezmorim (Manhattan); Wholesale Klezmer Band (Western Massachusetts); Yale Klezmer Band (New Haven, big band); and Yiddishe Cup Klezmer Band (Cleveland). Furthermore, the reputation of new stars of klezmer music began to rival the fame of the older ones like Tarras, Schwartz, and Brandwein; among these performers, Andy Statman (originally a bluegrass mandolin player who came under the influence of Tarras and Tarras's Chassidic klezmer), Giora Feidman (clarinetist, originally from Buenos Aires, then Israel), David Krakauer and Walter Zev Feldman

---

[36] Cited in Ari Davidow, web page: http://www.well.com/user/ari/klezcontacts.html.

[37] This description of the revival of klezmer music is drawn partly from a lecture, "Radical Jewish Culture and the Klezmer Revival" by Kent Underwood, delivered at the Jewish Music Roundtable as part of the Annual Meeting of the Music Library Association, Los Angeles, 17 March 1999.

figure prominently. Nearly all these early stars and bands were out to resuscitate the moribund traditional klezmer sound as known from the 1920s; they did not consciously aim to alter it. As preservationists they wanted to save the old klezmer music before there were no more people left who knew what it should sound like. That changes to the traditional sounds occurred can be attributed to the fact that klezmer music was quickly back on its feet, and that to make it healthy, vibrant, and living it had to evolve. Even in those bands which were most tied to the old tradition, elements of change crept in. For example, on its fall 1997 tour to Europe, the Kapelye—one of the best traditional klezmer ensembles—utilized the traditional instruments of accordion (Lauren Brody), clarinet (Ken Maltz), tuba (Eric Berman), and keyboard (Pete Sokolow), but supplemented by vocals (Adrienne Cooper) and banjo (Henri Sapoznik), American nightclub additions to traditional klezmer sounds.

The necessity to be creative with klezmer music rather than just revive it had become blatantly clear by 1992 when the Klezmatics released their album *Rhythm + Jews*. The Klezmatics (led by Frank London) tried to modernize klezmer with electronics and other newer instruments and to fuse it with other genres of music. (Music which fuses at least two contrasting styles is termed "crossover music.") Coupled with its more youthful sound (the fusion of the kinds of music that appealed to young people) was the new klezmer's frequent attempts to go beyond simple dance music and make political statements. The youth were rebellious and less reverential, and so they treated this old traditional dance music with less than traditional awe. They felt compelled to make changes. Following the Klezmatics come a whole series of recordings by various Jewish klezmer groups throughout North America and England eager to change klezmer into all kinds of Jewish and other music. Other New York groups of jazzier, rockier, new wave klezmer include Hasidic New Wave, Paradox Trio, Naftule's Dream, and Modern Klezmer Quartet (fusion of bop and klezmer); modern stars now added Neshama Carlebach. Some groups, like Brave Old World, mix unfused traditional early twentieth-century klezmer with some of the sounds of the late twentieth century on the same concert program or on the same recording; among its members are Joel Rubin (clarinet), Stuart Brotman (string bass), Michael Alpert (fiddle), Hankus Netsky (piano), Moishe Yerushalimsky (trombone), and Lisa Rose (*tsimbal*), all of whom at one time or another played in some of the other bands. They typify a new type of klezmer band, the international rather than local sort; the members of the group live and work in different countries and cities when they are not actually playing in Brave Old World. "The only klezmer artist writing songs about contemporary topics in Yiddish, Alpert has penned tunes on the Chernobyl nuclear disaster, the Gulf War and the fall of the Berlin Wall."[38] Andy Statman and Yale Strom (violin) mix klezmer with jazz and bluegrass.[39]

By the beginning of the twenty-first century there were registered klezmer ensembles in twenty-nine states and the District of Columbia and in five Canadian provinces. Among the leading klezmer groups outside New York are Austin Klezmorim (Texas); Brave Old World (Boston); Maxwell Street Klezmer Band (Chicago, which mixes academic, folk theater, and jazz backgrounds); New Orleans Klezmer Allstars (combines rock, jazz, cajun); Twelve Corners Klezmer Band (Rochester,

---

[38] Jon Kalish, "A New Generation Gets Klezmerized," 18 May 1994.

[39] Other members of the group include Mark Dress (bass), Ismail Buttera (accordian), and Seido Salifoski (*dumbec*).

NY); and Tzimmes (Vancouver, which includes some Ladino texts and some synthesized sounds on one recording and American country music on another). There is fusion not only between traditional klezmer and various popular genres but also between klezmer and classical music. Classical Israeli violinist Itzhak Perlman has made several recordings and given concerts with various klezmer bands including the Klezmatics, the Klezmer Conservatory Band, Brave Old World, and the Andy Statman Klezmer Orchestra. The Boston Shirim have fused such classical works as Mahler's First Symphony with klezmer, as well as klezmer with hits from the Yiddish theater.

Once the revival of klezmer bands took hold in the United States and Canada, it was quickly picked up by musicians overseas. Although the revival of klezmer bands in England was led by Jews, klezmer revivals in Germany and elsewhere in Europe were, with few exceptions, initiated by non-Jewish groups. Berlin alone had twenty-five klezmer bands in the 1990s. Among the European groups today are Gojim (Austria); Budowitz (Austria); Klezmic noiZ (Belgium); Pressburger Klezmer Band (Czechoslovakia); Spielniks (Denmark); Burning Bush (England); Merlin Shepherd Klezmer Trio (England); Gregori Schecter's Klezmer Festival Band (England); Doina Klezmer (Finland); De Naye Kapelye (Hungary); Aufwind (Germany); Frejlechs (Germany); Jontef (Germany); Kasbeck (Germany); Klezmo-Copter (Germany); Massel Klezmorim (Germany); De Gojim (The Netherlands); Klezmokum (The Netherlands); Kroke (Poland); Herwig Strobl (Poland); Poza (Ukraine); Nano Peylet (France); Hadash Klezmer Orchestra (Italy); Klezroyin (Italy); Rony Micro Band (Italy); Sniper (Italy); Kandel's Kapell (Sweden); Klezmer Powwow (Switzerland); and Kol Simcha (Switzerland). Elsewhere, the Australian klezmer band Klezmania (from Oystralia) includes such modernized and localized pieces as "Tale of the Kangaroo Klezmer" and "Dunkin' Bagels," performed by vocals, guitar/mandolin, balalaika, *bayan*, clarinet, and soprano sax. Other bands in Australia are Closet Klezmer in Canberra and the Melbourne-based Klezmeritis. A klezmer band in Brazil is Zemer and a band in Argentina is the Faineklezmer Quintet.

In the Máramaros county of Transylvania before the Holocaust, Jewish klezmer musicians and non-Jewish Gypsy instrumentalists often played together at both Jewish and non-Jewish weddings, Purim celebrations, and dance parties. The latter two occasions seem to have been more typical in Hungary than in other Eastern European Jewish communities. After the War, several of the non-Jewish musicians survived and continued to play the music, though they did not understand its fullness. What they demonstrated, however, is that there was a Hungarian style of klezmer music that was part of the overall Eastern European style of klezmer but which "had its own genres and performing styles which are not identical with either the main Jewish or the Hungarian instrumental styles."[40] There were two types of pieces: duple meter dances called *czárdás* or *Hosid*, and pieces with *rubato* in an improvisatory style. The dances resemble closely the *freylakhs*, *shers*, and *khosids* of the non-Hungarian klezmer bands. The *rubato* pieces are different from the *doinas* of other klezmer groups in that the ornaments are slower, the improvisation more closely resembles liturgical recitative, and the lead violin's execution is similar to Gypsy playing.

To further development of new klezmer groups and reaffirm traditional klezmer style so that new groups can build upon it, several workshops were organized which have become virtual schools of klezmer music. "While working as a sound archivist at the prestigious YIVO Institute

---

[40] Most of the discussion of this version of klezmer music is based on Frigyesi's analysis; see above n. 31.

for Jewish Research, Henry Sapoznik founded KlezKamp, a well-attended Yiddish folk-arts convention (with a heavy emphasis on klezmer) that has been held in the Catskills annually since 1985."[41] Likewise, "Alpert, a former member of one of the West Coast's first klezmer groups, the Chutzpa Orchestra, back in the late 1970s, now plays fiddle in Brave Old World and helps run Buffalo on the Roof, a West Virginia retreat similar to KlezKamp."[42]

The unusual situation of Yiddish music at the end of the twentieth and at the beginning of the twenty-first century is that it is flourishing even though the Yiddish language is only spoken as a native tongue by a few persons. The challenge to Yiddish as a legitimate language, let alone as a universal Jewish language, is now understood in exactly the opposite way from how it was understood a century earlier. Then Yiddish was a living language just beginning to find its literature, theater, and music; millions spoke it despite its abasement by literary critics and the *maskilim*. A century later, though Yiddish is no longer spoken but by a handful of diehards, its literature, theater, and music are regarded by Jews and Gentiles alike as among the great contributions of Jews to the history of world culture.

Suggestions for Further Reading

Cahan, Y. L. *Yiddish Folksongs with Melodies*, ed. Max Weinreich. New York: YIVO, 1957.

Heskes, Irene. "Music as Social History: American Yiddish Theater Music, 1882-1920." In *American Music* 2 (1984): 73-87.

Kadison, Luba, and Joseph Buloff. *On Stage, Off Stage: Memories of a Lifetime in the Yiddish Theatre*, ed. Irving Genn. Cambridge: Harvard University Press, 1992.

Levin, Neil, ed. *Songs of the American Jewish Experience*. Chicago: Board of Jewish Education, 1976.

Rosenfeld, Lulla Adler. *The Yiddish Theatre and Jacob P. Adler*. New York: Thomas Y. Crowell, 1977; rev. ed. New York: Shapolsky Brothers, 1988.

Sandrow, Nahma. *Vagabond Stars: A World History of Yiddish Theater*. New York: Limelight Editions, 1986.

Sapoznik, Henry. *Klezmer! Jewish Music from Old World to Our World*. New York: Schirmer Books, 1999.

Silverman, Jerry. *The Yiddish Song Book*. Briarcliff Manor, NY: Stein and Day Publishers, 1983.

Slobin, Mark, ed. *American Klezmer: Its Roots and Offshoots*. Berkeley: University of California Press, 2002.

Slobin, Mark. *Old Jewish Folk Music: the Collections and Writings of Moseh Beregovski*. Philadelphia: University of Pennsylvania Press, 1982.

Strom, Yale. *The Book of Klezmer: The History, the Music, the Folklore*. Chicago: A Cappella Books, 2002.

Wiener, Leo. *The History of Yiddish Literature in the Nineteenth Century*. New York: Charles Scribner's Sons, 1899.

---

[41] Kalish.

[42] Ibid.

10 ‖ Secular Jewish Musicians of Modern Europe

Germany

Among upper-class Jews in Germany the *Haskalah* had the desired effect immediately in music, that is, by the early nineteenth century young German Jews from the enlightened families enjoyed and studied European art music and entered its professional ranks. However, a negative consequence was evident within a few years—nearly all young Jewish musicians had converted to Christianity.

The *Haskalah*'s purpose was to enable Jews to coexist with Christians in a tolerant state, and thus Jews were encouraged to modernize their life styles to conform to Christian Europe in the late eighteenth- and early nineteenth centuries. In the arts Jews were to accept the prevailing aesthetics of other Europeans, who—as was then widely believed—had brought the arts to a level unmatched by any other culture in the world. Jews' conversion to Christian art, however, was not meant to be their conversion to the Christian religion; but in most cases of professional musicians it came to be just this. German Jewish musicians found that they could enter the music profession, but everywhere they went they encountered hostile anti-Semitism. There were sneering remarks, social slurs, or discrimination against Jews. Since art replaced religion as the sacred trust for such musicians, they felt no need to carry on their backs the burden of being Jewish. Indeed, art became the new religion, and this art was historically, and still predominantly, Christian. Meyerbeer[1] was one exception, a true German *maskil* who remained fervently Jewish while dominating the European opera scene from 1830 to 1860; but most other European Jewish musicians of the first half of the nineteenth century were practicing Christians.

Among the first of these was Isaak Moscheles (1794-1870), who was born into a family of *maskilim* in Prague. His father, a clothing merchant with great interest in music, saw to it that his son had the best piano teachers in the city. When the father died in 1808, Isaak was sent to Vienna to study, and there he became a pupil of Salieri and one of Beethoven's most trusted

---

[1] See below, p. 219.

disciples. Six years later, when Vienna rejoiced in Napoleon's defeat, "the Jewish community to which Moscheles still belonged at that time, commissioned a cantata from him to celebrate the occasion. It was performed with great pomp and presented in a revised version to the public for a second time a year later at the Congress of Vienna."[2] Within a few years Moscheles was heralded as one of the greatest pianists of Europe, and he traveled throughout the continent with great success. From 1825 to 1846 his home base was London, and thereafter he lived with his family in Leipzig, where he was an esteemed professor of piano at the conservatory. He composed a great deal of music, most of it involving the piano, and he remained faithful to the style of middle-period Beethoven. Outwardly, however, he did not remain faithful to Judaism; early in his career he had converted to Christianity, and he raised his children as Christians.

Moscheles was not entirely ignorant of his Jewish heritage. As Smidak points out, he had begun to study the works of the philosopher Moses Mendelssohn by 1820,[3] and when he visited his mother in Prague in 1835, he recounted that "she had just finished her prayers from the family bible which I remember so well."[4] In 1849 he took his children to Prague to see the city of their father's origins and to visit his relatives. Yet he and his wife had converted to Christianity, they celebrated Christmas with her family in Hamburg, they christened their children in the Lutheran Church, and he changed his name from the Jewish Isaak to the German Ignaz. Moscheles started as a typical *maskil*, but by the time of his marriage he had already disassociated himself from the history of Jewish music.

Both Ferdinand Hiller (1811-85) and Stephen Heller (1813-88) were of Jewish descent, both were distinguished pianists and composers, and both were converts. Their reactions to their Jewish past were quite different, however. Hiller's family was well off, if not overly wealthy, and had integrated into German society in Frankfurt am Main. Typical of that period, the only way for Jews to have a successful career in business or the arts was to become Christians. Conversion was against the precepts of the *Haskalah*,[5] yet Hiller did not consider his conversion a rejection of Judaism; he thought of himself as a descendant of the *Haskalah* and his becoming a Christian an expediency. Hiller's father had decided that he would convert, and while his chosen career was then open to him, he faced the same problems that plagued Felix Mendelssohn, a close friend. Hiller felt at home among German Jewish converts to Christianity, but was never completely accepted by a large number of Christians.[6] When Wagner emerged in the mid-nineteenth century as the leading anti-Semitic musician, Hiller took special note that Wagner was not afraid to embrace him and "seemed not to fear the Jewish infection."[7] Like Mendelssohn,

---

[2] Emil F. Smidak, *Isaak-Ignaz Moscheles: The Life of the Composer and his Encounters with Beethoven, Liszt, Chopin, and Mendelssohn* (1st ed. Vienna: J & V Edition, 1988; trans. ed. Aldershot, Hampshire: Scolar Press, 1989), 15.

[3] Smidak, 20.

[4] Ibid., 104-05.

[5] Lowenthal, 227ff.

[6] For brief comments on Hiller's sensitivity to his Jewishness, see Joel Sach's introduction to Ferdinand Hiller, *Mendelssohn: Letters and Recollections*, trans. M. E. von Glehn (New York: Vienna House, 1972), xi-xii.

[7] Reinhold Sietz, *Aus Ferdinand Hillers Briefwechsel*, in *Beiträge zu einer Biographie Ferdinand Hillers*, 6, in Beiträge zur rheinischen Musikgeschichte, 70 (Cologne: Arno Volk-Verlag, 1968), 96. Hiller's remark appears in a letter to Hermann Levi from 17 January 1872.

when he turned to Jewish topics in his music—his opera *Die Zerstörung Jerusalems* (The Destruction of Jerusalem) and the cantatas *Israels Siegeszug* (Israel's Path to Victory) and *Rebecca* are his best known such works—he wrote without any consideration of Jewish music. Yet, as Reinhold Sietz, his biographer, has stated,

> That essentially he felt tied to the Jewish world is evinced not only by the large number of his friends and disciples who were of Jewish origins but also by the facts that almost all the texts he chose for his vocal music came from the Old Testament, that he had a deep knowledge of Jewish rituals and practices, and that he held the utmost respect for Jewish synagogue music. In 1827 when he was traveling to Vienna, someone asked him his religion,[8] and he responded, "I was never discrete enough to hide that I belong to one of the oldest races on Earth, one of whose beliefs I carry out each week when I give two Gulden to charity. *Noblesse oblige*." After he wrote his Mass, which was to be performed in a Cathedral, he wrote to M[oritz] Hartmann on May 28, 1872 that he "wanted the people to know how little faith was connected with making a beautiful mass."[9] Hiller considered himself bound to a rational, humane Deism following the philosophy of Moses Mendelssohn.[10]

Heller, born Jewish in Hungary, converted to Christianity while still a young man to make possible his concert career as a pianist in Germany. His conversion was probably hastened by sharp disputes with a tyrannical father, who tried to shape his career and then abandoned him. In 1838 he settled in Paris where he remained for the rest of his life, respected as a sensitive and intelligent pianist but not as a great artist. There is nothing Jewish in his music, and whatever contributions he may have made to the music of his people were lost because of the inherent anti-Semitism of German society. Even in liberal Paris he did not feel comfortable as a Jew because of his early German experiences. Unlike Hiller, who maintained very close ties to his family, Heller separated himself from his and thereby also excluded whatever feelings for Judaism he might have retained had his relationship to his parents been as close as Hiller's to his parents.

Similarly, Felix Mendelssohn, the great nineteenth-century German composer of Jewish lineage, can hardly be part of the history of Jewish music through his own compositions. While he chose some topics from the Old Testament, he chose just as many from the New Testament and produced many cantatas specifically for Protestant worship. His oratorio *Elijah* is considered his most Jewish work, yet his other principal oratorio is *St. Paul*, hardly a Jewish story. Nonetheless, Mendelssohn is part of the history of Jewish music not only because he was the grandson of the most important *maskil* in Jewish history, but because he inspired countless Jewish youth throughout the nineteenth century to become musicians, some of whom remained Jewish and devoted their talents specifically to Jewish music.

---

[8] Ferdinand Hiller, *Künstlerleben* (Cologne, 1880), 42-43.

[9] *Kölnische Volkszeitung*, 24 October 1911, no. 909.

[10] Sietz, 7:141.

Because of his grandfather's prominence in German Jewish history[11] and his own amazing talents, Felix became a central personality in the role of Jewish converts from the *Haskalah*, particularly in Germany. His father Abraham converted the family to Christianity not only to get ahead in the banking world and to satisfy his wife's social desires, but also because he believed that, while no religion has a corner on truth, "Christianity [is] the more purified form and the one most accepted by the majority of civilized people."[12] He felt that as a Christian Felix would be better able to have a career in modern Germany. While the agnostic Abraham maintained some ties to Judaism, he decided that Felix should be able to move freely in Christian society. He told his son to drop the name Mendelssohn and assume the name Bartholdy so as to escape immediate recognition as being of Jewish origins. The Bartholdy name had been adopted by his wife's brother when he converted from Judaism to Christianity, and Abraham had hyphenated it to his own name.[13] Felix, though he did not like his uncle, continued to use the name Bartholdy, and while he remained proud of his grandfather's name, he knew little of Judaism and was a practicing Christian. He was always aware of his grandfather and of his Jewish origins—anti-Semites would never let him forget it.[14] More than that, though, he was a deeply religious man and composed many religious pieces, usually with a clearly Christian purpose; but in all his many letters with their frequent exclamations of religious fervor, he seemed indifferent to Judaism except as it might have affected his relatives who were still Jews.[15]

Abraham Mendelssohn, whom Werner regards as the brightest of Moses's six children, had made friends among the intellectual and artistic elite in Paris and Germany. Through them he was able to hire the best possible teacher for Felix, Karl Friedrich Zelter (1758-1832), and through him, in turn, Felix met the most important writers and musicians, including Goethe. For a Jewish child (as *maskilim* in Europe considered him) to be accepted as an honored guest by the then greatest German writer highlighted to ambitious Jewish youths and parents the potential success of the *Haskalah*. It gave them hope that the degradation and exclusion Jews felt from ghetto life could be obliterated if one had talent and the breeding of a German, despite continued anti-Semitism and lack of political rights. Once he was raised to the level of a Jewish hero, Felix Mendelssohn's musical accomplishments were adored by Jews as products of a Jewish mind and soul even though, from a traditional standpoint, there was nothing Jewish about his music. Even in his great oratorio *Elijah*, when he brings in texts that are translations of Jewish prayers ("Lord God of Abraham, Isaac and Israel" for example), the music is Mendelssohn's own.

---

[11] His grandfather was the great Moses Mendelssohn, a prime mover in the *Haskalah* movement. See above, Historical Interlude, *Haskalah*, 153-57.

[12] In a letter from Abraham Mendelssohn to his son Felix, dated 8 July 1829, translated in Werner, *Mendelssohn*, 37. Despite our reliance on Werner's study for our understanding of Felix Mendelssohn the Jew, it has been pointed out that during the past several decades many faults have been found with this volume. See John Michael Cooper, "Knowing Mendelssohn: A Challenge from the Primary Sources," in *Notes: Quarterly Journal of the Music Library Association* 61 (2004): 35-95, esp. 70-71.

[13] Werner, *Mendelssohn*, 33.

[14] Ibid., 28; Jeffrey S. Sposato, "Creative Writing: The [Self-] Identification of Mendelssohn as Jew," in *The Musical Quarterly* 82 (1998): 193.

[15] Werner, *Mendelssohn*, 42, tries to show that Mendelssohn took great pride in his Judaism, but Sposato convincingly refutes much of Werner's position.

But, because this bass aria was regarded as Mendelssohn's private prayer as a Jew, the style and substance of the music was then copied by Jews everywhere as "Jewish" music. The Mendelssohn sound—a mixture of 1830s Biedermeier harmony with the sentimentalism of the period— became the ideal for the German reformers inside the synagogue (Louis Lewandowski's music is the most well-known), and once accepted there it became the new sound of Jewish music wherever it was performed.

In the generation that followed Mendelssohn, Friedrich Gernsheim (1830-1916) was one of the most important secular and enlightened Jewish musicians. Born the son of a Jewish physician in Worms, famous for its old Jewish community, he was a student of, among others, Marmontel in Paris, Moscheles in Leipzig, and Hiller in Cologne. He taught in a number of cities in Germany as well as in Rotterdam; then, from 1880 to 1904, he taught and conducted choral concerts at the Stern Conservatory in Berlin. In Paris he mingled with Saint-Saëns, Lalo, Rossini, and Heller, and he counted among his friends Johannes Brahms and Max Bruch (a pupil of Hiller). Engelbert Humperdinck (composer of the opera *Hansel and Gretel*) was his student. He was highly regarded as a pedagogue and conductor in his lifetime, though today he is all but forgotten.

Nearly all of Gernsheim's compositions fall outside any religious context and most have no Jewish connotation at all. He did write some church music—an early *Salve Regina* and an *Ave Maria* and *Te Deum* late in life, which were no doubt required of an important choral conductor in Berlin at the end of the nineteenth century. But what sets Gernsheim apart from Mendelssohn and the others is that he remained Jewish and that in 1882 he published *Elohenu, hebräischer Gesang* for violoncello and small orchestra or piano, and in 1888 brought out his Symphony No. 3 in C Minor, a tone poem entitled *Miriam*.[16] In 1884 Gernsheim wrote to Hiller, his revered and then retired teacher, that he would like to apply for Hiller's old position at the Conservatory in Cologne should Brahms and others turn it down.[17] Hiller responded confidentially to Gernsheim that it was not because he was Jewish that the city authorities would turn him down but because he was related to, and had close ties with, the richest and most influential Jews in Cologne.[18] Hiller later assured Gernsheim that no one in Cologne had said anything anti-Semitic against him;[19] it was only Hiller's instinct that led him very privately to suggest that, down deep, the Cologne authorities were suspicious of his Jewish ties. Thus Hiller, who had outwardly divorced himself from Judaism, could hold the position, but Gernsheim, who maintained his Judaism publicly, would not be accepted.

Gernsheim's close friend Hermann Levi (1839-1900) was another Jewish member of this generation to achieve considerable success in music.[20] During the last third of the nineteenth century he was one of the two or three most important orchestral conductors in Europe. His background is somewhat different from other German Jewish musicians who were scions of

---

[16] Willi Kahl, "Gernsheim," in *Die Musik in Geschichte und Gegenwart*, 1st ed., vol. 4 (Kassel: Bärenreiter, 1955), cols. 1821-24.

[17] Sietz, 5:72, in *Beiträge zur rheinischen Musikgeschichte*, 65 (Köln: Arno Volk-Verlag, 1966).

[18] Ibid., 7:20.

[19] Ibid., 7:21, in a letter dated 12 May 1884.

[20] Frithjof Haas, *Zwischen Brahms und Wagner: der Dirigent Hermann Levi* (Zürich/Mainz: Atlantis Musikbuch-Verlag, 1995), esp. 44, 56.

assimilated Jews or recent converts. Levi's father, Benedikt Levi (1806-99), was the Reform rabbi of Giessen, and it is hard to imagine Hermann's early years being anything but soaked in Judaism. However, Benedikt Levi was a true *maskil* who combined his Talmudic studies with a university education culminating in a doctorate in philosophy; so when his son aspired to a career in music, he encouraged him at age thirteen to enter a regular German Gymnasium in Mannheim. Two years later Hermann entered the Leipzig Conservatory. Despite having composed some when he was young, including setting Psalm 24 in 1862, he quickly realized that he was not on a level with Brahms and Wagner, and he concentrated on a career as a conductor. He held several posts in Saarbrücken, Rotterdam, and Karlsrühe, where Jews were fully accepted[21] and where he gained a considerable reputation for his interpretion, especially of the works of Brahms, whose friendship he quickly cultivated.[22] But his primary interest was in the operas of Wagner, whose music he conducted in Karlsrühe, Bayreuth, and Munich, in which city he held important opera posts from 1872 to 1896. Much has been written about Levi's importance for the promotion of Wagner's music and the continual anti-Semitic insults he endured from Wagner.[23] Cosima Liszt, Wagner's second wife, liked Levi for his urbaneness and talent, and despite Wagner's continual harassment of him, noted that her husband could not do without him. When Wagner wanted his operas performed, he relied on King Ludwig of Bavaria to finance and promote them. This Ludwig did, but by the early 1880s, with the premier of *Parsifal*, Wagner's last opera, Ludwig demanded that Levi conduct; Ludwig appreciated the genius of his house conductor and, despite Wagner's continual anti-Semitic diatribes against Levi and all other Jews, he did not knuckle under to Wagner's prejudices. Wagner then pleaded with Levi to convert to Christianity so as not to defile his great Christian opera; of course, Levi, who remained in close contact with his rabbinical father all through this episode, did not do so. As a gesture to Wagner, however, Levi (who may have been ill) allowed Wagner to conduct the last three scenes during the first performance of the opera.

Levi's loyalty to Wagner and late-nineteenth-century German culture conflicted with Levi's loyalty to his family. Though at times he toyed with the idea of converting, especially when he married a non-Jew and when his older brother converted to Catholicism and changed the family name to Lendeck, he realized that that step would not grant him any more security, since baptized Jews were then not accepted as full Christians. Wagner and his circle joked incessantly about Joachim and other highly-regarded musicians who were born Jewish and,

---

[21] When Levi signed his contract for his second season in Karlsruhe, in which he swore allegiance to the Grand Duke Friedrich, he specifically crossed out words that made his oath dependent on the Christian bible (Haas, 103); that this was allowed by Friedrich is a sign of his liberality toward Jews, and it further emphasizes Levi's loyalty to his father's faith.

[22] Since Brahms was a member of the liberal artistic class in Germany, and fully accepted Jews, Levi had no problems being a close friend. But with regard to Wagner, anti-Semitism affected not only Levi but Brahms as well. "Brahms highly respected Wagner as a composer but detested the man, especially because of his anti-Semitism"; Haas, 151. When Levi succumbed to the Wagnermania that affected so many Germans and was ready to accept the man Wagner despite his anti-Semitism, Brahms broke off all further personal relations with Levi. Other members of the Brahms-Levi circle also questioned Levi's motivations, such as the poet Paul Heyse (Haas, 222).

[23] See Robert W. Gutman, *Richard Wagner: The Man, His Mind, and His Music* (New York: Harcourt, Brace & World, 1968), esp. 410-13.

despite conversion, were inherently unable to be real German musicians. Levi was the most tragic of the Jewish musicians of the *Haskalah* since, in the same sense as the Jewish-born German poet Heinrich Heine, who chose to live in the more accepting social climate of France, he was caught in the abyss of self-hatred caused by his simultaneous love for his ancestors (there had been fourteen generations of rabbis in his family ending with his father, with whom he was always very close) and for those whose culture he adored but who hated his ancestors.[24] As his career developed, Levi feared that he would be rejected because he was Jewish, yet he refused to give up either his religion or his career. Even after Wagner died, Levi was plagued by doubts about his ability to conduct great German works because Wagner and others had implanted in his mind their continual assertions that a Jew was genetically incapable of understanding the true spirit of German masterpieces. Cosima Wagner fueled Levi's dilemma with her brutal attacks on his Jewishness both before and after her husband died; as she explained, Levi "achieved his greatness through his own efforts despite his evil genes, while she—born of good genes—achieved what is bad through her own efforts."[25] At times Levi explained Wagner's anti-Semitism as the sentiments of a German nationalist whose ideals remained pure,[26] but inwardly he knew better. Levi was quite aware of the tragedy of his situation and that of all Jews in Germany,[27] and he eventually collapsed in a nervous condition that ended his career. Then, and only then (1896), did he convert to Christianity, largely to accommodate his second wife, and when it was clear that he did not do so to promote his career; we do not know how his conversion affected his relationship to his father, who was then still alive.

What Levi experienced was the result of the particular social situation of Jews in Germany during the nineteenth century. Long after France had granted political equality to Jews, the German states treated Jews as second-class citizens. Never having enjoyed the strong political union that had made France so prosperous, Germans, divided into many independent states, suffered from an inferiority problem that had deep psychological effects. Jews were an easy scapegoat for the ills of the German people. A handful of Jews had achieved enormous wealth, and now more and more Jews (even if converted) were showing their talents in the arts. The assumption was that Jewish wealth deprived Germans of wealth, and Jews in high positions in the arts deprived Germans of those positions.

Wagner, who struggled to get his new operas produced, had to find a scapegoat to explain his commercial failures, and presaging the Nazis, he turned on the Jews as the source for his and Germany's woes. The problem of Wagner dominated the last half of the nineteenth century and well into the twentieth. After disappointments in Paris in the 1840s, where the transplanted German Jew Meyerbeer held sway over the opera world, Wagner voiced his feelings against all

[24] Haas, 243-44, 366-69.

[25] Ibid., 345.

[26] Ibid., 255.

[27] Ibid., 286, cites a letter written after Wagner's death from Levi to the anti-Semitic conductor Julius Kniese, in which Levi wishes to avoid Kniese in Bayreuth so as to avoid memory of Kniese a few years before asking Wagner to get rid of Levi because a Jew cannot understand Wagner's music. In 1894 Levi iterated his discomfort in remaining with the Wagnerites at Bayreuth since as a Jew he was continually attacked no matter how much he contributed to the Wagner cause (ibid., 348-49).

Jews in a notorious essay, "Judaism in Music" ("Das Judenthum in der Musik"), which he brought out in 1850 under the pseudonym "Freigedank" and then republished nineteen years later under his own name. Wagner's operas were immensely popular with the German people. Caught up in an irrational nationalism that culminated in World War II, Germans regarded Wagner's essays on social as well as operatic matters as gospel truth rather than as the offensive meandering of a disturbed xenophobe.

Thus, however great their musical contributions and however much they tried to hide their Jewish roots, German musicians of Jewish origins were outcasts. A number of Jewish musicians, such as Levi and Gernsheim, came to recognize that no amount of denial of their Judaism would make the Germans accept them as Germans, so they remained faithful to their roots while they took advantage of the *Haskalah* to step outside the ghetto and participate in music in Germany and elsewhere. Wagner respected Levi for remaining steadfast in his beliefs despite provocations,[28] and even before he met Levi, Wagner had come to admit that some Jews were artistically acceptable if they were sensible enough to agree with Wagner's ideas.[29]

As the nineteenth century drew to a close, the leading musical personality in Europe was Gustav Mahler (1860-1911). Born an assimilated Jew in Bohemia, he entered the Vienna Conservatory in 1875, and by 1880 had begun his conducting career in an Austrian village. After short stays in Yugoslavia, and in the cities of Kassel, Prague, Leipzig, and Budapest, among others, he was named conductor of the Hamburg Opera (1891-97), then of the Vienna Staatsoper (1897-1907), and finally of the New York Metropolitan Opera (1907-11). He also regularly conducted the Vienna Philharmonic (1898-1901) and the New York Philharmonic (1909-11). His lasting fame is due to his ten symphonies and his songs, which have become immensely popular with concert audiences since the 1950s.

Mahler's relationship to his Judaism was essentially negative, and there is nothing Jewish about his compositions. He put his conducting and his compositions above everything else; only the death of his small daughter and the realization that he was dying young slowed him down. That he was born Jewish in an anti-Semitic world became a thorn in his side. To his younger Jewish friend, the conductor Oskar Fried, who was denied a permanent position in Frankfurt, he is said to have commented: "And don't forget that we can do nothing about our being Jewish, our chief mistake."[30] Mahler could only sense the tragedy of his position as a Jew who reached higher and higher to gain acceptance as an artist while never being able to achieve true social and political acceptance no matter how much he turned against his Judaism. He continually confronted prejudice, such as when he sought to conduct Wagner's operas at Bayreuth and was turned down because he was Jewish.[31] When the most important conducting job in Central

[28] Cosima Wagner, *Diaries 1869-1877*, ed. Martin Gregor-Dellin and Dietrich Mack, trans. Geoffrey Skelton (New York: Harcourt Brace Jovanovich, 1978), 214, 441.

[29] Haas, 152. In his life-long habit of using people for his own end, Wagner had no compunction against using Jews whenever they could further him and his cause; see ibid., 265.

[30] Herta Blaukopf, ed., *Mahler's Unknown Letters*, trans. Richard Stokes (Boston: Northeastern University Press, 1987), 55.

[31] Despite Cosima Wagner's interest in Mahler, he was passed over by the most influential resident conductor at Bayreuth, Felix Mottl, with the comment "Everyone has told me how very gifted he is, but he is unfortunately a Jew." Hermann Levi, another resident conductor, apparently had no say in the matter. See Blaukopf, 200. Cosima's

Europe became vacant, at the Vienna Staatsoper, and only his Judaism stood in his way, Mahler converted to Catholicism. According to his wife Alma, whom Mahler married in 1902 in the Church of St. Charles Borromeo,

> Mahler . . . stood up for Jesus Christ in so many of our early arguments. He truly believed in Christ. He loved the Catholic mysticism, the Gregorian chant, the smell of incense; he rarely passed a church without entering. . . . [Mahler] was the curious paradox of a Jew championing Christ against a Christian [Alma was a non-believing Catholic].[32]

Yet, in perhaps weaker moments, he was still tied to his origins. He was pleased when Alma gave some coins to a poor Polish Jew at the railway station in Warsaw—a feeling of guilt?—and he turned to the Bible when he feared he was losing his wife to Walter Gropius.[33] He identified his own suffering with the eternal suffering of Jews and recognized this essential trait in Ossip Gabrilowitch (1878-1936), the Russian Jewish pianist.[34] But at no time did he take the stance of his American friend Dr. Joseph Fraenkel, who refused baptism that would have allowed him to become a physician in Austria and who then moved to the United States, where religion was not a great barrier to his receiving a medical education.[35]

The list of other Jewish musicians involved in the preservation and promotion of central European art music during the nineteenth century and into the 1930s is long, even if confined to only the most well-known. Prominent among these musicians are composers Karl Goldmark (1830-1915) and Alexander Zemlinsky (1871-1942); violinists Heinrich Wilhelm Ernst (1814-65), Joseph Joachim (1831-1907), Gustav Hollaender (1855-1915), Bronislaw Huberman (1882-1947), and Joseph Szigeti (1892-1973); pianists Ignaz Friedman (1882-1948), Harold Bauer (1873-1951), and Artur Schnabel (1882-1951); singers Lola Beeth (1864-1940), Selma Kurz (1875-1933), Sophie Braslau (1892-1934), and Friedrich Schorr (1888-1953); and conductors Eduard Lassen (1830-1904), Siegfried Ochs (1858-1929), Oskar Fried (1871-1941), Leo Blech (1871-1958), and Bruno Walter (1876-1962). Some converted to Christianity, some remained at least nominally Jewish, and all owed their ability to take part in general middle-European art music to the *Haskalah*.

At the end of a century of Jewish participation in Central European art music the situation came to a head in the years between the two World Wars. However great their integration into the mainstream of European art music, Jews as Jews felt ostracized and Jews who converted, however satisfied they were with being Christian, felt just as ostracized.

The case of Arnold Schoenberg (1874-1951; fig. 10.1), at the end of the *Haskalah* experiment in Germany and Austria, is different: Schoenberg was a little younger and lived on into the Nazi period. Like his mentor Mahler, Schoenberg converted to Christianity (in 1898), but unlike

curious relationship with Mahler continued when Mahler agreed to conduct an awful opera written by Wagner's son, Siegfried; the opera's failure was attributed to the "Semites." Yet Cosima appreciated Mahler's efforts on behalf of her late husband. Ibid., 205-07, 214.

[32] Alma Mahler Werfel, *And the Bridge is Love*, ed. E.B. Ashton (New York: Harcourt, Brace, 1958), 24.

[33] Ibid., 23-24, 53.

[34] Ibid., 35.

[35] Ibid., 67.

FIG. 10.1   Arnold Schoenberg,
photograph by Florence Homolka
Courtesy of the Arnold Schoenberg Center, Vienna

Mahler, Schoenberg did so as a Protestant in Catholic Vienna and out of conviction, rather than as an expediency to promote his career. Also unlike Mahler, he emphatically returned to the Jewish fold a short time later. Born in Vienna, where he spent most of his life, he came from an integrated family and had little Jewish upbringing. He was fascinated by Wagnerism and first gained fame in 1902 with the premier of his *Verklärte Nacht* (*Transfigured Night*), written three years before, which was an outgrowth of his feeling for the German Romanticism of Wagner and his successors. This was followed by his *Gurrelieder* (*Songs of War*), written over ten years and premiered in Vienna in 1913. But Wagnerism was a dead end for him.

Schoenberg became the European leader among composers in a turn away from several centuries of harmonic tradition. His first atonal work, the piano composition Opus 11, no. 1, shocked everyone in 1909. Eventually, he developed his dodecaphonic system of composition, in which each note of the tempered scale is of equal importance. Schoenberg wrote a basic harmony book (1911), which he dedicated to Mahler shortly after his death, out of a debt to Mahler's interest in his music. Yet, as Schoenberg developed his new system, counterpoint rather than harmony came to be the primary focus. He worked in Berlin briefly in 1901-03 and 1911, and had a more substantial appointment at the Prussian Academy of Arts, 1925-33.

The Nazi takeover of Germany in 1933 forced Schoenberg to leave the country immediately, both because he was a Jew and because the new music he espoused was regarded by the National Socialists as antithetical to the great tradition of German Romanticism. He was keenly aware of what the Nazis were up to and was under no delusion that Austria was any different from Germany. The only way he knew how to protest the barbarism of the Nazis was to return to Judaism officially and become an outspoken proponent of an international movement to save the Jews of Europe. His was not a token return to the Jewish religion forced upon him by the Nazis, however. He had a deep-seated commitment to Judaism that was evinced in some of his earlier music; and he became an interested Zionist in the first few years of the twentieth century while Theodor Herzl was still alive. His conversion to Protestantism, obviously, was a youthful venture that quickly disappointed him. Schoenberg's concern for the Jewish people came to affect his later music profoundly, particularly after his family experienced a personal anti-Semitic attack in 1921. He escaped temporarily to Paris in 1933 and then immigrated to the United States, where he taught in Boston (1933-34), at the University of Southern California (1934-36), and at the University of California in Los Angeles (1936-44), whose music building is named in his honor. He became an American citizen in 1941.

Schoenberg is important for Jewish music not only because he became an ardent Zionist and was intensely involved with the biblical mission of the Jews as the chosen people. Far more significant is that he imparted to his art music Jewish musical and philosophical traits that changed the course of the history of European art music.[36] Schoenberg's approach to composition fundamentally changed the way composers of art music conceived their art and craft; from a basically harmonic approach, favored from at least the seventeenth century to the beginning of the twentieth, Schoenberg moved to a basically contrapuntal approach. Jewish musical tradition is essentially monophonic and non-metrical, and feeling this instinctively, Schoenberg reintroduced melodic thinking rather than harmonic thinking into contemporary composition, together with a much more subtle approach to rhythm. His system eventually led to a theory of atonal and linear composition that gradually during the twentieth century attracted most of the younger composers. While the theory is not observed as rigorously as it was through the 1960s, it has had a lasting effect on all twentieth-century composition. A part of this theory was Schoenberg's concern for hexachordal structures (the twelve notes of the tone row divided into two groups of six) which, according to Alexander Ringer, related to Schoenberg's understanding of Jewish mysticism (Chassidic numerology).[37] Thus, while previous Central European Jewish composers entered into the mainstream of European music by adopting the aesthetics of non-Jewish music, Schoenberg transformed that European music into a new music based to a considerable extent on his Jewish perspective.

This thinking is manifest in nearly all his compositions, but especially in those that are clearly Jewish. With compositions and torsos of compositions like the opera *Moses und Aron*, *Der biblische Weg* (*The Biblical Path*), the oratorio *Die Jakobsleiter* (*Jacob's Ladder*), *Kol Nidre* (commissioned by a synagogue in Los Angeles), the Hebrew psalms Schoenberg wrote for Israel at the end of his life, and *A Survivor from Warsaw*, he brought Jewish subjects into the concert hall not only in the abstract but also in concrete ways. Many of these Jewish works are political and religious statements of a Jew to the Christian world, and the Christian world has listened. While throughout the nineteenth century Jewish musicians were grudgingly accepted in Germany and Central Europe as imitators of non-Jewish music, thanks to Schoenberg, since the end of the Second World War Jewish musical thinking has been accepted as playing a central part in the European heritage.

---

[36] For a thorough discussion of Schoenberg's importance as a Jewish composer, see Alexander L. Ringer, *Arnold Schoenberg: The Composer as Jew* (Oxford: Clarendon Press, 1990). See also Gradenwitz, esp. 212-32.

[37] Ringer, chapter 10.

France

Since the *Haskalah* movement developed differently in France and Germany, so too did the role of musicians. In France, Jews had achieved political equality at the time of the French Revolution. Within a generation French Jewish musicians were basically treated fairly and as equals of non-Jewish French musicians. They did not have to convert to achieve this equality, and most remained loyal to their origins. The pianist Alkan and the composer Halévy were the most successful, along with the German composers Meyerbeer and Offenbach, who immigrated to Paris. Alkan and Halévy achieved success by being Jewish in their music as well as in their lives, while Meyerbeer and the young Offenbach made minor contributions. Only Offenbach followed the German course of converting and disappearing from the *Haskalah*, though not until after his early life as a klezmer musician; once a Christian he did not suffer subtle ostracism from French society because of his Jewish origins.

Jacques-François-Fromenthal-Élie Halévy (1799-1862) was the son of a leading French *maskil*, Elias Levy (d. 1826), who in 1818 founded the journal *L'Israëlite français* upon the motto of the *Haskalah*: "Be loyal to your country and preserve your faith."[38] A German Jew, he had come to Paris to take advantage of the political emancipation of Jews there, and he instilled in his composer son a strong pride in both his French and Jewish heritages. Early in his life Fromenthal wrote a *Marche Funèbre et De Profundis en Hébreu* (Funeral March and Out of the Depths in Hebrew) in commemoration of the death of the Duc de Berry, a state occasion celebrated in the Jewish Temple in Rue St. Avoie and sung by the famous cantor Israel Lövy with choir and orchestra. While he continued his affiliation with the Jewish community in Paris and was an important member of the head consistory that made important musical decisions for the Jews of France, Fromenthal's main attentions were focused on opera, on the Paris Conservatory where he was a professor, and on the Institute of France which he served as both secretary and vice president.

It is in his most famous work, the opera *La Juive*, that Halévy made the clearest Jewish statement of the French nineteenth-century *Haskalah* movement. It quickly became a standard repertory piece. In the opera Halévy portrayed the ugliness of Christian intolerance of Jews through a violent story that sees the hero and heroine—both Jews—die a horrible death because of their religion. Halévy was able to dramatize emphatically the frustrations of his co-religionists as he and his family had experienced them in post-Revolutionary France. Yet the work is not an entirely negative opera portraying only anti-Semitism. At the opening of the second act Halévy presents a token Seder, which attempts to picture the warmth of a family gathering on this great occasion, and for it Halévy suggests Jewish chant. In the entire French *Haskalah* no one conveyed to the general French population more convincingly and poignantly the Jews' unique calamity of being accepted politically but not socially. The mere fact that such an opera could attain fame and be one of the country's most popular operas, however, is a tribute to the success of the *Haskalah* in opening up French culture to a Jewish voice. Not until the twentieth century did the Jews of Central and Eastern Europe achieve what Halévy did in this opera.

Charles-Henri Valentin Alkan (1813-88) was regarded in France as one of Europe's greatest pianists and composers for the piano, but he never achieved the fame of a Chopin or a Liszt

---

[38] J. Baron, "A Golden Age," 30-51.

because of his eccentric behavior. His father, Elkanan Morhange (d. 1855) was a solfège teacher in Paris, and among his pupils was Antoine-François Marmontel (1816-98), later professor of piano at the Conservatory and rival of Alkan. After a very successful early career, Alkan withdrew from public eye in the 1860s, only to re-emerge in the 1870s. During this time away from the public he translated the Hebrew Bible into French, and then also the New Testament into French. He composed prolifically for the piano and also for the organ, and in several cases there are elements of Jewish chant and Jewish tunes in his compositions.[39] He served with Halévy on the Consistory's committee to find a chief cantor for Paris in the 1840s and helped select Samuel Naumbourg for that position. In appreciation, Alkan was asked by Naumbourg to join Halévy, Meyerbeer, and others in contributing synagogue music to Naumbourg's publications. Except for not gaining a professorship at the Conservatory, which Alkan attributed to anti-Semitism, he seems never to have confronted any of the problems that German Jewish composers and performers faced. He did not have to convert to obtain a position (Alkan's excuse that it was his Judaism that kept him from the Conservatory job is suspicious since Halévy remained staunchly Jewish while teaching at the Conservatory), and he was never ostracized for his beliefs. Despite the fact that his eccentricities led to gossip and problems with his full acceptance, there is no immediate evidence that this was tied to his religious beliefs.[40]

Giacomo Meyerbeer (1791-1864) was undoubtedly the most successful German Jewish musician of the first half of the nineteenth century, but he achieved his success primarily in Paris, not in his native Berlin. The son of a leading German *maskil*, Judah Hertz Beer (1769-1825), who helped found Berlin's Reform community, Meyerbeer swore allegiance to his people and never wavered from that commitment. He wrote synagogue music for Naumbourg in Paris, and other music in Hebrew for Paris and for Berlin. His fame, however, did not rest on anything Jewish; rather he became the principal composer of opera in Paris from the 1830s to the 1860s. He chose no Jewish subjects, as had his friend Halévy; the closest he came was his *Les Huguenots*, which is an opera dealing with religious intolerance of Catholics against Protestants. His wealth and power in Paris were used beneficently on behalf of Jewish charities and artists of different faiths. Both the Jewish-German poet Heinrich Heine and the struggling young Richard Wagner came to him for help, and after he assisted both, they turned on him—Wagner most emphatically by aiming his notoriously anti-Semitic treatise *Das Judenthum in der Musik* squarely at Meyerbeer. Meyerbeer received state funerals both in Paris and in Berlin—in both places performed by rabbis in front of Christian royalty.

While Jacques Offenbach started out as a klezmer musician and seemed to be following Alkan, Halévy, and Meyerbeer as a product of the *Haskalah*, his career and life took a sudden turn in a different direction in 1844, and he left Judaism forever. Born in Germany, he was sent to Paris by his very traditional father to live with a cantor and become a bar mitzvah. He and his younger brother, both string players, entertained as dance musicians in Paris. For his band Offenbach wrote at least one Jewish piece, a waltz entitled "Rebecca, based on Jewish melodies of the fifteenth century." Upon his marriage to a Catholic woman, however, he converted to Christianity, then,

---

[39] Ibid., 45-47.

[40] The wildest rumor, completely unfounded, concerned Alkan's death. Legend had it that Alkan was killed when he reached for a volume of the Talmud on his bookshelf and the entire collection of Talmud volumes fell on him.

in the 1850s followed a career as composer of operettas which would make him famous. His satiric and hilarious musical comedies spawned the French and Viennese operettas of the next half century, the English Gilbert and Sullivan musical comedies, and the American musical theatre.

The generation after that of Halévy, Alkan, and Meyerbeer did not achieve the fame or importance of its predecessor. Jewish composers continued to compose, but with the possible exception of Paul Dukas, were no longer central figures in French music. There were several non-Jewish composers who wrote a work or two on a Jewish theme (the opera *Le Juif Polonais* [The Polish Jew] in 1900 by Camille Erlanger [1861-1919], for example), and some musicians had personal ties with the Jewish community (Bizet's wife was Halévy's daughter, for example).

Not until the 1920s, however, was there once again a French Jewish composer of major stature: Darius Milhaud (1892-1974; fig. 10.2). Milhaud stemmed from an old Jewish family in Provence and remained faithful to his Sephardic heritage. He entered the Paris Conservatory in 1909, where he was a pupil of some of France's leading composers: Widor, d'Indy, and Dukas. While still a student he became associated with the Parisian avant garde, including Satie, Cocteau, and Claudel. The last was appointed to a diplomatic post in Brazil in 1917, and Milhaud joined him there until late in 1918. In 1920 a French critic (Henri Collet) referred to six young French composers as *Les Six*, which forever afterward linked Milhaud to the careers of Honegger, Poulenc, Auric, Durey, and Tailleferre. He visited the United States in 1922 and returned there from 1940 to 1947 to escape the Nazi occupation of France; he continued to visit America regularly until 1971. While in America he taught at Mills College in Oakland, California, and was part of the new summer music festival in Aspen, Colorado.

FIG. 10.2   Photograph of Darius Milhaud
*Courtesy of the Milken Archive of
American Jewish Music, New York*

Milhaud was a prolific composer who wrote in many different genres. Many of Milhaud's works are based on his early fascination with jazz and other American popular idioms; chief among these is his ballet of 1923, *La Création du Monde* (*The Creation of the World*). There are works with decided Brazilian flavor, and numerous works in tribute to his French and American experiences. Of his sixteen operas, *Christophe Colomb* (1930) is probably the most often performed. There are twenty string quartets, of which nos. 14 and 15 can be played either separately or simultaneously as an octet.

Of particular interest is the virtually unknown last quartet, Op. 442, which utilizes ten melodies once sung by the Jews of the county of Venaissin, an old Sephardic Provençal community where Milhaud's ancestors had lived for hundreds of years[41] and which was destroyed by the Nazis. The tunes form "a cycle of festive prayers for the liturgical year as observed in the Sephardic rite in Venaissin."[42] Milhaud's source was a collection of melodies from Comtat Venaissin published in 1887 (*Chants Hébraïques Comtadins*). In addition, there are many sonatas and other chamber works, symphonies for large and small orchestras, concertos, songs, and piano works. While most of these have no Jewish connotations, a significant number have Jewish subjects, Hebrew texts, and/or borrowings from his Sephardic musical background such as found in the twentieth string quartet. Chief among these are his operas *Esther de Carpentras* (1925)[43] and *David* (1954),[44] *Cain and Abel* (for narrator and orchestra, 1945), *Ouverture méditerranéenne* (Mediterranean Overture, 1954), *Ode pour Jerusalem* (Ode to Jerusalem, 1972), *Le Candélabre à sept branches* (The Seven-branch Candelabra, piano suite, 1952), many songs and choral works, such as *Huit poèmes juifs* (Eight Jewish Poems, 1916), *Six chants populaires hébraïques* (Six Popular Hebrew Songs, 1925), *Cantate nuptiale* (Song of Songs, 1937), *Kaddisch* (voice, chorus, and organ, 1945), *Promesse de Dieu* (God's Promise, 1971-72), and *Ani Maamim* (I Believe, for soprano, chorus, orchestra, and four speakers, 1972), numerous settings of psalms, and his setting of the entire *Sabbath Morning Service* (1947).[45]

As in the case of Halévy, Milhaud was able to participate as a Jew in the general musical scene in France, but while the former was limited primarily to one work, Milhaud composed Jewish art music throughout his career and did not write specifically identifiable Christian music. Like Schoenberg, the premier of whose *Pierrot Lunaire* Milhaud had conducted in 1913,[46] he expressed himself as a Jew from the early years of his career until his very last works, but unlike Schoenberg he did not throw away traditional European art music in order to establish a new system. In conjunction with his famous five French colleagues, he wrote in a neo-classical

---

[41] Milhaud has recounted the history of his family in his *My Happy Life: An Autobiography*, trans. Donald Evans, George Hall, and Christopher Hall (London/New York: Marion Boyars, 1995), chapter 1.

[42] For information on this quartet cf. Paul Cherry, "A Hidden Mahzor in an Unknown String Quartet by Darius Milhaud," in *The Darius Milhaud Society Newsletter* 13 (1997): 15-17. In 1939 Milhaud had also utilized a Palestinian tune "The Queen of Sheba" in a setting for string quartet (Opus 207).

[43] The plot of the opera is summarized briefly in Milhaud, 132-33. For a brief analysis of the opera cf. Paul Collaer, *Darius Milhaud*, trans. Jane Hohfeld Galante (San Francisco: San Francisco Press, 1988), 93-102.

[44] Ibid., 149-54.

[45] Ibid., 179-81 for Henri Barraud's brief analysis of the service.

[46] Milhaud, 104-05.

style that remained tonal and easily accessible to the average classical audience. And he remained a *maskil* all his life; as he stated at the opening of his autobiography, "I am a Frenchman from Provence, and, by religion, a Jew."[47]

Mention might also be made of the German emigrant to Paris Jean Berger, whose original name was Arthur Schlossberg.

While Switzerland was not a leading center for the *Haskalah*, it enters this history because of Ernest Bloch (1880-1959). With the ability of Jewish composers to express their Judaism in the setting of European art music, Bloch was able to participate fully in the fruits of the *Haskalah*. He was encouraged as a child in his native city of Geneva to study music, to continue violin under the great master, Eugene Ysaye in Brussels, and to study composition.[48] He undertook further study in Frankfurt am Main at the end of the century, and composed his first symphony. After some disappointments in Paris, Bloch returned home in 1904 and entered his father's business, all the while composing, among other things his opera, *Macbeth*. At this time Bloch also lectured on music and began to write a series of Jewish art compositions which would soon place him in the center of the musical *Haskalah*. Milhaud recounted that when he visited Bloch in Switzerland during these years, he enjoyed Bloch's enthusiasm for these Jewish works; the visits no doubt inspired Milhaud to pursue this kind of composition, too.[49]

With the economic disasters that befell even Switzerland during the First World War, Bloch took advantage of an offer to conduct an orchestra for the tour of a dancer in the United States. When the tour fell through, Bloch concentrated on developing his reputation in America as a composer. He also gained a reputation as an outstanding composition teacher, at the Mannes School in New York (1917-20), the Cleveland Institute of Music which he organized (1920-25), the San Francisco Conservatory which he directed (1925-30), and finally, after time spent in Switzerland (1930-39), at the University of California in Berkeley (1940-52). After his retirement from teaching Bloch spent his last years in Oregon.

Bloch's approach to Jewish art music was not derived from some a priori scheme. Rather, in his own testimony, it flowed naturally from his Jewish soul. He did not consciously copy Jewish folk song or synagogue chant, but he felt both and created art music in an atmosphere that allowed him to express his Jewishness naturally as part of his overall musical style. As he stated in 1917,

> I hold it of first importance to write good, genuine music, my music. It is the Jewish soul that interests me, the complex glowing agitated soul that I feel vibrating throughout the Bible; the freshness and naiveté of the patriarchs; the violence which is evident in the prophetical books; the Jew's savage love of justice; the despair of the preacher in Jerusalem; the sorrow and immensity of the Book of Job; the sensuality of the Song of Songs. All

---

[47] Ibid., 23.

[48] The outline of Bloch's biography here is based on Alex Cohen, "Ernest Bloch - A Biography," in Leah M. Jaffa, ed., *The Music of Ernest Bloch: A Program Manual* (New York: National Jewish Music Council of the National Jewish Welfare Board, 1955), 44-48.

[49] Milhaud, 56.

this is in us, all this is in me, and it is the better part of me. It is all that
I endeavor to hear in myself and to transcribe in my music. The venerable
emotion of the race that slumbers way down in our souls.[50]

In *Schelomo, Hebrew Rhapsody* (1915-16), for violoncello and orchestra, Solomon of the
Bible speaks wisely to the audience in a pseudo-cantillation that sounds Jewish, sounds Biblical,
and reaches audiences of all religions and cultures. The three movements of the suite *Baal
Shem* (*Three Pictures of Chassidic Life*, 1923), among the most popular concert works for violin
written in the twentieth century, are soaked in Yiddish folklore and mystic innuendoes.

Although he lived in the United States half his life, Bloch wrote nearly all his Jewish art music
in Switzerland (various psalms in 1913-14, the *Israel Symphony* in 1912-16, *Three Jewish Poems*
in 1913, and *Schelomo*). Most of what he wrote in America is specifically American or without
any national or religious context (Bloch would have said "racial" context). He was the first to
compose for an American synagogue an artistic oratorio whose text is a complete Jewish service—
Avodat Hakodesh (1930-33), yet this work, too, was written in his native country. Thus, while
like Schoenberg and Milhaud he came to the United States, unlike either of them his Jewish soul
seems harbored in Europe, where he felt the spirit of the *Haskalah*. Schoenberg and Milhaud
knew little or no Hebrew and were fully assimilated into German and French culture respectively,
yet their alienation from Germany and France was such that America stimulated their Jewish
creativity. Not only assimilated but completely at home in Switzerland, Bloch apparently felt
more comfortable in expressing his Jewish soul there than in America.

Poland

The German *Haskalah* came to Poland early in the nineteenth century and its manifestations
there paralleled much of its development in its western neighbor. The major difference, however,
was that Poland had the largest Jewish population in Europe in the nineteenth century, and
the battles between assimilationists and traditionalists were waged in greater intensity.

Before the *Haskalah* movement entered Poland, enlightened Jews had no recourse to
secular Polish art except if they converted. Among the earliest Jewish composers of secular
Polish music was Maria Szymanowska (1789-1831), who converted to Catholicism as a child
and thereupon was allowed to study music. She was a successful pianist who toured France
as well as Poland and Russia; among her few compositions are songs and chamber music in a
pre-romantic style.

From 1815 to 1830—a period of relative liberalism in Poland—individual enlightened Jews
were able to mix with the Polish intelligentsia with ease. Some became very successful, very rich,
and well respected in Polish society while maintaining ties to their Jewish heritage, among them,
Joseph Wolff, a physician "who hosted a well-known musical salon" and whose descendants
included the pianist Edward Wolff (1816-80) and the violinist Henri Wieniawski (1835-80), Poland's
most famous violinist of the nineteenth century. Later in the century, despite the worsening

---

[50] Cited in Abraham W. Binder, "A Review of the Recording of Ernest Bloch's 'Israel Symphony,'" in Jaffa, 36.

of Jewish-Christian relations, Jewish musicians—whether practicing Jews or not—were highly regarded and participated fully in Polish musical life. During the first four decades of the twentieth century, Jewish musicians continued to occupy a significant role in Polish orchestras. The Warsaw Philharmonic was founded by the Jew Aleksander Reichman, and many of its members were Jews, including the conductor Grzegorz Fitelberg (1879-1953). Among the leading Polish-Jewish concert artists were violinists Pawel Kochanski (1887-1934), Bronislaw Huberman (1882-1947), and Henryk Szeryng (1918-88), pianists Artur Rubinstein, Moritz Rosenthal (1862-1946), Leopold Godowsky (1870-1938), and Ignaz Friedman (1882-1948), conductors Paul Kletzki (1900-73) and Roman Ryterband (1914-79), harpsichordist Wanda Landowska (1879-1959), and cellist Gregory Piatigorski (1903-76). Polish Jewish composers include Adolf Sonnenfeld (1837-1914) and Leopold Lewandowski (1831-96), both of whom wrote many operettas and dances, Henry Vars (1902-77), an important composer of film scores, and members of the musical avant garde, including Jozef Koffler (1896-1944), Karol Rathaus (1891-1954), Szymon Laks (1901-83), and Aleksander Tansman (1897-1986).[51]

Russia

In Russia, the fate of Jewish composers of art music paralleled the development of the Russian *Haskalah*. Jews did not matter in the history of Russian music prior to the mid-nineteenth century when the Rubinstein brothers began to make their careers. By the beginning of the twentieth century, however, Jews began to dominate the area of classical music performance. Jewish art music was stimulated by Jewish music students who entered conservatories and combined their Jewish roots with mastery of technique and style. Despite the obliteration of much of Jewish life in the aftermath of the Revolutions of 1917 and 1918, Jewish musicians who by then were a part of Russia's mainstream musical culture were able to make out just as those modern Jews of the *Haskalah* were able to enter the Russian political mainstream with much less trauma than Orthodox Jews faced.

Foreign musicians and foreign art music had prevailed in Russia until the 1830s and 1840s when, during the reign of Nicholas II, Russians had been encouraged to develop nationalistic traits. Mikhail Glinka and his contemporary Alexander Dargomizksy introduced specific Russian elements into their works. Glinka's two operas stressed not only Russian peasant life, legend, patriotism, language, costumes, and scenery but also gradually built the music around Russian scales and instruments. Dargomizsky developed Russian recitative. These pioneers of Russian nationalist music were followed in the 1860s by a group of amateur nationalists, three of whom placed Russian national music in the forefront of European art music: Modest Mussorgsky, Alexander Borodin, and Nicholay Rimsky-Korsakov. None had conservatory training,[52] but their talents overshone their technical deficiencies (though it could be argued that we might have had more of

---

[51] Marian Fuks, "Musical Traditions of Polish Jews," abstract in *Polish/Jewish Music! International Conference November 15-16, 1998, Los Angeles*, pp. 8-9.

[52] By the 1870s Rimsky-Korsakov, unlike the others, had devoted considerable study to the techniques of musical composition and had become one of the finest teachers of harmony, counterpoint, and orchestration in Russia.

the fruits of their talents had they been better trained). On the other hand, two Jewish musicians of their generation in Russia who received solid musical training were the brothers Anton and Nicholas Rubinstein.

Anton Rubinstein was born in Vichvatinetz near Berdichev in 1829. His father, unwilling to be tied to a life of poverty and degradation, baptized the family into the Russian Orthodox faith and moved to Moscow (which was not permitted to a practicing Jew), where he entered the leather tanning business, and made a small fortune. Anton's mother was from a German-Jewish family that had integrated into German society. Determined that her children should have a thorough education in Western European art music so that they would be accepted by Christian society, she started teaching them herself. Anton was soon sent to the best private teacher of piano in Moscow, Alexander Ivanovich Villoing. By the age of eleven, as Villoing's best student, Anton traveled with him to Paris, then one of the most important musical capitals of Europe and the city where Jews easily gained entrance into the professional musical world. With his debut there in 1841, Anton proved himself to belong to the group of top concert artists, and from then on he moved in the circles of Chopin, Liszt, Berlioz, Meyerbeer, Henri Vieuxtemps, Friedrich Kalkbrenner, Moscheles, and Mendelssohn. During the 1840s Rubinstein concertized extensively, stopping just long enough in 1844 to study composition in Berlin with Siegfried Wilhelm Dehn (1799-1858).

When Anton Rubinstein tried to return to Russia in 1849, he encountered problems at the border of the country because he stated his profession on his passport as "musician," which was not a recognized profession in Russia at that time. During the 1850s, he nurtured the idea of establishing music as a profession, and, in 1858, with the support of the tsar's sister-in-law, Helena Pavlova, he founded the Russian Musical Society. Then, in St. Petersburg in 1861, Rubinstein opened the first music conservatory in Russia. Some of the best professionals he could find were the first instructors: Davidov (cello), Wieniawski and, upon his death, Auer (violin), Leschetizky (piano), and Zaremba (composition); the first student was a young lawyer who really wanted to be a composer—Piotr Il'yich Tchaikovsky.

In 1867, having achieved success in this area, Anton Rubinstein resigned as director of the conservatory and began an extensive concert tour, which even took him to America (1872-73). He held numerous posts in Russia, including director of the Imperial Theatre, and he was ennobled by the tsar in 1877 for his efforts on behalf of the country. From 1886 to 1888 he again directed the St. Petersburg Conservatory. Two years later Rubinstein started an international piano competition, perhaps the first such event in the world; after his death in 1894, it was named the Rubinstein International Competition (later succeeded by the Tchaikovsky Competition).

Technically, Anton Rubinstein cannot be considered a *maskil*, because while he was a small child he was converted to Christianity. The Russian *maskilim* wanted emancipation of the Jews as Jews, not their assimilation into a Christian world.[53] But Rubinstein's conversion did not end his relationship with his people. Everyone knew his origins, and he took special pride that as a Jew (at least by birth) he was honored by the anti-Semitic Russian court. His often cited quotation that "The Russians consider me a German and the Germans consider me a Russian, the Christians call me a Jew and the Jews call me a Christian" was indeed the very dilemma in

---

[53] Greenbaum, 115.

which many *maskilim* and Jewish converts to Christianity found themselves, hovering between different societies and cultures, uncertain where they belonged. It mattered little to Russians or Germans, Christians or Jews what denomination Rubinstein was so long as his piano playing was sublime and his compositions satisfied. He did write some Jewish music or at least Biblically-inspired music, such as the operas *The Maccabees* (1875) and *Sulamith* (1883), the oratorios *The Tower of Babel* (1870) and *Moses* (1892), and two concert scenes *Hecuba* and *Hagar in the Desert*. But his oratorios *Christ* and *Paradise Lost* clearly did not express his Jewishness. Thus, to some extent Anton Rubinstein was a *maskil*: he retained some consciousness of being Jewish, did not practice Christianity, and was no less religious as a Jew than many unconverted Jewish *maskilim*.

Anton's younger brother Nicholas Rubinstein (1835-81) was also a fine pianist, but he never achieved the international renown of his brother, in whose shadow he lived. Although as a young man he toured as a pianist, he is best remembered as a pedagogue whose students dominated the scene at the end of the nineteenth century. He founded the Moscow branch of the Russian Musical Society a year after his brother founded the parent organization in St. Petersburg, and in 1866 he founded the Moscow Conservatory, which today is the Tchaikovsky Conservatory in Moscow. Needing a composition teacher for the new school, Nicholas had asked his brother, who had recommended Tchaikovsky, the first graduate of the St. Petersburg school. During his tenure as director of the Conservatory Nicholas Rubinstein was the unquestioned leader of the musical scene in Moscow. From 1860 until his death he was also conductor of the Moscow concerts of the Imperial Music Society. Like his brother, he was an assimilated Jewish artist in Russia at a time when such artists were so highly regarded that local anti-Semitism could not displace them.

By the end of the century, a number of talented Jews had graduated from the conservatories and begun careers in Russian music. In the same period the Jewish nationalist movement was taking shape under the leadership of Saul Ginsburg (1866-1940) and Pesach Marek (1862-1920), who began collecting Jewish folk song as the true voice of the Jewish people.[54] The Jewish nationalists' work, inspired by the Russian nationalists of a generation before, was an attempt to save Jewish folk song from extinction and to promote it in artistic settings in concert halls. Joel Engel (1868-1927) was asked to write down the melodies of the folk songs which Ginsburg and Marek collected, and in 1905 he published the first of these in his own, artistic arrangements in Moscow.

Meanwhile, as Weisser recounts, Mili Balakirev invited the young Polish-Jewish musician Ephraim Skliar (1871-1943) to St. Petersburg in 1901 to study with Rimsky-Korsakov.[55] Skliar, the son of a cantor and himself a former itinerant singer and cantor, organized a Jewish folk song club at the Conservatory, though he apparently knew very few folk songs. When Skliar wrote a Yiddish song for Rimsky-Korsakov's composition class, the composer called on Jewish composers in the class to stop writing Russian and European nationalistic music and concentrate on developing a specifically Jewish music. During the next few years Jewish students at the Conservatory continued Skliar's initiatives, with the participation of Engel who "repeatedly came to St. Petersburg and kept the flames burning with private conversations with the students."

---

[54] Albert Weisser, *The Modern Renaissance of Jewish Music: Events and Figures, Eastern Europe and America*, reprinted with new introduction by Eric Werner (New York: Da Capo Press, 1983), 26-27.

[55] Weisser, 41-44.

Then in 1908 they organized the Society for Jewish Folk Music, which they hoped would spread through Russia. Particularly active at the beginning besides Engel and Skliar were Lazare Saminsky (1882-1959), Solomon Rosowsky (1878-1962), Leo Nesviski (1885-1984, whose Hebrew name was Arie Abileah), and Tomars, followed in the next few years by Michael Fabinovitch Gnessin (1883-1957), Pesach Lvov, Alexander M. Zhitomirski, Moshe Shalit, Joseph Achron (1886-1943), Alexander Krein (1883-1951), Jacob Weinberg (1879-1956), Maximillian Steinberg (1883-1946), Moses Michael Milner (1882-1952) and L. Streicher. In addition, poets and writers also joined, and patrons were found to support the Society's program. By the year 1912 the Society had 389 members (249 in St. Petersburg, the rest in other parts of Russia). Under the Society's auspices, art music and a volume of Jewish folk music were published, and in that year five large concerts were given, featuring both young Jewish musicians (Jascha Heifetz, Ephraim Zimbalist, Joseph Press) as well as non-Jewish musicians (Feodor Chaliapin).[56] When the Society finally disbanded at the time of the Revolution, most of the members fled to America or Palestine; a few others, among them Gnessin, who tried his hand at living in Palestine but was disappointed by musical opportunities there, returned to Russia to play major musical roles in the new Soviet country.

Of all the musicians who were affected by the *Haskalah*, only composers Ernest Bloch, Arnold Schoenberg, and Darius Milhaud did as much for the cause of Jewish music during the first half of the twentieth century as, collectively, the members of the Society for Jewish Music in Russia did. The Russians built a vast repertoire of art music based on Jewish folk music, religious music, and dance, and on extra-musical Jewish topics. Engel's works, for example, include settings of Jewish folk songs for voice and piano, settings of poems by Shaul Tchernikovsky, two vocal duets for Sholom Aleichem's play *Divorce*, "Habad Nigun" and "Freilachs" for violin and piano, and, after he emigrated to Palestine, children's songs for the pioneers as well as incidental music for An-ski's *The Dybbuk* and for several plays by Y. L. Peretz. Joseph Achron's *Hebrew Melody* (only one among many of his Jewish compositions) was composed in 1911 and soon became a standard violin work performed and recorded by Jewish (and Gentile) violinists from Mischa Elman, Jascha Heifetz and Achron himself to Pinchas Zuckerman and Itzhak Perlman.[57]

Michael Milner, who had the strongest ties of any of the Society's members to Jewish folk music in the Pale of Settlement, is particularly famous for his Yiddish art songs (especially "In Cheder" [In School] of 1914). His Jewish art works extend as well to piano music and music for orchestra (for example, his *Symphony on Jewish Themes*).[58] Lazare Saminsky's contributions include not only his Jewish compositions but also his arguments for "what is Jewish" in music; in stressing the purity of Biblical cantillation as true Jewish music as opposed to the corruption of Yiddish music with its extensive borrowings from Polish and Russian non-Jewish music, he provoked avid discussion of what everyone was trying to do. This self-criticism within the Jewish Music Society was an impetus to the healthy maturing of Jewish art music, manifested in moves away from simple imitations and arrangements to integrations of a Jewish melos into

---

[56] Ibid., 48.

[57] For a catalogue of Achron's works, see Weisser, 89-91.

[58] For a catalogue of Milner's works, see ibid., 101-02.

composers' own styles. As Weisser points out, Saminsky as well as Michael Gnessin wrote art music in which their own "personal styles" are "welded [into] a synthesis in which both the Jew and the universalist are able to speak with one voice."[59] Thus Saminsky is Jewish not only in early works such as his *First Hebrew Song Cycle* (1909), *Chassidic Dance* (1909), and *Two Hebrew Lullabies* (1908-14), but also in his ostensibly non-Jewish works such as the five symphonies, his other symphonic works, and his chamber music.

Gnessin, in turn, was the most eclectic composer of the entire Society: a disciple of Scriabin, a favorite pupil of Rimsky-Korsakov, and a close friend of the most talented new generation of poets, playwrights, and directors (including Vsevolod Meyerhold) in all of Russia. He composed in the post-Romantic style associated with early Schoenberg, and his themes centered on "Greek Drama, English Romantic poetry, and Russian contemporary art and poetry."[60] Yet Gnessin was the son of a rabbi associated with the *Haskalah*, and a close family friend was Eliezar Gerovitch, then cantor in Rostov and later in Odessa at the Brody Synagogue. He felt entirely Jewish and, despite his interests in non-Jewish art music initially, he could not escape the draw of his religious heritage. When the Society was organized, Gnessin was one of the first to join. From 1914 into the 1920s he wrote specifically Jewish pieces, but without abandoning his earlier style. Just as Saminsky welded his Jewishness to his general artistic style, so did Gnessin.

In terms of Jewish music, the most important consequence of the *Haskalah* in Russia was the establishment of the Society for Jewish Music. It encouraged the collection, preservation, and promotion of Jewish folk music, the development of different styles of art music based on that heritage, and it encouraged the spread of a specifically Jewish musical heritage throughout the world. For individual Jews, the most important consequence of the *Haskalah* in Russia was the encouragement of Jewish youth to enter conservatories, receive premier professional training, and to go out into the world as performers of art music. While the *Haskalah* unleashed Jewish performers into the mainstream throughout the continent, Russia alone in Europe produced (and continues to produce) skilled performing musicians in such large numbers who are Jewish.

In tsarist Russia Jews were rarely allowed to live in St. Petersburg or Moscow, but some larger cities within the Russian Empire, such as Vilna and later Odessa,[61] did permit Jews to be residents. Many trades and professions were forbidden to Jews. Poverty was widespread, though a small number of Jews, some in the *Haskalah* movement and some belonging to the more Orthodox group, were able to become secure in their livelihoods, if not actually rich. For the average Jewish child growing up in Russia in the nineteenth century, however, only religious studies gave rewards (not material ones, though) and, except for those believing in the *Haskalah*, there was little chance for fame and fortune. Later in the nineteenth century a drive to improve

---

[59] Weisser, 105.

[60] Ibid., 125. A catalogue of Gnessin's earlier works are on pp. 128-30. Gnessin was one of the few members of the Society to remain in Russia after the Revolution, where he became a professor at the Moscow Conservatory (1923-35), Leningrad Conservatory (1935-45), and Gnessin School (1945-51), which had his family name. Because of political necessities, he seems to have little to do with Jewish music after 1926.

[61] Odessa was hospitable to Jews from its founding at the end of the eighteenth century, and even had Jewish town officials; see Emanuel Rubin, "David Nowakowski (1848-1921): A New Voice from Old Odessa," *Musica Judaica* 16 (2001-02): 20-52.

the lot of Jews was launched, though in actuality very little improvement occurred. An occasional university or professional school opening went to a token Jew or two, but this only frustrated the many who were not admitted. The future for a Jewish child remained bleak—unless, of course, that child had a musical gift. With hard practice a musical *Wunderkind* could gain admittance to the conservatories in St. Petersburg and Moscow or study privately with a great teacher. The Rubinsteins (even if they were converted) had forged the way, and there were some Jewish professors in the conservatories—for example, Karl Davidov and Leopold Auer—who certainly had sympathy for talented Jewish youngsters. By the beginning of the twentieth century many Jewish children studied violin and piano with great diligence in the hope that their talents were sufficient for them to break through the anti-Semitic barriers and be accepted at a prestigious conservatory, study with a celebrated teacher, and then go on to world fame and fortune. A number did just this, such as violinists Mischa Elman (1891-1967), Jascha Heifetz (1901-87), Mischa Mischakoff (1895-1981), Nathan Milstein (1904-92), and David Oistrakh (1908-74);[62] pianists Arthur Friedheim (1859-1932), Moritz Rosenthal (1862-1946), Ossip Gabrilowitch (1878-1936), Artur Rubinstein (1887-1982), and Vladimir Horowitz (1903-89); conductors Felix Blumenfeld (1863-1931) and Serge Koussevitzky (1874-1951); and others. When the Soviet government took over in 1918, many Jewish children continued to look to music as a way to be accepted in the reigning society without political repercussions and with a relatively satisfying degree of personal security.

Consequences of the *Haskalah*

The accomplishments of Schoenberg, Milhaud, Bloch, and the Russians opened the door for many other Jewish composers to express themselves both artistically and in a Jewish manner. Among these were Ernst Toch (1887-1964), Kurt Weill (1900-50), Mario Castelnuovo-Tedesco (1895-1968)—all of whom immigrated to America, as well as the less well known Moses Pergament (1893-1977) from Sweden and Linda Phillips (b. 1899) from Australia, both of whose works manifest strong Jewish identities. Pergament was a critic and composed such works as *Adon Olam* for chorus and orchestra, *Rapsodia Hebraica* (1935) for orchestra, *Kol Nidre* for baritone, mixed choir and organ, and *Dybuk* (1935) for violin and orchestra.

Phillips was a concert pianist as well as prolific composer. Her compositions include the songs *Three Songs from Hebrew Sources* ("Ash Trees" or "Elisheva"; "The Golden Bird" on a text by Chayim Nachman Bialik; and "The Yemenite Bride"); *Judge me, O God*, an anthem for mixed voices on a text from Psalm 43; *Chanukah Dance* for piano; and considerable chamber music on Jewish subjects: *Feast of Dedication* (trumpet, piano trio); five piano trios entitled *The Feast of Weeks* (1934), *Purim Festival* (1935), *Music from Lamentations* (1935), *Trio Yigdal*, and *Trio Adon Olam*; the piano quintet *Kol Nidre* (1933), *Festival Trio in D Minor: The Song of Dew and The Song of Songs* (flute, violoncello, piano, 1939), *Exaltation* (Chassidic air and dance for oboe, violin, violoncello, piano, 1939), *Yemenite Wedding Dance* (flute, piano), *Maccabean Song* (violoncello, piano), *Olenu*

---

[62] In addition to these superstars, many fine Russian-Jewish violinists populated the orchestras of the world, led chamber ensembles, and had successful careers even if they never achieved stardom.

(violoncello or viola, piano), *Yigdal* (violin, piano), *The Purim Festival* (violin, piano), *Chanukah-Dance for Festival of Lights* (violin, piano), *Two Jewish Folk Melodies* (violin, piano), *Eili, Eili* (soprano, piano trio) and *Hebraic Elegy* (violin, piano). Besides these examples, the many Jewish composers and performers active in America, Britain, and Israel since the second half of the twentieth century are further testimony to successes obtained following the achievements of Schoenberg, Milhaud, Bloch, and the Russian musicians mentioned.

Finally, alongside the emergence of proud Jewish musicians in these years, another fundamental development occurred and should also be noted. It is the clear influence of Jewish music on non-Jewish composers. Probably the most famous example of Jewish music by a non-Jew is Max Bruch (1838-1920's) *Kol nidrei*, composed for the Jewish community of Liverpool in 1880. However, there are several other notable cases, for instance, involving Glinka, Mussorgsky, Saint-Saëns, Ravel, and Prokofiev. Mikhail Glinka (1804-57) included "Hebrew Song" in his collection *Proshchaniye s Peterburgom* (A Farewell to St Petersburg), 1840. Modest Mussorgsky (1839-81's) musical characterization of Jews in *Pictures at an Exhibition* is an attempt to capture the vocalization and idiomatic inflections of Russian Jews in heated conversation; while on his tombstone Mussorgsky requested Jewish music. Saint-Saëns (1835-1921's) *Samson et Delilah* revolves around a Jewish story and also aims at a sort of Jewish musical ethos. In *Two Hebrew Melodies*, for violin and piano of 1914, Maurice Ravel (1875-1937) introduces "Kaddish" and "The Eternal Enigma."[63] One last example is Sergei Prokofiev (1891-1953), whose *Overture on Hebrew Themes*, written while he was in New York, utilizes a klezmer band.[64]

Suggestions for Further Reading

Gradenwitz, Peter. *The Music of Israel: From the Biblical Era to Modern Times.* 2nd ed. Portland, OR: Amadeus Press, 1996.

Ringer, Alexander L. *Arnold Schoenberg: The Composer as Jew.* Oxford: Clarendon Press, 1990.

Rubin, Emanuel. "David Nowakowski (1848-1921): A New Voice from Old Odessa." *Musica Judaica* 16 (2001-02): 20-52.

Weisser, Albert. *The Modern Renaissance of Jewish Music: Events and Figure, Eastern Europe and America.* Reprint, with new introduction by Eric Werner. New York: Da Capo Press, 1983.

Werner, Eric. *Mendelssohn: A New Image of the Composer and His Age.* London: The Free Press of Glencoe, Collier-Macmillan, 1963.

Werner, Marc A. *Richard Wagner and the Anti-Semitic Imagination.* Lincoln: University of Nebraska Press, 1995.

---

[63] There is some speculation that both Saint-Saëns and Ravel had Jewish ancestry.

[64] This comprehensive survey of the influence of the *Haskalah* on European Jewish music is not a complete survey. Thus, for example, there were significant Jewish musicians in England in the nineteenth and early twentieth centuries who took part in European musical life as a result of their acceptance of the non-ghetto life, such as Isaac Nathan (1791-1864; see above, p. 150), John Barnett (1802-90), Henry Russell (1812-1900; see below, p. 268), Charles Kensington Salaman (1814-1901), George Henschel (1850-1934), Frederic Hymen Cowen (1852-1935), and Julius Benedict (1804-85). But the ultimate significance of the *Haskalah* was in enabling Jews to express themselves in general European music as Jews with a specifically Jewish voice, and that is where the focus of this survey has stayed.

11 | The History and Development of Jewish Liturgical Music in America

The Jewish community in North America today comprises representatives of most Jewish communities from the rest of the world. Because they have experienced religious freedom and far better treatment than on any other continent, Jews in the New World have flourished, taking in much from the various Old Worlds from which they came and at the same time creating new institutions not conceivable elsewhere. Jewish immigrants brought with them their traditional synagogue music, which differed from one part of the world to another; some elements of the music were retained and others thrown out, some of one tradition were merged with another tradition, and the whole was continually bombarded by non-Jewish influences, both sacred and secular. The history and present situation of synagogue music in the United States and Canada, which can be called *Minhag* America (that is, the American tradition) is therefore a volatile story, one that is growing and changing as we write.

The majority of the Jews in North America during the seventeenth and eighteenth centuries were Sephardic. They settled primarily on the East Coast or in New Orleans where the men were successful merchants. During this time and until the 1840s small numbers of German Ashkenazic Jews also came and wandered from the East Coast to the West Coast, often as peddlers, shopkeepers, and adventurers; by the early nineteenth century they outnumbered the Sephardim. Polish Jews trickled in, too—most were also small-time peddlers. During the 1840s and for the next thirty years much larger numbers of German Ashkenazim came to America to escape the disillusionment of the German *Haskalah* and to seek better economic opportunities. Then, with the assassination of Tsar Alexander II in 1881 and the subsequent violent pogroms in Russia, around two million Russian and Polish Ashkenazim immigrated; they quickly outnumbered both the Sephardim and the German Ashkenazim in North America. In 1924, the United States government eliminated such large scale Jewish immigration. After that, America's shores only occasionally reopened to further Jewish immigration: when extreme political events in the world caused dire consequences for Jews. Thus, in the 1930s primarily refugees from Nazi Germany were let in, and in the 1970s and 1980s, refugees from Communism. Meanwhile, small numbers of Jews from various other parts of the world also came here: a second major wave of Sephardic Jews from the crumbling Ottoman Empire between 1900 and 1924, Latin American Jews from Cuba in the 1960s, Persian Jews in the 1970s, and Jews from Ethiopia in the 1980s.

In the early nineteenth century it was widely thought that Judaism would eventually die out in North America because the Jewish population here was not large and because of the strong temptations of assimilation—a fear that has remained alive in the United States because of general acceptance of the Jew as an American citizen equal to a Christian. Certainly, to many American Jews in the nineteenth century, Jewish music had already died. Yet beginning in the twentieth century Jewish communities experienced a rebirth of Jewish identification, and since then Jewish music has become a more vibrant form of expression than ever before.

Early American Sephardic Synagogues (1654-1830s) and Their Music

By 1776 there were five synagogues in America: in New York, Newport, Philadelphia, Charleston, and Savannah, all following the Sephardic rite. The oldest Jewish community in the United States was established by Sephardic Jews in New York in 1654 just prior to *Rosh Hashanah*; by the following spring there were regular Sephardic Sabbath services. The services no doubt were chanted in a way familiar to Dutch/English Sephardim, and those who led the prayers were simply ordinary members of the community. When Dutch rule gave way to British rule in 1664, however, Jews were forced to discontinue regular services.[1] By the 1680s, despite an official British ban on Jewish public worship, there is evidence that Jews were again holding services, under the leadership of a voluntary cantor. The first known cantor in the city of New York was Saul Brown, a Dutch Jewish merchant who had arrived in New York in 1685 and served as cantor at Shearith Israel, the oldest Jewish congregation in America, until 1702. Beginning in 1728 a Jewish religious school was associated with Shearith Israel. In 1762, a full-time position was created for a cantor who was to spend part of the time as principal teacher at the school. Among the first trained there was Gershon Seixas (1746-1816), the first American-born cantor and probably the most important cantor in America in the eighteenth century. From 1768 to 1816 he served Shearith Israel (with brief interludes in Philadelphia and Connecticut during the Revolution), where, besides his cantorial duties, his responsibilities included keeping the children under control.

On 2 December 1763, the synagogue in Newport, Rhode Island, was opened. Today it is the oldest synagogue building in America and once again in use as a synagogue. At the opening ceremonies

---

[1] Jacob R. Marcus, *The Colonial American Jew 1491-1776* (Detroit: Wayne State University Press, 1970), 232-33 and 864. Most of the following discussion on American synagogue music before 1800 is based on this study and also on Marcus's *United States Jewry 1776-1985* (Detroit: Wayne State University Press, 1989), vol. 1.

> ...several portions of Scripture and of [the] service with a prayer for the royal family were read and finely sung by the priests and people.... [T]he harmony and solemnity of the musick ... could not but raise in the mind a faint idea of the majesty and grandeur of the ancient Jewish worship mentioned in Scripture.[2]

A year later the dozen and a half Jewish families in Newport boasted a cantor from Amsterdam, Isaac Touro, who as a full-time cantor for two decades gave the Newport synagogue an anchor not enjoyed by most of the other Jewish communities at that time. But then, Newport was one of the major ports on the Atlantic Coast and one of America's most prosperous cities. Although most of the Newport Jews were Ashkenazic, the synagogue was founded primarily as a Sephardic synagogue. Likewise, religious services held in Savannah, Georgia began in 1733, also following the Sephardic rite. Because of the number of Ashkenazic Jews in the congregation, though, squabbling over the melodies to be sung by the cantor prevented construction of a permanent synagogue building. The first synagogue in Philadelphia was established as a Sephardic synagogue in 1771. There, in 1776, Ezekiel Levy served not only as reader but as *shochet* and Hebrew teacher as well.

In the early American synagogue the cantor was the chief officiant. Often he was equivalent to the modern rabbi. He performed marriages, funerals, and circumcisions, taught in Hebrew schools, and in addition chanted prayers. Yet he was the employee of the lay leadership, who controlled the affairs of the synagogue without cantorial interference. Cantors were not held in the same esteem as rabbis from Europe. Local aristocratic Jews who were the wealthy directors of synagogue boards tended to treat cantors as servants. Even the experienced cantors serving in New York and Newport, many of Sephardic background, remained under the control of the laity. In many cases this was all to the good since a number of cantors were failures in business and were not of leadership quality. But all in all, it needs to be said that really good cantors and rabbis avoided emigrating from Europe to America until the 1830s. There were powerful cantors in Charleston from around the time the congregation was organized in 1756 on,[3] but, even though Charleston was the leading Jewish community in America to ca. 1820, rarely was there a full-time cantor; moreover, the power of the cantors came more from their non-synagogue activities as business-men or the school master. Only one cantor there, Abraham Alexander, is known to have been a paid professional, and he also spent considerable time at Shearith Israel in New York as cantor. Beginning in 1830 some cantors were also expected to preach sermons at some of the services.

Each congregation had its own peculiarities, which then were modified by each new cantor, whose style included improvisation as part of traditional Jewish music. Jacob Raphael Cohen, who served as cantor in Montreal in 1778-81, moved on to New York, and then to Philadelphia, where he died in 1811. In 1807-08 *Chazzan* Cohen was ordered by his Philadelphia congregation to conduct services even without a *minyan*. The congregation in Philadelphia hired other cantors when they could be found, such as Emanuel Nunez Carvalho, who left Charleston to serve in

[2] Stanley F. Chyet, *Lopez of Newport: Colonial American Merchant Prince* (Detroit: Wayne State University Press, 1970), 56-60.

[3] Abraham Wolf Binder, *Studies in Jewish Music: Collected Writings of A.W. Binder*, ed. Irene Heskes (New York: Bloch Publishing Co., 1971), 157; and Marcus, *Colonial American Jew*, 885-86.

Philadelphia in 1815-17. Abraham Israel Keys, who also served in Philadelphia (from 1824 to 1828), was, like Cohen and Carvalho, from England. Keys was no intellectual but had manners, could chant well, and applied himself to teaching his congregants to sing in unison. It is reported that when the new synagogue building was dedicated on 1 January 1825,

> Keys was assisted by the *chazzan* from New York; both men wore robes. There was a well-trained Jewish choir of male and female voices . . . [though] one pious Jew tried unsuccessfully to restrict the women singers to the gallery.[4]

In the early nineteenth century Shearith Israel in New York helped struggling congregations around the country locate cantors.[5] In Richmond's Sephardic synagogue in 1824 Isaac Leeser, a young Ashkenazic immigrant who on occasion assisted the reader, managed to learn traditional Spanish-Jewish chants so that a few years later, when he was called to be cantor at Sephardic Mikveh Israel in Philadelphia, he was fully acquainted with that rite. Leeser was of such stature that, under his tenure as cantor in the 1830s and 1840s, Mikveh Israel in Philadelphia was the leading congregation in the United States. Lesser (1807-68), generally a strict Orthodox Jew, was a fighter for many Jewish causes, among which were the rights of a cantor to make decisions on personal matters and to receive benefits. In 1850 he left Mikveh Israel, and seven years later became cantor of Beth-El Emet in Philadelphia, where his duties also included preaching.

The fusion of rabbi (preacher) and cantor (singer) in Leeser is only the most famous case because Leeser became one of the first great leaders of Judaism in the United States; the fusion, however, was widespread. Since they were fully accepted by their communities, they took on the titles of *Chazzan*, Dr., and Reverend. The "Reverend Dr." Joseph Yesuran Pinto, a cantor in New York, was the first to do so. By the 1780s the cantor/reverend in Newport even dressed as the Christian clergy in order to accommodate himself to the non-Jewish community. Until the 1840s the cantor was often the *rebbe* to his Jewish congregants and a member of the collared clergy to his Christian neighbors. As Charleston's synagogue board had ruled, a cantor should "be a kind, affable man, . . . be dignified, a good teacher, and an educated gentleman, who could hold his own in good Christian society."[6] Most cantors were not celebrated persons, yet they were visible spiritual leaders. On the one hand, the cantor was the model Jew for the Jewish community, so he had to keep kosher. On the other hand, Jews wanted to be like everyone else, so they expected their cantors to be like Christian clergy. The cantor was always on exhibit to the Christians as to what it meant to be a Jew. While Jews looked up to Seixas in New York as a truly competent cantor, other cantors with mediocre voices and dubious knowledge were tolerated because of this visibility to the non-Jewish community. Jacob Lippman, for example, a part-time cantor at Rodeph Shalom in Philadelphia, was otherwise a local merchant; he was not a learned leader, but he was better than having no cantor at all. Dr. Jacob De La Motta (1789-1845), leader of the Savannah

---

[4] Marcus, *United States Jewry*, 1:239.

[5] Ibid., 1:651.

[6] Ibid., 1:252-53.

Jewish community and an amateur cantor, was professionally a botanist and physician, and in those capacities thereby showed that he served not just Jews but the entire community as well.

Only after the Revolution—in 1786—was the first Ashkenazic synagogue founded in Charleston. Between 1654 and 1801 the number of congregations in America grew to eight, including one in Montreal (Shearith Israel founded in 1768) and one in Lancaster, Pennsylvania. Despite their small numbers, there were three distinct rites in American synagogues by the early nineteenth century: Spanish-English-Dutch Sephardic, Polish Ashkenazic, and German Ashkenazic. The first prayer books were printed for traditional Sephardic services. The services in Sephardic synagogues were chanted entirely in Hebrew; the exception to Hebrew was for sermons which were usually in English. In the 1760s there were already some English translations provided for the prayers, but these would have been for informational purposes only and were not actually recited. The first full edition of a Sephardic prayer book in 1826 had Hebrew and English translations on facing pages; whether by this time the English was actually recited instead of or alongside the Hebrew remains doubtful. Only in Sunday Schools in the 1830s was it standard practice to sing hymns in both Hebrew and English. The first American Ashkenazic prayer book was published in 1848, but many Ashkenazim were altering their services and going a different route from the Sephardic.

Since the Sephardic congregations were traditional Orthodox, no permanent choirs were established. An attempt to create a choir in 1818 at Shearith Israel was strongly opposed by its leadership because it sounded too Protestant and too much like practices in the nascent German Reform synagogues. Rather, the early American congregations preferred congregational singing to singing by a choir. Nevertheless, the idea of a choir was attractive enough in New York so that two other congregations—Anshe Chesed and Emanu-El— soon introduced choirs.[7]

German and Polish Ashkenazic Synagogues from the Late Eighteenth Century to 1870

The first German congregation in the United States was founded in Charleston, South Carolina in 1786, but existed for only a few years.[8] Moses Levy, an immigrant from Galicia who became rich in the New World and was the chief supporter of the congregation, officiated as voluntary cantor. After the congregation's demise and until 1795, German and Polish Jews in America worshipped in Sephardic synagogues.

In 1795 an Ashkenazic synagogue was established in Philadelphia: Rodeph Shalom (Seeker of Peace), which still exists. In 1819 Rodeph Shalom hired Jacob Lippman as cantor.

> He made a living not by intoning the services but through his eloquence in selling second-hand clothing, and he supplemented his income through ritual slaughter, circumcision, collecting dues, and probably, by teaching the children their Hebrew abc's.[9]

---

[7] Binder, *Studies*, 158.

[8] Marcus, *United States Jewry*, 2:219.

[9] Ibid., 2:219.

The second permanent Ashkenazic congregation in America, B'nai Israel, was established in Cincinnati in 1824, and the following year an English Ashkenazic synagogue by the same name (B'nai Israel) was started in New York City. By 1840 the number of Jews in America was somewhere between 10,000 and 15,000, which was up from the 1776 count of about 1,500 to 2000. By 1840 there were at least twenty-one congregations in sixteen cities. By then only six were Sephardic, the rest Ashkenazic.

Ashkenazic Jews initially found little difficulty worshipping in Sephardic synagogues, but eventually this posed a problem. The rites were different, and as their numbers grew, Ashkenazim wanted their own prayers and melodies. As long as both groups worshipped together, there were squabbles, so that inevitably the two groups separated and formed two distinct congregations. Before 1840 the Germans and Poles—the Ashkenazim—separated from the Sephardim with the blessing of the Sephardim, but afterwards the Poles separated from Germans. Each wanted a cantor who would cater to their particular ethnic background and sing the melodies peculiar to a particular region of Europe with which they were familiar. Thus, before 1840 the early Cincinnati congregation found both Poles and Germans together. After 1840, however, there were enough Ashkenazim to form separate congregations. In Chicago the strictly Orthodox congregation Kehilath Anshe Maariv (ever since known as KAM, founded in 1847) originally housed both Polish and German Jews, but in 1852 the Polish segment withdrew and founded its own congregation Kehilath B'nai Sholom.[10] Once separate Ashkenazic synagogues were founded, communication and cooperation existed among the different groups. When the Sephardic cantor Peixotto died, for instance, the entire Jewish community in New York, including Ashkenazic Jews, mourned.

Elsewhere in the country the Ashkenazim circulated widely, usually in small numbers, often as peddlers. During the Gold Rush in California many Jews made their way to San Francisco and to the tiny mining communities eastward in the mountains. In Nevada City, California, a Gold Rush boom town, there were enough Jews to have a *minyan* and conduct High Holiday services in 1852; a Mr. H. Leo, whose brother was a rabbi, "acted as Hazan, and was assisted by several others."[11] In 1855 the Nevada City group purchased a shofar. In nearby Grass Valley another *minyan* lost its shofar in a fire in 1856 and had to purchase another one.[12] The first congregation in Memphis was Congregation B'nai Israel founded in 1853. Among the duties of its first rabbi, hired at the end of 1858, was "to lead the choir." Shortly afterwards the congregation split: the rabbi followed the Orthodox segment into a new congregation and the original B'nai Israel became Reform.[13] Bene Jeshurun in Columbus, Ohio, had as "minister" (*shaliach tzibbur*), first, Simon Lazarus, who from 1851 to 1855 led services as a volunteer, succeeded by Joseph Goodman, a businessman, who was paid for his duties, and then by Meyer Wetterhan.[14]

---

[10] Irving Cutler, *The Jews of Chicago: From Shtetl to Suburb* (Urbana: University of Illinois Press, 1996), 10, 15.

[11] Robert E. Levinson, *The Jews in the California Gold Rush* (New York: Ktav, 1978), 93.

[12] Ibid., 108-09.

[13] Selma S. Lewis, *A Biblical People in the Bible Belt: The Jewish Community of Memphis, Tennessee, 1840s-1960s* (Macon, GA: Mercer University Press, 1998), 9-10.

[14] Marc Lee Raphael, *Jews and Judaism in a Midwestern Community: Columbus, Ohio, 1840-1975* (Columbus: Ohio Historical Society, 1979), 58-59.

Only in 1868, when most of the members of Bene Jeshurun resigned to form a new synagogue, B'nai Israel (Children of Israel), did Columbus hire its first ordained rabbi.

When the Hebrew Benevolent Congregation of Atlanta held its first services in 1860, the service was chanted entirely in Hebrew by knowledgeable laity without instruments; the influence of Leeser was predominant at first.[15] After 1868 Isaac Mayer Wise exerted greater influence on the Atlanta congregation and reforms were introduced, such as a *melodeon* (a portable organ) and a mixed choir. The first Jewish congregation in Milwaukee (1849) Emanu-El (God is with us) was already split by 1854 over disputes as to whether Polish or German *Minhag* (tradition) should be used. The following year another split over the same issue occurred among the members of the Polish synagogue, and S. Strauss was hired as the *shochet* (ritual slaughterer), teacher, and cantor of a new Polish synagogue with more empathy to German custom than in the other Polish synagogue in Milwaukee. In 1856 the first and third synagogues merged under the name B'nai Jeshurun and hired a rabbi, who served until 1860; he was followed by a cantor who kept the services going until another rabbi was hired in 1863. Once they had a rabbi, the Milwaukee congregation sought a cantor to "cooperate in divine services with choir and organ and give religious instruction at the congregational school,"[16] as the archival notices report.

Ashkenazic Cantors of the Nineteenth Century to 1870

In the small villages of Germany and Poland the *chazzan* was often the main person in charge of religious services; he often also functioned as *melammed*, *shochet*, and *mohel*. Rabbis, who tended to reside only in the major Jewish centers, were Talmudic scholars and judges, whose wisdom was sought when a matter of Jewish law was at stake and who preached only a few times a year. They did not regularly conduct religious services or participate in life-cycle events, whereas the cantor did. Therefore it comes as no surprise that, when the Ashkenazic communities were first organized in America in the nineteenth century, the majority of the religious leaders of these communities also were not rabbis but *chazzanim*. Samuel M. Isaacs (1804-78) was typical.[17] He was born in Holland, raised in England, and was called to become cantor at Congregation B'nai Jeshurun in New York in 1839. He was contracted to read the service (i.e., chant it) and preach a few times a year; his title was Reverend. Six years later, when a splinter group from B'nai Jeshurun was formed, Isaacs joined the new group which took the name Sha'arey Tefila. Isaacs continued to chant most of the prayers at Sha'arey Tefila, but he also had as voluntary assistants a *ba'al tefillah* (reader of prayers), a *ba'al kri'ah* (reader of Torah), various congregants as readers of the *haftarah*, and during the High Holidays various other members of the congregation as prayer singers. When the congregation agreed to hire

---

[15] Steven Hertzberg, *Strangers within the Gate City: The Jews of Atlanta 1845-1915* (Philadelphia: Jewish Publication Society, 1978), 57-58.

[16] Louis J. Swichkow and Lloyd P. Gartner, *The History of the Jews of Milwaukee* (Philadelphia: Jewish Publication Society, 1963), 46.

[17] The following information on Isaacs is from Simon Cohen, *Shaaray Tefila: A History of Its Hundred Years 1845-1945* (New York: Greenberg, 1945), 2-12.

a professional assistant, they appointed a man who could sing but not do cantillation. During his nearly forty years at this synagogue Isaacs was referred to as Reverend, *Chazzan*, and Rabbi, and indeed he was in fact all three. He was a respected clergyman in the company of Christian ministers and frequently preached as they did, he sang much of the regular Sabbath and holiday service and at weddings and funerals, and he was regarded as the authority in Jewish religious matters. When he participated in the dedication of Beth El Synagogue in Buffalo, New York, in 1850, he was referred to as Reverend Isaacs, he sang some of the service, and he delivered the principal "oration."[18] By 1870 Isaacs was considered the rabbi of Sha'arey Tefila and his paid assistants included Mr. Phillips as reader and Mr. E. M. Myers as assistant reader; he also had a paid choir. When he began to reduce his activities toward the end of his life, the congregation hired, not an assistant cantor, but an assistant rabbi—Frederick de Sola Mendes (like Isaacs, an Englishman)—who became the head rabbi in 1877 upon Isaacs's retirement.

In Buffalo, New York, Rev. Ansell and Isaac Moses Slatsky were cantors at Beth El in 1847-48 and were followed by Mr. Marks in 1856—all before the first ordained rabbi, Samson Falk, arrived in 1860. Ansell chanted most of the prayers, read the Torah, and blew the shofar, while Slatsky substituted for him at the morning and *mincha* (late afternoon) services. Marks not only sang but preached. Cantors had been the main spiritual leaders in Milwaukee, too, before 1857 when Rabbi Isador Kalisch (1816-86) became the city's first ordained rabbi, and by 1863 the cantor was a secondary personage.[19]

There were numerous other early Ashkenazic cantors in America, both professional and lay. The Baltimore Hebrew Congregation, for example, had thirteen cantors from 1835 to 1844, and there were many small *minyans* (prayer groups) in the city, where individual laymen acted as cantors.[20] Abraham Rice, the first ordained rabbi to leave Europe for a post in America, came to Baltimore in 1840, where he was surprised to discover that in the United States the cantor was the most highly regarded Jewish ecclesiastical personage. When he opened his own small, strictly Orthodox synagogue in 1851, he was rabbi, preacher, and cantor all at once.[21] Mayer Klein was the first cantor in Chicago sometime in the later 1840s.[22] Simson Hopfermann (or Hoffman) was the first cantor and *shochet* in Cleveland in 1846-47.[23] A few years later Gustavus M. Cohen (1820-1902), who had been trained in music and Hebrew in his native Saxony, became the first professionally-trained cantor in Cleveland; he remained a major force for Jewish music there as cantor, rabbi, and composer for the rest of the century, despite being replaced by an ordained rabbi after only a few years of trying to be both cantor and rabbi. Jacob Frankel (1808-87) was appointed cantor of Rodeph Shalom in Philadelphia in 1848. During the Civil War he

---

[18] Adler and Connolly, 64.

[19] Swichkow, 46.

[20] Isaac M. Fein, *The Making of an American Jewish Community: The History of Baltimore Jewry from 1773 to 1920* (Philadelphia: Jewish Publication Society, 1971), 108, 112.

[21] Ibid., 54, 57.

[22] Cutler, 9.

[23] Lloyd P. Gartner, *History of the Jews of Cleveland* (Cleveland: Western Reserve Historical Society; New York: Jewish Theological Seminary of America, 1978), 17.

is known to have sung to soldiers in hospitals in Washington, D.C.[24] The Little Rock, Arkansas Congregation hired Jonas Levy for its cantorship in 1853,[25] while at Ahavas Chesed in New York Samuel Welsh (1835-1901) was employed in the post from 1865 to 1880, before returning to Prague.[26] These cantors served also, at times, as *shochet*, *mohel* (ritual circumciser), and teacher. Until 1870 Jewish children in Baltimore studied at Jewish day schools run by the synagogues in which the cantors did most of the teaching. Whereas women teachers were hired for the newly formed Sunday schools in the Sephardic synagogues from the 1850s on, teaching posts in the Ashkenazic schools were limited to men, and for these positions few with knowledge of Jewish education besides the cantors were available. Adding to all these duties, most of the cantors continued working in other careers to make a living. Cantor Davidson, of Baltimore Hebrew Congregation, for example, was a dentist in his spare time, and Simson Hopfermann was a peddler.[27]

American Reform Music and the Development of Reform Music and Liturgy to 1932

Worldwide, the first Reform temple was established in 1810 in Seesen, Germany. From the beginning it banned cantillation and *nusach ha-tefillah*; everything was *read* in German and Hebrew. At the dedication ceremony, an organ was used, probably played by Gerson Rosenstein (1790-1851), the organist there.[28] The music consisted of Protestant-like hymns in German or Hebrew, so that no cantor was needed. When the temple in Seesen was banned, the Reform congregation in Hamburg quickly assumed leadership in 1818; the music in the Reform service there consisted of choral singing with organ accompaniment. Until 1879 it had no cantor; only in that year was cantillation restored and a cantor hired. Sulzer himself was against cantillation, but he differed from the North Germans in his reworking of traditional *nusach* into choral and cantorial singing rather than wholesale borrowing of Protestant chorales.

American Reform synagogues were influenced by the early German reformers. Cantillation was not widely accepted, and Wise, who had studied with Sulzer in Vienna, eliminated it in Albany when he first arrived there. Before the introduction of the music of Sulzer and Naumbourg in America, the American Reformers understood Jewish music to be that which was heard in the North German temples. The American Reformers in the 1820s "employed art music, and a choir; they sang the psalms together with both Jewish and Christian hymns. Some thirty hymns, borrowed from the Protestants, were appended to the *Sabbath Service*. . . . Worshippers were abjured to chant in harmony with the reader."[29] Congregational singing was emphasized

---

[24] Marcus, *United States Jewry*, 3:44, and Binder, *Studies*, 159.

[25] S. Lewis, 9.

[26] Binder, 160.

[27] Fein, 113, and Gartner, 19.

[28] Frühauf, 25.

[29] Marcus, *United States Jewry*, 1:630.

by the German Reformers and thus by their descendants who came to America in the 1840s and 1850s. Since that was also the musical style of American Protestant churches, assimilationist American Jews eagerly accepted both congregational singing of hymns and organ accompaniment. Penina Moïse (1797-1880) was an American Jewish poetess who composed 200 hymns; they could have been sung just as easily by Protestants, but she was devoutly committed to Judaism, and meant for the hymns to be sung in synagogues. As of 1940 the *Union Hymnal*, the official hymnal of Reform Jews at that time, still included some of her hymns. Early Reform Jews in Charleston in 1824-25 had no daily prayers; they limited their observances to the Sabbath, Shevu'ot, and the High Holidays. In imitation of their esteemed Protestant neighbors they demanded decorum and down-played any idea of a return to Zion. In 1825 they organized the Reform Society of Israelites, which consisted of laymen ignorant of tradition who felt no qualms about abandoning 1800 years of rabbinic Judaism. After the laymen founded the Society, a rabbi was hired in 1841—the first American Reform rabbi—who was to support the insurgents but at the same time to try to connect them with their Jewish past.[30]

The first half of the nineteenth century found organs and Christian choirs introduced to Reform synagogues.[31] Gustavus Poznanski, temporary cantor at Beth Elohim in Charleston, introduced the organ into the American synagogue in 1838, and its use spread rapidly. When Oheb Shalom Congregation of Baltimore—which was neither Reform nor Orthodox—wanted to install an organ in 1858, the officers contacted Rabbi Isaac M. Wise who gave *halachic* approval; a *shabbos goy* pumped the bellows.[32] In 1861 when Sinai was established as the first Reform synagogue in Chicago, acquisition of an organ and choir was among the first requirements. The cantors at B'nai Jeshurun in Milwaukee in the 1860s and following had to sing with an organ, according to the job description. The *melodeon*, a portable organ, was used in Atlanta from 1870 on, and when they built a new synagogue there in 1877, an organ was installed. Likewise Temple Sinai of New Orleans had an organ from its inception in 1871. Few organists were Jewish, but this was in keeping with the fact that most choirs, too, were Christian; there simply were not enough Jewish musicians to carry out the desires of congregations that wanted organs and choirs. At Anshe Chesid in Cleveland, when the organ was first installed in 1878 the choir had only one Jew in it, a lady. In Columbus, Ohio, B'nai Israel's "gentile choir" in fact enjoyed city-wide renown in the 1880s.[33] In the early 1890s in Akron, Ohio, a Gentile was even hired to blow the shofar in a Reform congregation after none of the Jews there could do it. Right wing reformers (who were nearest Conservatives) tolerated organs during the 1890s to the 1920s, though one major leader, Judah Magnes (1877-1948) opted for modern music, but not an organ, in the synagogue.

Choirs were at first only volunteer and therefore were regarded as aids to congregational singing. During the 1840s Max Lilienthal, who hailed from Munich and earlier had played an important role in Russia, introduced a choir and "good music" into New York City synagogues.[34]

---

[30] Ibid., 1:625, 637.

[31] Ibid., 3:74.

[32] Fein, 117. A "shabbos goy" is a non-Jew who performs tasks for Jews that Jews are forbidden to perform on the Sabbath.

[33] Raphael, 71.

[34] Marcus, *United States Jewry*, 3:98.

But once a choir became professional and sang *to* rather than *with* the congregation, the two practices—choral and congregational singing—proved antithetical. When Temple Emanu-El was founded in New York, its prayer book was Orthodox, its amateur choir was all male, and its cantor was to "chant in the ancient traditional way."[35] Then came Cantor Leo Merzbacher, who in 1842 organized a choir there to lead congregational responses and introduce the contemporary music of Sulzer, Naumbourg, and Lewandowski. To handle the more demanding works of European choral composers, however, not amateurs but professionals were required, and in many cases these professionals were not Jewish. By 1848 when the choir director of Emanu-El was paid $75 a year and each of the singers paid $25 per year, we know that for the Sabbath service there was an organ, a mixed choir of men and women, Jews and Gentiles.[36] The following year Leon Sternberger became cantor of neighboring Anshe Chesed in New York, and he also immediately introduced the music of Sulzer and Lewandowski.

Traditional Jews in the United States, as in Europe, were opposed to choral music except for special occasions, when singing appropriate hymns in Hebrew was permitted. For example, documents reveal that for the dedication of KAM's (Kehilath Anshe Mayriv) new synagogue in Chicago in 1851, "the Choir, consisting of a large number of ladies and gentleman, did honor to the occasion and to the denomination,"[37] and in 1853 that a concert of choral music accompanied by organ at Temple Emanu-El in New York raised money for the new organ there.

As the old century drew to a close and the new century dawned, many congregations continued the practice of using a professional choir. A congregant described the music of the service in the Temple in Atlanta in 1885 thus:

> [It is a] handsome temple, fine organ . . . and the best trained and best-voiced choir the city affords for the money. The only thing that dampens our ardor is that the choristers, who sing "Sh'ma Yisrael" and "Ayn Kaylohaynu" in our temple on Shabbos, sing "Jesus Lover of My Soul" in the Episcopal and Presbyterian churches, on Sunday. However, the young element in our Jewish circle is, at best, not very religiously inclined and rather listens to fine music . . . than do the performing itself.[38]

But the situation was not universally that. Some Reform congregations, aware of their Orthodox roots, retained a cantor who carried the burden of the music and either did not have a choir or kept the amateur Jewish choir as accompaniment to the cantor. In Gates of Prayer Reform Synagogue in New Orleans in 1908, for example, where the men still wore hats, a *chazzan* led the services and there was no choir.[39] Nonetheless, in Reform synagogues the professional choir became widespread, and by 1920 when most Reform congregations had shifted their main service from Saturday morning to Friday night, the professional choirs were for the most part employed

---

[35] Binder, *Studies*, 162.

[36] Marcus, *United States Jewry*, 3:688.

[37] Cutler, 13.

[38] *Atlanta Constitution* (1 October 1886), 5, as quoted in Hertzberg, 67.

[39] Marcus, *United States Jewry*, 3:688.

for the *Kabbalat Shabbat* services (the preliminary Friday night service). In non-Reform synagogues, however, in the years just prior to World War I, the Young Israel Movement introduced lectures and congregational singing on Friday nights. This latter approach to Friday night synagogue music involving full congregational participation and no professional choir would become an important practice late in the twentieth century, one affecting many Reform congregations. Today *Gates of Prayer*, for example, has a cantorial soloist Victoria May who also leads a volunteer choir.

The musical changes which the early reformers had brought in included the use of an organ, mixed choir, and an occasional hymn sung in English, but by the 1850s the reforms were much more radical. Mr. Lowenberg, president of Vicksburg's Reform congregation, served from 1866 as rabbi, cantor, *mohel*, and whatever else the Jewish community needed. Services had Protestant-like hymns purposely modeled on Christian hymns so that the Jews' Protestant neighbors would find the modes of Jewish worship suitable to a Christian society.[40] In many other Reform congregations of that time the emphasis was on good music and technically-trained singers, which meant, for most of them, Christian music and Christian musicians. When Rebecca Gratz founded the first Jewish Sunday school in Philadelphia in 1818, school children were expected to sing these hymns regularly so that within a short time the Jewish community thought only of the hymns as typifying Jewish liturgical music. A few knowledgeable cantors tried to stem the tide, but they were primarily in New York and had only minor success.[41] Elsewhere in the country the cantors were not the most musical or well trained.[42] Thus, with only relatively mediocre cantors trying to maintain a non-Protestant tradition, nothing really impeded the wide acceptance of Protestant hymnology in the Reform synagogue.

In 1900 there were 791 Jewish congregations in the United States: fifty formally Orthodox, ninety belonging to the Union of American Hebrew Congregations (Reform), and the rest conservative and unaffiliated Orthodox. German and Bohemian Jewish immigrants comprised the Reform congregations, and Russian and Polish immigrants, the Orthodox ones. In 1900 there were about 525 rabbis in the United States; by 1917 the number had grown to 1,500. By 1920-21 in New York City alone there were over 700 Orthodox congregations and thirty Conservative congregations; in the entire country there were more than 220 Reform congregations. Altogether by 1920 there were about three million Jews in the United States. By then several musical service settings, hymnals, and songbooks were in use.[43] Within ten years New York was the largest Jewish city in the world, followed by Warsaw, and then by Chicago; most American Jews in 1930 were Orthodox and were heavily steeped in their European past. A generation or so later most American Jews had become Reform or Conservative. While traditional Ashkenazic music was retained by the Orthodox communities, as more and more Jews became Conservative or Reform they accepted the American brand of Jewish music.

Thus, a tradition of Christian-like music for the Reform Synagogue was well-established in America during the nineteenth century and formed the basis of Reform music until World War II. Local composers abounded. Edward Woolf, who came from England to Mobile, Alabama, in 1837,

---

[40] Ibid., 3:132.

[41] Among the important cantors in New York City were Leo Merzbacher and G. M. Cohen at Emanu-El; Jonas Hecht, Leon Steinberger, and Ansel Leo at Anshe Chesed; and Ignatius Ritterman and Judah Kramer at B'nai Jeshurun.

[42] Binder, *Studies*, 158.

[43] Marcus, *United States Jewry*, 3:618.

eventually settled in New York in 1841 and shortly thereafter composed a service. A few years later another Jew in Mobile, Sigmund Schlesinger (1835-1906), who had come from Germany, composed a series of services for the Reform synagogue whose style copied German Protestant traditional chorales and arias from Verdi, Donizetti, and other opera composers, which thrilled his congregation.[44] E. Roget, a Jew in Philadelphia, was another who used borrowed material for a synagogue hymn, in his case a popular Italian air by F.G. Bertoni.[45] Max Braun of Newark, New Jersey, wrote *Sabbath Evening Service* in 1891 with text in German, Hebrew, and English following the prayer books of Szold and Hübsch; his music is entirely Protestant in harmony, though some of the melodies suggest Sulzer. Frederick Kitziger (1844-1903) came from Germany to New Orleans just after the Civil War and served as music director at Touro Synagogue from 1881 until his death. During this time, Kitziger, who was not a Jew, wrote and published more synagogue music than anyone else in America, including two complete settings of the Sabbath service, sometimes adapting well-known melodies to fit the prayer (such as *Moon Light* Sonata as "O What Is Man?" from the Yom Kippur Memorial Service).[46] James H. Rogers, another non-Jew, wrote a Sabbath service for the Reform congregation in Cleveland where he was musical director in the 1930s.

Gradually in Reform temples during the second half of the nineteenth century the cantor was discarded, to be replaced by a choir hidden in a loft, and the rabbi replaced the cantor as the central leader of worship. After 1900 Reform congregations increased their budgets for music so that they could accommodate bigger choirs and perform large choral works inspired by the oratorios and operas of Gounod and Wagner. Atlanta's Rabbi David Marx, a typical Reform rabbi at the turn of the century, had no qualms at the dedication of his new temple building in 1902, by having the choir perform Jules Massenet's "The Last Sleep of the Virgin."[47]

Almost from the beginning Reform Jews accepted women in their worship services. In 1850 Wise brought girls into his choir so that he could introduce his congregation to Sulzer's music and works of other modern European cantors as well as to German hymns. Cantor Merzbacher of Temple Emanu-El in New York organized a mixed choir in 1842 to lead congregational responses and to introduce the music of Sulzer, Naumbourg, and Lewandowski. When Leon Sternberger from Warsaw became cantor of Anshe Chesed in 1849, he was so disappointed in the music he found there that he immediately sent for Sulzer's and Lewandowski's music, which required women as well as men. From this point forth, Reform Judaism has not questioned the presence of women in the music of the service, though it took another century before the cantorate was opened to women.

In an attempt to unify all the different Reform congregations in North America, the Central Conference of American Rabbis decided to publish a single prayer book that would replace the many different prayer books in use during the nineteenth century. The *Union Prayer Book* first came out in 1892 and codified the use of a predominantly English-language service. The principal changes in Jewish music rendered by the Reform movement, which had included adding the

---

[44] Ibid., 2:60.

[45] Ibid., 1:349.

[46] Ibid., 3:388. Christians were often hired as organists and to sing in synagogue choirs. There was influence in the other direction; also, for example, in this period a Jew was employed by the Mobile Presbyterian Church.

[47] Hertzberg, 69.

organ and mixed choir and stressing Friday night services, now involved recomposing most of the traditional liturgy. Old music was no longer suited to the English prayers in the new prayer book. At this time most Reform synagogue choirs and organists were Gentile; these Gentiles had to provide the new music and did so easily by simply changing words to known Protestant chorales.

Many Jews, too, tried to compose music that would suit the taste of the American Reform Jew for things Protestant. The first hymnal for the Reform movement, modeled on Protestant hymnals, was published in 1842; another published in 1876 by Otto Loeb had hymns in German and some tunes taken directly from Protestant hymnals. Another early hymnal was edited by Simon Hecht in 1878. Gustav Gottheil's hymnal of the 1880s included Christian hymns, while the songbook of Isaac S. Moses, which went through fourteen editions between 1894 and 1920, included music by Mozart, Beethoven, and Schumann. The first *Union Hymnal* of the Reform movement was published in 1897 under the leadership of Alois Kaiser, and further editions came out in 1911 and 1914. All the hymns in these first editions were similar to Protestant hymns. Only in the much later edition of 1932, under the editorship of Abraham Binder (fig. 11.1), Jacob Singer, and James Heller were traditional tunes and *piyyutim* brought back, though many of the hymns in the older editions were retained. Meanwhile attempts were made to provide musical settings for the specific services in the Reform prayer books. Sigmund Schlesinger wrote the first complete musical setting of the *Union Prayer Book*, but there was nothing traditional about it and, according to Binder, "it had a deleterious effect on Reform Jewish music."[48]

FIG. 11.1   A. W. Binder

Courtesy of Hadassah Binder Markson

---

[48] Binder, *Studies*, 163.

While Reform Jews had dropped cantillation, other Jews kept it central in their liturgy. In the early years of the country, the Sephardic Jews brought their chants from Europe, and some of these chants are still heard in Shearith Israel in New York. German cantors who came before 1840 brought their cantillations and their melodies to America, too. As the music of Naumbourg and Sulzer gained popularity in America, however, and German Reform spread to the new country, the cantillation was dropped in the Reform synagogues. From 1846 to 1900 fighting continued over the use of traditional chants.

A few isolated but important American cantors tried to hang on to the Ashkenazic *nusach*. Alois Kaiser (1840-1908) was born in Hungary and studied with Sulzer. After serving as a cantor in Vienna (1859-63) and Prague (1863-66), he immigrated to Baltimore, where he served Congregation Ohav Shalom for the next forty-two years. His synagogue compositions include "Zimrat Yah" (1871-86), *Confirmation Hymns* (1873), "Yizkor" (1879), and a cantata for *Simchat Torah* (1890). He was one of the editors of the first *Union Hymnal* (1897) for which he contributed some of his own works. William Sparger (1860-1904) was cantor at Temple Emanuel in New York. Besides his contributions to the first *Union Hymnal* and a two-volume collection of settings of the Sabbath Service (1901), he also published essays on Jewish music. Edward Stark (1863-1918), the son of a traditional German cantor, grew up in New York and then moved to San Francisco, where he succeeded Daniel Levy (1826-1910)[49] as cantor of Temple Emanuel from 1893 to 1913. Besides numerous works for Jewish choirs and children, he contributed to the *Union Hymnal* editions of 1909 and 1911 as well as to the official reform song books for *Rosh Hashanah* (1910) and *Yom Kippur* (1913). When Stark composed his own setting of the *Union Prayer Book*, he used traditional elements—the first to do so in America. This inspired other Jewish musicians to set the Reform service with what is understood as traditional Jewish music.

But all the efforts of Kaiser, Sparger, and Stark were countered by the work of many others featuring hymns in a Protestant manner. Early in the twentieth century the battle continued. The National Council of Jewish Women sponsored projects on synagogue music ca. 1910 to try to reintroduce traditional Jewish music because many Jewish women could not tolerate "Ave Maria" and other Christian melodies in Jewish services. In recognition of the need to bring back Jewish music into the service, the Central Conference of American Rabbis (Reform) in 1921 created standing committees on music. The same year the Hebrew Union College purchased the *Birnbaum Collection*, which brought to America one of the largest and most important collections of written examples of traditional Ashkenazic music. Shortly thereafter, in 1922, Binder reintroduced cantillation into a Reform synagogue—Stephen Wise's Free Synagogue in New York—and then taught it on a regular basis to rabbinic students in the Jewish Institute of Religion and later at the Hebrew Union College-Jewish Institute of Religion and its cantorial school. Binder published his manual for cantillation in 1959, by which time much of the Reform movement had begun a shift back to more traditional liturgy and music. A similar manual is Samuel Rosenbaum's *A Guide to Haftarah Chanting* (1973); Rosenbaum was cantor of Temple Beth El in Rochester, New York.

---

[49] Information on Levy kindly supplied by Paula B. Freedman of Congregation Emanu-El, San Francisco. Fred Rosenbaum, *Visions of Reform: Congregation Emanu-El and the Jews of San Francisco 1849-2000* (Judah L. Magnes Museum, 2000).

Art Music for the Reform Synagogue: Immigrant Composers and Their American Disciples ca. 1930-70

During the period from ca. 1930 to ca. 1970 a number of exceptional European-born and European-trained musicians who were Jews came to America and wrote for the American synagogue—usually for Reform congregations. Some, such as Ernst Bloch and Kurt Weill, made their living as composers apart from the synagogue and made only occasional contributions to the synagogue, while others, such as Herbert Fromm and Heinrich Schalit, were employed as synagogue musicians and wrote primarily for the liturgy. Most came to America to escape the Nazis, but some, like Bloch, came earlier. Because they were great composers, not simply hack musicians, and because they were deeply imbued with traditional European Jewish music, they brought a new dimension to American synagogue music: their music was art music as much as functional synagogue music.

The pioneer in this group was Ernest Bloch (fig. 11.2), whose career as a Jewish musician is discussed in chapter 10.[50] From 1925 to 1930 he was director of the San Francisco Conservatory of Music and became known to the leadership of Reform Temple Emanu-El in that city. Aware that he had such a great composer of Jewish music in his midst, Cantor Reuben Rinder (1887-1959) arranged for his synagogue to commission Bloch to write a setting of the Saturday morning liturgy for the Reform synagogue according to the *Union Prayer Book*.[51] Entitled *Avodath ha-Kodesh* (Sacred Service), it was written from 1932 to 1933 and premiered in 1934 in Rinder's synagogue. Shortly thereafter it was performed at Temple Emanu-El in New York, conducted by Lazare Saminsky. *Avodath ha-Kodesh* is scored for baritone and mixed chorus, accompanied by either organ or orchestra, and it is suitable for performance in a Reform synagogue as part of a service or in a concert hall. It has been performed widely throughout the world and established a precedent which would soon be imitated by many other gifted composers; a composer could write a single piece that would satisfy his/her needs for religious expression and at the same time be true to his/her artistic standards. For congregations with organs and raised on the music of Sulzer, Lewandowski, and Naumbourg, this was a logical continuation of that great nineteenth-century European tradition.

Those who followed Bloch differed from him in one main respect. While Bloch used no specific quotations of traditional synagogue song in his service, the others frequently quoted well-known *missinai* tunes or imitated cantillation or prayer modes. Following the theories of Joseph Yasser (1893-1981) and Isadore Freed, who recognized the modal nature of traditional synagogue music and developed a harmony based on that, these new synagogue/art composers were able to go further than the nineteenth-century masters in synthesizing the inherited synagogue oral tradition with the new art music.

Among the followers of Bloch was Heinrich Schalit, who was born in Vienna in 1886 and graduated from the Conservatory there in 1906. He served as organist of the Great Synagogue of Munich from 1927 to 1933 and the Great Synagogue in Rome from 1933 to 1939. Arriving in the

---

[50] Bloch came to America in 1916 but returned to Europe; he came again, permanently, in 1917, and became an American citizen in 1924.

[51] On the commissioning of this work, see Heskes, *Passport*, 284.

FIG. 11.2   Ernest Bloch in Roveredo (Ticino),
Switzerland in 1931,
photograph by his daughter,
Lucienne Bloch

Courtesy of Lucienne Allen and the Bloch family

United States in 1940, he then served Reform congregations in Rochester, Providence, Hollywood, and Denver. For the American synagogues, following Bloch's example, he composed *Sabbath Morning Liturgy* (1952) and *Sabbath Eve Liturgy* (1959), though without the elaborate orchestration.

Another follower of Bloch was Herbert Fromm (1905-96), who was born in Bavaria and graduated from the Academy of Music in Munich. Escaping the Nazis in 1937 he was at first organist and music director of Reform Temple Beth Zion in Buffalo and from 1941 until his death he was associated, as organist, choir director, and composer, with Reform Temple Israel in Boston and Brookline, Massachusetts. Among Fromm's many liturgical compositions are his Friday evening service *Adath Israel* (1943), *The Kiddush through the Jewish Year* (date unknown), *Ma-ariv* (evening devotion: three prayers and a hymn for baritone, reader, mixed choir, and orchestra, 1976), *Chag ha-matsot* (1967), and *Atonement Music* (1948).

Herman Berlinski was born in Leipzig in 1910 and studied in Paris before coming to New York where he continued his education at the Jewish Theological Seminary. He served as organist at Temple Emanu-El in New York and from 1963 until his death in 2002 was Minister of Music to the Washington Hebrew Congregation. He composed many organ preludes based on *Missinai* tunes, an *Avodat Shabbath* commissioned by the Conservative Park Avenue Synagogue, and many other liturgical as well as non-liturgical Jewish compositions.

Max Janowski (1912-91), who was the musical director of KAM Isaiah Israel Congregation in Hyde Park, Illinois from 1938 to 1991, is especially renowned for his setting of "Avinu Malkeynu," which has become standard in most Reform synagogues in America and has frequently been recorded by cantors and Jewish pop stars. Born in Germany, he arrived in America in 1937 and was commissioned by the United Synagogue of America to compose his *Compassion* Cantata, which brought him recognition in his new country. Subsequently he composed an enormous amount of synagogue works including *Avodath Hakodesh shel Kehilath Anshe Maariv* (Sacred Service of Congregation Anshe Maariv) in 1947 for mixed choir and optional organ, a *Sabbath Evening*

Seder (third edition, 1975), and *On That Day: Sabbath Music* in 1978 for cantor, soloists, choir and organ. His works are characterized as attractive, artistic, easily comprehended by lay congregants, and always mindful of traditional European *chazzanut*.[52]

Zavel Zilberts (1880-1949) was born in Russia, trained at the Warsaw Conservatory, and was active in Lodz and Moscow before immigrating to New York in 1920. In addition to composing basic traditional Orthodox cantorials, he also published, in the year of his death, *Neginoth Yisroel*, a setting of a service in the *Union Prayer Book*.

Julius Chajes (1910-85) was born in Lvov, Galicia, studied in Vienna, and immigrated to Israel in 1934. He moved to New York in 1937 where he taught, and then he became music director of Temple Beth El in Detroit. Among his liturgical works is a Sabbath evening service from 1946 for cantor, mixed choir, and organ.

Lazar Weiner (1897-1982) was born near Kiev and immigrated to America in 1914. From 1929 to 1975 he was Musical Director of Central Synagogue in New York; he also taught and conducted Jewish music in various institutions in New York and was a prolific arranger of Yiddish songs. His principal synagogue compositions are *Likras Shabos*, a Sabbath evening service for solo voice, with piano or organ (date unknown) and *Shir l'yom hashabos*, a Sabbath evening service for cantor, choir, and organ (1972).

Frederick Piket (1903-74) is another prolific composer of art music for the synagogue who came to New York in 1940 to escape the Holocaust. Born in Constantinople, he was a music student in Vienna and Berlin. In America Picket became Music Director of the Free Synagogue in Flushing, New York, and taught at several New York schools including New York University and the School of Sacred Music of Hebrew Union College. Among his works are *The Seventh Day*, a Friday evening service for cantor, mixed voices, and organ (1961); *Kavod La-Torah*, a Torah service for Friday evening (1962); *Midnight Penitential Service (S'lichos)*, for cantor, reader, mixed choir and organ (1968), *Memorial Service* for cantor, mixed choir and organ (1969), *Shalosh R'galim*, a complete musical liturgy for the evening and morning services of Pesach, Shavuoth, and Sukkoth according to the *Union Prayer Book* (1970), *Shire Bet Sinai* for Friday evening (1970), *Music for Yom Kippur Evening and Morning* (1973), and *Shire B'ne YeShurun*, for Sabbath morning (1969).

Benjamin Grobani's *Shire Tefilah*, a Sabbath evening service for cantor, mixed voices, and organ (1966), has found a secure place in the repertories of numerous Reform synagogues. Unlike the others, who were primarily composers, organists, and choir directors, Grobani was a cantor at Temple Oheb Shalom in Baltimore from 1941 to 1970. He received his musical training at the Cincinnati Conservatory of Music and at the Curtis Institute in Philadelphia.

Kurt Weill (1900-50), on the other hand, was so successful as a composer of theater music and music for the movies that he could be independent of any regular synagogue appointment. His best-known liturgical work is a setting of the Friday night *Kiddush*. Stefan Wolpe (1902-72), who came to the United States in 1938 after a few years in Palestine, wrote his one liturgical work, *Yigdal*, in 1945 for a Sabbath Evening service at Park Avenue Synagogue in New York. Robert Starer, born in 1924 in Vienna, has written numerous works for cantor, choir, unison congregation, and organ, including a complete *Sabbath Evening Service* (1970) and isolated hymns and psalms.

---

[52] Deborah L. Felder, "Liturgy and Drama: Max Janowski: A Case Study," Hebrew Union College-Jewish Institute of Religion, Cantorial School thesis, 1996.

Besides Ashkenazic Jews there have been several very important Sephardic Jews who have contributed art music to the American synagogue. Chief among these are Darius Milhaud (see chapter 9) and Mario Castelnuovo-Tedesco. Castelnuovo-Tedesco (1895-1968) was born in Italy and came to America in 1939. He worked mostly in Los Angeles and wrote for the movies as well as for the concert stage. Inspired by some Hebrew songs composed by his father, he wrote numerous sacred works including his *Sacred Service for Sabbath Eve* (1943) and *Lecho Dodi* (1936).

A number of American-born composers, influenced by Bloch and by the immigrants who followed, also contributed art music to the synagogue. Frederick Jacobi (1891-1952) hailed from San Francisco where he received his basic music education, and he studied directly under Bloch. Although he never held a regular synagogue appointment, he composed a *Sabbath Evening Service* (1931) before Bloch's *Avodath ha-Kodesh* and wrote *Six Pieces for the Organ for Use in the Synagogue* (1933). Maurice Goldman (1910-84) wrote two Friday evening services according to the *Union Prayer Book: Friday Evening Service* (1933) and *Sabbath Eve Service* (1949), the latter for cantor, choir and organ. Reuven Kosakoff (1898-1987) was a native of New Haven and was trained at the Yale Music School, the Julliard School of Music, and in Berlin. In addition to writing much Jewish music for the concert hall, he set the Reform liturgy for the Friday evening service.

Max Helfman (1901-63) was actually born in Poland but came to America as a child in 1909. Trained in Jewish academies and at the Curtis Institute of Music in Philadelphia, he held appointments in synagogues in Hollywood, Los Angeles, Newark, and Paterson. He was the first dean of the School of Fine Arts at the Jewish Theological Seminary in New York. His main contribution to synagogue art music is his *Shabbat Kodesh* (1942).

Like Helfman, Isadore Freed (1900-60) was born in Europe (Brest-Litovsk, Russia) and came to Philadelphia while still a child. Also a pupil of Bloch, he studied at the Curtis Institute and in Paris and had as teachers Josef Hofmann, Arthur Honegger, and Vincent d'Indy. He served Keneseth Israel Temple in Philadelphia from 1933 to 1946 and Temple Israel in Lawrence, New York from 1946 to 1960. He wrote no fewer than six services for the Reform synagogue. His study, *Harmonizing the Jewish Modes* (1958), codifies the theory of Jewish harmony as practiced by most of the synagogue composers of this generation. David Amram (b. 1930) composed a *Friday Evening Service* with organ in 1960, and David Diamond wrote *Mizmor David* (Sacred Service) in 1951.

Conservative and Orthodox Synagogues and Their Music in the Nineteenth and Twentieth Centuries

As Jewish immigrants spread westward through the United States they took their practices with them. During the first half of the nineteenth century, most of the Ashkenazic congregations organized in America were initially Orthodox. The pressures for assimilation were strong, however, and many Jews opted for changes in the ritual that would lead to the formation of Reform or Conservative congregations. Some remained Orthodox either by splitting away from more reform-minded Jews or by driving the reformers out. In many cases, however, such as in Columbus in 1868 when the reformers left the Orthodox Bene Jeshuren, there were not enough Orthodox left to maintain a *minyan* and the Orthodox synagogue dissolved. Those Orthodox who were determined to maintain their rites were faced with great difficulties in the American wilderness. By 1858 there was a congregation in Portland, Oregon, whose cantor not only chanted the service but also taught the children Hebrew and some secular disciplines. So highly valued was he that he was paid $1,000, a rather substantial salary for that time.[53]

The obstacles to observing strict orthodoxy, however, were not only the relatively open and inviting Christian society around Jews, but also the types of Jews who were in America. During the 1840s and 1850s some rabbis and cantors circulated around America, but they were often quite disreputable; there was no control over standards nor any certification process for them. Such certification was needed to encourage moral young American men to become cantors, men who would be comfortable in English as well as German. Talmudic scholars from Europe did not come to America until Jewish communities were well established (Leeser was practically the lone exception), though cantors and preachers did.[54] From the 1840s to 1860s in the absence of trained leadership, laymen led services, some of whom had fine voices and went on to become cantors despite their inferior knowledge of Jewish law and custom. As in Sephardic congregations, there were others who occupied ministerial or rabbinical roles who lacked moral standing. Most congregations, unlike that in Portland, wanted a single person who could do everything but offered him little security in return. A cantor in Wilkes-Barre, Pennsylvania, for example, could not make ends meet by simply being a cantor, so he taught guitar to supplement his income.[55] Conservative congregations barely tolerated Christian-like music that was rampant in Reform congregations, but did little to provide for knowledgeable cantors who would secure traditional *nusach*.

As Eastern Europeans began to arrive in America en masse from the 1880s on, they brought over a Jewish *nusach* that was different from German Ashkenazic music, let alone from German Reform hymnody. They were moved mostly by Yiddish and Hebrew songs and by cantorial floridity. Some continued without change the liturgical music they were accustomed to in the *shtetls* in the old country; those who could maintained the *meshorerim* popular in Eastern Europe instead of the modern Orthodox choir, not to speak of the American Christian choir. At Anshe Emeth in Cleveland, a Polish Orthodox synagogue, the Yom Kippur services in 1887 were led by the traditional *chazzan* accompanied by the congregation which "prayed and sang in a softer tone."[56] On the other hand at B'ne Jeshurun in Cleveland on the very same Yom Kippur, the *chazzan* was accompanied by a quartet of boys, and the congregation every once in a while would join in and repeat prayers and chants in a loud voice. B'ne Jeshurun was already showing signs of change from Europe in that men and women by 1887 were sitting together and not all the men wore *talitot*, but there was no organ, cantillation was retained without exception, and the prayers were all in Hebrew, which distinguished this synagogue from the Reform synagogues in Cleveland at the time. In Atlanta during the first two decades of the twentieth century the East European immigrants chanted their traditional services, initially without the assistance of a cantor, but then with immigrant cantors. In Milwaukee Orthodox children were drilled by

---

[53] Marcus, *United States Jewry*, 2:125.

[54] Ibid., 3:230.

[55] Ibid., 2:228.

[56] Gartner, 163-69.

rote in the prayers by *shochtim* or cantors who were men of little learning; that situation changed in 1901 and following when the highly regarded chief rabbi, Solomon Scheinfeld (1860-1943), was appointed, who demanded a higher level of competency. Shortly after Scheinfeld's death the young, unknown Richard Tucker, later to become a major Metropolitan Opera star, conducted High Holiday services at Scheinfeld's Teutonia Street synagogue.[57]

The custom in America of the cantor assuming the role of the rabbi was not limited to Reform Jews and to the nineteenth century. Julius T. Loeb served as both cantor and rabbi at Conservative congregation Beth Israel in Atlanta from 1907 to 1909. Since there continued to be a shortage of traditional rabbis in America during the early years of the twentieth century and an abundance of cantors, many congregations had only cantors who, in emergency cases, served the role that the Reform rabbi was serving as minister to the life cycle needs of the congregation. From the 1880s until 1908, Agudas Achim in Columbus was served by an assortment of cantors, *mohels*, and other lay persons; in that latter year the first ordained rabbi arrived. The first *Chassidic* congregation in Atlanta, Beth Hamedrash Hagadol Anshe Sfard (founded in 1913), was served for a number of years by a cantor, not a rabbi.[58] An Orthodox congregation in Cincinnati, Adath Israel, in 1910 had as permanent officiant a cantor whom it paid $35 per month.

The quality of the cantors improved greatly during this time because of the quality of the new Eastern European immigrant cantors and the pressure for improvement felt by each cantor competing against so many others for the limited number of positions. Instead of a musically illiterate singer, the cantor was rapidly becoming a modern, trained musician. By 1920, as some of the changes in Eastern European Ashkenazic music became known and as the popularity of some Reform changes in the liturgy were experienced first hand, in Conservative synagogues there were all-Jewish choirs of males and females, and some congregations had an organ. In Philadelphia in the 1920s, young Conservative Jews who had become Americanized and were entering into the mainstream of American professional life began to demand mixed seating and to organize mixed choirs for late Friday night services.[59]

Loosely defined, the Orthodox community is a heterogeneous one comprising traditional Orthodox, several genres of Chassidic, Young Israel, and others. Each has its own idea of Jewish liturgical music—both the repertoire and the means for performing it. The population shift to America from Europe and the dependency of American-born and American-trained Orthodox musicians upon the European tradition led to the necessity of preserving what had been a predominantly oral tradition by writing it down. As a result, it was the work of the few knowledgeable immigrants whose variant versions of orally transmitted conventions soon became fixed as *the* tradition.

Among the most important of these were Gershon Ephros (1890-1978) and Max Wohlberg (1907-96). Both were authorities on Eastern-European Ashkenazic *nusach*, and both taught these to countless students—Reform as well as Conservative—some of whom became prominent rabbis,

[57] *The Books of Rabbi S. I. Scheinfeld*, trans. David Kuselewitz, ed. Amram Scheinfeld (Chicago: Scheinfeld Foundation, 1977), 2-3, 10-12.

[58] Hertzberg, 87, 93.

[59] Robert Tabak, "Orthodox Judaism in Transition," in Murray Friedman, ed., *Jewish Life in Philadelphia* (Philadelphia: Ishi Publications, 1983), 55.

cantors, choir directors, choristers, and musicologists. Among Ephros's works are *Hallel V'Zimrah* (1968), a complete Sabbath morning service for cantor, choir, and organ, according to the Reform *Prayer Book*; *Lel Shabbat* (1967) and *L'Yom Hashabbat* (1966), Sabbath evening and morning services for cantor, choir, and organ according to the Conservative prayer book; *Manginot Shabat* (1948 and 1957), a Friday night Conservative service which includes congregational songs added by Harry Coopersmith; *Services for Weekday Evening and Morning* (1952), and numerous other compositions. Ephros also compiled his monumental anthology of synagogue music for cantor, choir, and organ (1929-69, with several later editions of individual volumes) which has served as a source for traditional chant and *nusach* for several generations of synagogue musicians in America. Only one major work, his "Birchath Kohanim" (1925), contains no organ and is scored only for cantor and choir.

Wohlberg, on the other hand, wrote primarily for unaccompanied singers, though he, too, included the organ in a few publications. In his *Arvit L'hol* (1972), for example, a complete evening service for weekdays and several holidays, Wohlberg included an optional organ part added by Charles Davidson, whereas in his "Chemdat Shabbat" (1971) and his "Yachad b'Kol" (1975) he wrote only for cantor and congregation without organ. Works like *Shakar Arakeshkha* (1974) and *Shirei Zimiroh* (1947), settings of the entire weekday and Sabbath morning services respectively, were designed for traditional Conservative synagogues without any instrument. Wohlberg also left to the Jewish Theological Society Library a vast manuscript and recorded collection of cantorials and cantillation which he compiled from dozens of cantors active during his lifetime.

Besides Ephros and Wohlberg there were other European-born cantors and choir directors who transmitted the Ashkenazi *nusach* to twentieth-century American Orthodox and Conservative synagogues. Zavel Zilberts, who came to the United States in 1920, was one of these. Among his works are a popular setting of the Saturday evening service (*Havdalah*) and *The Complete High Holiday Liturgy for the Hazzan*. Until well into the second half of the twentieth century, the Orthodox synagogues made few changes in their music inherited from the likes of Ephros, Wohlberg, and Zilberts, but Conservative congregations were almost as flexible as Reform congregations.

Two contemporary Conservative congregations can be contrasted in their musical establishment. North Shore Suburban Beth El in Highland Park, north of Chicago, is a traditional Conservative congregation.[60] Founded in 1948, it has a rabbi and a cantor. During the service all the prayers are sung in Hebrew unaccompanied by any instrument. On a typical Saturday morning there often are laymen who chant all the prayers up to the "Sh'ma," at which point the cantor enters and continues until the end. He leaves the Torah Service to be conducted by the laity, who take over for the benedictions, and often for the cantillation; at this point women also participate (the congregation has mixed seating). The only English is the spoken portions of the service which are translations of the Torah and Haftarah, the sermon, and announcements. Congregational singing occurs at certain favorite moments during the prayers and of course for those prayers traditionally recited by the congregation. A non-professional choir, made up of members of the congregation, joins the cantor not on Sabbaths but on holidays.

Another Conservative congregation is Park Avenue Synagogue in New York, founded in 1882. Served during the twentieth century by three of the most prominent cantors in the Conservative movement (Abraham Sukoenig, David Putterman, and David Lefkowitz), Park Avenue

---

[60] The following is according to informant Stuart Dorf, a member of this congregation.

Synagogue differs in three important respects from North Shore Suburban Beth El: it has a professional choir that sings year round, the music is accompanied by an organ played by a professional organist, and there are some prayers recited and even occasionally sung in English. Cantor Sukoenig composed his own music, including some pieces without accompaniment and some with organ; his *Sabbath Evening Service* (1929), composed with his son, Sidney Sukoenig, even used the *Union Prayer Book* as the source of its texts. Furthermore, over the years Park Avenue Synagogue has commissioned new art music for the liturgy from distinguished Jewish secular composers, thus introducing the congregation to music to which it is unaccustomed, a practice that contrasts with North Shore Suburban Beth El's, where traditional chant is always heard.

Just as in the Reform synagogue, today special services in Conservative synagogues try to appeal to special groups of persons. Cognizant of the loss of many young Jews through assimilation, in March 1999, Sinai Temple in Los Angeles, for example, held a *Kabbalat Shabbat* service entitled "Friday Night Live," in which a rock band played not only for the social hour following the service (*Oneg Shabbat*) but for the entire service as well; apparently it worked since over two thousand young adults attended. This type of service has appeared occasionally in other Conservative synagogues, including similar *Friday Night Live* in New York City.

In the Chassidic tradition the individual tunes (*nigunim*) of particular *rebbes* have served as the chief musical contributions. Just prior to the Second World War Chassidic sects in America were bolstered by the arrival of some rabbis from Europe, who then continued to invent *nigunim*, some of which spread to all Chassidic groups throughout North America and even to other groups of Jews.

Perhaps the most creative of all these teachers was Rabbi Shlomo Carlebach,[61] who was born in Berlin in 1925, the son of Rabbi Naftali Carlebach, a mitnagged rabbi in Germany and eventually the chief rabbi of Baden. Reb Naftali was open to all kinds of people and did not shy away from Chassidic Jews; he introduced his sons to the great *rebbes* of his generation, and was friends with the Tchortkover, the Shiniver, and the *Alte Rebbe* of Lubavitch, about whom later he said, "I inhaled them." As a young boy, Carlebach joined the choir in Baden. In 1939 the Carlebach family fled the Nazis, stopping en route to the United States at the yeshiva in Telz, Lithuania, where Carlebach learned Torah in the style of the Telzers for a few weeks. In New York they settled in Crown Heights, where Reb Naftali became the rabbi, moving to Manhattan in 1949 when Naftali took over Congregation Kehillath Jacob, which is now the Carlebach Synagogue on West 79th Street. The following year, Menachem Mendel Schneerson, then chief rabbi in the Chassidic Lubavitch sect, arranged for Shlomo Carlebach to travel to various yeshivas to see how others were teaching. Upon Carlebach's return to New York in 1956, he was invited to give a class on *Chassidism* at Columbia University, received the highest degree of *smicha* (ordination), and obtained his doctorate of philosophy at Columbia.

Carlebach's first pulpit was in Dorothy, New Jersey, where he was a rabbi for the egg farmers, most of them Holocaust survivors. Aside from giving the *drashot* (Torah commentary) on *Shabbat*, there wasn't much to do, so Reb Carlebach started doodling little melodies on an old piano. In 1958 he asked a performer he heard singing and playing a guitar in a café in Greenwich

---

[61] The following remarks on Carlebach are based on the biographical materials on the Carlebach Web Page edited by Jeanette Friedman with the assistance of Neila Carlebach.

Village to teach him a few chords, then "went out and bought himself a little *guitareleh*," having decided to compose songs and sing them in public. After he cut his first album *Haneshama Lach* in 1960, he began receiving invitations to sing all over the world. (He liked to say he was the first *frum* [religious] Jew in show business.) Carlebach preceded the guitar-song composers of the Reform movement by more than a decade, but his guitar songs were for non-synagogue religious occasions; the tunes by themselves, without accompaniment, soon were accepted in most Orthodox synagogues. Carlebach composed hundreds of original melodies over a thirty-six year period ending with his death in 1994, and he performed these not only to live audiences but on many audio cassettes, CDs, and videos. Most of these *nigunim* were published in *The Shlomo Carlebach Anthology* and *Shlomo Carlebach Songbook II* (both edited by Vevel Pasternak for Tara Publications), and *The Shlomo Shabbos Songbook* (*Kehilat Jacob Book*). Among many of his popular Chassidic tunes are "Esah Eini," "Od Yishama" (he began and ended his career with two settings of this wedding song), "Am Yisroel Chai," "L'ma'an Ahai" (in 1995, a New Jersey church choir sang a hymn with this melody for a visit by the Pope), "Mkimi," "Tov l'Hodos," "Ein Kelukeinu," "Asher Boro" (a melody for the traditional wedding liturgy), "Unvenei" (Carlebach's final musical composition), and "Niggun." Other composers of popular *nigunim* sung by American Chassidim include Chaim Banet, Moseh Laufer, Baruch Chait, Ben Zion Shenker, Shmuel Brazil, Seymour Rockoff, Yigal Calek, and Shlomo Simcha.

Importation of European Cantors 1880-1950 and American-born Cantors

By the mid-nineteenth century a few well-trained European cantors began to arrive in America. Chief among these were Leon Sternberger from Warsaw, who went to Anshe Chesed Synagogue in New York in 1849; Ignatius Kitterman from Cracow, who was hired by B'nei Jeshurun in 1855, and his successor Judah Kramer from Vilna, who came to B'nei Jeshurun in 1858. The first important Eastern European cantors to arrive in America were Baruch Schorr from Lvov, Poland, who worked in New York from 1891 to 1896; Pinhas Minkowsky from Odessa, who first spent the year 1897 to 1898 in New York and then, after returning to Europe, came back to America (Boston) from ca. 1919 to 1924; Israel Cooper who came from Vilna to America in 1900; Abraham Frachtenberg (1861-1927) who came from Galicia to America in 1901; and Zeidel Rovner (*né* Margovsky, 1856-1946) who arrived in America in 1912. Each came with his own compositions and rarely performed the works of others.

At the beginning of the twentieth century Eastern European synagogues in America had star cantors who overshadowed their rabbis; congregations hired the star cantor to attract new immigrants. These cantors sang opera-like arias as well as traditional *chazzanuth*. A cantor was often more valuable than a rabbi because, if he had a good voice, he would bring in a crowd who could help pay the mortgage. Many immigrant Jews were apathetic to their religion in Europe but through sentiment, stirred by the beautiful and nostalgic voice of the great cantor, they could be lured into a traditional American synagogue. This was true not only in New York, but even in such outlying cities as Milwaukee before World War I.

The immigration of such cantors continued until the outbreak of World War II. Among their number who settled in New York and achieved legendary status were Berele Chagy (1892-1954), Mordecai Hershman (1888-1940), Adolph Katchko (1886-1958), Pavel Kwartin (1874-1953), Moshe Koussevitzky (1899-1966), David Roitman (1885-1944), Lieb Glantz (1898-ca. 1970; Glantz also served Sinai Temple in Los Angeles), and Joseph Shlisky (1894-ca. 1954). Chicago boasted its own brilliant cantors who, despite lacking the fame of those who worked in the New York area, could match the latter in all other matters.[62] These included Joseph Giblichman (1887-1954) who was born in Volotshisk, studied *chazzanuth* as well as musical theory, voice, and harmony in Vienna, and came to Chicago in 1923, where he served the Sfardishe Shul and later the South Side Hebrew Congregation; Todros Greenberg (1893-1976), a prolific composer of chant, who was born in a village near Berdichev, served as a *meshorer* with his uncle, then came to Chicago where he continued to sing after he developed blindness, though he held no regular post; Aaron Kritz, baritone, who was born in Kremenitz in 1886, studied in London and came to Chicago in 1915, where he worked at several synagogues; Tevele Cohen, who came from Ekaterinoslav Russia, to Chicago at a young age and sang in his father's synagogue choir at Congregation Poal Zedeck Anshe Sfard; A. Manovitz, who possessed a bass-baritone voice with a brilliant upper register; Pavel Slavensky, cantor at Temple Sholom from 1952 to 1964, who learned his craft in his native Hungary; Moses Silverman (d. 1986), a lyric tenor, who as a boy was in the choirs of Roitman, Hershman, and Rosenblatt, and who later was cantor at Conservative Anshe Emet Synagogue for forty-six years; and Joshua Lind (1890-1973), a pupil of Zeidel Rovner, who first immigrated from Russia to New York just before World War I and then to Chicago in the 1930s.

As time went on new rabbis with credentials arrived from Europe. The rise of the American rabbinate started as a tug-of-war with the *chazzanim*, who had achieved status within American communities before rabbis were on the scene. The rabbis were beginning to win when the wave of star cantors began arriving at the end of the nineteenth century. Despite the intrigues of small congregations that sought to hire star cantors to raise memberships and pay off mortgages, rabbis at most larger and more established American congregations had by this time passed their cantor in their congregation's esteem. The rabbinate had achieved a new image on a par with the Protestant clergy, and by the 1950s the cantorate had lost much of its earlier status in comparison to the rabbinate. Just as the earlier *chazzan* and the subsequent rabbi had altered their beings to suit the peculiar needs of American Jewish communities, so the newer cantor had to change to be a leader of the new kind of American Jews of the late twentieth century.

By the 1980s the last of the great Golden Age cantors were either dead or retired, and there were no more cantors coming from the decimated Jewish communities of Europe. American boys were no longer trained in the Orthodox choirs of devoted immigrants that were so common at the beginning of the twentieth century. Only a handful of younger cantors emerged. Rather, young Jewish boys with good voices, as a rule aimed not at a career in a synagogue but rather in opera, pop music, or other forms of secular music. The examples of Jan Peerce (Jacob Pincus

---

[62] The history of Chicago's cantorate may be found in Moses A. Silverman, "The Cantorate," in *The Sentinel's History of Chicago Jewry 1911-1986* (Chicago: Sentinel Publishing Co., n.d.), 184-86; Bea Kraus, "The Cantors: Gifted Voices Remembered," in *Doris Minsky Memorial Fund Publication*, no. 3 (Chicago: Chicago Jewish Historical Society, n.d.); and in Zaludkowski. Special thanks to Dan Sharon and Joy Kingsolver, Archivist, Chicago Jewish Archives, Spertus Institute of Jewish Studies.

Perelmuth, 1904-84) and his brother-in-law Richard Tucker (Reuben Ticker, 1913-75), both stars at the Metropolitan Opera in New York and occasional cantors in various locales, were the most renowned. The barriers to such careers that characterized Europe in the eighteenth and nineteenth centuries did not exist in America. A new means for continuing the tradition of the cantor, therefore, had to be established by the late 1940s and early 1950s: the cantorial schools of America.

American Jewish Religious Musical Organizations and Institutions

Before World War I American Jews relied on European-trained cantors and music directors or on the Christian musicians in their communities. The need to come together to discuss common issues and to deal with the dichotomy between a European tradition and an American tradition caused cantors, the purveyors of Jewish liturgical music, to form organizations through which to share their problems. The most significant such group in the nineteenth century was the Jewish Ministers Cantors Association of America (in Yiddish: *Chazonim Farband*) which was founded in 1894 in New York and which helped bring together cantors mostly from the East Coast, including Reform, Conservative, and Orthodox. This group continued well into the twentieth century and produced an important history of the cantorate in 1924.[63] By the 1950s, however, it was largely replaced by the new denominational organizations mentioned below. At the turn of the century, in 1903, the Conservative Synagogue movement founded the Cantor's Association of America as another such group.

During the two decades between the two world wars, the synagogue musicians in America, now considerably more numerous than before the Second World War, expanded their efforts to organize themselves. The cantors, whether ordained in Europe or not ordained at all, formed national and regional groups. By 1920 Reform congregations appealed to the Hebrew Union College to train not only rabbis but Jewish cantors, organists, and choirs as well, and while little was accomplished at the time in those areas, the school hired one of the most prominent Jewish musicologists, Abraham Idelsohn, to teach at the College and, in 1925, the Reform cantors did organize their own Board of American Hazzan Ministers. Rabbi Stephen Wise responded more positively, bringing Binder to teach cantillation at his New York school, the Jewish Institute of Religion. At the end of the decade, in 1930 the Cantors Cultural Organization was founded to promote Jewish education.

After World War II it became apparent that American Jews could no longer delay in organizing themselves if they were to have synagogue music in the future—the endless source of European Jewish musicians had dried up. The first need was to have certified, trained cantors to lead the way. Those who were already in the profession needed to be certified so that synagogues would have some assurance that a newly hired cantor really knew his profession. The cantors needed to decide what criteria were essential for a certified cantor and they needed a forum to establish these criteria. Thus, in 1947 the Conservative cantors of America organized the Cantors Assembly of America, in 1953 the Reform cantors organized the American Conference of Certified Cantors, and in 1960 the Orthodox cantors organized the Cantorial Council of America.

---

[63] Rosen, ed., *History of Hazanuth.*

In addition, new schools were organized to train new generations of cantors. After World War II it became imperative that America train its own cantors. At first an attempt was made to open a non-denominational school for Jewish cantors to fill the void created by the Holocaust in Europe, which had provided America with its trained cantors prior to the War. But the different denominations could not agree on some points, so the three main groups opened their own schools.

The Hebrew Union College-Jewish Institute of Religion, the Reform rabbinical school which combined the Cincinnati Hebrew Union College with the New York Jewish Institute of Religion, organized its School of Sacred Music in New York in 1948 with the express purpose of training Reform cantors and certifying them. The school was established under the leadership of Eric Werner who had become Idelsohn's successor; Abraham Franzblau was its first director. By 1998 it had trained, certified, and placed over two hundred American cantors. Yeshiva University's Cantorial Training Institute (renamed The Philip and Sarah Belz School of Jewish Music) trains Orthodox cantors, and the Cantors' Institute (since 1952) and the College of Jewish Music of the Jewish Theological Seminary of America train Conservative cantors.

Furthermore, to disseminate and perpetuate the great traditions of Jewish music at the local synagogues it was necessary after World War II to publish Jewish music which could then be purchased by certified cantors, organists, choir directors, and any person responsible for the music of the service. The most important publisher of this music has been Transcontinental Music Corporation, founded by Joseph Freudenthal (1903-64), who was born in Germany and came to America in 1938.

The situation at Reform Temple Emanuel B'ne Jeshurun (1200 families) in Milwaukee was typical of the immediate post-War period. This leading Milwaukee synagogue had had no cantors since the late nineteenth century[64] and had instead a professional Christian organist and choir. In 1948 it hired an uncertified immigrant cantor. While he knew much of the liturgy, he had no advanced training in *nusach* and no awareness of American traditions, and proved to be incapable of adjusting to the needs of an American Reform congregation. After his release in 1951, a new cantor was sought—this time one of the first graduates of the Reform school, Sol Altshuler (1917-64). An American-born tenor who turned from a promising opera career to the synagogue, Altschuler proved ideal for a congregation redefining and rediscovering Jewish liturgical music. He was trained to work with this kind of situation and was educated in traditional *nusach*, as well as in all the developments in American Jewish music of the previous hundred years.

After half a century of the existence of the cantorial schools and of the certification processes, the situation of the cantorate in America changed radically from that before 1945. By the 1990s the vast majority of professional cantors were in the Reform and Conservative movements, with only a handful serving Orthodox synagogues. In the Chicago area, for example, of sixty-four synagogues studied in 1998,[65] twenty-three had at least one cantor alongside the rabbi (one of those, Conservative synagogue Anshe Emet, had two cantors) and two additional synagogues had a cantor and no rabbi, two congregations had a cantorial soloist, and thirty-seven synagogues

---

[64] Instead it had two to three ordained rabbis and a separate educator.

[65] This represents slightly more than half the Chicago-area synagogues listed by Rachel B. Heimovics, *The Chicago Jewish Source Book* (Chicago: Follett, 1981), 90-113, which, though not complete, gives enough cross section to give a good picture of the situation in Chicago.

had no professional cantor or cantorial soloist. Only two traditional or Orthodox synagogues had cantors while the remaining twenty-four cantors were split nearly evenly between employment in Reform and Conservative synagogues. Twenty-five Orthodox Synagogues, as opposed to six Reform, four Conservative, and two other, had no cantors. Almost all the Conservative and Reform cantors—especially the younger ones—were trained in the cantorial schools in New York, and there is considerable uniformity among them in repertory and in approach to the functions of being a modern American cantor (see chapter 7).

Organists and Choirs ca. 1920-70

Since organs were brought into the synagogue over the protest of more traditional Jews only in the mid-nineteenth century, there was not a tradition of Jewish organists. In Berlin in 1815, Israel Jacobson caused a sensation when he used the organ in services in private homes, but from 1818 on, when Hamburg's Reform temple included an organ, there is a continual history of the use of the organ by some Jews in their worship services. In France there were a number of Jews who played the organ in temples; probably the most distinguished was the concert pianist and composer Charles-Henri Valentin Alkan (1813-88), who was offered the position of organist at the temple rue Notre Dame de Nazareth in Paris in 1851 and again in 1854 but declined.[66]

In America nearly all synagogue organists even into the late twentieth century were Christian. One exception was Max Braun, organist of Oheb Shalom synagogue in Newark at the turn of the twentieth century. Other noted exceptions during the later twentieth century included immigrants Berlinski, Fromm, Sargon and some of the other music directors who are not cantors. Jacobi, also not a cantor, was the rare American-born Jewish organist. Jacob Beimel (1880-1944), on the other hand, was a famous cantor, choir director, and professional secular musician, first in Europe and then in New York and Philadelphia, who composed *Organ Music for Jewish Worship* (New York: Transcontinental, 1951). To help direct these organists in choice of repertory and in other problems associated peculiarly with Reform synagogues, the Guild of Temple Musicians was founded. One of the rare American-born Jewish organists was Henry S. Jacobs (1907-64), who was music director of Temple Sinai in New Orleans from 1939 until his death. Later in the twentieth century composers of organ music for the synagogue included Robert Starer, Jack Gottlieb, Michael Isaacson, Mary Jeanne Van Appledorn, and Robert Strassburg, among others.

Orthodox congregations in America had, since the 1880s, many cantors who were competent choir directors and who modeled their choirs on either the *meshorerim* of Eastern Europe or on the four-part choirs of the large synagogues in such centers as Berlin, Vienna, or Odessa. Choir directors in Reform synagogues often were not cantors and not even Jewish. Beginning in 1922 under the leadership of Abraham Binder, American Reform rabbis were taught the importance of Jewish music and the need to hire Jewish musicians to restore the tradition. During the 1920s there was a gradual improvement in the quality of choir directors in Reform synagogues. Some of these during this time were Herman Wohl, Jacob Margulies, Meyer Machtenberg, and Abraham Binder himself. The traditional *nusach* was restored through the hiring of Eastern European Jewish musicians who then directed the music of the services. The old melodies were

---

[66] J. Baron, "A Golden Age," 145.

brought back and the concept of synagogue rhythm—much freer than that in the Protestant Church—was again made the cornerstone of new Jewish music. Binder and Beimel worked for the revival of congregational singing.[67] At first this seemed a natural part of the revival of traditional Jewish music, but then the concepts of choir and congregational singing were recognized as antithetical. This antithesis remains a problem today for American synagogues, particularly Reform and Conservative ones.

New Sephardim (Oriental Jews) and Their Music

When the new Sephardim arrived in America at the end of the nineteenth century and beginning of the twentieth, they did not feel at home worshipping in Ashkenazic synagogues because of differences in liturgy, pronunciation of Hebrew, and music.[68] Among the Eastern Sephardim in this group were not only those from Greece and Turkey but also those commonly referred to as "Oriental" Jews, that is, Jews from Iraq, Iran, Syria and other areas east of the Mediterranean Sea, who shared many characteristics with the other Sephardim but did not actually trace their ancestry to Spain. They were also ostracized by old, established Sephardim in such congregations as Shearith Israel in New York because they physically were different (darker complexions), they were far less educated and skilled in modern occupations, and their music was conditioned by centuries of exposure to Islamic and Middle Eastern musical styles and melodies which the older Sephardic Jews had not experienced. In New York, where the number of new Sephardim was the largest, each group of Sephardim formed its own synagogue or place of worship based on the common origins of its members. Gradually over the twentieth century the Sephardic community—both old and new—has come together for common cultural and religious purposes, though sharp divisions still exist particularly where the immigrants are the most recent to arrive.

The Jews who left Aleppo, Syria, and settled in New York in the early twentieth century brought with them their traditional music and musical practices, which they have retained to the present despite the assimilationist tendencies of many Ashkenazic Jews in New York. There is little difference between their music and that of the Aleppo Jews who, at the same time, migrated to Mexico or Israel.[69] Cantors lead the services in the synagogue and while in the past they were mostly traditional *shaliach tzibbur* (i.e., not professional or paid), today they are frequently professional cantors imported from Israel. Just as in Orthodox Ashkenazic services, while women often attend services and even, as little girls, sit with the men, the men constitute the *minyan* and are responsible for all aspects of the service.

The most unusual feature of the Aleppo service is the singing of *pizmonim* or *piyyutim*, whose tunes mostly originated in secular, non-Jewish (mostly Arabic) sources. Jewish poets

---

[67] Binder, *Studies*, 161.

[68] For specifics on the New Sephardic community see Joseph M. Papo, *Sephardim in Twentieth Century America: In Search of Unity* (San Jose, CA: Pelé Yoetz Books, 1987).

[69] The most thorough study of the musical practices of these Aleppo Jews is by Kay Kaufman Shelemay, *Let Jasmine Rain Down: Song and Remembrance among Syrian Jews* (Chicago/London: University of Chicago Press, 1998); see also her extensive bibliography.

take the tunes and add stylized Hebrew poems which suit a particular family and occasion; the most highly regarded poets were Raphael Taboush (1873-1919, born in Aleppo and died in Cairo), Moses Ashear (1877-1940, born in Aleppo, immigrated to Brooklyn in 1912, where he died), Eliyahu Menaged (1890-1964, immigrated to New York in 1912), and Naphtali Tawil (1902-63, born in Jerusalem, immigrated to New York in 1912). The highly personal nature and pervasiveness of these tunes and their texts affect both liturgical music and the music of social activities outside the synagogue and often in the home. The tunes are usually sung by a group of men in unison or in responsorial style, and many women know the tunes as well. Some of the tunes are so popular that regular parts of the liturgy, such as the Kaddish, are sung to them; cantors, including Isaac Cain in Mexico, have added to the Arabic tunes popular Western melodies, even raiding Broadway musicals, Beethoven sonatas and Rachmaninov concertos— reenacting the trends in nineteenth century Reform synagogues. Whereas the Reform used the borrowed sources without essential change, the Syrian-American singer demonstrates his creativity by improvising around the tune in Arabic fashion.

The Arabian theories of *maqam* have been adapted to all aspects of chanting in the Syrian synagogue, and there are strict practices of cantillation based on the *maqam* suitable for a particular time of year or for a particular life-cycle event. Another unusual aspect of the Syrian ritual are the *bakkashot* (paraliturgical hymns in Hebrew sung in early Sabbath morning hours) by members of the congregation as they arrive in the synagogue, as much as six hours before the service proper begins.[70] The American Syrian Jews, especially in Brooklyn, enjoy a festive *Sebet* (literally, Sabbath), which is a lengthy celebration in the home following *Shabbat* morning services consisting primarily of the singing of *pizmonim*.[71]

Despite their small numbers—some 30,000 arrived from 1900 to 1924—the New Sephardim have spread throughout the country, in large measure owing to specific relocation plans. Although none of these communities has been studied in such detail as the Syrians in New York, we can make a few observations on them. In all cases the first order of business of any congregation was to have a knowledgeable prayer and Torah chanter, which was often done by a lay person, by a rabbi, or by a cantor. For example, in Detroit, where there were only a handful of New Sephardim before 1935, the laity ran its own services in the spaces provided by the Ashkenazim. Cincinnati boasted a much larger community of fifty families; from 1900 to 1933 services were led by Rabbi Gaigir, and from 1933 to 1945 lay persons sang the service. Indianapolis started receiving the New Sephardim in 1912 and their services were led by Rabbi Michael Albagli, who served as cantor and teacher until 1948. In Seattle Rev. David Behar was originally both a cantor and teacher at Congregation Ezra Bessaroth until 1939; today that congregation's cantor, Isaac Azose, keeps the tradition intact. Cantor Jack Maimon served the Sephardic community of Portland, Oregon (founded 1909) for over forty years. When the Moroccan synagogue of Los Angeles was established in the 1970s, congregation Em Habanim in North Hollywood was served by Chazzan Solomon Ben Shitreet.[72]

---

[70] Shelemay, *Let Jasmine*, 255.

[71] In Mexico City the Syrian Jews do not celebrate an elaborate *Sebet* on *Shabbat* but rather on special joyous occasions such as a wedding.

[72] Papo, 294-95.

Developments since 1970

While the development of art music for the American synagogue was primarily in the hands of composers and music directors, only a few cantors also participated in this. Most notably, Max Wohlberg, who by the 1970s was regarded as the dean of American cantors, composed his service *Chemdat Shabbat* in 1970 primarily for use in the Conservative synagogue. It was, like Binder's services, an attempt to involve the congregation in song with the cantor.

Perhaps the most prolific composer of synagogue music in an artistic, yet traditional, vein during the decade before 1970 is Cantor Charles Davidson. Born in 1929, he is cantor at Conservative Congregation Adath Jeshurun in Philadelphia. Among his works are *Chassidic Sabbath* (1961) for cantor, mixed choir, and organ; *And David Danced Before the Lord* (1966), a Sabbath service for cantor, mixed choir, and orchestra (or piano or organ); *Libi b'mizrach* (1972), a *Sephardic Service for the Sabbath* for cantor, congregation, unison and part choir, with optional organ, flute, and Israeli drum; *Kol Ya'akov* (1978), a Sabbath eve service for cantor, congregational choir (sopranos, altos, and men), and accompaniment; *The Hush of Midnight Music: an American S'lichot Service* (1986) for cantor, congregation, keyboard, lead guitar, fender bass, and percussion; a "Kedushah" (1994) on a text from the Reform prayer book *Gates of Prayer*; and many other works.

Another prolific composer of American synagogue music is Samuel Adler (b. 1928). During his tenure in Dallas from 1953 to 1966 as synagogue music director he wrote *Shir Chadash*, a Sabbath evening service for two or three-part choir (1960), *Be-Sha'aray Tefila* (1963), and *Shiru Ladonoy*, a solo service for Friday evening (1965). Adler wound up at the Eastman Conservatory of Music, where he taught composition and became a distinguished theorist. He continues to write synagogue compositions, such as *Shiray Yeladim*, a collection of synagogue songs for young children sponsored by the Union of American Hebrew Congregations (1970), *Yamim Noraim*, for Yom Kippur (1972), *Havdalah* (1986) for mixed choir and keyboard with two optional flutes, *L'Chah Dodi* (1987) for cantor, mixed choir, organ and flute (based on the text from the Reform prayer book *Gates of Prayer*), *Twelve Songs of Praise* (1988) for unison choir or congregation and organ, *Psalm 146* (1989) for mixed choir and organ, *Y'varechicha* (1990) for mixed choir and organ, *Yamim Noraim* (1990) for cantor, choir and organ, and *Mah Tovu* (1994) for cantor, mixed choir and organ. He also has the semi-liturgical choral works for Hanukah, "Praise Thy Saving Power" and "The Flames of Freedom," both from 1984.

One of the most popular synagogue compositions of the late twentieth century is Ben Steinberg's *Sholam Rav*. Steinberg was born in 1930 in Winnipeg, Canada, and educated in Toronto. For many years he has served as Director of Music for Reform Temple Sinai in Toronto and has written many liturgical works, including five services for solo, choir and organ (for example, *Pirchay Shir Kodesh* [1964] and *Simchat Hashabbat* [1976]). Among his works are *A Ben Steinberg Solo Collection* (1988), for high or medium voice and keyboard (including "Mah Tovu," "Ahavat Olam," "Lo yareiu," "R'tzei vim'nuchateinu," "Yism'chu," "Vayomer David l'Avigayil," and "Hinei yamim baim"); *Kol shalom*, settings for the Sabbath evening service (1991) for cantor, choir, and organ with optional string orchestra; *Avodat Hakodesh*, settings for the Sabbath morning service (1992) for cantor, choir, and organ with optional woodwind quartet accompaniment; *Meditation and Mah y'didot mishk'notecha* (1990) for cantor, mixed choir, and organ; *Shomeir Yisrael*, settings for the Sabbath evening service (1995) for cantor, narrator, choir, and organ with optional chamber orchestra; and Psalm 24: *S'eu sh'arim* (1995) for mixed choir and organ. In addition Steinberg has written a religious cantata, *The Crown of Torah* (1993) for cantor, narrator, mixed choir, children's choir, and instrumental ensemble (flute, oboe, cello, harp, organ); and the religious concert pieces *Z'mirot* (1994) for two voices, flute, and piano. In 1961 he published a manual for directors of junior choirs in synagogues: *Together Do They Sing* (Union of American Hebrew Congregations, 1961).

Robert Starer, whose contributions to art music in the synagogue date from well before 1970, continued with such works as *Lecha Dodi* and psalms for chorus, violin, violoncello, and harp (1988). Jack Gottlieb, who stepped out of the synagogue as a music director before 1970, has continued writing art music for Reform or Conservative synagogue worship in such pieces as *Four Affirmations* (1983) for choir, soloist (alto or baritone) and brass sextet (or organ), Invocation-*Tsur Yisrael*, Declaration from "On a note of triumph" by Norman Corwin, and *Celebration-Half-Kaddish*); *Ma Tovu* (1979) for medium voice and piano; *Shachar Avakesh'cha* on words by Solomon ibn Gabirol (1979) for medium voice and piano; and Psalm 23 from *Psalmistry* (1985) for mixed choir, two flutes, and organ (or piano). William Sharlin (b. 1920) was in the first graduating class of the Reform cantorial school in 1951 and served Leo Baeck Temple in Los Angeles for many years as cantor. Trained to utilize the various traditions of Reform music in his services, Sharlin also began composing his own music for the liturgy, though it remained in manuscript until after 1970. In 1973 he published a setting of *Sholom Aleychem* for two-voice choir with optional accompaniment of guitar (letter notation is provided). *Elohai n'shamah* (1992), a portion of *Gates of Prayer*, the Reform prayer book of the 1970s, is a setting for cantor, mixed choir and keyboard, and *Shir Hashirim* (Song of Songs, 1985) is scored for solo voice and keyboard.

Cantor Stephen Richards was born in New York City in 1935, educated at Columbia University, and trained at the School of Sacred Music of the Hebrew Union College. He has served congregations in Rochester, Indianapolis, Phoenix, and San Francisco (Congregation B'nai Tikvah); in addition he was an editor for Transcontinental Publishing Company and was a faculty member of the School of Sacred Music. Among his many liturgical works is *Echad*, a Friday evening service for cantor, choir, congregation, and instrumental ensemble with no spoken words, which was premiered at Central Synagogue in New York in May 1997 and repeated at Larchmont Temple in March 1998. Simon Sargon, who has been Director of Music at Temple Emanu-El in Dallas since 1974, also has an extensive career composing for the synagogue. Born in Bombay, India, in 1938, raised in Boston, educated at Brandeis University and at Julliard, Sargon has lectured extensively and is also a pianist; among other engagements, he was singer Jennie Tourel's accompanist from 1963 to 1971. Richard Wernick (b. 1934) is among a group of concert hall composers who after 1970 also wrote for the liturgy, in Wernick's case *And on the Seventh Day*, a service for cantor and percussion, in 1979.

A little younger than the above is Michael Isaacson (b. 1942) who has written many interesting liturgical compositions, often with instruments other than organ. The works with the most unusual settings are *Hegyon Libi*, a Sabbath evening service for cantor, two-part choir, string quartet and organ (1969); *Nishmat Chayim*, a Sabbath evening Reform service for cantor, treble choir, organ and woodwind quintet (1984); *Kol Sasson*, a marriage service for cantor, organ, soprano recorder and percussion (1972); *Bayom Hahu* for cantor (medium voice), unison choir, flute, keyboard, and optional guitar (1982); and, in keeping with the folk song liturgies of the 1970s, *Avodat Amamit*, a folk service for voice with guitar (1974). More traditional settings are *Enosh* for the High Holidays, for cantor, woman's choir and organ (1990); *Sim Shalom*, a Reform service for Sabbath morning and the High Holidays, for solo (medium voice), mixed choir (SATB) and keyboard (1986); and his *Kaddish* for *S'lichot*, scored for cantor, mixed choir and piano (1979). He also composed special liturgical works with original text by Kerry Baker for his son and daughter: *B'ni* (1978) and *Biti* (1982), both for medium voice and harp with alternate guitar chording. In addition to composing, Isaacson has also produced *Ten Lessons in Composing Jewish Music*, commissioned by the Jewish Music Commission of Los Angeles, designed to help would-be composers of Jewish music acquire a basic understanding of what makes a good piece of Jewish music and what cliches are to be avoided. Isaacson teaches a course on this subject at the University of Judaism in Los Angeles.

Bonia Shur was born in Latvia in 1923 and came to the United States via Israel in 1960. He was well established as a composer of orchestral music, movie music, and music for television when, in 1974, he was appointed Director of Liturgical Arts at Hebrew Union College-Jewish Institute of Religion in Cincinnati. As a teacher of many rabbis he has had a large influence on the course of Reform synagogue music during the last quarter of the twentieth and into the twenty-first century. Among his many compositions are a *Sabbath Eve Service* (1980), a *Sabbath Morning Service* (1984), *Four Settings of Mi Chamochah* (1984), *Yesh Kochavim* (1995), and many individual items included in anthologies. The folk-like character of his settings, particularly his *Vshomru*, have made his music popular with many congregations.

What was particularly new in the development of art music in the synagogue since 1970 was the introduction of women composers. Miriam Gideon (1906-96) was the first major woman composer of Jewish art music for the synagogue. Born in Colorado, she studied in New York and Boston with, among others, Roger Sessions and Lazare Saminsky, and taught at the Jewish Theological Seminary in New York as well as at the Manhattan School of Music. Her first *Sacred Service* was written for David Good, Music Director of The Temple (Reform) in Cleveland, Ohio, in 1970; it is scored for four soloists, mixed choir, and an instrumental ensemble of flute, oboe, bassoon, trumpet, viola, cello and organ. The text, mostly in Hebrew, is based on the Friday evening Sabbath service. Gideon's later Sabbath service, *Shirat Miriam L'Shabbat* (Miriam's Song for the Sabbath) was commissioned by Conservative Park Avenue Synagogue of New York in 1974 and is scored for cantor, mixed choir, and organ.[73] In that composition Gideon circumvents the free serial techniques adopted in her earlier liturgical music for a diatonic idiom, and she culls traditional elements, for example, prayer modes, cantillations, and even folk songs from the Middle East.

Shortly thereafter Judith Lang Zaimont in Minneapolis wrote her *Sacred Service* (1976). Much younger than Gideon (she was born in 1945), Zaimont studied with Hugo Weisgall, Otto Luening, and Andre Jolivet. The 1976 work is based on the third service of the Reform *Union Prayer Book* and is scored for baritone solo, mixed chorus, and orchestra. Zaimont also has written *A Woman of Valor* for mezzo soprano and string quartet in memory of Bronia Kwartin, wife of the famous cantor.

[73] Information on five Jewish women composers comes from Emily Freeman Brown, "Jewish Liturgical Music by American Women Since 1945," in *Proceedings of the First International Conference on Jewish Music*, ed. Steve Stanton and Alexander Knapp (London: City University Department of Music, 1997), 19-25.

Maxine Warshauer wrote her *Shacharit* as a doctoral dissertation for the University of South Carolina; it is scored for soprano and tenor soloists, narrator, mixed choir, and orchestra (with an enlarged percussion section). Because she is an Orthodox Jew, she could not consider writing this work for performance as part of the traditional synagogue service, and as a result she does not quote the liturgy exactly, but in fact the composition could be performed in Conservative and Reform synagogues. Warshauer, who graduated from Harvard University and the New England Conservatory of Music, studied under Mario Davidovsky, William Thomas MacKinley, and Richard Goodwin.

In addition to synagogue services and prayers composed as classical art music, there are also jazz settings and settings that use other modern, popular musical idioms. Jack Gottlieb, for example, has written jazz-oriented synagogue compositions, Michael Isaacson writes in a Hollywood style, Sherwood Goffin (a New York cantor) composes in a pop music style of the 1980s, Cantor Martin Davidson also writes in a pop music style, Ralph Schlossberg is a singing rock cantor, Deborah Katchkoo-Zimmerman (a conservative cantor) mixes blues and pop with Jewish styles, and Yeduda Julio Glantz prefers to mix Latin American, South African, European, and Israeli styles. Conservative Cantor Sol Zim created a rock service *David Superstar* in 1974 which, despite intense disapproval by his colleague Cantor David Putterman, Zim hoped would move from revolutionary to traditional within a generation.[74] Margot Stein, head of New Legends, is the co-founder of *Shabbat Unplugged* and also founded the group Miraj with Geela Rayzel Raphel and Juliet Irene Spitzer, with whom she has produced the CD, *A Moon Note*. Canadian Hanna Tiferet combines Hebrew and English folk ballads with calypso, Hassidic, and jazz styles in her Jewish liturgical music. A country music cantorial soloist in Los Angeles is Doug Cotler, whose songs include new lyrics and adaptations of traditional Hebrew designed primarily for children. His inspiration was Kinky Friedman, the most well-known Jewish country singer. Cross-over music (classical art music mixed with popular) is represented by Cantor Charles Davidson's *The Hush of Midnight Music: An American S'lichot Service* (see above). Ben Sidran of Madison, Wisconsin, a jazz musician who attends High Holiday services at Gates of Prayer, the oldest synagogue building in Wisconsin, has composed music for the alternative services which was recorded in the early 1990s and released in 1993. Sidran sings, along with the congregation's children's choir and a few other voices, accompanied at times (but not all at once) by various instruments such as guitar, percussion, vibes, piano, harmonica, bass clarinet, clarinet, flute, steel drums, percussion, trumpet, violin, shofar, electric keyboard, and accordion. The tone color and style are his own version of modern jazz, but the language is that of the synagogue and he incorporates some traditional melodies and motives.

While the art composers have written primarily for professional musicians and expect their liturgical music to be performed for the congregation, rabbis have felt a greater need to bring the congregation back into singing the services. Ever since Binder's efforts to reestablish traditional Jewish music in the American Reform synagogue, there have been some composers who have concentrated on providing practical compositions for use at regular worship services where the congregation participates. Some art composers have written practical services with amateur choirs in mind, and while many of these compositions are "artistic," their main raison

---

[74] Slobin, *Chosen Voices*, 216-17.

d'être has been functional. Max Janowski, for example, wrote a large collection of synagogue music for the entire liturgical year designed to be sung by members of a junior congregation (high schoolers). Many such pieces have come and gone, but a few have become standards alongside the familiar responses and prayers of Sulzer, Lewandowski, and Naumbourg. Among these are Janowski's *Avinu Malkenu* and Steinberg's *Shalom Rav*. One of the most successful composers of functional music in the 1990s has been Benjie-Ellen Schiller, a Reform cantor. She has written a complete Hebrew service (1991) for soprano cantor, amateur choir, and piano which was premiered in a synagogue in New Jersey. Most of her works are for life-cycle events.

The establishment of the National Federation of Temple Youth summer camps during the 1950s and into the 1970s brought a large number of Reform Jewish young people together in an informal Jewish setting. By the early 1970s the need for campfire songs to accompany religious services was satisfied by several talented composers, most notably Debbie Friedman, Louie Dobin, and the team of Cantor Jeff Klepper and Rabbi Dan Freelander. Their music served initially a very limited function: to provide young people with easy-to-sing songs based on popular folk styles of the 1970s with liturgical words or paraphrases of the liturgy in Hebrew or English. As the young people returned to their homes after camp sessions were over and attended their local synagogues, they wanted to continue singing their campfire liturgical songs rather than the more artistic songs their elders were singing or hearing as part of the standard synagogue liturgy. A generational split occurred, often according to taste, and certainly conditioned by familiarity. Young people consciously and willingly learned the new folk song liturgy, whereas they were not being taught the older Jewish music; whatever exposure they had to traditional music of whatever kind occurred when they were very young children. When the young people of the early 1970s became adults and began determining the music of the adult synagogues, their treasured campfire songs began to replace Sulzer, Bloch, and traditional *chazzanuth*. By 1990 Reform and some Conservative cantors were sought out also for their ability to play the guitar and lead favorite Debbie Friedman songs in the synagogue, not only for their ability to chant cantillation or psalmody monophonically or with any sort of choir.

A reaction has set in against this wholesale erasure of all former Jewish music, so that as the twenty-first century begins, a new kind of synthesized music prevails. For example, on 20 February 1998, Congregation Kol Ami of White Plains, New York, held a Friday night service typical of many Reform and some Conservative synagogues in America today. Cantor Annie Bornstein-Howard, sometimes accompanied by an organ and four-voice mixed choir, sang six traditional liturgical melodies in Hebrew or English, a *Sh'ma* by Sulzer and a *Kiddush* by Lewandowski, Ephros' *L'cha Adonai*, six prayers or responses by American art composers Binder, Freed and their more recent disciples, Debbie Friedman's *Mi Shebeirach* and Klepper's *Bayom Hahu*. Meanwhile, according to Cantor Linda Blumenthal of Congregation Temple Israel in St. Louis, Missouri, "at any given service here . . . you will most likely [hear] prayers set to music by Salomone Rossi, Soloman Sulzer, A.W. Binder, Louis Lewandowski, Max Janowski (our traditionalists), Jeffrey Klepper, Daniel Freelander, Debbie Friedman (our contemporary up-tempo composers), and Michael Isaacson, Rachel[le] Nelson, Stephen Richards, Benjamin Steinberg, Charles Davidson (our contemporary composers in a traditional style)." To the list of contemporary composers should be added Meir Finklestein (b. 1951), author of *L'dor Vador*, and Robert Solomon (b. 1947). At the 1997 biennial convention of the Union of American Hebrew Congregations in Dallas, the

Sabbath services included works by Lewandowski, Mordecai Zeira, Charles Davidson, Leon Algazi, Rachelle Nelson, Sol Zim, Doug Cotler, Richard Silverman, Jeff Klepper, Moshe Rothblum, Stephen Richards, Ben Steinberg, Jeff Klepper, Debbie Friedman, William Sharlin/Max Helfman, Simon Sargon, Ernest Bloch, David Schiff, Gershon Kingsley, Richard Cohn, David Goldstein, Andrea Jill Higgins, Michael Isaacson, and Bonia Shur. The variety would leave every congregant finding something spiritual during the service even if the music of the entire service was to some unappealing in places or without coherence. The question now is whether this mélange of musical styles is too heterogeneous for a Jewish service or whether it enhances the liturgy; the basic rule—that the liturgy and its spiritual content are the crux of the service and the music is there only to abet them—is open to scrutiny. The debate that raged a century before—Protestant church music versus traditional Ashkenazic *nusach*—has now been reformulated as popular secular music versus any traditional Jewish music (Sephardic, Yemeni, and others, as well as Ashkenazic), and the resolution seems to be to keep it all.

Suggestions for Further Reading

Binder, Abraham Wolf. *Studies in Jewish Music: Collected Writings of A.W. Binder*, ed. Irene Heskes. New York: Bloch Publishing Co., 1971.

Brown, Emily Freeman. "Jewish Liturgical Music by American Women Since 1945." In *Proceedings of the First International Conference on Jewish Music*, ed. Steve Stanton and Alexander Knapp, 19-25. London: City University Department of Music, 1997.

Heskes, Irene. *Passport to Jewish Music: Its History, Traditions, and Culture*. Westport, CT: Greenwood, 1994.

Shelemay, Kay Kaufman. *Let Jasmine Rain Down: Songs and Remembrance Among Syrian Jews*. Chicago and London: University of Chicago Press, 1998.

Slobin, Mark. *Chosen Voices: The Story of the American Cantorate*. Urbana: University of Illinois Press, 1989.

12 ‖ Secular Jewish Music and Musicians in North America

When Jews began to migrate to North America in large numbers at the end of the nineteenth century, many of them were drawn to music as a profession. Perhaps it was because the entertainment industry in the United States was relatively new and not closed to Jews, whereas most universities, banks, large companies, and other professions restricted, or even denied, entry to Jews. Jobs were scarce as millions of new immigrants poured into New York, Boston, Philadelphia, Baltimore, Chicago, Cleveland, and other cities of the East Coast and Middle West, and many impoverished newcomers, unwilling or unable to enter the sweatshops, turned to music as a way to earn their livelihood. Perhaps, too, it was because the creative musical talent of many Eastern-European Jews could not reach fruition in Eastern Europe where even the entertainment industry was blatantly anti-Semitic. In the new world, the Jewish immigrants could finally exercise their pent-up musical energies without restraint.

As we have seen, a traditional profession for musically talented Jews in Europe who did not want to become cantors or who did not have the preparation to be so was the *badchan*, the comic musician, but the life of the *badchan* in Europe was hard and with little financial returns. In America, the *badchan* became the Jewish singer or comedian who was much appreciated by all Americans and eventually saw financial remuneration commensurate with his or her talents. Whatever the cause, Jews emerged in the 1890s as a dominant force in much of America's new popular music and continued to play a major role throughout the twentieth century.

Before the 1890s, when the Jewish population in the U.S. was relatively small, Jews emigrating from Western Europe were able to find work in business and industry, and music was only a luxury to be patronized but not adopted as a profession. There were exceptions, however, and some Jews were involved in the popular musical culture of the nineteenth century. The most famous American musician of the nineteenth century, Louis Moreau Gottschalk (1829-69), was half Jewish. His father came from England in 1828 and may have been related to a rabbinical family there, but his mother was Roman Catholic, descended from an aristocratic Haitian family, and Louis Moreau seems never to have been involved with the Jewish communities of the many places where he was active. His father identified with the Jews of New Orleans, where he lived and where his son was born, and made regular contributions to Jewish causes there, but that seems to have been the end of it. There was nothing Jewish about any of Gottschalk's compositions, although they had a marked influence on some later American styles. His music was influenced by Chopin, Liszt, African-American rhythms and French Creole melodies, not Jewish motives.

Another important Jewish personality in American music was Henry Russell (1812-1900). Born in London into a Jewish acting family, Henry Russell was a star from childhood on. He came to the U.S. and Canada only from 1836 to ca. 1841 and again from 1843 to ca. 1845, but during these brief years he toured extensively and made major changes in American popular music. He was a one-man show, playing the piano while singing ballads of his own creation, some seventy-five being written in America. The ballads ranged from sweet, sentimental songs, which Americans loved at that time, to political and social satires and diatribes which woke his audiences up to the evils of their society. Stephen Foster was in the audience in a Pittsburgh concert in 1843 and learned much from Russell's example of sweet, simple melodies coupled with words either of sentimentality or of clever humor. Once again, there is nothing Jewish about Russell's music, but his engagement in social causes as part of musical entertainment seems to have been a Jewish trait, since that was the fare of Yiddish *badchanim* in Europe.

Tin Pan Alley

The situation changed dramatically in the 1890s. In 1892 Charles K. Harris (1867-1930), a Jew living in Milwaukee, published a new song entitled "After the Ball," which revolutionized American popular music. The sheet music edition of "After the Ball" set new records for the number of copies sold—well over a million—and brought both fame and wealth to Harris. Harris soon moved to New York, where he continued to write songs, though he never was able to equal his first great success. By setting an example of shrewd business acumen in marketing the songs, he set the stage for the creation of a sheet music industry in New York that soon became known as Tin Pan Alley.

Immigrant Jews, especially in New York, saw in Harris's prosperity the chance to market their own songs and entertainment with the possibility of realizing the American dream of financial security. "After the Ball" was not a Jewish composition, but Harris did write another song that is specifically Jewish, entitled "The Rabbi's Daughter." This work deals with a common phenomenon which American Jews faced daily. The rabbi's daughter of the title has fallen in love with a Gentile, but because of her loyalty to her father and her faith, she cannot marry him. Thereupon she wilts away and dies of grief over a love that had no chance of fruition. The mood and story are similar to those in "After the Ball," but the scene has been removed from the universal to the particularly Jewish.

Tin Pan Alley flourished from 1892 until the 1940s, with a few carry-overs into the 1950s. It derived its name from a beat-up old piano in the music publishing studio of the Von Tilzer brothers on 28th Street in Manhattan, which was the heart of the music industry in New York from the 1890s until well into the twentieth century. Monroe Rosenfeld, a magazine writer, coined the term "Tin Pan Alley" to refer to this music district where the tinny sounds of pianos like that in the Von Tilzer firm could be heard.

While most of the music of Tin Pan Alley cannot be regarded as Jewish, a disproportionate number of the players in the creation of this vital form of American music were Jewish. Their names and their songs are more a part of American musical history than Jewish musical history. Among the Jewish composers of American popular music are Gus Edwards (1879-1961), famous for "By the Light of the Silvery Moon" (1909), "School Days" (1907), and "In My Merry Oldsmobile" (1907); the brothers Harry Von Tilzer (1872-1946) and Albert Von Tilzer (1878-1956) (their original name was Gumm), who between them wrote "I Want a Girl Just Like the Girl Who Married Dear Old Dad" (1911), "A Bird in a Gilded Cage" (1899), "Take Me Out to the Ball Game" (1908)—the theme song of America's national sport—and "Wait 'till the Sun Shines, Nellie" (1905); Nora Bayes (1880-1928), a popular singer whose real name was Dora Goldberg and who claimed to have written at least part of "Shine On, Harvest Moon" (1908) with her husband Jack Norworth; Louis Wolfe Gilbert (1886-1970), whose "Waiting for the Robert E. Lee" (1912) describes a South whose geography he confuses; the oft-married Joe E. Howard (1867-1961), whose wild life-style with women is immortalized in "Hello My Baby" (1899), "I Wonder Who's Kissing Her Now" (1909), and "Goodbye My Lady Love" (1904); Irving Berlin (1888-1989), the most prolific of all the Tin Pan Alley composers, whose "Alexander's Ragtime Band" (1911), "Oh How I Hate to Get Up in the Morning" (1918), "A Pretty Girl is Like a Melody" (1919), "Let's Take an Old Fashioned Walk" (1949), "God Bless America" (1938), "White Christmas" (1940), and "Easter Parade" (1933) are only a few of his most successful songs; George Gershwin (1898-1937), Berlin's only equal, whose many masterpieces include "Swanee" (1919), "Someone to Watch Over Me" (1926), "I've Got Rhythm" (1930), and "Bidin' My Time" (1930); Jerome Kern (1885-1945), famous for "Look for the Silver Lining" (1920), "Smoke Gets In Your Eyes" (1933), "Sitting Pretty" (1924), "All the Things You Are" (1939), and "Long Ago and Far Away" (1944), among others; Sam Lewis (1885-1959), known for "Dinah" (1925), "I'm Sitting On Top of the World" (1925), "Rock-A-By Your Baby with a Dixie Melody" (1918), "Five-Foot-Two, Eyes of Blue" (1925), and "My Mammy" (1920); Gus Kahn (1886-1941), whose most famous songs are "Yes Sir, That's My Baby" (1925), "Toot, Toot, Tootsie" (1922), and "Carolina in the Morning" (1922); Sammy Cahn (1913-93), among whose songs are "Shoe Shine Boy" (1936), "Can't You Just See Yourself" (1947), "Its Been a Long, Long Time" (with the refrain "Kiss Me Once, Kiss Me Twice, Kiss Me Once Again") (1945), "Let It Snow" (1945), "Five Minutes More" (1946), "Papa Won't You Dance With Me" (1947), and "Love and Marriage" (1955) popularized by Frank Sinatra; the lyricist Jack Yellen (1892-1991), whose "Happy Days Are Here Again" (1929) became the theme song of the Democratic Party of the United States; Harold Arlen (1905-86), most famous for the music to the movie *Wizard of Oz*, whose numerous songs included "I Love A Parade" (1931), "Between the Devil and the Deep Blue Sea" (1931), "I've Got the World On a String" (1932), "Stormy Weather" (1933), and "Cabin in the Sky" (1943); Frank Loesser (1901-88), whose "Once in Love with Amy" (1948), "Jingle Jangle Jingle" (1942), and "Praise the Lord and Pass the Ammunition" (1942) were among the most popular songs of the middle twentieth century; Billy Rose (1899-1966), an alias for William Rosenberg, who achieved immortality with his "Its Only a Paper Moon" (1933), "Me and My Shadow" (1927), "Barney Google" (1929), and "That Old Gang of Mine" (1923); and the lyricist E.Y. Yip Harburg (1896-1981), among whose many works is the Depression Era theme song "Brother Can You Spare a Dime," made famous by Bing Crosby. Many of these composers were also involved with shows on Broadway and with Hollywood films.

The Jewish composers and lyricists sought to create an American style of song, not a Jewish one, and they succeeded very well. Buoyed on by the new sounds of ragtime and jazz emanating originally from New Orleans and eventually from Chicago, Kansas City, and New York's African-American communities, the Tin Pan Alley musicians helped establish what has been regarded as one of America's main contributions to musical art in the twentieth century. In the process, the Jewish composers consciously avoided sounding Jewish in order to escape the demeaning atmosphere of the European ghetto and *shtetl*. Yet there were exceptions.

In his early years and even after he had established himself as one of the leading practitioners of Tin Pan Alley, Irving Berlin wrote a few songs evocative of his European and Yiddish-American background, such as "Yascha Michaeloffsky's Melody" (1928), "Yiddisha Professor" (1912), and "Cohen Owes Me Ninety Seven Dollars" (1915). In 1954 he wrote his last great song, "Count Your Blessings," which was premiered by Eddie Fisher at the American Jewish Tercentenary banquet to commemorate three hundred years of Jewish settlement in America. Although his second wife was not Jewish and he did not especially identify himself as a Jew, Berlin died as a Jew and had a Jewish funeral.

Another who felt secure enough in his North American environment to express his Jewish background was Sammy Cahn. Cahn heard a Yiddish song by Sholem Secunda sung by African-Americans in Harlem, and he was so moved by it that he redesigned the text and sought to bring it before the general American public. He managed to interest the Andrews Sisters into performing it in 1937, and immediately "Bei mir bist du sheyn" (1933) became a smash hit. A third songwriter to make clear his Jewish identity was Jack Yellen, whose Jewish songs include "Mr. Siegal, You Gotta Make It Legal," "My Mother's Sabbath Candles," and especially his greatest hit, "My Yiddishe Mama" (1925). Although Berlin, Cahn, and Yellen wrote songs with Jewish subjects, the musical style remained that of Tin Pan Alley.

American Musical Theater

Many Jewish immigrants who came to America from Eastern Europe after 1881 had experienced the new Yiddish theater in their homelands (see chapter 9). New York quickly became a new center for Yiddish theater because it was where the mass of poor Jewish refugees could feel at home, hear their own language with all its subtle nuances, and witness actors mimicking the particular experiences which they had endured. Non-Jewish American theaters posed several problems, beginning with language, but also including the high price of tickets and an ambiance with which the immigrant could not yet identify. In its greatest period, from 1890 to 1940, the New York Yiddish theater produced a remarkable array of artists, including composers and singers, whose heirs would eventually move over to the American theater and transform it.

At the turn of the twentieth century the American light musical theater—a genre regarded for many years as entirely apart from opera—consisted of two basic types of performance: the operetta and the musical revue or vaudeville. The source for the operetta was in Europe, from Offenbach's wonderful Parisian satires to the works of Vienna's Johann Strauss and London's

Gilbert and Sullivan. Offenbach had started the genre in the 1850s. The most important American composers of operettas were the non-Jew Victor Herbert (1859-1924), a native of Ireland, and Sigmund Romberg (1887-1951), a Jew born in Hungary. Romberg came to the United States in 1909 and within a few years became Herbert's chief rival and successor. His first successful operetta was *The Midnight Girl* (1914), and among his seventy such works the most famous are *Blossom Time* (1921), *The Student Prince* (1924), *The Desert Song* (1926), and *The New Moon* (1928). The writers and performers of operetta were highly trained musicians and actors, and those immigrants coming from Western and Central Europe who had conservatory and university training were at home in the operetta.

That was not the case with Russian and Polish Jews. For these immigrants, who had little or no training in the high art of music, operetta was not an option. Rather, the many musical individuals among them gravitated toward revues and vaudeville. The various individual acts of a revue could range from well-constructed, creative songs and dances composed and performed by trained artists to slapstick vignettes improvised by inspired, skilled artisans. The immigrant Jew without conservatory or university credentials found that such brief sketches did not require the structural skill or training of sustaining a large-scale composition such as a sophisticated opera or operetta. The immigrant Jew could demonstrate, however, enough inspiration and skill to entertain a low-brow audience. The *badchan* was perfect for vaudeville; a clown with dancing and singing and juggling skills, he was equipped to joke with and entertain an audience. With a long tradition of the *badchan* among the Jewish people, it was a short step for young Jewish immigrants or the children of recent immigrants to seek musical fulfillment in vaudeville and revues. They changed their names to sound more American, but their accents, their sense of humor, their identity with the average American, and their spicy Yiddish vocabulary helped change American vaudeville into a Jewish genre.

Among the many Jews who helped to shape vaudeville and revues were Eddie Cantor (= Isidore Itzkowitz, 1892-1964), Fanny Brice (= Fannie Borach, 1891-1951), Joe Smith (= Joe Sultzer, 1884-1981), Charlie Dale (= Charles Marks, 1881-1971), Al Jolson (= Asa Yoelson, 1886-1950), Sophie Tucker (Sophie Abuza, later Kalish, 1888-1966), Irving Berlin (= Israel Balin, 1888-1989), Jack Benny (= Benjamin Kubelsky, 1894-1974), and Phil Silvers (= Philip Silversmith, 1912-85). By the beginning of the twentieth century the country was linked through circuits of theaters, usually owned by a family of entrepreneurs such as the Shuberts, and these vaudeville stars would tour the nation by putting on stands of a few days to months at a theatre in one town, then another, then yet another. Most cities had buildings which would house the visiting revues or vaudevilles, and through these tours America adopted the Jewish stars as true American entertainment.

New York, as the largest American city and the one with the largest Jewish population, inevitably was the focal point of the whole vaudeville movement. Within the city successful performers often moved freely from Second Avenue's Yiddish stage to 14th Street's vaudeville. One entrepreneur played an especially important role in the history of the revue through his business genius and his recognition of the talents of many of the Jewish stars. Florenz Ziegfeld (1867-1932) was born in Chicago but concentrated his energies in New York. After producing a number of early musicals between 1899 and 1906, he decided in 1907 to begin a series of annual "Follies" or revues glamorizing the American woman. From 1907 to 1925 and again in

1927 he presented the "Ziegfield Follies" (he added his name in 1911), which gave many Jewish vaudeville stars (including most of those just listed) a start into their careers and fame.

With the help of Ziegfield a monumental change in the American musical theater came with the opening of Jerome Kern's masterpiece *Show Boat* in 1927. Kern (1885-1945) was the son of a German Jewish immigrant who belonged to and worked at Temple Emanu-El, the prominent Reform congregation in New York. As a member of the German Jewish community, Kern was brought up in an atmosphere of the academy—i.e., thoroughly trained in music and the arts in general. Among Kern's music teachers was Selma Franko, a Jew and a member of a very distinguished family of symphonic and band musicians. Thus, unlike the Russian Jewish immigrants, Kern was ready to work in operetta, but he also was attuned enough to contemporary American music—specifically the music of Tin Pan Alley and vaudeville—to integrate these American sounds into his operetta. By combining vaudeville-like music and an operetta-like story, Kern created in *Show Boat* the prototype of the modern American musical theater.

Another milestone in the development of the American musical theater was created by George Gershwin (= Jacob Gershvin or Gershovitz, 1898-1937). Born in New York to Russian Jewish immigrants, he studied the rudiments of piano and theory in a haphazard fashion and began his career at sixteen as a pianist hawking new sheet music in music stores. In 1918-19 he wrote his first revues, *Half Past Eight* and *La La Lucille*, but it was his song "Swanee," sung by Al Jolson in the revue *Sinbad* (1919) that made him famous. In the next few years he poured out numerous revues as well as a few musical comedies, and then from 1924 on he concentrated on musical comedies such as *Lady Be Good* (1924), *Strike Up the Band* (1927 and 1930), *Girl Crazy* (1930), *Of Thee I Sing* (1931), and *Let 'em Eat Cake* (1933).

Despite his obvious genius as a tunesmith, Gershwin felt somewhat insecure with his musical training, which he deemed was not adequate for him to write music that would be accepted by the high-brow musical establishment. The Jews who had made a success in operetta, opera, and symphonic music were Germans or other Central and Western Europeans, and since Gershwin was Russian, he had to prove that his origins were not a handicap to this kind of composition. In his early revues Gershwin had concentrated on cultivating the jazz idiom to which he naturally and easily related. His ambition, however, was to write highbrow art music in which he could utilize his own jazz style. He sought out music teachers to help him throughout his adult life, including Maurice Ravel and Arnold Schoenberg, in order to equip himself with the necessary tools for writing art music. His first attempt—and probably his best-known—at "serious" concert music was his 1924 *Rhapsody in Blue*, which he composed for piano and jazz band for the leading New York band director Paul Whiteman.[1] Subsequently he composed a piano concerto (1925), *Three Preludes for Piano* (1926), *An American in Paris* (1928), *Second Rhapsody* (1931), and *Cuban Overture* (1932).

The most important composition of Gershwin's drive to integrate classical and both Tin Pan Alley and African-American music for highbrow audiences was his opera *Porgy and Bess* (1935) based on a work of DuBose Heyward. Following Kern's "Show Boat," which shows Jewish compassion for the downtrodden African-American, Gershwin, too, shows empathy with the plight of poor Southern Blacks. A Jew could identify with the victims of racial prejudice because

---

[1] *Rhapsody in Blue* was also composed by Gershwin for solo piano and for two pianos. The orchestral version is an arrangement of the original jazz band score by Whiteman's composer-arranger Ferde Grofé.

he, too, had suffered a similar fate for more than a millennium. The highbrow audience of Italian, French, and German opera was not yet ready for an American opera, however, especially one sympathetic to African-Americans that dealt with drugs and illicit sex, and it took thirty years before *Porgy and Bess* was finally accepted as opera, and then often imitated. Gershwin's music for this opera took America by storm and was soon among the most beloved music any American had yet produced. It is the most frequently produced American opera in the world.

The immediate historical effect was the establishment of serious drama, heretofore limited to opera, in the arena of the American musical theater with its cast of ordinary, even poor, Americans and its jazz and ragtime rhythms set in a classical framework. Kern's *Show Boat* had challenged the non-dramatic vaudeville and revue, though not with the large orchestral sounds and remarkable harmonies of Gershwin, and the only rival on the operatic stage to a dramatic story set in America and enacted by low-class Americans—Giacomo Puccini's *Girl of the Golden West*—was an Italian opera (albeit based on an American play by David Belasco). Both *Show Boat* and *Porgy and Bess* signaled the beginning of the new American musical theater, and what Gershwin proved to himself and his immediate milieu—that Russian-American Jews could carry on this next stage alongside German-American Jews—heralded the arrival of the great Jewish-American creators of the American musical theater.

The Golden Age of the American musical began in earnest in 1943 with the premiere of Richard Rodgers and Oscar Hammerstein II's masterpiece *Oklahoma*. Richard Rodgers (1902-79), a native of New York, was trained at Columbia University and the Institute of Musical Art (now the Juilliard School of Music). Although he was raised a Jew and was a *bar mitzvah*, he ignored the vibrant Yiddish theater of the time and quickly gravitated to the traditional American revues and musical comedies and collaborated with the lyricist Lorenz Hart in creating some of the finest American songs of the 1920s and 1930s. Their most successful stage works include *On Your Toes* (1936), *Babes in Arms* (1937), and *Pal Joey* (1940). After Hart's death in 1943, Rodgers began a partnership with Oscar Hammerstein that produced the first real classics of the American musical theater: *Oklahoma!* (1943), *Carousel* (1945), *South Pacific* (1949), *The King and I* (1951), and *The Sound of Music* (1959). Until 1960 Rodgers had shown no interest in his Jewish background, but that would change later.

Both Kurt Weill (1900-50), a German-Jewish refugee from the Nazis, and Irving Berlin were also contributing to the growing musical theater repertory both before and after *Oklahoma!* Weill had written his *Dreigroschenoper* (*Three-Penny Opera*) in 1928 and his German opera *Aufstieg und Fall der Stadt Mahagonny* (*Rise and Fall of the City Mahagonny*) in 1927, both in Berlin, and when he arrived in the United States in 1935 he brought with him his experience as one of the leading satiric writers of the time. His Broadway contributions include *Knickerbocker Holiday* (1938), *One Touch of Venus* (1943), and *Love Life* (1948). Weill, the son of a cantor, demonstrated nothing Jewish in these works; he saved that for his Biblical drama *Eternal Road* (1935), in which he used "old synagogal music for the first time for a large theatrical work"[2] and in his liturgical *Kiddish*. Irving Berlin continued to write revues (for example, *As Thousands Cheer* (1933) and *This Is the Army* (1942), but after *Oklahoma!* he, too, turned to the musical with *Miss Liberty* (1949), *Call Me Madam* (1950), *Mr. President* (1962), and above all, *Annie Get Your Gun* (1946).

---

[2] Weill in a letter printed in Philip V. Bohlman, *The World Centre for Jewish Music in Palestine 1936-1940* (Oxford: Clarendon, 1992), 28.

The list of composers comprising the Golden Age of the musical (1943-70) is, once again, dominated by Jews. Among those not yet mentioned are Jule Styne (1905-94) for *Gentlemen Prefer Blonds* (1949), *Bells Are Ringing* (1956), *Gypsy* (1959), *Funny Girl* (1964), *Peter Pan* (1954), and many others as composer and/or librettist; Leonard Bernstein (1918-90; fig. 12.1) for *Candide* (1956) and *West Side Story* (1957); Frederick Loewe (1901-88) for *Brigadoon* (1947), *My Fair Lady* (1956), and *Camelot* (1960); Frank Loesser (1910-69) for *Where's Charley* (1948), *Guys and Dolls* (1950), *The Most Happy Fella* (1956), and *How to Succeed in Business Without Really Trying* (1961); and Stephen Sondheim (b. 1930) for *A Funny Thing Happened on the Way to the Forum* (1962), *Company* (1970), *Follies* (1971), *A Little Night Music* (1976), *Into the Woods* (1987), *Sweeney Todd* (1979), and others.[3]

Until 1964 these Jewish composers felt constrained to separate their Jewishness from their work on Broadway. Broadway symbolized American musical entertainment as well as legitimate American theater. To be Jewish meant Second Avenue theater, which until the 1940s had been the center of the Yiddish theater. A number of Yiddish actors, such as Paul Muni, Fanny Brice, and Mollie Picon, had traversed the barrier between the two theatrical zones, but they were careful to keep their theaters distinct: Yiddish on Second Avenue and American on Broadway. By 1964, however, Yiddish theater on Second Avenue was already dead. Furthermore, in literature Jews were beginning to express their Jewish values and ideals in English to the general American public rather than in Yiddish to a solely Jewish audience. In this setting, Jerry Bock (b. 1928) produced on Broadway the first Yiddish musical, albeit in English, that became one of the Golden Era classics: *Fiddler on the Roof*. For the first time on Broadway, a Jewish story by one of the greatest Jewish story tellers (Sholem Aleichem), in a Jewish setting, including Jewish jokes and Jewish prayers with Jewish music, was presented to a general American audience, and everyone loved it. It had over three thousand performances on Broadway before closing, has been in numerous road shows, has been staged by many regional American theaters including by high schools and even grammar schools, and was made into a film which ensured its lasting acceptance by audiences throughout the world. It has also been translated into many different languages—including Hebrew.

The significance of *Fiddler on the Roof* for all the Jewish composers of Broadway musicals was clear. The fear that the Jew had of not being accepted as a Jew was now dispelled. While Bernstein was clearing the way for Jewishness to be accepted in the concert hall, Bock had done the same for the American musical theater. Only a handful of composers, however, tried to follow Bock, since the obvious monumentality of *Fiddler on the Roof* made it risky for anyone else to try to emulate it. Bock himself was unable to follow his success with another; his attempt, *The Rothschilds* (1970), fell flat, and he retired from the scene.

Richard Rodgers, on the other hand, had a modest success with the hilarious musical comedy *Two By Two* (1970) starring Danny Kaye. Based on the Biblical story of Noah, *Two By Two* makes Noah a modern man, with all his weaknesses and foibles, who reluctantly takes on God's command to build an ark and set sail. The other characters are also made to be "real" which thereby makes the story of Noah into a plausible tale. Rodgers thus returned to his roots for one of his last shows and evinced the change that had taken place on Broadway since his earliest works in the 1930s.

---

[3] Sondheim is also a librettist and was involved in many great musicals where he was not the composer, most notably in Bernstein's *West Side Story*.

FIG. 12.1   Photograph of Leonard Bernstein,
David Putterman, and Max Helfman on the
bimah in Park Avenue Synagogue, New York

Courtesy of the Milken Archive of American Jewish Music, New York

New composers, who did not experience the insecurity of being Jewish on Broadway and knowing the success of Bock, had no trouble putting positive Jewish characters on the Broadway stage. John Kander's *Cabaret* (1968) portrayed the ominous scene in Berlin's bohemian life just prior to the Nazi takeover, and his characterization of Herr Schultz, the Jew, is extraordinarily sensitive and sympathetic. On the other hand Marvin Hamlisch's characterization of Greg (whose real name is Sidney Kenneth Beckenstein, or in Hebrew Rochmel Lev Ben Yokov Meyer Beckenstein) in *A Chorus Line* (1975) is straightforward, without any attempt to make the Jew anything other than a normal hopeful in a Broadway tryout. More recently Charles Strouse, the composer of the Broadway hits *Annie* and *Titanic*, also wrote the musical *Rags* (1987) which depicts a Jewish woman named Hershkovitz who immigrates to America with her ten-year-old son. Evoking the sounds and experiences of the Jewish immigrant to New York early in the twentieth century, Strouse includes a little klezmer music and "Kaddish" among other musical numbers.

Other American Popular Music

In addition to Tin Pan Alley and the Broadway musical theater, other areas of popular American music have had Jewish participation, although not in the same numbers. In jazz, for example, where the African-American musician has contributed the greatest share, Jews have played only a peripheral role, but nonetheless Jewish performers have abounded. In New Orleans there were Jews in some of the earliest white bands, such as "Mike" Caplan (trumpeter), Bob Stein (drummer), Joe Wolfe (pianist), Marty or Monty Korn (clarinetist), Marcus Korn (trombonist) and others.[4] The Korn brothers were the children of a rabbi, and Caplan, the last survivor of the French Opera Orchestra in New Orleans, blew the shofar at Temple Sinai in New Orleans every *Rosh Hashanah* until his death. When jazz spread to other cities, there were more Jews who filled important secondary roles, such as Willie "the Lion" Smith (1897-1973), whose father was Jewish and whose mother was African-American. Smith was an important jazz pianist in New York from the 1920s until his death; he composed stride piano music, which he recorded, and when Artie Shaw and Tommy Dorsey played arrangements of his music, he became famous. In the meantime, he also served as a cantor during the 1940s.

The most important Jewish musician in this vein was Benny Goodman (1909-86). Goodman began his musical training in Chicago at the Kehelah Jacob Synagogue and eventually had important instruction in clarinet from a classical player. But New Orleans jazz was his main inspiration in his youth, and he opted for a career in vaudeville playing jazz clarinet. Because by the early 1920s many of the greatest jazz performers, such as King Oliver, Louis Armstrong, and especially Johnny Dodds and Bix Beiderbecke, were performing regularly in Chicago, he was able to hear the best early jazz. Goodman played in numerous bands and finally formed his own band in 1934. By now the big band had replaced the smaller jazz ensemble, and he hired the great African-American band leader and pianist Fletcher Henderson—a major racial breakthrough at that time—to arrange earlier jazz works for the larger group. In 1935 he established a new style of "swing" music,

---

[4] Bruce B. Raeburn, "Jewish Jazzmen in New Orleans, 1890-1940: An Overview," *The Jazz Archivist* 12 (May 1997): 1-12.

which came to dominate American dance band music for the next fifteen years. During that time he helped promote the careers of many young musicians, such as Gene Krupa (drummer), Lionel Hampton (xylophonist), and Harry James (trumpeter). With both his big band and with small jazz ensembles Goodman traveled all over America establishing new dimensions for American popular music, and, at the same time, he created a career in classical music as America's most famous clarinetist. He brought his bands to Carnegie Hall in New York in 1938, which was the first time that august citadel of classical music housed jazz, and he himself performed a recital in Town Hall in 1938, for which he commissioned Bela Bartók to write *Contrasts*. He recorded Mozart's Clarinet Quintet with the Budapest String Quartet, the most highly regarded string quartet of the time, and later he commissioned clarinet concertos from Aaron Copland (1947) and Paul Hindemith (1947). During the 1940s to 1970s Goodman appeared in classical concerts with many of the country's leading symphony orchestras, and he continued to be active on the stage until he died.

Goodman was clearly a Jewish musician, but he also expressed himself occasionally in Jewish musical idioms. The most celebrated case was his collaboration with Ziggy Elman (1914-68), a klezmer trumpeter, who was part of Goodman's big band in the late 1930s and with whom Goodman recorded *And the Angels Sing*, a klezmer work composed by Elman. Goodman was surely aware of klezmer music when he was a child in Chicago, and since he played an instrument that in the twentieth century has been closely associated with klezmer, it was only natural that at some point in his vast career he would include the klezmer clarinet. The affinity between klezmer and jazz bands in the early part of the century—popular dance music emphasizing the clarinet and trap set and with a violin[5]—was only enhanced as klezmer musicians took up playing jazz in the 1920s.

Another band leader and clarinetist of the mid-twentieth century who sometimes rivaled Goodman is Artie Shaw (= Abraham Isaac Arshawsky, 1910-2004). Born in New York of impoverished Jewish immigrants from Austria and Russia, Shaw first confronted his Judaism when as an eight-year-old he experienced his first anti-Semitism in a school in New Haven, Connecticut. As he says in his 1952 autobiography, "this had more to do with shaping the course and direction of my entire life than any other thing."[6] He decided then and there that he would always live as a Jew, though he also admits being ashamed of his Jewish name which he changed to his famous stage name while he was still a teenager. Shaw's principal fame rests on his moving clarinet style, on several short-lived bands, and on a few recordings that were among the all-time best-sellers (such as his band's rendition of Cole Porter's "Begin the Beguine" [1938], *Frenesi* [1940], and his one recording with Billy Holiday).

Alongside the big band leaders were the composers, arrangers, and side men in the bands. Some of these were Jewish. For example, one of the main arrangers for Goodman, Shaw, the Dorsey Brothers, Stan Kenton, and Boyd Raeburn's big band (popular in the 1940s), was George Handy (1920-97), whose real name was Joseph Hendleman. Among the Jewish drummers for such bands as those led by Coleman Hawkins, Dizzy Gillespie, Boyd Raeburn, Charlie Parker, Ray Anthony and others were Lee Abrams (b. 1925), Stan Levey (b. 1925), Mel Lewis (b. 1929) and Tiny (Norman) Kahn (1924-53). Lou Levy (b. 1928), Mel Stitzel (1902-52), Milt Raskin (1916-77)

---

[5] The earliest jazz bands frequently had a violin; Piron's band, for example, one of the most important in New Orleans in the 1920s, was led by a violinist.

[6] Artie Shaw, *The Trouble with Cinderella [An Outline of Identity]* (New York: Farrar, Straus and Young, 1952), 26.

and Hal Schaefer (b. 1925) were famous pianists with the big bands, while Ray Abrams (b. 1920), Al Cohn (1925-88), and Frankie Socolow (1923-81) were distinguished saxophone players with the bands of Gene Krupa, Tommy Dorsey, Artie Shaw and Woody Herman, among others. Wilbur Schwartz (b. 1918) played clarinet with Glenn Miller and Boyd Raeburn, Sonny (Saul) Berman (1924-47) played trumpet with Woody Herman, Si (Simon) Zentner (b. 1917) was a distinguished trombone player with Les Brown, Raeburn, and even Mickey Katz,[7] while string bass players Artie Shapiro (b. 1916) and Sandy (Sidney) Block (b. 1917) played for Paul Whiteman, Benny Goodman, and Tommy Dorsey. Red Rodney (b. 1927) was a trumpeter for Krupa, Goodman, Jimmy Dorsey, Charlie Parker and Woody Herman; a Jew from Philadelphia, he played "Jewish gigs" when he was not playing with the major bands, and recorded *Sophisticated Yenta* on Elektra.

Besides jazz and the big bands, there are many other situations in American popular music where Jews have played a role. Among the crooners was Mel Tormé (Melvin Torme, b. 1925). The salon piano style that has been so popular in America since the 1930s has had several leading Jewish practitioners, the most famous of whom was Eddy Duchin (1910-51). Among the folk music specialists especially popular in the 1960s and 1970s are Bob Dylan (= Robert Allen Zimmerman, b. 1941), Paul Simon (b. 1941), and Simon's singing partner, Art Garfunkel (b. 1941). Dylan, the greatest of all poets of the American folk song era, has had various religious experiences, the last, it seems, being his return in the 1980s to the Judaism of his birth. While his texts are not specifically Jewish, the general tenor of his poetry reflects a Jewish sense of morality. Simon, too, is primarily a protest singer and songwriter, but in at least one song— "Silent Eyes" (1975)—he stands in awe before Jerusalem who "calls my name." The salsa music tradition is Latin American and would seem to have little prospects for an American Jew, but Larry Harlow, a Jew from Brooklyn, known among the salsa performers as "el Judio Maravilloso" (the Marvelous Jew), was one of salsa's greatest and most influential stars from the 1950s to the 1970s. Perhaps the most interesting of these musicians from a Jewish standpoint is Kinky Friedman (b. 1944), whose country music is so mixed with Jewish commentary that it disarms any unbeliever. Friedman was born in Texas and found that "Cowboys and Jews have a common bond. They are the only two groups to wear their hats indoors and attach a certain importance to it." Friedman named his band The Texas Jewboys ca. 1970 and cut his first record in 1973 in Nashville (*Sold American*). Among his songs are "Ride 'Em Jewboy" and "They Ain't Makin' Jews Like Jesus Anymore." Much of his music is like Dylan's and Simon's in its adherence to the protest movement of the 1960s and 1970s. He disbanded his band and started a solo career in 1977, and then in the 1980s deserted the concert hall for a writing career. In 2005 he moved into politics by announcing his candidacy for governor of Texas.

Among the most distinguished popular American Jewish singers of the second half of the twentieth century are Neil Diamond and Barbra Streisand. Diamond was born in Brooklyn in 1941 and broke into the recording business in 1960. He devoted himself to writing songs after he graduated from college in 1962. His first successful recording came in 1965, and he has poured out popular-selling discs on LP and then CD ever since. His style is mildly country and gospel. Diamond's production is geared toward mass consumption, and he has produced nothing that is Jewish— on the contrary, he has probably had the best-selling Christmas albums each year during the 1990s.

---

[7] Katz was a klezmer, an arranger for Spike Jones, and the father of the actor Joel Grey.

Barbra Streisand, on the other hand, has become the foremost Jewish entertainer of her time. Born in New York in 1942 to a poor Hebrew scholar who died young, Streisand has devoted much of her work to the memory of her father and to his causes. After various early personal triumphs in shows that were not successful, she produced her first solo vocal album in 1962 which had astounding success, and in 1963 she started performing on Broadway as the lead in *Funny Girl*, the life of Fanny Brice, who as a fearless and successful Jewish woman was clearly one of her role models. Through this show and the many shows and films which followed, Streisand has emphasized her devotion to her religion and to various causes important to most Jews: gay rights, women's rights, Israel, Jewish education, political liberalism, and the environment. She is without equal as a singer and comedian, and amazingly has also achieved stardom as a serious actress and director. In her movie *Yentl* (1983) she portrayed life in a Russian/Polish *shtetl* in the early twentieth century and the particular problems women faced; the story has a similar girl-dressed-as-boy situation as the 1936 Yiddish film classic *Yidl mit dem Fidl* by Joseph Green, starring another of Streisand's icons, Molly Picon. In the 1970s she recorded a telephone conversation with former Prime Minister Golda Meir in which both of them sing "Hatikvah," the Israeli national anthem. In 1997 she produced another album with one of her favorite synagogue works, Max Janowski's "Avinu Malkeinu."

Jews have also been involved in rock bands and in the various bands that stem from the rock tradition. Usually there is nothing Jewish about these bands, but during the 1990s one—Phish—reveled in Jewish content. Among its hit pieces are "Avenu Malkenu," "Jerusalem City of Gold," "Scent of a Mule" (with "klezmer jam"), and "Oh Kee Pah Ceremony."

While a disproportionate percentage of Jews have commanded the field of American musical entertainment in all aspects—including composition, performance, and promotion, the reason for this cannot lie in talent alone. As stated at the opening of this chapter, economic and social conditions led to the preponderance of Jews in Tin Pan Alley and later the musical theater. Since the mid-twentieth century the glamour, financial rewards, and half a century or more of expectations have helped young Jews decide to continue pursuing musical careers. In many ways this situation was the culmination of centuries of the *badchanim*, who despite starvation, prejudice and persecution, kept Jews laughing until, in America, they could realize their talents to the fullest before a peaceful world community.

American Jews in Classical Music in the Twentieth and Twenty-First Centuries

Just as few Jews were involved in popular American music prior to the 1890s, only a handful of Jews participated in the classical musical life of the country before then. In cities such as Cincinnati, New Orleans, Boston, Buffalo, St. Louis, and of course New York, Jews occasionally played in orchestras or conducted them, participated in chamber music, taught music, sang professionally or in amateur choruses. But the impact that Jews would have on the field of classical music in the twentieth century was nowhere in evidence. In Europe, as we have seen, most of the Jews who were professionally active in classical music were assimilationist, and when these Jews came to America on concert tours—for example, Anton Rubinstein in the early 1870s—they were not identified as Jews.

Two particular Jewish families did have a major impact on American classical music during the last few decades of the nineteenth century, however, and the repercussions have had a lasting influence until the present day. The sire of the first of these was Hamman (Herman?) Franko, who emigrated from Germany to New Orleans in the 1840s and was a successful jeweler.[8] Franko's family name in Germany was Holländer, and among his close relatives back in the old country were the violinist Gustav Holländer and the composer Victor Holländer.[9] At least eight of Franko's children became performing musicians, among them, Selma (1853-1932), Jeanne (1855-1940), Sam (1857-1937), Rachel (1860-?), and Nahan (1861-1930). In 1862, Hamman lost his business and was imprisoned by the Union Army for smuggling ammunition to the Confederate army. Pardoned by Lincoln, he took his family back to Germany until 1869. There, son Sam Franko studied violin with Joachim in Berlin and both he and his sister Jeanne also studied violin with Vieuxtemps in Paris. After the family's return to America, they started playing concerts as a family in New York and then in New Orleans. While the siblings went their own way in pursuit of their careers, they continued to perform together through the 1890s. Sam Franko later had a distinguished career as a violinist (soloist of the Mendelssohn Quintette Club of Boston, concertmaster of the Theodore Thomas Orchestra, solo violist with the New York Philharmonic Society) and became an important conductor and composer. Jeanne Franko appeared as violin soloist with orchestras led by Theodore Thomas, Anton Seidl, John Philip Sousa, and others, and was actively engaged in chamber concerts and solo recitals. During one recital in 1884 she performed on both the violin and the piano, in virtuoso works by Chopin and Liszt. Nahan became concertmaster and conductor of the Metropolitan Opera Orchestra and played in a string quartet with cellist Victor Herbert. Pianist Selma was the music teacher of Jerome Kern; her second son Edwin Franko Goldman became, after Sousa, the most famous band master in twentieth-century America. Members of the Franko family remained nominally Jewish, and they made no effort to express themselves as Jews in their music.

The other family whose significance was felt well into the twentieth century was headed by Leopold Damrosch (1832-85), who came from a Polish-Jewish family in Posen committed to the *Haskalah*. Leopold was determined to be a German musician, even after he immigrated to the United States in 1871, and he hid his background successfully; he married a Lutheran woman and brought up his children as Christians.[10] Despite occasional outbursts of anti-Semitism against them and their own published admission that they were half Jewish, both Frank Damrosch (1859-1937) and Walter Damrosch (1862-1950) considered themselves Christian. They were among the most important conductors in this country in the early twentieth century, as earlier their father had been. Their sister Clara (1869-1948), a pianist, and her Jewish violinist husband David Mannes (1866-1959), founded the Mannes College of Music in 1916. Though raised as a pious Jew, Mannes broke with his religion and accepted the assimilationist attitude of the Damrosch family.

---

[8] John H. Baron, "Franko, Jeanne," in *Jewish Women in America: An Historical Encyclopedia*, ed. Paula Hyman and Deborah Dash Moore (New York: Carlson Publishering, Inc., 1997).

[9] Hamman Holländer had two brothers, Benjamin and Isaac. Benjamin was the father of Gustav (head of the famous Berlin Stern Conservatory from 1894 to 1897) and Victor (composer of operettas). See Kirby Reid Jolly, "Edwin Franko Goldman and the Goldman Band" (D.Ed. diss., New York University, 1971), 15.

[10] George Martin, *The Damrosch Dynasty: America's First Family of Music* (Boston: Houghton Mifflin Company, 1983), esp. 20-21 and 317-20.

The Franko and Damrosch families are typical of the American Jews who were active and successful musicians in late nineteenth- and early twentieth-century North America. Except for the accident of birth, they were American or German musicians first and foremost, and their Jewish origins were of no consequence, except in so far as they had to endure occasional anti-Semitism. As public figures, they found it prudent to hide their Jewishness, in order to steer clear of possible danger and in order to advance their careers. No Jewish elements have been noted in any of their music.

A third family that remained vibrantly Jewish and achieved success in music, though not of the variety of the Frankos and Damroschs, is the family of Cantor Heschel Singer of Buffalo. Three of Singer's children were involved in music in one way or another,[11] as were his grandchildren and great-grandchildren. The Singer family portrait is more typical of average Jewish musicians in America. Singer's son Jacob Singer (1884-1964) became a rabbi and was one of the leaders of the Reform music movement during the first half of the twentieth century. Jacob's brother, the violinist Julius Singer (1878-1934), went to Bratislava in 1903-04 to study with the great teacher Otakar Ševčik(1852-1934). After a short time in the Cincinnati Symphony he became a member of the Buffalo Symphony, a position he retained until his death. He was a renowned teacher and he remained devoted to his religion. His sister, Ann, a pianist, married the violinist-violist Ivan Shapiro, who also was a member of the Buffalo Symphony. His most distinguished pupil was their daughter, Eudice Shapiro.

While an increasing number of American Jews entered the field of classical music just before World War I, it was with the stimuli, first of Ernest Bloch, who came here in 1916, later of Russian performers of unusual ability who arrived after the Russian Revolution, and then, a few years later, of the German Jewish musicians fleeing the Nazis who settled in the U.S., that American Jews began to participate in the classical music field in large numbers.

Composers of Jewish Art Music in North America

That major European Jewish composers were a catalyst to developments in the U.S. cannot be overemphasized. Besides Bloch we have already cited the famous immigrant composers Arnold Schoenberg (1874-1951), Mario Castelnuovo-Tedesco (1895-1968), and Ernst Toch (1887-1964). Schoenberg's importance to the history of Jewish art music has been discussed above. Once in America he produced many works on Jewish themes, from operas to cantatas to psalm settings, and he took an active part in assisting the settlement of refugees streaming out of Europe. Castelnuovo-Tedesco wrote *3 Corali su Melodie Ebraichi for Piano* (1926) and his second violin concerto *I Profiti* (1935) before he arrived here (in 1939), and, once in America, four oratorios on Jewish themes, *Ruth* (1949), *Jonah* (1951), *Esther* (1962), and *Tobias and the Angel* (1964-65); as well as *Three Sephardic Songs for Soprano and Harp; The Divan of Moses-Ibn-Ezra*, a cycle of songs for voice and guitar (1966); *Prayers My Grandfather Wrote;* six preludes for organ or piano on themes by Bruto Senigaglia (1962); and *Song of Songs* (1963). Toch, who arrived in 1934, wrote a number of Jewish secular works in the United States, including *Jephta, Rhapsodic Poem* (his

---

[11] The fourth child's grandchildren are excellent, well-trained amateur musicians.

Symphony no. 5, 1962), *Cantata of the Bitter Herbs* for solo soprano, alto, tenor, bass-baritone, mixed chorus, orchestra, and narrator (1941); and *Vanity of Vanities* (1954) for soprano, tenor, flute, clarinet, violin, and violoncello.

These four composers already had reputations in Europe in both general music and Jewish music, and, when they arrived in this country, they were immediately regarded by the public as important artists. That they also divulged themselves as Jews meant that the public listened and showed consideration to the Jewish elements in their music, which, broadly speaking, American Jewish composers until then had been apprehensive would not happen if their compositions expressed Hebraic qualities. These were decades in which powerful American anti-Semites, such as the critic, composer and Columbia University Professor Daniel Gregory Mason and the automobile manufacturer Henry Ford, cognizant of the prominence of Jewish musicians in America, feared for the purity of what they perceived to be true white Protestant American music. Ford's in-house newspaper stated in 1921:

> The Jewish influence on American music is, without doubt, regarded as serious by those who know anything about it. Not only is there a growing protest against the Judaization of our few great orchestras, but there is a strong reaction from the racial collusion that fills the concert stage and popular platform with Jewish artists to the exclusion of all others.

Jewish composers were sensitive to the insults and vicious attacks, and, feeling insecure as Jews in America because of the plight of Jews for over one thousand years in Europe, on the whole they tended initially to assimilate and hide any Jewish identity in their music. Schoenberg, Toch, Castelnuovo-Tedesco and Bloch encouraged Jewish composers and performers to do otherwise.

By the early 1940s, it became acceptable to be a composer of Jewish art music in America. This is especially seen in the case of Leonard Bernstein, who was both proud of his heritage and inspired by the immigrants. Born and raised in Boston, Bernstein (1918-90) attended Harvard University at a time when it was just beginning to shed its three centuries of anti-Semitism, and he was one of the first to study at Tanglewood's Berkshire Music Center, a school associated with the summer home of the Boston Symphony Orchestra, when it opened in 1940. His talent as a conductor was immediately recognized by Serge Koussevitzky, the conductor of the Boston Symphony and himself a Russian Jew. Koussevitzky recommended that Bernstein change his name because it sounded too Jewish, but Bernstein refused, determined to be Jewish in whatever he did. Over a fifty-year career Bernstein conducted major orchestras, from the Boston Symphony and the New York Philharmonic to the Vienna Philharmonic and the Israel Philharmonic, and wherever he went he was honored and respected for his musical abilities and for his pride in his Judaism. But his lasting fame rests on his compositions, which in the classical area include such overtly Jewish works as the *Jeremiah Symphony* (1942), *Kaddish Symphony no. 3* (1963), *Chichester Psalms* (in Hebrew, 1965), *Dybbuk* Ballet and Suites (1974), *Simchu Na* and *Reena*, Jewish folk songs (1947), *Halil* for flute and orchestra (1981), and the Concerto for Orchestra (1986-89). This last work is a composite of *Jubilee Games*, written for the fiftieth anniversary of the Israel Philharmonic; *Diaspora Games*, based on the Hebrew number 18 (*chai*) that signifies life; and *Benediction*, with text of the traditional priestly benediction.

In the realm of Jewish art music there were professional Jewish composers in America before Bernstein. Some were immigrants whose reputations were acquired only after they settled here. An early example is Nicolai Berezowsky (1900-53), who was born in Russia, came to the United States in 1922 as a violinist, and wrote *Suite Hebraïque* for orchestra in 1928. Another was Leo Ornstein (1892-2002), who emigrated from Russia to the United States in 1907, and is the author of *Hebraic Fantasy* for violin and piano (1929). Frederick Jacobi (1891-1952) composed a *Sabbath Evening Service* and *Hagiographa: Three Biblical Narratives* (1938) for string quartet and piano. Erich Zeisl (1905-59) had written no works with Hebraic elements while in Vienna, but once he emigrated to America, he rediscovered his Jewish background with such works as *Requiem Ebraico* (Psalm 92, 1945), *Prayer* (for soprano and either keyboard or orchestra, 1945), the opera *Job* (1939-58), and the Biblical ballets *The Vineyard* (= *Naboth's Vineyard*, 1953) and *Jacob and Rachel* (1954). Another composer is Maurice Goldman (b. 1910), whose cantata *Song of Ruth* dates from the pre-World War II years.

Immigrants of the next generation who arrived in America while still young, and then made their careers here, include Robert Starer (b. 1924), Hugo Weisgall (1912-97), and Lukas Foss (b. 1922). Starer left his native Vienna in 1938 for Israel and settled in the United States in 1947, eventually teaching at the Cantor's Institute of the Jewish Theological Seminary (1962-63). His two Jewish ballets, both from 1960, are *The Story of Esther* and *The Dybbuk*; other Jewish pieces include *Kli Zemer* (1985) for clarinet and orchestra, *Proverbs for a Son* (1992) in Hebrew and English for mixed chorus, *Nishmat Adam* (*The Soul of Man*, 1992) for speaker, soprano, violoncello and piano, and *Yizkor or Anima Aeterna* (1992) for flute and harpsichord. Starer has also written several pieces for the synagogue, including a *Sabbath Evening Service* in 1970. Weisgall came to the U.S. in 1920 and later taught at the Cantor's Institute of the Jewish Theological Seminary. His major secular Jewish work, the opera *Esther*, premiered in 1993. Among his other compositions of Jewish art music are *Holiday Dance, no. 1 (Hanukkah)*, from *Graven Images*, no. 4 for woodwind quintet (flute, oboe, clarinet, bassoon, horn [1979]); *Holiday Dance, no. 2 (Purim)*, from *Graven Images*, no. 5 for mixed ensemble (flute, oboe, clarinet, bassoon, horn, trumpet [1979]); *Tekiatot: Rituals for Rosh Hashana* (1985) for chamber orchestra (whose movements are "Malkhuyyot," "Zikhronot," and "Shofarot"); "Loves' Wounded," two songs for baritone and orchestra on a Hebrew text of Judah Halevi (1987); "V'ohavto" for unison chorus, baritone solo, and strings (1994?); and *Psalm of the Distant Dove*, a canticle for mezzo-soprano and piano on texts translated from Hebrew by Raymond P. Scheindlin (1995). Lucas Foss emigrated from Germany before World War II. He has composed *Song of Songs* (1946), *Psalms* (1956), *Odon Olom* (1951), and *Solomon Rossi Suite* (1975).

Among the native-born Americans, besides Bernstein, are Bernard Rogers (1893-1968), who contributed *Psalm 114* (1968) and earlier *The Prophet Isaiah* (1950); Aaron Copland (1900-90), who wrote *Vitebsk, Study on a Jewish Theme* (1928); Miriam Gideon (1906-96), who wrote *Biblical Masks* for violin and piano or organ (1960); Edwin Gerschefski (b. 1909), whose Jewish works for the concert hall include *The Lord's Controversy with His People* (1949) and *Psalm 100* for soprano, bass, chorus, percussion and piano (1965); Arthur Cohn (b. 1910), author of *Hebraic Study* for bassoon (1944) and *Kaddish* for orchestra (1974); Morton Gould (b. 1913), who composed *Jericho* for band (1939) and the score to the film *Holocaust*, which appeared on TV (1978) and which he then orchestrated as a suite (1979) and reorchestrated for band (1980); David Diamond (1915-2005), who wrote *Psalm* for orchestra (1936) and the children's opera *Golden Slippers* (1967), based in part on *Der Zivug* by I. L. Peretz; George Rochberg (1918-2005), author of *Three Psalms in Hebrew* (1954), *David the Psalmist* (1954), and *Mizmor L'Piyus* (1970); Harold Shapero (b. 1920), composer of a *Hebrew Cantata* (1954) for solo voices, chorus, flute, trumpet, violin, harp, and organ; Leo Smit (b. 1921), whose *Tzadik* is for saxophone quartet (1983); Ezra Laderman (b. 1924), who has written two television opera-cantatas, *The Questions of Abraham* (1973) and *And David Wept* (1972), two dances entitled *Song of Songs* (1960) and *Esther* (1960), and two symphonies nicknamed *Jerusalem* (1973) and *Isaiah* (1982); and Yehudi Wyner (b. 1929), son of Lazar Weiner, the prominent synagogue composer and member of the Russian Jewish circle, who has composed *Passover Offering* for flute, clarinet, trombone, and violoncello (1959). Among the more recent composers are Joel Spiegelman (b. 1933), a former professor of music at Sarah Lawrence College, author of *Mystery of the Sabbath* (1969) and *How Lovely Is Thy Dwelling Place* (1982) for bass, chorus, and organ; and Richard Wernick (b. 1934), of the University of Pennsylvania, who has written *Kaddish Requiem* (1971, a secular service for the victims of Indochina), *Visions of Terror and Wonder*, which includes some Hebrew text (1976), and *The Oracle of Shimon Bar Yochai*, for violoncello, piano and soprano (1982).

Special mention must also be made of Steve Reich (b. 1936), one of the leading exponents of minimalism, whose orchestral version of his *Tehillim* for singers and chamber group opened the 1982 New York Philharmonic subscription season. He has also written the extraordinarily poignant *Different Trains* (1988) for tape and string quartet, which juxtaposes the boring train rides he—the spoiled American child—took in the early 1940s across the United States and the train rides that his fellow Jewish children in Europe were forced to take at the same time. Reich's opera *Cave* (1993) is based on the fatherhood of Abraham.

Other North-American born composers include the Canadian Alexander Brott (1915-2005), composer of *Israel* for chorus and orchestra (1956); Meyer Kupferman (b. 1926) whose Jewish works include *Images of Chagall* (1987) for clarinet, bassoon, trumpet, trombone, violin, bass and percussion, *And Job's Wife* (1990), a cycle of three songs for soprano, flute and harp, and *The Shadows of Jerusalem* (1992) for mezzo, clarinet, violoncello, and piano; Seymour Shifrin (1926-79) whose early songs "Chronicles" are in Hebrew; and Elie Siegmeister (1909-91), one of the founders of the American Composers Alliance in 1937 and the composer of two Jewish operas, *The Lady of the Lake* and *Angel Levine*, based on Jewish stories by Bernard Malamud (this last has a synagogue scene). One of Siegmeister's most prolific pupils is Leonard J. Lehrman (b. 1949), who has written seven operas on Jewish topics, several also on subjects by Bernard Malamud; in addition, he has several sets of songs, such as "The Bourgeois Poet" (1970) on poems by Karl Shapiro, "Ein Wanderer durch Deutschland" (1984) on texts by Heinrich Heine, and "Jewish Voices in Germany" (1986), as well as individual songs, such as "I'd Like to Go Away Alone" (1991), "Kererte a Ti" (Ladino, 1997), and "In der Fremd" (Yiddish, 1983).

Composers of Jewish art music have also made contributions to the synagogue (for example, Diamond, Lehrman, Siegmeister, and Wernick). Other composers, such as David Amram (b. 1930), and Jacob Druckman (b. 1928), have not written compositions with Jewish elements for the concert hall but have composed for the Jewish liturgy (Amram's *Friday Evening Service* with organ [1960], Druckman's *Sabbath Eve Service* [198-?], and Jacobi's *Sabbath Service* [1931]).

Professional synagogue composers have also composed Jewish art music. Among the earliest of these was Lazare Saminsky (1882-1959), formerly a member of the St. Petersburg

Society for Jewish Music who emigrated to the United States in 1920, where he became director of music at Temple Emanu-El in New York. His works for the secular concert hall include the opera-ballet, *The Daughter of Jeptha* (1928), a *Lament of Rachel* (1922), and *Jerusalem, City of Solomon and Christ* (1930). Lazar Weiner (1897-1982), who served the Free Synagogue in Flushing, New York, composed *Amos*, a sacred cantata for baritone, tenor, mixed chorus, piano or organ (1972). Herman Berlinski (1910-2001), affiliated with congregations in New York and Washington, D.C., produced three Jewish oratorios, *Kiddush Ha-Shem* (1960), *Job* (1972), and *The Trumpets of Freedom* (1988); four Jewish cantatas, *The Earth Is the Lord's* (1966), *Sing to the Lord a New Song* (1978), *The Beadle of Prague* (1983), and *The Days of Awe* (1985); as well as *Chazoth* for string quartet and ondes martenot (1938), and *Prayer for the Night* (1968). Three recent composers are Cantor Stephen Richards, whose *Prayer: Suite for Oboe and Strings* (1997) the composer indicates has a Hebraic flavor, Samuel Adler, and Jack Gottlieb. Samuel Adler (b.1928) was born in Germany and came to the United States in 1939; he served as music director at Temple Emanuel in Dallas from 1953 to 1966, and then taught at the Eastman School of Music. Early in his career he composed *The Feast of Lights* (1957), a Hanukah suite for orchestra. In 1975 he wrote both his Symphony no. 5: *We Are the Echoes* for mezzo soprano and orchestra as well as *We Believe: a Hymn of Faith* for four soloists, mixed chorus, and eight instrumentalists; subsequently he added *L'Olam Vaed* (1978), a meditation for violoncello and piano, *Rededication* (1985) for four part male chorus and brass quintet (on texts from the Psalms and the Hanukah prayer, *Haneroth Halalu*), *Concerto Shir Hama'a lot* (1991) for woodwind quintet and orchestra, *Lullaby* (1992) based on an old Hebrew folk tune and set for violin and piano, *Ports of Call: A Mediterranean Suite* (1994) for two violins and guitar which includes a musical picture of Haifa, and various songs. Jack Gottlieb (b. 1930), who served Temple Israel in St. Louis and then was composer in residence at the Hebrew Union College School of Sacred Music in New York, wrote *The Song of Songs, Which is Solomon's* (1976).

American Jewish Performers of Classical Music

By the end of the First World War, the number of Jewish musicians in America was considerable. There were hundreds of orchestral musicians, chorus singers, and piano teachers spread across the country. In some cases these professionals also participated in Jewish liturgical or secular functions, though many others did not participate, in the wake of such anti-Semitic attacks as those launched by Henry Ford. In addition, there were performers and conductors of worldwide reputations. They had trickled into the United States before 1918, but after World War I and the Russian Revolution, many of the exceptionally talented performers remaining in Europe chose to leave the uncertainties there for the freedoms of America. With the outbreak of World War II and the clear danger the Nazis posed for European Jews, a great many more Jewish professionals, including many of the remaining European Jewish superstars, came to this country. As a result America became for the first time one of the world centers of classical music. As in the case of the composers, the immigrant performers were a stimulus to the American-born musicians, and this had an effect on all young American performers, Jew and Gentile alike.[12]

---

[12] Gdal Saleski, *Famous Musicians of Jewish Origin* (New York: Bloch Publishing, Co., 1949).

Among the many prominent European Jewish orchestral conductors who emigrated were Serge Koussevitzky (1874-1951), Pierre Monteux (1875-1964), Bruno Walter (= Bruno Walter Schlesinger, 1876-1962), Fritz Stiedry (1883-1968), Otto Klemperer (1885-1973), Jascha Horenstein (1887-1973), Fritz Reiner (1888-1963), Vladimir Golschmann (1893-1972), Joseph Rosenstock (1895-1985), George Szell (1897-1970), William Steinberg (1899-1978), Efrem Kurtz (1900-95), Josef Krips (1902-74), Kurt Herbert Adler (1905-88), Erich Leinsdorf (= Landauer, 1912-93), and Walter Susskind (1913-80). Among their many American disciples are the Jews Leonard Bernstein, Leonard Slatkin (b. 1944), Lukas Foss, James Levine (b. 1943), Lorin Maazel (b. 1930), and Michael Tilson Thomas (b. 1944, who is the grandson of Boris Thomashefsky, one of the greatest actors on the old Yiddish stage). Meanwhile the first American to become conductor of a major American orchestra was Alfred Wallenstein (1898-1983) in Los Angeles. A few other prominent Jewish conductors of American orchestras have been Georg Solti (1912-97) and Daniel Barenboim (b. 1942) in Chicago, and André Previn (b. 1929) in Houston, Pittsburgh, and Los Angeles.

Besides conductors, Jewish performers either born in America or who have made America their home include the violinists Jascha Heifetz (1901-89), Fritz Kreisler (1875-1962), Joseph Szigeti (1892-1973), Yehudi Menuhin (1916-99), Oscar Shumsky (b. 1917), Mischa Elman (1891-1967), Mischa Mischakoff (1895-1981), Richard Burgin (1893-1981), Nathan Milstein (1904-92), Joseph Achron (1886-1943), Leopold Auer (1845-1930), Isaac Stern (1920-2001), Louis Kaufman (1906-94), Eudice Shapiro (b. 1914), Alexander Schneider (1908-93) and, in recent times, the Israelis Pinchas Zukerman (b. 1948) and Itzhak Perlman (b. 1945). Jewish pianists in this category have been Artur Rubinstein (1887-1982), Josef Hoffman (1876-1957), Rudolf Serkin (1903-91), Vladimir Horowitz (1903-89), Gary Graffman (b. 1928), Leon Fleisher (b. 1928), Murray Perahia (b. 1947, Separdi), Josef Lhévinne (1874-1944), Rosina Bessie Lhévinne (1880-1976), and Lorin Hollander (b. 1944). Others are violist Joseph Fuchs, violoncellists Emanuel Feuermann (1902-42), Nathanial Rosen (b. 1948), and Leonard Rose (1918-84), flutists Samuel Baron (1927-97) and Eugenie Zukerman (b. 1944), oboists the brothers Harold Gomberg (1916-85) and Ralph Gomberg (b. 1921), clarinetists David Openheim and Benny Goodman, bassoonists Leonard Sherrow and Sol Schoenbach, harmonica-player Larry Adler (1914-2001), percussionist Harold Farberman (b. 1929), and many others. The number of Jewish musicians in chamber ensembles is also large; Jews make up all or most of the seats in some ensembles, for example, the Budapest Quartet, Fine Arts Quartet, Julliard Quartet, Beaux Arts Trio, New York Woodwind Quintet, American Arts Quartet, Hollywood Quartet.

Among the most famous Jewish singers who sang at the Metropolitan Opera in New York are Roberta Peters (= Petermann, b. 1930), Judith Raskin (1928-84), Regina Resnik (b. 1922), Robert Merrill (b. 1917), Richard Tucker (1913-75), Jan Peerce (1904-84), and Leonard Warren (1911-60). Beverly Sills (= Belle Miriam Silverman, b. 1929) sang most of her career at the New York City Opera. All these singers also sang in synagogues or participated in Jewish music in one way or another. Many also sang guest engagements at other American opera houses in Chicago, Houston, Seattle, Santa Fe, San Francisco, New Orleans, and elsewhere.

The phenomenon of the predominance of Jewish musicians during much of the twentieth century can be explained by several factors already alluded to. Through much of that century the elitist and moneyed patrons of music cherished classical music above all other types of music and had a tendency to put musical genius on a pedestal. Already in Russia at the beginning of the twentieth century Russian Jews recognized—as we have seen in the cases of Anton and Nicolas Rubinstein—that one way out of the Pale of Settlement or ghetto was to become a virtuoso performer. All other studies and interests could be put aside as anxious parents rushed their children into musical careers. When these same Russian Jews came to America, the initial reaction was the same. The best possibility for Jewish children to get out of the sweatshops and out of the ghettos, particularly in New York, Philadelphia, Boston, Chicago and other industrialized cities, was through a career in music. Many universities had a quota (*numerus clausus*) restricting the number of immigrants, the language was strange, many businesses and neighborhoods were closed to Jews . . . but a musician could surmount all these barriers. Just as in the second half of the twentieth century African-American athletes—through sheer physical talent—were able to transcend racial barriers and become accepted in businesses, neighborhoods, and universities which were otherwise closed to them, so in the first half of the century musical talent was an avenue of acceptance available to Jews. Of course, the parallel stops there, because the Jew could intermarry and disappear as a Jew, whereas an African-American cannot escape his or her skin color. And to some extent many Jewish musicians did lose interest in their heritage, in about the same proportion as other American Jews have, but many other Jews, as we have seen above, have remained consciously Jewish while pursuing their musical careers.

While it is clearly a social phenomenon that Jews have played such a large role in the performance of American classical music, it does not mean that Judaism has played an aesthetic role. To what extent has a Jewish music resulted from this large participation of Jews in the performance of music? In the twentieth and twenty-first centuries composers have convincingly shown that they can express themselves in a Jewish manner. In addition, there are cases where Jewish performers are involved in performances of Jewish dance or theatrical music, such as Itzhak Perlman's recording *In the Fiddler's House*,[13] where he plays klezmer music, or such as Isaac Stern's fiddling in the movie version of *Fiddler on the Roof*. Despite the fame of both violinists in the classical concert hall, such performances here by Perlman and Stern are not regarded as "classical" but rather as popular. Do Jewish performers play Beethoven or Brahms differently from non-Jewish performers? Legend has it that in the late nineteeth century when Russian classical performers began to rival performers in Germany, France, England and Italy, they brought a pathos and emotionalism to their music that revolutionized how audiences responded to classical music; since so many of the Russian performers were Jewish (the Rubinstein brothers, Leopold Auer, Carl Davidoff, to mention just the leaders), it is possible that the extremely emotional rendition of classical music was a Russian-Jewish way of performing. This is impossible to prove since we have no recordings of the earlier non-Russian musicians with whom to compare the Russians, we would be hard pressed to demonstrate that Russian Christians play differently from Russian Jews, and we certainly cannot compare how German Jews played vis-á-vis Russian Jews. The mere presence of Jews on stage, the Yiddish spoken or Jewish jokes cracked during rehearsal, the facial expressions of the Jewish musicians give a Jewish aura about some performances of classical music, but the actual music that is heard during the performance is more the personal expression of the individual artist communicating non-Jewish music to a universal

---

[13] Angel Records, 72435-55555-2, 1995.

audience. Despite the impossibility of defining a Jewish aesthetics of classical music, the large participation of so many Jews in this kind of music all out of proportion to their numbers in the overall population of America is important for the history of Jewish music because it demonstrates the importance of music to Jews, even in a society where Jews have largely assimilated with their non-Jewish neighbors.

Suggestions for Further Reading

Benarde, Scott R. *Stars of David: Rock 'n' Jewish Stories*. Hanover: Brandeis University Press, 2003.
Billig, Michael. *Rock 'n' Roll Jews*. Syracuse: Syracuse University Press, 2000.
Friedman, Lester. *The Jewish Image in American Film*. Secaucus, NJ: Citadel Press, 1987.
Gottlieb, Jack. *Funny, It Doesn't Sound Jewish: How Yiddish Songs Influenced Tin Pan Alley, Broadway, and Hollywood*. State University of New York Press, 2004.
Kanter, Kenneth. *The Jews of Tin Pan Alley*. New York: KTAV, 1982.
Most, Andrea. *Making Americans: Jews and the Broadway Musical*. Cambridge: Harvard University Press, 2004.
Oseary, Guy. *Jews Who Rock*. New York: St. Martin's Griffen, 2001.
Sobel, Bernard. *A Pictorial History of Vaudeville*. New York: Bonanza Books, 1961.

HISTORICAL INTERLUDE | *Trauma and Triumph in the Middle Twentieth Century*

Not since slavery in Egypt and the Babylonian Captivity had Jews experienced such tragedy as occurred in Europe in the second quarter of the twentieth century. Since the Crusades of the Middle Ages, European Jews had been murdered at will—sometimes in response to natural disasters such as plagues and crop failures, sometimes in imagined retribution for mythical religious injustices such as the "betrayal" of Jesus and the scurrilous charge of using Christian children's blood to make *matzahs* (the unleavened bread which Jews eat during Passover, which in fact contains no blood of any sort). None of the accusations against Jews were substantiated, but by 1933 it was ingrained in some minds that only the extermination of all people who were at least one quarter Jewish would rid society of all its basic ills. While the Germans led the way, they had eager followers in other countries of Europe.

A number of distinguished European musicians held some prejudice against Jews. It was the German composer Richard Wagner (1813-83), however, who became the symbol of musical anti-Semitism. As discussed in chapter 10, Wagner published a treatise in 1850 which attacked Jewish composers of European art music, and in a number of operas he satirized Jews in pernicious ways. By the end of his life, and for the next sixty years, Wagner's words and operas held a leading position in European and world cultural life.

In 1925 Adolf Hitler (1889-1945) published *Mein Kampf* (*My Struggle*), in which he called for the extermination of Jews. Though he plotted the "final solution" that was intended to rid Europe of Jews once and for all, most Jews laughed him off at the time. But when Hitler was elected to power in Germany in 1933 Jews took alarm, particularly in Central Europe. Gradually but steadily Jews lost their rights and possessions in Germany. 9 November 1938 riots broke out, synagogues and other Jewish institutions were burned, Jewish places of business were destroyed, and many Jews lost their lives. This night of rioting, looting, burning, and window-smashing staged by Hitler's followers—the Nazis—was termed *Kristallnacht* (The Night of Broken Glass). Meanwhile, Hitler had rebuilt the German army—which had been dismantled at the end of World War I—into the strongest army in Europe, and in 1938 he began what he had hoped would be the takeover of all Europe. He nearly succeeded. Countries like Austria, Czechoslovakia, Poland, France, The Netherlands, Denmark, Belgium, Lithuania, and Latvia were completely gobbled up by the Nazis, and others, like the Soviet Union, were invaded and largely occupied. Furthermore, some countries were allied to Germany, such as Italy and Hungary. All the captured territories and the countries allied to Germany had sizable Jewish populations, and the "final solution" was brought to those lands. A few thousand Jews managed to escape, but millions of Jews were either killed outright or were herded into concentration camps in towns like Auschwitz, Treblinka, Terezín (= Theresienstadt), Dachau, Bergen/Belsen, and Buchenwald, where they perished through slave labor and in gas ovens. Even in neutral countries like Switzerland, Jews were put into concentration camps where many died.

With the combined efforts of anti-Nazi freedom fighters in Europe and the armies of the Soviet Union, England, Canada, the other members of the British Commonwealth, and the United States, Hitler was finally defeated in May 1945. Many Jews fought against the Germans, including those among the freedom fighters of the occupied countries known as Partisans. As the armies of the free world pushed the Germans back, Jews were liberated from camps, but they had nowhere to go. Most had lost their families, their home towns were destroyed, and they had no possessions; they were called Displaced Persons (DPs). Some eventually made new lives in new places in Europe, and others—particularly from Western Europe—returned to their native homes. But the majority left Europe, chiefly for the United States, Palestine, and Canada.

The result of the Nazi attempt to annihilate the Jews—termed the Holocaust, or *Sho'ah*, in Hebrew—was the complete destruction of the European center of the Ashkenazic tradition. Instead of millions who lived in Europe before the War, now only a few thousand, broken and lost, were left in Europe. The center of Jewish population shifted to the United States, where the Jewish community was just beginning to establish institutions capable of carrying on its traditions for its five million inhabitants. A million Jews survived in the Soviet Union, but they were severely restricted and virtually no synagogues or other Jewish institutions were tolerated by the Communist government. Eighty thousand Jews survived in Budapest, Hungary, the only city in Eastern Europe where Jews were permitted synagogues and a kosher restaurant after 1945, but Hungary was not a free country and Jews were still subjugated with little chance to develop a Jewish life. In 1945 there was another hope, namely the establishment of a homeland in Palestine— the realization of a dream which had lasted two millennia, not as a center of Ashkenazic Jewry but of world Jewry. Thus, from the destruction of *Minhag Ashkenaz* in Europe would come forth two new *minhagim*, or customs: *Minhag America* and *Minhag Israel*—both influenced by, and descended from, the Ashkenazic, but different from it and going their own ways.

Jewish settlement in the land of Israel was already under way prior to World War II, and the nation of Israel was officially sanctioned as a free, sovereign state on 15 May 1948; it was able to be a viable Jewish country by then because of a series of developments which went back many years.

While the majority of Jews of the world lived in the Diaspora for two thousand years, a Jewish presence in *Eretz Yisrael* continued throughout this period. This old community, whose forebears never left the country or lived there prior to 1881, is referred to as the "old *yishuv*" (= settlement). The Jewish population in the Holy Land remained small until the end of the nineteenth century, though it gradually grew as Jewish immigrants, mostly religious pilgrims, trickled in.

With the start of the pogroms in Russia in 1881 and the subsequent popularity of Theodore Herzl's Zionism, Ashkenazic Jews began to move to *Eretz Yisrael* in increasing numbers. The new *yishuv* (settlement), then, refers to all Jews arriving in Palestine after 1881, mostly through the impetus of the Zionist movement. In the years from 1882 until 1948, there were six basic waves of immigration from Europe; each wave is called an *aliyah*. The first *aliyah* consisted of East Europeans fleeing the tyrannical rule of the tsar and the notorious pogroms of 1881; these tended to be worldly Jews, members of the *Haskalah*, rather than traditional Jews.

East Europeans also dominated the second *aliyah*, from 1904 to 1913. 35,000 to 40,000 East Europeans fled a new, violent series of pogroms in Kishinev, but among these Jews were many who were socialists, and they idealistically created collective farms—the *kibbutzim*. In addition, during the period of the second *aliyah* a difference of opinion arose in one important farm community, Rishon Le'Zion, as to how the schools were to be organized, and this dispute led to the founding of Israel's largest city. One group preferred to teach children in modern European vernacular languages, while another group split off and created a new high school (gymnasium) in a suburb of Jaffa where only Hebrew would be used for instruction. This occurred in 1909, and the new suburb would become Tel Aviv.

By the end of World War I, Turkey was replaced by Great Britain as the political power controlling the land. A third *aliyah* came after World War I and the Russian Revolution, lasting from 1919 to 1923; its participants were Russian and Polish refugees who were escaping the ravages of war in Europe. Jerusalem was the religious center of the Jewish settlers, while Tel Aviv had become its secular center.

The fourth *aliyah*, from 1924 to 1926, included the largest group until then, mostly urban Jews, not farmers, from the major cities of Poland, and they were attracted primarily to the new city of Tel Aviv rather than to the Kibbutzim, to the old farm settlements, or to the religious cities (especially Jerusalem). Now Ashkenazic Jews outnumbered their Sephardic co-religionists. A fifth *aliyah* was caused by the rise of violent anti-Semitism in Central Europe from 1928 to 1939; the population of European Jews in Palestine went from 150,000 to 445,000 during these twelve years, with about eighty-five thousand just from Germany. The German Jews were mostly university educated, highly organized, modern technocrats whose presence in Palestine significantly changed the nature of that country and its institutions. From 1940 to 1945 the British authorities, fearful of an Arab uprising stirred up by the Germans, barred official immigration to Palestine. The sixth *aliyah*, from 1945 to 1949, brought in the refugees from the Second World War and Nazi persecution, which occurred simultaneously with the final push to the creation of the State of Israel. After Independence in May 1948, additional *aliyot* occurred, which by 1961 had brought the Jewish population of Israel to about two million, and by 2005 to about 5.4 million out of a total population of 6.5 million.

After fifty years, Israel is a vibrant country with a musical life all its own. Not only Europeans, but also Persians, Iraqis, Egyptians, Moroccans, Indians, Bukharans, Ethiopians, Yemenites, and Kurdistanis, have settled there and intermingled. While each group maintains its own musical traditions, they all also share a common musical culture which they have experienced together during the country's first half-century.

13 || *Music of the Holocaust*

Nazi Discrimination and Jewish Reaction in Germany to 1940

Although Jews had lived in Germany for almost two millennia by the outbreak of World War I, many Gentile Germans still regarded Jews as foreigners. The seeds of the Holocaust itself were planted in Germany a millennium ago during the Crusades when Germans along with other Europeans assumed that it was permissible to kill Jews. Anti-semitism had increased during the sixteenth century when Martin Luther lashed out at Jews for refusing to accept his brand of Christianity. With the defeat of the German army in World War I, right-wing Germans sought a scapegoat for their loss rather than looking at themselves, and Jews were a vulnerable target. Small in number but extremely successful in all aspects of German culture, business, and science, they were easily noticed and politically weak.

In music Jews had taken two paths at the opening of the twentieth century that were not traditionally German: they became committed to a universal European style of music and, in so doing, they became leaders in the musical avant-garde. Mahler and Schoenberg were the central Jewish figures who pushed German music beyond Wagner and into an international arena. Hans Pfitzner (1869-1949), a leading conservative composer in Germany, published an article in 1920 entitled "Die neue Aesthetik der musikalischen Impotenz. Ein Verwesungssymptom?" (The New Aesthetic of Musical Impotence: a Symptom of Decay?).[1] In it Pfitzner drew a parallel between the decay of German society which led to the military defeat and the decay in musical taste which would lead to the end of the German hegemony in music. From Bach to Wagner Germans had dominated classical music. Pfitzner asserted that it was not German Gentiles who were responsible for this decay; rather, it was Jews and their sympathizers (chief of whom was the great twentieth-century German composer Paul Hindemith [1895-1963]).

---

[1] Erik Levi, *Music in the Third Reich* (New York: St. Martin's Press, 1994), 4.

Pfitzner's article was followed by a number of others in various anti-Semitic papers and journals and in widely-read books. Karl Storck's posthumous volume *Die Musik der Gegenwart* (Music of the Present, 1922) specifically named Schoenberg and Mahler as the culprits—not Mahler as a conductor but as a composer. Two years later one of the most revered musicologists of the era, Hans Joachim Moser (1889-1967), equated music and race: Jews and Germans were inevitably opposed in matters of culture.[2]

Until this point the Nazis were insignificant in this debate, but two important musical events gave them an opportunity to take up the cause of the arch-conservatives. In 1927 Ernst Krenek's opera *Jonny spielt auf!* (Jonny Sounds Off) made a sensational debut because for the first time African-Americans were highlighted in a European opera. Krenek (1900-91), a non-Jew, was a member of the avant-garde and was fascinated by jazz and other Negro music. The next year saw the premier of Kurt Weill's *Die Dreigroschenoper* (*The Threepenny Opera*), in which the outcasts of society are highlighted. Weill, a Jew, wrote in a cabaret style heavily influenced by jazz. Both operas were condemned for their subject matter and for their use of modern compositional techniques. At this time Alfred Rosenberg (1893-1946) was one of Hitler's chief propagandists, and in his Nazi journal of culture in January 1929, he traced the cultural decline of the time to an international conspiracy led by Jews and manifested in these two operas.

The growth of sound movies at the end of the 1920s brought unemployment to many German musicians, and coupled with the general, extreme economic depression in the country at the time, the plight of these musicians became desperate. They saw some very talented Jewish musicians who were working, and they saw those musicians involved in the international avant-garde. They hated the style, and so were ready to vent their frustration on these Jewish musicians. The Nazis seized the opportunity and led the German musicians in riots against the Jewish musicians with the aim of ridding Germany of Jews and their influence.

When Hitler gained control of the German government in January 1933, the Nazis were in a position to carry out what previously had only been a threat. Jewish and anti-Nazi conductors were immediately bullied and their concerts had to be cancelled; this affected such luminaries as Bruno Walter (Bruno Walter Schlesinger, 1876-1962), Otto Klemperer (1885-1973), Fritz Stiedry (1883-1968), Jascha Horenstein (1898-1973), Joseph Rosenstock (1895-1985), and William Steinberg (1899-1978). Jews were removed from radio and press positions in March, which put Germany's leading music critics—Paul Bekker (1882-1937), Oscar Bie (1864-1938), Alfred Einstein (1880-1952), and Hugo Leichtentritt (1874-1951)—out of work; and by April the Nazis passed a law which effectively prohibited Jews from holding any teaching positions in conservatories or most positions in opera houses.

Among the earliest Germans to rally to the Nazi cause was the excellent violinist Gustav Havemann, who had been a pupil of Joachim and whose string quartet had promoted the chamber music of Schoenberg and Hindemith in the 1920s. Perhaps out of fear for his own safety, Havemann became a staunch supporter of Hitler and took a leadership position in expelling Jews from the most important musical organizations in Germany. When Joseph Goebbels (1897-1945), Hitler's chief propagandist and rival of Rosenberg, founded the Reichsmusikkammer (Government Office

---

[2] For an assessment of Moser's activities on behalf of the Nazis, see Pamela Potter, *Most German of the Arts: Musicology and Society from the Weimar Republic to the End of Hitler's Reich* (New Haven: Yale University Press, 1998), *passim*.

of Music) in 1933, he placed Havemann in charge along with Germany's most famous composer, Richard Strauss (1864-1949), and its most famous conductor, Wilhelm Furtwängler (1886-1954). All three were anxious to restore Germany's reputation as the world's foremost country for classical music, but none of the three envisioned the terror which Goebbels and Hitler were unleashing physically against Jews. By 1935 all three had been fired by the Nazis and replaced with rabidly anti-Semitic Nazis.

The final solution, as it affected German Jewish musicians, could now be carried out. "The Nazis were committed to carrying through their programme of anti-semitism, its ultimate goal being the complete removal of Jewish influence from German music."[3] To find all these Jewish musicians, musicologist Herbert Gerigk published his *Lexikon der Juden in der Musik* (Lexicon of Jews in Music, 1940) which gave details about who among musicians was Jewish, whether a practicing Jew or a Jew by accident of at least one-fourth Jewish blood. To help the Arian German distinguish Jewish art from non-Jewish art, a musical exhibition was opened in Düsseldorf in May 1938, on the theme *Entartete Musik* (degenerate music), modeled on a similar exhibit the year before dedicated to degenerate visual arts.[4] The musical exhibit consisted of portraits of Jewish and anti-Nazi musicians coupled with slogans defaming their works; six booths made it possible for visitors to listen to some of the music of these unfortunate artists. Should a musical work by a Jew be performed in public or a Jewish performer accidentally make an appearance, the printed program and the newspaper review were required to place a (J), an abbreviation for *Jude* (German for Jew), after the citation to make it clear to the listener or reader that a Jew was involved; musicologists writing histories had to do the same thing lest an unsuspecting Arian fall under "corrupt Jewish influence."

As soon as the Nazis came to power, some Jewish musicians with foresight immediately left the country. Among these were the violinist Fritz Kreisler (1875-1962), the bass singer Emanuel List (1888-1967), the pianist Artur Schnabel (1882-1951), and the violinist Szymon Goldberg 1909-93). They had the advantage that they were not German citizens—the first two Austrians, the latter two Poles—and their allegiance to Germany where they had pursued their careers was not as binding as it was for many native-born German Jews who naively considered themselves safe.[5] It also helped that they were internationally famous and could command audiences in any foreign country to which they moved. Of course, the avant-garde, already under fire, realized the danger, so artists like Weill, Schoenberg, and Hindemith fled at once.

Over the next few years many other Jewish musicians came to realize the hopelessness of staying in Germany and emigrated. In 1935 some of the best orchestral musicians went to Palestine to join Bronislaw Huberman's new Palestine Symphony, while others went to England, America, or even Tokyo and Shanghai. Despite some skepticism by Jews that Furtwängler was a Nazi-sympathizer, he in fact helped many of his orchestral musicians to escape.[6] The esteemed

---

[3] Levi, 39.

[4] Ibid., 94-98.

[5] Michael H. Kater, *The Twisted Muse: Musicians and Their Music in the Third Reich* (New York and Oxford: Oxford University Press, 1997), 88.

[6] Fred K. Prieberg, *Trial of Strength: Wilhelm Furtwängler in the Third Reich*, trans. Christopher Dolan (Boston: Northeastern University Press, 1994), explains this conductor's strange role under the Nazis.

conductor stood up to the Nazis on numerous occasions, largely because he felt that politics had no place in art, but as soon as he realized the physical danger in which his Jewish musicians were, he actively arranged for their departure from Germany.

Under international pressure to assist Jewish artists who had lost their jobs and were now starving, the Nazis decided to help Jews organize their own performance venues throughout Germany. It was a clever political move that fooled some into believing that the Nazis were not all bad. On 23 June 1933, the Kulturbund deutscher Jüden (Cultural Society of German Jews) was officially sanctioned, and the psychiatrist Kurt Singer (d. 1944)—who had prior experience as deputy director of the Berlin State Opera—took over as director.[7] Any city in Germany with a sizeable Jewish population could arrange for performances of plays, operas, and concerts with the proviso that the audiences must be Jewish, the funding must come from Jewish sources, and the programs must be approved first by Nazi censors. In Berlin alone, with a large Jewish population, there were during the first few years of the Kulturbund many opera performances and nearly one concert a day. The other principal cities with active chapters of the Kulturbund were Munich, Frankfurt, Hamburg, Stuttgart, Mannheim, Breslau, and Cologne. At first the repertories were just about the same as what non-Jewish audiences were hearing, with occasional whimsical censoring by inconsistent Nazi officials; this contradicted the Nazi party line since Jews were supposed to be tied to some international avant-garde conspiracy and not capable of the same taste as ordinary Germans.[8] True, Mendelssohn's music, which was performed much less frequently by non-Jews in Germany, was frequently programmed by the Kulturbund, but the works of the avant-garde, now banned by the Nazis, were also heard infrequently by Jewish audiences, who were not interested. Although they no longer had the best instruments and could not play in the best concert halls or opera houses, by and large the quality of the Kulturbund performances was as high as in the non-Jewish musical organizations.

By 1938, however, as many of the best German Jewish musicians had left the country and persecution began to reduce Jewish means to support such endeavors, the rapid decline of the Kulturbund was inevitable. *Kristallnacht* (Night of broken crystal),[9] on 9 November 1938, signaled the beginning of the massive German extermination of the Jews. What had been occasional violence against Jews, continual humiliation, deprivation of legal and economic rights, and a war of words, turned into mass killings and destruction of what was left of Jewish property. 30,000 Jews were immediately deported to concentration camps where they perished, and terror now reigned. Singer himself left Germany for Holland (where he was later captured by the Nazis and murdered in a gas chamber), and despite gallant efforts by the remaining few Jews to have some opera and concert performances, the Kulturbund was officially shut down by the Germans in September 1941. The musicians were sent to concentration camps where most died.

The most important legacy of the Kulturbund was the effort by many members of the organization to look inward and become involved with Jewish music. By being shut out from

[7] Levi, 49-57.

[8] Michael Meyer, *The Politics of the Music in the Third Reich* (New York: Peter Lang, 1993), 76-77.

[9] On the nights of 9-10 November 1938, Nazi hooligans wandered through Jewish neighborhoods in Germany, breaking windows of businesses, synagogues and homes, looting, burning, and rounding up Jews to be sent to concentration camps.

the non-Jewish musical world, the German Jews were forced to notice their own composers and music which, before 1933, they had largely ignored. In terms of classical music, attention was now given to living Jewish composers such as Ernst Toch (1887-1964) and Karol Rathaus (1895-1954), and "at least 155 works by over 70 Jewish composers were performed during the eight years of the Kulturbund's existence."[10] Most were in an old-fashioned late romantic style, however. A highlight of the opera productions was a performance in September 1938 in Berlin of Weinberg's Zionist opera *The Pioneers*, since Zionism now appeared as a salvation to those facing death in Germany. In addition to concert music, there was also revived interest in Jewish folk music and synagogue music.

Chief among the organizers of such music was Chemjo Winawer (= Vinaver, 1900-74) who formed the choir *Ha-nigun* in July 1933, and continued performing both traditional synagogue music and new choral works in concert halls and in synagogues until forced to emigrate to America in 1938. Two others were important in spreading Jewish folk music both before 1933 and afterward within the Kulturbund. Arno Nadel (1878-1943), born in Vilna, settled in Berlin and was a synagogue choir director in Berlin from 1916 to 1941. He founded there the Jüdische Volksheim (Jewish People's Home) in 1916 and took advantage of the presence of the over 80,000 East European Jews who came to Germany, mostly to Berlin, from 1917 to 1920, to amass a large collection of Jewish folksongs. He published some of these pieces and tried to make German Jews aware of Jewish folksong. He was a follower of Alexander Eliasberg (1878-1924) but, whereas Nadel dealt with Eastern European song as an Eastern European phenomenon, Eliasberg tried to make German Jews accept Jewish folksong as their own. The second folklorist in the Kulturbund was Jacob Schönberg (1900-?), who had published *Die traditionellen Gesänge des Israelitischen Gottesdienstes in Deutschland* (Traditional Songs of the Israelite Liturgy in Germany) in 1926. This Schönberg went one step further: German Jews should accept not only Eastern Jewish folksong but also the folksong of Jews in other parts of the world, and he incorporated such folksongs in his own compositions.

The Holocaust in the Rest of Europe 1938-45

The 1930s were times of hope and panic for the Jews of the rest of Europe. At first many such Jews did not consider a Nazi threat in Germany to affect them. Jews in other central European countries, such as Czechoslovakia and Hungary, and in Western Europe found their host countries basically friendly and open to Jewish musicians and to the avant-garde associated with them. They continued to carry on their musical activities as before, though with increasing bullying by Nazi sympathizers. By 1938, however, with the *Anschluss* (annexation) of Austria and, a year later, Czechoslovakia to Germany, Jews had real reason to fear for their lives, and many of them who had fled their country to other lands in Europe now looked to North America, South America, and Palestine as the only safe places of refuge. Austrian and Czech Jews immediately came under the same laws and restrictions as German Jews, and Jewish musicians were suddenly unemployed,

---

[10] According to Prieberg, 88, as cited in Levi, 53.

boycotted, and deported to concentration camps. When the Germans invaded Poland in 1939, it was clear to the few remaining disbelievers that Hitler was on his way to destroy Judaism in all of Europe. While many Western and Central European Jews had the means and connections to emigrate, Eastern European Jews on the whole did not, and therefore were quickly rounded up by the invading Nazis and exterminated. Jewish musical life came to a quick and decisive conclusion.

Musical activities were so important to so many Jews, however, that as they moved into concentration camps they were able, in certain cases, to pursue some semblance of musical activities. Songs were transportable and were sung everywhere; they reflect every aspect of the ghettos prior to deportation and also every aspect after deportation to the camps. Once in the camps, Jews found that in some cases musical performances were encouraged by the Nazis. Fania Fenelon, for example, describes her experience as a member of the women's orchestra in Auschwitz from January 1944 to liberation. Fenelon states that even though she had clean clothes and daily showers, she had to play "gay, light music and marching music for hours on end while our eyes witnessed the marching of thousands of people to the gas chambers and ovens."[11] Even musical theater occurred in some camps. The Terezín concentration camp in Czechoslovakia was set up as a showcase camp for outsiders as part of Nazi propaganda, and the Nazis, in order to make it seem reasonably normal, encouraged artists of all sorts to work their trade. Distinguished performers and composers came there, including Karel Ancerl (1908-73), a gifted orchestral conductor, who was one of the few who survived the war and thereafter became his country's leading symphonic director.

Holocaust Songs

The Holocaust tragically brought a last flourishing of Yiddish song. As World War II approached and the Yiddish-speaking world was led back into the ghettos and then into the concentration camps, Jews poured out their agony in song. While the pre-Holocaust Yiddish song dealt with all the topics one finds in the songs of any people, the Holocaust songs dealt with the despair of torture and annihilation and the eternal hope that there would be a future. However much empathy one has for the trials and agony of earlier Yiddish-speaking Jews as expressed in their songs, the horrors of the Holocaust as reflected in the songs of its victims is far more painful to contemplate. The songs, after all, are among the most poignant testimonials of the Holocaust, whose authors were always facing death as they composed. They are witness to the Jewish will to survive even in the face of cruel, senseless German bestiality (emulated by Poles and many other Christians when they had a chance).

As Rubin points out, the songs often show that the authors did not fully comprehend the Nazi determination to extinguish the Jewish spirit forever.[12] Songs composed in Poland in 1939 after the German invasion are full of optimism and joke that the oppressor would soon be liquidated. As the war lingered, however, the songs took on an ominous tone.

[11] Fania Fénelon, *Playing for Time*, trans. Judith Landry (Syracuse: Syracuse University Press, 1977).

[12] Ruth Rubin, *Voices of a People: The Story of Yiddish Folksong* (Philadelphia: The Jewish Publication Society of America, 1979), 423-24.

Many categories are represented in the songs of World War II: lullabies, work songs, satirical songs and ballads, prayer songs, songs of pain and anguish, shame and humiliation, songs of ghetto life, concentration camp and death camp songs, songs of courage and heroism, bitter hatred for the enemy, songs of faith and hope, struggle and joy in victory. Almost entirely absent are the songs of normal times: love and marriage, children, joy in work and study, humor and merriment. The occasional drinking and dance song has the macabre quality of the seventeenth-century dance of death; the rare love song pines away beneath the gray ghetto walls, yearning for the sight of a green blade of grass and a bit of blue sky. . . . Through all the songs, however, there flows the singleminded will to live, to survive, to preserve wherever and as long as possible every vestige of dignity, self-respect, the traditions and customs cherished for centuries, the precious habits of learning and teaching, the creative urge to write, sing, and even put on plays and concerts.[13]

Ruth Rubin describes in great detail the types of Yiddish songs sung during the Holocaust and the sordid conditions under which they were sung. She points especially to Gebirtig, whose "Minutn fun b'tochn" (Moments of Confidence) was written a year after the Nazi invasion, on 2 October 1940, in which he tries to bolster Jewish faith: "Don't relinquish for a moment your weapon of laughter and gaiety, for it keeps you united." Yet two years before that he wrote one of the most famous Holocaust songs, in which he predicted what would come ("Es brent") and demanded that Jews fight back:

> It's burning, brothers, it's burning!
> Oh, our poor little town is aflame! . . .
> And you stand there looking on
> With folded arms,
> And you stand there looking on
> While our town goes up in flames. . . .
> Quench [the fire] with your own blood.
> Show that you can do it.
> Do not stand there looking on
> With folded arms.

And street beggars, which many Jews became a short time after occupation, sang ditties as they lined the streets of the ghettoed cities before deportation:

Vos darfn mir veynen, vos darfn mir klogn,
Mir veln noch frankn a kadish noch zogn.

(Why should we weep, why should we mourn,
We'll live to say the prayer of the dead for Frank.)[14]

---

[13] R. Rubin, 424.

[14] A Jew named Frank was appointed governor of German-occupied Poland in 1939 and served as the quisling of the Polish-Jewish community.

or:

Lomir zayn freylech un zogn zich vitsn,   (Let us be gay and tell jokes,
Mir veln noch hitlern shive noch zitsn.   We'll yet live to see Hitler dead.)

The plight of the children was recounted not only by mothers and fathers torn from their infants and youngsters but by the youngsters themselves before being handed the candy that was their ticket to the gas chambers. One boy wrote a march which was picked up by other youths as they marched wherever:

Mir zingen a lidl fun hayntiger tsayt   (We sing a song of modern times
Fun yidishe tsores, fun yidishe layd,   Of Jewish troubles and Jewish suffering,
Un chotsh mir zenen yinglech kleyn   And though we are still very young lads
Mir veysn dem hunger, mir knonen dem payn.   We know of hunger, we know of pain.)

A twelve-year-old girl fights her fate by doggedly believing in her people:

Eyns, tsvey, dray,   (One, two three,
Der tog vil nit farbay,   The days seem to drag by,
Shlepn tsigl, breter, shteyner,   Lugging bricks and boards and stones,
Un fun toyte mentshn beyner,   And of dead corpses, the bones,
Got! vi tut dos vey!   God! How painful it is!

Eyns, tsvey, dray,   One, two three,
Her tsu mayn geshrey!   Listen to my cry!
Fun umbakante masn-kvorim   Of unmarked mass graves
Kleyne kinder fun chadorim   Of children from the Hebrew schools
Kayn mames do mit zey.   Without their mothers here.

Eyns, tsvey, dray,   One, two, three,
Gloybn mir getray,   We faithfully believe,
Vartn mir un hofn   As we wait and hope
Vi du host undz farshprochn,   As you have promised us:
Am yisroel chay!   That Israel lives!)

Those Jews who were able to escape and fight back had their own folk songs, too. The songs of the *Yidn-Partizaner*—the Jewish partisans—form a large repertory. "Veynik zaynen mir in tsol, drayste vi milionen" (We are very few in number, But our courage is of millions) was sung by the Voroshilov brigade in White Russia. The most famous of the partisan songs was Hirsh Glik's (1920-ca. 1944) "Zog nit keynmol az du geyst dem letstn veg" (Never say that you are treading the final path) set to a melody by brothers named Pokras from the Soviet Union. Many other Yiddish folk texts were set to Soviet tunes or to other folk melodies, and unless there were survivors to sing them after the war, only the texts survived.

Yaakov Rotenberg (born in Lodz in 1926) was interviewed by Gila Flam in Israel forty-five years after the war for his remembrances of the music of the ghetto and camps, and he recalled the importance of the street songs for his survival.

> . . . A human being always strives for something. So I found the songs. A song is also something. It is a relaxing drug for people. It was something like that for me. At that time I did not understand the significance of these songs. Now I do; when one listens to a song he escapes from everyday life, he escapes from his despair.[15]

Rotenberg also reflected that "[These songs] served in place of newspapers, radios, and other forms of entertainment." Flam has interviewed a number of the survivors from the Lodz ghetto and published the songs which they sang. These songs describe the daily experiences in the ghetto. In some cases the songs are parodies of earlier Yiddish classics, such as "Ver klapt dos azoy shpet bay nakht?" (Who knocks here so late at night?) (Flam no. 30), which is an adaptation of a song by the same title in Cahan's 1957 anthology (nos. 104-05) and Beregovski's collections (Slobin no. 327). What was a love song between a man and a woman in an idealistic world becomes in the Lodz ghetto during the Holocaust an impassioned dialogue about the basic need for food.

Concerts and Yiddish Theater in the Occupied Cities and Camps

During the war many Polish Jews were first herded into ghettos in one of the larger cities—Warsaw's Jewish population alone went up to 450,000, not spread throughout the large city but now confined to the tiny old ghetto—and to some extent music and musical theater continued, though under severely impoverished conditions. The masses spoke Yiddish, so Yiddish was the language of nearly all performances, but this caused some problems for assimilated Jews who, if they were older, had forgotten their Yiddish or, if they were younger, had never known any Yiddish. Many performances were in private apartments of those Jews who still had some money, and others were in children's play areas (schools were officially banned). Beggars, often former stage performers, lined the streets, and begged for anything while they fiddled or sang. Vilna had a theater that performed Sholom Aleichem, Goldfaden, Hirschbein, Pinsky, and others from January 1942 to June 1943, when massive deportation ended Jewish life there.

There were also little cabaret theater companies throughout Poland and Lithuania which entertained wherever they could. In Vilna the composer Kasriel Broyde wrote songs for such cabarets, and for his efforts he was arrested and died in a camp in Estonia. Pinchas Shaar, a designer for the Revue Theater in the Lodz ghetto, fared better. Along with other survivors from there he recalls that most of the songs were from before the war, and that the most successful

---

[15] Gila Flam, *Singing for Survival: Songs of the Lodz Ghetto, 1940-45* (Urbana and Chicago: University of Illinois Press, 1992), 53.

at the time in Lodz was the duet "Ver der ershter vet lakhn?" (Who will laugh first?) by Gebirtig.[16] The revues were like cabarets in that there was no story, just a collection of Yiddish songs. David Beyglman (1887-1944) composed for the revue a lullaby "Makh tsi di eygelekh" (Close your eyes) on a text by Isaiah Shpigl (1906-90), which, after it was sung for the Jewish governor of Lodz, caused the poet to be transferred and nearly killed because it was a pessimistic song.[17]

In Warsaw, the largest ghetto in Europe, Jews were able to have orchestras and choruses after the Nazis took control of the city in 1939, most of which remained in operation until the famous Warsaw Uprising from April to May 1943 led to the slaughter of hundreds of thousands of Jews.[18] Before the invasion, many Jewish orchestral musicians had been distinguished members of Polish orchestras, not only of Warsaw but of other cities and towns as well. Now they were part of the Warsaw ghetto orchestras. The best orchestra was formed by composers Adam Fumanski and Marion Neuteich in 1940; a second orchestra was organized in 1941. Of the three active choruses, one was a children's chorus and another was a youth chorus; there was also an all-female chorus. Performance venues were scarce, so many concerts were held in synagogues and outdoors.

In addition to classical concerts there were many cabarets and cafes in which distinguished musicians performed in Yiddish, Hebrew, and Polish; Marysia Ajzensztat, known as the "Nightingale of the Ghetto," was probably the most highly regarded of such singers.[19] Menahem Kipnis and his wife, Zimrah Zeligfeld, gave concerts of Jewish folk music, and Warsaw's leading cantor, Gerson Sirota (1874-1943) sang with the orchestra in the library of the Tlomacki Synagogue. Warsaw had five Jewish theaters during the first two years of occupation, but after summer, 1941 most of the actors had been deported and they had to close. On the streets poor musicians begged for alms, and after they sold their instruments for food, they sang as best they could. Many died of starvation and disease. Yet, however sad their conditions were, many ghetto performers helped distract the populace from the tragedy that awaited them, at least for a while.

From the ghettos those Jews who were not already murdered were sent to concentration camps, where in utter desperation to survive, the inmates sang of hope and encouraged interred professional musicians to perform. Individual accounts from the few survivors tell of efforts by exhausted, humiliated, sick prisoners who composed or performed until their last breath. One who survived Auschwitz related how the German commandant wanted to be entertained by violin music; the first violinist who was brought forth could not play a popular waltz, so he was shot, but the survivor, who was called next, somehow could play the tune and survived. In some camps larger performances took place, such as symphony and oratorio concerts for the enjoyment primarily of the German guards; composers such as Viktor Ullmann in Theresienstadt sometimes composed new works for such performances.

[16] Flam, 131-35.

[17] Ibid., 146-48.

[18] For a description of musical life in Nazi-occupied Warsaw, cf. Stephen Powitz, "Musical Life in the Warsaw Ghetto," *Journal of Jewish Music and Liturgy* 4 (1981-82): 2-10.

[19] Alexander Donat, *The Holocaust Kingdom: A Memoir* (New York: Holt, Rinehart and Winston, 1965), 43, as quoted in Powitz, 8.

Composers Under and Against the Nazis

Some non-Jewish composers expressed their opposition to Hitler before the war began. One of the most significant musical statements against the Nazis came from Paul Hindemith (1895-1963), a non-Jew married to a Jewess. Hindemith had achieved great fame prior to 1933 as one of the leaders of the German avant-garde, and he held an important teaching post at the Berlin Hochschule für Musik. When the Nazis took over, he was attacked both for his choice of a wife and for his eclectic music. Deprived of support and income, he left for Turkey in 1934, then Switzerland, and finally the United States in 1937. His opera *Mathis der Maler* (Matthias the Painter, written 1934-35, premiered in Switzerland 1938) is a clear attack on the Nazis who interfere with the arts; it reaches a zenith of protest against Hitler during a book-burning scene reminiscent of the many book burnings instigated by Hitler's ministers that took place in Germany in the 1930s.[20] While the opera does not single out Jews as the victims, it makes clear that Jewish artists are the ones to suffer from this debased German regime. Other anti-German works which appeared during the next few years included Sergei Prokofiev's opera *War and Peace* (1941-52) in Russia and Michael Tippett's (1905-98) oratorio *A Child of Our Time* (1939-41) in England. The latter was inspired by Herschel Grynspan, a Jewish youth, who assassinated a Nazi embassy official in Paris in 1938.

It was difficult for Jewish composers to write concert music about the Holocaust while it was going on, but in the camps several composers managed to do so, especially in Terezín. The situation in that Czech camp was different from that in the others in that the Nazis enabled the inmates to have musical organizations, including an orchestra. The outside world was to be tricked into believing that concentration camps were merely detention camps, and therefore artistic creativity was encouraged in Terezín, the show place for the duping of the International Red Cross. Since outstanding performers and conductors were also in the camp, the situation lent itself to composers whose urge to give musical testimony to the atrocities in the camp could be realized by actual performances. A distinguished group of Czech composers were sent there, including Viktor Ullmann, Pavel Haas, Hans Krása, Gideon Klein, Zikmund (= Siegmund) Schul, and Karel Berman.[21]

Viktor Ullmann (1898-1944), a pupil of Schoenberg in Vienna, was one of the bright young stars of the avant-garde movement. Half Jewish, Ullmann was banished by the Nazis from Stuttgart, where he was living in 1933, to Czechoslovakia, where he held citizenship. He then taught at the Prague Conservatory and worked at the opera as accompanist and conductor. After the *Anschluss*, he lived in great poverty. In 1942 he and his wife and one of their children were shipped to Theresienstadt (the German name for Terezín) where he was very active organizing concerts and composing for two years before he and his family were gassed in Auschwitz. While interred in the camp he wrote thirty-five works, including three piano sonatas (the final sonata dedicated to his lost children), several song cycles, and an opera *Der Kaiser von Atlantis* (The Emperor of

---

[20] The reluctance of post-Nazi German opera directors to stage this scene is incomprehensible since it is the most powerful in the entire opera.

[21] The basic study of the music in Terezín concentration camp is Joza Karas, *Music in Terezín 1941-1945* (New York: Beaufort Books & Pendragon Press, 1985).

Atlantis), which deals with an emperor who outlaws death but later begs for its return to relieve humanity from the horrors of life.[22] The opera is a vocal setting of a work by the great German poet Rainer Maria Rilke (1875-1926). Ullmann also arranged many Yiddish songs for chorus to be sung in the concentration camp.

Pavel Haas (1899-1944) studied in Brno and later in Prague where he was a pupil of Janáček, the most important Czech composer of the early twentieth century. Haas was much less intrigued by the avant-garde than many of his contemporaries and turned instead to settings of Bohemian and Jewish folk songs and American jazz. He was also a composer for the theater and film. While in Terezín he composed a song cycle *Four Songs on Chinese Poetry* (1944) and a *Study for String Orchestra* (1940-41), which has become one of his best-known works.

Hans Krása (1899-1944) worked under Alexander von Zemlinsky (1871-1942) in Prague and had an early interest in Schoenberg's music. He composed only a few works but achieved considerable success with them; a symphony was performed by Koussevitzky and the Boston Symphony Orchestra in 1926, and George Szell conducted his opera *Verlobung im Traum* (The Dream Betrothal) (1933) in Prague after it won a state prize. When he was deported to Terezín in 1942, he revised an earlier opera *Brundibár* (1938) for performance in the camp in 1943, and it was performed an amazing fifty-five times in the camp. When the International Red Cross visited the camp, the Nazis filmed the opera for propaganda purposes, and the surviving film is a rare glimpse today of what was going on then. The opera is designed to be performed by children and was originally written in 1941 for the children in the Hagibor orphanage in Prague. By the time of its Prague premier in 1942, the composer and some of the others involved in its production had been deported to Terezín. Shortly thereafter, nearly everyone else connected with the production was in the camp, too, so it was decided to reproduce the opera there. Despite this success, however, or maybe because of it, Krása was sent to Auschwitz Concentration Camp in 1944 and shot. The children, including Honza Treichlinger, a fourteen-year-old who caused a major sensation for his gifted portrayal of the title role, were subsequently shipped to Auschwitz and gassed to death.

The three youngest composers of outstanding ability in Terezín were Gideon Klein, Zikmund Schul, and Karel Berman. Klein (1919-45) was a child prodigy and graduated as a star pianist from the Prague conservatory at twenty in 1939. A pupil of Alois Hába (1893-1973) and an admirer of Janáček (1854-1928), Schoenberg, and Alban Berg (1885-1935), Klein was a modernist who had the misfortune of embarking on a career just as he was being rounded up for deportation. Once in Terezín he quickly became a leader of the concerts there, but once Terezín was no longer the Nazi showcase, he was deported to Auschwitz and executed. He had little time to compose, but he did manage to write a *Fantasy and Fugue for String Quartet and String Trio* and a *Partita for String Orchestra* (1943).

Zikmund Schul (1916-44) was born in Germany and started his advanced compositional studies with Hindemith. Because of the Nazi takeover, however, he was forced to flee and went to Prague where he was immediately taken as a pupil by Hába. He was incarcerated by the Nazis in Terezín at the end of 1941 and spent the remainder of his brief life there. Schul's compositions

---

[22] Nicolas Slonimsky, *The Concise Baker's Biographical Dictionary of Musicians*, 8th ed. (New York: Schirmer, 1994), 1052.

written in the camp had a Jewish orientation, starting with *Two Chassidic Dances* for viola and cello, opus 15 (1941-42) and continuing with *Ki tavou al-ha-eretz* (Go to the land) for boys' chorus, 1942, a fugue for cantor solo with male choir (1942), and an incomplete *Duo for Violin and Viola* (1943).

When Karel Berman arrived in Terezín in 1943, he had not yet completed his studies, but he did have several compositions to his credit. While in the camp he wrote *Terezín* for piano and *Poupata*, a song cycle for voice and piano. Berman was the only one of the group of composers to survive the war. After he was freed, he continued his studies in Prague and became an important figure in opera in Czechoslovakia. He was a highly regarded vocal teacher and taught at the Conservatory in Prague until his retirement in 1991. Other composers, such as Carlo Taube (1897-1944), Viktor Kohn, Frantisek Domazlicky (b. 1913), Ilse Weber (1903-44) and Karel Reiner (1910-79), wrote music which is either lost or not of the same outstanding caliber as by the others; they, too, helped keep Jewish music alive in the concentration camps.

Meanwhile some other composers were interned in other camps. Aleksander Kulisiewicz, who was freed at the end of the war, spent five years in Sachsenhausen concentration camp near Berlin, where he composed many songs. He also memorized the songs sung and composed by others who did not survive the war, and afterwards he wrote them out. Comprising an amazing 100,000 pages of text, his collection is now housed at the Holocaust Museum in Washington, D.C.

Erwin Schulhoff (1894-1942), who was a socialist and who tarried too long deciding whether or not to emigrate to the Soviet Union, was caught by the Nazis and deported to Wulzburg concentration camp near Munich, where he died of tuberculosis. He was a pupil of Max Reger and Hába and was identified during the 1920s and 1930s as one of Europe's major avant-garde composers. After becoming a communist in the mid-1930s, his style changed to a slick, superficial transparency that he did not deal with very well. This is in keeping with the Communist belief that music should be simple and directly appealing to the masses. The resulting late compositions, therefore, do not live up to the success of his earlier ones. He was beginning his Eighth Symphony when he died.

After the war both Jews and non-Jews began to memorialize the many Jews killed by the Nazis. Among the first was Arnold Schoenberg, who was commissioned by Serge Koussevizky in 1946 to commemorate the Warsaw Ghetto Uprising. The resulting piece, *A Survivor from Warsaw* (unison male chorus, orchestra, narrator, 1947), is a no-holds-barred account of the horrors faced by the Jewish martyrs of the Polish capital. Russia's greatest post-war composer, Dmitri Shostakovich (1906-76), set to music various anti-fascist and anti-tyranny poems in his Symphony No. 14. More specifically, the first movement of his Symphony No. 13 (1962), a musical setting of Yevtushenko's poem "Babi Yar," is both a commemoration of the Jews shot near Kiev by the Nazis and a protest against the Soviet government that it did not place any memorial on the spot. By writing these two symphonies and also a setting of Jewish songs Shostakovich placed his life and career in jeopardy; the Thirteenth Symphony was actually performed clandestinely in Moscow and a tape copy was then sent to America for public performance. Another specific event that was memorialized in music is *Kristallnacht*, the remembrance of which was composed in Samuel Adler's *Stars in the Dust* (1986) for soprano, tenor, baritone, narrator, chorus, and seven-piece instrumental ensemble. This is a cantata whose text was written by Samuel Rosenbaum (1919-97).

Some post-war composers wrote works commemorating the entire Holocaust. For example, the Catholic, Polish composer Krzysztof Penderecki (b. 1933) dedicated his setting of the Latin sequence *Dies Irae* (1967)—a part of the Catholic Requiem Mass for the dead—to the memory of those murdered at the Polish village, Auschwitz. A work for mixed chorus, soloists, and orchestra, it had its premier at the site of the Auschwitz Concentration Camp. A few years later Lazar Weiner wrote a musical *Kaddish in Memory of the Six Million* (1971), scored for mixed choir, tenor solo, and piano.

The Israeli composer Aharon Harlap (b. 1941) composed *The Fire and the Mountains* (*Ha-eish veheharim*, 1980) for mixed chorus, soloists, narrator, and orchestra. Simon Sargon's first symphony (1985) is entitled *Holocaust*; it is scored for male chorus, baritone solo, and orchestra. By far the most common subject of Holocaust music is the relics of the 15,000 children who were interred in Theresienstadt from 1942 to 1944, of whom only a hundred survived the war. When not performing slave labor for the Nazis, the children were allowed to draw and write poems. Some of these poems have been set to music.

Srul Irving Glick (b. 1936), a cantor in Toronto, set "I Never Saw Another Butterfly" for choir, as did Cantor Charles Davidson in 1968 (published in 1971) for one or two voices or three-part choir with piano; Davidson subtitles his work "A musical memorial to the 15,000 children who passed through Teresienstadt on their journey to Auschwitz." Robert Stern wrote his chamber work *Terezín* for violoncello, piano, and voice, with texts by the Terezín children. Special settings of these poems for children performers include Joel Hardyk's "I Never Saw Another Butterfly" ("When a New Child Comes") for soprano, alto, and oboe (1980) and Jeanie Brindley-Barnett's *Butterfly Songs* for mixed chorus and orchestra (1993); Hardyk is an administrator in the Peabody Conservatory Preparatory Division in Baltimore, while Brindley-Barnett teaches voice to younger children in a Catholic school in Minnesota. Brindley-Barnett's work was premiered in Minneapolis with the Minnesota Symphony and with one of the few survivors reading her poem that she wrote as a child in Terezín. Ronald Senator also based his *Holocaust Requiem: Kaddish for Terezín* (1986) on poems and diaries of the children. At the London premiere in 1986 he arranged for musicians who had survived that camp to play his piece.

Several composers have expressed their own feelings about the Holocaust without having been in it or without using the poetry of those who were. Probably the most well-known such work is Steve Reich's *Different Trains* (1989). This is a piece for string quartet (which imitates the sound of trains) and taped voice (which eerily represents train conductors on American trains and European Jewish children on their way to concentration camps). Reich is ruefully comparing his long, boring train rides across the United States during the Holocaust to the frightening train rides Jewish children his age were taking simultaneously in Europe. Michael Horvit (b. 1932), a distinguished composer, theorist, and teacher in Houston, Texas, explores the meaning of the Holocaust in his *Even When God Is Silent* for mixed choir (1993).

The malicious, senseless torture and slaughter of six million men, women, and children for no reason other than their Jewish birth looms as one of the most evil acts in history. It is almost impossible to grasp emotionally. Both Jewish and non-Jewish composers, as well as literary figures and other artists, have grappled with trying to find some meaning in that incomprehensible disaster, and it is likely that artists will continue to do so. For Jewish composers, though, it has been a particularly difficult challenge, yet one which they have had to face.

Suggestions for Further Reading

Fénelon, Fania. *Playing for Time*. Trans. Judith Landry. Syracuse: Syracuse University Press, 1977.

Flam, Gila. *Singing for Survival: Songs of the Lodz Ghetto, 1940-45*. Urbana and Chicago: University of Illinois Press, 1992.

Karas, Joza. *Music in Terezín 1941-1945*. New York: Beaufort Books & Pendragon Press, 1985.

Kater, Michael H. *The Twisted Muse: Musicians and their Music in the Third Reich*. New York and Oxford: Oxford University Press, 1997.

Levi, Erik. *Music in the Third Reich*. New York: St. Martin's Press, 1994.

Newman, Richard with Karen Kirtley. *Alma Rosé: Vienna to Auschwitz*. Portland, OR: Amadeus Press, 2000.

Potter, Pamela. *Most German of the Arts: Musicology and Society from the Weimar Republic to the End of Hitler's Reich*. New Haven: Yale University Press, 1998.

Powitz, Stephen. "Musical Life in the Warsaw Ghetto," *Journal of Jewish Music and Liturgy* 4 (1981-82): 2-10.

Shirli, Gilbert. *Music in the Holocaust. Confronting Life in the Nazi Ghettos and Camps*. Oxford: Oxford University Press, 2005.

14 || Creation of a National Music Prior to Israeli Statehood

Music of the Old Yishuv and the First and Second Aliyot

The members of the Old Yishuv (the Jewish settlement in Palestine prior to Zionist immigration) were mostly Sephardic Jews who had no acquaintance with the *Haskalah* movement or any other strain of liberalism. For these people no instruments of any kind, other than the *shofar* on prescribed occasions, were allowed in the synagogue. In the Old Yishuv the music of the synagogue was chanted without the colorful coloraturas and other operatic intrusions common in Orthodox Ashkenazic liturgies, but it did have its own kind of ornamentation, closely reflecting the Palestinian pronunciation of Hebrew. The chanting paralleled Muslim singing, with many nasal sounds and subtle throat trills, quarter tones. In their music outside the synagogue Sephardic Jews had instruments, which they played primarily during the seven days of festivities following weddings. In earlier times, Ashkenazic settlers in Palestine also had klezmer bands; however, beginning in 1859 the bands were prohibited, out of respect for the destruction of Jerusalem almost two thousand years before. Folk music, when allowed, was similar to that heard among other peoples of the area. In the Old Yishuv, European art and music did have a presence, though in the private homes of the Turkish and British colonial occupiers.

The New Yishuv (the Jewish settlement in Palestine resulting from Zionism) brought many secular Jews into Palestine, and, as a result, Palestine experienced a growth of Jewish secular music, both vocal and instrumental. As more religious Ashkenazic Jews settled in the country, European and, eventually, American synagogue music of all kinds found its way into Eretz Yisrael as well. Orthodox Jews, however, whether Sephardic, Ashkenazic, Yemenite, Persian, Syrian, or other, quickly became the minority in Palestine, and remained so throughout the twentieth century. In this century Jewish secular music experienced the most significant development.

The first *aliyah* (wave of Jewish immigration to Palestine or Israel; pl., *aliyot*) from Europe introduced Ashkenazic secular and religious music that for the most part had been the folk and synagogue music the new settlers had known in their native Russia. Influenced by the *Haskalah*, however, they had broken out of *shtetl* life; therefore, in addition to their traditional Jewish music, they were eager to hear the music of the Christian European world. Many of them had settled on farms away from Jerusalem so they would not be in direct conflict with the traditionalists there, who would not tolerate any change. Accordingly, in 1895, in the Rishon L'Tzion settlement sponsored by Baron Edmond de Rothschild, the pioneers established the first community orchestra in Palestine. It consisted of twenty-five to thirty people, mostly wind players. The orchestra lasted until 1905 and was revived briefly in 1912, then again in 1924. In the next few years orchestras were also established in some other settlements, such as Zichron Ya'akov and Petach Tikvah. In these early years of rebuilding the country from sand, the pioneers had so much else to do and think about that the formation of any musical ensembles, whatever their artistic standards, was a monumental achievement and a sign of the importance which the settlers gave to music as spiritual refreshment.

Also a part of the first aliyah were the Yemenite Jews who had lived in the South Arabian peninsula for over a thousand years. Many of them had immigrated to Palestine beginning about 1882, and they rigorously retained their musical and liturgical identity. The rest of the Yemenite Jews moved permanently to Israel after Statehood. The Yemenites did not borrow Arab tunes for sacred texts, as Syrian Jews did, but, rather, each man who recited the liturgy had to invent his own tunes.

The second aliyah introduced the socialistic kibbutz, in which everyone belonged to the community and each individual shared possessions with everyone else. In these surroundings music became a community affair. Music remained simple so that everyone could participate. Rather than large instrumental ensembles, the kibbutzim created choral groups in which anyone, whether trained as a musician or not, could sing. These choral groups have remained popular to the present day. There were no professional musicians in the early days, since the professions of the kibbutz were directed toward farming and the manual labor necessary to creating settlements, yet relaxation by means of singing in choirs and simple folk music had their place, too. Religious music, too, was of little concern, though basic Jewish religious holidays were celebrated with the help of modern cantors or *shlichei tzibbur.*

During the first few decades of the Second Yishuv, Palestine saw the importation of various Jewish folk musics. The Jews of Poland had their folk music, such as klezmer dances and Yiddish songs, which differed from that of the Jews of France or Germany, or for that matter, of Yemen, Iraq, Syria, South Africa, or Palestine. The most idealistic members of the second aliyah decided to forget all imported folk music and seek a new folk music, but this could not happen overnight, just as the parallel elimination of vernacular Jewish tongues such as Yiddish, Ladino, and other dialects took time. Gradually, over the first half century, a common Israeli folk music emerged, based on common experiences: the kibbutz life (whether experienced first hand or treated idealistically), reclaiming the land, building a new country, immigration, war, interaction with Arab neighbors, and interaction with world folk music as heard on the radio and recordings, from such stars as Pete Seeger. But the fruits of this new folk music were apparent only after Statehood.

Not everyone who made aliyah from 1904 to 1913 went to a kibbutz. There were always some who were devoutly religious and preferred the established Jewish settlement in the Old City of Jerusalem. Others went to the older settlements, such as Rishon L'Tzion, or to Jaffa (Tel Aviv-Jaffa) where secular Judaism was in vogue. The importance of music in Tel Aviv-Jaffa was clear from the start, since the gymnasium, which was the first institution built in the new city, included music as part of the curriculum. In 1907 the first music store opened there, and soon there were concerts.

Among the early settlers of Tel Aviv-Jaffa were those who preferred to live in cities where they could continue to cultivate their interests in European, particularly German, culture. Since they did not find the basic institutions for the kind of music they knew in late nineteenth-century Central Europe, they started to create them based on European models. One of the first such institutions was the Violin of Zion Society, founded in Jaffa in 1904, with a branch in Jerusalem in 1908. This Society brought foreign artists to perform in Palestine, beginning with the Russian pianist David Schor (1867-1942) in 1907. Jaffa was the preferred site for such a society since the zealously religious Jews of the First Yishuv in Jerusalem made it very difficult for other Jews to perform secular music of the European type there, but modern Jews living in the New City of Jerusalem were able to follow Tel Aviv's model. The aims of the Society were to spread art music, both Jewish and non-Jewish, among the settlers through concerts and education.[1] They arranged for a community orchestra and children's concerts not only in Tel Aviv and the New City of Jerusalem but also in the farm settlements Petach Tikvah and Rishon L'Tzion; there were no concert halls, so the concerts were in hotels, schools, private homes, and embassies.

In addition, the new settlers of German background approached Jewish music not from the standpoint of its religious function, but rather as an anthropological and sociological phenomenon to be studied and classified as any other *Wissenschaft* (science). The early leader of this Germanic propensity to organize, study, and classify Jewish music was Abraham Zvi Idelsohn (1882-1938), who had learned *chazzanut* in his native Latvian community and had studied music both in the Stern Conservatory of Berlin and in Leipzig. After a short time as cantor in Bavaria and in South Africa, he arrived in Eretz Yisrael in 1906, where he began his systematic study of Jewish music, starting first with the Yemenites. He earned his living teaching music to children in a *Hilfsverein* (aid society) school. The following year, 1907, he founded the first Hebrew chorus, and in 1910 he organized an Institute for Jewish Music with two aims: the study of the music of all the various Jewish ethnic communities in Palestine, and the synthesis of Ashkenazic, Yemenite, Sephardic, Halebis (Syrian), and all other Jewish musics into a unique song of Israel. He and his assistant, Cantor Shlomo Zalman Rivlin (1884-1962), created choirs led by the cantors of the various ethnic groups and brought them all together to sing in a concert in 1910. Opposition from the First Yishuv, however, ended this project, and no further combined concerts took place. Thereafter Idelsohn continued his choral activities only with his own Ashkenazic chorus. In 1915 Idelsohn notated a familiar Chassidic melody from Sadgora in Bukovina, and fit it with a Hebrew text, "Havah Nagilah," probably by Moshe Nathanson; he rearranged the song in 1918 for his chorus and published it in 1922, after which it became the most popular hora ever produced.

Over the next two decades and more, Idelsohn became the most important scholar of Jewish music from a historical, sociological, and anthropological standpoint. The fruits of his work—primarily his two volumes, *Jewish Music in Its Historical Development* (1929) and *Jewish Liturgy and Its Development* (1932), and his extraordinarily valuable ten-volume *Thesaurus of Hebrew-Oriental*

---

[1] Stated in the newspaper *Hashkafa*, ed. Ben-Yehuda (1908), as cited in Jehoash Hirshberg, *Music in the Jewish Community of Palestine 1880-1948: A Social History* (Oxford: Clarendon Press, 1995), 31.

Melodies (1914-33)—remain the cornerstone of Jewish studies to the present day. In 1913 Idelsohn presented his initial findings to the Imperial Academy of Sciences in Vienna. He taught at the Jerusalem School of Music (1919-21), a conservatory he helped establish, and moved to Hebrew Union College in Cincinnati (1924-34).

Other developments during the second decade of the twentieth century began to bring Palestine closer to the European ideal of a musical center. In 1910 pianist Shulamit Ruppin (1873-1912) founded the first conservatory of music, which she located in Jaffa just as the German settlers there moved out to the garden suburb of Jaffa, which they named Tel Aviv. Although this conservatory would not last until the formation of Statehood, it was reasonably successful during this early period. Seventy-five students, mostly women, formed the first class, half of whom emigrated from Europe. From 1911 to 1914 there was also a branch in Jerusalem. The following year a member of the Shulamit faculty, pianist Miriam Levit, opened the first piano studio in Palestine, and within a few years instruction in other instruments and voice was also offered. With training grounds for future musicians in place, it was possible for Jewish musicians and theorists to begin to think of a new Hebrew art based not on European models but on the particular experience in Eretz Yisrael. In 1917 a treatise by Mark Golinkin (1875-1963) called for just such a new aesthetic, of which opera would be the cornerstone, as it had been in Russia a century earlier. Golinkin's plea was endorsed by no less a figure than the leading Hebrew poet of the time, Chayim Nachman Bialik (1873-1934), who sought a new art, a Zionist melos.

Another Hebrew poet who had just immigrated to Palestine from Romania, Naftali Hertz Imber (b. Galicia, 1856-d. New York, 1909), author of a number of Zionist-inspired poems in Hebrew, fashioned "Hatikvah," on a familiar Romanian tune—the poem which soon became the national anthem of all the Jewish settlers. "Nobody ever actually chose 'Hatikva' as Israel's national anthem," wrote Carl Schrag; "[t]he state inherited the song, as it were, along with other treasures of the Zionist movement."[2] "Hatikvah" began its life as "Tikvatenu" (Our Hope) in Jassy, Rumania, in 1877. Five years later, when Imber visited the land of his dreams, he was moved to expand the poem to nine verses. It is a fervent vision of Zionism's hope for the Jews' return, after two thousand years, "to be a free people in their own homeland," as the poet wrote. The first attempt to set Imber's poem to music seems to have been made by Leon Igly, a farmer on the pioneering settlement, Zichron Ya'acov. When Igly gave up farming and returned to Russia his melody was lost.

A new melody—the one familiar today—emerged a short while later in Rishon L'Zion, and this is the melody that is heard today. Its roots are unclear. It has been traced to various Eastern European folk sources; it also appears in a piano variation by Mozart, in Giovanni Battista Viotti's Violin Concerto no. 22, and it is a principal theme in Bohemian composer Bedřich Smetana's nationalist tone poem *The Moldau* (1888). In 1890, the people from Rishon L'Zion who were then building the new community of Rehovot chose "Tikvatenu" as their theme song, and the workers who set out each morning to Rehovot did so singing "Tikvatenu" on their way. By 1898, when Theodore Herzl visited Rehovot, the folk melody had achieved such status that the settlers greeted the founder of Zionism by singing it at his arrival.

---

[2] Carl Schrag, "The Hope of a Wandering Poet: The Story Behind Israel's National Anthem," *Israel Review* 21, no. 2 (April 1996), issued by the Embassy of Israel in Singapore. I am indebted to Israeli scholar David Halperin for calling my attention to this concise history of "Hatikva." (ER)

There were other settings of the poem as well. The synagogue composer David Nowakowski was asked to write a setting for the Fifth Zionist Congress held in Odessa in 1901, and responded with a cantata for chorus and solo voice.[3] It was a lengthy, sophisticated composition setting each verse to increasingly complex music, and whatever its virtues, it did not have the appeal of the simple European folk melody that had already won favor among the pioneers. Thus, it was the folk melody that was chosen as the official anthem of the Zionist movement for the 1933 Zionist Congress, and which was later employed as a national anthem at the founding of the state in 1948. Through its widespread popularlity it has triumphed over all other contenders, though no formal adoption as a national anthem has ever taken place.

Music of the Third and Fourth Aliyot

Before World War I there were three Jewish music schools in Palestine: the Shulamit School and the Levit School in Tel Aviv and the branch of the Shulamit School in Jerusalem. Only the first of these was able to stay in continual operation during the war, though it had to move to a settlement outside Tel Aviv to do so while fighting raged in Jaffa/Tel Aviv. After the war Levit reopened in Tel Aviv in 1919 and expanded her school in 1921 to include other instruments besides piano. Meanwhile two new music schools opened: one in Haifa in 1918 under the direction of Dunya Weizmann, and the other, in which Idelsohn had a part, in Jerusalem in 1919. The music schools were at the center of all musical activities in Palestine, and their importance for educating the musicians who would lead the country in the future cannot be overestimated. A large percentage of Jewish youth in Palestine took courses in music at their regular schools, and the number of students enrolled in the music schools, when compared to the total number of students in the country, was considerable. Only one group of Jews remained hostile to the music schools, namely the members of the Old Yishuv in Jerusalem. This antagonism changed somewhat, however, when the distinguished cantor from Riga, Solomon Rosowsky, arrived in Jerusalem in 1925 and helped organize a cantorial division as part of Idelsohn's school (which Idelsohn had long since abandoned).

The third aliyah brought into Palestine mostly Russian and Polish Jews, including for the first time numbers of artists and musicians. When they arrived, some of these were already trained and had been productive in music in their native lands. They had developed their own styles of composition and their own ideals of performance based on their European backgrounds. They confronted their new environment by remaining loyal to their European heritages and challenging those in Palestine to equal their standards. For the most part, their music was not conditioned by Palestinian music. Some of these immigrants were able to survive because they were willing to live on a meager income and to teach, while others became disillusioned and emigrated, either back to Europe or elsewhere. On the other hand, other immigrants arrived who were sufficiently young and at the beginning of their careers, so they were open to interact with the music they found in Palestine. Thus, two lines of development followed from this aliyah that would impact the future of Israel: a strong European line interested in developing

---

[3] See E. Rubin, "David Nowakowski," 20-52, esp. 31.

artists and institutions that could compete with the best that Europe had to offer, and another, Israeli line interested in developing a new folk music and an art music that would be specific to the settlers' new surroundings and different from general European music.

The German immigrants of the second aliyah had already begun the Europeanization of the Palestinian musical environment, and they continued to do so but with the addition of the new Russian and Polish immigrants. The interests of the Germans versus the Polish-Russians greatly overlapped during this early period when basic institutions of music had to be started. In 1919 the German Idelsohn founded the Jerusalem School of Music, and shortly afterwards the British pianist Thelma Yellin-Bentwich (1895-19?) and her sister, the violinist Margery Bentwich, established the Jerusalem Music Society (1921-36), which sponsored concerts of chamber music, the keystone of which was the Jerusalem String Quartet. The audiences for these concerts were the European aristocracy of Palestine, and the concerts were often held in their homes. The Russian Mark Golinkin (1875-1963) did not arrive in Palestine until 1923, but his essay of 1917 (mentioned above) led to the creation of the Hebrew Musical Association in 1921, which encouraged opera in Hebrew. Eventually there were conflicts between the Central Europeans and the Eastern Europeans over taste; for example, the Central Europeans worshipped Wagner, Brahms, and Bruckner, whereas the Russians' icons were Rimsky-Korsakov and Tchaikovsky. These differences remained throughout the pre-Statehood years.

Following the fourth aliyah, which consisted primarily of urban Jews, music became much more professional among the Jews in Palestine. Tel Aviv was now growing as the musical center of the land. On 25 December 1923, an orchestra of forty-five players gave the first symphonic program in Tel Aviv, with an all-Beethoven concert. There were enough musicians in the country by 1924 to support the founding of the Union of Workers in Art. Most of them were in Tel Aviv during the 1920s, playing in the growing number of cafes that hired musicians to entertain customers or in the silent picture theaters where many musicians were needed to perform the background music. In 1925 the Hebrew Music Society was established for chamber music concerts in Tel Aviv, and an elitist chamber music society that corresponded to the Jerusalem Musical Society of the Bentwich sisters was also initiated; the latter society played the German-Austrian classical repertory almost exclusively. Before long there were more good professional musicians than there were jobs for them, and some were forced to go back to Europe. Some of the best associates of the Russian Society for Jewish Folk Music, such as Leo Nisvitzky, Joel Engel, Joseph Achron, and Michael Gnessin, came to Palestine at this time, but only Engel and Nisvitzky remained. Meanwhile, in the mid-1920s, famous Jewish and non-Jewish soloists began to perform in Palestine for the eager European immigrants, among them, Jascha Heifetz, Ossip Gabrilowitz, Jan Kubelik, and Arthur Rubinstein.

At about the same time efforts to create a Hebrew opera were begun. Upon his arrival, Golinkin took over the Hebrew Musical Association, which until then had been responsible for opera in concert performances only, using students from the Shulamit School. On 26 July 1923, he conducted the first complete, staged opera ever to be performed in Palestine, Verdi's *La Traviata*, in Hebrew translation; the first performance was in Tel Aviv, with subsequent performances in Jerusalem and Haifa. Mikhail Gnessin, too, came in 1923 to Palestine and at once began to compose an opera inspired by the mountains there; *Abraham's Youth*, which was to be the title of a five-act opera, was left incomplete when he returned to Russia. In 1925 Jacob Weinberg composed *Hechalutz* (The Pioneer), the first original Hebrew opera, but it was too expensive to be put on in Palestine at the time; its premiere took place instead in New York City in 1934. Golinkin's opera company was always in financial trouble, and closed in 1927. He revived his company in 1932 and continued to put on operas until 1940, though the critics pointed to the mediocrity of the productions. By 1927 the difficulties of producing expensive operas led to increased interest in oratorios, and in July of this year the Bible Chorus under Fordhaus Ben-Tzisi (1898-1981) gave Haydn's oratorio, *The Creation*.[4] Meanwhile, music criticism evolved. Weinberg earned part of his living by writing for the newspaper *Doar Ha-yom* (Daily Mail) from 1925 to 1927, before he left the country. Two other music critics also emerged in 1925, the German David Rosolio (1898-1963) who wrote for *Ha-aretz* (The Nation) and the Russian Menash Rabinowitz (1899-1968) who wrote for *Davar* (Word); both had long, distinguished careers in Palestine and Israel.

At the very end of 1923 Joel Engel arrived from Berlin with his publishing house, Jubal Verlag (Yuval),[5] which became the first Jewish music publishing house in Palestine. It was devoted to bringing out the music of the composers of the Russian Jewish Folk Music Society. After Engel's early death, his Berlin colleague M. Rosenstein tried to keep the press operating, using Universal Edition in Vienna as printer, which worked until 1938, when the political situation turned sour. Engel also brought with him the goals of the Russian Society for Jewish Folk Music. He had been interested in gathering folk music from Jews in Russia, harmonizing it, and presenting it to concert audiences. Once in Palestine, he took an interest in the new Jewish folk music created by the pioneers. The early settlers, particularly in the kibbutzim, wrote about their everyday life: shepherding, plowing, building, and interacting with the Bedouins and Arabs. Engel took these simple songs and set them not only for concert performance with piano accompaniment but also for use by all Jews in Eretz Yisrael, whether on kibbutzim or in the three bigger cities of Jerusalem, Haifa, and Tel Aviv. Through Engel's efforts some of these songs became national folk songs. In turn, some of the songs were sent back to Europe to be performed by Jewish singers before Jewish and non-Jewish audiences.

The exuberance and idealism expressed in the songs began to serve another purpose: they were used as propaganda to lure European Jewish youth to "make aliyah" (meaning emigrating, or "coming up" to the Land of Israel).[6] The Jewish Agency, formed in 1929, and the Jewish National Fund made conscious use of song as a tool for mastering the language as well as a means of inculcating Zionist values. As early as 1926 the Jewish National Fund established a Youth Section, whose purpose was to capture the imagination of young people in the Diaspora. New songs with Zionist content were commissioned to encourage young people to learn their heritage and how it might be practiced in a land of their own. The first song written with that purpose in mind may have been "Shirat ha-emek" (Song of the [Jezre'el] Valley), written by Engel. By 1927

---

[4] Oratorios by amateur groups had been featured in Tel Aviv from time to time as early as 1925; see Hirshberg, *Music*, 93.

[5] Yuval is named in the Bible as the first musician.

[6] By the early 1930s some of the finest European and American Jewish composers continued Engel's efforts by arranging folk songs which had the same Zionist aim. On the contributions of Kurt Weill, Darius Milhaud, Paul Dessau, Aaron Copland, Ernst Toch, Stefan Wolpe, Erich Walter Sternberg, and Arthur Honegger, see Hans Nathan, ed., *Israeli Folk Music: Songs of the Early Pioneers* (Madison, WI: A-R Editions, 1994).

the Youth Section printed its first songbook under the editorship of Shlomo Rosovsky, assembled at the invitation of the Hashomer ha-Tza'ir (Young Guard) movement in Poland. A letter sent to musicians and poets by the Youth Section stated, "song is capable of disseminating Zionist culture better than a speech [or] a pamphlet."[7] The creation of a collection of high-quality original songs was urged, rather than "street ditties," as Rosovsky scornfully called them. The resulting anthology, *Mi-Zimrat ha-aretz* (Songs of the Land) appeared in April 1929. It was the first of a flood that followed, inexpensively printed and designed for mass distribution.[8]

Adolescents and young adults were brought to the yishuv from communities all over the world and trained to return to their homes imbued with a zeal for aliyah. Those emissaries (*shlichim*) were inspired to pass their enthusiasm along through social and political activism, encouraging friends and acquaintances to come "build the land" with them. One of the principal means for achieving that was through songs and dances praising the life of *chalutzim* (pioneers) who traded the comfort of an assimilated life in the diaspora for the sacred duty of turning alkali deserts and mosquito-ridden marshes into a vital, modern country. Bold and optimistic songs praised those with the fortitude to become pioneers and envisioned a new world, indeed, a new kind of Jew: free, independent, and no longer dependent on the tolerance of others for existence. Typical was the song "Nivneh artzeinu" (We will build our land), which begins

> We will build our land, our native land,
> For this land is ours.
> We will build our land, our native land:
> This is the command of our blood.

New songs were continually issued by the Center for Education and Culture of the *Histadrut* (National Labor Federation). Composers sang of the pioneering spirit, of the beauty of the land, and of love, all in Hebrew. Many songs became so popular that they virtually became folk tunes, shaping a unifying culture for a polyglot society. "Ro'eh v'ro'ah" (Shepherd and Shepherdess) by Matityahu Shelem (1904-75) was typical of the genre:

> Somewhere in the distance among the mountains,
> Are a shepherd and shepherdess with their flock.
> He is hers, she is his;
> Two eyes of love.

Most of this music was written by composers with East European roots, and bears characteristics of that culture's music. Many songs specifically stressed the values idealized by the Jewish Agency. There was a focus on agricultural life and the collective settlement (*kibbutz*). "We came to the

---

[7] Letter of 14 November 1927, cited in Natan Shahar, "The Eretz Yisraeli Song and the Jewish National Fund," *Modern Jews and the Musical Agendas*, ed. Ezra Mendelsohn (New York: Oxford University Press, 1993), 79.

[8] "It was not artistic inclination or inherent creative drive that made [the pioneer composers] turn to the popular song. . . . It was rather the recognition of a very real national need." See Michal Smoira, "Homage to Yedidya Admon," *IMI News* (1992): 2-3, 8.

country" (*Anu banu artzah*) ran one of them, "to build the land and be built by it." *Artzah alinu* (We immigrated to the country), sang youngsters in America, Poland, and France, and indeed, many of them were moved to become pioneers in the Land of Israel.

Agricultural festivals, relegated to minor status for centuries of landless exile, were given new prominence in collections such as *Classified Palestine Songs*.[9] This was issued in five slim, paper-bound volumes, each devoted to a specific type of song: "Camp Songs," "Songs of Valor and Heroism," "Children's Songs," "Nature Festivals," and "Shabbat, Pesach, Succoth." The volume devoted to "Nature Festivals" (e.g., *Tu b'Shvat*, *Lag b'Omer*, gathering of the harvest, etc.) would probably never have appeared in the Diaspora. It was as much aimed at indoctrinating Diaspora youth as providing recreational music for the settlers themselves. Texts were presented in Hebrew and English in parallel columns, with transliterations given for the Hebrew as well; that is, it was prepared for non-readers of the language. Similarly propagandistic songs included the rousing "El yivneh ha-galil" (God will build the Galilee), set by Julius Chajes (b. 1910) to the declarative poem of Yitzchak Katznelson.

Some of the country's most prominent composers of art music were enlisted in the effort to create a body of national song where none had existed. Included among them was Emanuel Amiran-Pugatchov (1909-93), a musician of no small merit who arrived in Palestine in 1924, became the Chief Supervisor of Music Education, and devoted himself enthusiastically to song composition. He wrote over five hundred, a great part of them for children and young adults. Amiran wanted to break free of the East European tradition from which he had come, and looked to Bedouin and Arab melodies for inspiration, influencing others to do the same. The list of gifted songwriters included some of the best-known composers of the generation, such as Marc Lavry, Joel Engel, Paul Ben-Haim, and Alexander Boskovitch. Others in that group were the gifted melodist Sarah Levy-Tanai (founder of the Inbal Yemenite Dancers), Efraim Ben-Hayim, Moshe Bick, Nissan Cohen Melamed, Avraham Daus, Yitzchak Edel, Yedidia Gorochov (Admon-Gorochov), Zvi Kaplan, Issachar Miron, Nachum Nardi, Sholom Postolsky, Menashe Rabina, Moshe Rapaport, Daniel Sambursky, Yehuda Shertok (Sharett), Vardina Shlonsky, Yoel Walbe, Mattityahu Weiner, David Zahavy, Emanuel Zamir, and Mordecai Ze'ira, to name only a few of the most productive of them.

Thus, gradually, during the fourth aliyah, the necessary components of a vibrant musical society were being established. It was during the next large aliyah, however, that the country experienced its most significant growth in musical activities.

Fifth and Sixth Aliyot

With the increase in violent anti-Semitism in Europe in the late 1920s and early 1930s, the fifth aliyah began to take shape. It did not lead at once to a large wave of European Jews moving to Palestine; until 1933 when Hitler took over Germany, emigration from Europe was not urgent. For example, in 1932 one hundred and fifty German Jews immigrated to Palestine; in 1933 5,750 refugees fled there from Hitler's Nazi Germany. While the Germans were an important

---

[9] *Classified Palestine Songs* (Jerusalem: Overseas Youth Department of the Jewish National Fund, December 1946).

part of the fifth aliyah, the majority still came from other parts of Europe, mostly from Poland and Russia. In the early years of this aliyah efforts were made to build on what had just preceded. The 1920s saw the immigration of large numbers of elite musicians and the creation of national institutions to support a music industry. While not all these institutions were able to survive, some did and the seeds were planted for others. The size of the music industry increased in the 1930s, with the arrival of tens of thousands of Western and Middle European Jews, whose standards were the highest in the world for classical music. Professionalism in music was developed to such an extent that, by the end of the 1930s, the growth of the music institutions changed Palestine from a country interested in attracting great artists from around the world to a country producing great Israeli artists who went out into the world.

In 1929 *Ha-Nigun* ("melody"; The Universal Society for the Promotion of Jewish Music) was founded by David Schor (1867-1942); it attempted to turn Engel's European approach to a new national folk music into a more Middle Eastern-oriented effort. Its three principal activities were in line with what Engel (by then deceased) had tried to do: recognize the folk music that was everywhere among the people of the country as well as in the diaspora, research and compile the music, and create art music based on folk music by encouraging composers of Hebrew music and disseminating these works into all Jewish homes.[10] But *Ha-Nigun* went further by creating an Institute for the Promotion of Music among the People, whose aim was to bring music and music education everywhere in Palestine with the latest techniques in music education developed in Europe. This kind of education was to make every individual in the country sensitive to music, not to train virtuosos. Schor's dream proved to be too lofty for the country at that time; these were idealistic proposals supported by the Communist Jews of the Yishuv, but the majority of Jewish settlers did not take up the challenge and most of the students expected to be trained to be virtuosos, not simply to be given music appreciation courses. Nonetheless, the fledgling Hebrew University, founded in 1925, took in *Ha-Nigun* as part of the school, which included lectures on music by Schor, Cantor Rosowsky, and critic Rabinowitz, along with a university chorus directed by Schor. The University also created a Music Department in its National Library, which was allied with *Ha-Nigun*.

Also in the year 1929 the Russian conductor Zinovy Kompaneetz founded the Concert Ensemble, originally a group of fifteen musicians who played better-known classical compositions as well as new Jewish works by Engel and Krein to large audiences. Unfortunately, the lack of an appropriate concert hall, unmet salary expenses, and rioting by Arabs cut short its initial season. Its only full season (1931-32) with an expanded group of twenty-five players met with popular success, but it proved too costly. The ensemble disbanded and Kompaneetz returned to Russia.

By the end of the 1920s the makings of a professional European musical community in Palestine had been set up. Music education existed at various levels, music critics set standards of expectation, libraries and stores provided musical scores and instruments,[11] and there was a slowly-growing elite of first-rate musicians living there. The 1930s would solidify this, thanks not in the least to the horrifying events in Europe beginning in 1933.

---

[10] Hirshberg, *Music*, 84-85.

[11] Whereas earlier music stores catered to all aspects of music, in 1933 the country had reached sufficient sophistication that S. Kleinmann opened a store that sold only pianos.

Seeing that the concerts of the Jerusalem Music Society were aimed only at an elite, wealthy audience, the Bentwich sisters founded the Saturday Evening Pops. These were concerts of mostly serious music but played specifically for the general public at prices which they could afford. The Jerusalem Pops lasted, however, only from 1930 to 1932.

In 1931 one of the leading Jewish theaters of Europe, the Habimah Theatre, immigrated *in toto* to Palestine from Europe. Suddenly the Jews in Palestine had a high quality, professional acting troupe performing both old and new plays in Hebrew. Such a theatre opened up positions for theatre musicians and set an example for first-class professional music organizations.

As the Nazi persecutions rose in Germany and Jews were systematically excluded from everyday affairs, thousands of German Jews, including many top-notch musicians, sought ways to emigrate. Among these immigrants to Palestine were some composers who were to flourish in the coming years in their new environment (see chapter 15 for discussion of their careers in Israel), while others, such as Stepan Wolpe and Yehuda Bernstein (later Julian Bern, 1911-89, who went to Palestine in 1939 but left for the United States in 1953), were not able to do so and left for other places.[12]

By 1936 some major musical institutions had come into being. Among the first was *Agudat Compositorim U-Mehabrim* (ACUM), a society of composers and authors, similar to the American ASCAP, which protected the rights of all these new composers. It was formed initially in 1934 and became an official organization in 1936. A small number of Jewish musicians in Palestine organized the Palestine branch of the International Society for Contemporary Music in 1938, which linked the Palestine composers as a distinct entity with their contemporaries throughout the world. In addition, the number of professional music critics increased from the three pioneer critics of the 1920s to sixteen critics by the mid-1930s.

Throughout the 1930s chamber music was an important aspect of musical life in Palestine. With the arrival of Emil Hauser in 1932, Europe had to be aware that chamber music was now a factor in Eretz Yisrael. Hauser had been first violinist of the Budapest Quartet, and upon his arrival he immediately joined the Jerusalem Quartet in the same capacity. By the mid 1930s there were three other professional string quartets performing regularly in the country, one of which included the composer Ödön Partos, who was principal violist of the Israel Philharmonic. In addition, at least eight chamber music societies presented concerts throughout Palestine. The repertories and the audiences, like the performers, were almost exclusively Central European. One of the most interesting chamber musicians to arrive was harpsichordist Frank Peleg (formerly Pollack, 1910-68), who upon his aliyah in 1935 became one of the sparks of the musical scene in Palestine.

In 1933 Emil Hauser opened the Palestine Conservatory of Music and Dramatic Art in Jerusalem, which became the leading music school in the country. In 1944 a branch was formed in Tel Aviv under the leadership of Partos, Alexander Boskovitch, and others, but very soon thereafter it became independent of the Jerusalem school. The Tel Aviv Conservatory became known as the Samuel Rubin Israeli Academy of Music (which since 1965 has been part of the University of Tel Aviv), and the Jerusalem Conservatory was replaced by the Jerusalem Rubin Academy of Music and Dance in 1947. Meanwhile the Shulamit School continued and the studios

---

[12] For a brief discussion of these composers and their principal compositions, see Gradenwitz, 343-86.

of various local musicians survived, though most of the smaller schools in Tel Aviv (four in all) merged by the late 1930s into the Hebrew Conservatory under the directorship of Leo Kestenberg. One other music school of great importance was the first music teachers' training school in Tel Aviv, which opened in 1945.

Two major events in the musical life of Eretz Yisrael in 1936 forever changed the course of music in that region of the world: establishment of the Palestine (later Israel) Symphony Orchestra and of the Palestine Broadcasting Service (later Kol Israel radio). Before 1936 there had been orchestras in the country, but they suffered from several fundamental problems. The musicians, struggling to make a living in the cafes and movie theaters, only had a limited amount of time for rehearsals and performances in a symphony orchestra, and the pool of talent for such an orchestra was limited. Both the Jerusalem String Orchestra and the Symphonic-Philharmonic Union tried, but audiences and especially critics were harsh in their evaluations. Political events in Europe and the hard work of one man changed the situation and created the new orchestra, which quickly became a world-class orchestra.

Bronislaw Huberman (1882-1947) was one of Europe's finest violinists in the first four decades of the twentieth century. A child prodigy, he had studied with Joseph Joachim in Germany. He was at first no Zionist, but he did plan a pan-European Jewish orchestra that would unite all Europe in one outstanding ensemble. After he gave violin concerts in Palestine in 1929 and 1931, on his third visit in 1934 he finally realized that a pan-European Jewish orchestra would be best if stationed in Eretz Yisrael, away from fascist anti-Semites. Fired up with enthusiasm for this project, Huberman set about raising the necessary money, and because of his fame as a star violinist, he was taken seriously by many patrons in Europe. When in 1936 the Nazis removed Jewish musicians from German orchestras, Huberman and his associates immediately recruited the best of them to come to Palestine with their families to join the handful of outstanding musicians who had already immigrated. Auditions were held, a group of outstanding conductors (William Steinberg, Michael Taube, and Issay Dobrowen) was enlisted to work with the winners, and no less a personage than Arturo Toscanini was brought in to inaugurate the first concert on 26 December 1936 in Tel Aviv. The concert was repeated in Haifa and Jerusalem, and then the orchestra went on a tour of Egypt.

During the first season conductor Malcolm Sargent joined the resident conductors, and in the next several seasons Toscanini returned and the anti-Nazi German conductor Hermann Scherchen also was featured. Some orchestral members were recruited by American orchestras and left after a season or so, but the majority remained to ensure the consistently high quality of performances. A survey of the orchestra's repertory during its first ten years shows a preponderance of German-Austrian masterpieces but also attention to other repertories, including contemporary music and music by Jewish composers in Palestine.[13]

The other main musical institution founded in Eretz Yisrael in 1936 was the Palestine Broadcasting Service. The British officials established the station, the only one in the region, with three departments: English, Arabic, and Hebrew. Most of the music performed on the radio was live music under the direction of Karl Salomon (1899-1974), a composer and singer, who had arrived in 1933. Initially there were seven players who performed in a studio band conducted

---

[13] Hirshberg, *Music*, 137.

by Philip Sharp, an Englishman. By 1938 the orchestra had expanded to forty players. In addition to playing pieces over the radio, weekly public concerts in the Y.M.C.A. Auditorium were broadcast throughout the country. Since Huberman did not approve of radio broadcasts for his Palestine Symphony Orchestra, the Palestine Broadcasting Service orchestra developed on its own into a major ensemble, the second orchestra of the country. While both orchestras were part of the transplanted European tradition, the Jews from other parts of the world, especially from Yemen, Syria, and East of Palestine, had their music played on the radio as well. Thus, the radio played an important part in making Jews from one part of the world aware of the music of Jews from other parts, and acquainted them all with the music of the Arabs.

With the arrival of so many outstanding professionals, it seemed time for the revival of opera in Palestine. In 1934 a chamber opera company was organized by the conductors Hans Schlesinger and Karl Salomon and the stage director Beno Frankel, which produced Pergolesi's *La Serva Padrona* and Mozart's *The Abduction from the Seraglio*, both in Hebrew. After it failed in 1935 the next attempt at opera, Offenbach's *The Tales of Hoffmann*, occurred in 1939 under the leadership of Alexander Boskovitch, but it, too, closed after only one production. Golinkin tried one more time in 1940 with Halevy's *La Juive* as an anti-Nazi statement, but could not keep the company going. More successful was the Palestine Folk Opera, which ran from 1941 to 1946 with seventeen different opera productions, mostly of the light-opera variety. Its greatest triumph came with Marc Lavri's *Dan the Guard* (*Dan ha-shomer*), the first original Hebrew opera premiered in Palestine.

The German-Jewish community maintained its separate musical identity throughout this pre-Statehood period.[14] It transplanted not only the great institutions of German culture to the new land—the symphonies, the operas, the academies—but it also brought with it its middle class milieu. It was common in Germany and Austria during the early twentieth century for families to come together for an evening of *Hausmusik* (music played at home by amateurs) and *Abendessen* (small evening meal), and when German families found themselves in Tel Aviv, they continued this practice. On Friday evenings German Jews in Israel gathered for small chamber music sessions in one of their homes, with meals and social intercourse sprinkled between quartets and piano trios of Haydn, Mozart, and Beethoven. Many members of the group would take turns performing, while others listened intently to the music no matter how amateurishly performed. Since German Jews were generally not synagogue-goers, these evening soirées were substitutes for Friday night worship services as practiced in Russian and more observant homes.

One of the most grandiose schemes for Jewish music in Palestine was initiated by the German dentist Salli Levi (1894-1951) when he immigrated to Eretz Yisrael in 1935. Active in his native Frankfurt am Main as a patron of Jewish music, he published there in 1929 an essay *Das Judentum in der Musik* (Judaism in Music)[15] in which he tried to define Jewish music as "the music of the Jews." In 1936 he organized the World Center for Jewish Music in Palestine with goals of collecting Jewish compositions, unifying all Jewish composers around a publishing house and journal, and focusing Jewish musical activities from all over the world on Eretz Yisrael by holding

---

[14] Philip V. Bohlman, *"The Land Where Two Streams Flow": Music in the German-Jewish Community of Israel* (Urbana and Chicago: University of Illinois Press, 1989).

[15] The book's title is a clear reference to Wagner's notorious anti-Semitic essay of the same name.

scholarly congresses and music festivals there.[16] Initially Levi met with some success: he contacted and received general encouragement from many Jewish patrons, composers, and performers throughout the world including such composers as Milhaud, Weill, Wolpe, and Bloch (and even from non-Jews like Bartók), he published two issues of a scholarly Jewish journal *Musica Hebraica*, which was and is highly regarded, and many Jewish composers sent him scores, often in manuscript.

But while this grand enterprise was well worthy of fulfillment, Levi failed by 1940 because he could not establish a firm financial basis for his organization, he was unable to form strong ties with other Jewish musical institutions in Palestine (notably the Palestine Orchestra and the Music Department of Hebrew University),[17] and events in Europe made it impossible for world Jewry to concentrate on music. Indeed, many Jewish musicologists, performers, and composers tried to use the World Center for Jewish Music as a means to escape from Nazi Germany; in only one case, however, did this benefit the Center directly. The cellist, composer, and former member of the Russian Jewish School around Engel, Joachim Stutschewsky (1891-1981) found himself stranded in Switzerland in 1937 as a stateless person, and with the help of Levi and the Center, Stutschewsky was able to come to Palestine in 1938, where he soon took charge of many concerts on behalf of the organization. Although the World Center for Jewish Music disbanded in 1940, its goals were eventually realized after the modern State of Israel was created.

Non-European Music in Palestine before 1948

Palestine proved to be a fruitful zone for ethnomusicological study since Jews were gathering there from so many different world cultures. Idelsohn's seminal studies were followed by Robert Lachmann (1892-1939), a distinguished Jewish ethnomusicologist who had been librarian at the Berlin State Library. While he tried to preserve Yemenite music through recordings, much of his work is flawed because he also at times dictated to the Yemenite musicians telling them to play as he wanted and not as they were accustomed. Lachmann was succeeded by Edith Gerson-Kiwi (1908-92), who had been trained in Germany and taught at the Palestine Conservatory in Jerusalem from 1942 on. She traversed the land with her recording machines and created oscilloscope-like gadgets to read non-Western music. Every attempt of hers was to keep the original music in its original setting, played by natives on their own instruments or sung with their own accents and styles. Great effort was made not to tinker with the sources. She, more than her two predecessors, modernized the discipline of ethnomusicology.

At the same time some of the non-Western musicians from those societies made inroads into the Ashkenazic communities of the country. The most famous of these was Bracha Tzfira (1910-90), a Yemenite Jewess, who carried her musical tradition not only within Palestine but outside as well, in Europe, Egypt, and elsewhere. She attracted attention initially for singing her native songs as she had learned them, without Western editing. For a while, though, she

---

[16] Bohlman, *World Centre*, 8.

[17] Levi objected to the orchestra's concentration on non-Jewish classics, while the University did not consider the non-academic Levi the proper person to establish archives and manage scholarly projects.

succumbed to the popularization of her folk tradition by giving concerts of the melodies harmonized and otherwise arranged by her husband Nachum Nardi (Naroditzky), a Russian Ashkenazic Jew (1901-70), who accompanied her on the piano. She was criticized by Yemenites and Sephardim for distorting the music, but Europeans preferred these arrangements. When she met Alberto Hemsi (1897-1974) in Egypt in the late 1930s, she became aware of how a sensitive non-Ashkenazic musician could render her folk songs in a way that did not distort them. From then on she used only his arrangements of Sephardic songs. Hemsi was a Sephardic Jew originally from Turkey who was a synagogue choir director in Alexandria. Most notable among those who followed Tzfira as non-Ashkenazic folk singers were Esther Gamlielit, Naomi Tzuri, and Yehiel Adaqi.

Ezra Aharon (b. 1903), was an Iraqi *ud* player who worked with Robert Lachmann in Cairo initially, and then after 1934 in Eretz Yisrael. The Palestine Broadcasting Service hired Aharon in 1936 to give recitals on the radio, and eventually he joined some of the other, Western instrumentalists at the studio to produce a synthesis of the sounds of the two cultures. Aharon played both *ud* and *kanun* while the studio musicians played Western harmony on the violin, flute, and violoncello. In keeping with the traditional Iraqi practice of improvisation Aharon's music was rarely written down. Various other Iraqi Jewish musicians in Palestine played the *ud*, flute, and *darbukkah* (drum).

Summary

The obstacles to a Jewish art music representative of all the people were seemingly insurmountable at this time. The public and the major Zionist institutions put an emphasis on folk, rather than art music. Many Jewish musicians from Eastern Europe and the Middle East had no training in Western art music, and in general there was a lack of a common denominator, so diverse were the backgrounds of the new settlers and the Middle Eastern community. All the institutions of art music that grew up were geared toward the European concert repertoire, not promulgation of a national folk melos. Only in the many choral groups, nearly all amateur, which flourished throughout the country in both the smallest kibbutz and the largest metropolitan area from the earliest days of the first aliyah to 1948, was there an attempt to reach the people with a new folk music in an artistic setting.

Those considerations were swept aside with the flood of first-rate German performers, teachers, scholars, and composers who arrived during the 1930s, fleeing from the Nazis. They brought with them their urbanized Jewish music and urbanized German musical organizations. Many of these musicians embraced the indigenous sounds of their new country and started a synthesis of all Jewish types, as well as promoted an understanding of the diversity that would keep Israel's musical culture vibrant. Whereas the earlier Russian immigrants moved to farming communities and had little formal musical training, the German Jews came from and moved to cities and had considerable musical sophistication. The German immigrants had the following options: remain fixed in their German tastes (e.g., Stepan Wolpe), give in wholly to some as yet-to-be fully defined Israeli taste, or compromise (Ben-Haim and Tal). The Russian Jews were seeking national cultural unity, but most Germans resisted this; Israel could sing in many musical styles. What came to unify all these people as Israelis was their common language (Hebrew), their roots in the Bible, and their common history since the 1930s. Starting in May 1948, it became Israel's responsibility to determine its own folk and art music.

Suggestions for Further Reading

Bohlman, Philip V. *"The Land Where Two Streams Flow": Music in the German-Jewish Community of Israel*. Urbana and Chicago: University of Illinois Press, 1989.

Bohlman, Philip V. *The World Centre for Jewish Music in Palestine 1936-1940: Jewish Musical Life on the Eve of World War II*. Oxford: Clarendon Press, 1992.

Gradenwitz, Peter. *The Music of Israel from the Biblical Era to Modern Times*. 2nd rev. ed. Portland, OR: Amadeus Press, 1996.

Hirshberg, Jehoash. *Music in the Jewish Community of Palestine 1880-1948: A Social History*. Oxford: Clarendon Press, 1995.

Nathan, Hans, ed. *Israeli Folk Music: Songs of the Early Pioneers*. Madison, WI: A-R Editions, 1994.

15 || *Music in Modern Israel*

The Jewish State Reborn

A new chapter in Jewish history began when the United Nations endorsed the partition of Palestine into Jewish and Arab states on 29 November 1947. Six months later, on 14 May 1948, the provisional government declared its independence and the yishuv became the State of Israel, reclaiming Jewish nationhood for the first time since the destruction of the Temple. While it might be argued that the music of Israel is ipso facto Jewish, that is not necessarily the case. Moslem or Christian Israeli citizens would probably not want their music identified as Jewish, and pop music by an Israeli composer, even with Hebrew words, need not be intrinsically "Jewish," as we have already seen. Some might even object to calling the country a "Jewish state," which implies that it is a theocracy. Others would aver just as strongly that not only is the state of Israel Jewish, but all its intellectual products are, by definition, informed by Jewish spirituality. It appears that even in Israel—or perhaps especially there—the same conundrum faces us and the same yard-stick applies. Each composition must be judged individually as to whether it "meets Jewish needs."

This chapter will survey the social, religious, and economic factors that shaped musical life in modern Israel, then go on to look at the country's music and the composers who created it. We will begin by singling out two factors unique to Israeli culture that have had a commanding influence on Israel's music: the renaissance of the Hebrew language and the ingathering of the exiles. The first impacted the rhythm and inflection of Hebrew-speaking composers; the second, their immersion in non-Western, as well as Western, musical traditions.

Renaissance of the Hebrew Language

Hebrew alone of the ancient languages has been successfully revived as a national tongue, more than two thousand years after it had ceased to be a demotic expression. By contrast, Latin remains isolated today in the province of scholarship, in spite of continuing use in the Roman

Catholic Church and sporadic efforts to revive it. Other attempts to renovate "lost" languages—Gaelic or Welsh, for instance—generated a certain amount of interest, but have not risen to the level of primary daily use. There were several reasons for the successful reinvigoration of Hebrew. One was the continuing use of Hebrew in prayer, which injected the language deep into Jewish consciousness. Hebrew had never truly "died." There was always at least a small proportion of the Jewish population who read and wrote the language, using it for religious study and legal purposes, if not for day-to-day speech. The foresight of the medieval Masoretes, as was seen in chapter 4, prevented the language from becoming just another unspoken ancient tongue, as happened to other once widely-used languages like Akkadian and Ugaritic. Another element was the influence of the Bible, whose idioms, stories, and even words, became part of the thought and speech patterns of many cultures. Hebrew idioms such as "finding favor in one's eyes," or key words like "Sabbath," "Amen," or "Hallelujah" found their way into the speech of many nations through the Bible. A debt is also owed to modern pioneers such as Eliezer Ben-Yehuda (1858-1922), who almost single-handedly built up the modern Hebrew lexicon, or literary figures of the *Haskalah* like Hayyim Nachman Bialik (1873-1934), or Ahad Ha'am (Asher Ginzberg, 1856-1927), who stimulated the creation of modern literature in Hebrew.

As a result, Hebrew is the language of the Israeli populace today, used for everything from advertising to zoology. Israeli school children can read the source texts of their culture directly, unlike their counterparts in Greece, who need special instruction to grapple with Homer in the original. While English speakers have difficulty with writers as recent as Shakespeare, and are virtually cut off from Chaucer without special instruction, when the Lamentations of Jeremiah are read on Tishah b'Av in Israel, the ancient poetry can be understood by every Israeli school child with all the power of its original expression.

This has musical implications, two of which we will focus on here. The first might be called "acclimatization." Each language has a rhythm and intonation of its own. The musical ear of a young composer raised hearing a particular linguistic pattern is uniquely educated. There is a recognizable "music" to German, Russian, Chinese, or Swedish: a distinctive melodic curve and rhythm for each. Even within the same language there are regional or national differences in intonation. Within the United States, for example, there are easily identifiable differences between the speech of people from Maine and Georgia. Modern Hebrew shapes the musical idiom of Israel; but its influence is complicated by the large percentage of non-native speakers. During the formative first half-century of the state, Hebrew was still a second language for more than half the adult population. Later we will look at the cultural influence of those societies in shaping the Israeli melos (musical idiom), but here we are just talking about the different intonations and rhythm of Hebrew speech.[1]

The artificially-created folk music that had characterized the yishuv was transmuted into a true folk melos as the pre-state songs sank into the consciousness of Israelis until, for most people, they were indistinguishable from a musical heritage of centuries. Spreading abroad, they became popular in other countries as well, where they were widely accepted as Israeli

---

[1] A valuable discussion of this topic can be found in Zvi Keren, *Contemporary Israeli Music: Its Sources and Development* ([Tel Aviv]: Bar-Ilan University Press, 1980); see esp. chapter 4, "The Influence of the Hebrew Language and Israeli Folk Songs."

folk music. Mordecai Ze'ira's haunting melody for Ya'akov Orland's poem, "Shnei shoshanim" (Two Roses), remains one of the era's loveliest songs, while Issachar Miron's rousing, "Tze-na, tze-na" (Go out, Girls, and Greet the Soldiers) made the American Hit Parade in 1950.[2] Fluid melodies, modal harmonies, and a sensitive fit of words and music set an initial high standard for national song that has for the most part been maintained to the present.

The population mix of urban Europeans with peasant folk from the farthest reaches of the Atlas Mountains, of Muscovites and Baghdadis, Holocaust survivors and adventurers, the idealistic and the desperate, the religious and the atheistic, could not have become a nation without commonalities to bind them together. Music played an important role in creating such unifying experiences precisely because, while it could be enjoyed non-verbally, it could also serve as a vehicle for wrapping one's tongue around a new language. Song and dance formed an attractive counterpoise to communal work as an experience shared by all.

Ingathering of Exiles: A Cultural Mosaic

One of the principles laid down at the founding of the state was that Israel should be a haven for Jews from anywhere in the world. *Kibbutz galuyot* (ingathering of the Exiles) was seen as a moral imperative, not just a political need. As a result, Israel was composed of ethnic groups from Diaspora cultures all over the world. To facilitate that, any Jew who immigrated to Israel could be granted citizenship upon request.[3] Tens of thousands of Holocaust survivors made their way to the country, bringing with them memories not only of the horrors they had been through, but nostalgia for the better aspects of the life they had left behind. They hoped for a land such as Theodore Herzl had envisioned in his novel *Altneuland*: democratic and free, the image of pre-Nazi Europe at its best. That vision did not take the true extent of the Diaspora into account. For every Jew that came from the Western world, another was to come from North Africa or the Middle East. "In 1948," wrote Prittie and Dineen, "there were approximately 837,000 Jews living in Arab countries. By 1973 there were fewer than 50,000. In 1948 one Israeli in ten was an Oriental. . . . [By the mid-1970s it was] one in two."[4]

Driven from their homes in Arab countries by anti-Jewish riots, economic oppression, or religious idealism, so-called "Oriental" Jews—those from Arab lands—flocked to Israel where they encountered their European cousins in mutual culture shock that, by the beginning of the

[2] Miron's song, first written in 1941, was rewritten by Julius Grossman (Michrovsky) in 1947 for the collection *Songs of Israel*. That latter version was translated by Mitchell Parish and became a best-selling record (Decca) by the Weavers with the Gordon Jenkins Orchestra in 1950.

[3] This so-called "Law of Return" does not, as some would suggest, preclude citizenship for non-Jews, who are welcome as citizens through the usual naturalization process. What it does is to guarantee citizenship automatically to Jews who request it. Its primary purpose is to assure that there would never again be a circumstance such as occurred during the Nazi reign of terror, when Jews attempting to flee were turned away from one country after another, only to be cast back into the Holocaust for lack of acceptance outside the countries in which they were being persecuted.

[4] Terence Prittie and Bernard Dineen, *The Double Exodus: A Study of the Arab and Jewish Refugees in the Middle East* (London: Goodhart Press, n.d. [ca. 1975]), 20.

twenty-first century, was not yet completely resolved. Add to that volatile mix the later immigration of large communities from Ethiopia and Russia, and it became evident that, despite the imaginings of European Jewry, neither Ashdod nor Tel Aviv would emerge from their first century looking much like pre-World War II Vienna. Israel is situated at the crossroad of East and West, culturally as well as geographically. Recorded music from New York, Beirut, Cairo, and Paris fill the air at any Israeli marketplace, mingling in the ears of shoppers. As one Israeli composer put it, "What is more natural than for an Israeli composer to be attuned to the sounds engulfing him wherever he goes in his country, and whenever he turns on the radio? Israel is at the heart of the Middle East and there is no way and no use to escape that fact."[5]

From the point of view of creating a unified musical culture that fact has proven problematic. Eastern and Western cultures brought different tastes and practices for virtually every parameter of musical style. The Oriental community saw little point to the social ritual of the concert that played so important a role in European tradition, while Europeans could perceive no beauty in the microtonal modes and rhythmic subtleties beloved by the Orientals. At first it seemed that there would be no musical interaction between the two communities. While a handful of performers of Oriental extraction gained acceptance among Europeans in the early days of statehood, as we shall see, they did so by adopting a Western musical stance and importing features of their own culture as exoticisms.

Place of Music in Israeli Society

The State of Israel has demonstrated its high regard for music through an ongoing policy of economic support. Even while the country was beset by aggression, struggling under political pressure, and faced with the formidable socio-economic problem of absorbing unprecedented numbers of immigrants, the performing arts still received a laudable amount of attention and financial support. Every metropolitan center boasts professional groups that present a wide variety of concerts with the help of government support. A mixture of public and private funding has not only created schools for the study of music, but brings the world's finest artists to the country to teach and take part in internationally renowned festivals. Similarly, a publishing house, the Israel Music Institute, is specifically subsidized to publish and disseminate the works of Israeli composers. To get some insight into the country's many musical activities, we will look briefly at the Israel Festival-Jerusalem, one of the most visible public faces of Israel's musical efforts.

The Israel Festival began in 1961 with performances in the magnificent open-air theater at Caesaria built by Herod two thousand years ago, but it has been centered in Jerusalem since 1987. The festival's performances, though, take place throughout the country so that every Israeli can have an opportunity to participate. While it was first conceived as a showcase for the country and its artists, the festival has educational dimensions as well.

Israel Festival-Jerusalem provides opportunities for Israeli music to be performed before an international audience. While the festival may not always have been as aggressive as some would like in giving exposure to its nationals, still, the performance of a certain number of new

---

[5] Menachem Wiesenberg, correspondence to author, 5 October 1999.

compositions has been undertaken every year. In 1998 and 1999, for example, new orchestral pieces by Josef Bardanshvili, Gil Shochat, and Betty Olivero were introduced. In the field of popular music recognition is given every year to Israelis who have made major contributions to the musical scene. The festival of 1999 paid tribute to Shalom Hanoch, a pioneer of Israeli rock music, and the previous year to composer Naomi Shemer, whose body of popular music includes the single best-known song to come out of the country, "Jerusalem of Gold." Another group recently selected for such an honor was Tarnegolim, which was popular in the 1950s and 1960s under the leadership of Noemi Polani; a retrospective of her music was performed.

As an educational institution, Israel Festival-Jerusalem has contributed enormously to making Israeli concert life more richly varied. For years it served as a bulwark against the kind of artistic provinciality that might have enveloped a country closed off from ready access to the rest of the world. "We saw our mission as exposing the Israeli public, the artists, and the younger generations to what is happening in art all over the world," explained Joseph (Yossi) Tel-Gan, the festival's general manager.[6] One of the aims in bringing in outstanding musicians from throughout the world was to keep the public and the country's own musicians abreast of the latest developments in concert music. The practice was soon extended also to the fields of jazz, world music, dance, and theater. That same educational outlook dictates some of the festival's admission policies. As many as three or four events every day are free to the public, and some of those performances are specifically aimed at families and children. Performers ranging from classical Japanese ensembles to current pop groups are featured in free outdoor events as well as their major appearances.

Every year for three weeks musicians from China, India, or Turkey, as well as from the Western world, appear in joint performances with Israeli musicians. The personal interaction provides opportunities for Israeli musicians to absorb aspects of world music at first hand and fosters contacts that lead to opportunities abroad. Additionally, by recognizing the music of representative artists from Israel's own "oriental" (i.e., non-Western) communities, the festival plays a role in upgrading public acceptance of those styles. "Now," as the festival's director puts it, "there is an opening of many Israelis to these two waves [of musical style] coming from different places."[7]

This priority for the festival at a time when one might think that politics or engineering would have a more pressing claim on this small country's resources, demonstrates a profound appreciation for the art of music—an appreciation that dates back to the Bible. If, as has been said, the ultimate test of values is the allocation of resources, the Jewish state has demonstrated without a doubt that music is highly valued by its people.

Role of Music Education

Public school music teachers played an unusually important part in unifying the country. Taking a leaf from the music education practices of central Europe, where so many Israeli music teachers had their roots, two features of music education were widely employed that saw little

---

[6] Joseph (Yossi) Tel-Gan, General Director, Israel Music Festival, in an interview with the author, 21 July 1999.

[7] Tel-Gan, personal interview cited.

use in American schools at that time. The first was use of the recorder as a basic instrument for all children; the second was the practice of eurythmics, or musical training through movement, as pioneered by Swiss educator Emile Jacques-Dalcroze (1865-1950). For most people, though, access to music comes most naturally through singing. In addition to being a basic tool for music training, song was viewed as a powerful vehicle for unifying the disparate immigrant populations and composers were encouraged to write pedagogical music for schools as well as social and art songs. The majority of public school students were from immigrant families that did not speak Hebrew at home, so singing was a tool in accustoming them to their new language. In the process of teaching those songs music teachers implanted a lifelong love of their art into the next generation. To give some idea of that process we will take a brief look at the story of music education in one of the children's villages during and immediately after the Second World War. Children's villages were an Israeli response to a whole complex of social problems produced by displaced persons, broken homes, unwed mothers, orphans, and family poverty. They were a blend of work camp and boarding school. Moshe Jacobson, now retired as a supervisor of music in the public schools, described them:

> The system included a half-day of classes—five classes, and four hours a day of work for every child. It was like a little autonomous village for the children. They had farming, carpentry, metal shop, vegetables, a bakery.[8]

In 1942 Jacobson, then a twenty-one-year-old violinist, became the music teacher of the Meier Shafira children's village. There was no money to buy instruments—there was hardly money to buy food—but together with the children he fixed some broken, cast-off mandolins, built music stands, and began teaching the children to play. Within a short time a choir was organized, too, and soon half of the two hundred children in the village sang in the choir. Music classes for everyone included singing, music reading, basic theory, and music appreciation, with well-known composers such as Yitzchak Edel administering examinations. A mandolin ensemble soon developed among the children, with instruments of all sizes. Jacobson compiled a teaching method for the instrument, commissioning etudes and small concert pieces from Israeli composers such as Haim Alexander, David Zehavy, Joel Walbe, and Uri Givon, and including folk songs from many nations, as well as compositions by non-Israeli contemporary composers such as Luciano Berio and Béla Bártok. Such achievements, multiplied by the number of talented and determined teachers in mid-twentieth century Israel, shaped the importance that music came to have in Israel's cultural life. The result can be seen today in the high percentage of concert attendance, the burgeoning of locally-sponsored recitals, and the extraordinary number of fine professional orchestras that characterize the musical scene in Israel.

---

[8] The quotations and information in the following three paragraphs are taken from a personal interview with Moshe Jacobson, 14 July 1999.

Laying the Groundwork

With a rising inflow of European immigrants at the close of the Second World War, new institutions began to appear. In 1948 the new state created a Ministry of Education and Culture, in effect giving music a seat in the deliberations of the government. In 1949 Israeli Music Publishers began operations, and in 1952 the first International Choral Festival (*Zimriah*) was held in Jerusalem. Before the end of the decade the infrastructure was sufficiently well-developed that by 1959 a Museum of Ancient and Oriental Music and Ethnology could be founded in Haifa.

The first generation of composers to be heard as Israelis attempted to write music that contributed in some way to the definition of a unique Israeli identity. They chose one of two principal routes to accomplish that: transplanting an existing musical style with Jewish associations, or constructing a new style appropriate to their new nation.

The first of those choices led to the adoption of an Eastern European melos already established in the popular mind as "sounding Jewish." Syncopated rhythms of the hora[9] and augmented seconds common to the *selicha* and *magen-avot* modes[10] became the basis for a musical style that had much in common with the klezmer rather than the music of contemporary Europe. Ödön Partos (fig. 15.1), who first came to the country in 1938 as principal violist of the Palestine Symphony Orchestra, wrote a joyous hora as the last movement of his First Viola Concerto. Like cellist-composer Joachim Stutschewsky (1891-1982), who immigrated under similar circumstances, Partos concertized and made arrangements of East European folk songs, many of which he integrated into his compositions. His works included many references to Eastern European

FIG. 15.1   Ödön Partos
Courtesy of the Israel Music Institute

music, and one of his most-performed pieces, *Yizkor* (In Memoriam) for viola and orchestra, incorporated Ashkenazi cantillation motives. Alexander Boskovitch, who also came in 1938, based his early compositions in the country on East European folk motives, although, as we shall see, he later changed his musical direction.

The other route toward defining an Israeli musical language involved creating a pseudo-Oriental guise by adopting stylistic mannerisms of Arab music. Such music tended toward asymmetrical rhythms, marked presence of percussion (especially drums and cymbals), scales featuring augmented seconds, and frequent melismatic passages in more-or-less free rhythm. More often than not the harmony was modal or tonally ambiguous, producing a studied kind of Mideasternism. Paul Ben-Haim and Alexander Boskovitch were among the leading composers who sought to create a Middle Eastern sound that would make the music of the Jewish state

---

[9] A dance that originated in and around Rumania.

[10] See chapter 6.

singularly identifiable. Other important composers working in this style included Menachem Avidom (1908-95) and Yitzchak Edel (1896-1973). The author and composer Max Brod seems to have been the one who dubbed this the "Mediterranean," or "Eastern Mediterranean" style.

Looking back on those efforts it might appear tempting to denigrate both paths as synthetic. In today's intellectual climate the search for ethnomusicological authenticity would scorn them as equally artificial; but it would be anachronistic to impose today's attitudes on the first half of the twentieth century. A great deal of well-crafted music was written in one or another of those styles by composers engaged in an honest search for a new musical identity. Trained in the conservatories of Europe, they immigrated with their compositional technique already in hand. Many had earlier established successful careers using a standard European musical vernacular that did not seem to suit the needs of their adopted country. For that generation the question, "What is Jewish music?" was not an abstruse academic concern, but a practical problem demanding immediate solution. Their creative response resulted in an outpouring of songs and symphonic pieces with either an Eastern European or quasi-Middle Eastern style, which met the country's needs and laid a strong foundation for the generations to come.

Max Brod (1884-1968), although born earlier than most of the others, was one of the last of this group to arrive, escaping from Prague on the last train to leave before the German army's arrival in 1939. Paul Ben-Haim (1897-1984) came in 1933. Other pioneer composers, writers of both concert and light music, included Erich Walter Sternberg (1891-1974), Yedidya Admon-Gorochov (1894-1982), Ephraim Ben-Haim (1895-1981), Baruch Kobias (1895-1964), Yitzchak Edel (1896-1973), Karl Salmon (Salomon) (1897-1974), Joel Walbe (1898-1980), Yehuda Leib Glantz (1898-1964), Menashe Ravina (1899-1968), Moshe Bick (1899-1979), Nachum Nardi (1901-77), Yehuda Shertok (Sharett) (1901-79), and Marc Lavry (Lavritzki) (1903-67). Two others, Sara Levy-Tanai (b. 1911) and David Zehavy (1910-77), should be mentioned here, although their birthdates would seem to put them into the next group. Born in Israel, they made their presence felt earlier than colleagues of the same age who immigrated later.

From among those Paul Ben-Haim (fig. 15.2) might be chosen as representative. Ben-Haim belongs with this group chronologically, but it might be more meaningful to think of him as straddling this generation and the next, for the defining fact of his career was not the date of his birth, but that of his arrival in pre-state Palestine. Born Paul Frankenberger in Munich, Germany, 5 July 1897, he graduated from the Academy of Arts in that city in 1920, then served as assistant conductor to Bruno Walter and Hans Knappertbusch before taking a podium of his own in Augsburg (1924-31). In 1931 he returned to Munich, where he began to build a reputation as a pianist and composer. By 1933 the rise of Nazism forced him to leave Germany and settle in Palestine. The thirty-six-year-old composer had already written several well-received compositions before leaving

FIG. 15.2 **Paul Ben-Haim**
Courtesy of the Israel Music Insitute

Germany: a *String Trio* (op. 10), a *Concerto Grosso*, a male-chorus setting of Psalm 126, several large orchestral pieces, and a large three-part oratorio, *Yoram*.

Tel Aviv in 1933 was not the active musical center it has become today, and Ben-Haim's initial work was on quite a different scale from his life in Europe. His first musical undertaking after immigration was to arrange traditional songs for concerts of the Yemenite singer, Bracha Tsefira. He worked as a pianist and teacher, establishing himself before the end of the decade as a musical force to be reckoned with. Ben-Haim grappled with the problem of writing music that embraced his new surroundings, and by adopting features of Arabic and Jewish-Oriental music into his own distinctive expression, established himself as the leading composer of the Eastern Mediterranean school. His music blends Oriental modes and cantorial melismas, minutely-notated rhythms, an underlayer of unpitched percussion, and the use of non-traditional, but still tonal, harmony. His *First Symphony*, written in 1940 as he watched the Nazi war machine rolling over Europe, is a powerful work whose turbulent outer movements are separated by a tranquil, hauntingly beautiful "Psalm." *In Memoriam*, dating from 1942, and the *Second Symphony* (1943-45) established Ben-Haim as a composer of international stature. Sonatas, concertos, songs, and chamber music pieces continued to pour from his pen. In 1957 he was awarded the prestigious Israel Prize in recognition of his work. Some of his important later works include *The Sweet Singer of Israel*, *To the Chief Musician—Metamorphoses for Orchestra*, a *Concerto for Violin*, *Capriccio for Piano and Orchestra*, *Symphonic Metamorphoses on a Bach Chorale*, and sonatas written for a number of his friends, including many performing artists.

Cultivating an Israeli Style

The generation of composers following the pioneers, and to a great extent overlapping with them chronologically, was a larger group and was more widely dispersed stylistically. They consolidated the musical language of the pioneer generations and established new directions in which the nation's composers would move. The biggest single factor influencing their immigration was the Holocaust, from which most of them had fled.

Some representative composers, with their countries of origin, ranging across styles from the concert hall to the *kumzitz* (campfire songfest), include Stefan Wolpe (1902-72: Germany), Benjamin Omer (Hatuli) (1902-76: Poland), Avraham Daus (1902-74: Germany), Israel Brandman (1902-93: Poland), Ezra Aharon (1903-95: Iraq), Miriam Shatal (1903: Holland), Moshe Rapaport (1903-68: Poland), Joseph Kaminski (1903-72: USSR), Shabtai (Siegmund Leo Petrushka) (1903-97: Germany), Yehuda Wohl (1904-88: Germany), Mattityahu Shelem (Weiner) (1904-75: Poland), Baruch Lifman (1905-70), Franz Crzellitzer (1905-79: Germany), Mordechai Zeira (1905-68: Russia), Verdina (Rachel) Shlonsky (1905-90: Ukraine), Nissan Cohen-Melamed (1906-83: Iraq), Dov Ginzburg (1906-89: Poland), Alexander Uriah Boskovitch (1907-64: Rumania), Ödön Partos (1907-77: Hungary), Meir Ben-Uri (1908: USSR), Aviassaf Barnea (Bernstein) (1908-57: Poland), Menachem Avidom (1908-95: Poland), Daniel Sambursky (1909-77: Germany), Bernd Bergel (1909-69: Germany), Hanoch (Heinrich) Jacoby (1909-90: Germany), Dan Aronovicz (1909-81: Poland), Shlomo Yoffe (1909-95: Poland), Emanuel Amiran-Pugatchov (1909-93: Ukraine), Josef Tal (1910: Poland), Frank Peleg (Pollack) (1910-68: Czechoslovakia), Moshe Wilensky (1910-97: Poland), David Zehavy

(1910-77: Israel), Werner Fabian Sussman (1910-72: Germany), Julius Chajes (1910: Poland), Yehuda Bernstein (later Julian Bern) (1911-89), Sarah Levy-Tanai (1911: Israel), Zvi Nagan (1912-86: Germany), Uri Givon (1912-74: Yugoslavia), Artur Gelbrun (1913-85: Poland), Yochanan Boehm (1914-86: Germany), Alexander Argov (1914-95: Russia), Zvi Menachem Eliar Ben-Yossef (1914-48: Poland), Haim Alexander (1915: Germany), Giora Schuster (1915: Germany), Abel Ehrlich (1915: Germany), and Herbert Brün (1919-2001). Altogether fourteen composers came from Germany, the same number from Poland, several from Eastern Europe (Russia, Latvia, Lithuania, the Ukraine, Czechoslovakia, Yugoslavia, Hungary, Rumania), one from Holland, and two from Iraq.

The increased immigration of established European composers during the late twenties and thirties was symptomatic of what was happening on a larger scale throughout the country. The earlier trickle of immigrants became a flood because of the turmoil in Europe. The influx of composers was matched by a proportional increase in performing musicians. Where the pre-state society had a scarcity of excellent performers, this generation was blessed with many, so that composers had far less trouble finding skilled professionals to play and sing their works. That circumstance not only encouraged composers to write more, but also to dare more in their writing. Persuasive performances played a large part in making their music known, not only to their countrymen, but to concert-goers around the world.

Some continued exploring Middle Eastern models. In part, this was of a piece with a general tendency in Israel to reject European traditions such as the Yiddish language as symbols of the Diaspora; but their attitude also grew out of positive attraction to the fresh sounds of the East, not simply revulsion from an oppressive past. These composers found novel approaches in the techniques of the Middle East that lifted their compositions out of the rut into which they felt European music had fallen. Western music itself was then involved in confused self-examination, and the absorption of non-Western ideas offered a positive alternative to such movements as Schoenberg's hyper-intellectual "System of Composing with Twelve Tones" or the experiments of Western colleagues with computer-generated music.

The music of the Mediterranean School has much to recommend it. The compositions make rewarding listening for their mastery of the post-Romantic and national modernist idiom; however, they are not reliable ethnomusicological guides to the Middle East. Their tonal language was that of Hungary's Kodaly, Russia's Prokofiev, or in America, composers like Samuel Barber. They were, to a great extent, European composers striving to adapt to a new environment, to appreciate and absorb its sounds. Even though they represent essentially an outsiders' view of the Middle East, their works remain towering monuments in the chronicle of Israeli music. An outstanding example of this style can be heard in Paul Ben-Haim's orchestral composition, *Scenes from Israel*. Karl Salomon (1897-1974) was another of the early generation of composers who followed suit in such pieces as his symphonic *Nights in Canaan* or the "Jerba" movement of *Partita for Strings* of 1948. In the next generation, Mordecai Seter (Staronimsky) (1916-94) picked up this tradition with his Yemenite-influenced music for Sarah Levy-Tanai's Inbal Dance Theatre, culminating in the oratorio *Tikkun chatzot* (Midnight Vigil) in 1961.

Not all composers agreed that it was necessary or even wise to establish a unique Middle Eastern sound. Some felt that the idea of musical nationalism was an outmoded concept, and should be discarded along with other ideas that smacked of nineteenth-century Romanticism. Israel was an established fact, and it did not seem as necessary to them to make an identifiably

"Israeli" statement, as it had a generation earlier. This group expressed their nationalism by choosing Hebrew texts or Jewish subjects, but made use of all the modernist resources found in the music of their western contemporaries, eschewing folk idioms.

Others devoted themselves to the creation of *Gebrauchsmusik* (functional music), a term coined by the German musicologist Heinrich Besseler to denote music designed for amateur music-makers that did not make virtuoso performance demands. Such an approach had long been well-received in the socialist ethic of the kibbutz, where participation was valued more than professional execution. Some maintained a foot in both camps, adopting sophisticated techniques such as polytonality or twelve-tone writing when it seemed desirable, but also writing music that could be performed by children or amateurs as their way of supporting the growth of musical culture.

Many composers turned to the new techniques their post-war colleagues were exploring in Europe. Stefan Wolpe, a musician of great originality and rigorous discipline, lived in Israel for only five years, from 1933 to 1938, but during that time he taught a number of those who would become the leading composers of the next generation. Among the important works he produced then, the "starkly expressive"[11] *Twelve Palestinian Songs* (1936) and an oratorio, *Israel and His Land*, stand out. Another composer subscribing to European models was Bernd Bergel (1909-69), who wrote tonally-centered but non-harmonic music in a contrapuntal texture similar to that of Paul Hindemith. A leading example of this group was Joseph Tal (b. 1910) (fig. 15.3). Tal had been an adherent of Arnold Schoenberg's twelve-tone technique, a musical philosophy he saw no need to change when he fled to Palestine in 1934. Establishing himself as a pianist,

FIG. 15.3 Joseph Tal
Courtesy of the Israel Music Institute

he joined the staff of the new Jerusalem Conservatory at its founding in the concert season 1936-37, and in 1948 became the school's director, a post he held until 1952. His music has been described as having "broad, dramatic gestures and driving bursts of energy." Tal would later extend his interest in the abstract manipulation of tones to electronic music, producing a number of powerful compositions in that medium, including six operas: *Ashmedai* (1968) and *Masada 967* (1972), *The Temptation* (1975), *Der Turm* (The Tower) (1983), a chamber opera called *Der Garten* (The Garden) (1987), and his last opera, *Josef* (1993).

As the country began to take shape, popular culture also began to thrive, trailing behind it the vigorous musical venues of radio, television, and film. Skillful composers of pop music began to make their voices heard in a lighter style. One of those was Moshe Wilensky (1910-97), who had come to the country in 1932 and became music director of *Matateh* (Broom) satirical theatre. A writer on music and pioneer of Israel's recording industry, Wilensky also composed the first song to be commercially recorded in Eretz Yisrael, "Oh Auntie, Do Say Yes," recorded in 1933.

---

[11] This descriptive term is taken from Gradenwitz, 356.

Composers already working in the country were gradually attracted to one or another of the preceding approaches. Alexander Boskovitch and Ödön Partos were, perhaps, two of the most important who modified their thinking to integrate the newer techniques. Alexander Boskovitch (fig. 15.4), who had studied with Paul Dukas in Paris, came to Tel Aviv in 1938 and lived there until his death in 1964. While still working in his native Transylvania he wrote a suite based on East European Jewish folk melodies, believing, as Eric Werner had put it, that "All 'national' art is music based upon some identifiable substance of folk music, or on a stylization of it."[12] In a 1937 essay refuting Wagner's scurrilous *Das Judentum in der Musik* (Judaism in Music), Boskovitch had defined Jewish music as "the expression of the Jewish spirit and mentality in sound."[13] His early orchestral suite, *The Golden Chain*, provided a sophisticated transmutation of East European melodic style into a richly orchestrated texture. After relocating in Israel he thought it only logical, at first, to incorporate folk music of the Middle East into his

FIG. 15.4   Alexander Boskovitch
Courtesy of the Israel Music Institute

compositions. While his fellow émigrés longed to perpetuate the cultural milieu they had left behind, Boskovitch, rather than trying to recreate Paris or Berlin in Tel Aviv, formulated a style based on fusing the musical resources of the Middle East with European compositional techniques.[14] Boskovitch undertook a systematic study of Middle Eastern music, and investigated the possibilities of exploiting this lore of the orient into his own and Israel's style of music.[15] One frequently performed example of that style is his *Semitic Suite* for orchestra. He is reputed to have said that his dream was to create "Asiatic symphonic music."[16] That goal would change, though, over the following years. From 1945 to 1959 Boskovitch, shaken by discovery of the murder of his parents at the hands of the Nazis, composed nothing. In 1959 he began writing again, beginning with a symphonic poem, *Shir ha-Ma'alot* (Song of Ascents, or Pilgrim's Song; see chapter 2, p. 32), followed by a fresh outpouring of new music, including a cantata, *Daughter of Israel* (1960), the *Concerto da Camera* for violin and chamber ensemble (1961), and *Kinah* (Lament) for cello and piano (1964). In the last years of his life he turned to more mathematical structures,

---

[12] Eric Werner, "Identity and Character of Jewish Music," in *Proceedings of the World Congress on Jewish Music* (Jerusalem, 1978), 2.

[13] Quoted by Jehoash Hirshberg in "Alexander U. Boskovitch and the Quest for an Israeli Musical Style," *Modern Jews and Their Musical Agendas*, vol. 9, ed. Ezra Mendelsshon (New York and Oxford: Oxford University Press, 1993), 95.

[14] Yehuda Yannay, "Encountering the Boskovitch Legacy—A Generation Later," *IMI [Israel Music Institute] News* (1997, no. 2-1998, no. 1), 8.

[15] Habib Hassan Touma, "Alexander Uriyah Boskovitch, My Teacher," *IMI News* (1997, no. 2-1998, no. 1), 8.

[16] See Keren, 82.

blending his earlier attachment to nationalist expression with a growing interest in serial compo-sition. He masterfully wove the two approaches into a balance of tightly-knit works that integrate oriental sonorities into a web of serial construction. This phase of his thought can be seen in the *Concerto da Camera* of 1962 and his last composition, *Ornaments*, a concerto for flute and orchestra of 1964, the year of his death.

In the 1970s Ödön Partos also began to incorporate more abstract techniques into his music, moving away from the folk themes that permeated his earlier compositions and developing an intellectualized structural premise for his works. Roman Haubenstock-Ramati (1919-98) shunned East European and Mediterranean references entirely in favor of complex, highly structured music, and developed new graphic notational resources to express it, transforming his multi-colored scores into works of visual art as well as directions for musical performance. He left Israel to take a post as professor at the Vienna Conservatory and editor for Universal Editions. Other composers adopting a European stance included Menachem Avidom (1908-95) (fig. 15.5), who advocated accessibility in contemporary music and exploited both Mediterranean and European influences, Hanoch Jacoby (1909-90), who employed Hindemithian sonorities and structures, and Abel Ehrlich (b. 1915).

FIG. 15.5   Menachem Avidom
Courtesy of the Israel Music Institute

In Israeli popular music of the 1950s two performance groups in particular stood out as establishing an "Israeli" sound: the soloist Shoshana Damari, a Yemenite singer, and the male trio *Shelishiat Aravah* (Trio Aravah).[17] Shoshana Damari (b. 1922, Damar, Yemen; d. 2006, Tel Aviv, Israel) was gifted with a rich, throaty alto unlike anything heard among vocalists of the West. Her performance of lyrical songs of the first and second generation composers, especially those of Moshe Wilensky, conferred on them a depth and elegance that elevated their folk-like melodies to the level of high art. This remarkable performer remained in the front ranks of the Israeli musical world until the end of the twentieth century. The Trio Aravah took their name from the

---

[17] Arie Lavie, Shimon Israeli, and Zvi Borodovski.

area known as the *Aravah*, or Jordan Rift, which runs below sea level from Lake Kinneret (The Sea of Galilee) to the Gulf of Eilat. They cultivated a distinctive sound based on modal harmonies, either unaccompanied or accompanied by a simple hand drum with occasional rhythmic guitar chords. Their high tenor, baritone, and deep bass voices combined in open harmony featuring parallel fourths and fifths that gave their arrangements a uniquely Eastern sound—again, unlike anything heard in the West. Both Shoshana Damari and the Trio Aravah became as popular outside Israel as inside.

1967-80: An Emotional Roller Coaster

On 5 June 1967, Israelis found themselves once again at war against overwhelming odds. They surprised the whole world—and themselves—by defeating the combined Arab forces in only six days and recapturing the Old City of Jerusalem, which had lain largely neglected in Jordanian hands since 1948. In the aftermath of such an overwhelming triumph, they felt, peace would be theirs at last. It was a time of optimism and national pride, a time for acceptance as an equal among the nations, for economic growth and individual success. That, of course, was not the straight line taken by history, but as apparent certainties, they colored Israeli vision in those years and were reflected in the world of music.

A single song, "Yerushalayim shel zahav" (Jerusalem of Gold), characterized Israel's triumphant spirit at that time. It was a song that would become known the world over, and was even suggested as the country's national anthem. In the summer of 1967, as in the three preceding summers, a national song festival and competition was scheduled for May 15, Israeli Independence Day. Naomi Shemer (1930-2004) (fig. 15.6), one of the country's best-loved writers of popular songs,[18] had consistently walked off with prizes in the earlier contests, so she declined to compete that year; but responding to the request of Jerusalem's mayor, Teddy Kollek, she wrote words and music to be presented at the festival's beginning as a theme song for that city. It was an immediate hit, quickly selling thousands of copies and going into overseas editions that would eventually run into the millions. Only three weeks later, when war broke out again, that song was on the

FIG. 15.6   Naomi Shemer
Courtesy of Israel Music Institute

---

[18] To cite only a handful from the catalogue of her hit songs: "Ahavat poalei binyan" (1964), "Al ha-derech etz omed, Al kol eileh" (1980), "Biglal masmer" (1958), "Chamsinim bamishlat" (1958), "Ha-chagigah nigmeret" (1976), "Ha-kol patuach" (1993), "Ir levanah" (1960), "Leil emesh" (1960), "Lu yehi" (1973), "Machar" (1963), "Or" (1988), "Sapanay Shlomo ha-melech" (1972), "Shir ha-shuk" (1961), "Shir he-asor" (1959), "Yerushalayim shel zahav" (1967), "Zamar noded" (1958).

lips of the Israeli soldiers who fought their way to the Western Wall of the Temple Mount on June 7, and with verses rewritten to accommodate the astonishing fact of Jerusalem's reunification, it became Israel's hymn expressing love for her capital. Artfully ambiguous harmonically, the song shifts back and forth between major and minor modes, changing key centers in mid-phrase, and only committing itself to its home key at the very end. Shemer's lovely poem, with its biblical resonances, captured the hearts of Jews and non-Jews everywhere, and the intense, folk-like melody could be heard in Nairobi as frequently as Tel Aviv or New York.

That ebullience was short-lived. "The triumph of the 1967 'Six-Day War' may have done more damage to the values of Zionism than any other single event. Culturally, it was a Pyrrhic victory."[19] As the populace grew accustomed to an inflated self-image, what had been confidence decayed into egotism, optimism degenerated to giddy expectations, and materialism began to edge out Zionist idealism. Israel's playwrights railed against the megalomania, in a movement elsewhere called the "Theatre of Confrontation." By the early 1970s the country's mood was changing again under a steady onslaught of terrorism, and the bubble burst in 1972, when eight Israeli athletes were murdered by terrorists in a dramatic standoff at the Olympic games and the world showed the level of its "concern" with blasé continuation of the games the next day.

In October 1973 Egypt and Syria attacked unexpectedly on Yom Kippur, the most solemn day of the year. Israeli forces managed to defeat the attackers after a three-week struggle, but only at great cost. The aftermath of the war brought political turmoil. Prime Minister Golda Meier and her cabinet resigned under popular pressure, to be replaced by another Labor government led by Yitzchak Rabin. The unresolved discontent, though, led to Rabin's defeat in the next election, when for the first time in Israel's brief history, the opposition party (Likud) took power, with Menachem Begin at the helm. Israel's spirits turned upward once again in November 1977 when, in a daring move, President Anwar al-Sadat of Egypt flew to Jerusalem to address the Knesset (legislature) and called on the Begin government to begin peace talks. Another period of national euphoria was reached when a peace treaty with Egypt was signed on 26 March 1979. The emotional roller coaster of those turbulent years was reflected in the country's music. Israel's composers, like its other citizens, fought and died in those wars, which played no little part in their introspective attitude as they struggled to understand the place of their art in the nation's life.

Sowing the Seeds of Change

Composers reaching maturity around the time of the Six-Day War were born between 1920 and 1948. Immigrants who came immediately following the upheavals of the Second World War made up the largest group. Those included such composers as Jacob Gilboa (b. 1920 in Czechoslovakia), Issachar Miron-Michrovsky (b. 1920 in Poland), Levi Wachtel (b. 1920 in Germany), Chaya Arbel (b. 1921), Edmond Halpern (b. 1921 in Poland), Yitzchak Barsam (b. 1922 in Austria), Yehezkel Braun (b. 1922 in Germany), Moshe Lustig (b. 1922 in Germany), Benjamin Bar-Am (b. 1923 in Germany), Theodore Holdheim (b. 1923 in Germany), Yehoshua Lakner (b. 1924 in

---

[19] Emanuel Rubin, "Israel's Theatre of Confrontation," *World Literature Today* 60, no. 2 (spring 1986): 242.

Czechoslovak), Sergiu Natra (b. 1924 in Rumania), Robert Starer (b. 1924 in Austria), Yehuda Engel (b. 1924 in Austria), Moshe Kilon (b. 1925 in Hungary), Arie Rufeisen (b. 1926 in Hungary), Ben-Zion Orgad (Bueschel) (b. 1926 in Germany), the conductor Gary Bertini (b. 1927 in Bessarabia), Tzvi Avni (Steinke) (b. 1927 in Germany), Lev Kogan (b. 1927 in USSR), Sarah Feigin (b. 1928 in USSR), Moshe Gassner (b. 1929 in Hungary), Mark Kopytman (b. 1929 in Ukraine, USSR), Ram Da-Oz (Avraham Daus) (b. 1929 in Germany), Bruno Reinhardt (b. 1929 in Rumania), and Asher Ben-Yohanan (b. 1929 in Macedonia).

Many of those, immigrants like Ben-Zion Orgad and Tzvi Avni, or native Israelis Noam Sheriff and Ami Ma'ayani, went abroad to study, and brought back the idea of a new internationalism from such places as Darmstadt, New York, and Paris. Luigi Nono and Luciano Berio, they reasoned, did not "sound Italian," the music of Karlheinz Stockhausen or Boris Blacher was not identifiably German, and Pierre Boulez or Olivier Messiaen could not be picked out as French from the sound of their compositions. Why, then, should Israeli music require a national identity? They believed that their compositions should not be dependent solely on such superficial elements as Oriental modes or Arab melodies, and searched for a deeper expression of what made their music Israeli. For some, the congruity of "Israeli" and "Jewish" became a pressing question. They found no single answer, though, and through the late sixties and seventies several different streams can be discerned in Israeli music, crossing, diverging, and rejoining in confusing ways.

One such direction can be found among those who can be called internationalists, in that they wished to free themselves from what many felt were artificially imposed European or Middle Eastern features. A leading figure who chose that path was Joseph Tal, whose music explored compositional techniques such as serialization, atonality, aleatoric music, and electronically-processed or computer-generated sound.[20] Music was universal, such composers felt, and it would be parochial to shackle it to a national identity. The use of folk melodies, in particular, was rejected or downplayed, although preference for Jewish texts and subject matter continued to find a place in their music.

Others who also avoided overt imitation of Mediterranean or Eastern European style characteristics, still felt that they had something specifically Jewish to say, and sought new ways to express it with contemporary, rather than folk, resources. Ben-Zion Orgad (fig. 15.7) was one of those. Born in Gelsenkirchen, Germany in 1926, his family fled to Tel Aviv in 1933. "For me," he has said, "being an Israeli composer enables a certain tendency. . . . I declare 'I belong.'"[21] "Belonging," to Orgad, means "acknowledgement of a tradition, of collective memory . . . [and]

---

[20] "Serialization" is a method of composing developed by the twentieth-century composer Arnold Schoenberg, in which all the notes of the chromatic scale are arranged in a predetermined series that forms the structural basis of a composition. "Atonality" refers to music that avoids any feeling of a tonal center, using other techniques to create whatever sense of harmony, phrase, and cadence the composer wishes his music to have. "Aleatoric music" is music composed in such a way that some elements—or even all of its elements—are left to chance. "Electronically processed" music may use conventional music or recorded non-musical sounds (waterfalls, for example, or the sounds of crickets chirping) as a sound source to be manipulated electronically. "Computer-generated music," on the other hand, is created by using the computer itself as an instrument to generate sounds, musical structure, or both.

[21] This and the subsequent quotes by Ben-Zion Orgad in this paragraph are taken from Robert Fleisher, *Twenty Israeli Composers: Voices of a Culture* (Detroit: Wayne State University Press, 1997), 131-32.

FIG. 15.7   Ben-Tzion Orgad
Courtesy of the Israel Music Institute

the landscape, with all the emotional layers and history that it bears." His compositional style, he says, is rooted in "the people . . . a heterogeneous society, whose real common denominator is the language, so strongly connected to the Bible, and to the book of prayers. . . . This kind of spiritual common denominator serves like a territory . . . very specific to the Hebrew language." As one might expect from that outlook, Orgad has been deeply influenced by cantillation and prayer, which he weaves through his compositions in spoken, as well as sung, voices, sometimes as the principal focus of the music, sometimes as background. Textural surprises, which can occur in dense, overlapping layers of sound or in ethereal, almost rootless melodies, are an integral part of his music.

Yitzchak Sadai (b. 1935), who immigrated in 1969 from Bulgaria, and Leon Schidlowski (b. 1931), who emigrated from Chile that same year, took quite a different tack, leaning toward experimentalism with abstract sound. They felt no need to explain themselves or their culture in their music. Schidlowsky often employed aleatoric music, in which some elements were left to chance, and used a system of notational pictographs that allowed the performer great freedom, but at the same time kept the overall sonority within the composer's control. Sadai, more conservative in the appearance of his scores, wrote jagged melodies accompanied by richly dissonant harmonies and used neutral, abstract subject matter. Others, such as Yehuda Yannay (b. 1937), whose earlier music is sometimes satirical or deliberately provoking, located themselves in the experimental vanguard. Over time, though, many of them sought spiritual underpinning for their compositional approach. Yannay, for example, was moved by Buber's notion of "inner Hebraic revelation or inner radiance . . . [as] a powerful lens through which he viewed the world-at-hand and his career as a composer,"[22] in such later works as his *Ha-nigun ha-ganuz* (The Hidden Melody) of 1994.

---

[22] Burt J. Levy, Liner notes for the compact disc *Hidden Melodies, Compositions by Yehuda Yannay* (St. Paul, MN: American Composers' Forum, innova 531, 1999), [2].

Tzvi Avni (fig. 15.8), whose musical style has changed more than once in reflection of his wrestling with those questions, was born in 1927 at Saarbrucken, Germany. Coming to Israel in 1935, he developed a love for both painting and music. It was music that won out, and in his late teens Avni studied with Abel Ehrlich (1945-2003), and Mordecai Seter (1916-94). He feels today that Seter was "the person who opened my eyes and ears to what is in that chorale you are harmonizing."[23] Avni was composing in the "Mediterranean" idiom when he left for further study in the United States in 1962. He worked with Aaron Copland and Lukas Foss at Tanglewood, then delved into electronic music with Vladimir Ussachevsky at Columbia University and Myron Shaeffer at the University of Toronto. The two years he spent in North America were an important watershed in his musical thought. His *Vocalise*, written at that time, featured waves of electronically-generated sound supporting a wordless singing voice. Returning to Israel in 1964 Avni found no facilities for electronic composition, and returned

FIG. 15.8   Tzvi Avni
Courtesy of the Israel Music Institute

to writing for conventional instruments, but now with an electronically-inspired freedom. When the Jerusalem Academy acquired its first synthesizer in 1971, he was appointed as teacher of electronic music.

For all of his interest in technology, Avni was not so much an experimentalist as a colorist. He eclectically absorbed influences from both East and West, fusing them into a personal style that sounds like neither, yet has overtones of both. Waves of sound sweep through his music. Bold melodies with acrobatic leaps are offset by small gestures that bring to mind Middle Eastern arabesques. He identifies Israeli and non-Western elements in his own music, though they are not always as evident to others as the orientalisms of preceding generations. He wrote of his piano piece, *Triptych*, "Some of the characteristics of east and west, which have characterized my other piano works . . . exist here as well."[24] Avni creates lucid, rather than frantic, music—the sounds of Apollo, not Dionysus. His characteristic rationalism has remained constant through four decades of maturity and change, producing a body of work as satisfying to perform as to hear.

An almost political motivation can be seen in many composers of different styles who agreed that Israeli music needed some audible identity. They had lived through the Holocaust and its aftermath, suffering themselves, as well as losing loved ones and friends. There was a debt to be paid, not by revenge, but by demonstrating that in defiance of Hitler's plan and Europe's accession to it, there was now a proud Jewish state. Their response was a return to setting classical Hebrew texts from the *Tanach*, the *paytanim*, or the *Siddur*. It would be too simplistic

---

[23] Fleisher, 139.

[24] Composer's note on the composition, *Triptych* (Tel Aviv: Israel Music Institute, 1994).

to think of this as an entirely separate group. It was a moral conviction, not a musical one, that bound these composers together, and they ranged all over the map stylistically.

In recent years even composers who seemed quite abstract in their approach have adopted a more Jewish orientation. Tzvi Avni, as an example, has lately begun to instill a new element of Jewish spirituality into his music. Avni, once an internationalist, now believes that there is such a thing as Jewish music. "Israeli composers live in a specially charged atmosphere," he says. "The common denominator is spiritual content—some connection to the Bible, to the Israeli experience."[25] Avni explains that he himself has changed since the seventies. "Before, I thought in terms of what is an Israeli. My music is more 'Jewish' these days than it was then." He is concerned about the cultural assimilation of the Jews and what that might mean. While many think that living in Israel is the ultimate way to avoid assimilation, Avni is not so sure. "The majority of Israeli secular society is assimilating culturally," he fears. Perhaps that is the reason he has turned to more Jewish texts for his music, taking an interest in the mystical writings of Rabbi Nachman of Bratslav.

Native-born Ami Ma'ayani (b. 1936) settled on a midpoint between East and West in his music. Although he, too, spent time in New York studying with the electronic music pioneer Vladimir Ussachevsky, he did not find that suitable for his own musical expression. One analyst has described Ma'ayani's music as "Post-Eastern-Mediterranean,"[26] a term that tries to capture the fusion of Near Eastern elements with Western instrumental and harmonic colors. Ma'ayani strives for universality, but without divesting himself of Oriental influences. One does not feel he is trying to paint a particular locale in the manner of Paul Ben-Haim. Instead, he integrates the Arab musician's approach to improvisation and structure found in the *maqam*, style features of Yemenite folk music, and European musical forms such as sonata, variation, and rondo. Unlike many of his generation, Ma'ayani is comfortable treating Yiddish texts, too, as in the song cycle, *Yiddische Lieder* for alto and orchestra. His music does not replicate the external musical imagery of Yiddish or Arab culture, but rather fuses disparate elements found in his own. He argues, "Music that comes from Israel has to represent something special and unique that comes from this zone . . . I don't believe in the international style,"[27] yet at the same time he has said, concerning his *Symphony no. 3*, that he was "part of the French school."[28]

Such apparent contradictions led some composers to seek a more focused identity in Israel's cultural sub-groups. After the mid-seventies they began to seek individual ethnic voices—tiles within the mosaic of Israeli society. This cohort was the first to have a significant number of native-born Israelis, some of whom came from clearly defined ethnic roots within the culture. At least one of those was not even Jewish, although he was certainly an Israeli. Habib Hassan Touma (1934-98) was an Israeli Arab from Nazareth who became a significant composer and authored an important book on Arab music.[29]

---

[25] Interview with the author, 19 July 1999. This and the succeeding quotes from Tzvi Avni are taken from that same interview.

[26] Keren, 101.

[27] Fleisher, 156-57.

[28] Interview with Uri Toeplitz in the program notes of the Israel Philharmonic of 1969, quoted in Fleisher, 151.

[29] Habib Hassan Touma's *The Music of the Arabs*, originally issued in German, is now available in English (Portland: Amadeus Press, 1996).

The Ashkenazi religious wing also found their musical voice in the seventies. After years of scorning music not directly connected with Jewish ritual, composers of religious music turned to a more contemporary style to win the attention of younger people. They did not storm the symphony halls, but concentrated on spiritual songs in a popular idiom, accompanied with simple guitar chords or lightly orchestrated. With attractive melodies, clear harmonies, and texts chosen from the prayer or *piyyut* literature, these songs swept to popularity on the wings of three Chassidic Song Festivals, founded as a counterpoise to the secular Israeli Song Festival. Composers such as David Weinkranz, with "Y'varechecha" (He will bless you), Akiva Nof, with "Sisu et Yerushalayim" (Celebrate Jerusalem), Ehud and Sarah Zweig with "Yedid nefesh" (Soul mate), Nurit Hirsh with "Oseh shalom" (Make Peace), and others picked up the movement initiated by the charismatic Rabbi Shlomo Carlebach, himself the composer of countless religious "hits" such as "David, melech Yisrael" (David, King of Israel) and "Od avinu chai" (Our Father Lives On).

The next group of immigrants, those born between 1930 and the founding of the state, included Joan Franks-Williams (b. 1930 in U.S., later returned there), Sergiu Shapira (b. 1931 in Rumania), Leon Schidlowsky (b. 1931 in Chile), Aryeh Levanon (b. 1932 in Rumania), André Hajdu (b. 1932 in Hungary), Zvi Snunit (b. 1933-66, in Germany), Dov Carmel (b. 1933 in Hungary), Teodor Broder (b. 1933 in Poland), David Ori (b. 1934 in Hungary), Shimon Shachal (b. 1934 in Morocco), Yitzchak Sadai (Sidi) (b. 1935 in Bulgaria), Dov Seltzer (b. 1935 in Rumania), Frederick Kaufman (b. 1936 in the U. S.), Yehuda Yannay (b. 1937 in Rumania), Avraham Amzalag (b. 1941 in Morocco), Aharon Harlap (b. 1941 in Canada), Yoram Paporisz (b. 1944 in Poland), Daniel Galay (b. 1945 in Argentina), Gabriel Iranyi (b. 1946 in Rumania), Max Stern (b. 1947 in U.S.), and Dan Yuhas (b. 1947 in Hungary).

The number of native-born (*sabra*) composers of concert music has, as might be expected, been growing continuously. The pre-state composers were largely from Eastern Europe, while the second and much of the third generations were dominated by European-trained refugees who shaped the musical environment with imported tools. The native composers born in the forties and after, though, were products of an Israeli environment. Hebrew was their first language, with all the musical implications of that fact, and the sonorities of modern Israel surrounded them from their earliest days. They were products of Israeli schools and conservatories, and if they went abroad for advanced studies, they did so as Israelis.

One such *sabra* was Noam Sheriff (b. 1935) (fig. 15.9). Composer, conductor, and educator, Sheriff has left an indelible imprint on twentieth-century Israeli music that few can match. His children's concerts with the Israel Philharmonic and Jerusalem Symphony Orchestras reflected a teacher's imagination wedded to musical thought, as, for example, when he demonstrated the construction of Beethoven's Fifth Symphony

FIG. 15.9 **Noam Sheriff**
Courtesy of the Israel Music Institute

by showing a fascinated audience of children how the rhythmic kernel of the work is structured into the different movements by using Lego blocks. A student of Paul Ben-Haim, he made his debut at the age of twenty-two with the *Festival Prelude*, in a concert conducted by Leonard Bernstein that inaugurated the famous Mann Auditorium, home of the Israel Philharmonic. He went on to study composition with Boris Blacher in Berlin, returning to Israel in 1963, where he joined the faculties of the Music academies in both Jerusalem and Tel Aviv. In addition to numerous orchestral and chamber music works, he has written music for films and festivals. In 1971 he was honored by the city of Tel Aviv and in 1987 his powerful memorial to the victims of the Holocaust, *Mechayeh ha-meitim* (The Revival of the Dead), was premiered by the Israel Philharmonic Orchestra in Amsterdam. *Mechayeh ha-meitim*, conceived while the composer was in Germany, was based on the prayer from the daily *Amidah* (see chapters 1 and 3): "Blessed are You, O Lord, Ruler of the universe, who revives the dead." To commemorate the 500th anniversary of the expulsion of the Jews from Spain, his symphonic oratorio *Sephardic Passion* was performed by the Israel Philharmonic in Toledo, Spain, on 4 May 1992, with tenor Placido Domingo and soprano Esther Kenan-Ofri as soloists. Sheriff's compositions are romantic in nature, and while he stretches the bounds of tonality with rich dissonances, there is always a feeling for a tonal center that helps to make his music accessible. Combining large-scale harmonic logic with his own finely-honed sense of drama and lush orchestration, Noam Sheriff may well be the most popular of the Israeli composers of concert music. As a conductor Sheriff fought tirelessly to have the works of Richard Wagner and Richard Strauss performed in Israel, where Wagner's outspoken anti-Semitism and Strauss's membership in the Nazi party were held to be sufficient reason for refusing to play their music. With the support of conductor Zubin Mehta, Sheriff eventually carried the day, and such musical censorship is no longer automatic in Israel today.

It is instructive, though, to stop here and consider the controversy in Israeli concert life over those two composers closely identified with the Nazi regime. Conductor Mendi Rodin led the Rishon Le-Tzion orchestra in Wagner's *Siegfried Idyll* at a concert in October 2000, and was taken to task by many for doing so. During the Israel Festival of 2001, Argentine-born Israeli conductor Daniel Barenboim announced at the end of his July 8 concert that he would perform the Prelude to Wagner's opera *Tristan und Isolde* as an extra encore, and that those who chose to leave the hall could do so before the piece began. A number of the audience did, some voicing their displeasure with shouted epithets. Most, though, stayed to hear the piece, and many applauded Barenboim for daring to conduct it—and with a German orchestra, at that. Zipi Shohat, in an article in the newspaper *Ha'aretz* ("Wagner Gets In Through the Back Door," 9 July 2001, p. 9), stated that Yossi Tel-Gan, director of the Festival, was furious, for he had specifically asked Barenboim not to play Wagner, which had been submitted on the original program, and the conductor had agreed to the change. Barenboim, for his part, felt that he had not breached his contract, but had simply added an optional additional encore to the concert. He told the audience what he was going to do, and had given an opportunity to leave for those who wished to do so. A few days later Tel-Gan, having had a chance to think about the matter, backed off and assured Israeli music lovers that while he did not support Barenboim's act, he would not keep an artist of that stature from participating in future festivals.

This is not an issue with an easy resolution. Many feel that the argument revolves around artistic freedom and aesthetic value: great music deserves to be played, and it is not the government's role to decide what is acceptable art. Others take the position that it is a question of ethics and sensitivity; that is, musicians should not bestow the honor of performance on composers who declared hatred for them, nor should the audience be insulted by music representing the system that had inflicted such monstrous suffering upon them. Survivors of the Holocaust are deeply offended by attempts to perform the music of those two composers. The only common ground between the two positions is their agreement on the importance of music to society.

That appreciation of music's place in the social order can be seen in the proportion of Israelis taking up the serious study of music, crowding the concert halls, and participating in amateur music groups. A comparison of the number of native-born musicians in each of the generations of composers demonstrates the growth of a vigorous Israeli compositional school. The number of native-born composers born before 1930 was just six: David Zehavy (1910-77), Sarah Levy-Tanai (b. 1911), Mordecai Seter (1916-94), the tragically short-lived Daniel Friedlander (1918-36), Nira Chen (b. 1924), Emanuel Zamir (Pescner) (1925-62), and Gil Aldema (b. 1928). By the middle of the century a noticeably increasing number were visible. Seven were born in the decade of the thirties: Yardena Alotin (1930-94), Reuven Yaron (1932-56), Habib Hassan Touma (1934-98), Noam Sheriff (b. 1935), Ami Ma'ayani (b. 1936), Shimon Cohen (b. 1937), and Uri Sharvit (b. 1939). The next decade saw the birth of seventeen composers that we know of: Josef Mar-Haim (b. 1940), Eitan Avitzur (b. 1941), Menachem Zur (b. 1942), Arie (Arik) Shapira (b. 1943), Ron Levy (b. 1944), Yair Rosenblum (1944-1996), Rami Bar-Niv (b. 1945), Tzipora (Tzippi) Fleischer (b. 1946), Yishai Knoll (b. 1946), Arad Atar (b. 1947), Shulamit Ran (b. 1947), Yael German (b. 1947), Oded Assaf (b. 1948), Vered Shilony (b. 1948), Noa Guy (b. 1949), and Naphtali Wagner (b. 1949). That number increases with time, and it is possible to list twenty-three native Israeli composers born since 1950 who have made a name for themselves: Benny Nagari (b. 1950), Lior Shambadal (b. 1950), Joseph Peles (b. 1950), Yoni Rechter (b. 1951), Moshe Zormen (b. 1952), Naftaly Lahav (b. 1952), Avner Kenner (b. 1952), Ron Weidberg (b. 1953), Yinam Leef (b. 1953), Daniel Akiva (b. 1953), Ella Lazar-Sheriff (b. 1954), Ari Ben-Shabetai (b. 1954), Betty Olivero (b. 1954), Moshe Rasiuk (b. 1954), Yuval Shaked (b. 1955), Eitan Steinberg (b. 1955), Yehudit Ravitz (b. 1956), Dror Elemelech (b. 1956), Hagar Kadima (b. 1957), Michael Wolpe (b. 1960), Oded Zehavi (b. 1961), Alex Wasserman (b. 1963), and Tomer Lev (b. 1967).

Added to those is a new wave of Russian and East European immigrants whose sensibilities were honed in a different climate. Leading this group is Mark Kopytman (b. 1929), who arrived in 1972 with a background in both medicine and music, and became a powerful new voice as a composer and teacher at the Rubin Academy of Music in Jerusalem. Lev Kogan (b. 1927), who had received the title "Honored Artist" in the USSR, came to Israel the same year, to be followed by a host of others: Sarah Feigin (b. 1928), Joseph Dorfman (b. 1940), Jan Freidlin (b. 1944), Meir Mindel (b. 1946), Boris Pigovat (b. 1953), Yuri Povolotsky (b. 1962), Josef Bardanshvili, Anatoly Boyarsky, Michael Burshtin, Ilya Dimov, Eduard Gazarov, Ruben Kazhiloti, Vladimir Levitt, and Elmar Fel, to name only a few of the more prominent of them.

In addition, Israel has become a net exporter of musicians. Given the exponential growth of institutions for advanced musical training in Israel and the long tradition of music making in Jewish society, it was inevitable that the number of composers, singers, instrumentalists, and conductors in the country would grow to exceed the ability of the country to absorb their talents. The better-known Israeli performing artists, such as Daniel Barenboim or Itzchak Perlman, became international transients—it is the nature of their vocation; but even below the superstar level, Israeli conductors, singers, and instrumentalists can be found in orchestras and opera houses all over the world in disproportionately large numbers, considering the size of their country. The count is augmented by a growing number of expatriate composers retaining Israeli identity while living and working in other countries. Among those are Daniel Oppenheim, Jan Radzynski, Shulamit Ran, Amnon Wolman, and Yehuda Yannay, all working in the United States. Until his recent death Habib Hassan Touma taught in Berlin, where Gabriel Iranyi is also located, while Betty Olivero resides in Italy.

Ethnic Awareness

Three principal factors shaped the increasing awareness of the music of Israel's many ethnic subdivisions. One was certainly the sense of physical, political, and spiritual isolation imposed by Arab intransigency after 1948. The physical isolation was caused by the difficulty and expense of leapfrogging the encircling ring of Arab countries that would not allow Jews to cross their borders. Political isolation came out of Israel's pariah status as much of the world succumbed to the pressure of the Arab economic boycott. Spiritual isolation was due to the anti-Israeli bias reflected in such international degradations as the "Zionism equals racism" canard forced on the United Nations by the Arab States. The net result was to focus Israel's vision inward.

The second circumstance that spotlighted Israel's ethnic groups was an international resurgence of interest in the music of non-Western cultures. Earlier in the century, Jewish scholars had been among the leaders of those studying non-Western music. Abraham Zvi Idelsohn, who lived in Jerusalem from 1906 to 1921, was among the first to make use of the phonograph for field recordings of non-western music. Robert Lachman (1892-1939), considered one of the fathers of modern ethnomusicological study, was a member of the Hebrew University faculty. Edith Gerson-Kiwi (1908-92) one of his students, became one of the world's leading scholars of Middle Eastern music. In 1963 French-trained scholar Israel Adler came to the Hebrew University, where he created the National Jewish Music Research Centre the following year, containing such invaluable material as Lachmann's 322 original wax cylinders, 1,378 ethnomusicological recordings on metal disks made by A. Z. Idelssohn, and some 8,300 items from the Kiev Library thought to have been lost when Jewish music researcher Moshe Beregovski was exiled to Siberia in 1949. The Jewish Music Research Centre houses thousands of field recordings from disappearing Jewish communities all over the globe. It is presently housed on the campus of Hebrew University in Jerusalem and is under the direction of Israeli scholar Edwin Seroussi.

In Europe and the United States the twentieth century was marked by a gradually increasing interest in music of the non-Western world. Beginning as early as 1889, when the Paris World's Fair introduced African and Asian music to fascinated westerners, composers as different as Maurice Ravel and Colin McPhee found themselves drawn to those sounds. Although that development was somewhat interrupted by the two world wars, composers of the 1960s began to reexamine non-Western music. Important ethnomusicological studies had been conducted throughout the first half of the century, but non-Western music only began to be widely disseminated after the Second World War. In the last third of the twentieth century popular musicians found fresh new sounds in the music of Asia, Africa, and the Middle East, resulting in a movement toward what came to be called "World Music." Musicians in Israel had been greatly taken with non-Western music early on, but their interest had become diffuse by the sixties. In the 1980s Israeli musicians discovered that the focus of earlier generations on Middle Eastern music had been visionary, though parochial.

The third factor was the political maturation of Israel's non-Western majority. Shut out of the major political parties in the early years and often ignored in the rough-and-tumble of politics, the Sephardic population began to find its own voice in the seventies and eighties, making its considerable presence felt in civic and political activism. That led to increased recognition of the interests of Israel's Oriental communities in government and culture, with the result that it soon became impossible for dominant Ashkenazi interests to ignore the music of the Sephardic world any longer.

With a handful of exceptions, the music of Israeli Arabs and the various Jewish Oriental communities had been unrepresented or grossly underrepresented in the Israeli mainstream well into the 1970s. It was little heard on Israeli radio, invisible on television, and not performed at all in concerts. "Essentially," wrote one Sephardic advocate, "popular . . . Ashkenazi music delegitimatized Jewish ethnic music . . . [whose] major voice was one of uneducated Oriental pop stars."[30] For most Israelis of European extraction, such sounds were heard—if at all—only while scrolling across radio and television stations from the surrounding Arab states. In addition to being unfamiliar, Oriental music bore the stigma of association with the enemy. Music of Moroccan or Kurdish Jews was heard only at their own communal celebrations. Even there, as Gerson Yonah, director of a Kurdish-Israeli dance troupe mourned,[31] more young people were electing Western-style weddings while fewer were willing to invest in mastering traditional instruments, songs, or dances of a far-off homeland fading from memory.

In spite of such marginalization, music of the Middle Eastern communities had a lively underground existence. A "cassette culture" evolved, with the best performers of non-Western styles circulating among faithful audiences in tape-recorded form. The great Egyptian popular singer Umm Kalthoum had a larger audience in Israel than the American Bruce Springsteen. It was a powerful subterranean river that was bound to surface sooner or later, and its rise was first felt in popular music, where nightclubs founded by such ethnic groups as the Yemenite or Iranian Jews for their own pleasure began attracting young Israelis of Western origin. Ethnic dance troupes—Greek, Bulgarian, Kurdish, Moroccan—found wide popularity, and the employment of ethnic musicians at weddings and other celebrations spread the sound of this music to a slowly growing public.

The result, by the 1980s, was a movement in popular music that came to be known simply as *musikah mizrachit* (Oriental Music). Almost ignored by the pop establishment at first, *musikah mizrachit* elbowed its way into popularity almost entirely by word of mouth. Yemenite singer Ofra Haza shot to the top of the charts, first in Israel, then in Europe, singing modern pop

---

[30] Yitzchak Kerem, personal communication, 27 September 1999.

[31] Personal conversation of June 1993.

versions of traditional songs from the Yemenite *Divan*, a collection of *piyyutim* by the sixteenth-century Rabbi Sholem Shabazi. Middle Eastern melody became fashionable, and could soon be heard infusing aspects of isolated Western-oriented pop songs.[32] Middle Eastern musicians began to be heard on the radio, and their recordings were sold in slowly increasing numbers all through the seventies and eighties. Pop singers like Yehoram Gaon, with a repertoire of Andalusian songs, and Yehuda Polikar, with Greek, gained enthusiastic followings. In the nineties Yemenite pop star Noa (Achinoam Nini) wove Middle Eastern motives through her thoroughly Westernized songs, while groups such as the band *Ha-Breirah ha-Tivit* (Natural Gathering)[33] of Moroccan-born Shlomo Bar, with its sophisticated blend of Western pop and North African traditions, received increasing attention.

"I think it's a wave that goes all over the world," observed Yossi Tel-Gan with evident enthusiasm, "but here [in Israel] it has deep roots because you hear Arab music on the radio. . . . You don't have to go to East Jerusalem (the Arab sector) . . . you can hear every other night a celebration of weddings . . . and after twenty years it is not strange any more."[34] By "it," this thoroughly Westernized Israeli meant the music of the Middle East, of the Arab world, and of the greater part of the Israeli population, which had come from that world. Immersed for fifty years in broadcasts from Egypt, Jordan, Lebanon, Syria, and Saudi Arabia, to all but the most isolationist Israelis or the most recent Western immigrants such music "is not strange any more."

This led to a revival of interest that went beyond the descriptive, exotic orientalism of the pioneer generations. It was appreciation of a new sound-world for its own sake. The building blocks of a new musical culture, in which Eastern and Western training may be united, are now beginning to take shape. A school of Middle Eastern Music with a baccalaureate program, for example, has been established in the Musrara neighborhood of Jerusalem under the patronage of the Sephardic pop star Yehoram Gaon.

The movement has not been restricted to popular music alone. Increasingly, young Israeli composers of art music, some of whom come from Middle Eastern heritage, are turning to that sound-world as the basis for sophisticated treatment in concert works. Avraham Amzallag (b. 1941), of Moroccan birth, founded and conducted the Israel Andalusian Ensemble. He has drawn on his heritage for a number of compositions, including *Taqsim* for flute, and *Tariq—Three Moroccan Piyyutim*, for tenor and mixed choir. Haifa-born Tzippi Fleischer (fig. 15.10) also availed herself of Middle Eastern sonorities to good effect in several compositions, including the cantata, *Like Two Branches* for chamber choir, two oboes, *kanun*, and a supplemented set of *tar* drums, or her Oratorio for mixed choir with an ensemble of guitars, mandolas, and orchestra. She writes that her early song cycle, *Girl-Butterfly-Girl*, "reflects the inception of the Oriental stylistic tendency"[35] in her music. The cycle of four songs was originally written for the *ud* and

---

[32] As early as the mid-1970s an Israeli rock song called "Al titen li ye'utz" (Don't give me advice), had a typical cynical-adolescent, shoulder-shrugging chorus that opened with a *taqsim*-like free introduction reminiscent of the *ud*—but on the electric guitar.

[33] A literal translation might be "Natural Selection"; however, Bar chooses to have the group's name appear in English as "Natural Gathering" on his compact disc, *Shoreshim* (lit., Roots), given in English as "Origins."

[34] Joseph (Yossi) Tel-Gan, General Director, Israel Music Festival, in an interview with the author, 21 July 1999.

[35] Tsippi Fleischer, composer's notes on "Girl-Butterfly-Girl," *IMI News* (1991, no. 4-1992, no. 1), 25.

FIG. 15.10   Tzippi Fleischer
Courtesy of the Israel Music Institute

FIG. 15.11   Menachem Wiesenberg
Courtesy of the Israel Music Institute

nay, but has been transcribed by the composer for soprano, renaissance recorder, and harpsichord, the recorder replacing the *ney* while the harpsichord mimics the *ud*.

Even composers who had emigrated from Western countries gravitated to the eastern melos, while native Israelis found a legitimacy in those sonorities that brought their Western intellectual training into harmony with their environment. Perhaps the attitude is best exemplified by a composer of Western orientation who turned to the East for inspiration. Menachem Wiesenberg (b. 1950) (fig. 15.11) has written a great deal of music integrating the techniques of both worlds. His motet, "Go to the Ant, Thou Sluggard," was "built on a symmetrical scale reminiscent of the Indian raga," according to the composer's notes, and he has composed chamber music for piano, cello, and *ud* incorporating a virtuoso *taqsim* like that which traditionally prefaces Arabic solo compositions featuring that lute-like instrument. He was influenced by the virtuoso Arab *ud* player Taiseer Elias, who helped Wiesenberg to learn the style and technique of his instrument. The composer suggests two reasons for his merging of Eastern and Western styles. The first is purely musical: "As a part of my artistic development I'm always looking for new sonoric possibilities that will serve as a kind of raw material [through which] I express my own musical ideas."[36] The second reflects an idealism in which the fusion of musical styles is precursor to the fusion of cultures: "It is important for me to find a way . . . to respect the tradition of my Arab fellow citizens and neighbors, while at the same time being faithful to my own individual language . . . I really think that the arts can bridge between peoples and cultures,

---

[36] This and the following quote are taken from a personal communication with M. Wiesenberg, 5 October 1999.

and even if it is to a very small degree, it's worthwhile for me to try it as a human being, and especially as a Jew."

Tzvi Avni, who teaches composition at the Jerusalem Academy, mused that the immigration from so many different cultures has had a positive effect on young composers. "In the '60s and '70s," he said, we thought folk music had run its course—was over. Today that is clearly not the case."[37] The return to folk material is a two-edged sword, though. Some Israeli composers are also seeking cultural roots in the once-scorned European diaspora for material, as native-born Shulamit Ran (b. 1947) did in her opera of 1998, *The Dybbuk*, a new setting of an old European Jewish folk tale originally collected by S. An-Ski (Shloyme Zanvl Rappoport, 1863-1920) on a 1912 field trip to gather folk material. Ran, who teaches at the University of Chicago, had previously been writing in a lyrically dissonant style of abstract music, as in her effective *String Quartet no. 1* (1988), that evidenced little interest in folk material.[38] Aryeh Levanon (b. 1932) also reached back to Eastern Europe with his *Freylachs* for string orchestra, as did Haim Permont (b. 1950) with his *Nigun* for flute and string orchestra. While Israeli composers have clearly not turned their backs on their European heritage, the present trend is that fewer composers are looking toward European folk song, while interest in non-Western styles is growing.

Israeli music at the turn of the twenty-first century is a heady blend. Increased awareness of the internal ethnic communities, fascinated absorption of Middle Eastern musical ideas, and mastery of the technical apparatus of Western composition all indicate that something exciting is brewing. Those streams have not yet blended into a unified musical style, and they may not do so. Instead, they may combine like the swirls of a marble cake, blending into a unified whole, but retaining recognizably separate identities.

Suggestions for Further Reading

Danto, L., A. Rigai, et al. *Israeli Composers*. New York: Musical Heritage Society, 1973.

Fleisher, R. J. *Twenty Israeli Composers: Voices of a Culture*. Detroit: Wayne State University Press, 1997.

Gradenwitz, Peter. *The Music of Israel: From the Biblical Era to Modern Times*. Portland: Amadeus Press, 1996.

Hirshberg, J. "Alexander U. Boskovitch and the Quest for an Israeli Musical Style." In *Modern Jews and Their Musical Agendas*, ed. E. Mendelsohn, 9:92-109. New York: Oxford University Press, 1993.

---

[37] Ibid.

[38] An-Ski had turned the tale into a Russian play in 1914, then translated it into Yiddish two years later (see chapter 9). It was first performed in Warsaw in 1920, then as Yiddish productions in New York and Moscow in 1922, with music by Joel Engel, who in 1926 assembled those pieces into a suite as his opus 35. In 1938 the play was made into a powerful film in Poland, with music by Henech Kon. Other composers also found the story a suitable subject. Bernard Sekles wrote an orchestral prelude on that theme in 1929. *The Dybbuk* was also set as an opera by Lodovico Rocca, premiered at La Scala in 1934, and as a ballet by Max Ettinger (1947). Other operas based on the Dybbuk story were composed by David Tamkin in 1951 and Michael Whyte in 1962.

Israel Music Institute. Website. List of composers, available recordings, and events: http://www.imi.org.il.

Keren, Zvi. *Contemporary Israeli Music: Its Sources and Stylistic Development*. Tel Aviv: Bar-Ilan University Press, 1980.

Lyman, D. *Great Jews in Music*. Middle Village, NY: J. David Publishers, 1986.

National Jewish Music Council. *Music of Israel Today: An Annotated List of Musical Compositions about the Land and the People of Israel*. New York, 1963.

Ravina, M., S. Skulski, et al. *Who is Who in ACUM; Authors, Composers and Music Publishers, Biographical Notes and Principal Works*. [Tel Aviv]: ACUM ltd. Société d'auteurs compositeurs et editeurs de musique en Israel, 1965.

Tischler, Alice. *A Descriptive Bibliography of Art Music by Israeli Composers*. Detroit Studies in Music Bibliography, no. 62. Warren, MI: Harmonie Park Press, 1988.

POSTLUDE ‖ *What We Have Seen*

During some four millennia the Jewish people have had a rich and varied musical history. While ritual has changed and those who today regard themselves as Jews have varied cultural origins, all Jews consider their religious ideals to be descended from Abraham, Isaac, and Jacob through Moses to the Kingdom of Saul, David, and Solomon, as related in the *Tanach*. Those ideals, the words of the *Tanach*, and the several thousand years of interpretation expressed in the *Mishnah* and Talmud are paramount in creating a peoplehood of Jews.

How Jews sing those words or otherwise express Jewishness in their music is of secondary importance to the religious texts themselves. That music should occupy a secondary position can perhaps be partly understood because until recently the music was preserved only through oral tradition. But several aspects of the music do go back to Biblical times and have been preserved. The sound of the shofar has not differed much in three thousand years. Likewise the idea of singing the scripture—cantillation—has not changed since it was initiated millenia ago, though the actual melodies and rhythms cannot be traced with any degree of certainty for more than five hundred years. These are the two most important elements in what is a Jewish sound in music; they have been preserved with many alterations and variants based on the cultural diversity of different Jewish communities around the world.

All the other kinds of music which Jews have sung and played, inside and outside the synagogue, are Jewish insofar as they have served the ends of the Jewish community. When the Israel Philharmonic plays Beethoven's Fifth Symphony for a preponderantly Jewish audience in Tel Aviv, the music serves a general middle-European cultural milieu and not a specifically Jewish one. On the other hand, when that same audience listens to Schoenberg's *A Survivor from Warsaw*, specific aspects of the Jewish experience are part of the music, the text, and especially the textual theme of the piece, and the catharsis created in the audience occurs because of the Jewish experience that particular music evokes.

Present Situation

Jewish musicians who passed from the world of an isolated Jewish community onto the concert stages and dance halls of Europe and America in the nineteenth and early twentieth centuries carried their Judaism with them like a snail carries its shell. It was the spiritual home they never left behind but could not retreat into if they wanted to better their lot. Some, like Gustav Mahler, yielded to outside pressure in those countries where it was greatest, and converted. Others, like the American Harold Arlen, or the Rubinstein brothers of Russia, as we have seen, kept their identities as Jews but often were unsure of the relevance of that identity to their artistic life. Still others found no inconsistency between their spiritual and creative selves, and like Jacques Fromenthal Halévy, Charles Valentin Alkan, or, in a later generation, Arnold Schoenberg, Darius Milhaud, and Leonard Bernstein, they intermixed the two comfortably. As Jewish musicians became part of a more tolerant Western culture, they began to perceive that Jewish needs were congruent with the needs of the larger audience, and as time went on the distinction that was once quite clear grew less so. Thus, in the United States in the first half of the twentieth century it did not seem incongruous that Jews could write patriotic songs (Berlin's "God Bless America") or shows decrying the plight of African-Americans (Kern's *Showboat*, Gershwin's *Porgy and Bess*) or Puerto Ricans (Bernstein's *West Side Story*), or even songs celebrating the secular aspects of nominally Christian holidays (Berlin's "White Christmas" and "The Easter Parade"). Jewish indebtedness to the freedoms of America and Jewish concern for the downtrodden were consistent with Jewish beliefs from Biblical times, and music served those ends.

The Future

Inasmuch as the future grows out of the present, we might surmise what is in store for Jewish music through study and recollection of what has constituted Jewish music until now. Since, in all likelihood, the Jewish people will continue to live in diverse cultures, different forms and styles of music will continue to be used. As we discussed, one problem that arose in the late twentieth century was the introduction of music that until then was foreign (guitar-accompanied camp songs) into the Reform and many Conservative synagogues in North America. The songs themselves did not pose a problem, for, as we have seen, many favorite synagogue tunes were borrowed from distinctly non-Jewish sources and became, over centuries, an integral part of the synagogue service. The new songs are in the tradition of the sixteenth-century *Paytan* Israel Najara, who wrote paraliturgical poetry in a popular style for singing to borrowed or original music. But, under the pressure of falling synagogue attendance, the rush to adopt youth-oriented music overwhelmed other styles. Many Jewish youth of the 1970s and 1980s heard only camp songs as Jewish religious music when they were growing up and now have no feeling for, or knowledge of, the centuries of Jewish traditional music. As we noted, new music needs to be encouraged and the best of it absorbed within the framework of the synagogue music's rich tradition, though not to completely replace the melodies of the past.

The paths of Jewish music seem more assured now, in part because Jews recognize the appeal music has, and in part because, through knowledge of their music from the past four thousand years, Jews have a great deal more to express. Tastes will inevitably change as music conveys the text and ideals of Judaism to new ages of Jews with distinctive problems and different interpretations of tradition. But there is no reason why Jewish music should not continue to thrive, to the extent that the Jewish people become increasingly aware of their vibrant musical heritage and supportive of those who would graft new musical expressions onto the flourishing trunk of the existing tree.

A Note on Translation, Transliteration, and Pronunciation

For the reader's convenience, important foreign words are translated at their first appearance in the text and are defined again in the alphabetical glossary that follows. Standard dictionary meanings have been given for most of those words, but in some cases translations specific to the musical context have been supplied.

A separate but related problem is the transliteration of words originally written in non-Roman alphabets such as Hebrew, Arabic, Yiddish, Ladino, or Russian. Of necessity this book contains many such transliterated words. While linguists have developed separate, scientific transliterations for each of the above-mentioned languages, their use would present readers with the problem of mastering a separate orthography for each language. That only seemed to put an additional barrier between the reader and key words in the text.

To avoid that, the authors have transliterated non-Roman alphabets with a single, consistent Romanized spelling. No such attempt, though, is made to phoneticize languages using the Latin alphabet. French *"au revoir"* is written as is, without phoneticizing it into *"o vwa"* or some such approximation. What such an approach lacks in precision is more than offset by its convenience and readability, which were key considerations in this context.

The transliteration system used here can be summarized as using English consonants with Italian vowel values. In this simple system single consonants have normal English values; e.g., w = w as in water, j = j as in joy, z = z as in zebra, etc. Consonant clusters that can be rendered with English consonants follow that same rule; e.g., sh = sh as in ship, tch = tch as in latch. Foreign consonants that do not have English equivalents are transliterated to the nearest approximation of their sound according to the table below. An example of this is our resolution of the sound of "ch" as in the German word *Nacht*, which is found in several of the languages occurring in this book, but is not found in English. After much soul-searching it was decided to use "ch" throughout as the clearest English rendering of, for example, two different Hebrew consonants ("chet" and "chaf"). There is, in fact, a fine distinction between those sounds to a good Hebrew speaker, but that distinction was lost in Europeanized Hebrew, and it is not represented here. A Hebrew word such as " חַזָּן " (cantor) can be found in various sources transliterated as "chazzan," "chazin," "hazan," "hasan," "ḥazzan," and numerous other possibilities. While continuing to use the original authors' transliterations in quotations and titles, all occurrences in the book's text are represented as "chazzan." Thus all the variant readings for those letters are combined into the single consonant cluster, "ch." Vowels, as mentioned, have unambiguous Italian values. Diphthongs are transliterated by two vowels that blend their stand-alone Italian values, as shown in the table below.

Two different Hebrew spellings that, for practical purposes produce a similar effect for the English reader, have been combined into a single sign with the apostrophe ('). One of those is the glottal stop that we use in English at the beginning of both syllables of "uh-oh." The other is the *shvah*, a short, indeterminate vowel sound that occurs in English as the "a" in "a dog," or at the beginning of such words as "another," or "enough" in ordinary speech. Such dual use might seem to be problematical, but in practice it makes easier reading for the non-Hebrew speaker. The first (the glottal stop) is represented by an apostrophe preceding a vowel, while an apostrophe following a consonant signifies the second, a pronounced *shvah*. If a consonant directly precedes a vowel, the effect is the same for the reader: a truncated "uh" sound. Thus, the four-syllable Hebrew word for "until we meet again" is rendered as *l'hitra'ot*, with the first apostrophe representing a pronounced *shvah* and the second one a glottal stop separating the two vowels. In any instance where a *shvah* is followed directly by a glottal stop the two signs are elided into one for simplicity's sake; e.g., the Hebrew for "in a ship" is represented as *b'oniah*, not *b"oniah*.

Table A.1, below, summarizes the pronunciation key for vowels and certain consonants used in transliteration. All other letters have standard English pronunciation.

TABLE A.1
Pronunciation Key for Hebrew and Arabic Transliterations

Letter	Pronounced as in . . .	Letter	Pronounced as in . . .
a	father or not	o	post or bone
ai	buy or sigh	oi	boy or oil
au	out or down	u	pull or soup
e	pen or set	j	joy or gem
ei	day or weigh	k	can or king
i	short, as in pin, but can also be long, as in eager	ch	(Scottish) loch or (German) nacht
tch	Dutch or change	tz, ts	nuts
'	Glottal stop as in "uh-oh"; also, indeterminate vowel (shva) as in enough *or* alone		

GLOSSARY

a cappella. Voices without accompaniment (Italian).

Adar. The sixth month of the Jewish calendar (Hebrew).

adonai malach. One of the synagogue modes (Hebrew), or, in Yiddish, *Shteiger*. Also found transliterated as *adonoy moloch* in older Ashkenazic Hebrew.

aeolian. Natural minor scale (e.g., the "white note" scale on the piano going from the pitch "a" up to the next "a.").

ahavah raba. A musical mode used frequently in Ashkenazic music which is characterized by the augmented second; named after a prayer sung in this mode (Hebrew).

alamot. An obscure term that may possibly mean "with psalteries" (Hebrew).

aleatoric. Music of chance, without design.

aliyah. Arising or going up, such as to read the benedictions for the Torah; also, to immigrate to Israel (Hebrew).

Amidah. "Standing," the central prayer of the synagogue service which is recited while standing (Hebrew).

Anschluss. "Annexation," refers specifically to the Nazi annexation of Austria and Czechoslovakia in 1938 (German).

antiphonal performance. Alternation between two performing bodies of relatively equal size.

Ashkenazic. Pertaining to those Jews who lived in Europe north of the Alps whose vernacular language was Yiddish.

aulos. Ancient reed instrument (Greek).

Av. The eleventh month of the Jewish calendar (Hebrew).

avodah. Prayer service (Hebrew).

avodat Shabbat. Prayer service for the Sabbath (Hebrew).

ba'al kri'ah. Master of reading the Torah (Hebrew).

ba'al tefillah. Leader in the recitation of prayers in the Synagogue (Hebrew).

badchan. Entertainer, often a comic and a singer, primarily appearing at weddings (Yiddish).

bakkasha (pl., *bakkashot*). Prayer of request (Hebrew).

Banu Amalik. Jewish tribe in Arabia (Arabic).

bet ha-mikdash. Solomon's Temple (Hebrew).

bet knesset. Congregational house; i.e., synagogue (Hebrew).

biblios. Book (Greek).

bimah. The pulpit in the synagogue (Hebrew).

bobbe. Grandmother (Yiddish).

brachot. Blessings sanctifying acts and experiences of daily life (Hebrew).

briss. See *brit milah*.

brit milah. Circumcision ceremony (Hebrew); also found as *briss* (old Ashkenazic Hebrew and Yiddish).

bulgar. A klezmer dance coming from Bulgaria (Yiddish).

cantigas. Medieval Spanish songs (Spanish).

cantillation. Chanting (of the liturgy).

canzone. A metrical rhymed song (Italian).

centonization. Musical improvisation based on a group of pre-existing melodies.

chalil. Flute (Hebrew).

chalutzim. Pioneers, specifically settlers in the pre-state holy land (Hebrew).

Chassid (pl., **Chassidim**). Righteous man; also, a follower of the Baal Shem Tov (Hebrew); also found as *chosid* (Yiddish).

Chassidic. Adjective pertaining to those Jews whose mystical faith was inspired by the founder of Chasidism, the Baal Shem Tov (English, derived from Hebrew).

chatzotzerah. Trumpet (Hebrew).

chazzan (pl., *chazzanim*). Prayer leader in the synagogue (Hebrew).

chazzanut. Vocal style developed by the *chazzanim* (Hebrew).

cheder. Religious school for Jewish boys (Yiddish).

cheironomy. Musical hand-signs indicating how the music is to be sung.

chibur. Musical structure or shape according to Isaiah ben Isaac (Hebrew).

chidduyot. Wedding songs (Hebrew).

chomer. Matter out of which melodies are constructed according to Isaiah ben Isaac (Hebrew).

chosid. A klezmer dance (Yiddish, from the Hebrew).

christos. Messiah (Greek).

Chumash. Five books of the law (Hebrew).

commedia dell'arte. A type of Italian theater in the Renaissance using stock characters (Italian).

consistoire. A political region of France (French).

contrafactum. New song set to an existing melody (Latin).

contratenor. A high male voice.

conversos. Jews converted to Christianity by force in Spain in the fifteenth century (Spanish).

czárdás. A Hungarian dance (Hungarian).

darbukkah. Drum made of a membrane stretched over a clay vase-shaped frame (Arabic).

dhimmi. Religious minority living under Islamic rule (Arabic).

diaspora. Dispersion; the Jewish community outside the land of Israel.

diegetic. Cinema music in which the music is a realistic part of the story, not just background or incidental.

Dies Irae. "Day of Wrath," a lengthy poem that is part of the Roman Catholic Mass for the Dead (Latin).

divan. Poetic anthology (Arabic).

dodecaphonic. Compositional system exploiting all 12 tones of the chromatic scale in its structure, developed by Arnold Schoenberg.

doina. Florid, improvised klezmer music (Yiddish).

dorian. The first of the eight church modes.

doxology. Profession of faith.

drash. Sermon or interpretation of scripture (Hebrew).

duff. Drum (Arabic).

ebreo. Jew (Italian).

ekphonetic. A musical notation in which each musical motive is represented by a sign inserted into the text.

entartete Musik. Degenerate music, music not accepted by the Nazis (German).

Essenes. A zealot group of monk-like Jews who lived in the desert of Israel in Greco-Roman times.

ethnomusicology. The study of the music of particular ethnic groups.

etnachta. *Ta'am* which marks the middle of a verse (Aramaic).

exilarch. Ruler of the Jewish community in Baghdad.

freylachs. Wedding dances (Yiddish).

gabbai. Beadle; the person responsible for the arrangements for synagogue ritual and sometimes for the physical condition of the synagogue (Hebrew).

gamba, or *viola da gamba*. Bowed string instrument held between the thighs (Italian).

ga'on. Title designating an outstanding rabbinic leader (Hebrew).

garin. Nucleus of a *ta'am*; the part that carries the distinctive musical motive (Hebrew).

Gebrauchsmusik. "Practical music"; music written for a specific function (German).

Gemeinde. Society (German).

genizah. A place for storing Torah scrolls and other religious objects that are no longer usable (Hebrew).

ghayta. See *zurna*.

gleeman (pl., *gleemen*). Medieval English term for lower-class popular entertainers. See also *jongleur*, *juglar*.

haftarah (pl., *haftarot*). Weekly reading from the prophetic books (Hebrew).

haggadah. "Retelling"; the book containing the stories, songs, hymns, and prayers for the Seder of Pesach (Hebrew).

hagiographa. Holy writings (Greek).

halachah. Jewish religious law (Hebrew).

halachah mi-Sinai. "The law from Sinai"; phrase used to indicate purported antiquity, especially of hymn melodies whose origins are lost (Hebrew).

halebis. Syrian.

hallel. Songs of praise (Hebrew).

Hashomer ha-Tza'ir. Young Guard movement (Hebrew).

Haskalah. Jewish Enlightenment (Hebrew).

Hausmusik. Music to be made in a private home (German).

hazzan. Overseer, source of the Hebrew word *chazzan* (Assyrian).

hexachordal. As a part of the 12-tone system, the grouping of six notes to form a melodic unit.

Histadrut. Israeli National Labor Organization.

Holocaust. Systematic extermination of the Jews of Europe by the Nazis.

hora. Originally a Rumanian dance used by klezmer musicians and later transferred to Israel as its national dance (Hebrew).

Hoshana Rabbah. Great Hosannah; a holiday falling on the 21st day of Tishrei featuring, among other things, synagogal song (Hebrew).

intermedia. Musical entertainments during the intermission of a larger entertainment (Italian).

Janissary bands. Turkish bands.

jongleur (pl., *jongleurs*). Medieval French term for lower-class popular entertainers. See also *gleeman*, *juglar*.

juglar (pl., *juglares*). Medieval Spanish term for lower-class popular entertainers. See also *gleeman*, *jongleur*.

Juif. Jew (French).

kabbala. Jewish mysticism, particularly of the late Middle Ages and Renaissance (Hebrew).

kabbalat Shabbat. "Welcoming of the Sabbath," the initial section of the Friday Evening Service (Hebrew).

kaddish. Sanctification of God's name, recited several times during the synagogue service and once at the end in commemoration of the dead; also recited privately by mourners (Hebrew).

kadosh, kadosh, kadosh, adonai tzeva'ot. Opening phrase of the *Kedushah* (sanctification) (Hebrew).

kamil. The fast rhythmic modes (Arabic).

Kara'ite. Jewish sect that adheres solely to the written text of the Torah, rejecting all rabbinic interpretation.

kasat. Cymbals (Arabic).

kasher. Bound by the law of the Torah (Hebrew); also found as *kosher* (Yiddish).

Kedushah. The prayer sanctifying God's name ("Holy, holy, holy . . .") (Hebrew).

keren. Horn (Hebrew).

Ketubim. Holy writings; the third division of the Tanach (Hebrew).

kibbutz. Collective settlement in Israel, usually, but not necessarily, a farming collective (Hebrew).

kibbutz galuyot. "Ingathering of the exiles," the Israeli mission to bring back all Jews to Israel (Hebrew).

kiddush. The blessing over wine (Hebrew).

kidomet. Unaccented syllable preceding the accent in a cantillation *ta'am* (Hebrew).

kinah. Lamentation; prayer of mourning (Hebrew).

kinnor. In ancient Hebrew: lyre; in modern Hebrew: violin (Hebrew).

Kislev. The third month of the Jewish calendar (Hebrew).

kithara. Ancient lyre (Greek).

klal Yisrael. "Community of Israel," referring to the unity of the Jewish people (Hebrew); also found as *klal Yisroel* (Yiddish).

klezmer. As a noun: dance musician; also, as an adjective: Jewish dance music (Yiddish).

knesset. Israeli parliament (Hebrew).

ko'ach pisuk. Separating power of disjunctive *te'amim* (Hebrew).

kohen (pl., *kohanim*). Hereditary priest of the ancient Temple (Hebrew).

Kol isha ervah. "A woman's voice is forbidden"; the doctrine that a woman's singing is forbidden to men outside her own family (Hebrew).

Kol Nidre. Special prayer asking for forgiveness for religious vows taken under duress during the past year, recited on the eve of Yom Kippur (Hebrew).

kontakia. Metrical Greek Christian hymns (Greek).

Kristallnacht. "Night of broken glass"; 9 November 1938, when the Nazis pillaged Jewish buildings (German).

krummhorn. A double reed instrument of the Renaissance (German).

Kulturbund deutscher Jüden. German Jewish Culture Society formed to keep Jewish musicians active during the early years of the Nazis (German).

Ladino. Judeo-Spanish language (Ladino).

Lag b'omer. Minor festival falling on the 33rd Day of the "counting of the omer"; i.e., the six weeks between Pesach and Shavuot (Hebrew).

lahanim. Melodies (Hebrew).

"**L'cha dodi**." "To You, My Beloved," hymn sung early in the Friday evening service that joyously welcomes the incoming Sabbath, envisioning it as a bride (Hebrew).

Levites. The tribe of Levi; one of the twelve tribes of Israel.

logogenic. Music whose structure is determined by the words to which it is set.

ma'amadot. Representatives; here, specifically those sent to participate in the sacrifices in the ancient Temple (Hebrew).

Ma'ariv. Evening Service (Hebrew).

machol. Dance (Hebrew).

mafsiqim. "Disjunctives"; *te'amim* that terminate in a brief silence, or musical rest (Hebrew).

magen avot **mode**. One of the synagogue modes, loosely resembling the natural minor mode (Hebrew); also found as *mogen ovos* (old Ashkenazic Hebrew and Yiddish).

maqam (pl., *maqamot*). Arabic musical modes (Arabic).

Marranos. Disparaging term for Jews converted to Christianity by force in fifteenth-century Spain who continued to practice their Judaism in secret (Spanish).

maskil (pl., *maskilim*). "Enlightened" Jew of the *Haskalah* (Hebrew and Yiddish).

masorah. Tradition (Hebrew).

Masoretes. Early medieval scholars who determined the correct reading of the Torah.

mechabrim. "Conjunctives"; i.e., *te'amim* that do not terminate with a musical rest (Hebrew).

melamed. 1) teacher in a Jewish elementary school (Yiddish); 2) teacher (Hebrew).

melismas. Florid melodies sung on a single syllable.

melismatic. Setting of a text in which each syllable is set to many notes.

melos. Special common quality of a group of melodies.

meshorer (pl., *meshorerim*). Singer who accompanies the cantor (Hebrew); also found as *meshoyrer* (Yiddish).

messa di voce. A vocal ornament involving gradual increase and decrease in the volume of a sustained tone (Italian).

metallophones. Percussion instruments made of metal.

metziltayim. Cymbals (Hebrew).

microtonal. Tuning with musical intervals narrower than a half-step.

Minchah. Afternoon service (Hebrew).

minhag. Practice or tradition (Hebrew).

Minnesinger. Fifteenth-sixteenth century German singer-composer of popular melodies (German).

minyan. Group of ten Jewish adult men required for an Orthodox service (Hebrew).

Mishnah. Jewish law interpreting the Torah, later enlarged and explained by the *Talmud* (Hebrew).

mi-sinai (also found as *missinai*). Designation for old Ashkenazic melodies which, according to inaccurate legend, dated from the time of Moses on Mt. Sinai (Hebrew).

mitpallelim. Ancient prayer leaders (Hebrew).

mixolydian. Seventh of the eight Gregorian modes.

mohel. Man who is qualified to perform ritual circumcision (Hebrew).

mujwiz. Single-reed instrument (Arabic).

musica humana. Music of the soul; the "harmony" of a person with the environment, or within himself— not actually sounding music (Latin).

musica instrumentalis. All audible music (Latin).

musica mundana. Music of the celestial spheres; the "harmony" of heavenly bodies in their orbits— a theoretical sound that can only be heard by the deities (Latin).

musikah mizrachit. Oriental (i.e., Middle Eastern) music popular in Israel (Hebrew).

muwwasha. A form of Arab song (Arabic).

Nadhir. Medieval Jewish tribe of the Arabian peninsula (Arabic).

nashid. The opening section of a *muwwasha* (Arabic).

nay. Flute (Arabic).

neginah. Playing by touching the strings (Hebrew).

ne'imot. Musical tones, according to Avicenna (Hebrew).

neumatic. A setting of the text in which each syllable has a few notes.

nevel. Harp (Hebrew).

nevi'im. Prophets (Hebrew).

nevi'im acharonim. "Later" prophets (Hebrew).

nevi'im rishonim. "Early" prophets (Hebrew).

nigun. A textless melody created by *Chassidim* for exultation; a melody (Hebrew).

Nissan. The seventh month of the Jewish calendar (Hebrew).

nogenim. (String) players (Hebrew).

nusach. Musical style characteristic of a group.

nusach tefillah. Musical style of prayer.

pa'am (pl., *pa'amonim*). Bells (Hebrew).

parashah. Section of the Torah recited each week (Hebrew).

paytan (pl., *paytanim*). Poet-singers who created *piyyutim* (Hebrew).

Pesach. Passover (Hebrew).

Pharisees. Ancient scholars of the Torah; later to give birth to the rabbinic movement.

phrygian. Third of the eight church modes.

piyyut (pl., *piyyutim*). Religious poem (Hebrew).

precentor. Reader of the prayers.

psallein. To pluck (a string instrument) (Greek).

pseudepigrapha. Writings excluded from the Hebrew Bible because of questionable authorship (Greek).

Purim. Feast of Lots (Hebrew).

purimshpil. Popular plays written to be performed during Purim (Yiddish).

qaina. Singing girl (Arabic).

Quraiza. Jewish tribe (Hebrew).

rav. Rabbi (Yiddish).

rebab. A one-string violin-like instrument played with a bow (Arabic).

rebbe. Learned Jew, especially among Chassidim (Yiddish).

Reichsmusikkammer. Government Office of Music during the Nazi Period (German).

responsorial performance. Alternation between a soloist and a choral response.

responsum. Learned opinion (Latin).

romanceros. Popular Spanish ballads or story-songs (Spanish, Ladino).

Rosh Chodesh. Beginning of the new moon (Hebrew).

Rosh Hashanah. New Year (Hebrew).

rubato. A temporary flexibility in the otherwise regular beat of a piece (Italian).

sabra. Native-born Israeli (Hebrew).

Sadducees. An assimilationist party of Jews in Greco-Roman times made up primarily of the wealthy and priestly class.

sajat. See **sunuj**.

Sanctus. Part of the Roman Catholic Mass which is a translation of Hebrew *Kedusha* (Latin).

Sanhedrin. Ancient Jewish parliament (Aramaic, from the Greek, *sunedrion*).

Schelomo, Shelomo. Solomon (Hebrew).

schola cantorum. School of singers founded by Pope Gregory the Great (590-604) (Latin).

Sefer Nevi'im. Book of Prophets (Hebrew).

Sefer Tehillim. Book of Psalms (Hebrew).

selicha mode. Mode used for prayers of pardon (Hebrew).

Selichot. Penitential prayer service (Hebrew).

Sephardic. Pertaining to Jews of Spanish origin (Sephardim) and their descendants.

s'firat ha-Omer. Counting of the Omer (the days between Pesach and Shavu'ot) (Hebrew).

Shabbat. Sabbath (Hebrew); also found as *Shabbos* (Yiddish).

shabbos goy. A non-Jew who performs tasks forbidden to Jews during *Shabbat* and other Holy Days (Yiddish).

Shacharit. Morning service (Hebrew).

shaliach (pl., *shlichim*). Emissary, such as those sent from Palestine to recruit Polish Jewish youth (Hebrew).

shaliach tzibbur. Chazzan; precentor, or one who leads synagogue prayer (Hebrew).

shalosh regalim. The three pilgrimage holidays of *Pesach*, *Sukkot*, and *Shavu'ot* (Hebrew).

shatz. Prayer leader (abbreviation of *shaliach tzibbur*).

Shavu'ot. Feast of Weeks, takes place seven weeks after Pesach (Hebrew).

shawm. Double-reed wind instrument, precursor to the oboe in Europe.

Shemini Atzeret. Eight Day Assembly (Hebrew).

sheminit. Musical performance direction, possibly meaning to perform at the octave (Hebrew).

sher. A klezmer dance (Yiddish).

sherele. Another (diminutive) name for a *sher* (Yiddish).

shigu. Dirge (Assyrian).

shir. Poem or song (Hebrew).

Shir chanukat ha-bayit. "Song for the Dedication of the House," Psalm 30 (Hebrew).

shira. Song or main section of a *muwwasha* (Hebrew).

Sh'ma Yisrael. "Hear Oh Israel," the most basic prayer of Jews, affirming the one-ness of God (Hebrew).

Sh'moneh esrei. "Eighteen benedictions," another name for *Amidah* (Hebrew).

shochet. Ritual slaughterer (Hebrew).

shofar. Trumpet-like wind instrument made from an animal horn (Hebrew).

shpilman. Community entertainer (Yiddish).

shtetl. Jewish village in Eastern Europe (Yiddish).

shul. Local synagogue (Yiddish).

Shushan Purim. Extra day of Purim for walled cities (Hebrew).

Sh'va 'Asar b'Tammuz. Fast of the Seventeenth Day of *Tammuz* (Hebrew).

siddur. Prayer book (Hebrew).

Sifrei Emet. Collective designation for the books of Job, Proverbs, and Psalms (Hebrew).

silluk. A disjunctive *ta'am* marking the end of a verse in cantillation (Hebrew).

Simchat Torah. (Rejoicing in the Torah) holy day when the reading of the Five Books of the Law comes to an end and is started over (Hebrew).

simsimyya. Harp (Arabic).

sistrum. A rattle with a wooden handle and disks that jangle.

Sivan. The ninth month of the Jewish calendar (Hebrew).

sof pasuk. Another name sometimes used for the *silluk*. (Actually, this more properly designates the colon-shaped sign designating the end of the verse, not the *ta'am*.) (Hebrew).

sonata da chiesa. Instrumental sonata "for the church" of the Baroque era, usually in four movements, slow-fast-slow-fast in tempo (Italian).

Steiger, shteiger, or *shtayger*. Generic designation for a synagogue mode (German, Yiddish).

submediant. Sixth degree of the Western scale.

Sukkot. Festival of booths or harvest (Hebrew).

sunuj. Finger cymbals (Arabic).

ta'am (pl., *te'amim*). Sign in the Torah which indicates music (Hebrew).

Ta'anit Esther. Fast of Esther (Hebrew).

tachanun. Same as **techinah**.

taksim. Improvised instrumental prelude in Turkish and Arabic music (Arabic).

Tanach. The complete Torah, including all three divisions (Hebrew).

tannaim. Great teachers of the Sanhedrin (Hebrew).

taqil. The slow rhythmic modes (Arabic).

Targum. Aramaic translation of the Bible purportedly by Oukelos (Hebrew).

tchines. Blessings and devotional prayers for women (Yiddish).

Te Deum. A Roman Catholic hymn of praise to God (Latin).

techinah. Prayers of petition (Hebrew).

Tefillah. Prayer, also applied specifically to the *Amidah* (Hebrew).

tenuto. A mark over a musical note that indicates holding it slightly longer than indicated by its written value (Italian).

Tevet. The fourth month of the Jewish calendar (Hebrew).

tip'cha. Name of one of the *te'amim* (Hebrew).

Tishah b'Av. "The ninth day of *Av*," a solemn fast day of mourning for the destruction of the Temple (Hebrew).

Tishre. The first month of the Jewish calendar (Hebrew).

tof (pl., *tuppim*). Hand drum (Hebrew).

tofefot. Timbrels (Hebrew).

Torah. 1) The Five Books of the Law; 2) the *Tanach*; i.e., the entire three divisions of the Bible; 3) all Jewish learning (Hebrew).

troubadour. A medieval poet and singer thought to be a noble person.

trouvère. Troubador from Northern Europe (French).

tsimbl. Hammered zither common in Eastern European klezmer bands (Yiddish).

Tu b'Shevat. "New Year of the Trees" (Hebrew).

tzafat. Wedding procession (Hebrew).

tzni'ut. Elaborate code of modesty (Hebrew).

Tzum Gedalya. Fast of Gedalia (Hebrew).

Tzum Tevet. Fast of Tevet (Hebrew).

ud. Lute-like instrument (Arabic).

ugav. Ancient: double reed instrument; modern: organ (Hebrew).

Viddui. Prayer of confession (Hebrew).

yeshivah. School for religious study (Hebrew, also used in Yiddish).

yiddishkeit. Yiddish culture, "Jewishness" (Yiddish).

Yigdal elohim chai. "Praise the Living God," a synagogue hymn.

yishuv. Jewish community in pre-state Palestine (Hebrew).

Y'mei ha-Nora'im. Days of Awe (Hebrew).

Yom ha-Atzma'ut. Israel's Independence Day (Hebrew).

Yom ha-Sho'ah. Holocaust Commemoration Day (Hebrew).

Yom ha-Zikaron. Memorial Day (Hebrew).

Yom Kippur. Day of Atonement (Hebrew).

Zamar sh'eri. An elegiac song (Assyrian).

zamr. See *zurna*.

Zimriah. International Choral Festival held in Israel (Hebrew).

Zionism. The political movement to return Jews from the diaspora to the Holy Land.

z'mirot. Religious songs sung at home (Hebrew).

zurna. Oboe-like instrument (Arabic).

BIBLIOGRAPHY

A bisl yidishkayt. http://www.yiddishmusic.com.

Abrahams, Israel. *A Companion to the Authorized Daily Prayerbook: Historical and Explanatory Notes*. New York: Hermon Press, 1966.

_____, and Cecil Roth. *Jewish Life in the Middle Ages*. London: E. Goldston Ltd., 1932.

Adler, Israel. *Musical Life and Traditions of the Portuguese Jewish Community of Amsterdam in the XVIIIth Century*. Yuval Monograph Series, 3. Jerusalem: Magnes Press Hebrew University, 1974.

_____. "The Notated Synagogue Chants of the 12th Century of Obadiah, the Norman Proselyte." In *Contributions to a Historical Study of Jewish Music*, ed. Eric Werner, 168-99. New York: Ktav Publishing House, 1976.

_____. "Le traité anonyme du manuscrit hebreu 1037 de la Bibliothèque Nationale de Paris." *Yuval: Studies of the Jewish Music Research Centre* 1 (1968): 1-47.

_____. *Trois chants synagogaux du XIIe siécle*. Tel Aviv: Israeli Music Publications, 1969.

_____, Christian Joseph Lidarti, et al. *Oeuvres du répertoire de la communauté portugaise d'Amsterdam*. Musique Synagogale Ancienne. Tel Aviv: Israeli Music Publications, 1965.

Adler, Selig, and Thomas E. Connolly. *From Ararat to Suburbia: The History of the Jewish Community of Buffalo*. Philadelphia: The Jewish Publication Society of America, 1960.

Aleichem, Sholem. *The Nightingale; or, The Saga of Yosele Solovey the Cantor*, trans. Aliza Shevrin. New York: Putnam, 1985.

Altmann, Alexander. *Jewish Medieval and Renaissance Studies*. Brandeis University Studies and Texts, 4. Cambridge, MA: Harvard University Press, 1967.

Armistead, Samuel G., Joseph H. Silverman, and Israel J. Katz. *Judeo-Spanish Ballads from Oral Tradition*. Folk Literature of the Sephardic Jews, 2-3. Berkeley: University of California Press, 1986.

Avenary, Hanoch. *Ashkenazi Tradition of Biblical Chant Between 1500 and 1900*. Jerusalem: World Congress on Jewish Music, 1978.

_____. "A Genizah Find of Saadya's Psalm-Preface and Its Musical Aspects." In *Contributions to a Historical Study of Jewish Music*, ed. Eric Werner, 37-54. New York: Ktav Publishing House, 1976.

Badt, B. *Die Lieder des Süsskind von Trimberg*, ed. Karl Schwarz. Jüdische Bücherei, 6. Berlin: Fritz Gurlitt, 1920.

Baker, H. W., William Henry Monk, and Charles Steggall. *Hymns Ancient and Modern*. London: W. Clowes and Sons, 189-?.

Baron, John H. "Additional Thoughts on the Golden Age of French Jewish Composers." *Musica Judaica: Journal of the American Society for Jewish Music* 14 (1999): 153-58.

_____. "Franko, Jeanne." *Jewish Women in America: An Historical Encyclopedia*, ed. Paula Hyman and Deborah Dash Moore, 472-73. New York: Routledge, 1997.

_____. "A Golden Age for Jewish Musicians in Paris: 1820-1865." *Musica Judaica: Journal of the American Society for Jewish Music* 12 (1991-92): 30-51.

_____. "Music as Entertainment and Symbol in the Yiddish Cinema from the 1920's and 1930's." In *Musik und Szene: Festschrift für Werner Braun*, ed. Bernhard R. Appel, Karl W. Geck, and Herbert Schneider. Saarbrücker Studien zur Musikwissenschaft, new series, 9 (2001): 413-28.

Baron, Salo. *A Social and Religious History of the Jews*. Philadelphia: Jewish Publication Society of America, 1957.

_____. *The Russian Jew Under Tsars and Soviets*. 2nd ed. New York: Macmillan Publishing Co., 1976.

Belcove-Shalin, Janet S. *New World Hasidim: Ethnographic Studies of Hasidic Jews in America*. SUNY Series in Anthropology and Judaic Studies, ed. Walter P. Zenner. Albany: State University of New York Press, 1995.

Ben-Yehudah, Barukh, and Ben-Zion Orgad. *Ta'ame ha-Mikra le-vate ha-sefer*. Ramat-Gan: Masada, 1968.

Benarde, Scott R. *Stars of David: Rock 'n' Jewish Stories*. Hanover: Brandeis University Press, 2003.

Beregovski, Moshe. *Old Jewish Folk Music: The Collections and Writings of Moshe Beregovski*, ed. Mark Slobin. Publications of the American Folklore Society, new series, 6. Philadelphia: University of Pennsylvania Press, 1982.

Bernal, Martin. *Black Athena: The Afroasiatic Roots of Classical Civilization*. London: Free Association Press, 1987.

Bikel, Theodore. *Classic Jewish Holiday Songs* (cassette). Van Nuys, CA: Nimmer Productions, 1987.

Billig, Michael. *Rock 'n' Roll Jews*. Syracuse: Syracuse University Press, 2000.

Binder, Abraham W. *Biblical Chant*. New York: Philosophical Library, 1959.

_____. *The Jewish Music Movement in America: An Informal Lecture*. New York: Jewish Music Council of the National Jewish Welfare Board, 1975.

_____. "A Review of the Recording of Ernest Bloch's 'Israel Symphony'." In *The Music of Ernest Bloch: A Program Manual*, ed. Leah M. Jaffa, 36-40. New York: National Jewish Music Council of the National Jewish Welfare Board, 1955.

_____. *Studies in Jewish Music: Collected Writings of A. W. Binder*, ed. Irene Heskes. New York: Bloch, 1971.

_____. *Union Hymnal: Songs and Prayers for Jewish Worship*. [Cincinnati]: Central Conference of American Rabbis, 1940.

Birnbaum, Eduard. "The High Holydays: The Koenigsberg Tradition (*Yamim nora'im mesorat kehilat Kenigsberg*)". In *Jewish Musical Heritage* (sound disc). Tel Aviv: Beth Hatefutsoth, 1990.

Blaukopf, Herta. *Mahler's Unknown Letters*, trans. Richard Stokes. Boston: Northeastern University Press, 1987.

B'nei Teman Group. *Ahavat Hadasa: Songs of the Jewish-Yemenite Diwan; Manakha Tradition (Ahavat Hadassah: Shirim me-divan yehude Teman; masoret Manakhah)* (sound disc BTR 9001). Tel Aviv: Beth Hatefutsoth, 1990.

Bohlman, Philip V. *"The Land Where Two Streams Flow": Music in the German-Jewish Community of Israel*. Urbana: University of Illinois Press, 1989.

_____. *The World Centre for Jewish Music in Palestine 1936-1940: Jewish Musical Life on the Eve of World War II*. Oxford: Clarendon Press, 1992.

Bradshaw, Paul F. *The Making of Jewish and Christian Workship*. In *Two Liturgical Traditions*, ed. Lawrence A. Hoffman. Vol. 5, part 1. Notre Dame: Notre Dame University Press, 1991.

Braun, Joachim. *Jews in Soviet Music*. Hebrew University of Jerusalem Soviet and East European Research Centre, no. 22. Jerusalem: Hebrew University of Jerusalem Soviet and East European Research Centre, 1977.

_____. *Music in Ancient Israel/Palestine: Archaeological, Written, and Comparative Sources*, trans. Douglas W. Stott. Grand Rapids/Cambridge (UK): William B. Eerdmans Publishing Company, 2002.

Breuer, Mordechai. *Te'ame ha-Mikra be-21 sefarim uve-sifre emet*. Yerushalayim: Mikhlalah, 1981.

Brown, Emily Freeman. "Jewish Liturgical Music by American Women Since 1945." In *Proceedings of the First International Conference on Jewish Music*, ed. Steve Stanton and Alexander Knapp. London: City University Department of Music, 1997.

Burney, Charles. *The Present State of Music in Germany, Netherlands, and the United Provinces or, A Tour Through Those Countries, Undertaken to Collect Materials for a General History of Music*. London: J. Robson, and G. Robinson, 1775; reprint, New York: Dover Publications, 1957.

Burton, Jack, ed. *The Blue Book of Hollywood Musicals: Songs from the Sound Tracks and the Stars Who Sang Them Since the Birth of the Talkies a Quarter-Century Ago*. Watkins Glen, NY: Century House, 1953.

_____. *The Blue Book of Tin Pan Alley: A Human Interest Anthology of American Popular Music*. Watkins Glen, NY: Century House, 1950.

_____. *The Index of American Popular Music: Thousands of Titles Cross-Referenced to Our Basic Anthologies of Popular Songs*. Watkins Glen, NY: Century House, 1957.

Cahan, Yehuda Leyb. *Yidishe folkslider mit melodyes: gezamlt fun Y.L. Kahan; tsunoyfgenumen un fun dos naye aroysgegebn durkh Maks Vaynraykh* [Yiddish Folksongs with Melodies, ed. Max Weinreich]. New York: Yidisher Visnshaftlekher Institut, 1957.

Cantorial Council of America. *Journal of Jewish Music and Liturgy*. [New York]: Cantorial Council of America, 1976.

Cherry, Paul. "A Hidden Mahzor in an Unknown String Quartet by Darius Milhaud." *The Darius Milhaud Society Newsletter* 13 (1997): 15-17.

Chyet, Stanley F. *Lopez of Newport: Colonial American Merchant Prince*. Detroit: Wayne State University Press, 1970.

Cohen, Alex. "Ernest Bloch - A Biography." In *The Music of Ernest Bloch: A Program Manual*, ed. Leah M. Jaffa, 44-48. New York: National Jewish Music Council of the National Jewish Welfare Board, 1955.

Cohen, Miles. "Masoretic Accents as Biblical Commentary." *The Journal of the Ancient Near Eastern Society of Columbia University* (January 1972): 2-11.

_____. *The System of Accentuation in the Hebrew Bible*. Minneapolis: Milco Press, 1969.

Cohen, Simon. *Shaaray Tefila: A History of Its Hundred Years 1845-1945*. New York: Greenberg, 1945.

Cohon, A. Irma, and Council of Jewish Women (U.S.). *An Introduction to Jewish Music in Eight Illustrated Lectures*. New York: Bloch, 1923.

Colbert, Warren E. *Who Wrote That Song? or, Who in the Hell is J. Fred Coots? An Informal Survey of American Popular Songs and Their Composers*. New York: Revisionist Press, 1975.

Collaer, Paul. *Darius Milhaud*, trans. Jane Hohfeld Galante. San Francisco: San Francisco Press, 1988.

Cooper, John Michael. "Knowing Mendelssohn: A Challenge from the Primary Sources." *Notes: Quarterly Journal of the Music Library Association* 61 (2004): 35-95.

Coopersmith, Harry, and Board of Jewish Education (Chicago, IL). *Jewish Community Songster*. New York: Hebrew Publishing Co., 1937.

_____, National Jewish Welfare Board, and American Association for Jewish Education. *Selected Jewish Songs for Members of the Armed Forces*. New York: Jewish Welfare Board, 1943.

Corenthal, Michael G. *Michael G. Corenthal Presents "Cohen on the Telephone": A History of Jewish Recorded Humor and Popular Music, 1892-1942*. Milwaukee: Yesterday's Memories, 1984.

Cowell, Henry. *Music of the World's Peoples*. In Ethnic Folkways Library (5 containers, 10 sound discs, FE 4504-FE 4508). New York, NY: Folkways Records, 1951.

Cutler, Irving. *The Jews of Chicago: From Shtetl to Suburb*. Urbana: University of Illinois Press, 1996.

Danto, Louis, et al. *Israeli Composers*. New York: Musical Heritage Society, 1973.

Davidow, Ari. Website. Available at http://www.well.com/user/ari/klezcontacts.html.

Dawidowicz, Lucy. *From That Place and Time: A Memoir 1938-1947*. New York: Norton, 1989.

Deutsch, Moritz. *Vorbeterschule: Vollständige Sammlung der alten Synagogen-Intonationen*. Breslau: Julius Hainauer, 1871.

Donat, Alexander. *The Holocaust Kingdom: A Memoir*. New York: Holt, Rinehart and Winston, 1965.

Donin, Hayim. *To Be a Jew: A Guide to Jewish Observance in Contemporary Life*. New York: Basic Books, 1972.

Edelman, Marsha Bryan. *A Bibliography of Jewish Music: Resource Materials for Educators*. New York: Hebrew Arts School, 1986.

_____. *Discovering Jewish Music*. Philadelphia: Jewish Publication Society, 2003

Ehrlich, Hermann. *Praktischer Stufengang zur Gründung und Bildung zweck- und zeitgemaesser Synagogenchöre, zugleich als theoretischpraktische Gesanglehre für höhere israelitische Lehranstalten und Volksschulen*. Meiningen: Keyssner, 1859.

Eisenstein, Judith Kaplan. *The Gateway to Jewish Song*. New York: Behrman's Jewish Book House, 1939.

_____. *Heritage of Music: The Music of the Jewish People*. New York: Union of American Hebrew Congregations, 1972.

_____. "Medieval Elements in the Liturgical Music of the Jews of Southern France and Northern Spain." *Musica Judaica: The Journal of the American Society for Jewish Music* 14 (1999): 9-29.

_____. "The Mystical Strain in Jewish Liturgical Music." In *Sacred Sound: Music in Religious Thought and Practice*, ed. Joyce Irwin. Chico, CA: Scholars Press & American Academy of Religion, 1983.

Elbogen, Ismar. *Jewish Liturgy: A Comprehensive History*, trans. Raymond P. Scheindlin, ed. Joseph Heinemann, et al. Philadelphia and Jerusalem: Jewish Publication Society of America, 1993.

Eldar, Ilan. *Torat ha-kriah ba-Mikra: sefer horayat ha-kore u-mishnato ha-leshonit*. Yerushalayim: ha-Akademyah la-lashon ha-Ivrit, 1994.

Elon, Amos. *The Pity of it All: A History of the Jews in Germany, 1743-1933*. New York: Henry Holt & Co., 2002.

Ewen, David. *The Life and Death of Tin Pan Alley: The Golden Age of American Popular Music*. New York: Funk and Wagnalls Co., 1964.

Farmer, Henry George. *A History of Arabian Music to the Thirteenth Century*. London: Luzac, 1967.

Fein, Isaac M. *The Making of an American Jewish Community: The History of Baltimore Jewry from 1773-1920*. Philadelphia: The Jewish Publication Society of America, 1971.

Felder, Deborah L. "Liturgy and Drama: Max Janowski: A Case Study." Thesis, Hebrew Union College - Jewish Institute of Religion, 1996.

Feldman, Zev, and Andrew Statman. *Zev Feldman & Andy Statman*. Shanachie Records 21002. [New York?], 1979.

Fellerer, Karl Gustav. "Jewish Elements in Pre-Gregorian Chant." In *World Congress on Jewish Music, Jerusalem 1978*, ed. Judith Cohen, 115-18. Tel Aviv: The Institute for the Translation of Hebrew Literature Ltd., 1982.

Fenelon, Fania. *Playing for Time*, trans. Judith Landry. Syracuse: Syracuse University Press, 1977.

Flam, Gila. *Singing for Survival: Songs of the Lodz Ghetto, 1940-45*. Urbana: University of Illinois Press, 1992.

Fleisher, Robert Jay. *Twenty Israeli Composers: Voices of a Culture*. Detroit: Wayne State University Press, 1997.

Flender, Reinhard. *Der biblische Sprechgesang und seine mündliche Überlieferung in Synagoge und griechischer Kirche*, ed. Richard Schaal. Quellenkataloge zur Musikgeschichte, 20. Wilhelmshaven: Heinrichshofen-Bücher, 1988.

_____. *Hebrew Psalmody: A Structural Investigation*. Yuval Monograph Series, 9. Jerusalem: The Magnes Press & Hebrew University, 1992.

Freed, Isidore. *Harmonizing the Jewish Modes*. New York: Sacred Music Press of the Hebrew Union College, 1958.

Freeman, David, and Miles Cohen. "The Dual Accentuation of the Ten Commandments." *Proceedings of the International Organization of Masoretic Studies* 1 (1974): 7-20.

_____. "The Masoretes as Exegetes: Selected Examples." *Proceedings of the International Organization of Masoretic Studies* 1 (1974): 35-46.

Friedmann, Aron. *Lebensbilder berühmter Kantoren*. Berlin: C. Boas Nachfolger, 1918.

Friedman, Lester. *The Jewish Image in American Film*. Secaucus, NJ: Citadel Press, 1987.

Frigyesi, Judit. "The Historical Value of the Record 'Maramaros—the Lost Jewish Music of Transylvania'." *Muzsikas—The Lost Jewish Music of Transylvania*. Recording booklet. Rykodisc USA HNCD1373. Salem, Mass, 1993.

Fromm, Herbert. *On Jewish Music: A Composer's View*. [New York]: Bloch, 1978.

Frühauf, Tina. "Louis Lewandowski's 'Five Festival Preludes' Op. 37 for Organ." *Journal of Jewish Music and Liturgy* 21 (1999): 20-40.

Fuks, Marian. *Muzyka ocalona: judaica polskie*. Warsaw: Wydawnictwa Radia i Telewizji, 1989.

Fuld, James J. *The Book of World-Famous Music: Classical, Popular, and Folk*. New York: Dover, 1985.

Galambush, Julie. *The Reluctant Parting: How the New Testament's Jewish Writers Created a Christian Book*. New York: Harper, 2005.

Galeen, Henrik, Paul Hermann Wegener, et al. *The Golem (Der Golem)*. Sandy Hook, CT: Video Images, 1982.

Gartner, Lloyd P. *History of the Jews of Cleveland*. Cleveland and New York: Western Reserve Historical Society & Jewish Theological Seminary of America, 1978.

Gelbrun, Artur, Willy Haparnas, et al. *Liturgy for the People: Essays in Honor of Gerald Ellard, S.J., 1894-1963*. Milwaukee: Bruce Publishing Co., 1963.

Geshuri, Meir Simon. *La-chasidim mizmor: me'asef sifruti ve-omanuti la-neginah datit-amamit shel ha-chasidim: im tavei-neginah, temunot u-faksimiliyot shel ishi ha-chasidut*. Yerushalayim: Chever Chovevim shel Neginat ha-Chasidim, 1935.

_____. *Yerushalayim ir ha-musikah: mi-tekufat Bayit Sheni*. Tel Aviv: ha-Menorah, 1968.

Glazerson, Matityahu. *Music and Kabbalah*. Jerusalem and Northvale, NJ: Jason Aaronson Inc., 1997.

Glückl (of Hameln). *The Life of Glückl of Hameln 1646-1724: Written by Herself*, ed. Beth-Zion Abrahams. New York: Thomas Yoseloff, 1963.

Golb, Norman. "Aspects of the Historical Background of Jewish Life in Medieval Egypt." In *Jewish Medieval and Renaissance Studies*, ed. Alexander Altman. Cambridge, MA: Harvard University Press, 1967.

Goldberg, Isaac. *Tin Pan Alley: A Chronicle of the American Popular Music Racket*. New York: The John Day Company, 1930.

Goldfarb, Israel, and Samuel E. Goldfarb. *The Jewish Songster: Music for Voice and Piano Part II*. Brooklyn: Religious Schools of Congregation Beth Israel, 1929.

Goldin, Mark, and Robert A. Rothstein. "On Musical Connections Between Jews and the Neighboring Peoples of Eastern and Western Europe." *Program in Soviet and East European Studies, Occasional Papers Series*, no. 18. [Amherst, MA]: International Area Studies Programs of The University of Massachusetts at Amherst, 1989.

Goren, Zekharyah. *Te'amei ha-Mikra ke-farshanut. Sifriyat Helal Ben-Chayim*. [Tel Aviv]: ha-Kibuts ha-me'uchad, 1995.

Goshen-Gottstein, M. H. "The Aleppo Codex and the Rise of the Massoretic Bible Text." *Biblical Archeologist* (summer 1979): 145-63.

Gottlieb, Jack. *Funny, It Doesn't Sound Jewish: How Yiddish Songs Influenced Tin Pan Alley, Broadway, and Hollywood.* State University of New York Press, 2004.

Gradenwitz, Peter. *The Music of Israel: From the Biblical Era to Modern Times.* Portland, OR: Amadeus Press, 1996.

_____. *The Music of Israel: Its Rise and Growth Through 5000 Years.* New York: W. W. Norton, 1949.

Grayzel, Solomon. *A History of the Jews from the Babylonian Exile to the Establishment of Israel.* Philadelphia: Jewish Publication Society of America, 1963.

Greenbaum, Masha. *The Jews of Lithuania: A History of a Remarkable Community 1316-1945.* Jerusalem: Gefen Publishing House, 1995.

Greenberg, Louis. *The Jews of Russia.* I: *The Struggle for Emancipation.* New Haven: Yale University Press, 1944.

Gutman, Robert W. *Richard Wagner: The Man, His Mind, and His Music.* New York: Harcourt, Brace & World, 1968.

Haas, Frithjof. *Zwischen Brahms und Wagner: der Dirigent Hermann Levi.* Zürich and Mainz: Atlantis Musikbuch-Verlag, 1995.

Haïk-Vantoura, Suzanne, and John Wheeler. *The Music of the Bible Revealed: The Deciphering of a Millenary Notation.* Berkeley, CA: BIBAL Press, 1991.

Hallo, William W., David B. Kuderman, and Michael Stanislawski. *Heritage: Civilization and the Jews, A Source Reader.* New York: Praeger, 1984.

Hamam, Abdel-Hamid. "Jordanian Music and Its Relationship to Western Music." Ph.D. diss., University of Wales, 1981.

Harrán, Don. *Salamone Rossi: Jewish Musician in Late Renaissance Mantua.* Oxford: Oxford University Press, 1999.

Harris, Hyman Hirsch. *Toldot ha-neginah veha-hazanut be-Yisrael.* Nyu-York: Hotsa'at "Bitsaron," 1950.

Heimovics, Rachel B. *The Chicago Jewish Source Book.* Chicago: Follett, 1981.

Hertzberg, Steven. *Strangers within the Gate City: The Jews of Atlanta 1845-1915.* Philadelphia: The Jewish Publication Society of America, 1978.

Heskes, Irene. "Music as Social History: American Yiddish Theater Music, 1882-1920." *American Music* 2 (1984): 73-87.

_____. *Passport to Jewish Music: Its History, Traditions, and Culture.* Westport, CT: Greenwood Press, 1994.

_____. *The Resource Book of Jewish Music: A Bibliographical and Topical Guide to the Book and Journal Literature and Program Materials.* Westport, CT: Greenwood Press, 1985.

_____, Lawrence Marwick, and Library of Congress. *Yiddish American Popular Songs, 1895 to 1950: A Catalog Based on the Lawrence Marwick Roster of Copyright Entries.* Washington, DC: Library of Congress, 1992.

_____, et al. *The Historic Contribution of Russian Jewry to Jewish Music.* New York, 1967.

Hiller, Ferdinand. *Künstlerleben.* Cologne: M. Du Mont-Schauberg, 1880.

Hirshberg, Jehoash. "Alexander U. Boskovitch and the Quest for an Israeli Musical Style." In *Modern Jews and Their Musical Agendas* 9, ed. Ezra Mendelsohn, 92-109. New York and Oxford: Oxford University Press, 1993.

_____. *Music in the Jewish Community of Palestine, 1880-1948: A Social History.* Oxford: Clarendon Press, Oxford University Press, 1995.

Hoffman, David Zevi. "The Use of the Organ in Responsa Literature." Trans. Winifred Wolfson. *Journal of Jewish Music & Liturgy* 18 (1995-96): 8-15.

Hoffman, Lawrence A., and Janet Roland Walton. *Sacred Sound and Social Change: Liturgical Music in Jewish and Christian Experience.* Notre Dame: University of Notre Dame Press, 1992.

Hoffman, Shlomo. *Miqra'ey musica*. Tel-Aviv: Israel Music Institute, 1974.

Holde, Artur. *Jews in Music: From the Age of Enlightenment to the Mid-Twentieth Century*. New York: Bloch, 1974.

Idelsohn, Avraham Zvi. *Jewish Liturgy and its Development*. New York: Sacred Music Press Hebrew Union College, 1932.

_____. *Jewish Music in its Historical Development*. New York: H. Holt and Company, 1929.

_____. *Sefer ha-shirim: Kovets shirim ivrim le-gane yeladim, le-vatei-sefer amamiyim ve-tikhonim*. Sifre-limud shel Chevrat ha-Ezrah li-Yehude Germaniyah, 2. Berlin: Chevrat ha-Ezrah li-Yehude Germaniyah, 1912.

_____. *Thesaurus of Oriental Hebrew Melodies*. Berlin: Harz, 1923. Translation of *Hebräisch-Orientalischer Melodienschatz, zum ersten Male gesammelt*. Leipzig: Breitkopf & Härtel, 1914.

_____, and Baruch Joseph Cohon. *The Jewish Song Book for Synagogue, School and Home: Covering the Complete Jewish Religious Year*. Cincinnati, OH: Publications for Judaism, 1961.

_____, and National Federation of Temple Brotherhoods. *The Ceremonies of Judaism*. Cincinnati: The National Federation of Temple Brotherhoods, 1929.

Isaacs, Ronald H. *Jewish Music: Its History, People, and Song*. Northvale, NJ: Jason Aronson, 1997.

Isaacson, Ben, and Devorah Wigoder. *The International Jewish Encyclopedia*. [Englewood Cliffs, NJ: Prentice-Hall, 1973.

Israel Music Institute. http://www.imi.org.il/.

Jacobs, Dick, and Harriet Jacobs. *Who Wrote That Song?* Cincinnati, OH: Writer's Digest Books, 1994.

Jacobson, Joshua R. *Chanting the Hebrew Bible: The Art of Cantillation*. Philadelphia: Jewish Publication Society, 2002.

_____. "What is Jewish Liturgical Music?" *Choral Journal* 38, no. 2 (1997): 39, 42-45.

Jeffery, Peter. "The Earliest Christian Chant Repertory Recovered: The Gregorian Witnesses to Jerusalem Chant." *Journal of the American Musicological Society* 47, no. 1 (1994): 1-38.

Jochsberger, Tzipora H., and Velvel Pasternak. *A Harvest of Jewish Song*. Cedarhurst, NY: Tara Publications, 1980.

_____, ed., and Israel Music Heritage Project. "Ashkenaz: Eastern Europe." In *A People and Its Music*, 3 (videocassette). Jerusalem and Teaneck, NJ: Israel Music Heritage Project, 1993.

_____. "Sepharad: Judeo-Spanish." In *A People and its Music*, 2 (videocassette). Jerusalem and Teaneck, NJ: Israel Music Heritage Project.

_____. "Teiman: Yemen." In *A People and its Music The Holocaust Kingdom: A Memoir*, 4 (videocassette). Jerusalem and Teaneck, NJ: Israel Music Heritage Project, 1993.

Jolly, Kirby Reid. "Edwin Franko Goldman and the Goldman Band." D.Ed. diss., New York University, 1971.

Kadison, Luba, and Joseph Buloff. *On Stage, Off Stage: Memories of a Lifetime in the Yiddish Theatre*, ed. Irving Genn. Cambridge: Harvard University Press, 1992.

Kahl, Willi. "Gernsheim." In *Die Musik in Geschichte und Gegenwart*. Kassel: Baerenreiter, 1955.

Kalish, Jon. "A New Generation Gets Klezmerized." *Newsday*, 8 May 1994, Fanfare Section, p. 13. Website http://home.wlu.edu/~blackmerh/klez/kalish.html.

Kanter, Kenneth Aaron. *The Jews on Tin Pan Alley: The Jewish Contribution to American Popular Music, 1830-1940*. New York: Ktav Publishing House & American Jewish Archives, 1982.

Kaplan, Mordecai Menahem, Eugene Kohn, et al. *The New Haggadah for the Pesah Seder (Hagadah shel pesah: seder hadash)*. New York: Behrman House, 1978.

Karas, Joza. *Music in Terezin 1941-1945*. New York: Beaufort Books & Pendragon Press, 1985.

_____. *The Terezín Collection: Music for String Quartet*. Bryn Mawr, PA: Excelsior Music, 1991.

Kater, Michael. *The Twisted Muse: Musicians and Their Music in the Third Reich*. New York: Oxford University Press, 1997.

Katsherginski, Sh. *Lider fun di getos un lagern: Tekstn un melodyes gezamlt, redaktirt, H. Leyvik*. [New York]: Tsiko, [ca. 1948].

Katz, Joshua Zeeb. *Moreh kriat ha-Torah*. Jerusalem, 1970.

Keren, Zvi. *Contemporary Israeli Music: Its Sources and Stylistic Development*. Tel Aviv: Bar-Ilan University Press, 1980.

Kisselgoff, Susman, Aleksandr Matveevich Zhitomirskii, et al. *Lider-zamelbukh far der yidisher shul un familye*. Berlin: Juwal, 1923.

Klezmer Pioneers: European and American Recordings 1905-1952. Rounder compact disc 1089. Cambridge, MA: Rounder Records, 1993.

Klingenstein, Susanne. *Enlarging America: The Cultural Work of Jewish Literary Scholars, 1930-1990*. Syracuse, NY: Syracuse University Press, 1998.

Kölnische Volkszeitung, 24 October 1911.

Kohn, Maier. *Vollständiger Jahrgang von Terzett- und Chorgesängen der Synagoge in München nebst sämtlichen Chorresponsorien zu den alten Gesangsweisen der Vorsänger (Chasunus)*. Munich: Johann Palm, 1839.

Koussevitzky, Moshe. *Cantor Moshe Koussevitzky Sings His Most Famous Synagogue Masterpieces* (3 sound cassettes: GRC 140, GRC 148, GRC 278). Brooklyn, NY: Greater Recording Co., 1973.

Kraus, Bea. "The Cantors: Gifted Voices Remembered." In *Doris Minsky Memorial Fund Publication*, no. 3. Chicago: Chicago Jewish Historical Society, n.d.

Kupfer, Ephraim. "Moellin." In *Encyclopedia Judaica*, 12:210-11. Jerusalem: Keter, 1972.

Lachmann, Robert, and Universitah ha-Ivrit bi-Yerushalayim. *Jewish Cantillation and Song in the Isle of Djerba*. Jerusalem: Archives of Oriental Music, Hebrew University, 1940.

Laks, Szymon. *Music of Another World*. Evanston: Northwestern University Press, 1989.

Landman, Leo. *The Cantor*. New York: Yeshiva University, 1972.

Levi, Erik. *Music in the Third Reich*. New York: St. Martin's Press, 1994.

Levien, John Mewburn. *The Singing of John Braham*. London: Novello and Co., Ltd., 1944.

Levin, Neil, ed. *Songs of the American Jewish Experience*. Chicago: Board of Jewish Education, 1976.

Levinson, Robert E. *The Jews in the California Gold Rush*. New York: Ktav, 1978.

Lewis, Selma S. *A Biblical People in the Bible Belt: The Jewish Community of Memphis, Tennessee, 1840s-1960s*. Macon: Mercer University Press, 1998.

Lichtenstein, Sabine. "Abraham Jacob Lichtenstein: eine jüdische Quelle für Carl Loewe und Max Bruch." *Die Musikforschung* 49, no. 4 (1996): 349-67.

Liptzin, Sol. *Eliakum Zunser, Poet of His People*. [New York]: Behrman House, 1950.

Lowenthal, Marvin. *The Jews of Germany: A Story of Sixteen Centuries*. Philadelphia: The Jewish Publication Society of America, 1936.

Lyman, Darryl. *Great Jews in Music*. Middle Village, NY: Jonathan David Publishers, 1986.

Mackerras, Catherine. *Hebrew Melodist: A Life of Isaac Nathan*. Sidney: Currawong, 1963.

Mahler, Raphael. *A History of Modern Jewry: 1780-1815*. New York: Schocken Books, 1971.

Marcus, Jacob R. *The Colonial American Jew 1491-1776*. Detroit: Wayne State University Press, 1970.

———. *United States Jewry 1776-1985*. Detroit: Wayne State University Press, 1989.

Margolis, B. *Dray Doyres*. [New York], 1957.

Marks, Paul F. *Bibliography of Literature Concerning Yemenite-Jewish Music*. Detroit Studies in Music Bibliography, 27. Detroit: Information Coordinators, 1973.

Martin, George. *The Damrosch Dynasty: America's First Family of Music*. Boston: Houghton Mifflin Company, 1983.

Masoret kehilat Danzig. Sound disc. Tel Aviv: Bet ha-Tefutsot 010956.

Master Digital, and Nimmer Productions. *The Jewish Holidays Video Guide* (videocassette). Santa Monica: Master Digital, 1987.

Memorial Foundation for Jewish Culture and Spector Films. *About the Jews of Yemen: A Vanishing Culture*. New York: Memorial Foundation for Jewish Culture, 1986.

Menasseh, Sarah. "A Song to Heal Your Wounds: Traditional Melodies of the Jews of Iraq." *Musica Judaica: Journal of the American Society for Jewish Music* 12 (1991-92): 1-29.

Mendelsohn, Ezra, and Universitah ha-Ivrit bi-Yerushalayim. *Modern Jews and Their Musical Agendas*. Studies in Contemporary Jewry, 9. New York: Oxford University Press, 1993.

Meyer, Michael. *The Politics of the Music in the Third Reich*. New York: Peter Lang, 1993.

Middleton, Ray, and Howard Barlow. *Ten Jewish Holy Days*. Sound disc. Candle Records, 1957.

Milhaud, Darius. *My Happy Life: An Autobiography*, trans. Donald Evans, George Hall, and Christopher Hall. London and New York: Marion Boyars, 1995.

Millgram, Abraham Ezra. *Jewish Worship*. Philadelphia: Jewish Publication Society, 1971.

‗‗‗‗‗‗‗, and Congregation Beth Israel (Philadelphia, PA). *Beth Israel Hymnal*. Philadelphia: Congregation Beth Israel, 1937.

‗‗‗‗‗‗‗, and Jewish Publication Society of America. *Sabbath, the Day of Delight*. Philadelphia: The Jewish Publication Society of America, 1944.

Mlotek, Eleanor Gordon. *Mir trogn a Gezang!* 3rd ed. New York: Education Department of the Workmen's Circle, 1982.

‗‗‗‗‗‗‗, and Joseph Mlotek, eds. *Pearls of Yiddish Song: Favorite Folk, Art and Theatre Songs with Yiddish Texts and Music, Parallel Transliterations, Translations, Historical Background, Guitar Chords*. New York: Education Department of the Workmen's Circle, 1989.

Morsch, Günter, Inge Lammel, and Akademie der Künste. *Sachsenhausen-Liederbuch: Originalwiedergabe eines illegalen Häftlingsliederbuches aus dem Konzentrationslager Sachsenhausen*. Berlin: Edition Hentrich, 1995.

Moses, Isaac S. *The Sabbath-School Hymnal: A Collection of Songs, Services and Responsive Readings for the School, Synagogue and Home*. New York: Bloch, 1928.

Most, Andrea. *Making Americans: Jews and the Broadway Musical*. Cambridge, MA: Harvard University Press, 2004.

Musikalische Volkskunst Spaniens. Sound disc. In *Hispaniae musica*, Archiv Produktion, 1969.

Nathan, Hans, ed. *Israeli Folk Music: Songs of the Early Pioneers*. Madison: A-R Editions, 1994.

Nathan, Issac. *Musurgia Vocalis*. London: G. and W. B. Whitaker, 1823.

National Jewish Music Council. *Music of Israel Today: An Annotated List of Musical Compositions about the Land and the People of Israel*, pt. 1. New York: National Jewish Music Council, 1963.

Naumbourg, Samuel. *Semiroth Israel [Z'mirot Yisra'el]*. 3 vols. Paris, [1847, 1852, 1857].

Ne'eman, Yehoshua L. *Kera be-ta'am*. Yerushalayim: Makhon ha-Yisraeli le-musikah datit, 1967.

‗‗‗‗‗‗‗. *Tselile ha-Mikra: yesodot ha-musikah shel ha-te'amim*. 2 vols. Tel Aviv: Moreshet be-siyua ha-Misrad le-inyene dat, 1955.

Neusner, Jacob. *Judaism's Theological Voice: The Melody of the Talmud*. Chicago Studies in the History of Judaism. Chicago: University of Chicago Press, 1995.

Newman, Richard, with Karen Kirtley. *Alma Rosé: Vienna to Auschwitz*. Portland, OR: Amadeus Press, 2000.

Nulman, Macy. *Concise Encyclopedia of Jewish Music*. New York: McGraw-Hill Book Co., 1975.

Olivestone, David. "Sirota." *Encyclopaedia Judaica*, 14:1620-21. Jerusalem: Keter, 1972.

Oseary, Guy. *Jews Who Rock*. New York: St. Martin's Griffen, 2001.

Padwa, Mia Diamond. "'For Your Voice is Sweet . . .': An Overview of *Kol isha*." *Jewish Orthodox Feminist Alliance Journal* 2, no. 1 (winter 2000): 4-5.

Palacín, Arcadio de Larrea. *Romances de Tetuan*. Madrid: Instituto de Estudios Africanos, 1959.

Papo, Joseph M. *Sephardim in Twentieth Century America: In Search of Unity*. San Jose: Pele Yoetz Books, 1987.

Paymer, Marvin E. *Facts Behind the Songs: A Handbook of American Popular Music from the Nineties to the '90s*. New York: Garland, 1993.

Peerce, Jan. *The Bluebird of Happiness*, ed. Alan Levy, 69. New York: Harper and Row, 1976.

Perlman, Michael. *Madrikh la-moreh le-limud "Te'ame ha-Mikra la-talmid."* Tel-Aviv: Zimrat, 1969.

Pfefferkorn, Eli, and United States Holocaust Memorial Council. *Commemorative Observances for Days of Remembrance.* Washington, DC: United States Holocaust Memorial Council, 1985.

Piattelli, Elio. *Canti liturgici ebraici di rito italiano.* Rome: Edizioni De Santis, 1967.

Potter, Pamela. *Most German of the Arts: Musicology and Society from the Weimar Republic to the End of Hitler's Reich.* New Haven: Yale University Press, 1998.

Powitz, Stephen. "Musical Life in the Warsaw Ghetto." *Journal of Jewish Music and Liturgy* 4 (1981-82): 2-10.

Prieberg, Fred K. *Musik im NS-Staat.* Frankfurt a/M: Fischer Taschenbuch Verlag, 1982.

_____. *Trial of Strength: Wilhelm Furtwaengler in the Third Reich,* trans. Christopher Dolan. Boston: Northeastern University Press, 1994.

Prior, Roger. "Jewish Musicians in the Tudor Court." *The Musical Quarterly* 69 (1983): 253-65.

Prittie, Terence, and Bernard Dineen. *The Double Exodus: A Study of Arab and Jewish Refugees in the Middle East.* London: Goodhart Press, n.d. [ca. 1975].

Qatib, al-Hasan ibn Ahmad, and Amnon Shiloah. *La Perfection des connaissances musicales.* Paris: P. Geuthner, 1972.

Raeburn, Bruce B. "Jewish Jazzmen in New Orleans, 1890-1940: An Overview." *The Jazz Archivist* 12 (1997): 1-12.

Raphael, Marc Lee. *Jews and Judaism in a Midwestern Community: Columbus, Ohio, 1840-1975.* Columbus: Ohio Historical Society, 1979.

Ravina, Menashe, Shelomoh Skulski, and Manasseh Rabinowitz. *Who is Who in ACUM: Authors, Composers and Music Publishers, Biographical Notes and Principal Works.* [Tel Aviv]: ACUM Ltd. (Société d'auteurs, compositeurs, et editeurs de musique en Israel), 1965.

Reif, Stefan C. "The Early History of Jewish Worship." In *The Making of Jewish and Christian Worship,* ed. Paul F. Bradhaw and Lawrence A. Hoffman. Notre Dame: Notre Dame University Press, 1991.

Ring, Mark M. "'Hashkiveinu No. 1,' David Nowakowsky (Choral Review)." *Choral Journal* 36, no. 7 (1996): 57.

Ringer, Alexander L. *Arnold Schoenberg: The Composer as Jew.* Oxford: Clarendon Press, 1990.

Robinson, Earl, Woody Guthrie, Joe Glazer, et al. *Songs for Political Action.* 2 sound discs. Hambergen: Bear Family, 1996.

Rogovoy, Seth. *The Essential Klezmer: A Music Lover's Guide to Jewish Roots and Soul Music, from the Old World to the Jazz Age to the Downtown Avant-Garde.* Chapel Hill: Algonquin, 2000.

Rosen, Aaron H. *The History of Hazanuth: Issued to the 30th Anniversary of the Jewish Ministers Cantors Association of America, Sunday, February 3rd, 1924.*

Rosenbaum, Fred. *Visions of Reform: Congregation Emanu-El and the Jews of San Francisco 1849-2000.* Judah L. Magnes Museum, 2000.

Rosenblatt, Samuel. *Yossele Rosenblatt: The Story of His Life as Told by His Son.* New York: Farrar, Straus and Young, 1954.

Rosenfeld, Lulla Adler. *The Yiddish Theatre and Jacob P. Adler.* New York: Thomas Y. Crowell, 1977; rev. ed., New York: Shapolsky Brothers, 1988.

Rosner, Fred. "Moses Maimonides on Music Therapy in His Responsum on Music." *Journal of Jewish Music and Liturgy* 16 (1993-94): 1-16.

Rosowsky, Solomon. *The Cantillation of the Bible, The Five Books of Moses.* New York: Reconstructionist Press, 1957.

_____, Shneur Zalman Zeitlin, and Haim Bar-Dayan. *Chamishah chumshe Torah u-keriatam: Sefer Shelomo Rozovski.* Yerushalayim: Mizrah u-Maarav, 1977.

Rossi, Salamone. *Complete Works,* ed. Don Harrán. Neuheusen: American Institute of Musicology, 1995-2003.

Rosten, Leo Calvin. *The Joys of Yiddish: A Relaxed Lexicon of Yiddish, Hebrew and Yinglish Words Often Encountered in English . . . from the Days of the Bible to Those of the Beatnik.* New York: McGraw-Hill, 1968.

Rothmüller, Aaron Marko. *The Music of the Jews.* Trans. H. S. Stevens. Cranbury, NJ: A. S. Barnes and Company, 1967.

Rubin, Emanuel. "Cantillation as a Key to 'Deconstructivist' Thought in the Masoretic Text of the Bible." In *Proceedings of the First International Conference on Jewish Music,* ed. Alexander Knapp. London: University Press, 1997.

_____. "David Nowakowski (1848-1921): A New Voice from Old Odessa." *Musica Judaica* 16 (2001-02): 20-52.

_____. "Israel's Theatre of Confrontation." *World Literature Today* 60, no. 2 (1986): 239-44.

_____. "Rhythmic and Structural Aspects of the Masoretic Cantillation of the Pentateuch." In *Eleventh World Congress of Jewish Studies,* Division D, 2 (1993): 219-26. Jerusalem.

Rubin, Ruth. *Voices of a People: The Story of Yiddish Folksong.* Philadelphia: The Jewish Publication Society of America, 1979.

Sachs, Joel. "Introduction." In Ferdinand Hiller, *Mendelssohn: Letters and Recollections,* trans. M. E. von Glehn, iii-xviii. New York: Vienna House, 1972.

Sadie, Stanley, ed. *The New Grove Dictionary of Musical Instruments.* London and New York: Macmillan Press, 1984.

Saleski, Gdal. *Famous Musicians of Jewish Origin.* New York: Bloch, 1949.

Saminsky, Lazare. *Music of the Ghetto and the Bible.* New York: Bloch, 1934.

Sandrow, Nahma. *Vagabond Stars: A World History of Yiddish Theater.* New York: Limelight Editions, 1986.

Sapoznik, Henry. *Klezmer! Jewish Music from Old World to Our World.* New York: Schirmer Books, 1999.

Sarna, Nahum M. *On the Book of Psalms: Exploring the Prayers of Ancient Israel.* New York: Schocken Books, 1993.

Scheinfeld, S. I. *The Books of Rabbi S. I. Scheinfeld,* trans. David Kuselewitz, ed. Amram Scheinfeld. Chicago: Scheinfeld Foundation, 1977.

Schulze, Kirsten E., Martin Stokes, and Colm Campbell. *Nationalism, Minorities and Diasporas: Identities and Rights in the Middle East.* Library of Modern Middle East Studies, 8. London: Tauris Academic Studies, 1996.

Sendrey, Alfred. *Bibliography of Jewish Music.* New York: Columbia University Press, 1951.

_____. *Music in Ancient Israel.* New York: Philosophical Library, 1969.

_____. *The Music of the Jews in the Diaspora (Up to 1800): A Contribution to the Social and Cultural History of the Jews.* New York: T. Yoseloff, 1971.

Shahar, Natan. "The Eretz Israeli Song and the Jewish National Fund." In *Modern Jews and Their Musical Agendas,* ed. Ezra Mendelsohn, 78-91. New York and Oxford: Oxford University Press, 1993.

Shamosh, Amnon. *Ha-Keter: Sipuro shel keter Aram-Tsovah.* Yerushalayim: Machon Ben-Zvi, 1987.

Shapiro, Nat, and Bruce Pollock. *Popular Music, 1920-1979: A Revised Cumulation.* Detroit, MI: Gale Research Co., 1985.

Sharoni, Nisan, Serayah Dablitski, et al. *Sefer em la-Mikra: kelalei ha-dikduk ve-te'amei ha-mikra ha-nogim la-halakhah le-ma'aseh, be-lashon kalah u-verurah; Ve-nilveh elav kuntres Imre fi: al ta'uyot ha-shekhihot ba-tefilah.* Bene Berak: N. Sharoni, 1993.

Shaw, Artie. *The Trouble with Cinderella (An Outline of Identity).* New York: Farrar, Straus and Young, 1952.

Shelemay, Kay Kaufman. *Let Jasmine Rain Down: Song and Remembrance among Syrian Jews.* Chicago and London: University of Chicago Press, 1998.

_____. *Song of Longing: An Ethiopian Journey.* Urbana and Chicago: University of Illinois Press, 1991.

Shepard, Thomas, and Lewis Ward Mudge. *Songs of Praise: With Tunes.* New York: A.S. Barnes, 1889.

Sherman, Pinchas. "Polische hazanut in fargangenheit un tzukunft." In *The History of Hazanuth Issued to the 30th Anniversary of the Jewish Ministers Cantors Association of America, Sunday, February 3rd, 1924*, ed. Aaron H. Rosen, 49-51. New York: The Jewish Ministers Cantors Association of America, Pinski-Massel Press, 1924.

Shiloah, Amnon. *The Dimension of Music in Islamic and Jewish Culture.* Aldershot, Hampshire, Great Britain, and Brookfield, VT: Variorum, 1993.

_____. *Jewish Musical Traditions.* Jewish Folklore and Anthropology Series. Detroit: Wayne State University Press, 1992.

_____. *Music in the World of Islam: A Socio-Cultural Study.* Detroit: Wayne State University Press, 1995.

_____. *The Theory of Music in Arabic Writings (c. 900-1900): Descriptive Catalogue of Manuscripts in Libraries of Europe and the U.S.A.* International Inventory of Musical Sources (RISM), ser. B, vol. 10. Munich: G. Henle Verlag, 1979.

_____, and Merkaz Moreshet Yahadut Bavel (Or Yehudah Israel). *The Musical Tradition of Iraqi Jews: Selection of Piyyutim and Songs.* Studies on History and Culture of Iraqi Jews, 3. Or Yehuda: Iraqi Jews' Traditional Culture Center Institute for Research on Iraqi Jewry, 1983.

Shiri, Gilbert. *Music in the Holocaust. Confronting Life in the Nazi Ghettos and Camps.* Oxford: Oxford University Press, 2005.

Shochet, Michael A. *The Cantor: A Calling for Today* (videocassette). New York: Thomas Kalamar, 1994.

Siegel, Richard, Michael Strassfeld, and Sharon Strassfeld. *The Jewish Catalog: A Do-It-Yourself Kit.* Philadelphia: Jewish Publication Society of America, 1973.

_____, and Carl Rheins. *The Jewish Almanac.* New York: Pacific Press, 1987.

Sietz, Reinhold. *Aus Ferdinand Hillers Briefwechsel (1826-1885): Beiträge zu einer Biographie Ferdinand Hillers*, 6. In *Beiträge zur rheinischen Musikgeschichte*, 70. Cologne: Arno Volk-Verlag, 1968.

Signer, Michael, ed. *The Itinerary of Benjamin of Tudela.* Malibu: Pangloss Press, 1983.

Silverman, Jerry. *The Yiddish Song Book.* New York: Stein and Day, 1983.

Silverman, Moses A. "The Cantorate." In *The Sentinel's History of Chicago Jewry 1911-1986*, pp. 184-186. Chicago: Sentinel Publishing Co., n.d.

Sitsky, Larry. *Music of the Repressed Russian Avant-garde, 1900-1929.* Contributions to the Study of Music and Dance, no. 31. Westport, CT: Greenwood Press, 1994.

Slobin, Mark. *Chosen Voices: The Story of the American Cantorate. Music in American Life.* Urbana: University of Illinois Press, 1989.

_____. *Old Jewish Folk Music: The Collections and Writings of Moshe Beregovski.* Philadelphia: University of Pennsylvania Press, 1982.

_____. *Tenement Songs: The Popular Music of the Jewish Immigrants The Theory of Music in Arabic Writings (c. 900-1900): Descriptive Catalogue of Music in American Life.* Urbana: University of Illinois Press, 1982.

_____, and Yosef Latayner. *Yiddish Theater in America: David's Violin (1897) and Shloyme Gorgl (189-).* Nineteenth-century American Musical Theater, 11. New York: Garland Publishers, 1994.

_____, ed. *American Klezmer: Its Roots and Offshoots.* Berkeley: University of California Press, 2002.

Smidak, Emil F. *Isaak-Ignaz Moscheles: The Life of the Composer and his Encounters with Beethoven, Liszt, Chopin, and Mendelssohn.* Aldershot: Scolar Press, 1989.

Sobel, Bernard. *A Pictorial History of Vaudeville.* New York: Bonanza Books, 1961.

Soltes, Avraham. *Off the Willows: The Rebirth of Modern Jewish Music.* New York: Bloch, 1970.

Spector, Johanna. "Chant and Cantillation." *Musica Judaica: Journal of the American Society for Jewish Music* 9, no. 1 (1986): 1-21.

Spiegel, Mira. "Kriah zimratit shel tekstim liturgiyim mekudashim mi-huts la-Mikra: ha-simunim ha-grafiyim shel ha-te'amim u-vitsu'ehem ha-musikaliyim," 2 vols. Diss., Hebrew University, 1997.

Spitzer, Harvey. "Samuel Naumbourg's Introduction to his *Agudath Schirim* (Paris, 1874)." *Journal of Jewish Music & Liturgy* 11 (1988-89): 17-34.

Sposato, Jeffrey S. "Creative Writing: The [Self-] Identification of Mendelssohn as Jew." *The Musical Quarterly* 82 (1998): 193-209.

Stainer, John, and Francis W. Galpin. *The Music of the Bible, With Some Account of the Development of Modern Musical Instruments from Ancient Types*. Da Capo Press Music Reprint Series. New York: Da Capo Press, 1970.

Stanislawski, Michael. *Tsar Nicholas I and the Jews: The Transformation of Jewish Society in Russia, 1825-1855*. Philadelphia: Jewish Publication Society of America, 1983.

Steinberg, Milton. *As a Driven Leaf*. Indianapolis and New York: Bobbs-Merrill, 1939.

Stillman, Norman A. *The Jews of Arab Lands: A History and Source Book*. Philadelphia: Jewish Publication Society of America, 1979.

Stillman, Yedida Kalfon, and George K. Zucker. *New Horizons in Sephardic Studies*. SUNY Series in Anthropology and Judaic Studies, ed. Walter P. Zenner. Albany: State University of New York Press, 1993.

Stonehill, Charles Archibald. *The Jewish Contribution to Civilization*. Birmingham: F. Juckes Ltd., 1940.

Strom, Yale. *The Book of Klezmer: The History, the Music, the Folklore*. Chicago: A Cappella Books, 2002.

Sullivan, Lawrence Eugene. *Enchanting Powers: Music in the World's Religions*. Religions of the World. Cambridge, MA: Harvard University Center for the Study of World Religions; distributed by Harvard University Press, 1997.

Sulzer, Salomon. *Schir Zion* 1 (1839); 2 (1865). Vienna: H. Engel.

_____. *Schir Zion*, ed. Joseph Sulzer. Frankfurt am Main: Kaufman, 1922.

Swichkow, Louis J., and Lloyd P. Gartner. *The History of the Jews of Milwaukee*. Philadelphia: Jewish Publication Society, 1963.

Tabak, Robert. "Orthodox Judaism in Transition." In *Jewish Life in Philadelphia 1830-1940*, ed. Murray Friedman. Philadelphia: Institute for the Study of Human Issues, 1982.

Taitz, Emily. "Kol Ishah—The Voice of Woman: Where was it Heard in Medieval Europe?" *Conservative Judaism* 38 (1986): 44-61.

Thomas, Michael Tilson. *Michael Tilson Thomas, Viva Voce: Conversations with Edward Seckerson*. London: Faber and Faber, 1994.

Tischler, Alice. *A Descriptive Bibliography of Art Music by Israeli Composers*. Detroit Studies in Music Bibliography, no. 62. Warren, MI: Harmonie Park Press, 1988.

Touma, Habib. *The Music of the Arabs*. Portland: Amadeus Press, 1996.

Tucker, Richard, and Sholom Secunda. *Cantorial Jewels: Ten Greatest Hebrew Prayers Sung by Richard Tucker*. Tel Aviv: CBS Records 72285 1975.

Underwood, Kent. "'Radical Jewish Culture' and the Klezmer Revival." Unpublished talk, Music Library Association Annual Meeting. Los Angeles, 17 March 1999.

United Jewish Appeal. *This Shall Tell All Ages: Art, Music and Writings of the Holocaust*. [New York]: UJA, 1981.

"Universitah ha-Ivrit bi-Yerushalayim. merkaz le-heker ha-musikah ha-yehudit." *Yuval* (Journal). Jerusalem: Magnes Press of Hebrew University, 1968.

Vinkovetzky, Aharon, comp. *Anthology of Yiddish Folksongs*, ed. Sinai Leichter with an introduction by Abba Kovner. Jerusalem: Magnes Press, 1983.

Wagner, Cosima. *Diaries 1869-1877*, trans. Geoffrey Skelton, ed. Martin Gregor-Dellin and Dietrich Mack. New York: Harcourt Brace Jovanovich, 1978.

Warembund, Morman, and Zalmen Mlotek, eds. *The New York Times Great Songs of the Yiddish Theater Arranged for Voice, Piano, and Guitar*. New York: Quadrangle & New York Times Book Co., 1975.

Wasielewski, Wilhelm Joseph von. *The Violoncello and its History*. English trans. Isobella S. E. Stigand. London and New York: Novello, Ewer and Co., 1894; reprint, New York: Da Capo, 1968.

Weil, Daniel Meir. *The Masoretic Chant of the Bible*. Jerusalem: Rubin Mass, 1995.

Weinberger, Leon J. *Jewish Hymnography: A Literary History*. London and Portland, OR: Littman Library of Jewish Civilization, 1998.

Weinberger, Moses. *People Walk on their Heads* (original title, *Jews and Judaism in New York*, 1887), trans. Jonathan D. Sarna. New York: Holmes & Mercier, 1982.

Weisser, Albert. *The Modern Renaissance of Jewish Music: Events and Figures, Eastern Europe and America*. New York: Bloch, 1954; reprint, New York: Da Capo Press, 1983.

_____, and National Jewish Music Council. *Bibliography of Publications and Other Resources on Jewish Music*. New York: National Jewish Music Council, 1969.

Weissler, Lenore E., and Archive of Folk Song (U.S.). *A Selected List of Material Relating to Hebrew and Israeli Folk Music*. Washington: Library of Congress Music Divison Archive of Folk Song, 1970.

Wellesz, Egon. *Eastern Elements in Western Chant*. Copenhagen: Munksgaard, 1974.

Werblowsky, R. J. Zwi, and Geoffrey Wigoder, eds. *The Encyclopedia of the Jewish Religion*. New York, Chicago, San Francisco: Holt, Rinehart, and Winston, 1965.

Werfel, Alma Mahler. *And the Bridge is Love*, ed. E. B. Ashton. New York: Harcourt, Brace, 1958.

Werner, Eric. *Contributions to a Historical Study of Jewish Music*. [New York]: Ktav, 1976.

_____. "Identity and Character of Jewish Music." In *Proceedings of the World Congress on Jewish Music, Jerusalem, 1978*, ed. Judith Cohen, 1-14. Tel Aviv: Institute for the Translation of Hebrew Literature, 1982.

_____. *Mendelssohn: A New Image of the Composer and His Age*. London: Collier-Macmillan, 1963.

_____. "The Oldest Sources of Synagogue Chant." *Proceedings of the American Academy for Jewish Research* 16 (1947): 225-32.

_____. *The Sacred Bridge: Liturgical Parallels in Synagogue and Early Church*. New York: Schocken Books, 1970.

_____. *The Sacred Bridge: The Interdependence of Liturgy and Music in Synagogue and Church During the First Millennium*. London and New York: D. Dobson, Columbia University Press, 1959.

_____. *Three Ages of Musical Thought: Essays on Ethics and Aesthetics*. Da Capo Press Music Reprint Series. New York: Da Capo Press, 1981.

_____. *A Voice Still Heard: The Sacred Songs of the Ashkenazic Jews*. University Park: Pennsylvania State University Press, 1976.

Werner, Marc A. *Richard Wagner and the Anti-Semitic Imagination*. Lincoln: University of Nebraska Press, 1995.

Wertheimer, Jack. *The Modern Jewish Experience: A Reader's Guide*. New York: New York University Press, 1993.

Wickes, William, and Aron Dotan. *Two Treatises on the Accentuation of the Old Testament*. 1881; reprint, New York: Ktav Publishing House, 1970.

Wickram, Jorg. *Der Goldfaden: Eine liebliche und kurzweilige Geschichte*. Munich: G. Hirth, 1923.

Wiener, Leo. *The History of Yiddish Literature in the Nineteenth Century*. New York: Charles Scribner's Sons, 1899.

Wigoder, Geoffrey. *The New Standard Jewish Encyclopedia*. New York: Facts on File, 1992.

Wohlberg, Max. "Significant Aspects of the Ashkenazic Hazzanic Recitative." *Proceedings of the World Congress of Jewish Music, Jerusalem, 1978*, ed. Judith Cohen. Tel Aviv: The Institute for the Translation of Hebrew Literature Ltd., 1982.

World Congress of Jewish Studies, 1985: Jerusalem Israel and World Union of Jewish Studies. 1986. *Proceedings of the Ninth World Congress of Jewish Studies, Jerusalem, August 4-12, 1985*. Publications of the World Union of Jewish Studies. Jerusalem: World Union of Jewish Studies.

World Congress of Jewish Studies, 1989: Jerusalem Israel and World Union of Jewish Studies. 1990. *Proceedings of the Tenth World Congress of Jewish Studies, Jerusalem, August 16-24, 1989*. Jerusalem: World Union of Jewish Studies.

Yardeini, Mordecai. *Vort un klang: eseyen, eseytn, eseytkes, poezye*. Nyu-York: Farlag "Malkah," 1979.

_____, and Jewish Music Alliance (New York, NY). *50 yor idish gezang in Amerike*. Nyu-York: Idishn Muzik Farband, 1964.

Yeivin, Israel. *Introduction to the Tiberian Masorah*. Missoula, MT: Scholars Press for Society of Biblical Literature and International Organization for Masoretic Studies, 1980.

_____. *Keter aram tsovah. Kitve mifal ha-Mikra shel ha-Universitah ha-Ivrit*. Jerusalem: Hotsa'at sefarim al shem Y. L. Magnes ha-Universitah ha-Ivrit, 1968.

Zahavy, Tzvee. "The Politics of Piety: Social Conflict and the Emergence of Rabbinic Liturgy." In *The Making of Jewish and Christian Worship*, ed. Paul F. Bradshaw and Lawrence A. Hoffman. Notre Dame and London: University of Notre Dame Press, 1991.

Zaludkowski, Eliyahu. *Kulturträger von der jüdischen Liturgie*. Detroit: Zaludkowski, 1930.

Zeitlin, Shneur Zalman, and Haim Bar-Dayan. *Megilat Ester u-kri'atah: masah, dikduk musikali, ha-Megilah be-tavei neginah*. Yerushalayim: Kiryat Sefer, 1974.

Zitron, Samuel Leib. *Barimte yidishe froyen: zayer lebn un virkn*. Varshe: "Ahisefer," 1928.

Zunser, Eliakum. *Verk*, ed. Mordkhe Schaechter. New York: YIVO, 1964.

Zylbercweig, Zalmen. *Avraham Goldfaden un Zigmunt Mogulesko*. Buenos Ayres: Farlag "Elisheva," 1936.

INDEX

ABOUT THE AUTHORS

EMANUEL RUBIN is Professor of Judaic Studies and Music History at the University of Massachusetts, Amherst, where he is also active as a composer. He has held teaching appointments and guest lectureships at a number of institutions in the United States and Israel. In addition to his studies on music of the Jews, Professor Rubin has published extensively on English and American music. He is the author of the recent monograph, *The English Glee in the Reign of George III* (Harmonie Park Press, 2003); of a critical edition of John Travers's *Eighteen Canzonets* of 1746 (A-R Editions, 2005); and a reprint and introduction (with Malcolm Nelson) to *A Collection of Catches, Canons, and Glees*, 4 vols. (Mellifont Press). Other essays have appeared in *Cultivating Music in America*, ed. R. Locke and C. Barr; *Opera and the Golden West*, ed. J. DiGaetani and J. Sirefman; *Dvořák in America*, ed. J. Tibbets; and in *American Music, Performance Practice Review*, *CMS Symposium*, *NASM Proceedings*, and *Musica Judaica*, among other journals.

JOHN H. BARON is Schawe Professor of Music and director of the graduate program in musicology at Tulane University in New Orleans. He has written widely about chamber music and is the author of *Chamber Music: A Research Guide*, Second Edition (Routledge, 2002) and *Intimate Music: A History of the Idea of Chamber Music* (Pendragon, 1998). In the area of American music he has produced an edition of piano music in New Orleans in the nineteenth century and edited Walter S. Jenkins, *The Remarkable Mrs. Beach, American Composer: A Biographical Account based on her Diaries . . .* (Harmonie Park Press, 1994). Professor Baron has also contributed editions of Spanish vocal music, French ballet music, and German keyboard music of the seventeenth century and a research guide to Baroque music (Garland, 1993). He has published extensively in musicological journals, including *American Music, Journal of the American Musicological Society, Musical Quarterly, Acta Musicologica*, and *Musica Judaica*.

Date Due

PRINTED IN U.S.A.   CAT. NO. 24 161   BRO DART